General Editors
W. J. F. JENNER and E. P. WILKINSON

Modern China
A CHRONOLOGY

20052

COLIN MACKERRAS
with the assistance of ROBERT CHAN

Modern China
A CHRONOLOGY
from 1842 to the present

W. H. Freeman and Company
San Francisco

© 1982 Thames and Hudson Ltd, London

First published in the United States in 1982 by W. H. Freeman and Company, 660 Market Street, San Francisco, California 94104.

Library of Congress Cataloging in Publication Data

Mackerras, Colin.
   Modern China.

    Bibliography: p.
    1. China—History—19th century—Chronology.
    2. China—History—20th century—Chronology. I. Chen, Robert.
II. Title.
DS755.M2 1982   951.04′02′02   81-19458
ISBN 0-7167-1411-6   AACR2

All rights reserved. No part of this publication may be reproduced or transmitted in any form or by any means, electronic or mechanical, including photocopy, recording or any information storage and retrieval system, without permission in writing from the publisher.

Printed and bound in Great Britain.

CONTENTS

Preface 6

Introduction 7

List of Abbreviations 21

Chronology 22

Maps 638

Glossary of Titles and Technical Terms 644

General Index 647

Geographical Index 695

PREFACE

This work is intended to serve as a reference for all those interested in modern Chinese history, either in a specialist or general way. While it makes no pretence at being complete, the compilers have hoped to cover events of fairly wide range and kind.

Several editorial matters require comment. Firstly we have used *pinyin* romanization throughout for Chinese names, except in very special cases where that course would create confusion (e.g., Peking, Amoy). We have designated Peking by that name except for the years 1928 to 1949 when it was formally called Beiping. For cities, we have, as far as possible, used the name preferred by the Chinese themselves. Thus we have consistently referred to Guangzhou, not Canton, Shenyang, not Mukden, except when quoting directly from a text or event which uses either of the latter names. For the sake of convenience we have shown in parentheses the province of all place-names but the most famous and common. Dates in the Qing period are given both according to the Western and, in parentheses, traditional Chinese lunar calendar; 'intercalary' is abbreviated to 'int.'. We have attempted rigid consistency in the translation of Chinese titles, as shown in the glossary of titles at the back.

We acknowledge with deep thanks the assistance of the Australian Research Grants Committee which provided a grant to cover two years' full-time work by the second of the authors. Numerous other people have given us encouragement, constructive criticism and help of various kinds, and to all we express our gratitude. In particular we should like to thank Dr Endymion Wilkinson and Dr William Jenner, who made numerous helpful suggestions on the conception and general layout of the chronology, as well as many detailed points regarding individual items. In addition we offer our thanks to Mr Dudley Nott and Mrs Lisa Ho, of Griffith University, who drew the maps, and to Mrs Lisa Ho, Mrs Wendy Smith and Mr Peter Chang for the enormous job of preparing the index.

Colin Mackerras
Robert Chan

INTRODUCTION

This book aims to present a classified and factually detailed chronology of modern China. It begins in 1842, that being the year of the Sino-British Treaty of Nanjing, the first of the unequal treaties. It is of course a matter of debate as to when 'modern' China commences, but it has seemed to us that 1842 is a convenient starting point and one which can be as well defended as any other to represent the beginning of modern China.

The classification of the events is generally self-explanatory. The major political or general incidents, be they military or civilian, or connected with foreign or domestic policy, are placed on the left-hand pages. The events of the right-hand pages are subdivided into six categories: A, ECONOMICS; B, OFFICIAL APPOINTMENTS, DISMISSALS, RESIGNATIONS ETC.; C, CULTURAL AND SOCIAL; D, PUBLICATIONS; E, NATURAL DISASTERS; and F, BIRTHS AND DEATHS. Events on the left-hand pages are not necessarily more important than those on the right and they include many which are there simply because they do not fit comfortably into any of the six categories of the right-hand pages, or because they belong equally well to several. Thus, a trade agreement comes under A, ECONOMICS, but a trade and culture agreement goes on the left-hand page.

Naturally many problems of classification have arisen, simply because many events can be legitimately placed in any of two or more categories. For instance, events connected with missionaries in the nineteenth century could have gone on the left-hand page because of their relation to politics and foreign affairs. However, we have decided to regard them consistently as social or religious events in the belief that this will be more convenient for the user.

'Appointments' have also raised a problem: whose appointments belong here? We have decided to place in this category all appointments by major self-proclaimed governments of clear historical significance. This applies to all periods of Chinese history covered here. For instance, appointments by the Taipings from 1851 to 1864 and those of the CCP from 1931 on are included here. For the Qing period we have included all appointments to the Grand Council, Grand Secretariat and *Zongli yamen* as well

7

Introduction

as regional viceroyships, but not provincial governorships or other appointments unless there is a special reason for so doing. We have not applied any rigid rules for inclusion or otherwise of appointments in the Republic or People's Republic periods, beyond our own decision of which are significant or illustrate an interesting and significant trend.

In general the classification of events becomes more complicated in the later period than in the earlier, partly because the history is itself more complicated. Some points need making. Firstly, associations, their foundation and activities are all placed under C, as being cultural and social entities. Political parties, on the other hand, go in the general section, unless the activity under discussion is primarily economic, social etc. The founding and activities of government organs go under A if they are economic etc.

The numerous demonstrations have also posed a classification problem. We have decided to categorize these according to their nature and their primary aims. Thus a demonstration over foreign policy or imperialism goes in the general left-hand pages; if its primary concern is over labour, then it goes under C as part of the labour movement; if the main point of the entry is police behaviour towards students, then the demonstration is considered part of society and goes under C. Normally the same criteria apply to strikes; if the issues are workers' rights, salaries etc., then they go under C as part of the labour movement; if they are to resist imperialism, then on the general left-hand page.

In the publications section D we have tried as far as possible to confine ourselves to first publication of any work. If a re-edition has been regarded as important enough to list, then we have made clear that it is not an original. In this section all titles are given in *pinyin* and English translation.

In the long run, many of our classifications of events are matters of value judgment which can be defended or attacked quite easily. We have decided, however, not to use this dilemma as a reason for abandoning the idea of classification altogether. We remain convinced that to categorize events simplifies the user's task of locating a particular one, and makes a chronology more generally useful, even if some incidents are of controversial classification.

More difficult than how to categorize the events has been the whole problem of which ones to include. A chronology does not aim to interpret or explain history, but to present accurate dates and information. This does not, however, completely solve the question of bias. The fact is that we are bound by our sources and

Introduction

the first qualification for the inclusion of any date is that it can be documented with reasonable certainty.

To some extent a view of history emerges from a chronology because which events are included and hence considered in some sense significant remains in the last analysis a question of the compilers' judgment. We have done our best to exercise historical objectivity, but on the other hand make no apology if some events are listed which others might consider not important enough to present. It is worth pointing out, also, that since there is no limit to the number of events, some have been included not so much for their own significance as for that of a trend which they represent or symbolize.

One clear policy-decision we have taken on the subject of what to include or exclude is to leave out all events in Taiwan from 1949 on, unless they are of vital relevance to the People's Republic of China (PRC) or concern the death of somebody of interest in the pre-1949 period. Events in Taiwan since 1949 would require a whole chronology by themselves. Already our work is fairly detailed yet only scratches the surface of events in China; to have added this further dimension we felt unnecessary and unbalanced. This decision does not imply a belief on the part of either compiler that Taiwan is anything but part of China.

The Sources; General Works

For the early period our basic sources have been Guo Tingyi's chronology *Zhongguo jindai shishi rizhi (Daily Chronology of Events in Modern Chinese History)* published in Taibei in 1963, and *Zhongguo jindai shishi ji (Chronology of Events in China's Modern History)*, compiled by a committee of the Normal University of Jilin province and published in Shanghai in 1959. Of these two works, Guo Tingyi's is the larger. Going down to the end of the Qing dynasty in 1911, it is a magnificent day-by-day presentation of events in China and it includes those of virtually all categories. A particularly good feature is the listing of events of special significance in the margins and major appointments in the appendices. The Jilin University chronology is also extremely valuable. Although not as detailed as Guo Tingyi's it does list virtually all events of any great importance. Its cutoff point, in accordance with the historical view prevalent in the PRC, is the May Fourth Movement (1919), not the end of the Qing. We have found it very useful to work from perspectives both from Taiwan and the PRC because the assessments of which events are important enough

Introduction

to be included in a chronology, as well as the way incidents are described, are bound to differ in some cases.

A third chronology we have used for the earlier period is *Zhongwai lishi nianbiao (Table of Historical Events in Chinese and Foreign History*, Hong Kong, 1971), by the famous historian Jian Bozan. This is a world chronology, not merely a Chinese, and so takes as its breakoff point a year of profound international significance: 1918, the end of World War I. It differs from the two chronologies noted above in that it does not generally list events by the day, but only by the month. Its great value for our chronology has been twofold. Firstly, it has helped us to assess whether a particular event is important enough to merit inclusion. Naturally it is in this sense a guide only and there are numerous occasions on which we have disagreed with Jian Bozan's judgment. Secondly, Jian Bozan has included a number of cultural and economic events which are not included either by the Jilin University committee or by Guo Tingyi.

We have made reference to several other less vital chronologies in dealing with the early period. One is Bansu's *Zhongshan chushi hou Zhongguo liushi niqn dashi ji (Chronology of China's History in the Sixty Years After the Birth of Sun Yatsen*, Shanghai), Bansu being a pen-name for the well-known historian Li Jiannong. As its name implies, this work begins with the birth of Sun Yatsen in 1866, and continues to 1928. It becomes more and more detailed as it proceeds and its major value lies in the post-Qing era; indeed for the Qing we have found it slightly unreliable. A second one to note is *Qingshi nianbiao (Table of Events in Qing History*, Taibei, 1966), but this work, although useful for cross-checking, cannot compete with Guo Tingyi's or the Jilin University's chronologies either in detail or accuracy.

Among non-Chinese-language sources two have been particularly useful for the Qing period. One is Hosea Ballou Morse's *The International Relations of the Chinese Empire* (Taibei reprint, 1971) in three volumes, the first prefaced October 1910 by the author, the second and third October 1917. This large-scale work not only contains a very brief chronology of its own but also gives many accurate dates based mainly on foreign sources. It thus adds a useful non-Chinese perspective, particularly important for correct foreign titles and other matters involving foreign relations. Of non-Chinese sources the one we have used most constantly, however, is A.W. Hummel, ed., *Eminent Chinese of the Ch'ing Period* (Washington, 1943–44), famous as an outstanding reference work on the Qing dynasty.

Introduction

The period of the Republic (1912–49) is a reasonably well documented one and there are several chronologies in the Chinese language. The largest in scale is *Zhongguo dashi ji (A Chronology of Twentieth-Century China 1904–1949)* published in six volumes by the Center for Chinese Research Materials Association of Research Libraries, Washington, DC, in 1973. This enormous work consists mainly of xerographic reproductions from original issues of the *Dongfang zazhi (Oriental Journal)*, a magazine which included a chronology of events in every issue. The *Oriental Journal* covers dates of every kind, political, cultural, social, economic and military, and is extraordinarily detailed. However, it concentrates mainly on events in areas controlled by the government of the day and for this reason has very little to say about the liberated areas. Moreover, during the Sino-Japanese War (1937–45), its material becomes increasingly scant, and from November 25, 1945 to December 31, 1946 there are no entries at all. It resumes reports from January 1, 1947 to November 24, 1948.

Fortunately in its sixth volume the *Chronology of Twentieth-Century China* has reproduced four other chronologies, the first two for the period 1941–1949, the last two in their entirety. They are Gao Yinzu's *Zhonghua minguo dashi ji (A Chronology of Significant Events of the Republic of China)*, Taibei, 1957; Wu Min and Xiao Feng's *Cong Wusi dao Zhonghua renmin gongheguo de dansheng (From the May Fourth Movement to the Birth of the People's Republic of China)*, Peking, 1951; *Disanci guonei geming zhanzheng dashi yuebiao (A Monthly Chronology of Significant Events of the Third Revolutionary Civil War)*, Peking, 1961; and Yang Bing'an's *Zhongguo renmin jiefang zhanzheng (The Chinese People's War of Liberation)*, Shanghai, 1955. The reason for the additional chronologies is to make up for the discontinuation of the *Dongfang zazhi* during the war.

Another important chronology written from the Nationalist Party (NP) point of view is the *Minguo dashi rizhi (A Day-by-Day Chronology of the Major Events of the Republic)*, compiled by Liu Shaotang and published in two volumes in Taibei in 1973 and 1979. The first volume covers the period 1912 to 1941; the second 1942 to 1971, ignoring the People's Republic as its title implies. This is a highly useful work which appears to seek to copy the magnificent achievements of Guo Tingyi. It is accurate and thorough but nevertheless biased in its manner and type of presentation. For the early period it is not nearly as rich in detail as the *Oriental Magazine*, but for the later it is much more copious. Moreover, it is wider in

11

Introduction

scope, including, for instance, a great deal of information on the dates of origin of newspapers, a subject almost totally absent in the *Oriental Magazine*. A chronology complementary to Liu Shaotang's is Gao Yinzu's *Zhonghua minguo dashi ji*, published by the World Press (*Shijie she*) in Taibei on October 10, 1957. This work extends from 1912 to 1956. It is narrower in range than Liu, but in general the two are fairly similar. Neither reaches the standard for its period that Guo Tingyi does for the Qing. That great scholar almost finished a chronology of the Republican period before he died. This work has now been published, but unfortunately not in time for us to use it for our own chronology.

Two further chronologies viewing events from the NP point of view are *Zhongguo Guomindang bashi nian dashi nianbiao* (*Chronology of the Major Events of the Eighty Years of the Chinese NP*), Taiwan, 1974; and Bansu's already mentioned *Zhongshan chushi hou Zhongguo liushi nian dashi ji*. Both of these chronologies have been partly copied from the *Oriental Journal* and neither can match it in wealth of detail. The first deals with events from 1894 to 1974, but since its focus is on the NP as suggested in its title, it follows that Party to Taiwan from 1949.

Looking at Republican history from the point of view of the Chinese Communist Party (CCP), the main chronology is that by Wu Min and Xiao Feng, mentioned earlier as included, in part, in the *Chronology of Twentieth-Century China*. The emphasis here is on the labour movement, the history of the CCP and activities in the liberated areas. It thus forms an extremely useful complement to Liu Shaotang's and Gao Yinzu's chronologies. The material is generally accurate, detailed and interesting and we have relied on this work heavily for the events concerning the left wing.

Among non-Chinese-language sources, three in English have been of the utmost use for the period of the Republic. They are (*i*) *The China Year Book*, (*ii*) *The Chinese Year Book*, and (*iii*) Howard Boorman and Richard C. Howard, eds., *Biographical Dictionary of Republican China*, published in four volumes by the Columbia University Press, New York and London, 1967–71.

The first two of these are serial publications, the former appearing almost annually from 1912 to 1939, the latter 1935–36 to 1944–45. The former presents the viewpoint of the British, the latter of the Chinese government. With that proviso, both are extremely useful, detailed and reliable, especially for economic matters. Both give the full texts of numerous treaties, agreements, and laws, and are really indispensable mines of information.

Introduction

Boorman's *Biographical Dictionary* provides a kind of counterpart to Hummel's work on the Qing, but is even more detailed and includes almost a full volume of source material. For our publications section we have frequently used Boorman as a guide to which works ought to be included, but the bibliographical volume of his *Dictionary* often lists late, not original, editions, making care necessary in its use for the compilation of a chronology. Because Boorman gives the birth and death dates of the biographees to the day, as far as they can be known, his work has been of great use for our section F, and we have rarely had reason to disagree with his dates.

The period of the PRC is up to now less well endowed with general chronological works than the Republican. On the whole the major sources of collected information cover shorter periods than those of the Qing or Republican eras. The basic source is the regular chronology in the *Xinhua yuebao* (*New China Monthly*) (renamed *Xinhua banyuekan, New China Semimonthly* from the beginning of 1956 to the end of 1960), which began on September 1, 1949. This consists of collected New China News Agency (NCNA) items. For the period to August 15, 1958, it is purely chronological, but thereafter the items are classified. The wealth of detail and accuracy make these reports of supreme value, even though they are all official material. The pre-Cultural Revolution section of this regular chronology section of the periodical has been collected, photographed and republished by the Center for Chinese Research Materials Association of Research Libraries, Washington, DC, under the title *New China Monthly Chronology of National and International Events of Significance* (1972) in three volumes. The first includes issues 1–62, covering events from September 1, 1949 to November 30, 1954, the second issues 63–194, events from December 1, 1954 to December 10, 1960, and finally the third issues 195–259, events from December 11, 1960 to April 30, 1966.

Another useful and comprehensive chronology for the early PRC period is that compiled by the History Department of the Nankai University in Tianjin. It is entitled *Zhonghua renmin gongheguo dashi ji* (*Chronology of Major Events of the PRC*). It is in two volumes, both published in Baoding in 1958, the first covering the period from 1949 to 1952 and the second from 1953 to 1956. This is an extremely comprehensive day-by-day chronology and although it is not classified it does cover events of most main kinds. It is based exclusively on Chinese newspapers and on sources from within the PRC.

Major chronologies in languages other than Chinese are some-

Introduction

what more copious for the PRC than for the earlier Qing and Republic. The most important is that by Peter Cheng, entitled *A Chronology of the People's Republic of China from October 1, 1949*, published in 1972 by Littlefield, Adams and Co., Totowa, New Jersey. This work goes down to the end of 1969. Mainly based on Chinese official reports, it also includes quite a few items relying on foreign news agencies and newspapers. Two other general English-language chronologies also exist for the PRC, albeit for the first period only. The more comprehensive is that in Peter Tang's *Communist China Today* (Washington, 1961), pp. 24–68, which goes down to July 1956. Less detailed, although broader in the period covered, is the official Chinese chronology in the *Peking Review* **38** (1959), pp. 22–5, **39** (1959), pp. 24–6 and **49** (1959), pp. 31–4. This focuses rather heavily on diplomatic events and is much less useful for economics than Tang.

Much of the major non-Chinese-language chronological work for the PRC is to be found in periodicals. Partly because we are still living in the period in question, these have not yet followed the examples of the *Dongfang zazhi* or *Xinhua yuekan* of being collected into a single or several volumes.

The first to mention is *Asian Recorder, A Weekly Digest of Asian Events*, which began publication in New Delhi in 1955. Although it covers the whole of Asia, it devotes a considerable amount of space to China. It contains extracts from the world's press, especially that of India, and this helps date events as well as find those not included in the Chinese sources or newspapers. Since press articles contain not only fact but also perspective, the entries in *Asian Recorder* have helped us to absorb various different points of view on particular events.

Another is the famous journal *The China Quarterly*, which began publication in London in 1960. From its first issue it included a 'Quarterly Chronicle and Documentation'. Initially this was fairly brief in every issue and the amount of material it contained very limited. As time has advanced, however, the information has become more and more detailed and the number of dates increased substantially. Moreover, the 'Quarterly Chronicle and Documentation' is categorized according to 'Internal Developments' and 'Foreign Relations'. The former are themselves subdivided in ways which are not standard in every issue but differ to suit the particular quarter. The events in 'Foreign Relations' indicate both how China stood in the general international situation and its relations with specific countries. We found *The China Quarterly* of immense

Introduction

use in developing our own chronology, especially since it is not purely a list of events but contains a good deal of analysis as well, based both on Chinese and foreign reports.

Asian Recorder and *The China Quarterly* are both regular publications and cover a fairly wide period. Both have continued without interruption since their inception and neither shows any sign of coming to an end.

Several other periodicals are more limited in time-range, though not necessarily in coverage for the periods under consideration. An early and a particularly useful one is *Contemporary China*, published in Hongkong. Successive issues of the journal contain chronologies covering the period from April 1957 to June 1964. The types of events listed are very wide-ranging, even though the chronology is itself not classified. Economic and foreign policy events are especially copious. The events are here based almost entirely on the Chinese press.

Three regular chronologies begun since 1969 are worth mentioning. By far the most useful is the section on China in the annual *Ajia dōkō nempō* (*Yearbook of Trends in Asia*), compiled by the Ajia kensei kenkyū jo (Asian Economic Research Institute) in Tokyo from 1970 on. The chronological section is extraordinarily detailed and, though not without mistakes, accurate and reliable, by far the most so among the three noted in this paragraph. The events are classified into political, economic, diplomatic and Sino-Japanese relations. Most are based on NCNA, but some on non-Chinese sources. Another regular chronology was in *Current Scene, Developments in the People's Republic of China*, a journal of the American consulate in Hongkong. From 1970 it included every month a day-by-day chronicle of events. It was very detailed and carried much interesting statistical material as well as the deaths of prominent people. On the other hand, it tended to focus on not very important diplomatic events, such as the arrival of ambassadors, at the expense of more interesting cultural or economic happenings. Its final issue unfortunately was published in August–September 1978. Beginning in October 1970, the Taibei English-language monthly *Issues and Studies* includes a detailed regular 'chronicle of events', the first covering the month August 16 to September 15. It is based entirely on NCNA reports.

Material for the PRC period is inevitably supplemented and checked through the Chinese and foreign press. It will be obvious to the reader that we have made considerable use of journals such as *Peking Review* and *Renmin ribao* (*People's Daily*), as well as foreign

Introduction

periodicals with China coverage, of which by far the most useful are the Hongkong-based *Far Eastern Economic Review* and *Ta Kung Pao*. One problem which is much more pronounced in the period of the People's Republic than in earlier years, is that the journals themselves often do not date economic and cultural events to the day. For this reason we have frequently listed an event not under the day when it actually happened, which we simply do not know, but under the day when NCNA or a Chinese newspaper reported it. Moreover, in the PRC, important press articles can herald new campaigns or political movements, so that a particular issue of a newspaper like *People's Daily* might itself qualify as an 'event'.

As with the Qing and Republican periods, there are biographical works which are in fact general because of the importance of a large number of leading figures in dating events. Among the most useful have been *Biographic Dictionary of Chinese Communism 1921–1965*, two volumes (Cambridge, Mass., 1971) and the Union Research Institute's *Who's Who in Communist China*, two volumes (revised edition, Hong Kong, 1969–1970).

Specific Topic Chronologies

In addition to the above chronologies, all of which cover events of various types, there are a number of useful chronological works which deal only with a single topic of history, either a particular aspect of a single period, or a single type of event.

Among those of the first classification, two deal with the Taiping uprising (1850–66). The more important is Guo Tingyi's two-volume *Taiping tianguo shishi rizhi* (*Day-by-day Chronology of Historical Events in the Taiping Heavenly Kingdom*), published in Shanghai in 1946. In clarity of presentation, wealth of detail, and accuracy of information this is a model chronology. The other is the English-language chronology of the Taipings on pp. 1573–1611 in the third volume of *The Taiping Rebellion* by Franz Michael and others. Michael's compendium has the great advantage also of containing translations into English of extended documents relating to the Taipings.

Another extended event well covered by chronological works is the war of liberation, as represented by *Yijiusiliu zhi yijiusijiu Guogong neizhan dashi yuebiao* (*A Month-by-Month Chronology of Major Events in the NP-CCP Civil War from 1946 to 1949*), compiled by the New Democracy Publishing House and prefaced March 1949 by the NCNA. Many entries in this work are word for word the same as in Wu Min's and Xiao Feng's chronology noted earlier, but for the period it covers it is more detailed and includes quite a few events of interest omitted in the book by Wu and Xiao.

Of all chronologies for the war of liberation, the most useful is *Disanci guonei geming zhanzheng dashi yuebiao*, noted earlier as included in *A Chronology of Twentieth-Century China 1904–1949*. This work is extremely detailed on CCP affairs and, despite its title, dates virtually every event to the day. It is also highly reliable. Its compilers have quite consciously followed the very copious dating in the notes of volume IV of *Mao Zedong xuanji (Selected Works of Mao Zedong)*, which is the one covering the period in question. We have found no instances where the dates disagree.

A third extended event is the Great Proletarian Cultural Revolution (GPCR) of 1966 to 1969. For this the essential source is Ding Wang, comp., *Zhonggong wenhua da geming ziliao huibian (Compendium of Materials on the Chinese Communist Great Cultural Revolution)*, published in six volumes by the Mingbao Monthly Company in Hongkong, 1969–72. Though not itself a chronology, this work contains so many accurately dated documents that it cannot but serve as an indispensable tool for anybody compiling one. A lesser, but still good, source is the chronology of the Cultural Revolution's first year (November 1965 to November 1966) on pp. 493–504 of *The Great Cultural Revolution in China* compiled by the Asian Research Centre in Hongkong and published in the same city in 1968. This traces the major stages of the movement well, especially from the political point of view.

Of those chronologies which cover only one aspect of history, a particularly important category is that covering the lives of individual great leaders. Among a number of significant and useful examples are Luo Jialun's *Guofu nianpu (Chronology of Sun Yatsen)* in two volumes (Taibei, 1965) and Huang Yuchuan's *Mao Zedong shengping ziliao jianbian yibajiusannian–yijiuliujiunian*, translated in the book itself as *Mao Tse-tung, A Chronology of His Life (1893–1969)*. This second work consists simply of verbatim quotations from sources on Mao's life, dated as accurately as possible. There is an enormous amount of invaluable information in this work, although it must be added that there are some important omissions. Many, but by no means the majority, of the entries are either quotations from or based on *The Selected Works of Mao Zedong*, itself a useful guide to events in the liberated areas because of the attention to chronological detail it contains.

A further classification of works on specific historical aspects

Introduction

is regional. The most useful example is the superb *Hunan jin bainian dashi jishu* (*Narratives of Major Events in Hunan over the Last Hundred Years*), published by the Hunan People's Publishing House in Changsha in 1959. This is not strictly speaking a chronology in that the entries narrate, discuss and judge events as well as chronicle them, but it does place them all in strict chronological order and also covers many events not found elsewhere. From the point of view of the revolution Hunan is a particularly interesting province and it is for revolutionary history that we found this work most useful.

Among other examples of works on regional history one could also add *Tibet 1950–1967*, Union Research Institute, Hong Kong, 1968, dealing with the single, yet unusually sensitive and interesting, area of Tibet. There are numerous documents here, as well as a chronology (in the strictest sense of the term) on pp. 765–825. While it is accurate and detailed, it provides no information outside standard NCNA reports.

Two chronologies of particular aspects of PRC history are Douglas M. Johnson and Hungdah Chiu, *Agreements of the People's Republic of China 1949–1967*, Harvard University Press, Cambridge, Mass., 1968; and Kenneth Lieberthal, *A Research Guide to Central Party and Government Meetings in China 1949–1975*, International Arts and Sciences Press Inc., White Plains, New York, 1976. Both of these are highly useful and the second in particular provides information and dating not found in standard NCNA reports. Both are excellent for cross-checking and ensuring against glaring lacunae.

Turning next to chronologies of specific relevance to one of our six right-hand-page categories, we begin with *Zhongguo meishu nianbiao* (*Table of Events of Chinese Fine Arts*), which deals with cultural matters, publications, archaeological finds etc., from the earliest times to 1911. Although only the last few pages are relevant to our period, the emphasis on culture makes this a very useful complementary chronology for our C subheading. For the same C subcategory a much larger and more precisely dated work is *Zhongguo jin qishi nian lai jiaoyu jishi* (*Records of Education in the Last Seventy Years in China*), published by the National Bureau of Compilation and Translation, and prefaced December 1933. This work is enormously detailed for all matters related to education. It covers the period 1862 to 1933 and deals with regional as well as central education. It cites its source in all cases.

Information for our category D on publications has been drawn largely by looking at the books themselves. One source, however, must be noted for the PRC period. That is the *Quanguo xinshu mu* (*National Catalogue of New Books*), which began publication in August 1951, but was suspended in 1966 during the Cultural Revolution. Fortunately it is among the numerous Chinese periodicals to have resumed publication in 1978. Though not exactly a chronology, it does specify the date of publication of every book to the month. It is extremely comprehensive, but does not always make clear if a particular book is being published or printed for the first time. It thus needs to be used with care.

Much more than publications, natural disasters (category E) find their way into standard general chronologies and yearbooks. A particularly useful supplement for cross-checking the main disaster years of the Qing and Republic is Deng Yunte's *Zhongguo jiuhuang shi* (*A History of Natural Calamities and Their Relief in China*), published in Peking in 1958. Though not a chronology, it is a superb aid for establishing which disasters were really major and which not.

Category F on births and deaths is also covered to some extent in general chronologies, especially deaths, famous people not yet being so when they are born. Apart from the biographical dictionaries already mentioned in the section on general chronologies, the outstanding work is Fujita Masanori's *Gendai Chūgoku jinbutsu hyō* (*Table of People in Modern China*), published by the Daian Company of Tokyo on May 25, 1969. This work tabulates the dates of births and deaths of well-known personages who died between 1919 and 1967 as well as other details such as place of origin, but it is in no sense a biographical dictionary. Its usefulness is greater than most tables of its kind in that it usually gives dates to the day, not merely the year, and also in its reliability, although it is not without mistakes.

The foregoing discussion is in no sense a comprehensive treatment of the sources we have used in the compilation of this chronology. In addition we have consulted numerous documentary works and primary sources. Perhaps just as significant are monographs and analytical works on a considerable variety of topics. In some cases these have helped us to fill in lacunae, but it is more important that they have helped to convey the feel of the period. Chronologies often fail in this respect and hence give no help in grasping the significance of incidents. There are hardly any events in the present chronology which have not been checked against secondary non-chronological sources of one kind or another, not only to double-

Introduction

check the date but to corroborate the significance or at least enable the compilers to judge the significance by placing the period or theme in an overall and general perspective. The monographs, biographies, general histories, articles and other secondary sources consulted are too numerous to list. They cover all years in our period, and a large number of topics. Although it is not the function of a chronology to convey a feeling for any particular period, we have found it necessary to achieve at least some understanding of events in order to date and describe them. It is in this way that the already good and increasing volume of monograph material on modern China is an indispensable aid to the compiler of a chronology.

LIST OF ABBREVIATIONS

APC	Agricultural Producers' Cooperative
CAAC	Civil Aviation Administration of China
CCP	Chinese Communist Party
CCPCC	Chinese Communist Party Central Committee
CEC	Central Executive Committee
CPG	Central People's Government
CPPCC	Chinese People's Political Consultative Conference
CPSU	Communist Party of the Soviet Union
CPSUCC	Central Committee of the Communist Party of the Soviet Union
CSC	Central Supervisory Committee
CSR	Chinese Soviet Republic
DPRK	Democratic People's Republic of Korea
DRVN	Democratic Republic of Vietnam
GAC	Government Administrative Council
GPCR	Great Proletarian Cultural Revolution
NCNA	New China News Agency
NEFA	North-east Frontier Agency
NG	National Government
NLF	National Liberation Front
NP	Nationalist Party
NPC	National People's Congress
NRA	National Revolutionary Army
PLA	People's Liberation Army
PRC	People's Republic of China
PRGSVN	Provisional Revolutionary Government of the Republic of South Vietnam
ROC	Republic of China
UN	United Nations
UNESCO	United Nations Educational, Scientific and Cultural Organization
UNRRA	United Nations Relief and Rehabilitation Administration
USA	United States of America
USSR	Union of Soviet Socialist Republics
WPRA	Workers' and Peasants' Red Army

1842 The Treaty of Nanjing

January 21 *(12/11)*. Yijing, a great-grandson of Qianlong and favourite of Daoguang, moves to Jiaxing (Zhejiang) to lead attacks against the British. Before this, the ships of the British expeditionary force had advanced from Guangzhou to the Zhejiang coast and several Chinese cities had already fallen in 1841.
22 *(12/12)*. Zhong Renjie of Chongyang (Hubei) leads an uprising of several thousand people, occupying the county city and killing officials.
March 3 *(1/22)*. Qing troops retake Chongyang and capture Zhong Renjie, whose rebellion collapses.
10 *(1/29)*. Qing troops under General Yijing launch an unsuccessful counterattack in eastern Zhejiang to retake Ningbo and other cities from the British.
15 *(2/4)*. The British expeditionary force attacks Cixi near Yuyao (Zhejiang). It meets fierce resistance west of the city but carries the day owing to the failure of Yijing's assistant commander Wenwei to send help.
28 *(2/17)*. Popular unrest erupts in Hangzhou, Huzhou, Shaoxing and other places over the British invasion.
April 14 *(3/4)*. British ships at Dinghai (Zhejiang) attacked and many small boats burned.
15 *(3/5)*. A post office is set up in Hongkong.
May 14 *(4/5)*. Dahonga and Yao Ying, two senior officials in Taiwan, execute some British prisoners from the British ships *Nerbudda* and *Ann*.
18 *(4/9)*. The British expeditionary force takes Zhapu (Zhejiang), but withdraws on May 22.
June 13 *(5/5)*. The British expeditionary force enters the mouth of the Yangzi River.
19 *(5/11)*. The British expeditionary force occupies Shanghai and pillages it.
22 *(5/14)*. Sir Henry Pottinger, British plenipotentiary at Guangzhou, joins the British expeditionary force at Shanghai.
July 21 *(6/14)*. The British expeditionary force takes Zhenjiang.
August 4 *(6/28)*. British warships reach Nanjing.
5 *(6/29)*. Pottinger reaches Nanjing.
14–15 *(7/9–10)*. Popular resistance in Jingjiang (Jiangsu) repels British onslaughts on the city.
20 *(7/15)*. Three specially appointed Commissioners, Qiying, Yilibu and Niu Jian, meet Pottinger on HMS *Cornwallis* for negotiations.
29 *(7/24)*. Qiying, Niu Jian, Yilibu and Pottinger sign the Treaty of Nanjing, thus ending the First Sino-British (Opium) War.
September 6 *(8/2)*. The Daoguang Emperor ratifies the Treaty of Nanjing.

Qiying becomes Viceroy of Liangjiang 1842

A ECONOMICS

February 16 *(1/7)*. Sir Henry Pottinger (1789–1856), British plenipotentiary at Guangzhou, declares Dinghai and Hongkong free trade ports.

B OFFICIAL APPOINTMENTS, DISMISSALS, TRANSFERS ETC.

January 19 *(12/9)*. Yang Guozhen becomes Viceroy of Minzhe (Fujian and Zhejiang) in place of Yan Botao.
February 16 *(1/7)*. Yiliang becomes Viceroy of Minzhe in place of Yang Guozhen.
March 18 *(2/7)*. The Qing court orders Lin Zexu into exile in Yili. He had been sent earlier but, owing to flooding in the Yellow River, had been ordered in the autumn of 1841 to assist in conservancy work at Kaifeng.
24 *(2/13)*. The Qing court appoints the imperial clansman Qiying as Tartar General of Guangzhou.
May 7 *(3/27)*. Funiyang'a becomes Viceroy of Shan'gan (Shaanxi and Gansu).
14 *(4/5)*. The court rewards Dahonga and Yao Ying for resistance against British following their claim to have sunk two British ships, the *Nerbudda* and *Ann*.
June 9 *(5/1)*. Yilibu is given the rank of a fourth-grade official and appointed assistant Military Commander at Zhapu.
October 17 *(9/14)*. Qiying replaces Niu Jian as Viceroy of Liangjiang (Jiangsu, Jiangxi and Anhui); Yilibu is appointed Tartar General of Guangzhou; Niu Jian is dismissed from all posts and arrested for his failures against the British.
November 13 *(10/11)*. Yijing and Wenwei are dismissed because of their defeat by the British.
21 *(10/19)*. Yijing and Wenwei are condemned to imprisonment awaiting execution.
December 24 *(11/23)*. Niu Jian is sentenced to prison pending execution.

C CULTURAL AND SOCIAL

November 25 *(10/23)*. Anti-British posters appear at the Minglun Hall in Guangzhou as part of a campaign led by Qian Jiang from Zhejiang to oppose British aggression. An anti-British manifesto is issued December 3.
December. Wang Shaoguang of the Guangdong gentry sets up the Dongping Association School.

1842-3

October 2 *(8/28)*. British warships begin withdrawal down the Yangzi.
6 *(9/3)*. British warships complete their departure from the Yangzi to sea.
17 *(9/14)*. Nian disturbances in Yongcheng (Henan), and on the border between Bozhou and Suzhou (Anhui).
November 6 *(10/4)*. An imperial order is issued that the three provinces Jiangsu, Henan and Anhui should cooperate to put down the Nian rebels.
23 *(10/21)*. Pottinger makes a demand to the Viceroy of Minzhe, Yiliang, for redress for the execution of British prisoners in Taiwan.
December 20 *(11/19)*. Rebellion having broken out among non-Han people in Qinghai, the court orders its suppression.
21 *(11/20)*. The court sends Yiliang to Taiwan to investigate the execution of the British prisoners there.
28 *(11/27)*. Britain ratifies the Treaty of Nanjing.

1843 Treaty of the Bogue

January 20 *(12/20)*. Pottinger and Yilibu meet in Guangzhou to discuss the affair of the execution of British prisoners in Taiwan and customs duty regulations.
February 23 *(1/25)*. Yiliang arrives in Taiwan to investigate the affair of the execution of British prisoners; he has Dahonga arrested for questioning.
March 3 *(2/3)*. An American merchant ship arrives in Wusong intending to proceed to Shanghai for trade, but it is refused permission.
April 5 *(3/6)*. Queen Victoria of England proclaims Hongkong a crown colony and creates Pottinger its Governor.
June 26 *(5/29)*. Qiying and Pottinger exchange ratification of the Treaty of Nanjing. The Hongkong government is formally set up.
30 *(6/3)*. The Qing court orders the Governor of Hunan, Wu Qijun, to send troops into Wugang prefecture (Hunan) to suppress a rebellion led by Zeng Ruzhu (who has killed the prefectural magistrate in order to prevent rice from leaving the region), and to arrest Zeng and other rebels. The rebellion is defeated by the end of July.
August 15 *(7/20)*. The Viceroy of Shan'gan, Funiyang'a, sends in a memorial that the rebellion in Qinghai has been suppressed (see December 20, 1842).
October 8 *(8/15)*. Qiying and Pottinger sign the Treaty of the Bogue (*Humen tiaoyue*) which contains details governing the operation of the Treaty of Nanjing.

1842-3

D PUBLICATIONS

May 4 (*3/24*). Completion of the *Menghua suobu* (*Fragmentary Notes on Dreams and Flowers*) by Yang Moujian, a vital early source book for the Peking theatre.
August 6–September 4 (*7*). Wei Yuan completes his account of the Qing rulers' military operations, *Shengwu ji* (*Records of Imperial Wars*) in fourteen chapters (author's preface dated the first month of autumn, August 6–September 4).

F BIRTHS AND DEATHS

July 9 (*6/2*). Wu Tingfang, Qing Minister to USA (1897–1901; 1907–09), b. in Singapore (d. 1922).

The Treaty Ports begin to open   1843

A ECONOMICS

July 22 (*6/25*). The Sino-British 'Tariff of Duties on the Foreign Trade with China' and 'General Regulations, under which the British Trade is to be conducted at the Five Ports of Canton, Amoy, Fuchow, Ningpo and Shanghai' are proclaimed and come into force.
27 (*7/1*). Guangzhou reopens for trade according to the new regulations.
November 17 (*9/26*). Shanghai opens for trade.

B OFFICIAL APPOINTMENTS, DISMISSALS, TRANSFERS ETC.

April 13 (*3/14*). The officials Dahonga and Yao Ying are dismissed from office and punished for executing British prisoners (see May 14, 1842).
22 (*3/23*). Yijing and Wenwei are both pardoned and given minor official posts.
June 23 (*5/26*). Liu Yunke replaces Yiliang as Viceroy of Minzhe.
October 12 (*8/19*). Qian Jiang is exiled to Xinjiang for his anti-British activities in Guangzhou.
18 (*8/25*). Dahonga and Yao Ying are pardoned by the Qing court.
December 1 (*10/10*). Qiying is ordered to return to his post as Viceroy of Liangjiang.

1843

26 (*9/4*). The British consul in Amoy, Henry Gribble, arrives in Amoy, a few days after which the port opens for trade.

November 8 (*9/17*). The British consul in Shanghai, George Balfour, arrives in the city.

9 (*9/18*). The French Foreign Office instructs its minister to China, Baron Théodose de Lagrené, to seek a treaty with China like the Treaty of Nanjing. De Lagrené leaves for China November 12.

December 19 (*10/28*). The British consul in Ningbo, Robert Thom, arrives in Ningbo.

1843

C CULTURAL AND SOCIAL

June. Having failed for the last time in the state examinations in Guangzhou, Hong Xiuquan, the future Taiping leader, studies the Christian pamphlet *Quanshi liangyan* (*Good Words to Admonish the Age*), causing him to believe himself the second son of God.
July 7 (*6/10*). Hong Xiuquan's preaching in his native Huaxian (Guangdong) leads to the baptism of his first converts, Hong Ren'gan and Feng Yunshan.
August 8 (*7/13*). The Viceroy of Liangguang (Guangdong and Guangxi), Qi Gong, sends in a memorial that every *xiang* in the two provinces should be provided with a Shengping *shexue* (School of the Association of Approaching Peace), to organize militia and provide a place where it could gather. The aim was to strengthen the provinces' defences against the British.
December 1 (*10/10*). Opium smoking is again banned by edict.

D PUBLICATIONS

Jiang Yong's *Lülü xinlun* (*New Discourse on Music*). Wei Yuan publishes his geography of foreign countries, *Haiguo tuzhi* (*Maps and Gazetteer of Maritime Countries*), in fifty chapters (author's preface dated January 1–29, 1843).
January 27 (*12/27*). The revision of *Da Qing yitong zhi* (*Comprehensive Geography of the Qing Empire*) is completed.

E NATURAL DISASTERS

August 2 (*7/7*). The Yellow River bursts its dykes at Zhongmou (Henan).
22 (*7/27*). Flooding occurs in Dongguang (Zhili).
September 1 (*int. 7/8*). The Yongding River in Zhili floods.

F BIRTHS AND DEATHS

March 4 (*2/4*). Yilibu d. aged 72.
September 4 (*int. 7/11*). Wu Dunyuan, known to foreigners as Howqua, d. aged 74.

1844 Treaties of Wangxia and Whampoa

February 24 *(1/7)*. US minister Caleb Cushing arrives in Macao, and three days later writes to Cheng Yucai, the Governor of Guangdong, announcing his intention to proceed shortly to Peking.

March 19 *(2/1)*. Cheng Yucai replies to Cushing preventing him from going to Peking.

May 5 *(3/18)*. The court issues an order that the authorities of Jiangsu, Shandong and Henan should arrest all Nian rebels.

8 *(3/21)*. Liu Yunke, the Viceroy of Minzhe, sends in a memorial announcing that the rebellion of the Heaven and Earth Society (Triads) in Jiayi in Taiwan has been defeated.

Sir John Francis Davis replaces Pottinger as British minister to China and Governor of Hongkong (taking up duties June 17).

18 *(4/2)*. Against the wishes of the people, British troops forcibly lease some land in Guangzhou south of the Pearl River, on which the city lies.

July 3 *(5/18)*. Cushing and Qiying, who had been negotiating since June 21, sign the Treaty of Wangxia (near Macao) giving to the USA all the privileges enjoyed by the British.

August 13 *(6/30)*. The French minister Théodose de Lagrené arrives in Macao.

September 1 *(7/19)*. The six-week-old revolt of Yang Dapeng of Leiyang (Hunan) against overtaxation is suppressed.

17 *(8/6)*. Following a memorial from Qiying, China sets Sanbamen as the border with Macao.

October 24 *(9/13)*. De Lagrené and Qiying sign the Sino-French Treaty of Whampoa on board the French corvette *Archimède*.

November 30 *(10/21)*. Hong Xiuquan returns to Huaxian.

The ban against the Catholic Church relaxed 1844

A Economics

January 1 (*11/12*). Ningbo opens for trade.
24 (*12/5*). The Qing court approves the establishment of the Chongqing ironworks in Yongning (Guangxi).
May 25 (*4/9*). Private silver mines are allowed in Yunnan, Sichuan, Guizhou and Guangxi.
June 30 (*5/15*). The court approves the opening of ironworks in Beiliu (Guangxi).
August 6 (*6/23*). An edict is issued encouraging merchants to run silver mines in Guangxi.

B Official Appointments, Dismissals, Transfers etc.

March 19 (*2/1*). Qiying becomes Viceroy of Liangguang; and Bichang acting Viceroy of Liangjiang.

C Cultural and Social

April 2 (*2/15*). Hong Xiuquan and Feng Yunshan leave Huaxian to begin preaching in Guangzhou and other places in Guangdong and Guangxi.
August 18 (*7/5*). The Board of Civil Appointment (*Libu*) memorializes, asking that honours be conferred on the Guangdong gentry who have contributed to the building of the Shengping Association schools.
25 (*7/12*). Robbery having become a serious problem in Guangdong, Qiying and others are ordered to do their best to arrest offenders.
November 11 (*10/2*). Following a memorial from Qiying, the Qing court approves the relaxation of the ban on Catholicism in the five treaty ports.
December 14 (*11/5*). The Qing court issues an edict relaxing the ban against the Catholic Church.

F Births and Deaths

July 7 (*5/22*). Qing administrator Zhao Ersun b. in Fengtian (d. 1927).
November 4 (*9/24*). Industrialist Sheng Xuanhuai b. in Changzhou (Jiangsu) (d. 1916).

1845 *Foreigners refused permission to enter the walled city of Guangzhou*

China's population for 1845 stands at some 421,340,000 people.

March 18 *(2/11)*. Three Englishmen are beaten on the city walls of Guangzhou. This was the beginning of the conflict over whether foreigners could enter the walled city of Guangzhou. The British demanded this right; the Chinese refused it.

22 *(2/15)*. British troops withdraw from Gulang Island in Amoy (Fujian).

May 7 *(4/2)*. The court orders the arrest of Li Yiyuan, the head of the Qinglian sect in Sichuan, Shaanxi and Gansu.

18 *(4/13)*. The Qing court orders the Governors of Zhili, Shandong and Henan to put down the Nian rebels of Daming (Zhili), one of their strongholds. There were several hundred Nian by this time.

June 13 *(5/9)*. Nian rebels ward off an official army at Juye in Caozhou (Shandong).

July 1 *(5/27)*. Baoxing, the Viceroy of Sichuan, sends in a memorial that Li Yiyuan has been arrested.

August 1 *(6/28)*. The court orders Qiying to arrest members of the Guangzhou Three Harmonies, Sleeping Dragon, and other societies who have been killing officials and resisting Qing rule.

14 *(7/12)*. The court grants permission for Denmark to set up a consulate in Guangdong and to carry on trade.

25 *(7/23)*. The Sino-French Treaty of Whampoa is exchanged in Macao.

October 2 *(9/2)*. A Moslem uprising breaks out in Yongchang (Yunnan); several thousand Moslems are killed.

13 *(9/13)*. The Moslems in Yongchang defeat a Qing army.

November 29 *(11/1)*. The British consul and the Intendant of Shanghai sign an agreement delineating the boundaries of the British Concession of the city.

December 21 *(11/23)*. An edict is issued that Qiying and others should forbid the British to enter the walled city of Guangzhou.

31 *(12/3)*. The Sino-American Treaty of Wangxia is exchanged in Guangzhou.

1845

A ECONOMICS

China's grain reserves for 1845 stand at some 32,300,000 piculs.
January 15 *(12/8)*. Lin Zexu is ordered to go to Kashgar to survey and supervise the opening up of wasteland.
July 8 *(6/4)*. The Qing court approves trade with Belgium.
August 26 *(7/24)*. A lead mine begins operations in Gongcheng (Guangxi).

B OFFICIAL APPOINTMENTS, DISMISSALS, TRANSFERS ETC.

May 18 *(4/13)*. He Changling becomes Viceroy of Yungui (Yunnan and Guizhou).
27 *(4/22)*. Huiji becomes Viceroy of Shan'gan.
October 28 *(9/28)*. As a reward for his merit in opening up land to cultivation in Yili, Lin Zexu is ordered back to Peking to await another appointment.
December 2 *(11/4)*. Buyantai becomes Viceroy of Shan'gan.

C CULTURAL AND SOCIAL

May 30 *(4/25)*. The *jinshi* degree is conferred on the following distinguished scholar-officials: Xiao Jinzhong (the *zhuangyuan* of 1845), Yan Jingming (1817–92), He Qiutao (1824–62), Wenxiang (1818–76), and Wei Yuan (1794–1856).
June 13 *(5/9)*. The court orders the arrest of robbers in the border regions of Shandong and Jiangsu; and especially of those who, in boats plying between Shanghai and Suzhou, carry weapons and traffic in opium.

D PUBLICATIONS

Completion of the first edition of the Peking guidebook *Dumen jilüe* (*Records of Peking*). Luo Zenan writes his *Mengzi jie* (*Explanations of Mencius*).
February 20 *(1/14)*. The *China Mail* begins publication, as a weekly in Hongkong.
August. The *Yixiang kaocheng xubian* (*Continuation of the Imperial Astronomical Instruments*) is completed.

1846 *Anti-British disturbances in Fuzhou and Guangzhou*

January 13 (*12/16*). Qiying issues a proclamation that foreigners may enter the walled city of Guangzhou. This so aroused the people of Guangzhou that a riot broke out on January 15 during which the prefectural offices were damaged and the magistrate fled.

16 (*12/19*). Qiying reverses his earlier ruling and issues a statement that the British may not enter the walled city of Guangzhou.

February 20 (*1/25*). Moslem disturbances again break out in Yongchang (Yunnan).

March 28–29 (*3/2–3*). The wounding of a Chinese by an Englishman leads to anti-British disturbances in Fuzhou (Fujian).

April 4 (*3/9*). Qiying and Davis sign a convention at the Bogue returning Zhoushan Island (Zhejiang), occupied by the British expeditionary force in 1841, to China; and agreeing to postpone the problem of entry to the walled city of Guangzhou.

June–July (*int. 5*). Disturbances among the non-Han people of Qinghai who kill officials and petty local soldiers. The government sends in troops to suppress them.

July 8 (*int. 5/11*). Two Englishmen beat up a Chinese hawker in Guangzhou, sparking a riot during which foreigners open fire, killing three Chinese.

25 (*6/3*). British troops withdraw from Zhoushan Island.

August 4 (*6/13*). The Viceroy of Shan'gan reports that the rebellion in Qinghai has been suppressed.

October 3 (*8/14*). The British Foreign Secretary, Lord Palmerston, instructs Davis to inform the Chinese authorities that the British government has ordered 'a ship of war' to be stationed in Guangzhou for the protection of the British subjects there.

13 (*8/24*). Davis writes to Palmerston informing him that the for-

1845-6

E Natural Disasters

February. An earthquake occurs in Zhanghua, Taiwan, which destroys more than 4200 houses and kills more than 380 people.
August 2 *(6/29)*. Flooding strikes Taoyuan (Jiangsu).

F Births and Deaths

January 8 *(12/1)*. Scholar Lin Botong d. aged 70.
October 22 *(9/23)*. Xu Jingcheng b. (d. 1900).

Further concessions to the Catholic Church 1846

B Official Appointments, Dismissals, Transfers etc.

April 25 *(3/30)*. Lin Zexu replaces Deng Tingzhen as Governor of Shaanxi.
October 12 *(8/23)*. He Changling is dismissed as Viceroy of Yungui because of his failure to quell the Yongchang Moslem rebellion, and replaced by Li Xingyuan. He is demoted to Financial Commissioner of Henan.

C Cultural and Social

February 8 *(1/13)*. An Imperial order is issued lifting all bans against the Catholic Church in every province, and returning churches built under Kangxi. This followed a request by de Lagrené and a memorial from Qiying.
March 18 *(2/21)*. The court issues a further proclamation relaxing the bans on the Catholic Church and ordering the return of churches built under Kangxi, but still prohibiting foreigners from going into the country to propagate religion.
August 5 *(6/14)*. The court orders the Governor of Shuntian Prefecture (Peking), and the Viceroys and Governors of the various provinces to arrest 'heterodox bandits' *(xiefei)*, that is, persons whose religious belief has led them to sedition or disturbing the peace.

D Publications

Liang Tingnan's *Haiguo sishou* (*Four Discourses on the Maritime Countries*) is published.

1846–7

eigners in Guangzhou 'have organized themselves in a species of armed body'.

November 5 (9/17). A rebellion led by Jin Deshun in Zhaowen (Jiangsu) is put down.

1847 The British attack Guangzhou

February 5 (12/20). Qiying sends in a memorial that the British have occupied Kashmir and made certain demands, including trade with Tibet, which have been refused.

11 (12/26). Disturbances break out between Moslem and Han Chinese in Shunning (Yunnan).

March 7 (1/21). The emigration of Chinese labourers in foreign ships begins when the British *Duke of Argyle* leaves Amoy for Havana, Cuba, with over 400.

12 (1/26). Six Englishmen and one American are subjected to volleys of stones in Foshan (Guangdong), resulting in a formal protest from Davis to Qiying on March 27, including a threat that the British government will 'punish' such 'outrages'.

April 3 (3/18). British ships of war make a surprise attack on Guangzhou. On April 1 Davis had ordered military action because of his dissatisfaction with Qiying's response (March 30) to his protest over the Foshan incident.

6 (3/21). Qiying agrees that the British may enter the walled city of Guangzhou after two years and guarantees punishment for any person harming an Englishman; the British warships then withdraw.

July 21 (6/10). Hong Xiuquan leaves Guangzhou for Guangxi.

22 (6/11). The Court of Colonial Affairs refuses a demand from Russia to increase trade with Tarbagatai, Yili and Kashgar.

August 12 (7/2). In Peking, Moslems from Yunnan bring accusations against the Yongchang rebels among their own people, notably Liu Shu (see October 2, 1845). Further similar accusations are brought on August 28.

September 6 (7/27). The Moslem rebellion of the Buruts breaks out in Kashgar with an attack on Yangi Hissar (Yingjishaer) not far south-south-east.

October 16 (9/8). The court orders the Viceroys and Governors of Zhili, Shandong and Henan to look for and arrest Nian rebels.

18 (9/10). A rebellion breaks out in the border areas of Hunan and Guangxi led by Lei Zaihao of the Yao Minority and the Han Chinese Li Hui.

F Births and Deaths

April 15 *(3/20)*. Governor of Shaanxi, Deng Tingzhen, d. aged 70.

1847

A Economics

March 20 *(2/4)*. Trade agreements signed with Norway and Sweden.
December. Reform of the salt monopoly in Hunan.

B Official Appointments, Dismissals, Transfers etc.

February 4 *(12/19)*. Qishan is appointed Viceroy of Sichuan.
April 30 *(3/16)*. Li Xingyuan is appointed Viceroy of Liangjiang; Lin Zexu of Yungui.
June 21 *(5/9)*. Chen Fuen is appointed to the Grand Council.
July 11 *(5/29)*. Zeng Guofan is appointed a sub-chancellor of the Grand Secretariat.
September 26 *(8/18)*. Wenqing becomes acting Viceroy of Shan'gan. Yishan and Buyantai are put in charge of suppressing the Burut rebellion.

C Cultural and Social

March 11–26 *(1/25–2/10)*. Hong Xiuquan and Hong Ren'gan go to Guangzhou, where they meet the American missionary I.J. Roberts.
June 7 *(4/25)*. The following distinguished men receive their *jinshi* degree: Zhang Zhiwan (1811–97), Li Hongzhang (1823–1901), Shen Baozhen (1820–79), Guo Songtao (1818–91), and Ma Xinyi (1821–70).
August 27 *(7/17)* Hong Xiuquan meets Feng Yunshan in Guiping (Guangxi). The God Worshippers Society by this time has some 2000 adherents.
October 26 *(9/18)*. Hong Xiuquan and Feng Yunshan destroy an idol in Xiangzhou (Guangxi), increasing Hong's prestige and resulting in an upsurge in recruitment for the God Worshippers.
November 10 *(10/3)*. In an attempt to revive the system, the court issues an edict that the capital and every province should organize and investigate *baojia*.
December 28 *(11/21)*. Feng Yunshan, earlier arrested, is rescued by the God Worshippers.

1847–8

November 29 (10/22). Government forces attack and defeat Burut troops, relieving the siege of Yangi Hissar. Yishan reports the suppression of the rebellion December 4.
December 3 (10/26). The Lei Zaihao rebellion is put down with Lei's capture.
5–6 (10/28–9). Six Englishmen are killed at Huangzhuqi, near Guangzhou.
12 (11/5). The British minister Davis leads a flotilla to Guangzhou, threatening reprisals unless Qiying takes action over the Huangzhuqi affair.
21 (11/14). Qiying has the four Huangzhuqi murderers executed. The following day Davis returns, satisfied, to Hongkong.

1848 The Court takes action against piracy off China's coast

January 6 (12/1). Strong anti-Moslem activities by Han Chinese erupt in Yongchang (Yunnan), including massacre of Moslems. Lin Zexu sends troops to settle the trouble.
17 (12/12). Feng Yunshan is again arrested.
February 13 (1/9). A Miao rebellion in Hunan over taxation is suppressed.
24 (1/20). Several Sichuanese and Yunnanese secret societies, having formed an alliance, rebel in Dali (Yunnan). They are suppressed March 7.
March 13 (2/9). The British consul in Shanghai, Rutherford Alcock, demands the arrest within two days of ten of the chief culprits who beat up Medhurst and the other missionaries. Later, after the failure of this measure, he orders the ten-gun brig *Childers* to dam the stream of food for the court.
19 (2/15). Alcock negotiates direct with the Viceroy of Liangjiang over the Qingpu incident.
22 (2/18). S.G. Bonham replaces Davis as British minister to China and Governor of Hongkong.
26 (2/22). Hong Xiuquan goes to Guangzhou to petition Qiying for Feng Yunshan's release. (Qiying had left for Peking so Hong returned to Guangxi.)
29 (2/25). Culprits of the Qingpu incident are sentenced to punishment.
May 2 (3/29). Lin Zexu sends in a memorial that disturbances among Han Chinese in Yongchang (Yunnan) have been settled.
14 (4/12). The court orders the Viceroys and Governors of Guangdong,

1847–8

E NATURAL DISASTERS

August. Drought in Henan province; relief work is carried out.

F BIRTHS AND DEATHS

April 23 *(3/9)*. Peking Opera actor Tan Xinpei b. (d. 1917).

Qiying becomes Grand Secretary **1848**

A ECONOMICS

The British Oriental Banking Corporation establishes a branch in Shanghai.
June 4 *(5/4)*. The Court of Colonial Affairs refuses a further Russian request for trade with Yili, Tarbagatai and Kashgar.
July 30 *(7/1)*. A Russian merchant ship calls in at Shanghai and asks for trade, but is refused.
September 17 *(8/20)*. Russians are forbidden to go to Shanghai for trade. (A further ship had arrived September 12.)
November 16 *(10/21)*. The first trial takes place of sea transport of grain from Shanghai to Tianjin.

B OFFICIAL APPOINTMENTS, DISMISSALS, TRANSFERS ETC.

February 3 *(12/29)*. Qiying is recalled to Peking. Xu Guangjin becomes acting Viceroy of Liangguang. Ye Mingchen becomes acting Governor of Guangdong.
July 4 *(6/4)*. Xu Guangjin confirmed as Viceroy of Liangguang, and Ye Mingchen as Governor of Guangdong.
December 4 *(11/9)*. Qishan is again made assistant Grand Secretary, maintaining his post as Viceroy of Sichuan. Qiying becomes Grand Secretary.

C CULTURAL AND SOCIAL

February 14 *(1/10)*. The court orders Qiying to tell the British not to

1848–9

Guangxi, Hunan and Jiangxi to arrest members of the Heaven and Earth and other secret societies.

June 7 (*5/7*). Bonham writes to Xu Guangjin, the Viceroy of Liangjiang, raising the old problem of foreign entry into the walled city of Guangzhou. Xu refuses immediate permission for entry June 20.

9 (*5/9*). The Governor of Guangxi sends in a memorial that the county magistrate of Tianbao (Guangxi) has been killed by bandits. (Banditry was becoming a more serious problem in Guangxi.)

October 1 (*9/5*). A Portuguese ship is sunk by pirates on the open sea between Shanghai and Zhapu (Zhejiang).

November. Hong Xiuquan arrives in Huaxian (Guangdong) to meet Feng Yunshan, by now released from prison.

12 (*10/17*). The court orders the arrest of local bandits and pirates in Zhejiang and Fujian. This order was followed, on November 15, by one demanding strict supervision of shipping on the coast of Jiangsu, Zhejiang, Fujian and Shandong and the arrest of pirates there.

27 (*11/2*). Rutherford Alcock concludes an agreement with the Chinese authorities under which the British Concession in Shanghai is enlarged to 470 acres.

December 30 (*12/5*). Lord Palmerston instructs Bonham not to use arms to force the issue of entry to the walled city of Guangzhou.

1849 *The Governor of Macao is assassinated; the Chinese deny the British access to the walled city of Guangzhou*

February 17 (*1/25*). Xu Guangjin holds an inconclusive interview with Bonham at the Bogue on the subject of entry into the walled city of Guangzhou, among other matters.

25 (*2/3*). A British naval officer in Hongkong, having raped a Chinese woman, is beaten up by the villagers and thrown into the water (but not killed).

March 17 (*2/23*). Because the magistrate of Songjiang (Jiangsu) has

go into private houses without reason, and the French that they may not go into the interior of the country to propagate their religion.

March 8 *(2/4)*. Three British missionaries, including W.H. Medhurst, are beaten up at Qingpu near Shanghai.

April 6 *(3/3)*. Yang Xiuqing claims in Guiping (Guangxi) that the Heavenly Father has descended to earth and is speaking through him. He thus assumes leadership of the God Worshippers in Hong Xiuquan's and Feng Yunshan's absence.

D PUBLICATIONS

Fang Dongshu's verse collection *Kaopan ji* (*Collection from the Seclusion Hut*); Liu Xihai's *Jinshi yuan* (*Metal and Stone Collection*) on the epigraphy of Sichuan; and Xie Chenglie's *Fuxian guan tihua shi* (*Poems Inscribed on Paintings from the Fuxian Hall*) are completed.

September. Xu Jiyu's geography of the world *Yinghuan zhilüe* (*Records of the World*) in ten chapters is completed.

E NATURAL DISASTERS

July 28 *(6/29)*. Serious floods occur in Xinghua and nearby counties in Jiangsu.

August 31 *(8/3)*. A serious typhoon strikes China's coast.

December 3 *(11/8)*. Large-scale earthquakes strike the Zhanghua and Jiayi areas of Taiwan, causing death and destruction.

F BIRTHS AND DEATHS

April 4 *(3/1)*. Historian Xu Song d. aged 67.
September 16 *(8/19)*. Sun Yirang b. (d. 1902).

Unusually serious natural disasters; death of Ruan Yuan   **1849**

A ECONOMICS

March 5 *(2/11)*. The Governor of Macao, João do Amaral, declares it a free port.

8 *(2/14)*. The Guangdong customs moves from Macao to Whampoa, many Chinese merchants moving also.

April. Repairs are carried out on the dykes of the Han River at Xiangyang (Hubei).

1849

placed a strict time limit and allowed no delays on the payment of taxes in a context of particularly bad conditions in the area, violence flares up among the people, who seriously damage the magistrate's offices; more than 100 people are killed or wounded.

April 1 (*3/9*). Xu Guangjin sends Bonham a copy of an Imperial rescript saying that the Emperor, unable to overcome the unanimous opposition of Guangzhou's people, was refusing the British permission to enter the walled city of Guangzhou.

6 (*3/14*). The French consul in Shanghai, L.C.N.M. de Montigny, settles the borders of the French Concession there with the Shanghai authorities.

22 (*3/30*). The Emperor orders Xu Guangjin and others to suppress a secret society uprising in Yangshan, Yingde and other counties of Guangdong. The uprising was suppressed by the end of July.

25 (*4/3*). The Portuguese Governor of Macao, João do Amaral, proclaims that any Chinese with landed property who leaves Macao without 'a previous licence from the Procurador's office' will have his property confiscated.

June 25 (*5/6*). The British Foreign Secretary, Lord Palmerston, orders Bonham to protest over the Chinese decision refusing foreigners permission to enter the walled city of Guangzhou, and over abrogation of the agreement of April 6, 1847.

August 18 (*7/1*). A rebellion in Minxian (Fujian) is suppressed with the arrest and execution of its leaders, Lin Shi and others.

22(*7/5*). The Portuguese Governor of Macao, Amaral, is assassinated because of his anti-Chinese policies.

24 (*7/7*). Bonham sends Xu Guangjin a formal protest over the decision on entry into the walled city of Guangzhou.

27 (*7/10*). Xu Guangjin denies official complicity in Amaral's assassination.

November 20 (*10/6*). An envoy is sent to grant ritual appointment to the new Korean King Cholchong.

27 (*10/3*). A rebellion, led by Li Yuanfa of the Heaven and Earth Society, breaks out in Xinning (Hunan), and rebels occupy the county city, killing officials.

19 (3/27). A memorial from Yili announces the opening up of 102,300 *mu* of new land.

B OFFICIAL APPOINTMENTS, DISMISSALS, TRANSFERS ETC.

April 26 (4/4). Lu Jianying replaces Li Xingyuan as Viceroy of Liangjiang.

May 7 (4/15). Xu Guangjin and Ye Mingchen are rewarded for their services in preventing the British from entering the walled city of Guangzhou, the former being made a hereditary viscount (zi), the latter a hereditary baron (*nan*).

September 10 (7/24). Lin Zexu retires because of illness and Cheng Yucai becomes the Viceroy of Yungui.

October 29 (9/15). Qishan becomes Viceroy of Shan'gan; Xu Zechun of Sichuan.

D PUBLICATIONS

Chen Sen's novel *Pinhua baojian* (*Precious Mirror of Theatrical Life*) on the lives of boy actors (author's preface undated) is completed.

June 11 (*int.* 4/21). Luo Zenan's treatise on Neo-Confucian philosophy *Ximing jiangyi* (*Commentary on the Ximing*) is completed.

September–October. Linqing's illustrated record of 240 incidents in his life *Hongxue yinyuan tuji* (*Pictorial Record of Rare Happenings*) is completed (Pan Shien's preface dated eighth month, September 17–October 15, 1849).

E NATURAL DISASTERS

Earthquakes and floods in Zhili, flooding in Hubei and Zhejiang, drought in Gansu and a plague epidemic in Zhejiang cause some 15,000,000 deaths.

February 8 (1/16). A large fire in Guilin burns down more than 7000 houses.

24 (2/2). Disastrous floods and earthquakes strike northern Taiwan.

June 2 (*int.* 4/12). A large-scale flood strikes Hubei, affecting 30 counties.

F BIRTHS AND DEATHS

August 8 (6/21). Scholar and official Liang Zhangju d. aged 74.
October 30 (9/16). Scholar Ye Changchi b. (d. 1917).
November 23 (10/9). Hong Xiuquan's first son, Tianguifu, b. (d. 1864).

1849-50

1850 *The God Worshippers win significant victories in Guangxi*

China's population reaches an estimated 430,000,000.

January 11 *(11/29)*. Li Yuanfa withdraws from Xinning (Hunan), in the face of attacks from the Hunan official forces. However, his men score a victory over the Qing army on January 16 west of the city.

March 9 *(1/26)*. As Yizhu ascends the throne, the following year is declared the first of the Xianfeng period.

May 1 *(3/20)*. The Governor of Jiangxi, Fei Kaishou, reports disturbances led by Yang Xitang of Luling over land taxation.

30 *(4/19)*. Bonham sends Walter H. Medhurst to Tianjin to deliver there a copy of the formal British letter of protest over China's refusal to allow British entry to the walled city of Guangzhou.

June. The Li Yuanfa rebellion is defeated with Li's arrest in Xinning.

2 *(4/22)*. P.A. da Cunha succeeds Amaral as Governor of Macao.

8 *(4/28)*. The Chinese representatives refuse to accept the British letter handed over by Medhurst, who returns to Shanghai June 11.

July. Groups of the God Worshippers gather in Jintian village, Guiping (Guangxi), to stage a revolt. In Xinyi (Guangdong), a group of several thousand God Worshippers under Ling Shiba fight against Qing forces, trying to join the main force.

4 *(5/25)*. The Emperor issues an edict describing 'the recent proceedings of foreigners at Tianjin' as 'contumacious and insulting in the extreme'.

6 *(5/27)*. Cunha dies of cholera.

August 15 *(7/8)*. The Heaven and Earth Society (also called Three Harmonies Society or Triads) in Guangxi occupies Taiping.

16 *(7/9)*. The Guangxi Triads occupy Ningming.

25 *(7/18)*. The Guangxi Triads occupy Zuozhou.

26 *(7/19)*. Chen Yagui of the Guangxi Triads takes Xiuren and Lipu.

September. Attacks by Qing troops against the God Worshippers in Jintian fail.

1 *(7/25)*. The court issues an edict forbidding Englishmen to live in the walled city of Fuzhou (Fujian).

12 *(8/7)*. The Guangxi Triads occupy Longzhou.

15 *(8/10)*. The Guangxi Triads occupy Qianjiang.

October. The God Worshippers in Luchuan (Guangxi) under Lai

1849-50

December 16 *(11/3)*. The famous scholar and official, Grand Secretary Ruan Yuan d. aged 85.
22 *(11/9)*. The scholar and historian Zhang Mu d. aged 44.

Accession of Xianfeng Emperor 1850

A ECONOMICS

February. The first steamship sails between Shanghai and London.
5 *(12/24)*. Following a Russian request for trade with Yili, Tarbagatai and Kashgar, the Emperor orders Saying'a, the Tartar General of Yili, to look into the matter and see if there are any obstacles.
May 2 *(3/21)*. The Tartar General of Yili, Saying'a, sends in a memorial that Russian trade should be permitted with Yili and Tarbagatai, but not with Kashgar.
August. The Russian Governor-general of Eastern Siberia, N. Muraviev, establishes a base at the mouth of the Amur, and calls it Nikolaievsk.
September 3 *(7/27)*. Lord Palmerston orders Bonham to open Suzhou, Hangzhou and Zhenjiang as trade ports, replacing Fuzhou and Ningbo.

B OFFICIAL APPOINTMENTS, DISMISSALS, TRANSFERS ETC.

February 25 *(1/14)*. The Daoguang Emperor's fourth son Yizhu becomes heir apparent.
28 *(1/17)*. Daoguang's sixth son Yixin is invested as Prince Gong.
March 9 *(1/26)*. Yizhu ascends the throne as Emperor.
June 15 *(5/6)*. Because of the suppression of the Li Yuanfa rebellion, the Viceroy of Huguang (Hunan and Hubei), Yutai, is rewarded with the rank of Grand Tutor to the Heir to the Throne.
July 10 *(6/3)*. The Grand Secretary Pan Shien retires at the age of 80 after a very distinguished official career. Qi Junzao becomes Grand Secretary and Du Shoutian assistant Grand Secretary.
September 30 *(8/25)*. Xiang Rong is appointed provincial Commander-in-Chief of Guangxi to deal with the rebels there.
October 17 *(9/13)*. Lin Zexu is appointed Imperial Commissioner to deal with the God Worshippers.
December 1 *(10/28)*. The Emperor issues a decree dismissing and condemning the Chief Grand Councillor Muzhang'a, and degrading Qiying, because of their pro-British policies and opposition to Lin Zexu. Saishang'a becomes assistant Grand Secretary.

1850-1

Jiu move to Yulin, and several thousand of them defeat the forces of the district magistrate Gu Xiegeng.

1 *(8/26)*. The Guangxi Triads occupy Yongkang.

3 *(8/28)*. Fighting breaks out in Guixian (Guangxi) between Hakkas and the native people, 'Puntis'.

6 *(9/2)*. The French ship *Albert* is robbed in Hongkong and its captain killed.

12 *(9/8)*. Troops are transferred from Hunan, Yunnan and Guizhou to Guangxi because of the disturbances there.

November. Several Triad leaders, including Luo Dagang, join the God Worshippers.

4 *(10/1)*. Qing troops besiege Hong Xiuquan and Feng Yunshan in Huazhou, Pingnan (Guangxi).

December 12 *(11/9)*. Ye Mingchen puts down a disturbance in Yingde (Guangdong), capturing and beheading over 300 people.

25 *(11/22)*. Yang Xiuqing and others break the siege by official forces of Hong Xiuquan in Huazhou, Pingnan. The armies of the two leaders join up and return to Jintian December 28.

28 *(11/25)*. The Guangxi Triads defeat the Yunnan Army in Guohua (Guangxi).

31 *(11/28)*. The Guixian Hakkas, who had been defeated by the 'Puntis', join the God Worshippers at Guiping.

1851 *The Heavenly Kingdom of Great Peace is proclaimed*

January 1 *(11/29)*. The God Worshippers under Hong Xiuquan, Hu Yihuang, Yang Xiuqing and others, win a major victory over the Qing forces in Guiping.

11 *(12/10)*. Hong Xiuquan declares himself the Heavenly King

1850–1

13 *(11/10)*. Yishan becomes Tartar General of Yili.
15 *(11/12)*. Li Xingyuan is appointed Imperial Commissioner, to suppress the God Worshippers.
21 *(11/18)*. Yutai is appointed Viceroy of Minzhe (Fujian and Zhejiang); Cheng Yucai of Huguang; and Wu Wenrong of Yungui.

C Cultural and Social

May 15 *(4/4)*. The Emperor receives a memorial that banditry is presenting a serious problem in virtually all provinces of China proper, in some places under the guise of heterodox religions. The Emperor issues an edict that all provincial governors and viceroys should take steps to arrest and punish offenders.

D Publications

July 25 *(6/17)*. A revised translation of the *New Testament* into Chinese is published.
August 3 *(6/26)*. The *North China Herald* begins publication in Shanghai under the editorship of the Englishman Henry Shearman.

E Natural Disasters

September 12 *(8/7)*. An earthquake strikes Xichang (Sichuan) killing more than 20,600 people and destroying offices and houses.

F Births and Deaths

February 25 *(1/14)*. The Daoguang Emperor d. aged 67.
May 18 *(4/7)*. The well-known scholar Qian Yiji d. aged 67.
September 22 *(8/17)*. The rebel Li Yuanfa is executed in Peking.
November 22 *(10/19)*. Lin Zexu d. aged 65.
December 17 *(11/14)*. Scholar Pi Xirui b. (d. 1908).

Hong Xiuquan becomes Heavenly King 1851

A Economics

February 1 *(1/1)*. The court remits all taxes from before 1850.
May 2 *(4/2)*. The Russian request for trade in Kashgar is refused.
July 20 *(6/22)*. The Tartar General of Yili, Yishan, comes to a trade

45

1851

and sets up the Heavenly Kingdom of Great Peace in Jintian.

13 (*12/12*). The Taipings fight against and defeat some Triad forces and occupy Dahuangjiang in Pingnan (Guangxi). The Guangxi Triad leaders, except for Luo Dagang, had surrendered to the Qing earlier the same month.

February 25 (*1/25*). Xu Guangjin is ordered to negotiate with Bonham the removal of some Englishmen who have been taking up unauthorized residence in the Ryukyu Islands.

March 2 (*1/30*). Two Americans are beaten up in Guangzhou.

10 (*2/8*). The Commander-in-Chief of Guangxi, Xiang Rong, and the Triads force the Taipings to retreat from Dahuangjiang.

19 (*2/17*). The Taipings defeat the forces of the Governor of Guangxi, Zhou Tianjue, and Xiang Rong in Wuxuan (Guangxi). At this time there were some 20,000 men in the Taiping army.

30 (*2/28*). The court orders the arrest of the three 'great kings' (*dawang*), leaders of 'heterodox' rebellious movements: Wu Guangmo of Xiangfu (Henan), Ma Wucheng of Qijiang (Sichuan), and Li Sanwen of Yingde (Guangdong).

April 3 (*3/2*). The Taipings again defeat Qing forces under Xiang Rong and others in Wuxuan.

May 5 (*4/5*). Qing troops break a month-long siege of Yulin (Guangxi) by the Taipings under Ling Shiba and Triad forces.

16 (*4/16*). Some 4000 Taipings enter the territory of Xiangzhou (Guangxi).

June 3 (*5/4*). The Nian stir up trouble in Nanyang and Nanzhao (Henan).

July 2 (*6/4*). Under pressure from Qing troops the Taipings retreat from Xiangshou to Wuxuan (Guangxi).

6 (*6/8*). Montigny, the French consul in Shanghai, demands that the Catholic church in Songjiang (Jiangsu) be handed back to the French. Two days earlier a French warship had arrived in Shanghai.

14 (*6/16*). Following the arrest of eight secret society leaders in Guangdong, some 3000 of their followers go west and join the Taiping army.

22 (*6/24*). The court orders the Governor of Anhui, Jiang Wenqing, to take action against the Nian, who have been very active in Shouzhou.

30 (*7/3*). The Guangdongese and Fujianese merchants of Shanghai post up signs denouncing the concession of territory to the British and to the French for Catholic churches.

August 15 (*7/19*). In Guiping (Guangxi), Hong Xiuquan proclaims the division of the Taiping forces into three armies to be commanded by Xiao Chaogui and Shi Dakai (vanguard), Yang Xiuqing (central) and

1851

agreement with the Russian E. Kovalevsky.

25 (*6/27*). Yishan signs with Kovalevsky the Treaty of Kuldja, under which Russian trade with Yili and Tarbagatai, but not Kashgar, is sanctioned and regulations for its prosecution laid down.

B   Official Appointments, Dismissals, Transfers etc. (Qing or Taiping)

February 5 (*1/5*). Saishang'a is appointed Grand Secretary.
March 23 (*2/21*). In Wuxuan (Guangxi), Hong Xiuquan formally ascends the Taiping throne as Heavenly King.
April 10 (*3/9*). Grand Secretary Saishang'a is appointed Imperial Envoy to deal with military developments.
11 (*3/10*). Saishang'a is appointed Imperial Commissioner; Muyin, Grand Councillor.
June 1 (*5/2*). Zhou Tianjue and Xiang Rong are punished because of the Taipings' entry into Xiangzhou.
16 (*5/17*). The Viceroy of Shan'gan, Qishan, is dismissed because of over-severe treatment of the native and Moslem peoples of Kokonor the previous year.
17 (*5/18*). Yutai becomes Viceroy of Shan'gan; and Ji Zhichang of Minzhe; Yucheng is appointed assistant Grand Secretary.
25 (*5/26*). Peng Yunzhang is appointed Grand Councillor.
October 22 (*int. 8/28*). Shuxing'a becomes Viceroy of Shan'gan.
December 17 (*10/25*). Hong Xiuquan institutes the king (*wang*) system. He appoints Yang Xiuqing as East King, Xiao Chaogui as West King, Feng Yunshan as South King, Wei Changhui as North King, and Shi Dakai as *Yiwang*; and ordains that the East King should exercise authority over the others.

C   Cultural and Social

The Jiangsu diocese of the Catholic church sets up an orphanage and a foundling hospital in Shanghai.
August 17 (*7/21*). The court bans two works, the Taoist book *Xingming guizhi* (*A Pointer to the Meaning of Human Nature and the Life Span*) and the novel *Shuihu zhuan* (*Water Margin*), and orders the destruction of their printing blocks, because of their association with secret societies, and 'religious bandits'.
September 26 (*int. 8/2*). The Viceroy of Liangjiang, Lu Jianying, memorializes asking that the Catholic Church be banned.

1851–2

Feng Yunshan and Wei Changhui (rear). The Taipings prepare for the march.

September 11 (*8/16*). The Taiping army breaks out of a Qing blockade along the Guiping border and moves north-east to Pingnan (Guangxi).

25 (*int. 8/1*). The Taipings take the district city of Yong'an (Guangxi); at this time there were more than 37,000 men and women in the Taipings.

27 (*int. 8/3*). The Guangdong Heaven and Earth Society defeats Qing forces in Xinyi (Guangdong).

October 1 (*int. 8/7*). Hong Xiuquan enters the district city of Yong'an and issues an edict that all captured goods be handed over to the Sacred Treasury of the Heavenly Court.

1852 The Taipings advance to Hubei

March 16 (*1/26*). The Viceroy of Minzhe, Ji Zhichang, sends in a memorial announcing the suppression of a rebellion in Jiayi, Taiwan, led by Hong Ji.

18 (*1/28*). Qing troops under Saishang'a attack Yong'an (Guangxi) with cannon.

21 (*2/1*). A British ship leaves Amoy to transport 475 Chinese workers to San Francisco.

April 5 (*2/16*). The Taipings, having abandoned Yong'an, break through the siege of the city and move north towards Guilin, the provincial capital of Guangxi.

8 (*2/19*). Violence breaks out on the British ship transporting the Chinese workers, and the captain is killed.

18 (*2/29*). The Taiping army arrives outside Guilin, and begins to attack it.

20 (*3/2*). The funeral of the late Daoguang Emperor takes place.

May 2 (*3/14*). The uprising of the Heaven and Earth Society and Abstinence Sect breaks out in Chenzhou (Hunan). They plunder the district city and kill the district magistrate; they break into the local prison and release the prisoners. The rebellion is soon put down.

1851-2

D PUBLICATIONS

Feng Guifen's *Xianfeng yuannian zhongxing biao* (*Table of Meridian Passages of Stars for 1851*) is completed.

E NATURAL DISASTERS

Widespread famine occurs.

F BIRTHS AND DEATHS

May 12 (4/12). Imperial Commissioner Li Xingyuan d. in Wuxuan (Guangxi) aged 53.
June 23 (5/24). Scholar Fang Dongshu d. aged 78.
December 22 (11/1). The Taiping Zhou Xineng is executed for plotting to betray the movement to the Qing.

Deaths of Feng Yunshan and Xiao Chaogui 1852

A ECONOMICS

April 4 (3/15). Yili and Tarbagatai open for external trade.

B OFFICIAL APPOINTMENTS, DISMISSALS, TRANSFERS ETC.

February 29 (1/10). Yucheng becomes a Grand Secretary; Naerjing'e an assistant Grand Secretary.
June 30 (5/13). Shao Can and Linkiu are appointed to the Grand Council.
September 7 (7/24). Ye Mingchen becomes acting Viceroy of Liangguang, replacing Xu Guangjin, who is sent to Hunan to manage military affairs against the Taipings. Yurui is appointed acting Viceroy of Sichuan.
October 14 (9/2). The Viceroy of Huguang, Cheng Yucai, is replaced by Xu Guangjin. Saishang'a is deprived of all ranks and arrested because of his failures against the Taipings.
November 26 (10/15). Wu Wenrong becomes Viceroy of Minzhe; and Luo Raodian of Yungui.
December 27 (11/17). Because of his failure to prevent the fall of Yuezhou, Xu Guangjin is degraded although retained in office.

1852

4 *(3/16)*. When the British ship (see above, March 21) arrives in the Ryukyus, twenty-three of the Chinese workers are arrested. On May 22, fifty-seven more are arrested.

19 *(4/1)*. The Taipings, unable to take Guilin, abandon the siege and march north-east towards Quanzhou (Guangxi).

21 *(4/3)*. Violence breaks out in Yinxian (Zhejiang) against taxation. The people destroy government offices and kill officials.

June 3 *(4/16)*. The Taipings take Quanzhou.

10 *(4/23)*. Local defence corps, organized by Hunanese gentry member Jiang Zhongyuan, defeat the Taipings between Quanzhou and Yongzhou (Hunan). This was their first defeat by a local defence corps.

12 *(4/25)*. The Taipings take Daozhou (Hunan). Thousands of secret society members join them; the provincial Commander-in-Chief Yu Wanqing and the district magistrate Wang Kuiyi flee the city.

July 25 *(6/9)*. Ye Mingchen's forces annihilate the Guangdong God Worshippers of Ling Shiba in Luojing, Gaozhou.

August 17 *(7/3)*. The Taipings take Chenzhou (Hunan); some 20,000 secret society members join them. This was one of several towns in the area the Taipings took in August.

26 *(7/12)*. Xiao Chaogui, Li Kaifang and Lin Fengxiang lead 1000 Taipings towards Changsha, the Hunanese capital.

September 11 *(7/28)*. The Taipings begin to besiege and attack Changsha.

November 12 *(10/1)*. Uprising of the Nian leader Zhang Luoxing begins in Bozhou (Anhui).

21 *(10/10)*. Two Englishmen are beaten up and wounded in Amoy because of the kidnap of the 475 Chinese workers.

24 *(10/13)*. British navy men go ashore in Amoy and shoot at Chinese, killing four and wounding five.

30 *(10/19)*. After several unsuccessful attacks on Changsha, the Taipings raise the siege of the city and cross the Xiang River under cover of rain.

December 3 *(10/22)*. The Taipings take Yiyang (Hunan), south of the Dongting Lake. They take several thousand boats to cross the lake towards Hubei.

13 *(11/3)*. The Taipings take Yuezhou, where they seize a great deal of ammunition.

23 *(11/13)*. The Taipings take Hanyang.

29 *(11/19)*. The Taipings take Hankou.

1852

C Cultural and Social

February 29 *(1/10)*. Hong Xiuquan orders strict investigation of those in the Taiping army who have broken the Seventh Heavenly Commandment (against adultery and lewdness); he orders that they be beheaded and their heads displayed to the crowd.

March 1 *(1/11)*. The court issues an edict against the wasteful or improper performance of dramas in Peking, such as including bad content, putting them on at night or inviting women.

April. Hong Xiuquan's cousin Hong Ren'gan visits Hongkong, where he meets the Swedish missionary Theodore Hamberg, who later wrote an account of the Taipings based on the conversation.

June 12 *(4/25)*. Pan Zuyin (1830–90) and Li Hongzao (1820–97) receive their *jinshi* degree.

September 13 *(7/30)*. Hong Xiuquan orders all Taipings to hand over all treasure to the Sacred Treasury of the Heavenly Court, forbidding the private hiding of gold and silver.

D Publications

Wei Yuan expands his *Haiguo tuzhi* (*Maps and Gazetteer of Maritime Countries*) to 100 chapters (author's preface dated 1852, no month given). Publication of the following Taiping works: *Banxing zhaoshu* (*Proclamations by Imperial Sanction*); *Sanzijing* (*The Trimetrical Classic*); *Taiping zhaoshu* (*The Taiping Imperial Declaration*); *Taiping lizhi* (*The Taiping Ceremonial Regulations*); *Taiping tiaogui* (*Taiping Rules and Regulations*); *Tianfu xiafan zhaoshu* (*The Book of Declarations of the Divine Will made During the Heavenly Father's Descent to Earth*); *Tianfu huangshangdi yanti huangzhao* (*Proclamation of Entitlement by the Heavenly Father, God*); *Tianming zhaozhi shu* (*The Book of Heavenly Decrees and Proclamations*); *Tiantiao shu* (*The Book of Heavenly Commandments*); and *Youxue shi* (*Odes for Youth*).

E Natural Disasters

Widespread famine continues.

May 26–June 10 *(4/8–4/23)*. Disastrous earthquakes strike Zhongwei (Gansu), destroying more than 20,000 houses, killing some 300 people and wounding over 400.

F Births and Deaths

May 8 *(3/20)*. Following wounds received defending Guilin from the

51

1853   The Taipings take Nanjing and declare it their capital

January 8 *(11/29)*. The Qing court sends Xiang Rong to the aid of Wuchang and orders Zeng Guofan to help in organizing local troops in Hunan.

12 *(12/4)*. The Taipings under Yang Xiuqing and others take Wuchang, the capital of Hubei.

Yang Xiuqing orders his followers to kill Qing officials but not to harm the common people.

29 *(12/21)*. Zeng Guofan arrives in Changsha to deal with the Taipings.

31 *(12/23)*. The American commissioner Humphrey Marshall arrives in Guangzhou demanding an interview with Ye Mingchen, but is refused. At this time Chinese policy made interviews with foreign representatives very difficult.

February 24 *(1/17)*. The Taipings under Shi Dakai take Anqing, the capital of Anhui.

March 4 *(1/25)*. The Taipings under Shi Dakai take Wuhu (Anhui).

15 *(2/6)*. On instructions from the Governor of Jiangsu, Wu Jianzhang, Intendant of Suzhou, Songjiang and Taicang, asks the British and French consuls in Shanghai for warships to defend Nanjing against the Taipings.

19 *(2/10)*. The Taipings take Nanjing, the capital of Jiangsu.

29 *(2/20)*. Hong Xiuquan enters Nanjing; he formally declares it the Taiping capital the same day and renames it Tianjing (the Heavenly Capital).

31 *(2/22)*. The Taipings under Luo Dagang take Zhenjiang. Xiang Rong's troops camp on the outskirts of Nanjing: the Jiangnan Command.

April 1 *(2/23)*. The Taipings under Li Kaifang and Lin Fengxiang take Yangzhou.

7 *(2/29)*. The British minister, S.G. Bonham, informs Wu Jianzhang that Britain will be responsible only for protecting the lives and property

Taipings on April 19, the assistant military commander of Guangzhou, Wulantai, d.

June 10 (*4/23*). Taiping leader Feng Yunshan d. in battle aged 30.

July 25 (*6/9*). Assistant Grand Secretary Du Shoutian d. aged 65. Rebel Ling Shiba killed.

Early October (*about 8/20*). Xiao Chaogui, seriously wounded during his attack on Changsha on September 11, d.

November 8 (*9/27*). Lin Shu, poet, painter and translator, b. (d. 1924).

Beginning of Lijin 1853

A Economics

March 10 (*2/1*). Bonham writes to the British Foreign Secretary, the Earl of Malmesbury, suggesting that to help protect Shanghai and assist the Qing would secure commercial profit.

April. The Qing court orders all provinces to try to locate mineral ores and find ways to mine them.

May. The Qing orders the opening of silver mines in Chengde and Pingquan (Zhili).

June 10 (*5/4*). The beginnings of the minting of a silver currency as a means of collecting revenue by the government to suppress the Taipings.

July. Lei Yixian, the Vice-President of the Board of Punishment, begins collecting around Yangzhou a new internal customs tax (*lijin*) to finance the operations against the Taipings.

3 (*5/27*). The first strings of ten large cash (*daqian*) are minted.

August 22 (*7/18*). The Qing government orders Yiliang to set up a customs house in Shanghai.

September 9 (*8/7*). The British and US consuls in Shanghai begin the collection of promissory notes instead of customs duties in cash.

14 (*8/12*). Following the request of Jiang Zhongyuan, the court issues an edict ordering Hunan and Hubei to build warships.

17 (*8/15*). The British and US consuls in Shanghai begin to collect customs duty from British and US merchants.

30 (*8/28*). The Qing court orders the minting of fifty strings of large cash.

October 28 (*9/26*). Shanghai maritime customs temporarily put a revenue cruiser on the Huangpu River. The imperial customs house in the foreign settlement had been demolished when the walled city had fallen. The American government forbids the US consul in Shanghai to levy customs duty in place of the Chinese authorities.

1853

of the British but will not send troops against the Taipings.

8 *(3/1)*. The British and Americans in Shanghai separately decide to set up volunteer corps to defend the foreign settlements.

12 *(3/5)*. A meeting of foreign consuls in Shanghai decides on a joint foreign volunteer corps to defend the foreign settlements.

14 *(3/7)*. Xiang Rong's Jiangnan Command forces begin to attack Nanjing.

16 *(3/9)*. Zhou Tianjue defeats the Nian near Shouzhou and captures the Nian leader, Lu Xialing.

The forces of Imperial Commissioner Qishan and others arrive outside Yangzhou: the Jiangbei Command.

22 *(3/15)*. Bonham, Captain E.G. Fishbourne and their interpreter T. Meadows leave Shanghai on HMS *Hermes* for Nanjing on a fact-finding and negotiating mission.

27 *(3/20)*. Bonham's party arrives in Nanjing and makes Britain's neutral stand towards the Taiping uprising clear.

30 *(3/23)*. Yang Xiuqing writes to Bonham explaining the politics and religion of the Taipings, and allowing the British to travel freely in Taiping territory and carry on trade.

May 5 *(3/28)*. Bonham's party arrives back in Shanghai.

8 *(4/1)*. The Taipings under Li Kaifang and Lin Fengxiang leave Yangzhou on their Northern Expedition.

14 *(4/7)*. The Double Sword Society (Triads) in southern Fujian under Huang Demei take Haideng.

16 *(4/9)*. The Taipings on their Northern Expedition take Chuzhou (Anhui).

18 *(4/11)*. The Triads under Huang Demei take Amoy (Fujian).

19 *(4/12)*. On Yang Xiuqing's orders, Hu Yihuang and Lai Hanying begin their Western Expedition along the Yangzi.

28 *(4/21)*. The Taiping Northern Expedition takes Fengyang (Anhui).

June 10 *(5/4)*. The Taiping Western Expedition reaches and occupies Anqing; the Northern Expedition takes Bozhou (Anhui).

18 *(5/12)*. The Manchu Grand Secretary Shengbao leaves the Yangzhou area for Henan to fight the Taipings there.

22 *(5/16)*. Jiang Zhongyuan reaches Nanchang to defend it against the Taipings.

24 *(5/18)*. The Taiping Western Expedition besieges and attacks Nanchang, capital of Jiangxi.

27 *(5/21)*. The Taiping Northern Expedition begins the crossing of the Yellow River and marches north.

July 28 *(6/23)*. The Taipings under Lai Hanying attack Nanchang but are beaten back by Jiang Zhongyuan's troops.

1853

November 27 *(10/27)*. The court orders that the land tax be levied ahead of time in the three provinces of Shanxi, Shaanxi and Sichuan.
December. The court orders the minting of strings of 1000, 500, 100, 10 and 5 large cash.
30 *(12/1)*. To organize water forces, Zeng Guofan sets up a factory in Xiangtan (Hunan) to build warships.

B Official Appointments, Dismissals, Transfers etc.

February 1 *(12/24)*. Ye Mingchen is confirmed as Viceroy of Liangguang.
3 *(12/26)*. Xiang Rong is appointed Imperial Commissioner to deal with the military situation. Xu Guangjin is arrested for failure to halt the advance of the Taipings. Zhang Liangji is appointed acting Viceroy of Huguang.
March 26 *(2/17)*. Yiliang becomes Viceroy of Liangjiang.
September 9 *(8/7)*. Wu Wenrong is appointed Viceroy of Huguang; Huichang of Minzhe; and Yurui of Sichuan.
October 6 *(9/4)*. Guiliang replaces Naerjing'e as Viceroy of Zhili.
21 *(9/19)*. Jiang Zhongyuan becomes Governor of Anhui.
November 7 *(10/7)*. The Qing court appoints Prince Gong (Yixin), and Ruilin as Grand Councillors.

C Cultural and Social

January 18 *(12/10)*. Hong Xiuquan sets up an office in Wuchang to accept tribute; Yang Xiuqing orders the establishment of separate women's quarters in Wuchang.
March 22 *(2/13)*. Yang Xiuqing orders that separate quarters be set up for men and women in Nanjing; and declares that the people of Nanjing must accept Taiping political authority and religious beliefs.
June 1 *(4/25)*. The distinguished official Ding Baozhen (1820–86) obtains his *jinshi* degree.
November 23 *(10/23)*. Some opium addicts are executed in Nanjing.

D Publications

Publication of the following official Taiping works: *Bian yaoxue wei zuili lun* (*Treatises on the Denunciations of the Demons' Den as the Criminals' Region*); *Jian tianjing yu Jinling lun* (*Treatises on Establishing the Heavenly Capital in Jinling*); *Jiuyizhao shengshu* (*Old Testament*); *Taiping jiushi ge* (*Taiping Songs on World Salvation*); *Tianchao tianmou zhidu* (*The Land*

1853

August 28 *(7/24)*. Detachments of the Hunan Army are defeated at Nanchang by the Taipings under Lai Hanying and others.
September 5 *(8/3)*. A Triad coalition led by Zhou Lichun of the Small Sword Society (Heaven and Earth Society) occupies Jiading (Jiangsu).
7 *(8/5)*. The Small Sword Society led by Liu Lichuan occupies the walled city of Shanghai.
16 *(8/14)*. The consuls of all countries in Shanghai declare their neutrality. Zeng Guofan leaves Changsha for Hengzhou to organize water forces.
24 *(8/22)*. The Taiping Western Expedition raises its siege of Nanchang and moves north.
25 *(8/23)*. Some 6000 Taiping troops under Shi Dakai arrive at Anqing.
29 *(8/27)*. The Taiping Northern Expedition enters Zhili. The Western Expedition takes Jiujiang (Jiangxi). Zeng Guofan arrives at Hengzhou.
October 15 *(9/13)*. The Taiping Western Expedition under Shi Zhenxiang defeats Jiang Zhongyuan's Hunan Army forces in Tianjiazhen (Hubei).
20 *(9/18)*. The Taiping Western Expedition under Shi Zhenxiang takes Hankou and Hanyang. This was the second time the Taipings had seized the cities.
30 *(9/28)*. The Taiping Northern Expedition attacks Tianjin.
November 6 *(10/6)*. The Taipings abandon Hankou and Hanyang and camp in Huangzhou to await reinforcements.
11 *(10/11)*. The Triads under Huang Demei withdraw from Amoy.
14 *(10/14)*. The Ryukyus send back to China 175 of the Chinese labourers who had left Amoy on a British ship on March 21, 1852. Many had died through sickness or suicide. See also April 8 and May 4, 1852.
December 6 *(11/6)*. The French representative A. de Bourboulon arrives in Nanjing, mainly to find out if stories of Taiping persecution of Catholics in Nanjing were true.
10 *(11/10)*. De Bourboulon sees Qin Rigang in Nanjing, who denies the stories of persecution of Catholics.
14 *(11/14)*. De Bourboulon leaves Nanjing for Shanghai.
23 *(11/23)*. The Taiping Northern Expedition defeats Imperial Commissioner Shengbao's Qing troops at Tianjin.
24 *(11/24)*. Yang Xiuqing publicly reprimands Hong Xiuquan.
26 *(11/26)*. The Taipings abandon Yangzhou, Qing troops of the Jiangbei Command under Imperial Commissioner Qishan reoccupying it on December 28.

1853

System of the Heavenly Kingdom); *Xinyizhao shengshu* (*New Testament*); and *Zhaoshu gaixi banxing lun* (*Treatises on Affixing the Imperial Seal on Proclamations and Books for Publication*).

August 1 (*6/27*). The Chinese-English language monthly *Xiaer guanzhen* (*Chinese Serial*) begins publication in Hongkong.

E NATURAL DISASTERS

Serious drought afflicts Anhui.

July 5 (*5/29*). The Yellow River overflows its banks. This was part of the process which eventually resulted in a change in the river's course. (See 1855).

26 (*6/21*). Serious floods occur in Taizhou (Zhejiang).

F BIRTHS AND DEATHS

March 19 (*2/10*). The Viceroy of Liangjiang, Lu Jianying, is killed on the Taiping occupation of Nanjing, aged 61.

July 1 (*5/25*). Zhang Jian, writer, industrialist and social reformer, b. (d. 1926).

October 16 (*9/14*). Mathematician Luo Shilin d. aged 69.

17 (*9/15*). Zhou Tianjue d. aged 81.

1854 *The Taiping Western Expedition ends in failure at the Battle of Tianjiazhen*

January 14 *(12/16)*. The Taipings under Hu Yihuang take Luzhou (Anhui).

February 5 *(1/8)*. The Taiping Northern Expedition under Li Kaifang, pressed at Tianjin by Qing troops under Senggelinqin and Shengbao, begins to retreat southward.

13 *(1/16)*. The British Foreign Secretary, the Earl of Clarendon, orders the new British minister to China and Governor of Hongkong, Sir John Bowring, to arrange for revisions in the Sino-British Treaty, the opening of all China, a resident ambassador in Peking and other matters.

16 *(1/19)*. The Western Expedition under Shi Zhenxiang takes Hankou and Hanyang, the third occupation of the cities by the Taipings, and besieges Wuchang.

23 *(1/26)*. Zeng Guofan forms ten camps of water forces in Xiangtan (Hunan), led by Zhu Ruhang, Peng Yulin and others.

25 *(1/28)*. Zeng Guofan's Hunan Army of some 17,000 men marches from Hengzhou to begin its offensive against the Taipings.

27 *(2/1)*. The Taiping Western Expedition under Shi Zhenxiang enters Hunan and takes Yuezhou.

March 9 *(2/11)*. The Taiping Northern Expedition retreats to Fucheng (Zhili).

21 *(2/23)*. The Taipings withdraw from Yuezhor which Zeng Guofan's forces reoccupy March 23.

April 4 *(3/7)*. The Battle of Muddy Flat, in which about 400 British and US troops, including the volunteer corps, drive Qing forces out of the concessions of Shanghai.

24 *(3/27)*. The Taiping Western Expedition takes Xiangtan (Hunan).

28 *(4/2)*. Zeng Guofan is defeated by the Taipings north of Changsha.

May 1 *(4/5)*. The Hunan Army under Taqibu and others inflicts its first decisive defeat on the Taipings and recovers Xiangtan. The Taipings retreat into Jiangxi under Lin Shaozhang.

4 *(4/8)*. Shi Zhenxiang and other Taipings retire to Yuezhou.

5 *(4/9)*. A Taiping army, sent north to reinforce the Northern Expedition, is defeated and retreats from Shandong.

21 *(4/25)*. The Governor-general of Eastern Siberia, Nikolai Muraviev, leads some 800 Russian troops in an attack on Heilongjiang.

27 *(5/1)*. An American delegation from Shanghai, led by Robert McLane, US commissioner to China, arrives at Nanjing, returning to Shanghai June 2.

30 *(5/4)*. The Taiping Northern Expedition under Li Kaifang occupies Gaotang (Shandong).

Qishan dies 1854

A ECONOMICS

January 20 (*12/2*). The US consul in Shanghai announces to US merchants that Shanghai is a free port.
February 9 (*1/12*). The Intendant of Suzhou, Songjiang and Taicong, Wu Jianzhang, sets up a provisional customs office in the concessions of Shanghai; the power of the Chinese authorities to collect duties is again acknowledged by foreign powers.
March 23 (*2/25*). Large cash is minted in strings of 100, 500 and 1000.
April. The court orders that the *lijin* tax be promoted.
May 9 (*4/13*). Britain, France and the US protest to China over the inland customs set up near Shanghai.
June 29 (*6/5*). Wu Jianzhang and the consuls of Britain, France and the USA in Shanghai reach agreement on the taxing of foreign trade. Wu would appoint and pay three foreign inspectors to take charge of the Shanghai customs house.
July 11 (*6/17*). The Municipal Council of the Shanghai concessions promulgates land regulations.
12 (*6/18*). The customs house set up under the agreement of June 29 begins operations.
21 (*6/27*). The Qing begins to mint aluminium coins.
August 12 (*7/19*). The Qing suspends the minting of large cash in strings of 1000, 500, 400, 300 or 200, and orders strict control over private minting.

B OFFICIAL APPOINTMENTS, DISMISSALS, TRANSFERS ETC. (QING OR TAIPING)

January 24 (*12/26*). Du Han is appointed to the Grand Council.
February 16 (*1/19*). Wang Yide becomes Viceroy of Minzhe.
March 10 (*2/12*). Taiyong becomes Viceroy of Huguang.
July 10 (*6/16*). Taiyong is dismissed and replaced as Viceroy of Huguang by Yang Pei in an acting capacity.
11 (*6/17*). Wu Jianzhang is dismissed and arrested for entering into partnership with an American firm which sold goods to the Taipings.
September 2 (*int. 7/10*). Because of Qishan's death, the court appoints Tuoming'a Imperial Commissioner and puts him in charge of military affairs in Yangzhou, headquarters of the Jiangbei Command.
October 26 (*9/5*). Yang Pei is confirmed as Viceroy of Huguang.
November 11 (*9/21*). Huang Zonghan replaces Yurui as Viceroy of Sichuan.

1854

June 14 (*5/19*). McLane writes to his home government that the Taipings cannot rule, and advocating that treaty rights be seized from the Qing court.

17 (*5/22*). The Guangdong Heaven and Earth Society (Red Turbans, Triads) under He Lu occupy Dongguan. This is the beginning of the Red Turbans revolt.

21 (*5/26*). In an interview with Yiliang, the Viceroy of Liangjiang McLane demands treaty rights in exchange for help against the Taipings.

26 (*6/2*). The Taipings take Wuchang for the second time.

July 5 (*6/11*). The Heaven and Earth Society (Triads) led by Chen Kai occupies Foshan (Guangdong).

11 (*6/17*). The Municipal Council of the Shanghai concessions set up.

20 (*6/26*). The Red Turbans (Triads) under the actor Li Wenmao besiege Guangzhou.

25 (*7/1*). The water forces of the Hunan Army under Zhu Ruhang inflict a decisive defeat on the Taipings at Yuezhou (Hunan), recapturing the city.

August 5 (*7/12*). The Guangdong Triads take Zhaoqing.

October 9 (*8/18*). The Guangxi Heaven and Earth Society under Hu Youlu and others occupies Guanyang and proclaims the Heavenly Kingdom of Ascending Peace.

14 (*8/23*). The Hunan Army retakes Wuchang; the Jingzhou Army retakes Hanyang.

15 (*8/24*). British, French and US envoys, including Bowring and McLane, arrive in Dagu near Tianjin to discuss treaty revision.

November 3 (*9/13*). Bowring and McLane hold talks at Dagu with Chonglun on their demands for treaty revision. These are finally rejected by the court on November 5 and Bowring and McLane leave Dagu for the south on November 10.

24 (*10/5*). The Hunan Army under Luo Zenan inflicts a serious defeat on the Taipings under Qin Rigang at Tianjiazhen (Hubei).

26 (*10/7*). The Nian leader Li Zhaoshou surrenders to the Qing in Huoshan (Anhui).

28 (*10/9*). The Taipings under Luo Dagang take Raozhou (Jiangxi).

December 2 (*10/13*). The Taiping defences at Tianjiazhen collapse, concluding the Battle of Tianjiazhen. Both sides had regarded this battle very seriously and thrown much into it. The Qing victory marked the effective end of the Taiping Western Expedition. The next day most of the defeated Taipings retreat into Jiangxi, some to Huangmei.

7 (*10/18*). Ye Mingchen writes to Bowring requesting help from British ships of war to quell the Red Turbans rebellion in Guangdong.

1854

C CULTURAL AND SOCIAL

Destruction of the Liuli Pagoda in Nanjing.
January 13 (*12/15*). Examinations are held by the Taipings in Nanjing for the selection of officials.
May 13 (*4/17*). The Taipings call for the support and service of medical men, promising them high positions and rewards.
September. The Taipings hold provincial examinations in Wuchang to select officials.
19 (*int. 7/27*). Women are allowed to leave the city of Nanjing because of the food shortage there. Rations to the women's quarters are stopped.

D PUBLICATIONS

Publication of the following Taiping works: *Tianqing daoli shu* (*The Book on the Principles of the Heavenly Nature*); *Tianli yaolun* (*Important Observations Regarding Heavenly Principles*); *Yuzhi qianzizhao* (*The Imperially Composed Thousand Word Edict*), plus calendars.

F BIRTHS AND DEATHS

January 8 (*12/10*). Scholar Yan Fu b. (d. 1921).
14 (*12/16*). Jiang Zhongyuan commits suicide after defeat by the Taipings, aged 41.
15 (*12/17*). Scholar and geographer Zou Hanxun d. aged 48.
February 12 (*1/15*). The Viceroy of Huguang Wu Wenrong, commits suicide after defeat by the Taipings.
May 16 (*4/20*). The famous official Pan Shien, who had been a Grand Councillor from 1834 to 1849, d. aged 84.
August 9 (*7/6*). Zhu Ruhang d. in battle against the Taipings.
11 (*7/18*). The Taiping minister Zeng Tianyang d. in battle aged about 60.
26 (*int. 7/3*). Imperial Commissioner Qishan d.

1854–5

Bowring refuses.

23 *(11/4)*. Following their defeat of the Taipings under Qin Rigang (December 20), the Hunan Army under Taqibu and Luo Zenan takes Huangmei.

1855 The Taiping Northern Expedition is defeated

January 17 *(11/29)*. Chen Kai's forces of the Heaven and Earth Society retreat from Foshan. Bowring orders Englishmen in China to maintain strict neutrality over the civil war.

31 *(12/14)*. Guangdong Qing forces defeat Li Wenmao's Triads and force them to abandon the siege of Guangzhou.

February 11 *(12/25)*. On the Yangzi River near Jiujiang (Jiangxi), the Taipings under Shi Dakai and Luo Dagang launch a surprise attack on Zeng Guofan's Hunan Army water forces and defeat them.

12 *(12/26)*. The court issues a proclamation that Russian boats be allowed to go home from Heilongjiang under escort and not allowed to return.

16 *(12/30)*. The Taipings under Qin Rigang, Wei Jun and Chen Yucheng inflict a serious defeat on the troops of the Viceroy of Huguang, Yang Pei, in Guangji (Hubei).

17 *(1/1)*. French troops and those of the Governor of Jiangsu, Jierhang'a, retake the walled city of Shanghai from the Small Sword Society, executing many of its leaders.

23 *(1/7)*. The Taipings under Qin Rigang and Chen Yucheng take Hanyang and Hankou for the fourth time.

April 3 *(2/17)*. The Taipings under Qin Rigang, Wei Jun and Chen Yucheng take Wuchang for the third time.

May 21 *(4/6)*. Guangdong Qing troops take Zhaoqing from the Triads Chen Kai and Li Wenmao, who move west towards Guangxi. Hu Youlu and Zhu Hongying of the Heavenly Kingdom of Ascending Peace abandon Guanyang (Guangxi) and move into Hunan.

31 *(4/16)*. In Renping (Shandong), Senggelinqin captures the Taiping Li Kaifang, leader of the Northern Expedition, which is thus effectively defeated.

June 5 *(4/21)*. Responding to Shi Dakai's call, forces of the Guangdong Heaven and Earth Society enter Hunan.

July. In Bozhou (Anhui), Zhang Luoxing becomes the chief leader of the Nian rebellion.

September. Bowring allows Chinese merchant ships registered in Hongkong to fly the British flag and receive British protection.

1854–5

The Yellow River changes course **1855**

A Economics

January. The Board of Revenue recommends the application of the *lijin* tax in provinces engaged in war. Imperial Commissioner Shengbao sends in a memorial advocating its wider application in the provinces.

June 27 (*5/14*). The Intendant of Taiwan and US Captain George A. Potter agree on allowing US merchants to Taiwan for trade.

December 13 (*11/5*). The court orders Ye Mingchen to buy 600 foreign cannon to be sent for use in Hubei.

B Official Appointments, Dismissals, Transfers etc.

January 11 (*11/23*). Hengchun becomes Viceroy of Yungui.

14 (*11/26*). Jia Zhen becomes Grand Secretary.

April 18 (*3/3*). Hu Linyi becomes acting Governor of Hubei.

June 2 (*4/18*). The right of perpetual inheritance is attached to Senggelinqin's princedom (granted March 9) because of his capture of Li Kaifang.

11 (*4/27*). Yang Pei is dismissed as Viceroy of Huguang and replaced by Guanwen.

September 2 (*7/21*). Wenqing, President of the Board of Revenue, becomes a Grand Councillor; Yixin is removed from the Grand Council.

November 4 (*9/25*). Guanwen becomes Imperial Commissioner, in charge of military affairs in Hubei.

C Cultural and Social

March. Yang Xiuqing permits marriages in Nanjing and does away with the women's quarters.

D Publications

Li Zhaoluo's *Hengxing chidao jingwei du tu* (*Map of the Fixed Stars according to Equatorial Co-ordinates*); and the Taiping work *Xingjun zongyao*

1855–6

7 (7/26). The beginning of the South-west Moslem rebellion. Du Wenxiu occupies Dali (Yunnan).

10 (7/29). Hu Youlu and Zhu Hongying of the Heavenly Kingdom of Ascending Peace are pursued south-east by Qing forces, and separate. Within a month Hu is captured.

26 (8/16). At a conference between Luo Zenan and Zeng Guofan on strategy, Luo agrees to go to the aid of Hu Linyi, who has been suffering defeats from the Taipings near Wuchang, and attempt to retake the city.

27 (8/17). The Guangdong Triads (Red Turbans) Chen Kai and Li Wenmao take Xunzhou (Guangxi) and make it the capital of a state called Dacheng.

October 24 (9/14). Zhang Xiumei of the Miao people in Guizhou rises in rebellion.

November 4 (9/25). Taiping forces under Shi Dakai, sent to relieve Wuchang, defeat Luo Zenan's Hunan army at Chongyang (Hubei), and take the town the following day.

10 (10/1). Qing forces under the Commander-in-Chief of Jiangnan, Hechun, retake Luzhou (Anhui).

11 (10/2). The uprising in Guizhou led by Xu Tingjie, known as the Honghao rebellion, begins with the capture of Tongren. This rebellion had taken several towns by the end of 1855.

25 (10/16). A Russian demand for the left bank of the Sungari River in Heilongjiang is rejected.

December 9 (11/1). Taipings under Shi Dakai take Xinchang (Jiangxi), having crossed from Hubei, and join up with some forces of the Guangdong Heaven and Earth Society.

23 (11/15). Shi Dakai's forces press on the Jiangxi capital, Nanchang.

1856 *The Arrow Incident*

February 1 (12/25). Taiping troops led by Qin Rigang, Chen Yucheng and Li Xiucheng leave Nanjing to relieve forces at Zhenjiang.

28 (1/23). The Hunan and Guizhou armies defeat the Honghao rebellion and retake Tongren (Guizhou); its leaders are killed or imprisoned.

March 28 (2/22). Shi Dakai's Taiping forces take Fuzhou (Jiangxi).

April 5 (3/1). Taiping forces under Qin Rigang, Chen Yucheng and Li Xiucheng, having scored a major victory over Qing forces under Imperial Commissioner Tuoming'a, take Yangzhou (Jiangsu).

(*Elements of Military Tactics for Troop Operations*) are completed.

August 15 (*7/3*). Pan Shihuang's *Xujing zhai yunyan guoyan lu* (*Glances at Clouds and Mists from the Xujing Studio*), on painting, is completed.

Late August. Zhang Dejian's *Zeiqing huizuan* (*Compilation on the Robbers' Situation*), a work compiled under the auspices of Zeng Guofan about the Taipings, is completed.

E   NATURAL DISASTERS

August 2 (*6/20*). Heavy rain and flooding cause the Yellow River to break its banks and change its course to follow the old Daqing River and empty into the sea just north of the Shandong Peninsula (its present course).

December 11 (*11/3*). The beginning of a series of earthquakes (which lasted until January 9, 1856) in Fengtian.

F   BIRTHS AND DEATHS

February 17 (*1/1*). Liu Lichuan, the leader of the Small Sword Society, is executed.

March 15 (*1/27*). Lin Fengxiang is executed in Peking, aged about 30.

April 3 (*2/17*). The Governor of Hubei, Tao Enpei, d. when the Taipings take Wuchang.

12 (*2/26*). Protestant Christian Liang Fa d. in Guangzhou aged 66.

June 11 (*4/27*). Li Kaifang is executed in Peking.

August 30 (*7/18*). Taqibu d. in Jiujiang aged 38.

October 23 (*9/13*). Xu Shichang, future President of the Peking Government, b. in Tianjin (d. 1939).

November 11 (*10/2*). Scholar and official Liu Baonan d. aged 64.

Assassination of Yang Xiuqing 1856

A   ECONOMICS

May. The court orders that silver and lead mines be opened in Urumchi.

July 4 (*6/3*). The court orders Yiliang, the Viceroy of Liangjiang, to plan the purchase of steamboats for use against the Taiping rebels.

October. Customs duty on opium is set at 20 *yuan* per box.

26 (*9/28*). Ye Mingchen closes the customs office in Guangzhou, thus stopping foreign trade.

December 14–15 (*11/17–18*). Angry Chinese set fire to and destroy the foreign factories in Guangzhou.

1856

17 (3/13). Qing forces under Imperial Commissioner Dexing'a retake Yangzhou.

May 2 (3/28). Taiping troops under Shi Dakai take Ningguo (Anhui).

19–21 (4/16–18). Several thousand people are killed in clashes between Han and Moslem people in Yunnan, the capital of Yunnan province.

June 1 (4/29). The Taipings under Qin Rigang, Chen Yucheng and Li Xiucheng defeat Qing forces near Zhenjiang.

19 (5/17). Qing forces under Yuan Jiasan take Zhiheji (Anhui), the base area of the Nian leader Zhang Luoxing.

20 (5/18). The first siege of Nanjing by Qing troops is broken when the forces of Shi Dakai, who had returned to defend the capital, in conjunction with those led by Qin Rigang, Chen Yucheng, Li Xiucheng and the Nian Li Zhaoshou, defeat Qing troops under Zhang Guoliang and Yang Xiuqing's troops attack and scatter the soldiers of the Jiangnan Command under Xiang Rong.

28 (5/26). A memorial from Heilongjiang reports that the Russians have again been moving down the Amur River and built houses on territory claimed to be Chinese.

July 1 (5/29). The American Commissioner to China, Dr Peter Parker, leaves Hongkong for the north, hoping to go to Peking to seek treaty revision. In fact he did not go further than Shanghai.

23 (6/22). Ye Mingchen having sent in a memorial that the envoys of the USA, Britain and France have asked to go to Peking to revise the treaties, an edict is issued preventing them from going to the capital.

25 (6/24). The French *chargé d'affaires*, Comte de Courcy, demands compensation from Ye Mingchen for Chapdelaine's death (See C).

August 13 (7/13). Zhang Guoliang defeats the Taipings under Qin Rigang and others in Danyang (Jiangsu).

20 (7/20). Ye Mingchen refuses the French demand of July 25.

24 (7/24). The Nian leader Zhang Luoxing retakes his base area in Zhiheji (Anhui).

28 (7/28). Shi Dakai's forces, having come to relieve Wuchang, combine with Taiping troops which have come out of the city. They attack Qing troops under Hu Linyi but are defeated.

September 1 (8/3). Wei Changhui returns to Nanjing from Jiangxi, the prelude to the slaughter of Yang Xiuqing and his relations and followers the next day.

24 (8/26). The Miao rebels in Guizhou take Taigong.

October. Shi Dakai returns to Nanjing to censure Wei Changhui for the assassinations. Wei therefore plans to kill Shi, who flees to Anqing. Wei slaughters all Shi's family members in Nanjing.

1856

B OFFICIAL APPOINTMENTS, DISMISSALS, TRANSFERS ETC. (QING OR TAIPING)

January 23 *(12/16)*. Wenqing and Ye Mingchen become Grand Secretaries, Guiliang and Peng Yunzhang assistant Grand Secretaries, Ye and Guiliang retaining their posts as Viceroys of Liangguang and Zhili respectively.
April 11 *(3/7)*. Tuoming'a is dismissed. Dexing'a becomes Imperial Commissioner and is put in charge of military affairs in Yangzhou.
27 *(3/23)*. Owing to the birth of her son, the future Tongzhi Emperor, Empress Xiaoqin, the future Empress Dowager, is promoted to second-class concubine with the title *Yifei*.
September 2 *(8/4)*. Wu Zhenyu becomes Viceroy of Sichuan.
8 *(8/10)*. The Commander-in-Chief of Jiangnan, Hechun, is appointed Imperial Commissioner in charge of military affairs in Jiangnan to replace Xiang Rong.
October 26 *(9/28)*. The Tartar General of Chengdu, Yuebin, replaces Yitang as Viceroy of Shan'gan.
November. Following Wei Changhui's death, Shi Dakai takes over the government in Nanjing under Hong Xiuquan.
28 *(11/1)*. Peng Yunzhang is appointed Grand Secretary and Weng Xincun assistant Grand Secretary.
December 15 *(11/18)*. Baisui is appointed to the Grand Council.

C CULTURAL AND SOCIAL

February 24 *(1/19)*. As part of a general policy of persecution of Christians in Xilin (Guangxi), the county magistrate Zhang Mingfeng has the French missionary Auguste Chapdelaine arrested.
29 *(1/24)*. Chapdelaine is decapitated on the orders of the magistrate in Xilin.
May 28 *(4/25)*. The writer, calligrapher, and official Weng Tonghe (1830–1904) receives the *jinshi* degree, topping the examinations.

D PUBLICATIONS

November 28 *(11/1)*. The *Da Qing Xuanzong Cheng huangdi shilu* (*Veritable Records of the Great Qing Daoguang Emperor*) is completed.

E NATURAL DISASTERS

July 27 *(6/26)*. The Yongding River floods.

1856–7

8 *(9/10)*. The lorcha *Arrow*, flying a British flag, is boarded by Chinese soldiers and officers in Guangzhou, who arrest the entire crew (twelve Chinese) on suspicion of piracy. The British consul in Guangzhou, Harry S. Parkes, protests to Ye Mingchen, demanding their release.
14 *(9/16)*. Ye Mingchen reports the release of nine of the arrested crewmen.
22 *(9/24)*. Ye Mingchen returns the twelve crewmen to Parkes but refuses to apologize.
25 *(9/27)*. British warships under Admiral Sir Michael Seymour seize the Haizhu Fort in front of Guangzhou city.
27 *(9/29)*. The British start to shell the city of Guangzhou, especially Ye Mingchen's *yamen*.
29 *(10/1)*. As Seymour enters his *yamen*, Ye Mingchen flees to the inner city of Guangzhou. He sends Wu Chongyue (like his late father Wu Bingjian, known to foreigners as Howqua) to talk peace.
November 11 *(10/14)*. Through Li Zhaoshou, Li Xiucheng makes formal arrangements to cooperate with the Nian under Zhang Luoxing.
20–22 *(10/23–5)*. US ships under Commodore Armstrong occupy and dismantle the five Barrier Forts in Guangdong, about four miles from Guangzhou.
December 19 *(11/22)*. Qing troops under Hu Linyi, the Governor of Hubei, retake Wuchang. The forces of Guanwen, Viceroy of Huguang, retake Hanyang from the Taipings.
30 *(12/4)*. Chinese on the Hongkong-bound British postal steamer *Thistle* capture the ship and kill all eleven foreigners on board.

1857 The British and French take Guangzhou

January 12 *(12/17)*. British troops burn down several thousand houses in Guangzhou.
14 *(12/19)*. Qing forces retreat from Jiujiang, having failed to drive the Taipings out of the city.
Seymour retreats from the foreign factory region of Guangzhou.
February 24 *(2/1)*. Chen Yucheng and Li Xiucheng defeat Qing forces under the Commander-in-Chief of Fujian, Qin Dingsan, at Tongcheng (Anhui).
March 3 *(2/8)*. Li Xiucheng and Li Zhaoshou, a Nian leader, defeat Qin Dingsan at Liuan (Anhui) and take the city.
15 *(2/20)*. Zhu Hongying's Heavenly Kingdom of Ascending Peace takes Liuzhou (Guangxi).
31 *(3/6)*. Taiping forces under Yang Fuqing move from Jiangxi

1856-7

F BIRTHS AND DEATHS

The historian and geographer Wei Yuan d. aged 62.
February 9 (*1/4*). Official and bibliophile Yang Yizeng d. aged 68.
April 12 (*3/8*). Luo Zenan d. from a battle wound, aged 48.
27 (*3/23*). The future Tongzhi Emperor b. (d. 1875).
May 23 (*4/20*). Former assistant Grand Secretary Tang Jinzhao d. aged 83.
June 1 (*4/29*). The Governor of Jiangsu, Jierhang'a, d. in battle near Zhenjiang.
August 9 (*7/9*). Xiang Rong d. through suicide in Danyang (Jiangsu) aged 55.
September 2 (*8/4*). Yang Xiuqing d. through assassination by Wei Changhui and others, aged 49.
November. With Hong Xiuquan's agreement, Wei Changhui d. through assassination.
December 14 (*11/17*). Grand Secretary Wenqing d. aged 60.

1857

A ECONOMICS

February. The court issues an order against the refusal in the markets to use the newly introduced iron coinage.
March. The Shanghai currency is changed from dollar to tael.
June. The court lays down regulations on the circulation of strings of large cash.
July. The court orders that plans be made for the opening up of waste land in Heilongjiang.

B OFFICIAL APPOINTMENTS, DISMISSALS, TRANSFERS ETC. (QING OR TAIPING)

January 21 (*12/26*). Guiliang is appointed Grand Secretary, Baisui assis-

1857

into Fujian and take Shaowu.

June 1 (*5/10*). A British force attacks Foshan (Guangdong), killing or wounding some fifty people.

Some 600 Russian soldiers march into Heilongjiang.

2 (*5/11*). Shi Dakai arrives in Tongling (Anhui) from Nanjing, which he had left because Hong Xiuquan no longer trusted him and Hong's brothers wanted to kill him.

28 (*int. 5/7*). Yang Fuqing's forces retreat into Jiangxi from Shaowu (Fujian).

July 2 (*int. 5/11*). The Earl of Elgin and Kincardine, British High Commissioner and plenipotentiary, arrives in Hongkong to negotiate with the Chinese.

12 (*int. 5/21*). The Moslem rebels of Yunnan under Ma Rulong attack the provincial capital Yunnan.

16 (*int. 5/25*). Qing forces under Zhang Guoliang retake Jurong (Jiangsu), and press on Nanjing. Zhang prepares for another siege of the city.

August 7 (*6/18*). The Russian envoy, Admiral Count Euphemius Putianin, arrives in Tianjin with trade and other demands. These are later refused. British troops blockade Guangzhou.

September 11 (*7/23*). Chen Yucheng, defeated in Hubei by Hu Linyi, retreats to Anhui.

October 2 (*8/15*). Qing forces defeat remaining Taiping forces in Hubei; the Qing regards it as 'pacified'.

5 (*8/18*). Shi Dakai leads his forces from Anhui to Jiangxi.

26 (*9/9*). The Hunan Army retakes Hukou (Jiangxi) from the Taipings after fierce fighting.

November 23 (*10/8*). Taiping forces under Li Xiucheng and Nian forces under Li Zhaoshou leave Luzhou (Anhui), having tried to take it, and press on Hezhou (Anhui), which they take November 28.

December 11 (*10/26*). Li Xiucheng, Li Zhaoshou and others move to the relief of Zhenjiang and face Qing forces under Zhang Guoliang.

12 (*10/27*). Elgin and the French Baron J.B.L. Gros, in simultaneous notes to Ye Mingchen, demand compensation for losses, and reparation for wrongs (for Gros including the death of Chapdelaine); the two also declare their forces will attack Guangzhou if they have not received satisfaction within ten days. The French join the blockade of Guangzhou.

14 (*10/29*). Ye Mingchen rejects the demands of Elgin and Gros.

27 (*11/12*). Qing forces under Zhang Guoliang and Hechun retake Zhenjiang from the Taipings. Li Xiucheng returns to Nanjing.

28 (*11/13*). Ye Mingchen having again rejected Anglo-French demands

1857

tant Grand Secretary. Tan Tingxiang becomes acting Viceroy of Zhili.

March 22 (2/27). Zeng Guofan is given three months' leave because of his father's death.

May 5 (4/12). He Guiqing becomes an acting Viceroy of Liangjiang, replacing Yiliang.

June?. With Shi Dakai's departure from Nanjing, Meng De'en takes over the Taiping government, under Hong Xiuquan, as Chief Commandant.

July 26 (6/6). He Guiqing is confirmed as Viceroy of Liangjiang.

August 8 (6/19). Zeng Guofan is allowed to retire temporarily for mourning.

15 (6/26). Wu Zhenyu becomes Viceroy of Yungui and Wang Qingyun of Sichuan.

October. Hong Xiuquan gives Chen Yucheng the title of Second Chief Commandant and Li Xiucheng that of deputy Commandant.

C   Cultural and Social

March 31 (3/6). In Shaowu (Fujian) the Taiping leader Yang Fuqing begins establishing women's quarters and having temples and images destroyed.

D   Publications

Alexander Wylie begins publishing the monthly Chinese-language *Liuhe congtan* (*Shanghai Serial*) in Shanghai. The Taiping *Tianfu shi* (*Poems by the Heavenly Father*) is published. A Chinese translation by Alexander Wylie and Li Shanlan of Books VII to XV of Euclid's *Elements* is published under the title *Jihe yuanben* (*Elements of Geometry*).

E   Natural Disasters

A plague of locusts in Zhili and Shaanxi; flooding in parts of Hubei, devastating drought and locust plague in Anhui and other provinces, flooding caused by breakages in the Yellow River dykes, and serious famine in Shandong, result in the death of some 8,000,000 people.

F   Births and Deaths

February 27 (2/4). Zeng Guofan's father, Zeng Linshu, d. aged 67.

July 21 (6/1). The Viceroy of Yungui, Hengchun, hangs himself because of his inability to cope with the Moslem rebellion in Yunnan.

October 18 (9/1). Liu E, scholar and writer, b. in Jiangsu (d. 1909).

1857-8

(December 25), an Anglo-French force of 5679 men, under Seymour, bombards Guangzhou.

29 *(11/14)*. Guangzhou falls to the Anglo-French force.

1858 The Treaties of Tianjin

January 5 *(11/21)*. Ye Mingchen is arrested by Parkes and others.
19 *(12/5)*. The forces of the Sparks from the Lantern Sect in Guizhou under Liu Yishun take Sinan. This was the beginning of the White Signal Rebellion.
February 22 *(1/9)*. Ye Mingchen leaves Hongkong for Calcutta, a prisoner on a British ship.
March 14 *(1/29)*. The Miao rebels of Guizhou take Duyun.
March. Li Xiucheng leaves Nanjing to gather relief forces against Qing troops besieging the city.
April 6 *(2/23)*. Chen Yucheng's forces move south from Henan to Hubei.
15 *(3/2)*. Shi Dakai moves into Zhejiang and takes Jiangshan.
May 17 *(4/5)*. Envoys of Britain (Elgin), France (Gros), USA (William Reed) and Russia (Putianin) having arrived outside Tianjin and requested entry to Peking to negotiate, the Emperor proclaims that their demands for the opening of further ports and the right to send envoys to reside in Peking and missionaries into the interior have been rejected.
19 *(4/7)*. Qing forces retake Jiujiang (Jiangxi).
20 *(4/8)*. British and French forces attack and occupy the Dagu Forts outside Tianjin to force agreement to the demands made on the court.
25 *(4/13)*. Qing troops under Shengbao and Yuan Jiasan retake Liuan (Anhui) and defeat the Nian leader Zhang Luoxing.
26 *(4/14)*. British and French warships reach Tianjin.
28 *(4/16)*. Yishan, Tartar General of Heilongjiang, and Nikolai Muraviev, Governor-general of Eastern Siberia, conclude the Treaty of Aigun under which the north bank of the Amur is recognized as Russian.
June 2 *(4/21)*. Guiliang and Huasha'na arrive in Tianjin to negotiate with the foreigners; Qiying arrives June 8.
13 *(5/3)*. The first of the four treaties with the powers, that with Russia, is signed in Tianjin. All four gave essentially the same concessions, i.e. the demands made by the foreigners and rejected on May 17.
18 *(5/8)*. Sino-US Treaty of Tianjin signed.

1857-8

Anglo-French Commission set up to run Guangzhou 1858

A Economics

January. Permission is granted for foreign merchants to pay the Fujian customs in silver dollars.
23 (*12/9*). The Russian Amur company is established.
May. People in Fuzhou (Fujian) go to the Viceroy's offices demanding that he allows the use of copper money (iron being inconvenient) and lowers the price of grain.
July 15 (*6/5*). The court sends Guiliang and Huasha'na to Shanghai to discuss the rates of tariffs on certain goods with He Guiqing, Viceroy of Liangjiang, and the British and French representatives.
October 12 (*9/6*). Sino-British discussions on tariffs begin in Shanghai.
November. The court strictly forbids speculation on the money markets. It grants permission for Yunnan to stop minting strings of large cash.
8 (*10/3*). Sino-British and Sino-US agreements on tariff and trade regulations are signed in Shanghai.
24 (*10/19*). A Sino-French agreement on tariff and trade regulations is signed in Shanghai.

B Official Appointments, Dismissals, Transfers etc. (Qing or Taiping)

January 9 (*11/25*). Parkes and others set up a three-man mixed Anglo-French commission to run Guangzhou.
27 (*12/13*). Ye Mingchen is dismissed because of the foreign occupation of Guangzhou; Huang Zonghan becomes the Viceroy of Liangguang.
February. Li Xiucheng takes over government in Nanjing.
March. It is agreed in Nanjing that court administrative affairs will be handled by Chief Commandant Meng De'en, Li Chunfa, and second deputy Chancellor of the Earth Department Lin Shaozhang, not by Hong Xiuquan's brothers Renfa and Renda.
April 25 (*3/12*). Tan Tingxiang is confirmed as Viceroy of Zhili.
June 2 (*4/21*). Senggelinqin is appointed Imperial Commissioner in charge of military affairs in Peking and Tianjin against further British and French attacks.

73

1858-9

24 (5/14). The Hunan Army takes Liuzhou (Guangxi), forcing Zhu Hongying and other leaders of the defeated Heavenly Kingdom of Ascending Peace to flee towards Guizhou.

26 (5/16). The Sino-British Treaty of Tianjin is signed.

27 (5/17). The Sino-French Treaty of Tianjin is signed.

August. Li Xiucheng, Chen Yucheng and other Taiping leaders meet in Congyang (Anhui) to plan the breaking of the siege round Nanjing.

18 (7/10). Taiping forces under Shi Dakai move from Zhejiang into Fujian.

23 (7/15). Taiping forces under Chen Yucheng take Luzhou (Anhui).

September 27 (8/21). Taiping forces under Chen Yucheng and Li Xiucheng defeat the Jiangbei Command under Imperial Commissioner Dexing'a, partly lifting the siege of Nanjing.

October 9 (9/3). Taiping forces under Li Xiucheng take Yangzhou, but Zhang Guoliang reoccupies it October 21.

15 (9/9). Qing forces under Duolong'a, Bao Chao and others begin attacking Anqing, the second most important of the cities held by the Taipings.

18 (9/12). Taiping troops under Shi Dakai move from Fujian into Jiangxi and take Ruijin.

November 1 (9/26). The Nian leader Li Zhaoshou surrenders to Shengbao in Chuzhou (Anhui).

15 (10/10). Taiping forces under Li Xiucheng and Chen Yucheng defeat the Hunan Army under Li Xubin, attacking the important supply centre Sanhe (Anhui).

27 (10/22). Qing troops abandon the siege of Nanjing.

December 29 (11/25). Lord Elgin, having sailed up the Yangzi as far as Hankou, meets Li Chunfa in Nanjing and tells him Britain will not assist the Qing in the war.

31 (11/27). The Chinese population of Hongkong stands at 74,041, including 23,920 boat people (statistics from the *North-China Herald*, April 16, 1859).

1859 Hong Ren'gan arrives in Nanjing

January 4 (12/1). Some 1000 British troops in Guangzhou attack the nearby village of Sanyuanli, but are driven out by local militia.

February 28 (1/26). Taiping forces under Xue Zhiyuan surrender to Qing forces led by Li Shizhong (in fact the new name of the former

1858-9

July 10 (*5/30*). Wenxiang and Kuangyuan are made Grand Councillors.
26 (*6/16*). Qingqi replaces Tan Tingxiang as Viceroy of Zhili.
August 31 (*7/23*). Shengbao is appointed Imperial Commissioner in charge of military affairs in Anhui.
October 16 (*9/10*). Baisui and Weng Xincun are appointed Grand Secretaries, Guanwen and Zhou Zupei assistant Grand Secretaries.

C Cultural and Social

October 16 (*9/10*). The Shanghai branch of the British Royal Asiatic Society is founded.

D Publications

Publication of the Taiping work *Xingshi wen* (*An Essay on the Awakening of the Age*) plus a calendar and the revised version of *Taiping lizhi*. The first Chinese-language daily, *Zhongwai xinbao*, the Chinese edition of the *Daily Press*, begins publication in Hongkong.
January 15–February 13 (*12*). Huasha'na's *De Zhuangguogong nianpu* (*Chronological Biography of Delengtai*) (Qi Junzao's preface dated January 15–February 13, 1858).

F Births and Deaths

March 19 (*2/5*). Kang Youwei b. in Guangdong (d. 1927).
June 29 (*5/19*). On Imperial orders, Qiying commits suicide because of the disastrous treaties with the powers.
November 15 (*10/10*). The Qing military commanders Li Xubin and Zeng Guohua, Zeng Guofan's younger brother, d. in battle at Sanhe (Anhui) (respectively aged 40 and 36).
21 (*10/16*). Etymologist and scholar Zhu Junsheng d. aged 70.

Death of Ye Mingchen 1859

A Economics

April 28 (*3/26*). Regulations are laid down for a *lijin* tax on opium.
October. The court issues an order strictly forbidding the private minting of money by melting down strings of large cash.

1859

Nian rebel Li Zhaoshou) and at the same time give up the city of Jiangpu (Jiangsu).

Early March. Shi Dakai's troops enter Hunan from Jiangxi.

2 *(1/28).* Li Shizhong lays siege to Nanjing.

4 *(1/30).* Elgin leaves Hongkong for home.

April 22 *(3/20).* Hong Xiuquan's cousin, Hong Ren'gan, arrives in Nanjing.

26 *(3/24).* The new British minister to China, Frederick Bruce, Elgin's brother, arrives in Hongkong.

May. Lan Chaogui and others of the Incense Burners' League rebel in Daguan, Zhaotong (Yunnan).

7 *(4/5).* Taiping forces under Shi Dakai defeat the Hunan Army under Liu Changyou at Xinning (Hunan) and advance to besiege Baoqing (Hunan).

June 20 *(5/20).* Bruce, de Bourboulon and J.E. Ward, representing Britain, France and USA respectively, arrive outside the port of Dagu, intending, despite an express Chinese wish to the contrary, to go to Peking to exchange the Treaties of Tianjin.

22 *(5/22).* Qing forces under Li Xuyi leave Wuchang for Baoqing to help defend it.

23 *(5/23).* Hengfu, the Viceroy of Zhili, asks that the ministers of foreign nations proceed to Peking through Beitang.

25 *(5/25).* British and French warships, under the command of British Admiral Sir James Hope, attack the Dagu forts, but are defeated by the Chinese garrison. US Commodore Josiah Tatnall assists the British to withdraw.

July 11 *(6/12).* British and French warships complete their withdrawal from Dagu, de Bourboulon and Bruce having already left for Shanghai on July 4 and 5 respectively.

14 *(6/15).* Qing forces under Zeng Guoquan defeat the Taipings under Yang Fuqing and conquer Fouliang (Jiangxi). The previous day Yang had withdrawn from Jingdezhen (Jiangxi).

August 14 *(7/16).* Shi Dakai's troops give up their siege of Baoqing and depart for Guangxi.

16 *(7/18).* Ward and Hengfu exchange the Sino-US Treaty of 1858 in Beitang.

27 *(7/29).* Shi Dakai's Taiping forces besiege Guilin, the capital of Guangxi.

September 16 *(8/20).* The Taiping forces of Wei Jun clash with Chen Yucheng's at Hezhou (Anhui).

October 3 *(9/8).* Lan Chaogui's Incense Burners' League occupies Yunlian (Sichuan).

November 15 (*10/21*). The court issues an edict allowing the USA to begin trading in Chaozhou and Taiwan.

December 20 (*11/26*). Taiping forces under Yang Fuqing, during an attack on Chizhou, are reported, for the first time, to be using foreign rifles.

B   OFFICIAL APPOINTMENTS, DISMISSALS, TRANSFERS ETC. (QING OR TAIPING)

January 1 (*12/28*). Zhang Liangji becomes Viceroy of Yungui.

March 9 (*2/5*). Because of his failure against the Taipings, Dexing'a is dismissed as Imperial Commissioner in charge of military affairs north of the Yangzi, and replaced by Imperial Commissioner Hechun.

25 (*2/21*). Hengfu becomes Viceroy of Zhili.

May 4 (*4/2*). Wang Qingyun is appointed Viceroy of Liangguang; Huang Zonghan of Sichuan.

11 (*4/9*). Hong Xiuquan appoints Hong Ren'gan as *Ganwang*.

24 (*4/22*). Qingrui replaces Wang Yide as Viceroy of Minzhe.

June 16 (*5/16*). Yishan is deprived of his rank of Tartar General because of the loss of Chinese territory in the Treaty of Aigun.

26 (*5/26*). Jia Zhen is appointed Grand Secretary to replace Wen Xincun, who retires.

Late June. Hong Xiuquan appoints Chen Yucheng as *Yingwang*.

October 7 (*9/12*). Lao Chongguang replaces Wang Qingyun as Viceroy of Liangguang.

29 (*10/4*). Zeng Wangyan becomes acting Viceroy of Sichuan.

30 (*10/5*). Kuangyuan is appointed to the Grand Council.

Mid–December. Li Xiucheng is appointed as *Zhongwang* of the Taipings.

C   CULTURAL AND SOCIAL

October 18 (*9/23*). Examinations are held in Nanjing, supervised by Hong Ren'gan, Chen Yucheng and Meng De'en.

November 16 (*10/22*). Hong Xiuquan officially revises the Taiping calendar system in accordance with Hong Ren'gan's proposals.

D   PUBLICATIONS

Hong Ren'gan's *Qinming wenheng zhengzongcai jingzhong junshi Ganwang baozhi* (*Writings of the Imperially Ordained Chief Examiner of the Literary Examinations, the Loyal Chief of Staff, the Ganwang*) is published.

1859–60

5 *(9/10)*. Shi Dakai's troops raise the siege of Guilin, after failing to take the city.

6 *(9/11)*. Lan Chaogui's Incense Burners' League occupies Gaoxian (Sichuan).

15 *(9/20)*. Taiping forces under Shi Dakai take Qingyuan (Guangxi).

November 21 *(10/27)*. Taiping forces under Chen Yucheng and Li Xiucheng take Pukou after a decisive victory over the Qing forces at Jiangpu.

December 8 *(11/15)*. Taiping troops under Yang Fuqing and others attack Chizhou (Anhui), defended by the Hunan Army under Peng Yulin and Wei Jun who had surrendered to the Qing a few days earlier.

23 *(11/30)*. The Taipings retake Chizhou.

1860 The British and French occupy Peking

January 7 *(12/15)*. Chen Yucheng joins forces with the Nian leader Zhang Luoxing in Tongcheng (Anhui).

28 *(1/6)*. Li Xiucheng leaves Nanjing for southern Anhui, planning to break the siege of Nanjing.

February 1 *(1/10)*. The Qing Jiangnan Command under Zhang Guoliang takes Jiangpu (Jiangsu) and tightens its siege of Nanjing.

24 *(2/3)*. Taiping troops under Li Xiucheng take Guangde (Anhui) and advance towards Zhejiang to break the siege of Nanjing.

March 8 *(2/16)*. The British and French ministers Bruce and de Bourboulon demand an apology and indemnities for the events of 1859; demand to be allowed to reside in Peking and to go to Peking to exchange the 1858 Treaties of Tianjin.

19 *(2/27)*. Taiping forces under Li Xiucheng take Hangzhou. Li aims to divide Zhang Guoliang's Jiangnan Command besieging Nanjing.

24 *(3/3)*. Li Xiucheng's forces abandon Hangzhou since the arrival of part of Zhang Guoliang's forces shows his plan has been successful.

April 5 *(3/15)*. The Viceroy of Liangjiang, He Guiqing, informs Bruce and de Bourboulon that their requests of March 8 have been refused.

May 6 *(int. 3/16)*. Taiping forces under Li Xiucheng, Li Shixian, Chen Yucheng, Yang Fuqing and others inflict a decisive defeat on the army of the Jiangnan Command and break the second major siege of Nanjing.

11 *(int. 3/21)*. At a major Taiping conference in Nanjing on strategy, attended by Hong Ren'gan, Li Xiucheng, Chen Yucheng and others, Hong's proposal to occupy the area along the Yangzi is adopted.

26 *(4/6)*. Taiping troops under Li Xiucheng and others take Changzhou

1859-60

Winter. Hong Ren'gan's *Zizheng xinpian* (*A New Treatise on Aids to Administration*) is published.

F Births and Deaths

January 7 (*12/4*). Feng Guozhang, acting President (1917–18) of the Peking Government, b. (d. 1919).
April 10 (*3/8*). Ye Mingchen d. near Calcutta aged 51.
September 16 (*8/20*). Yuan Shikai b. in Henan (d. 1916).
October 13 (*9/18*). Poet-official Zhang Weiping d. aged 79.

Destruction of the Old Summer Palace 1860

A Economics

January 1 (*12/9*). Chaozhou opens for trade.
July. Muraviev founds Vladivostok (meaning 'Rule of the East').
October 11 (*8/27*). At the British army headquarters in Peking, the artefacts looted from the Old Summer Palace are auctioned off.

B Official Appointments, Dismissals, Transfers etc.

June 8 (*4/19*). He Guiqing is dismissed as Viceroy of Liangjiang. Zeng Guofan replaces him as acting Viceroy.
August 10 (*6/24*) Zeng Guofan is confirmed as Viceroy of Liangjiang and appointed Imperial Commissioner in charge of military affairs in Jiangnan.
31 (*7/15*). Chongshi is appointed acting Viceroy of Sichuan.
September 8 (*7/23*). The Qing court appoints Zaiyuan and Muyin as Imperial Commissioners to negotiate with the British and French.
21 (*8/7*). The Qing court appoints Yixin, Prince Gong, as Imperial Commissioner to negotiate with the British and French, and dismisses Zaiyuan and Muyin.
October 12 (*8/28*). Senggelinqin and Grand Secretary Ruilin are dismissed because of their failures against the British and French.
November 9 (*9/27*). Senggelinqin is again made a prince of the second degree.
14 (*10/2*). Liu Yuanhao is appointed Viceroy of Yungui.
December 11 (*10/29*). Jiao Youying is appointed to the Grand Council.

1860

(Jiangsu). Bruce and de Bourboulon announce they will protect Shanghai from the Taipings.

27 *(4/7)*. Shi Dakai's army enters Guizhou.

30 *(4/10)*. Li Xiucheng takes Wuxi (Jiangsu).

June 2 *(4/13)*. Taiping forces under Li Xiucheng take Suzhou (Jiangsu). The American Frederick T. Ward begins to enlist foreigners into a rifle corps for the protection of Shanghai.

15 *(4/26)*. Taiping forces under Li Shixian take Jiaxing (Zhejiang), those under Li Xiucheng take Kunshan (Jiangsu).

26 *(5/8)*. The British and French governments notify the Western powers that a state of war exists with China.

July 1 *(5/13)*. Li Xiucheng takes Songjiang (Jiangsu).

15 *(5/27)*. Li Xiucheng announces that his forces will not injure foreigners in Shanghai.

16 *(5/28)*. Qing troops, assisted by the foreign Shanghai rifle corps under Ward and others, retake Songjiang.

22 *(6/5)*. Taiping troops under Lai Wenguang take Jiading (Jiangsu).

August 1 *(6/15)*. An allied British-French force lands at Beitang, near Tianjin.

12 *(6/26)*. Li Xiucheng retakes Songjiang.

18 *(7/2)*. Li Xiucheng arrives at Xujiahui (Zikawei), very near Shanghai, intending to take Shanghai.

19 *(7/3)*. Li Xiucheng's army is defeated by British and French forces at Shanghai, and retreats.

21 *(7/5)*. British and French troops take the Dagu forts.

24 *(7/8)*. Li Xiucheng's forces withdraw from Shanghai to relieve Jiaxing, besieged by Qing troops.

25 *(7/9)*. British ambassador extraordinary Lord Elgin and French ambassador Baron Gros arrive in Tianjin in the wake of an allied occupation of the city.

31 *(7/15)*. Grand Secretary Guiliang arrives in Tianjin to negotiate with Elgin and Gros.

September 8 *(7/23)*. Li Xiucheng's forces break the siege of Jiaxing.

18 *(8/4)*. Interpreter Harry S. Parkes and others in the British and French party are imprisoned. Allied British and French forces defeat a Qing army under Senggelinqin at Zhangjiawan just south of Tongzhou (Zhili).

21 *(8/7)*. British and French forces defeat a Qing army under Ruilin and others at Baliqiao, west of Tongzhou.

22 *(8/8)*. The Xianfeng Emperor leaves Peking for Jehol.

26 *(8/12)*. Taiping forces under Yang Fuqing and Li Shixian take Ningguo (Anhui).

1860

C CULTURAL AND SOCIAL

February 24 (*2/3*). Examinations are held in Nanjing for the selection of officials to conduct the Taiping provincial examinations.
April 22 (*int. 3/2*). The Qing court orders the Viceroy of Liangguang and Governor of Guangdong to ban the kidnapping and sale to foreigners of Chinese citizens; in Guangdong this practice had reached alarming proportions.
July 23 (*6/6*). The Sanqing Company, one of the great theatre troupes of Peking, performs at court as part of the celebration for the Emperor's thirtieth birthday, which fell on July 26. This was the first time a popular troupe had been invited to the court from the city. The new practice persisted until Xianfeng fled to Jehol later in the year.
28 (*6/11*). The famous Sixi Peking Opera Company performs at court.
August 2 (*6/16*). Hong Ren'gan meets the British missionaries Joseph Edkins and Griffith John at Suzhou.
October 6 (*8/22*). British and French forces occupy and pillage the Old Summer Palace (Yuanming yuan) outside Peking; the looting lasts several days.
13 (*8/29*). The American missionary I.J. Roberts arrives in Nanjing.
18–20 (*9/5–7*). On Elgin's instructions, the British burn the Old Summer Palace to the ground.
November 19 (*10/7*). Rong Hong (Yung Wing), the first Chinese returned student from the USA, arrives in Nanjing together with Griffith John and there advises Hong Ren'gan on improving the systems of administration, education, banking and others.
December 6 (*10/24*). Griffith John announces that Hong Xiuquan will allow foreign missionaries to work freely in Taiping territory.

D PUBLICATIONS

Publication of the Taiping work *Wangzhang cixiong qinmu qiner gongzheng fuyinshu* (*Gospel Jointly Witnessed and Heard by the Imperial Eldest and Second Eldest Brothers*). The *Jiangbei yuncheng* (*Transport North of the River*), an important work by Dong Xun on water transport north of the Yangzi, is completed.
January 23–February 21 (*1*). Completion of the early Peking Opera collection *Shuji tang jinyue* (*Contemporary Music from the Shuji Hall*) by Yu Zhi.
February 15 (*1/24*). He Qiutao presents his work *Shuofang beisheng* (*Historical Sourcebook of the Northern Regions*) to the Emperor.

1860-1

30 *(8/16)*. The Emperor and his court arrive in Jehol.
October. Li Xiucheng goes to Nanjing to discuss strategy with Hong Xiuquan. Li Xiucheng's forces begin a western expedition.
9 *(8/25)*. The Taipings under Li Shixian take Huizhou (Anhui).
13 *(8/29)*. British and French troops occupy Peking.
24 *(9/11)*. In Peking, Prince Gong exchanges the Sino-British Treaty of Tianjin with Lord Elgin and the two sign the Sino-British Convention of Peking.
25 *(9/12)*. In Peking, Prince Gong exchanges the Sino-French Treaty of Tianjin with Gros; the two sign the Sino-French Convention of Peking. China thus guarantees residence for foreign envoys in Peking and opens Tianjin as a treaty port.
November 1 *(9/19)*. French troops withdraw from Peking, followed by the British on November 7–8.
14 *(10/2)*. Prince Gong signs, with General Ignatieff of Russia, the Sino-Russian Convention of Peking by which China cedes all territory east of the Ussuri River, thus confirming and extending the Treaty of Aigun (May 28, 1858).
27 *(10/15)*. A Taiping siege of Hangzhou led by Li Shixian is broken by Qing troops under the Tartar General of Hangzhou, Ruichang.
December 3 *(10/21)*. Li Xiucheng is seriously defeated at Xiuning (Anhui) by the Hunan Army under Bao Chao.
28 *(11/17)*. Taiping troops under Li Shixian harass Zeng Guofan's army at Qimen (Anhui).

1861 *Establishment of the Zongli yamen*

January 13 *(12/3)*. Prince Gong and others send in a memorial suggesting the establishment of a general office to manage foreign affairs; the teaching of foreign languages to selected sons of bannermen; and the appointment of a superintendent of trade to take charge of the three northern ports of Niuzhuang in Liaodong, Tianjin (Zhili) and Dengzhou (Shandong).
20 *(12/10)*. An Imperial edict is issued to establish the *Zongli geguo tongshang shiwu yamen* (lit. 'office for the general management of affairs and trade with every country'), usually known as the *Zongli yamen*.
February 18 *(1/9)*. The Hunan Army under Tang Yixun defeats the Taiping forces attacking Qimen (Anhui).
March 7 *(1/26)*. Hong Ren'gan goes to Ningguo (Anhui) to seek recruits for the relief of Anqing.

1860-1

F BIRTHS AND DEATHS

March 21 (*2/29*). In Hangzhou the painter Dai Xi d. through suicide during the Taiping occupation of the city, aged 59.
May 19 (*int. 3/29*). The Commander-in-Chief of Jiangnan, Zhang Guoliang, d. by drowning aged 38.
26 (*4/6*). Imperial Commissioner Hechun d.
June 16 (*4/27*). The Qing military leader Xiao Qijiang d. in Sichuan.

Accession of the Tongzhi Emperor **1861**

A ECONOMICS

April 3 (*2/24*). Niuzhuang, in Liaodong, opens as a trade port.
5 (*2/26*). Kashgar opens for trade.
May 4 (*3/24*). US Commodore Stribling reaches agreement with the Taipings over the right of US ships to sail on the Yangzi for trade.
10 (*4/1*). Zhenjiang (Jiangsu) is opened as a trade port.
July 7 (*5/30*). Following the suggestion of the Britisher Robert Hart, Prince Gong sends in a memorial proposing the purchase of foreign ships and cannon for use against the Taipings.
August 22 (*7/17*). Yantai (Shandong) is opened as a trade port.
September 2 (*7/28*). A Sino-German trade treaty is signed in Tianjin.
December. Zeng Guoquan sets up an arsenal in Anqing to manufacture foreign weapons of war.

83

1861

9 *(1/28)*. The Nian Army takes Zhuxianzhen and threatens Kaifeng (Henan).
11 *(2/1)*. The *Zongli yamen* is formally established.
18 *(2/8)*. Taiping forces under Chen Yucheng take Huangzhou (Hubei).
21 *(2/11)*. The Shandong White Lotus sect rebels and takes Qiuxian (Zhili).
25 *(2/15)*. The first foreign minister, the Frenchman de Bourboulon, takes up residence in Peking.
29 *(2/19)*. The Shandong White Lotus sect takes Guanxian (Shandong).
April 9 *(2/30)*. The Taipings under Li Shixian take Jingdezhen (Jiangxi).
14 *(3/5)*. An attack on Huizhou (Anhui) by Qing forces under Tang Yixun and others is defeated by the Taipings.
20 *(3/11)*. Taiping forces under Li Xiucheng take Ji'an (Jiangxi).
22 *(3/13)*. Chen Yucheng leaves Hubei for Anhui, looking for a way to lift the siege of Anqing.
27 *(3/18)*. Taiping forces under Chen Yucheng attack the Hunan Army under Zeng Guoquan near Anqing.
May 3 *(3/24)*. Taiping reinforcements approach Anqing.
5 *(3/26)*. Zeng Guoquan leads troops to relieve the Qing army at Anqing.
16 *(4/7)*. The Shandong White Lotus sect takes Qinghe (Zhili).
28 *(4/19)*. Taiping troops under Li Shixian take Jinhua (Zhejiang).
June 10 *(5/3)*. Taiping forces again press on Qimen (Anhui).
15 *(5/8)*. Li Xiucheng's forces occupy Wuchang county (Hubei), and withdraw June 23 after gaining many new recruits.
July 24 *(6/17)*. One of the Shandong White Lotus sect leaders, Song Jingshi, surrenders to Imperial Commissioner Shengbao.
August 21 *(7/16)*. Qing troops retake Xunzhou (Guangxi), the Dacheng capital, and capture its leader, the Triad Chen Kai, whose troops later join Shi Dakai. (See also September 27, 1855.)
27 *(7/22)*. Taiping forces under Li Xiucheng attack the capital of Jiangxi, Nanchang, but are defeated. Chen Yucheng's forces attack the Hunan Army at Anqing, trying to break the siege, but are defeated.
September 5 *(8/1)*. The Hunan Army under Zeng Guoquan retakes Anqing, the Taiping defenders suffering appalling losses. The relief forces under Chen Yucheng and others retreat. Anqing was, apart from Nanjing, the Taipings' most important city and its loss was a decisive turning-point in the war.
16 *(8/12)*. At Qianshan (Jiangxi), some of Shi Dakai's followers and some Guangdong Triads, altogether some 200,000 men, join Li Xiucheng.

1861

B OFFICIAL APPOINTMENTS, DISMISSALS, TRANSFERS ETC.

January 16 *(12/6)*. The Qing court appoints the Englishman H.N. Lay as Inspector-general of Maritime Customs.

20 *(12/10)*. Prince Gong is placed at the head of the *Zongli yamen* with Grand Secretary Guiliang and Wenxiang as assistants; Chonghou is appointed Superintendent of Trade for Niuzhuang, Tianjin, and Dengzhou.

February 6 *(12/27)*. Zhou Zupei and Guanwen become Grand Secretaries and Sushun assistant Grand Secretary.

26 *(1/17)*. Wenyu becomes acting Viceroy of Zhili.

April 25 *(3/16)*. Chonglun and Hengqi are appointed to the *Zongli yamen*.

August 21 *(7/16)*. Emperor Xianfeng declares his five-year-old son Zaichun heir-apparent, and appoints eight regents: Zaiyuan, Duanhua, Sushun, Jingshou, Muyin, Kuangyuan, Du Han, and Jiao Youying.

23 *(7/18)*. Xiaoqin and Xiaozhen become Empresses Dowager.

25 *(7/20)*. Luo Bingzhang is appointed Viceroy of Sichuan; Fuji of Yungui.

October 4 *(9/1)*. The two Empresses Dowager Xiaozhen and Xiaoqin are given the honorary titles of Cian and Cixi respectively.

November 2 *(9/30)*. Jingshou, Muyin, Kuangyuan, Du Han and Jiao Youying are dismissed from the Grand Council. An edict is written (put into effect November 4) for the arrest of Zaiyuan, Duanhua and Sushun.

3 *(10/1)*. Prince Gong is appointed Adviser in the Administration of Government. He, Guiliang, Shen Zhaolin and Baoyun are appointed to the Grand Council, and Cao Yuying becomes a probationary Grand Councillor.

11 *(10/9)*. Zaichun ascends the throne as Emperor.

30 *(10/28)*. Baoyun and Dong Xun are appointed to the *Zongli yamen*.

December 2 *(11/1)*. The two Empresses Dowager become regents.

19 *(11/18)*. Fuji is dismissed as Viceroy of Yungui and replaced, in an acting capacity, by Pan Duo.

C CULTURAL AND SOCIAL

London missionaries set up a hospital in Peking.

D PUBLICATIONS

Publication of the following Taiping works: *Qinding shijie tiaoli* (*Imperial Regulations Governing Scholarly Ranks*); Hong Ren'gan's *Zhuyaoxiwen*

1861-2

Nian troops under Zhao Haoran press on Ji'nan (Shandong).
October 4 (*9/1*). The British and French forces begin their withdrawal from Guangzhou.
9 (*9/6*). The Nian Army is defeated in a fight against British and French forces in Yantai (Shandong).
26 (*9/23*). Shi Dakai enters Hunan from Guangxi.
30 (*9/27*). After a long siege, Miao Peilin takes Shouzhou (Anhui) for the Nian.
November 1 (*9/29*). The Taipings take Shaoxing (Zhejiang).
Zaichun, the heir-apparent, and the two Empresses Dowager, Cian and Cixi, return to Peking.
2 (*9/30*). The two Empresses Dowager and Prince Gong carry out a *coup* against the regents, and seize power at court.
7 (*10/5*). The next year is declared the first of Tongzhi.
24 (*10/22*). The Taipings take Yuyao (Zhejiang).
December 9 (*11/8*). The Taipings take Ningbo (Zhejiang).
23 (*11/22*). Troops of Lan Chaogui's Incense Burners' League move into Guang'an (Sichuan).
29 (*11/28*). The Taipings under Li Xiucheng take Hangzhou.

1862 *Foreign forces enter the war against the Taipings*

January 7 (*12/8*). The Taipings under Li Xiucheng advance from Hangzhou towards Shanghai. Li calls for support from the people and neutrality from the foreigners.
20 (*12/21*). Taiping forces under Tan Shaoguang attack Wusong and press on Shanghai.
26 (*12/27*). The court orders the *Zongli yamen* to negotiate with the British and French with a view to their offering troops to defend Shanghai against the Taipings.
February 10 (*1/12*). Li Xiucheng's Taipings are defeated by a force under the American F.T. Ward near Songjiang.
17 (*1/19*). Shi Dakai's forces enter Sichuan from Hubei.
March 1 (*2/1*). The Moslem rebel in Yunnan, Ma Rulong, surrenders to the Qing.
16 (*2/16*). The Governor of Jiangsu, Xue Huan, sends in a memorial

1861–2

(*Proclamations on the Extermination of Demons*); and a new calendar. Completion of the anti-Christian tract *Bixie jishi* (*A Record of Facts to Ward off Heterodoxy*).

April 11 (*3/2*). Completion of Hong Ren'gan's *Qinding yingjie guizhen* (*A Hero's Return to the Truth*).

September 20 (*8/16*). Completion of Hong Ren'gan's *Qinding junci shilu* (*Imperially Approved Veritable Records While Conducting Army Campaigns*).

November. Feng Guifen completes editing his *Jiaobin lu kangyi* (*Protests from the Jiaobin Hut*), a collection of some fifty essays on the social and economic problems of the time.

December. The *Shanghai xinbao* (*New Shanghai Paper*) begins publication as a weekly (see also July 2, 1872), the Chinese edition of the *North China Daily News*.

F Births and Deaths

April 20 (*3/11*). Duanfang b. (d. 1911).
August 22 (*7/17*). The Xianfeng Emperor d. in Jehol aged 30.
September 30 (*8/26*). The Governor of Hubei Hu Linyi d. in Wuchang aged 49.
November 8 (*10/6*). Sushun is executed, aged *c.* 46. Zaiyuan and Duanhua commit suicide.
December 3 (*11/2*). Tang Shaoyi b. (d. 1938).

Establishment of the College of Foreign Languages   1862

A Economics

January 1 (*12/2*). Hankou opens as a trading port.
February 19 (*1/21*). A foreign steamship purchased by Zeng Guofan arrives in Anqing.
Following a memorial from the *Zongli yamen* the court orders Jiangsu, Guangdong and other provinces to appropriate a total of 800,000 taels so that maritime customs can purchase ships, cannon and military equipment.
27 (*1/29*). The Viceroy of Liangguang, Lao Chongguang, finalizes negotiations with Robert Hart for the purchase of seven steamships from Britain for 650,000 silver taels.
March 27 (*2/27*). The American Shanghai Steam Navigation Company is founded in Shanghai.
August 13 (*7/18*). China signs a trade treaty with Portugal in Tianjin.

87

1862

that the foreign rifle corps defending Shanghai has changed its name to the 'Ever Victorious Army'.

April 8 (*3/10*). Li Hongzhang arrives in Shanghai from Anqing at the head of 6500 troops of the Hunan and Huai Armies.

11 (*3/13*). The Nian Army under Zhang Zongyu attacks Luoyang (Henan).

May 1 (*4/3*). Jiading near Shanghai is retaken from the Taipings by British and French forces, and the Ever Victorious Army.

9 (*4/11*). Shi Dakai's army enters Guizhou from Sichuan.

10 (*4/12*). Qing troops, assisted by British and French forces, retake Ningbo (Zhejiang).

13 (*4/15*). Qing troops under Duolong'a retake Luzhou (Anhui); Chen Yucheng flees to Shouzhou. The municipal council of the French Concession in Shanghai is established. The French thus organize a separate settlement.

15 (*4/17*). The Taiping leader Chen Yucheng is arrested in Shouzhou (Anhui) by Miao Peilin, a former Nian leader who had defected to the Qing in the spring.

17 (*4/19*). A Taiping north-western expedition, led by Chen Decai and Lai Wenguang, attacks Xi'an, the Shaanxi capital, but is repelled by General Tuoming'a, the Tartar General of Xi'an.

22 (*4/24*). Taiping forces under Chen Decai and Lai Wenguang seize Weinan (Shaanxi).

26 (*4/28*). Taiping troops under Li Xiucheng again take Jiading, driving out the British naval forces there, and press on Shanghai.

30 (*5/3*). Taiping troops under Tan Shaoguang take Huzhou (Zhejiang). Qing land troops under Zeng Guoquan and water forces under Peng Yulin arrive at the outskirts of Nanjing.

June 3 (*5/7*). Lan Chaogui of the Incense Burners' League moves from Sichuan to Shaanxi.

18 (*5/22*). Taiping forces under Li Xiucheng are defeated by the Huai Army on the outskirts of Shanghai.

29 (*6/3*). Following a Moslem-Han massacre, in which thousands died, Moslem rebels attack Xi'an: the beginning of the North-west Moslem rebellion.

July 5 (*6/9*). Lan Chaogui's troops occupy Yangxian (Shaanxi).

20 (*6/24*). The US Minister to China, Anson Burlingame, arrives to take up residence in Peking.

August 6 (*7/11*). Li Xiucheng calls a conference of Taiping leaders in Suzhou (Jiangsu) to plan the breaking of the siege of Nanjing.

23 (*7/28*). The Taipings, under Tan Shaoguang, again press on Shanghai but are defeated by Li Hongzhang four days later.

1862

B OFFICIAL APPOINTMENTS, DISMISSALS, TRANSFERS ETC.

January 30 *(1/1)*. Linkui and Zeng Guofan are appointed assistant Grand Secretaries.
February 14 *(1/16)*. Shen Zhaolin becomes acting Viceroy of Shan'gan.
August 14 *(7/19)*. Xilin becomes Viceroy of Shan'gan.
18 *(7/23)*. Qiling becomes Viceroy of Minzhe.
October 5 *(int. 8/12)*. Li Tangjie is appointed to the Grand Council.
7 *(int. 8/14)*. Li Hongzhang appoints H.A. Burgevine to succeed to Ward's command of the Ever Victorious Army.
9 *(int. 8/16)*. Woren is appointed Grand Secretary.
17 *(int. 8/24)*. Liu Changyou becomes Viceroy of Liangguang.
December 1 *(10/10)*. Cao Yuying is appointed to the Grand Council.

C CULTURAL AND SOCIAL

January 20 *(12/21)*. The American missionary I.J. Roberts leaves Nanjing after serious disagreement with Hong Ren'gan.
March 17 *(2/17)*. Local people destroy the Catholic orphanage in Nanchang (Jiangxi), as well as some shops and homes owned by Chinese Catholics.
18 *(2/18)*. Local people destroy the Catholic church outside Nanchang.
April 12 *(3/14)*. In Xiangtan (Hunan) a crowd of literati and commoners set fire to a new Catholic church.
13 *(3/15)*. A crowd pillages and demolishes the home of a well-to-do Christian family, burning five children to death.
July 11 *(6/15)*. Ten students enter the College of Foreign Languages at the *Zongli yamen*, Peking; this is the formal beginning of the College.
November 17 *(9/26)*. At the suggestion of the *Zongli yamen*, the court orders that selected military officials be sent to Shanghai and Ningbo to learn foreign military technology and methods.

D PUBLICATIONS

Publication of the *Taiping tianri* (*The Taiping Heavenly Chronicle*). The *Zhongwai zazhi* (*Shanghai Miscellany*) begins publication.
April 23 *(3/25)* Completion of the *Zhiping baojian* (*Precious Mirror of Good Government and Tranquillity*) by Zhang Zhiwan, Pan Zuyin and others, in which examples of good administration and regencies by empresses were gathered.

1862-3

September 21 *(8/28)*. The leader of the Ever Victorious Army, Ward, is fatally wounded in battle with the Taipings.
October 13 *(int. 8/20)*. An enormous Taiping force of some 100,000 men led by Li Xiucheng marches from Suzhou to relieve Nanjing. Heavy fighting breaks out with the Hunan Army under Zeng Guoquan.
26 *(9/4)*. Gansu Moslem rebels led by Ma Hualong attack Lingzhou.
November 3 *(9/12)*. The Taipings under Li Xiucheng and Li Shixian again attack the Hunan Army under Zeng Guoquan outside Nanjing, but are repulsed.
18 *(9/27)*. A combined British, French and Chinese force retakes Yuyao (Zhejiang) for the Qing.
December 1 *(10/10)*. Li Xiucheng's army crosses the Yangzi and prepares to move west, having failed to lift the siege of Nanjing.

1863 Suzhou falls to the Qing

January 9 *(11/20)*. A British order-in-council permits British naval and military officers to serve in the Qing forces.
11 *(11/22)*. Li Xiucheng returns to Suzhou (Jiangsu) from Nanjing.
16 *(11/27)*. Without authority from Peking, H.N. Lay concludes an agreement with Captain Sherard Osborn making the latter sole Commander-in-Chief of a naval force of several vessels bought by Lay for China.
22 *(12/4)*. The White Lotus leader Song Jingshi again revolts against the Qing and leads his troops from Shaanxi across the Yellow River east into Shanxi.
31 *(12/13)*. Shi Dakai's army moves from Sichuan to Yunnan.
February 7 *(12/20)*. Taiping troops under Chen Decai and Lai Wenguang occupy Xing'an (Shaanxi).
19 *(1/2)*. A combined Chinese, British and French force is defeated by the Taipings when they attack Shaoxing (Zhejiang).
March 4 *(1/15)*. Yunnan Moslem rebels occupy the provincial capital Yunnan. The Moslem Du Wenxiu later seizes the opportunity to

E   NATURAL DISASTERS

Summer. A cholera epidemic sweeps Shanghai.

F   BIRTHS AND DEATHS

May 17 *(4/19)*. The French admiral A.L. Protet d. in battle with the Taipings aged 54.
June 4 *(5/8)*. Chen Yucheng is executed in Henan aged 25.
30 *(6/4)*. The scholar and historian He Qiutao d., aged 38, in Baoding, where he was the director of the Lianchi Academy.
July 17 *(6/21)*. Grand Secretary Guiliang d. aged 76.
30 *(7/4)*. The Viceroy of Shan'gan, Shen Zhaolin, d. aged 61.
September 22 *(8/29)*. F.T. Ward d. aged 31.
December 12 *(10/21)*. Cao Kun, future President of the Peking government, b. (d. 1938).
17 *(10/26)*. The former Viceroy of Liangjiang, He Guiqing, executed for cowardice against the Taipings, aged 46.

Death of Shi Dakai **1863**

A   ECONOMICS

January 24 *(12/6)*. The Qing court orders the opening up of new land in Heilongjiang.
July 13 *(5/28)*. China and Denmark set up a trade agreement.
20 *(6/5)*. Li Hongzhang, the Governor of Jiangsu, refuses a request by British and American merchants in Shanghai to build a railway between Suzhou and Shanghai.
October 6 *(8/24)*. China and the Netherlands conclude a trade treaty in Tianjin.
16 *(9/4)*. Following Li Hongzhang's suggestion, the court orders Ding Richang to Shanghai to look after the manufacture of munitions. Li had already engaged some British and French minor officers and soldiers to manufacture them.
December 6 *(10/26)*. Rong Hong leaves Anqing for the USA. He had been commissioned by Zeng Guofan to buy machinery there for China's modernization. His purchases subsequently become the basis of the Jiangnan arsenal.

1863

take several cities.

11 (*1/22*). Shaanxi Moslem rebels again attack Xi'an.

15 (*1/26*). The combined Qing, French and British force retakes Shaoxing from the Taipings.

19 (*2/1*). Qing troops under Senggelinqin defeat the Nian leader Zhang Luoxing and take Zhiheji, his base area in northern Anhui. Cen Yuying and others re-establish Qing control in Yunnan.

23 (*2/5*). The Nian leader Zhang Luoxing is taken prisoner in Suzhou (Anhui) and soon executed.

26 (*2/8*). The Taipings Chen Decai and Lai Wenguang attack Hanzhong (Shaanxi) jointly with Lan Chaogui's forces.

May 11 (*3/24*). Li Xiucheng joins forces with the Nian leader Zhang Zongyu in an unsuccessful attack on Liuan (Anhui).

12 (*3/25*). Shi Dakai returns to Sichuan.

28 (*4/11*). The Ever Victorious Army under Gordon and the Huai Army retake Kunshan (Jiangsu).

June 13 (*4/27*). Zeng Guoquan's army takes Yuhuatai outside Nanjing. Shi Dakai surrenders to the Qing in Sichuan on the understanding that his life will be spared.

August 2 (*6/18*). H.A. Burgevine, recently dismissed as commander of the Ever Victorious Army, leaves Shanghai for Suzhou (Jiangsu) to join the Taiping forces under Tan Shaoguang there.

22 (*7/9*). Taiping forces under Li Xiucheng, using foreign rifles, attack the Hunan Army besieging Nanjing, but are defeated. The Huai Army under Cheng Xueqi begins to attack Suzhou.

September 21 (*8/9*). The British and American Concessions in Shanghai are formally amalgamated into the International Settlement.

23 (*8/11*). Li Xiucheng arrives in Suzhou, planning to break the siege of the city.

24 (*8/12*). Moslem rebels under Ma Hualong take Pingliang (Gansu).

October 2 (*8/20*). Taiping troops under Chen Decai and Lai Wenquang take Hanzhong (Shaanxi).

16 (*9/4*). Gordon writes to Li Xiucheng and Tan Shaoguang asking that foreigners in Suzhou be allowed to leave and not be harmed.

20 (*9/8*). Qing forces inflict a decisive defeat on the White Lotus sect under Song Jingshi in Kaizhou (Zhili). Song himself later flees south and joins the Nian rebels.

November 6 (*9/25*). The *Zongli yamen* refuses to accept Lay's action over the 'Lay-Osborn flotilla' (see January 16) and directs that its ships be returned. (They are later sold in India.)

17 (*10/7*). Lan Chaogui (Dashun) occupies Zhouzhi (Shaanxi).

27 (*10/17*). The Ever Victorious Army under Gordon attacks Suzhou

1863

B OFFICIAL APPOINTMENTS, DISMISSALS, TRANSFERS ETC.

January 3 *(11/14)*. Shengbao is arrested and examined. Duolong'a is appointed Imperial Commissioner in charge of military affairs in Shaanxi.
4 *(11/15)*. Li Hongzhang dismisses Burgevine from command of the Ever Victorious Army.
February 14 *(12/27)*. Wenyu is dismissed as Viceroy of Zhili and replaced by Liu Changyou.
March 25 *(2/7)*. Major Charles G. Gordon takes over command of the Ever Victorious Army.
May 5 *(3/18)*. Zuo Zongtang is appointed Viceroy of Minzhe; Zeng Guoquan Governor of Zhejiang.
26 *(4/9)*. Xue Huan is appointed to the *Zongli yamen*.
June 7 *(4/21)*. Lao Chongguang becomes Viceroy of Yungui.
July 6 *(5/21)*. Mao Hongbin becomes Viceroy of Liangguang.
November 15 *(10/5)*. H.N. Lay is dismissed as Inspector-General of Maritime Customs and replaced the following day by Robert Hart.

C CULTURAL AND SOCIAL

March 11 *(1/22)*. Li Hongzhang sends in a memorial asking for the setting up of a foreign languages school in Shanghai, on the model of Peking's College of Foreign Languages.
13 *(1/24)*. The people of Chongqing, angry at the prospect of handing over a temple to French missionaries, attack and destroy the Catholic church of the latter as well as the attached hospital and school.
22 *(2/4)*. The court receives a memorial from Chongshi urging action to ensure that Chinese officials treat cases involving Christians impartially; and that missionaries do not transmit their doctrine to disreputable persons.
28 *(2/10)*. Following Li Hongzhang's suggestion, a foreign languages school is set up in Shanghai called *Guang fangyan guan*.
April 23 *(3/6)*. The College of Foreign Languages in Peking begins French and Russian classes with ten students each.
June 11 *(4/25)*. Zhang Zhidong (1837–1909) and Huang Tifang (1832–99) receive their *jinshi* degree, Zhang coming third in the entire year.

D PUBLICATIONS

January. Gui Wencan presents to the throne his *Jingxue congshu* (*Collection on the Study of the Classics*).

1863—4

but is defeated by Taiping forces under Tan Shaoguang.
28 *(10/18)*. Cheng Xueqi meets with several Taiping generals inside the walls of Suzhou to discuss the terms of their surrender to the Qing.
30 *(10/20)*. Li Xiucheng abandons Suzhou, leaving Tan Shaoguang in charge of the city's defence.
December 4 *(10/24)*. Moslem rebels from Gansu, Ningxia and Shaanxi, led by Ma Yanbang and others, seize the Chinese city of Ningxia and kill many Chinese. Leading Taipings defending Suzhou hand the city over to Cheng Xueqi on the understanding that they would be given high military commissions in the Qing army. Li Hongzhang and Cheng Xueqi have them executed on December 6.
5 *(10/25)*. Moslem rebels led by Ma Zhaoyuan take Lingzhou (Gansu).
7 *(10/27)*. Gordon, furious at Li Hongzhang's perfidy in Suzhou the previous day, refuses to accept his orders. Li and Gordon remain estranged for several months.
12 *(11/2)*. The Huai Army retakes Wuxi (Jiangsu) from the Taipings.
20 *(11/10)*. Li Xiucheng returns to Nanjing. On this day or soon after, he advises Hong Xiuquan to flee; Hong refuses and orders Li to defend Nanjing.

1864 Nanjing falls to the Qing

February 10 *(1/3)*. Taiping forces under Chen Decai and Lai Wenguang leave Hanzhong (Shaanxi) for the east to try to relieve Nanjing.
March 25 *(2/18)*. The Huai Army under Cheng Xueqi retakes Jiaxing (Zhejiang); Cheng is seriously wounded.
30 *(2/23)*. Qing forces under the Tartar General of Xi'an, Duolong'a, make a fierce attack on Zhouzhi (Shaanxi). Doulong'a is seriously wounded.
31 *(2/24)*. Qing troops retake Hangzhou from the Taipings. The Ever Victorious Army is defeated at Jiangyin (Jiangsu) with the loss of more than 300 men. Qing troops retake Zhouzhi (Shaanxi) from Lan Chaogui (Dashun).
May 1 *(3/26)*. Nian troops under Zhang Zongyu, pursued by Senggelinqin, join the troops of Chen Decai and Lai Wenguang in Zaoyang (Hubei).
11 *(4/6)*. The Huai Army and the Ever Victorious Army retake Changzhou (Jiangsu) from the Taipings.
31 *(4/26)*. The Ever Victorious Army, having completed its task, disbands in Kunshan (Jiangsu).
June 3 *(4/29)*. The Xinjiang Moslem rebellion begins in Kucha, where

1863-4

F BIRTHS AND DEATHS

March 4 (*1/15*). The Viceroy of Yungui, Pan Duo, is killed by Moslem rebels in Yunnan, Yunnan Province.
August 6 (*6/22*). The Taiping Shi Dakai is executed in Chengdu aged 32.
8 (*6/24*). Yuan Jiasan d. of illness in Henan aged 57.
31 (*7/18*). Shengbao d. through suicide.
December 4 (*10/24*). Wu Chongyue d. aged 53. Tan Shaoguang is assassinated by Taiping colleagues.
6 (*10/26*). Miao Peilin is killed by his own soldiers.
8 (*10/28*). Qing military commander and official Li Xuyi d. aged 40.

Birth of Qi Baishi **1864**

A ECONOMICS

January. Li Hongzhang orders the Scotsman Halliday Macartney to purchase mechanical equipment for the Suzhou arsenal.
28 (*12/20*). In Anqing (Anhui) Zeng Guofan tries out a small steamship newly manufactured by Xu Shou and others.
June 2 (*4/28*). Li Hongzhang sends in a memorial calling for the investigation of all kinds of foreign machinery.
October 10 (*9/10*). China and Spain conclude a treaty of trade and navigation.

B OFFICIAL APPOINTMENTS, DISMISSALS, TRANSFERS ETC.

June 6 (*5/3*). Hong Xiuquan's son Tianguifu ascends the Taiping throne.
9 (*5/6*). Yang Yuebin replaces Xilin as Viceroy of Shan'gan.
August 1 (*6/29*). For their part in suppression of the Taipings, Zeng Guofan is made a Marquis of the first class and given the rank of Grand Guardian to the Heir to the Throne; Zeng Guoquan and Li Hongzhang are made Earls of the first class and Zeng given the rank of Junior Guardian to the Heir to the Throne.

1864

Burhanuddin is delared leader.

23 (5/20). Qing forces retake Pingliang (Gansu) from the Moslem rebels.

July 4–18 (6/1–15). The Hunan Army under Zeng Guoquan mounts fierce attacks on Nanjing.

15 (6/12). Moslem rebellion under Tuoming flares up in Xinjiang when Moslems in Urumchi burn and loot the Han section of the city.

17 (6/14). Moslem rebels seize the southern city of Manas (Xinjiang).

19 (6/16). The Taiping capital Nanjing falls to the Hunan Army under Zeng Guoquan.

19–22 (6/16–19). Fire destroys Nanjing. Some 100,000 Taipings in Nanjing either commit suicide or are slaughtered by Zeng Guoquan's troops.

20 (6/17). Li Xiucheng flees from Nanjing with Hong Tianguifu. The two get separated.

22 (6/19). Li Xiucheng is captured outside Nanjing.

24 (6/21). Hong Ren'gan flees with Hong Tianguifu and others to Guangde (Anhui).

28 (6/25). Zeng Guofan arrives in Nanjing.

29 (6/26). Hong Tianguifu and his party arrive in Huzhou (Zhejiang), still in Taiping hands.

Moslem rebels under Tuoming take the Chinese city of Urumchi.

August 14 (7/13). Zeng Guofan cuts the Hunan Army by 25,000 men.

24 (7/23). Qing troops under Senggelinqin defeat a Taiping-Nian coalition under Chen Decai, Lai Wenguang and Zhang Zongyu at Macheng (Hubei). Chen's troops move east while Lai Wenguang's and Zhang Zongyu's move west. (The fall of Nanjing had forced the Taiping leader Lai Wenguang to merge with the Nian.)

28 (7/27). Huzhou (Zhejiang) falls to the Qing.

September 22 (8/22). Hong Ren'gan and Hong Tianguifu, having fled from Huzhou into Anhui, enter Jiangxi.

October 3 (9/3). The Tartar city of Urumchi falls to Moslem rebels under Tuoming.

7 (9/7). The Russo-Chinese Protocol of Chuguchak (Tarbagatai) delimits the north-western frontiers.

9 (9/9). Hong Ren'gan is captured in Guangchang (Jiangxi).

14 (9/14). Taiping forces under Li Shixian take Zhangzhou (Fujian).

25 (9/25). Hong Tianguifu is captured in Shicheng (Jiangxi).

31 (10/2). Gansu Moslems seize Hezhou after a long siege.

November 7 (10/9). A large Taiping force of more than 70,000 under Chen Decai surrenders to Senggelinqin at Huoshan (Anhui).

December 7 (11/9). Nian troops under Lai Wenguang defeat Seng-

1864

November 6 *(10/8)*. Li Hongzhang becomes acting Viceroy of Liangjiang.

9 *(10/11)*. Zuo Zongtang is made an Earl of the first class and Bao Chao a Viscount of the first class for their part in the suppression of the Taipings.

C Cultural and Social

June 2 *(4/28)*. At the suggestion of the *Zongli yamen* the court sends forty-eight soldiers and officers from Peking to Jiangsu to learn about the manufacture of bombs and other munitions.

23 *(5/20)*. The Guangzhou College of Foreign Languages opens.

D Publications

Printing is completed of Li Zuoxian's *Guquan hui* (*Compendium of Ancient Coins*) (author's preface undated). The *Huazi ribao* begins publication in Hongkong as a Chinese edition of the *China Mail*. Zhao Zhiqian's *Bu Huanyu fangbei lu* (*Supplement to* [*Sun Xingyan's*] *Records on the World's Stone Inscriptions*) (author's preface dated first month, February 8–March 7, 1864), containing nearly 2000 stone and bronze inscriptions, is published.

July 1 *(5/28)*. The *North China Daily News* begins publication under this name.

July 30–August 7 *(6/27–7/6)*. Li Xiucheng writes his confession, his own account of the Taiping uprising and his role in it, for Zeng Guofan.

F Births and Deaths

January 1 *(11/22)*. Painter Qi Baishi b. in Xiangtan (Hunan) (d. 1957).
March 31 *(2/24)*. Lan Chaogui (Dashun). d.
April 15 *(3/10)*. Cheng Xueqi d. aged 34.
May 18 *(4/13)*. Duolong'a, the Tartar General of Xi'an, d. aged 47.
June 1 *(4/27)*. Hong Xiuquan, the Heavenly King of the Taipings, d. aged 51.
August 7 *(7/6)*. Li Xiucheng executed in Nanjing aged 41.
October 19 *(9/12)*. Li Yuanhong b. in Huangpi (Hubei) (d. 1928).
November 7 *(10/9)*. Chen Decai d. by suicide.
18 *(10/20)*. Hong Tianguifu executed by lingering death in Nanchang (Jiangxi) aged 15.
23 *(10/25)*. Hong Ren'gan executed by lingering death in Nanchang aged 42.

1864–5

gelinqin at Xiangyang (Hubei).
12 (*11/14*). Nian troops under Lai Wenguang and others defeat Senggelinqin at Dengzhou (Henan).
25 (*11/27*). Tuoming's Moslem troops occupy Turfan.

1865 The North-west Moslem rebellion gathers momentum

Early January. Buzurg Khan, a descendant of a former ruling house of Kashgar, Yakub Beg, his chief of staff, and other Moslems enter Xinjiang from Khokand.

Mid-January. Yakub Beg and Buzurg Khan occupy the Moslem city of Kashgar, and Buzurg Khan declares himself King of Kashgar.

18 (*12/21*). The court orders the *Zongli yamen* to ask the ministers of all the foreign countries in Peking to direct their consuls in Fujian to try to prevent contact with the Taipings in Zhangzhou.

29 (*1/3*). The Nian Lai Wenguang, Zhang Zongyu and others defeat Senggelinqin in Lushan (Henan).

February 18 (*1/23*). Riots break out in Liangzhou (Gansu); they last three days and three nights and result in the slaughter of many Moslems.

March. In Urumchi, Tuoming declares himself the Pure and True King.

23 (*2/26*). Gansu Moslem rebels under Ma Wenlu seize Suzhou (Gansu).

April 2 (*3/7*). Nian troops under Zhang Zongyu and Lai Wenguang move into Shandong from Henan. Moslems rebel in the city of Ganzhou (Gansu) but are forced to retreat to the countryside.

11 (*3/16*). Yakub Beg's forces take Yangi Hissar (Xinjiang).

May 15 (*4/21*). Qing troops retake Zhangzhou (Fujian) from the Taipings under Li Shixian.

18 (*4/24*). Combined anti-Qing forces under Lai Wenguang, Zhang Zongyu, Song Jingshi and others defeat Senggelinqin at Caozhou (Shandong).

July 4 (*int. 5/12*). The Qing army retakes Qianxi (Guizhou) from the White Signal sect which has held the city since 1859.

25 (*6/3*). Zhang Zongyu and Lai Wenguang split forces after an attempt to retake the Nian base area of Zhiheji ends in defeat.

August 7 (*6/16*). Moslem troops under Buzurg Khan and Yakub Beg seize Kucha and Aksu (Xinjiang) and take Burhanuddin prisoner.

29 (*7/9*). The Taipings under Lu Shunde occupy Changle (Guangdong).

September 7 (*7/18*). Yakub Beg's Moslem forces take the Han Chinese

The Jiangnan arsenal set up **1865**

A ECONOMICS

January. China borrows £1,430,000 from Great Britain – the beginning of China's international debt.
April. The Hongkong and Shanghai Banking Corporation is established in Hongkong.
June. Zeng Guofan sets up a machinery bureau (arsenal) in Shanghai.
September. The Jiangnan arsenal is set up in Shanghai.

B OFFICIAL APPOINTMENTS, DISMISSALS, TRANSFERS ETC.

March 13 (*3/16*). Ruilin becomes acting Viceroy of Liangguang.
April 2 (*3/7*). Prince Gong is deprived of all his offices for showing partiality to his relatives and for carelessness of conduct at court.
11 (*3/16*). Prince Gong is reinstated as head of the *Zongli yamen*.
May 8 (*4/14*). Prince Gong is reinstated as head of the Grand Council.
23 (*4/29*). Zeng Guofan is appointed Imperial Commissioner to suppress the Nian rebellion.
November 20 (*10/3*). Xu Jiyu is appointed to the *Zongli yamen*.
December 20 (*11/3*). Tan Tingxiang is appointed to the *Zongli yamen*.
28 (*11/11*). Li Hongzao is appointed a probationary member of the Grand Council.

C CULTURAL AND SOCIAL

February 20 (*1/25*). The French minister in Peking, Jules Berthemy, signs a Convention providing that land bought by missionaries in China's interior must be held in the name of the Catholic mission, not in that of an individual or individuals.
March 25 (*2/28*). At the suggestion of Shen Guifen, Governor of Shaanxi, the Qing court forbids the planting of the opium poppy.
June 19 (*5/26*). The Qing court orders every province to re-establish the *baojia* system.
August 29 (*7/9*). The French missionary François Mabileau is killed in Youyang (Sichuan).

city of Kashgar. Slaughter and plunder continue for a week, costing some 4000 Han Chinese their lives. Within the next six months or so after this Yakub Beg wins a power struggle against Buzurg Khan and assumes leadership over the Moslems of the area.

20 *(8/1)*. Qing forces recapture Changle from the Taipings and take Lu Shunde prisoner.

October 8 *(8/19)*. The White Signal sect takes Guangshun and Dingfan (Guizhou).

November 29 *(10/12)*. The forces of the Nian leaders Zhang Zongyu and Lai Wenguang merge again in Henan.

December 8 *(10/21)*. The Taipings under Wang Haiyang take Jiaying (Guangdong).

1866 Final defeat of the Taipings

January 23 *(12/7)*. Nian troops under Lai Wenguang take Huangpi (Hubei) as they press towards Hankou.

February 7 *(12/22)*. The Hunan Army under Bao Chao recaptures Jiaying (Guangdong). This action saw the final destruction of the

September 4 (*7/15*). The British Supreme Court of Shanghai is established.
17 (*7/28*). The Qing court issues an edict forbidding French missionaries to intervene in military affairs.

D PUBLICATIONS

January 27 (*1/1*). W.A.P. Martin's translation into Chinese under the title *Wanguo gongfa* of Henry Wheaton's *Elements of International Law* is presented to the throne.
February 2 (*1/7*). The *Zhongwai xinwen qiri lu* (*Chinese and Foreign Weekly News*) begins publication in Guangzhou.
June 23–July 22 (*int. 5*). Du Wenlan's *Pingding Yuefei jilüe* (*Records of the Pacification of the Guangxi Bandits*), a history of the Taipings, is completed (preface by Guanwen, Viceroy of Huguang, dated intercalary fifth month of 1865).
November 6 (*9/18*). Hart presents to the *Zongli yamen* his *Juwai pangguan lun* (*Discussions of a Bystander*) on various matters of domestic and diplomatic politics.

E NATURAL DISASTERS

Famine serious enough to cause the sale of human corpses for food occurs in southern Anhui and parts of Jiangsu.

F BIRTHS AND DEATHS

March 6 (*2/9*). Duan Qirui b. (d. 1936).
10 (*2/13*). Tan Sitong b. in Peking (d. 1898).
25 (*2/28*). Wu Jingheng (Zhihui), future member of the Western Hills group, b. in Wuxi (Jiangsu) (d. 1953).
May 18 (*4/24*). Senggelinqin d. in battle.
August 23 (*7/3*). Li Shixian is assassinated by Wang Haiyang, aged 31.
December 26 (*11/9*). Li Tangjie d. aged 67.

Birth of Sun Yatsen **1866**

A ECONOMICS

British merchants build a railway from Shanghai to Baoshan not far to the north-west.
July 14 (*6/3*). Following a memorial from Zuo Zongtang (June 25),

Taipings, apart from the forces of Lai Wenguang and others who had merged with the Nian.

15 (*1/1*). The White Signal sect again takes Qianxi (Guizhou).

March. Yakub Beg extends his control over Yarkand.

8 (*1/22*). Xinjiang Moslem rebels seize Yili.

April 11 (*2/26*). Xinjiang Moslem rebels take Tarbagataï.

17 (*3/3*). Moslem troops mutiny in Lanzhou, the capital of Gansu. They kill many officials and storm the Viceroy's offices.

June 10 (*4/28*). Du Wenxiu's Moslem rebel army of Yunnan takes Lijiang, Heqing and Jianchuan.

16 (*5/4*). The Commander-in-Chief of Gansu, Cao Kezhong, restablishes control in Lanzhou.

July 29 (*6/18*). Zeng Guofan sends in a memorial outlining his policy of defeating the Nian; it is to build dykes and walls along part of the Yellow River, the Grand Canal, the Huai and other rivers and contain the Nian within the area thus formed: the border regions of Henan, Anhui, Jiangsu and Shandong.

September 11 (*8/3*). Zhang Zongyu's and Lai Wenguang's forces reunite in Henan.

24 (*8/16*). Nian troops under Lai Wenguang and Zhang Żongyu break through river dykes near Kaifeng (Henan) and move east. The dykes had been built specially as part of Zeng Guofan's plan and the Nian action showed its failure.

October 3 (*8/25*). The court orders the arrest of Yang Wenzheng, the White Lotus sect leader.

20 (*9/12*). The Nian Army divides into two branches; the Eastern Nian under Lai Wenguang move towards Shandong, the Western under Zhang Zongyu towards Shaanxi. The two branches did not reunite again after this.

November 19 (*10/13*). Because of sickness and his failure against the Nian rebels, Zeng Guofan asks to be relieved of his posts of assistant Grand Secretary, Viceroy of Liangjiang, and Imperial Commissioner in charge of operations against the Nian.

December 2 (*10/26*). Qing troops under Liu Mingchuan defeat the Eastern Nian in Caoxian (Shandong), causing them to move back to Henan.

14 (*11/8*). The Western Nian under Zhang Zongyu press on Xi'an, the capital of Shaanxi.

22 (*11/16*). The Eastern Nian under Lai Wenguang enter Hubei from Henan and take Macheng.

1866

the court orders the establishment of a dockyard in Fuzhou.
August 19 (7/10). The Frenchman Prosper Giquel arrives in Fuzhou (Fujian) to discuss with and advise Zuo Zongtang in detail on the planned Fuzhou dockyard.
October 6 (8/28). The court accepts a proposal from Prince Gong and others to set up an arsenal in Tianjin and hands the matter over to Superintendent of Trade Chonghou.
26 (9/18). China and Italy conclude an agreement on trade regulations.

B Official Appointments, Dismissals, Transfers etc.

September 25 (8/17). Zuo Zongtang is made Viceroy of Shan'gan in place of Yang Yuebin, whose failure to cope with the Moslem uprisings had led to his resignation. Ruilin is confirmed as Viceroy of Liangguang. Wu Tang becomes Viceroy of Minzhe.
November 22 (10/16). Wang Yuanfang is appointed to the Grand Council to replace Li Hongzao.
26 (10/20). Li Hongzhang is made Imperial Commissioner in charge of the Hunan and Huai Armies.
December 7 (11/1). Zeng Guofan is ordered back as Viceroy of Liangjiang. Li Hongzhang is made Imperial Commissioner against the Nian rebels.

C Cultural and Social

December 11 (11/5). Following a memorial from Prince Gong and others, a scientific department of astronomy and mathematics is added to the College of Foreign Languages.

D Publications

April 15–May 13 (3). Liu Baonan's *Lunyu zhengyi* (*Orthodox Commentary on the Analects*) is completed.
April 30 (3/16). Li Yuandu's *Guochao xianzheng shilue* (*Brief Biographies of Former Worthies of the Qing*) is completed.

F Births and Deaths

February 1 (12/16). The Taiping leader Wang Haiyang d. aged about 35.
May 11 (3/27). Grand Councillor Cao Yuying d.
August 8 (6/28). Luo Zhenyu b. (d. 1940).

1866-7

1867 Rising of the 'night-bird bandits'

January. Yakub Beg extends his control to Khotan (Xinjiang).
11 (*12/6*). The Eastern Nian under Lai Wenguang defeat a Qing force under Commander-in-Chief Guo Songlin at Zhongxiang (Hubei); Guo is seriously wounded.
23 (*12/18*). The Western Nian under Zhang Zongyu defeat a Qing army near Xi'an (Shaanxi) and surround the city.
February 4 (*12/30*). Government reinforcements under Liu Songshan arrive at Xi'an, forcing Zhang Zongyu to move west.
March. Yakub Beg extends his control to Aksu, Kucha and Ush (Xinjiang).
23 (*2/18*). The Eastern Nian under Lai Wenguang defeat the Hunan Army in Qishui (Hubei).
April 19 (*3/15*). Qing forces under Liu Songshan take Linpingzhen (Shaanxi) from the Moslem rebels who join up with Zhang Zongyu, Western Nian and move to Xianyang (Shaanxi).
22 (*3/18*). The Moslem-Nian coalition presses on Xi'an.
May 27 (*4/24*). The Western Nian again attack Xi'an, but are repulsed.
June 13 (*5/12*). The Eastern Nian break the defences of the Grand Canal near Jining (Shandong) and press on Ji'nan, the provincial capital.
30 (*5/29*). The Eastern Nian press on Yantai (Shandong), but are repulsed by British and French troops.
July 5 (*6/4*). The revolt of the 'night-bird bandits', i.e. salt smugglers, erupts in Cangzhou, Yanshan, Bazhou and other parts of Zhili province.
10 (*6/9*). The French minister communicates with the *Zongli yamen* complaining of recent anti-foreign mass riots in Niuzhuang and other places and asking for tighter controls.
20 (*6/19*). In Guizhou, Qing troops under the Financial Commissioner of Yunnan, Cen Yuying, inflict a decisive defeat on the Miao rebels, seizing a major stronghold west of Bijie, killing some 20,000 of them and capturing the former Taiping military commander Tao Xinchun.
August 16 (*7/17*). Cen Yuying takes another stronghold of the Miao rebels, near Weining (Guizhou).
September 29 (*9/2*). The court orders the arrest of all members of the

1866–7

October 20 *(9/12)*. Grand Secretary Qi Junzao d. aged 73.
November 12 *(10/6)*. Sun Yatsen b. in Xiangshan (Guangdong) (d. 1925).

The China Shipping Company set up **1867**

A ECONOMICS

British merchants set up the China Shipping Company and American merchants the Shanghai Steamship Company.

January 10 *(12/5)*. Following on the change in course of the Yellow River, the court orders joint action in looking after the dykes among the three provinces Zhili, Shandong and Henan.
May. Li Hongzhang sets up the Jinling arsenal in Nanjing.
29 *(4/26)*. The Tianjin arsenal begins operations.
August 2 *(7/3)*. The *Zongli yamen* proposes the procurement of foreign rice.
December. Because of the lack of cash in Peking, the court orders all provinces to arrange for remittances to it.

B OFFICIAL APPOINTMENTS, DISMISSALS, TRANSFERS ETC.

February 15 *(1/11)*. Li Hongzhang replaces Guanwen as Viceroy of Huguang.
22 *(1/18)*. Zuo Zongtang is appointed Imperial Commissioner in charge of military affairs in Shaanxi and Gansu.
25 *(1/21)*. Xu Jiyu is appointed to the *Zongli yamen*.
April 2 *(2/28)*. Zhang Kaisong becomes Viceroy of Yungui.
June 10 *(5/9)*. Zeng Guofan is appointed Grand Secretary, retaining his post as Viceroy of Liangjiang, and Luo Bingzhang assistant Grand Secretary, also retaining his post as Viceroy of Sichuan.
November 9 *(10/14)*. Shen Guifen is appointed to the Grand Council.
26 *(11/1)*. The court confers on Zhigang and Sun Jiagu the rank of second-degree official.
29 *(11/4)*. Liu Changyou is dismissed as Viceroy of Zhili because of his failure to defeat the 'night-bird bandits' and replaced (in an acting capacity) by Guanwen.

C CULTURAL AND SOCIAL

May 7 *(4/4)*. The court allows young people from the Ryukyu Islands to come to China to study.

1867–8

Elder Brothers Society. This secret society had expanded considerably since the suppression of the Taipings.

November 19 *(10/24)*. The Huai Army under the Commander-in-Chief of Zhili, Liu Mingchuan, defeats the Eastern Nian in Ganyu (Jiangsu).

21 *(10/26)*. The Qing court sends the former American Minister to China, Anson Burlingame, to represent China as ambassador-at-large to Western countries.

22 *(10/27)*. In conjunction with Moslem rebels, the Western Nian under Zhang Zongyu occupy Suide (Shaanxi).

24 *(10/29)*. As part of their continuing campaign the 'night-bird bandits' again make trouble in Bazhou (Zhili).

26 *(11/1)*. The court sends Zhigang and Sun Jiagu as ambassadors-at-large to accompany Burlingame to the West. They were the first Chinese envoys sent to the West.

December 17 *(11/22)*. The Western Nian under Zhang Zongyu cross the Yellow River into Shanxi and take Jizhou.

24 *(11/29)*. Qing forces under Liu Mingchuan and Guo Songlin defeat the Eastern Nian under Lai Wenguang in Shandong. Qing troops recover Suide (Shaanxi).

1868 Final defeat of the Nian Army

January 2 *(12/8)*. The Western Nian enter Henan from Shanxi.

5 *(12/11)*. The Eastern Nian are annihilated near Yangzhou (Jiangsu). Lai Wenguang is captured.

7 *(12/13)*. The 'night-bird bandits' of Zhili are 'pacified'.

February 5 *(1/12)*. The Western Nian, having moved into Zhili (January 27), are defeated at Mancheng and move south-east.

19 *(1/26)*. Du Wenxiu's Dali Moslems occupy Fumin and Anning (Yunnan).

25 *(2/3)*. Burlingame, Zhigang and Sun Jiagu leave Shanghai for the USA.

March 8 *(2/15)*. The Dali Moslems and other anti-Qing groups besiege and attack Yunnan, the capital of Yunnan province.

April 1 *(3/9)*. Shaanxi Moslem rebels under Ma Zhenghe, Bai Yanhu and others enter Gansu and occupy Zhenyuan.

4 *(3/12)*. Shaanxi Moslem rebels under Ma Zhenghe and others seize Qingyang (Gansu).

17 *(3/25)*. The Western Nian under Zhang Zongyu enter Shandong.

27 *(4/5)*. The Western Nian approach Tianjin.

1867-8

D Publications

January 13 (12/8). The *Da Qing Wenzong Xian huangdi shilu* (*Veritable Records of the Qing Xianfeng Emperor*) and the *Da Qing Wenzong Xian huangdi shengxun* (*Edicts of the Qing Xianfeng Emperor*) are completed.

May 4–31 (4). Zhang Mu's *Menggu youmu ji* (*An Account of Pastoral Clans in Mongolia*) is completed (preface by Qi Junzao dated fourth month of 1859).

E Natural Disasters

March 13 (2/8). A major epidemic breaks out in Peking.
Early Summer. Drought causes a general crop failure.

F Births and Deaths

January 30 (12/25). Hengqi d. aged about 65.
February 21 (1/17). Viceroy of Yungui Lao Chongguang d. aged 65.
December 12 (11/17). Luo Bingzhang, assistant Grand Secretary and Viceroy of Sichuan, d. aged 74.

Birth of Cai Yuanpei 1868

A Economics

January 18 (12/24). The Fuzhou dockyard formally begins operating.
July 23 (6/4). Work is completed on the Jiangnan arsenal's first steamship; it is called the *Tianji*.

B Official Appointments, Dismissals, Transfers etc.

January 11 (12/17). Wu Tang is appointed Viceroy of Sichuan; Ma Xinyi of Minzhe.
  15 (12/21). Guo Baiyin becomes acting Viceroy of Huguang.
March 28 (3/5). The Viceroy of Yungui, Zhang Kaisong, is dismissed and replaced by Liu Yuezhao.
April 19 (3/27). Zhu Fengbiao is appointed Grand Secretary.
August 27 (7/10). Because of the suppression of the Nian, Zuo Zongtang and Li Hongzhang are given the title of Grand Guardian to the Heir to the Throne and Li is appointed assistant Grand Secretary, retaining his post as Viceroy of Huguang.
September 6 (7/20). Zeng Guofan is appointed Viceroy of Zhili, Ma

1868-9

May 21 (*4/29*). Zuo Zongtang and Li Hongzhang meet in Dezhou (Shandong) to discuss the suppression of the Nian Army.
26 (*int. 4/5*). The Hunan and Sichuan Armies under Xi Baotian conquer the base area of the White Signal sect near Sinan (Guizhou).
June 6 (*int. 4/16*). The Burlingame Mission has an interview with the US President Andrew Johnson.
July 15 (*5/26*). The *Zongli yamen* communicates with the British, French, US, Russian and other legations forbidding foreigners to dig for gold privately.
28 (*6/9*). The Sino-US 'Burlingame Treaty' is signed in Washington.
31 (*6/12*). Qing troops under the Financial Commissioner of Shandong, Pan Dingxin, inflict a decisive defeat on the Western Nian at Jiyang (Shandong).
August 16 (*6/28*). The Western Nian are annihilated near Renping (Shandong) by a Qing force under the Commander-in-Chief of Zhili, Liu Mingchuan. The Nian rebellion ends. The leader of the Guizhou White Signal sect, Liu Yishun, is captured; the White Signal rebellion is thus defeated. Qing troops under the Viceroy of Yungui, Liu Yuezhao, and others defeat Du Wenxiu's Moslem rebels and raise the siege of Yunnan city.
September 11 (*7/25*). The British consul in Shanghai, W.H. Medhurst, goes to Nanjing to negotiate with Zeng Guofan over the Yangzhou incident (see C, August 22).
19 (*8/4*). Burlingame arrives in London from New York.
November 9 (*9/25*). The British consul, Medhurst, leading four warships, arrives in Nanjing to negotiate over the Yangzhou incident. China's new steamship the *Tianji* is captured, thus forcing Zeng Guofan to accept all the British demands.
20 (*10/7*). The Burlingame Mission sees Queen Victoria.
December. Yakub Beg begins relations with Britain and Russia when Robert Shaw visits Yarkand and Kashgar from India and Shadi Mirza visits St Petersburg as Yakub Beg's representative.

1869 The Burlingame Mission in Europe

January 14 (*12/2*). The British Foreign Secretary, Lord Clarendon, reprimands Sir Rutherford Alcock, British minister in China, and Medhurst over their response to the Yangzhou incident and urges a

1868–9

Xinyi of Liangjiang and Yinggui of Minzhe.
November 28 (*10/15*). Li Hongzao is appointed a full member of the Grand Council.

C CULTURAL AND SOCIAL

May 17 (*4/25*). Among the 270 to gain their *jinshi* degree are Wu Dacheng (1835–1902), Baoting (1840–90), He Ruzhang (1838–91) and Xu Jingcheng (1845–1900).
August 22 (*7/5*). In Yangzhou some 10,000 people plunder and nearly destroy the residence of the missionaries of the China Inland Mission and hurt the occupants.
December 13 (*10/30*). The Mixed Court is set up in Shanghai.

D PUBLICATIONS

The prose works of the poet and scholar Gong Zizhen (1792–1841) are printed into two collections from manuscripts edited by Gong himself under the titles *Ding'an wenji* (*Collected Prose Works of Ding'an*) and *Ding'an xuji* (*A Further Collection of Ding'an's Works*) (joint introduction dated the intercalary fourth month, May 22 to June 19).
September 5 (*7/19*). The weekly *Zhongguo jiaohui xinbao* (*New China Missionary Review*) begins publication in Shanghai.

E NATURAL DISASTERS

August 12 (*6/24*). The Yellow River floods in Henan.
September 16 (*8/1*). The Yongding River floods.

F BIRTHS AND DEATHS

January 10 (*12/16*). Lai Wenguang is executed, aged 40.
    11 (*12/17*). Cai Yuanpei b. in Shaoxing (Zhejiang) (d. 1940).
March 4 (*2/11*). Lin Sen b. (d. 1943).
August 16 (*6/28*). The Nian leader Zhang Zongyu drowns himself.

The Execution of An Dehai **1869**

A ECONOMICS

Yinggui sets up the Fujian arsenal.
April 27 (*3/16*). China and Russia conclude overland trade regulations.

1869

more conciliatory attitude. (See November 9, 1868.)

20 (*12/8*). A clash between men from a British gunboat and the local people in a village near Chaozhou (Guangdong) results in the death of ten Chinese and the wounding of some British sailors.

24 (*12/12*). The Burlingame Mission has an audience with Napoleon III of France.

29 (*12/17*). British naval forces go ashore and plunder in several parts of Chaozhou. As a result of fighting, sixty-nine Chinese are killed and nearly 500 houses burned down.

March 18 (*2/6*). Shaanxi Moslem rebels, who had set up their base area in Dongzhiyuan (Gansu), attempt to move back into Shaanxi because of strong military pressure from Zuo Zongtang.

22 (*2/10*). Moslem rebels again press on Yunnan, the Yunnan capital.

24 (*2/12*). The British government expresses dissatisfaction over the British sailors' behaviour in Chaozhou on January 20.

April 4 (*2/23*). Qing troops under Zuo Zongtang take the Moslem rebel base of Dongzhiyuan.

5 (*2/24*). Qing forces defeat the Dongzhiyuan Moslems and retake Zhenyuan (Gansu).

6 (*2/25*). Qing forces retake Qingyang (Gansu) from the Dongzhiyuan Moslem rebels under Ma Zhenghe and others. Following their defeat, the surviving Shaanxi Moslem rebels flee to Jinjibao (Gansu), their other major base area.

May 3 (*3/22*). Miao rebels under Zhang Xiumei defeat the Hunan Army near Huangping (Guizhou).

22 (*4/11*). Miao rebels again occupy Duyun (Guizhou).

September 7 (*8/2*). The Governor of Shandong, Ding Baozhen, arrests An Dehai, the favourite eunuch of the Empress Dowager, Cixi, in Taian (Shandong). An had been sent by the Empress on a mission to Nanjing but arrogated privileges and power to himself, and also practised corruption. Ding's action was a very important move, curbing eunuch power.

8 (*8/3*). Zuo Zongtang's forces begin their attack on the Moslem rebels of Jinjibao (Gansu), led by the Gansu Moslem Ma Hualong and the Shaanxi Moslems Ma Zhenghe and Bai Yanhu.

11 (*8/6*). The Moslem Ma Hualong defeats a Qing army and takes Lingzhou (Gansu).

21 (*8/16*). Qing troops under Cen Yuying again relieve the siege of Yunnan city.

24 (*8/19*). The ministers of Britain, Russia, Germany, the USA and France set up in Peking the regulations governing the International Settlement in Shanghai.

June. The court accepts a suggestion from Li Hongzhang that China should purchase foreign copper to mint its currency.
10 *(5/1)*. The first steamship built by the Fuzhou dockyard, the *Wannianqing*, is launched.
September 2 *(7/26)*. China and Austria establish a trade and shipping treaty.
6 *(8/1)*. The court forbids Russian ships to enter the rivers of Jilin and Heilongjiang for trade and prohibits private trade with them.
December 6 *(11/4)*. The Fuzhou dockyard's second ship, the *Meiyun*, is launched.

B   OFFICIAL APPOINTMENTS, DISMISSALS, TRANSFERS ETC.

November 9 *(10/6)*. Zuo Zongtang takes over the office of Viceroy of Shan'gan.
12 *(10/9)*. Shen Guifen, Chenglin and Mao Changxi are appointed to the *Zongli yamen*.
26 *(10/23)*. The American missionary W.A.P. Martin becomes President of the College of Foreign Languages.

C   CULTURAL AND SOCIAL

January 2 *(11/20)*. In Youyang (Sichuan) militiamen burn a French missionary, Jean-François Rigaud, to death, together with a number of converts.
March 25 *(2/13)*. In Youyang, Catholics kill eighteen ordinary people and burn some ten houses in revenge for the January 2 incident.
April 22 *(3/11)*. In Youyang, converts again kill some hundred ordinary people and burn many houses to revenge the January 2 incident.
May 18 *(4/7)*. Anti-Christian disturbances occur in parts of Zhili.
June 14 *(5/5)*. The people of Zunyi (Guizhou) ransack and destroy French churches and other establishments and kill Catholic converts.
July 4 *(5/25)*. The *Zongli yamen* sends in a memorial that China should make a presentation of books to the USA. They include the enormous compendium *Huang Qing jingjie* (*Exegesis of Classics of the Imperial Qing*), and are still housed in the Library of Congress.
August 21 *(7/14)*. The Governor of Guizhou writes to the *Zongli yamen* and encloses the text of a letter distributed in the Zunyi area in mid-July in which the gentry show their intention to eliminate Catholicism entirely.
November 3 *(9/30)*. In Anqing (Anhui) two missionaries of the China

1869-70

October 6 *(9/2)*. The British minister, Rutherford Alcock, communicates with the *Zongli yamen* requesting that all foreign ministers resident in Peking be allowed audience with the Emperor.
12 *(9/8)*. Qing forces defeat the Shaanxi Moslem Bai Yanhu and other Moslem rebels near Guyuan (Gansu). Another defeat on October 21 forces Bai Yanhu, Ma Zhenghe and others to move west to Didao (Gansu).
November 2 *(9/29)*. The French *chargé d'affaires*, Count Julien de Rochechouart, demands speedy action over the several missionary incidents, and announces his plan to send warships up the Yangzi. Qing forces under Liu Songshan retake Lingzhou from Moslem rebels.
26 *(10/23)*. Shaanxi Moslem rebels under Bai Yanhu and others are defeated at Didao and move west towards Hezhou (Gansu).
December 2 *(10/29)*. The Burlingame Mission sees Kaiser Wilhelm I of Germany.
23 *(11/21)*. De Rochechouart leads four warships from Shanghai up the Yangzi to Nanjing to negotiate rapid settlements of all pending missionary difficulties.

1870 The Tianjin Massacre

January 23 *(12/22)*. Liu Songshan defeats the Shaanxi Moslem rebels in their Gansu base area Jinjibao.
27 *(12/26)*. Li Hongzhang arrives in Wuchang to negotiate over the Youyang incident with the French *chargé d'affaires* Rochechouart, who returns to Peking overland on January 29 after the negotiations.
February 2 *(1/3)*. The Burlingame Mission arrives in the Russian capital St Petersburg from Berlin.
6 *(1/7)*. A Moslem rebel army is defeated near Yunnan city.
14 *(1/15)*. Liu Songshan attacks the Moslem rebels near Jinjibao, as part of an overall attempt to seize their base area.
March 10 *(2/9)*. Qing troops under Liu Jintang (who has succeeded to the command of his uncle Liu Songshan) continue to attack the Jinjibao Moslem rebels.
May. Tuoming, 'Pure and True Moslem King' of the northern route of Xinjiang, based in Urumchi, sends troops to attack Kucha, but they are defeated by Yakub Beg of the southern route.
June 21 *(5/23)*. The 'Tianjin Massacre'. Popular anger against a French Catholic orphanage accused of kidnapping results in a mass siege of

Inland Mission are beaten up and their house ransacked; French Jesuit missionaries are beaten.

December 16 (*11/14*). The Jiangnan arsenal authorities are notified of authorization for Shanghai's *Guang fangyan guan* to move into the arsenal.

D PUBLICATIONS

February. Completion of *Yonglu xianjie* (*A Treatise on Snuff and Snuff Bottles*) by Zhao Zhiqian.

E NATURAL DISASTERS

September. Widespread flooding strikes Hunan.

F BIRTHS AND DEATHS

January 12 (*11/30*). Scholar Zhang Binglin b. in Yuyao (Zhejiang) (d. 1936).
September 12 (*8/7*). An Dehai is executed on Imperial order, aged 25.

Li Hongzhang appointed Viceroy of Zhili   1870

A ECONOMICS

June 6 (*5/8*). The *Zongli yamen* gives approval for the British to lay an undersea electric cable from Guangzhou to Shanghai.
November 4 (*10/12*). Chonghou and others memorialize announcing the completion of the Tianjin machinery bureau (arsenal).
December 23 (*11/2*). The imperial silk agencies of Hangzhou, Jiangning and Suzhou are ordered to manufacture 100,000 pieces of silk for the Emperor's wedding.

B OFFICIAL APPOINTMENTS, DISMISSALS, TRANSFERS ETC.

January 8 (*12/7*). Li Hanzhang is appointed acting Viceroy of Huguang.
June 28 (*5/30*). Chonghou is appointed Imperial Commissioner to go to France to convey China's apology for the 'Tianjin Massacre'.
July 14 (*6/16*). Zhang Guangzao, prefectural magistrate of Tianjin, and Liu Jie, the county magistrate, are both dismissed because of the Tianjin Massacre.
August 29 (*8/3*). Zeng Guofan is appointed Viceroy of Liangjiang, Li

1870–1

the church in the afternoon. The French consul Henri Fontanier shoots at, but misses, Superintendent of Trade Chonghou and Liu Jie, the county magistrate of Tianjin, and is himself killed by the crowd. It mutilates and kills every French person it can find and plunders and sets fire to the French consulate, the orphanage and the church. By nightfall over thirty Chinese converts and over twenty foreigners (seventeen French) are dead.

July 4 (*6/6*). Zeng Guofan goes to Tianjin to deal with the problems arising from the Tianjin Massacre.

August 22 (*7/26*). The Viceroy of Liangjiang, Ma Xinyi, is knifed by a former Taiping.

September. T. Douglas Forsyth, sent by the British Viceroy of India to establish contacts with Yakub Beg's administration in Xinjiang, leaves Yarkand for India.

October. Yakub Beg again defeats the forces of Tuoming and surrounds Turfan.

15 (*9/21*). The court expresses concern to Zuo Zongtang at the vast expense and slow speed of his suppression of the Gansu Moslem rebellion and orders quicker and more productive action.

24 (*10/1*). The Moslem rebel leader Ma Hualong is wounded as Liu Jintang bombards Jinjibao.

28 (*10/5*), Liu Jintang inflicts a serious defeat on Moslem rebels near Jinjibao (Gansu), killing 6000.

November 8 (*10/16*). Tuoming's forces surrender Turfan to Yakub Beg.

17 (*10/25*). A Qing force under Xi Baotian takes the main stronghold of the Miao rebels, Taigong (Guizhou).

18 (*10/26*). Zhigang and Sun Jiagu arrive back in Peking from the Burlingame Mission.

21 (*10/29*). Yakub Beg's troops begin to attack Dihua (Urumchi).

December 27 (*11/6*). As Yakub Beg continues to attack Urumchi, Tuoming surrenders to him, making Yakub Beg supreme leader of Moslems in Xinjiang.

30 (*11/9*). Qing forces retake Duyun (Guizhou) from the Miao rebels.

1871 *Sino-Japanese Friendship and Trade Treaty*

January 6 (*11/16*). The Moslem rebel Ma Hualong surrenders to Liu Jintang.

9 (*11/19*). Qing troops under Liu Jintang finally take Jinjibao (Gansu), the Moslem rebel base area.

Hongzhang of Zhili and Li Hanzhang is confirmed as Viceroy of
Huguang.
October 5 (*9/11*). The court orders that Zhang Guangzao and Liu Jie
be sent into lifelong exile because of the Tianjin Massacre.

C CULTURAL AND SOCIAL

Engraved dishes of the Zhou period are obtained by the British and
displayed in the British Museum, London.
January 1 (*11/30*). The ringleaders in the Youyang incident of January
2, 1869, are executed in Chongqing on orders from Li Hongzhang.
August 7 (*7/11*). The court issues an edict banning theatres of all kinds
in the Inner City of Peking.
18 (*7/22*). The Qing court orders every province to select talented
people from the forces guarding the coast to be sent abroad to study.
October 10 (*9/16*). Zeng Guofan sends in a memorial asking that intelligent young men be chosen to go to the West to study military
affairs, shipbuilding and so on there.

E NATURAL DISASTERS

August 4 (*7/8*). At Hankou the Yangzi River rises to a peak of 15.4
metres; the city floods.

F BIRTHS AND DEATHS

February 13 (*1/14*). Kang Zhilin, famous Sichuanese actor, b. (d. 1931).
14 (*1/15*). Liu Songshan d. in battle aged 37.
23 (*1/24*). Burlingame d. in St Petersburg aged 49.
August 23 (*7/27*). Ma Xinyi d. aged 49.

Death of Woren **1871**

A ECONOMICS

April 18 (*2/29*). The undersea electric cable between Shanghai and
Hongkong is completed.
June 3 (*4/16*). London is connected with Shanghai by undersea electric

1871

25 *(12/5)*. Chonghou arrives in Marseilles, planning to convey China's apology for the Tianjin Massacre to the French government.

February 27 *(1/9)*. Because of rebellious activity in Langson, Vietnam, just south of the Chinese border, the Commander-in-Chief of Guangxi, Feng Zicai, is sent to Taiping (Guangxi) to help deal with it.

March 21 *(2/1)*. After a long siege, Qing forces under Cen Yuying, the Governor of Yunnan, capture Chengjiang (Yunnan), from the province's Moslem rebels.

April 5 *(2/16)*. The Moslem rebellion in Ningxia is suppressed with the capture of its leaders, including Ma Wanxuan, and their headquarters.

May 30 *(4/12)*. The Hunan Elder Brothers Society seizes Yiyang (Hunan).

June 5 *(4/18)*. Qing troops retake Yiyang.

18 *(5/1)*. Some 3000 Russian soldiers advance toward Yili, ostensibly to suppress the rebellion of Yakub Beg and restore peace.

July 4 *(5/17)*. Russian troops occupy Yili.

September 1 *(7/17)*. In view of the Russian occupation of Yili, the court orders the Tartar General of Yili, Rongquan, to take action for its recovery; and that an overall plan be devised to retake all the cities of Xinjiang.

13 *(7/29)*. Li Hongzhang and the Japanese minister Date Munenari conclude the Sino-Japanese Friendship Treaty.

November 23 *(10/11)*. Chonghou, after several months' delay and a trip to England and the United States, at last sees French President Louis Thiers and delivers to him Chinese regret over the Tianjin Massacre.

27 *(10/15)*. Sixty-six Ryukyuan sailors go ashore in Taiwan after being shipwrecked; fifty-four are killed by aboriginal Taiwanese.

1871

cable via San Francisco.
September 13 (*7/29*). Li Hongzhang for China and Date Munenari for Japan conclude trade regulations.

B Official Appointments, Dismissals, Transfers etc.

April 17 (*2/28*). Ruichang is appointed Grand Secretary, and Wenxiang assistant Grand Secretary.
August 3 (*6/17*). Ruilin is appointed Grand Secretary.
October 19 (*9/6*). Zhang Zhiwan is appointed Viceroy of Minzhe.
December 14 (*11/3*). Li Henian replaces Zhang Zhiwan as Viceroy of Minzhe.

C Cultural and Social

June 23 (*5/6*). The court answers the memorial from Zuo Zongtang suggesting the suppression of the Moslem New Sect, which formed the ideological basis of Ma Hualong's rebellion, by vetoing his proposal for the time being.
July 25 (*6/8*). The court orders that the printing blocks of novels be destroyed.
September 3 (*7/19*). Zeng Guofan and Li Hongzhang send in a joint memorial suggesting that selected students be sent to the West to study subjects related to modernization and modern technology.
October 3 (*8/19*). An edict is issued that offices be set up in every province to look after homeless orphans.

E Natural Disasters

July 28 (*6/11*). The Yongding River floods.
August 9 (*6/23*). A cyclone strikes Taiwan.
29 (*7/14*). The Yongding River floods again.

F Births and Deaths

March 1 (*1/11*). Guanwen d. aged 73.
2 (*1/12*). Ma Hualong is executed.
June 8 (*4/21*). The famous conservative Grand Secretary Woren d. aged ?67.
August 14 (*6/28*). Zaitian, the future Guangxu Emperor, b, (d. 1908).
October 27 (*9/14*). Scholar and bibliophile Mo Youzhi d. aged 60.
November 27 (*10/15*). The Moslem rebel Tuoming d.

1872 The Guizhou Miao rebellion is crushed

January 21 (12/12). The Guizhou Army inflicts a defeat on the Miao rebels, beheading one of their leaders and capturing several others.

26 (12/17). Chonghou arrives back from France in Shanghai.

28 (12/19). The British minister to China, Thomas Wade, is beaten up in Peking.

April 30 (3/23). The Hunan and Guizhou Armies take the Miao rebel stronghold of Wuyapo near Kaili (Guizhou). Many thousands of Miao people are killed, including several leaders; many more surrender.

May 6 (3/29). A Japanese envoy arrives in Tianjin with a demand for changes to the Treaty of September 13, 1871. Li Hongzhong refuses the changes May 15.

12 (4/6). The seventeen-year-old Miao rebellion of Guizhou is finally suppressed with the capture of its main leader Zhang Xiumei. (See also October 24, 1855.)

June 8 (5/3). Yakub Beg signs a treaty with the Russians allowing them to come to Xinjiang for trade in return for their recognition of him as the leader of East Turkestan.

July 18 (6/13). The Russian minister, G. Vlangaly, announces that Russia will not hand Yili back to China for the time being, because of China's inability to protect it.

August 18 (7/15). Zuo Zongtang moves his headquarters to Lanzhou, the better to suppress the Moslem rebels of Gansu.

September 12 (8/10). Moslems of Xining (Qinghai) combine with Shaanxi Moslems under Bai Yanhu and others to resist Liu Jintang, and besiege Xining.

18 (8/16). The French minister, F.-L.-H. de Geofroy, demands that the Treaty of Tianjin be revised.

October 16 (9/15). Wedding of the Tongzhi Emperor. The ministers of the various countries request audience with the Emperor.

November 19 (10/19). Qing forces under Liu Jintang inflict a serious defeat on the Moslem rebels of the north-west by relieving the siege of Xining. Some 4000 Moslems are killed.

December 10–14 (11/10–14). Qing forces under Yang Yuke mine the south-eastern corner of the city walls of Dali, the capital of Du Wenxiu's rebel Yunnan kingdom, and force an entrance, though not yet to the Forbidden City within the city walls.

25 (11/25). Du Wenxiu personally leads troops out of the Forbidden City of Dali in a vain attempt to save his Moslem kingdom, but is intercepted by Yang Yuke.

26 (11/26). Du Wenxiu surrenders to the Qing.

A Economics

June 20 *(5/15)*. A memorial by Sub-Chancellor Song Jin of January 23 suggesting the discontinuation of shipbuilding is refuted by Li Hongzhang, who calls for further self-strengthening and modernization measures.
December 23 *(11/23)*. Li Hongzhang sends in a memorial suggesting an experimental merchant steamship company; this is the beginning of the China Merchants' Steam Navigation Company.

B Official Appointments, Dismissals, Transfers etc.

March 5 *(1/26)*. Chonghou and Xia Jiagao are appointed members of the *Zongli yamen*.
20 *(2/12)*. He Jing is appointed acting Viceroy of Liangjiang and Superintendent of Trade.
June 22 *(5/17)*. Li Hongzhang is appointed a Grand Secretary, retaining his post as Viceroy of Zhili.
July 16 *(6/11)*. Wenxiang is appointed a Grand Secretary and Quanqing an assistant Grand Secretary.
September 10 *(8/8)*. Danmaoqian is appointed Grand Secretary.
November 25 *(10/25)*. Zhang Shusheng becomes acting Viceroy of Liangjiang.

C Cultural and Social

An observatory is set up at the Catholic church in Zikawei near Shanghai.
August 12 *(7/9)*. The first group of thirty Chinese students to study abroad leaves Shanghai for the United States. It is led by Chen Lanbin and Rong Hong.

D Publications

Printing of Pan Zuyin's notes on the ancient bronzes he had collected, the two-volumed *Pangu lou yiqi kuanzhi* (*Inscriptions on Cups in the Pangu Studio*). Pan Zuyin prints Dai Xi's (1801–60) work *Guquan conghua* (*Collected Notes on Ancient Coins*), prefaced 1838.
April 30 *(3/23)*. The British Ernest Major initiates the *Shenbao* (*Shanghai Newspaper*), for many years the most influential of Chinese-language newspapers.
July 2 *(5/27)*. *Shanghai xinbao* becomes a daily.
September. The *Jiaoping Yuefei fanglüe* (*Strategies on Pacifying the Guangxi Bandits*) and *Jiaoping Nianfei fanglüe* (*Strategies on Pacifying the Nian*

1872–3

1873 *The Moslem rebellions of Yunnan and Gansu suppressed*

January 2 *(12/4)*. The Governor of Yunnan, Cen Yuying, arrives in Dali.

5 *(12/7)*. Qing forces, overcoming strong resistance, force Moslem troops to surrender and seize complete control of Dali's Forbidden City.

7–9 *(12/9–11)*. Qing forces carry out a large-scale massacre of many thousands of Moslems in Dali.

February 13 *(1/16)*. The Shaanxi Moslem rebel Bai Yanhu escapes from the Xining area to the north-west.

23 *(1/26)*. The Tongzhi Emperor takes personal control of the government from the regents.

24 *(1/27)*. The ministers of the various Western countries, Russia, Germany, the USA, Britain and France, write to the *Zongli yamen* demanding audience with the Emperor, now governing in his own right.

March 2 *(2/4)*. The leaders of the Moslem rebellion of Xining surrender to the Qing.

April 28 *(4/2)*. Qing forces under Yang Yuke retake Yunzhou (Yunnan) from the Moslem rebels.

30 *(4/4)*. Li Hongzhang and the Japanese minister, Soejima Taneomi, exchange the Sino-Japanese Treaty of 1871 in Tianjin.

May 29 *(5/4)*. The last embers of the Yunnan Moslem rebellion are crushed with the Qing capture of Tengyue (Yunnan).

June 29 *(6/5)*. The Japanese, Russian, American, British, French and Dutch ministers to China are received in audience by the Emperor and present their credentials; this was the first time any Chinese emperor had received foreign envoys in audience without demanding the *kowtow*.

Bandits) are completed by commissions, both headed by Prince Gong. These were official works containing memorials and similar documents on the Taiping and Nian rebellions respectively.

F BIRTHS AND DEATHS

March 12 (*2/4*). Zeng Guofan d. in Nanjing aged 60.
December 26 (*11/26*). Du Wenxiu is executed.

The China Merchants' Steam Navigation Company set up 1873

A ECONOMICS

January 14 (*12/16*). The China Merchants' Steam Navigation Company is set up.
April 28 (*4/2*). The court orders Li Hongzhang to have the waterworks near Peking repaired.

B OFFICIAL APPOINTMENTS, DISMISSALS, TRANSFERS ETC.

February 3 (*1/6*). Li Zongxi is appointed Viceroy of Liangjiang and Superintendent of Trade.
September 9 (*7/18*). Li Hongzhang puts Sheng Xuanhuai and Xu Run in charge of the China Merchants' Steam Navigation Company.
October 3 (*8/12*). Cen Yuying is appointed acting Viceroy of Yungui.
December 6 (*10/17*). Yakub Beg formally accepts the title of Amir Khan from the Sultan of Turkey. After this he is called Amir Mohammed Yakub Khan of Kashgaria.
14 (*10/25*). Zuo Zongtang is made assistant Grand Secretary.

C CULTURAL AND SOCIAL

March 24 (*2/26*). The French merchant Menard introduces rickshaws from Japan to Shanghai.
May 21 (*4/25*). An American church is damaged in Ruichang (Jiangxi).
June 12 (*5/18*). The second batch of thirty students leaves Shanghai bound for the USA.
September 5 (*7/14*). A French Catholic missionary and a Chinese convert are beaten to death in Qianjiang (Sichuan).

1873-4

August 1 (*int. 6/9*). A Qing army mounts a fierce attack on Suzhou (Gansu) held by Moslem rebels since March 23, 1865.

September 22 (*8/1*). The court orders Chen Lanbin and Rong Hong to head a commission to Cuba to investigate the conditions of Chinese workers there.

October 3 (*8/12*). Zuo Zongtang arrives in Suzhou to command the attack on the city against the Moslem rebels.

10 (*8/19*). Bai Yanhu occupies the Moslem city of Hami, but moves west six days later.

November 4 (*9/15*). The Moslem rebel leader of Suzhou, Ma Wenlu, surrenders to Zuo Zongtang.

12 (*9/23*). Zuo Zongtang takes Suzhou (Gansu) from the Moslem rebels. His troops slaughter many thousands of Moslems. The Gansu Moslem rebellion is thus ended.

December 11 (*10/22*). Yakub Beg formally receives in Kashgar Sir Douglas Forsyth, a British envoy sent from India, and expresses warm friendship for Britain.

21 (*11/2*). The Black Flag Army of Liu Yongfu defeats a French force under François Garnier in Hanoi, the citadel of which Garnier had taken on November 20, and Garnier is killed.

1874 The Japanese Taiwan Expedition

January 4 (*11/16*). The court, unwilling to surrender suzerainty in Annam to France, orders Ruilin, the Viceroy of Liangguang, to send in troops.

February 2 (*12/16*). Yakub Beg and Forsyth reach an agreement whereby Britain is allowed to station trading commissioners and set up consulates in Xinjiang in return for official recognition of Yakub Beg as Amir of Kashgaria.

March 15 (*1/27*). The Franco-Vietnamese Treaty of Peace and Alliance is signed in Saigon; French sovereignty over Cochinchina is thus recognized.

May 3 (*3/18*). Following the announcement by the French municipal council of its intention to build roads over the burial ground of the people of Ningbo in the French Concession of Shanghai, violence breaks out, resulting in the burning of some houses of foreigners and the death of several Chinese.

7 (*3/22*). The Japanese Taiwan Expedition, more than 3000 troops sent to punish the island's aborigines for the incident of November 27, 1871, land at Langjiao on the south-east coast.

1873–4

D PUBLICATIONS

Wang Tao publishes his *Pu Fa zhanji* (*Records on the Franco-Prussian War*).
April. Publication of *Xiguo jinshi huibian* (*Compilation of Recent Affairs of Western Countries*) compiled and printed by the Jiangnan Arsenal.

F BIRTHS AND DEATHS

February 23 (*1/26*). Liang Qichao b. in Xinhui (Guangdong) (d. 1929).
September 11 (*7/20*). Poet, painter and calligrapher He Shaoji d. aged 74.

Death of Feng Guifen 1874

A ECONOMICS

March 31 (*2/14*). The Qing court forbids individual provinces to set up *lijin* tax barriers privately.
April 9 (*2/23*). The court issues a prohibition against private minting in Peking.
June 3 (*4/19*). A machinery bureau (arsenal) is set up in Guangzhou.
September 1 (*7/21*). A suggestion by Shen Baozhen to borrow 2,000,000 taels from the Hongkong and Shanghai Banking Corporation for use in Taiwan is adopted by the court.
9 (*7/29*). The Emperor orders the permanent suspension of work on the rebuilding of the Yuanming yuan, the Summer Palace destroyed in 1860, because of the cost.

B OFFICIAL APPOINTMENTS, DISMISSALS, TRANSFERS ETC.

August 23 (*7/12*). Zuo Zongtang becomes Grand Secretary, retaining his post as Viceroy of Shan'gan. The Military Commander of Urumchi,

1874–5

    14 *(3/29)*. The Qing court sends Shen Baozhen to Taiwan to investigate conditions there.

June 2 *(4/18)*. The Japanese Expedition advances in Taiwan and sets some aboriginal settlements on fire.

    26 *(5/13)*. Li Hongzhang establishes a trade agreement with Peru and a settlement on the treatment of Chinese workers there.

July 1 *(5/18)*. Japanese destroy eighteen Taiwanese aboriginal villages.

    12 *(5/29)*. Because of the Japanese invasion of Taiwan, the court orders all coastal provinces to step up their defences.

August. Rong Hong is sent to Peru to examine conditions of Chinese workers there.

    22 *(7/11)*. Augustus Raymond Margary, a British interpreter, leaves Shanghai for the Burmese frontier to join an exploration mission led by Colonel H.A. Browne.

September 10 *(7/30)*. The Japanese Ōkubo Toshimichi arrives in Peking as plenipotentiary to negotiate with China over the Taiwan incident; negotiations begin with the *Zongli yamen* on September 14.

October 20 *(9/11)*. Chen Lanbin's and Rong Hong's Commission to Cuba presents a report to the *Zongli yamen* revealing extreme ill-treatment and suffering among Chinese workers in Cuba.

    31 *(9/22)*. A Sino-Japanese agreement is signed, settling the Taiwan incident; Japan agrees to withdraw from Taiwan; China concedes the Expedition was justified, and agrees to pay an indemnity of 500,000 taels and to restrain the Taiwan aborigines in future.

November 27 *(10/19)*. Ōkubo Toshimichi arrives back in Tokyo after the negotiations in Peking.

December 3 *(10/25)*. The Japanese Taiwan Expedition withdraws from Taiwan.

    23 *(11/15)*. Another Moslem rebellion breaks out in Gansu, centred on Hezhou and led by Min Dianchen.

1875 *The Margary Affair*

Postal services attached to maritime customs are opened.

January 22 *(12/15)*. The Hezhou Moslem rebellion is suppressed with the capture of Min Dianchen.

February 6 *(1/1)*. Browne's expedition leaves Bhamo, Burma, for China's Yunnan province. (See also August 22, 1874.)

    21 *(1/16)*. Several members of Browne's mission, all Chinese except

Jinglian, is made Imperial Commissioner in charge of military affairs in Xinjiang.

September 10 (7/30). Prince Gong, who had displeased the Emperor now ruling in his own right, is deprived of his rank. However, it is restored the following day.

October 17 (9/8). Yinghan is appointed Viceroy of Liangguang.

December 18 (11/10). The Emperor being ill with smallpox, the two Empresses Dowager again become co-regents. Baoyun is appointed Grand Secretary.

C CULTURAL AND SOCIAL

November 17 (10/9). A third batch of thirty students, including Tang Shaoyi, leaves for the USA to study.

D PUBLICATIONS

June 16 (5/3). Rong Hong and others begin the newspaper *Huibao* (*Reporter*) in Shanghai.

September 5 (7/25). The weekly *Zhongguo jiaohui xinbao* (*New China Missionary Review*) changes its name to the *Wanguo gongbao* (*The Globe Magazine*).

F BIRTHS AND DEATHS

March 17 (1/29). Zhang Ertian b. (d. 1945).
April 22 (3/7). Wu Peifu b. in Shandong (d. 1939).
May 28 (4/13). Scholar Feng Guifen d. aged 65.
October 21 (9/12). Chen Jiageng (Tan Kah Kee) b. (d. 1961).
November 4 (9/26). Jia Zhen d. aged 76.
     27 (10/19). Tang Hualong b. in Hubei (d. 1918).

The Guangxu Emperor ascends the throne **1875**

A ECONOMICS

January 20 (12/13). The British Jardine, Matheson and Co. begins the laying of tracks for the Wusong–Shanghai railway line.

August 14 (7/14). Following Shen Baozhen's suggestion, the Jilong coal mine is opened in Taiwan.

November 8 (10/11). Following the request of the Governor of Shan-

1875

Margary, are killed in the Yunnan jungle near the border with Burma. Next day the expedition is attacked by armed men and forced to go back to Burma.

March. In order to prevent the 'coolie trade', the Portuguese forbid Chinese 'emigration under contract as well as all free emigration' from Macao.

4 (1/27). The court accepts a proposal by Shen Baozhen to build a city and set up offices at Langjiao, Taiwan, and to bring aboriginal people under control.

10 (2/3). Li Hongzhang sends in a memorial suggesting that Zuo Zongtang's proposed expedition against Moslem rebels of Xinjiang should be stopped and the money spent on coastal defences.

19 (2/12). The British minister, Thomas Wade, having on March 11 received the news of Margary's murder, makes several demands, including an investigation into the affair in the presence of British officers, an indemnity of 150,000 taels, and the granting of Imperial audience to British diplomats.

May 25 (4/21). The acting French minister, de Rochechouart, asks Prince Gong to suppress the Chinese bands which often raided across the border into Tongking and to open a point of entry in Yunnan for trade.

June 10 (5/7). Japan declares it will station troops in the Ryukyu Islands.

15 (5/12). Prince Gong replies to de Rochechouart refusing both requests of May 25 and reaffirming China's suzerainty in Vietnam.

July 14 (6/12). Japan declares it will forbid the Ryukyus to send tribute to China.

15 (6/13). The acting Viceroy of Yungui, Cen Yuying, memorializes on the Margary affair. He states that Margary was murdered by native bandits.

August 7 (7/7). In Tianjin, Ding Richang exchanges with the Peruvian minister the treaty of June 26, 1874. Peru guarantees to abolish all abuses against Chinese workers there.

11 (7/11). In a memorandum to Li Hongzhang, Wade increases British demands over the Margary affair, including the trial of Cen Yuying and the despatch of an envoy to Britain to apologize.

28 (7/28). Following the receipt of Cen Yuying's memorial on the affair, Li Hanzhang is sent to Yunnan to investigate the Margary affair and Ding Richang and Li Hongzhang to Tianjin to negotiate with Wade.

September 7 (8/8). Xue Huan is sent to help Li Hanzhang with the investigations into the Margary affair.

20 (8/21). A Japanese ship surveying Kanghwa Bay in Korea is

dong, Ding Baozhen, the court agrees to set up a machinery bureau (arsenal) in Shandong and coastal forts in Yantai, Weihaiwei and Dengzhou.

December 5 (*11/8*). At the suggestion of the *Zongli yamen* the court increases customs duty.

B OFFICIAL APPOINTMENTS, DISMISSALS, TRANSFERS ETC.

January 12 (*12/5*). On the death of the Tongzhi Emperor, the Empress Dowager Xiaoqin (Cixi) adopts his cousin and her nephew Zaitian as her son and makes him successor to the throne. Liu Kunyi is appointed acting Viceroy of Liangjiang.
14 (*12/7*). The two Empresses Dowager, Xiaoqin and Xiaozhen, become co-regents for the second time, an announcement to that effect being made the following day.

February 25 (*1/20*). The Guangxu Emperor formally ascends the throne.

May 3 (*3/28*). Zuo Zongtang is appointed Imperial Commissioner in charge of military affairs in Xinjiang, and Jinshun military commander of Urumchi. The court thus decides in favour of the western expedition to reconquer Xinjiang.
30 (*4/26*). Shen Baozhen is appointed Viceroy of Liangjiang and is put in charge of the defence of the southern coast, Li Hongzhang of the northern.

August 28 (*7/28*). Guo Songtao is appointed as China's minister in England, the first formal appointment of a Chinese minister to reside as envoy in a foreign country.

September 1 (*8/2*). Liu Kunyi is appointed Viceroy of Liangguang.

December 1 (*11/4*). Guo Songtao becomes a member of the *Zongli yamen*.
2 (*11/5*). Liu Changyou replaces Liu Yuezhao as Viceroy of Yungui.
11 (*11/14*). The Qing court appoints Chen Lanbin and Rong Hong as Imperial Commissioners to represent China in the USA, Peru and Spain.

C CULTURAL AND SOCIAL

October 14 (*9/16*). A fourth batch of students leaves Shanghai to study in the USA.

D PUBLICATIONS

Printing of Weng Tongjue's *Huangchao bingzhi kaolüe* (*An Examination of the Dynasty's Military System*).

1875-6

fired on and two days later bombards and destroys the forts on the banks.

October 4 (*9/6*). Cen Yuying sends in a memorial that fifteen criminals involved in the Margary affair have been arrested.

November 27 (*10/30*). Following Shen Baozhen's suggestion, the court agrees that the Governor of Fujian should spend half the year (winter and spring) in Taiwan, the other half in the Fujian capital.

December 5 (*11/8*). Guo Songtao sends in a memorial suggesting that the blame for the Margary affair rests with Cen Yuying and that he should be punished.

1876 *The Sino-British Chefoo Convention*

January 15 (*12/19*). Japan declares to China, through its minister, Mori Arinori, that it recognizes Korea's independence so that Japan-Korean matters have nothing to do with the Sino-Japanese Treaty.

16 (*12/20*). The prefecture of Taibei is set up.

February 27 (*2/3*). Japan and Korea sign the Kanghwa Treaty, under which Japan recognizes Korean self-rule and Korea allows Japan trade. The Japanese minister officially communicates the signing of the treaty to the *Zongli yamen* on March 12.

April 7 (*3/13*). Zuo Zongtang arrives in Suzhou (Gansu), preparing to depart on his western expedition.

8 (*3/14*). Wade sends Forsyth to see Li Hongzhang, to seek peace on Yakub Beg's behalf.

June 10 (*5/19*). An uprising led by Hu Zhan'ao and others breaks out in Shunning (Yunnan); the rebels occupy the government offices, throw open the prisons and occupy the prefectural capital.

14 (*5/23*). Rebels under Hu Zhan'ao and others take Yunzhou (Yunnan).

15 (*5/24*). Wade leaves Peking in impatience over the delays in settling the Margary affair, and the following day the court orders Li Hongzhang to go and negotiate with him in Tianjin.

21 (*5/30*). Qing troops retake Yunzhou.

25 (*int. 5/4*). Qing troops retake Shunning.

August 3 (*6/14*). A man is crushed to death by a train on the Shanghai-Jiangwan Railway. Popular anger leads the Intendant of Wusong,

1875–6

September 29–October 28 (9). Zhang Zhidong completes his annotated bibliography of important Chinese works, *Shumu dawen* (*Answering Questions on the Catalogue of Books*).

F BIRTHS AND DEATHS

January 12 (12/5). The Tongzhi Emperor d. aged 18.
  30 (12/23). Min Dianchen is executed.
February 21 (1/16). A.R. Margary d. aged 29.
March 19 (2/12). Zhang Zuolin b. (d. 1928).
  27 (2/20). Tongzhi's wife, Empress Alute, commits suicide.
October 3 (9/5). *Zongli yamen* member Chonglun d. aged 82.

The Great Famine begins 1876

A ECONOMICS

February 1 (1/7). The court grants permission for Zuo Zongtang's foreign loan of 10,000,000 taels to finance his expedition against Yakub Beg.
March 26 (3/1). The court orders that Zuo Zongtang should raise only 5,000,000 taels through foreign loan, and should find the remainder in China itself.
April 1 (3/7). Qiongzhou, Hainan Island (Guangdong) opens as a trade port.
July 3 (int. 5/12). Business opens on a five-mile-long railway from Shanghai to Jiangwan, the beginning of the Shanghai–Wusong line.

B OFFICIAL APPOINTMENTS, DISMISSALS, TRANSFERS ETC.

January 15 (12/19). Li Hanzhang is appointed Viceroy of Sichuan in place of Wu Tang, and Weng Tongjue acting Viceroy of Huguang.
  19 (12/23). The court orders the dismissal of Colonel Li Zhenguo, believed to have ordered the attack on the British party which led to Margary's death.
April 9 (3/15). Jinglian is appointed to the Grand Council.
October 27 (9/11). He Jing becomes Viceroy of Minzhe, Li Hanzhang of Huguang, and Ding Baozhen of Sichuan.
December 11 (10/26). Li Hongzao and Jinglian are appointed to the *Zongli yamen*.

1876–7

Songjiang and Taicang, Ma Junguang, to ask the British consul in Shanghai, W.H. Medhurst, to have the line closed.

18 *(6/29)*. Qing forces under Liu Jintang and Jinshun retake Urumchi from the Moslem rebels after a long siege. This victory partly pacifies the northern route of Xinjiang. Bai Yanhu and other leaders flee south-east towards Turfan.

21 *(7/3)*. Wade and Li Hongzhang meet at Yantai (Chefoo); the negotiations reach a climax on August 31, when most issues are settled.

September 13 *(7/26)*. The Chefoo (Yantai) Convention is signed by Li Hongzhang and Wade. The Margary affair is settled with a compensation of 200,000 taels and a letter of apology to be sent by a mission to Britain; rules on the reception of foreign envoys are drawn up, and China agrees to open five new ports for trade: Yichang (Hubei), Wuhu (Anhui), Wenzhou (Zhejiang), Beihai (Guangxi) and Chongqing (Sichuan).

17 *(7/30)*. China ratifies the Chefoo Convention.

October 28 *(9/12)*. The *Zongli yamen* sets down rules governing the conduct of missions abroad.

November 6 *(9/21)*. The pacification of northern Xinjiang is completed with the conquest by Qing troops, under Jinshun and others, of the Southern City of Manas and the capture and execution of several main Moslem rebel leaders there.

December 3 *(10/18)*. The Chinese minister to Britain, Guo Songtao, and his deputy, Liu Xihong, leave Shanghai to take up their posts.

1877   *Yakub Beg is defeated*

February 8 *(12/26)*. Guo Songtao has audience with Queen Victoria of England and presents his credentials as well as the letter of apology over the Margary affair.

March. Yakub Beg sends an envoy seeking help from Russia but without success.

April 14 *(3/1)*. Liu Jintang leads his army south from Urumchi against Yakub Beg and towards the southern route of Xinjiang.

26 *(3/13)*. The Qing forces retake Turfan. Bai Yanhu flees west.

1876–7

C CULTURAL AND SOCIAL

March 29 *(3/4)*. Li Hongzhang writes to the *Zongli yamen* suggesting that seven men should be sent to a military academy in Germany to study.
April 15 *(3/21)*. Seven officers leave Tianjin for Germany to train in a military academy there, the first Chinese to study in Germany.
September 26 *(8/9)*. All provinces are ordered to ban absolutely the planting of the opium poppy – one of several such edicts at about this time.

D PUBLICATIONS

November 23 *(10/8)*. *Xinbao* (*Daily News*), the first bilingual (Chinese-English) newspaper in China, begins publication in Shanghai under the editorship of the English tea merchant Frederic Major.

E NATURAL DISASTERS

Drought and a locust plague in northern China devastate the crops; serious famine follows in Shaanxi, Gansu, Shanxi and other provinces.
Spring–Summer. Widespread flooding occurs in southern China, causing crop failure and famine.
June 7–10 *(5/16–19)*. Torrential rain and serious flooding occur in Fuzhou, the capital of Fujian.

F BIRTHS AND DEATHS

April 5 *(3/11)*. Zhang Boling b. (d. 1951).
May 26 *(5/4)*. Grand Secretary Wenxiang d. aged 57.

The first batch of Chinese students to study in Europe 1877

A ECONOMICS

January 18 *(12/5)*. The court accepts a proposal from Shen Baozhen that each province should give some money towards buying the steamships, wharves and godowns of the American Shanghai Steam Navigation Company and amalgamating them with the China Merchants' Steam Navigation Company.
April 1 *(2/18)*. Four cities open as ports: Yichang (Hubei), Wuhu (Anhui), Beihai (Guangdong) and Wenzhou (Zhejiang).

1877

Liu Jintang's forces having conquered most of Turkestan, Yakub Beg flees west.

May 23 *(4/11)*. Sa'id Yakub, representing Yakub Beg, arrives in London to seek British help.

June 13 *(5/3)*. The British Foreign Office authorizes Wade to try to mediate between Yakub Beg and the Chinese government.

15 *(5/5)*. Shanghai's first wired telegram is sent.

July 7 *(5/27)*. The British Foreign Office suggests to Guo Songtao conditions for settlement of the conflict with Yakub Beg, including that Yakub Beg should retain 'control over the country he now holds'.

16 *(6/6)*. News of Yakub Beg's death reaches London.

28 *(6/18)*. Zuo Zongtang sends in a memorial stating that after Xinjiang is reconquered the court should insist on Russia's returning Yili.

August 18 *(7/3)*. The court orders Zuo Zongtang to take charge of negotiations with Russia over the Xinjiang-Russian border.

October 7 *(9/1)*. Qing forces under Liu Jintang retake Karashar. Bai Yanhu abandons the city and flees.

18 *(9/12)*. Qing forces under Liu Jintang retake Kucha. Bai Yanhu flees west.

24 *(9/18)*. Qing troops under Liu Jintang retake Aksu. Some 100,000 Moslem rebels surrender.

26 *(9/20)*. Liu Jintang retakes Ush.

November 17 *(10/13)*. China and Spain conclude in Peking a treaty governing conditions of Chinese workers in Cuba.

December 17 *(11/13)*. Qing forces retake Kashgar and capture Bai Yanhu's deputy Wang Yuanlin.

24 *(11/20)*. Qing forces under Liu Jintang retake Yangi Hissar.

28 *(11/24)*. Bai Yanhu crosses into Russia and is given domicile by the Russians. At about the same time Yakub Beg's son Beg Kuli Beg takes refuge in Russia.

July 21 (6/11). Zuo Zongtang reports to the throne that the permitted loan of 5,000,000 taels (see A, March 26, 1876) has been raised from the Hongkong and Shanghai Banking Corporation.
October 21 (9/15). The Shanghai–Wusong railway is redeemed by the Qing and its tracks are torn up.

B OFFICIAL APPOINTMENTS, DISMISSALS, TRANSFERS ETC.

January 15 (12/2). He Ruzhang is appointed China's minister to Japan.
February 19 (1/7). Yinggui is appointed Grand Secretary and Zailing assistant Grand Secretary.

C CULTURAL AND SOCIAL

April 4 (2/21). Li Fengbao and Prosper Giquel, directors of the Fuzhou Dockyard Naval Academy, leave Hongkong with some thirty students and apprentices of the Academy, some bound for England, some for France, to study manufacturing and transportation. This is the first batch of Chinese students to study in Europe.

D PUBLICATIONS

Feng Guifen's literary collection *Xianzhi tang gao* (*Drafts from the Xianzhi Hall*) is published.

E NATURAL DISASTERS

Continuing drought in northern China causes serious famine. The *Qingshi* Basic Annals state: 'In Shanxi and Shaanxi there was great drought; people ate one another.'
May. Nanchang (Jiangxi) and nearby districts suffer flooding. Fuzhou (Fujian) is struck by a tidal wave and thunderstorm; the whole city is 6–10 feet under water.
June. Serious flooding affects Hunan, Guangxi, Jiangsu, Zhejiang, Fujian and Guangdong.
July 16 (6/6). Some 10,000 people having been drowned in flooding in Guangdong, the court orders the provincial authorities to take remedial action.
August. Hangzhou (Zhejiang) and nearby districts are devastated by great floods which cover most of the rice fields and drown many people.

1878 The Qing reconquest of Xinjiang is completed

January 2 (*11/29*). Qing troops complete their conquest of the southern route of Xinjiang with the capture of Khotan.

March 18 (*2/15*). The *Zongli yamen* communicates with the Russian minister in Peking, Eugene Butzow, requesting the return of Bai Yanhu and Beg Kuli Beg.

21 (*2/18*). Butzow replies to the *Zongli yamen* requesting that to settle the return of Bai Yanhu, Zuo Zongtang should get in touch with the Governor-general of Russian Turkestan, General K.P. Kaufman.

25 (*2/22*). Zuo Zongtang is ordered to send a despatch to Kaufman requesting the return of Bai Yanhu and Beg Kuli Beg.

May 6 (*4/5*). Guo Songtao, the first Chinese minister to France, presents his credentials.

June 22 (*5/22*). Irritated by the failure of its dealings with Butzow, the Qing court sends Chonghou to St Petersburg to negotiate the return of Yili, occupied by the Russians in 1871, the repatriation of Bai Yanhu and Beg Kuli Beg, and other questions.

September 3 (*8/7*). He Ruzhang, the Chinese minister in Tokyo, protests to the Japanese Foreign Ministry over Japan's preventing the Ryukyus from sending in tribute to China. He follows up with a similar protest on October 7.

16 (*8/20*). Bai Yanhu and his followers make a skirmish into Ush (Xinjiang) from Russia.

18 (*8/22*). Li Yangcai, a dismissed military officer originally from Guangdong, leads a force across the border into Vietnam.

October 31 (*10/6*). The court sends Feng Zicai to suppress the forces of Li Yangcai in northern Vietnam.

November 7 (*10/13*). Some Moslem rebels who had fled to Russia cross back into Xinjiang and advance towards Kashgar.

8 (*10/14*). Chonghou leaves Shanghai bound for Russia.

10 (*10/16*). Liu Jintang inflicts a great defeat on the Moslem rebels returning from Russia.

1877–8

F BIRTHS AND DEATHS

April 10 *(2/27)*. Shi Zhaoji b. (d. 1958).
May 29 *(4/17)*. Yakub Beg d. aged about 57.
December 3 *(10/29)*. Scholar Wang Guowei b. (d. 1927).
14 *(11/10)*. Peking Opera actor Yang Xiaolou b. (d. 1938).

Famine reaches catastrophic proportions in North China   1878

A ECONOMICS

July 11 *(6/12)*. The court strictly forbids private minting.
24 *(6/25)*. The Bureau for the Kaiping coal mines at Tianjin is formally opened. Work starts at the mines in October.
October 21 *(9/26)*. Li Hongzhang agrees to a request to set up the Shanghai cotton cloth mill; Shen Baozhen gives his approval November 14.

B OFFICIAL APPOINTMENTS, DISMISSALS, TRANSFERS ETC.

February 22 *(1/21)*. Guo Songtao is appointed minister to France (retaining his post to Britain).
March 15 *(2/12)*. Zuo Zongtang is made a second-class marquis and Liu Jintang a second-class baron to reward their reconquest of Xinjiang.
June 1 *(5/1)*. Zailing becomes Grand Secretary; Quanqing assistant Grand Secretary.
22 *(5/22)*. Chonghou is appointed Imperial Commissioner to go and negotiate in Russia.
August 21 *(7/23)*. Wang Wenshao and Zhou Jiamei are appointed to the *Zongli yamen*.
25 *(7/27)*. Zeng Jize is appointed Imperial Commissioner to Britain and France, Li Fengbao Imperial Commissioner to Germany.

C CULTURAL AND SOCIAL

May 5 *(4/4)*. The court rejects a proposal from Shen Baozhen to abolish the official examinations for military degrees.

E NATURAL DISASTERS

A locust plague afflicts north China.
April 11 *(3/9)*. More than 10,000 people are killed and innumerable

1878–9

December. The Customs Postal Department is opened in Peking and other places.

2 (*11/9*). Zuo Zongtang sends in a formal proposal that Xinjiang should be made into a regular province of prefectures, districts, counties and so on.

7 (*11/14*). The Viceroy of Liangguang, Liu Kunyi, receives a letter from the Vietnamese Emperor seeking military assistance against Li Yangcai.

31 (*12/8*). Chonghou arrives in St Petersburg for negotiations.

1879 *Japan annexes the Ryukyu Islands*

January 20 (*12/28*). Chonghou presents his credentials in St Petersburg to Tsar Alexander II of Russia.

March 8 (*2/16*). Chonghou begins negotiations over the return of Yili and other questions.

25 (*3/3*). Japan invades the Ryukyu Islands, and occupies the capital Naha.

April 4 (*3/13*). Japan formally declares that the Ryukyu Islands have been set up as its Okinawa Prefecture.

17–25 (*3/26–int. 3/5*). Wu Kedu composes, writes and sends to court a memorial denouncing the Empress Dowager Cixi for her infringement of precedent in selecting the Emperor.

May 10 (*int. 3/20*). The *Zongli yamen* protests to the Japanese minister in China, Shishido Tamaki, over the changing of the Ryukyu kingdom into Japan's Okinawa prefecture.

July 3 (*5/14*). An official from the Ryukyus sees Li Hongzhang and asks for help from China against Japan.

August 21 (*7/4*). At the suggestion of the *Zongli yamen*, the court orders Li Hongzhang to encourage Korea to establish treaties and trade with Western countries in order to curtail the growth of Japanese influence there.

September 20 (*8/5*). The *Zongli yamen* sends in a memorial reporting the view of the former US President Ulysses Grant that the Ryukyu problem be solved by dividing the islands into three, one part going

houses destroyed as a result of a typhoon in Guangdong.
25 *(3/23)*. Since severe drought continues to afflict Zhili, 160,000 piculs (*shi*) of rice are distributed as relief.

May. In Zhejiang, Jinhua and other prefectures are flooded and many people are drowned.

28 *(4/27)*. A British diplomatic despatch to Lord Salisbury, the Foreign Secretary, estimates that Shanxi lost about 5,000,000 people in the winter of 1877–78 owing to famine (about one-third of its population).

F BIRTHS AND DEATHS

January 13 *(12/11)*. Chen Jiongming b. in Guangdong (d. 1933).
   17 *(12/15)*. Chen Qimei b. in Zhejiang (d. 1916).
October 1 *(9/6)*. Huang Yanpei b. (d. 1965).

Last year of the Great Famine **1879**

A ECONOMICS

June 19 *(4/30)*. The Qing court gives formal approval for Shen Baozhen's suggestion that the Sichuan salt administration should have salt for sale transported by the government. Private transport had resulted in corruption and profiteering. (The new system had already been in operation more than a year.)

November 8 *(9/25)*. Because of troubles recently arising over inland trade the Western legations jointly request the *Zongli yamen* for reform of the inland customs system.

B OFFICIAL APPOINTMENTS, DISMISSALS, TRANSFERS ETC.

January 23 *(1/2)*. Wang Wenshao is appointed to the Grand Council.
November 6 *(9/23)*. Linshu and Chongli are appointed to the *Zongli yamen*.
December 27 *(11/15)*. Liu Kunyi is appointed Viceroy of Liangjiang in place of Shen Baozhen, and Zhang Shusheng of Liangguang.

C CULTURAL AND SOCIAL

June. Sun Yatsen goes from Macao to Honolulu to study.
August. The court orders Hubei to punish severely dealers who kidnap and sell women.

1879–80

to Japan, one to China, and the third to revert to the original Ryukyu kingdom.

October 2 (*8/17*). After long and complicated negotiations, Chonghou signs the Treaty of Livadia (on the Black Sea) without the prior approval of his government. Under the treaty, China regains Yili but cedes a considerable amount of territory, making Yili surrounded on three sides by Russia. China also agrees to pay 'an occupation fee' of 5,000,000 roubles and grants substantial trade and commercial concessions.

17 (*9/3*). The Commander-in-Chief of Guangxi, Feng Zicai, captures Li Yangcai and suppresses his uprising.

19 (*9/5*). Shen Baozhen sends in a memorial denouncing the Treaty of Livadia.

November 15 (*10/2*). A memorial from Li Hongzhang partly criticizes and partly defends the Treaty of Livadia.

December 4 (*10/21*). Zuo Zongtang denounces the Treaty of Livadia, and compares the cession of territory to 'throwing a bone to a dog'. He proposes that the treaty be renegotiated. Numerous comments on the treaty, overwhelmingly critical, were received at court about this time.

1880 *The Court renounces the Treaty of Livadia*

January 2 (*11/21*). The court issues an edict that the terms of the Treaty of Livadia and Chonghou's behaviour in leaving St Petersburg abruptly without imperial consent be seriously discussed.

3 (*11/22*). Chonghou arrives back in Peking.

16 (*12/5*). Zhang Zhidong sends in a memorial calling for Chonghou's execution and preparations for war against Russia.

21 (*12/10*). Li Hongzhang (who has now examined the complete text of the Treaty) and other senior officials send in memorials that

1879–80

D PUBLICATIONS

The *Zongli yamen* prints Huang Zunxian's *Riben zashi shi* (*Poems about Japan*) (completed autumn 1879); publication of the novel *Sanxia wuyi* (*Three Heroes and Five Gallants*) by Shi Yukun.

December. The *Da Qing Muzong Yi huangdi shilu* (*Veritable Records of the Great Qing Tongzhi Emperor*) and *Da Qing Muzong Yi huangdi shengxun* (*Edicts of the Great Qing Tongzhi Emperor*) are completed.

E NATURAL DISASTERS

According to Walter H. Mallory, from 1876 to this year serious drought results in 'hunger, disease, or violence' killing from 9,000,000 to 13,000,000 people in Shaanxi, Shanxi, Zhili, Henan and Shandong provinces.

May. More than 10,830 people are drowned when floods wash down the city walls of Wenxian (Gansu).

June 29–July 11 (*5/10–22*). Disastrous earthquakes strike south-eastern Gansu. Many houses are destroyed and people killed or injured.

F BIRTHS AND DEATHS

March 10 (*2/18*). Liao Zhongkai b. (d. 1925).
April 11 (*3/20*). Yu Youren b. in Shaanxi (d. 1964).
25 (*int. 3/5*). Wu Kedu commits suicide, aged 67, to ensure the transmission to the throne of the memorial he had just written.
September 26 (*8/11*). Danmaoqian d.
October 8 (*8/23*). Chen Duxiu b. (d. 1942).
December 9 (*10/26*). Hu Hanmin b. in Guangzhou (d. 1936).
18 (*11/6*). Shen Baozhen d. aged 59.

Chonghou is sentenced to death but then reprieved **1880**

A ECONOMICS

March 31 (*2/21*). At Li Hongzhang's suggestion, the court approves the purchase of two armoured ships for use along the Fujian coast.
July 11 (*6/5*). On Li Hongzhang's suggestion, the court approves the purchase from Britain of three further armoured ships, one for the south coast, two for the north.
September 5 (*8/1*). China and Brazil conclude a trade treaty in Tianjin.
16 (*8/12*). The Lanzhou mechanical woollen mill formally starts work.

1880

aspects of the Treaty of Livadia be rejected, including the border demarcation and the trade arrangements. The Empress Dowager holds a large conference, announces rejection of the border demarcation and trading arrangements in the Treaty, and calls for further debate. (A deluge of memorials denouncing the Treaty followed this call.)

February 19 (*1/10*). The court renounces the Treaty of Livadia and demands that it be renegotiated.

March 1 (*1/21*). Because of the Yili affair, the court orders military preparations and the strengthening of defences along the borders with Russia and the coast.

26 (*2/16*). The Japanese Takezoe Shinichirō negotiates with Li Hongzhang over the Ryukyus on the basis of Grant's suggestion. (See September 20, 1879.)

31 (*2/21*). Shen Guifen and Jinglian sign the Sino-German Supplementary Convention in Peking with the German minister, Max von Brandt.

June 8 (*5/1*). A concrete detailed proposal on the establishment of a new province in Xinjiang arrives at court from Zuo Zongtang.

15 (*5/8*). Zuo Zongtang arrives in Hami to prepare the north-western defences against the Russians. The *Zongli yamen* sends in a memorial asking for Chonghou to be pardoned.

July 30 (*6/24*). Zeng Jize arrives in St Petersburg to renegotiate the Treaty of Livadia.

August 4 (*6/29*). Zeng Jize sees Nikolai Giers, Russian assistant Foreign Minister, and others in St Petersburg and begins negotiations.

5 (*6/30*). Towards the end of a month-long visit to China, the former Commander of the Ever Victorious Army, Charles Gordon, submits twenty items of advice to Li Hongzhang, including moving the capital inland to be less accessible to foreign troops, and the urgent establishment of a telegraph service.

11 (*7/6*). A cable reaches Peking from Zeng Jize asking that Chonghou be set free. (See March 3, B.)

October 13 (*9/10*). Following anti-Chinese disturbances in the USA, a specially appointed commission, headed by James B. Angell of Michigan, begins negotiations with China over Chinese emigration to the USA.

26 (*9/23*). In Guangzhou a British customs officer, Edward Page, shoots a Chinese dead while on duty.

November 17 (*10/15*). In Peking Baoyun and Li Hongzao sign with Angell and others a treaty under which the USA are allowed to 'regulate, limit or suspend' Chinese immigration to America 'but may not absolutely prohibit it'.

1880

18 (*8/14*). Following a suggestion from Li Hongzhang, the Qing court orders him to set up a north-south telegraph cable from Peking to Shanghai.

November 17 (*10/15*). Baoyun and Li Hongzao sign a trade treaty with American Angell and others.

December 3 (*11/2*). Liu Mingchuan sends in a memorial suggesting the construction of a railway between Qingjiang (Jiangsu) and Peking.

B Official Appointments, Dismissals, Transfers etc.

February 17 (*1/8*). Li Hongzao is appointed to the Grand Council and the *Zongli yamen*.

19 (*1/10*). Zeng Jize is appointed Imperial Commissioner to Russia to conclude a new treaty.

March 3 (*1/23*). Chonghou is sentenced to imprisonment awaiting decapitation.

June 26 (*5/19*). Chonghou is reprieved.

August 12 (*7/7*). Chonghou is set free.

November 18 (*10/16*). Mao Changxi is again appointed to the *Zongli yamen*.

December 5 (*11/4*). Yang Changxun is appointed Viceroy of Shan'gan.

6 (*11/5*). Quanqing is appointed Grand Secretary and Linggui assistant Grand Secretary.

C Cultural and Social

Yang Shoujing goes to Tokyo where, as a secretary to the Chinese minister Li Shuchang, he collects many rare Chinese books, steles, inscriptions, paintings and printing blocks, and writes valuable notes on them.

August 22 (*7/17*). At Li Hongzhang's suggestion the court orders Wu Zancheng to organize the establishment of a naval academy at Tianjin.

October. A telegraph school is set up in Tianjin.

D Publications

Printing of *Wu Liutang xiansheng leiwen* (*Eulogies for Mr Wu Kedu*).

E Natural Disasters

November 2 (*9/30*). The Yellow River bursts the dykes at Dongming (Zhili), which are closed up again December 2.

1880–1

December 27 *(11/26)*. The French Foreign Minister Barthélemy Saint-Hilaire tells Zeng Jize that under the treaty of March 15, 1874, France recognizes the full independence of Vietnam.

1881 Treaty of St Petersburg

Installation of telephones in the Shanghai Concessions begins.

February 15 *(1/17)*. The trial of Edward Page opens at Guangzhou before Chief Justice French of the British Supreme Court at Shanghai (see October 26, 1880). The verdict was 'not guilty'. The case was a landmark in demonstrating the legal jurisdiction of foreign powers over their own nationals.

23 *(1/25)*. The court orders that Korean diplomatic affairs should come under the jurisdiction of the Superintendent of Trade for the northern ports (currently Li Hongzhang) and not, as previously, under the Board of Rites.

24 *(1/26)*. The Treaty of St Petersburg is signed, replacing that of Livadia. China gains a large strip of territory, changes are made in trade routes and customs and Russia's right to establish consulates in Turfan and Suzhou (Gansu) is secured; China agrees to pay 9,000,000 roubles' compensation.

March 12 *(2/13)*. A rebellion led by Lei Boli in Sichuan is put down.

17 *(2/18)*. A consulate is set up in Honolulu to look after overseas Chinese there.

May 15 *(4/18)*. The court approves the Treaty of St Petersburg.

June 30 *(6/5)*. A Vietnamese mission arrives in Peking and asks for help against the French.

August 19 *(7/25)*. The Treaty of St Petersburg is exchanged in the Russian capital.

22 *(7/28)*. Zeng Jize communicates with the Russian Foreign Ministry asking for the return of Bai Yanhu.

September 14 *(int. 7/21)*. Zeng Jize meets the French Foreign Minister Saint-Hilaire and tells him France should not hinder Chinese authority in Vietnam. He protests against the statement of December 27, 1880.

October. The Black Flag Army attacks two French merchants carrying goods from Hanoi to Yunnan at three points along the route.

3 *(8/11)*. China and Brazil conclude a treaty of friendship, trade and navigation (a revision of the trade treaty of September 5, 1880).

December 1 *(10/10)*. The Telegraph Administration is set up in Tianjin with branch offices in Shanghai, Suzhou (Jiangsu), Jining (Shandong) and other places.

1880–1

F BIRTHS AND DEATHS

March 8 (*1/28*). Huang Fu b. (d. 1936).

Birth of Lu Xun 1881

A ECONOMICS

February 14 (*1/16*). The court rejects Liu Mingchuan's suggestion of December 3, 1880, to build a railway from Qingjiang to Peking.
May 25 (*4/28*). The Kaiping coal mines in Zhili are set up as a government-supervised, merchant-operated industry.
June 9 (*5/13*). The short Tangshan–Xugezhuang (Zhili) railway line to transport coal from the Kaiping mines begins taking traffic.
August 9 (*7/15*). The cruisers *Chaoyong* and *Yangwei*, purchased on Li Hongzhang's instructions delivered by Ding Ruchang, leave Newcastle for China, arriving in Dagu (Zhili) on November 17.
October. British merchants found a running water company in Shanghai.
December 1 (*10/10*). The Shanghai–Tianjin telegraph line, constructed by the Danish Great Northern Telegraph Company, is completed (see September 18, 1880).

B OFFICIAL APPOINTMENTS, DISMISSALS, TRANSFERS ETC.

February 27 (*1/29*). Zuo Zongtang is appointed to the Grand Council and *Zongli yamen*.
   28 (*2/1*). Zeng Guoquan is appointed Viceroy of Shan'gan.
July 24 (*6/29*). Li Hongzao is appointed assistant Grand Secretary.
October 16 (*8/24*). Tan Zhonglin is appointed to replace the sick Zeng Guoquan as Viceroy of Shan'gan.
   26 (*9/4*). Zuo Zongtang is appointed Viceroy of Liangjiang.
December 5 (*10/14*). Linggui is appointed Grand Secretary and Wenyu assistant Grand Secretary.
   18 (*10/27*). Zhou Jiamei is again appointed to the *Zongli yamen*.

C CULTURAL AND SOCIAL

June 8 (*5/12*). The *Zongli yamen* decides to recall the Chinese students studying in America on the grounds that they are being denationalized.
December 2 (*10/11*). Li Hongzhang sends in a memorial asking to send

1881–2

6 (*10/15*). The *Zongli yamen* having received a cable from Zeng Jize saying that France is about to occupy the northern regions of Vietnam, the court orders that Zeng argue strongly with the French Foreign Ministry about the matter.

1882 *China intervenes in Korea*

January 1 (*11/12*). The French Foreign Minister, L. Gambetta, communicates with Zeng Jize, claiming full freedom of action for France as far as Vietnam is concerned.

March 7 (*1/8*). Zeng Jize sends in a memorial that Russia has agreed to imprison Bai Yanhu, thus solving the dispute over the former rebel.

22 (*2/4*). Yili is formally handed back to China.

April 25 (*3/8*). A French force under Henri Laurent Rivière occupies Hanoi, Vietnam.

May 3 (*3/16*). Zeng Jize protests to the French Foreign Minister over the French occupation of Hanoi.

30 (*4/14*). The court orders military preparations to defend China's southern border because of the French advances in Vietnam.

June 11 (*4/26*). Zhang Zhidong sends in a memorial advocating strong and concrete military action to strengthen China's ability to resist the French and preserve its position in Vietnam.

a second batch of students for training overseas from the Fuzhou Dockyard Naval Academy.

D PUBLICATIONS

Printing of the *Sichuan guanyun yan an leibian* (*Classified Compliation of Cases in the Officially Transported Salt of Sichuan*), reports on the salt administration in Sichuan for 1877 and 1878.

E NATURAL DISASTERS

July 14–15 (*6/19–20*). Disastrous typhoon and flooding in Taiwan cause serious crop damage and kill and injure many people.
20 (*6/25*). Earthquakes occur in southern Gansu.

F BIRTHS AND DEATHS

January 28 (*12/29*). The assistant Grand Secretary and Grand Councillor Shen Guifen d. aged 64.
April 8 (*3/10*). The Empress Cian d. aged 44.
September 25 (*8/3*). The famous writer Lu Xun (Zhou Shuren) b. in Shaoxing (d. 1936).

A strike at the Kaiping mines 1882

A ECONOMICS

April 18 (*3/1*). The Imperial Telegraph Administration is made into a government-supervised, merchant-operated body.
October 1 (*8/20*). China and Korea agree on trade regulations.

B OFFICIAL APPOINTMENTS, DISMISSALS, TRANSFERS ETC.

January 3 (*11/14*). Zhang Zhidong becomes Governor of Shanxi.
April 19 (*3/2*). Chen Lanbin is appointed to the *Zongli yamen*.
May 11 (*3/24*). Li Hongzhang obtains leave of absence to go into mourning for his mother.
   30 (*4/14*). Zeng Guoquan is appointed acting Viceroy of Liangguang because of the French advances in Vietnam.
June 22 (*5/7*). Because of the crisis in Vietnam, Cen Yuying is appointed acting Viceroy of Yungui.

1882–3

14 (4/29). A request by Korea to station an envoy in Peking is refused by the Qing court.

July 23 (6/9). A pro-Chinese conservative *coup d'état* occurs in Korea, directed against Japanese influence. The regent, the *Taewongun* (personal name Yi Si-eung) seizes power.

August 10 (6/27). Three Chinese warships, led by Ding Ruchang, arrive outside Seoul one day after a Japanese force arrives in Seoul harbour.

13 (6/30). The Qing court sends six battalions of the Huai Army under the Naval Commander-in-Chief of Guangdong, Wu Changqing, and accompanied by Ding Ruchang to Korea; they arrive August 17.

26 (7/13). Wu Changqing, Ding Ruchang and others kidnap the *Taewongun*, sending him by ship to Tianjin the following day.

30 (7/17). Without reference to China, Japan and Korea settle the dispute in a treaty between them. Japan is allowed to send troops and build barracks at her legation in Seoul.

September 5 (7/23). Li Hongzhang arrives in Tianjin from Hefei (Anhui), his leave of absence having been cancelled because of the Korean crisis.

22 (8/11). The court orders Tang Jiong, the Financial Commissioner of Yunnan, to lead troops into Vietnam to link up with Liu Yongfu's Black Flag Army and resist the French.

27 (8/16). Zhang Peilun of the Hanlin Academy sends in a memorial requesting a military campaign against Japan.

October 10 (8/29). In Kaihua (Yunnan) Liu Yongfu sees Tang Jiong, who agrees to give him munitions to fight the French.

29 (9/18). The Sino-Russian Yili border agreement is concluded.

December 15 (11/6). Zeng Guoquan sends soldiers to suppress an uprising in Qiongzhou, Hainan Island (Guangdong).

20 (11/11). Li Hongzhang and the French envoy F.A. Bourée sign at Shanghai a memorandum under which China agrees to withdraw troops from Tongking and France to take no action against the sovereignty of Vietnam; both guarantee Vietnamese independence.

1883 *France annexes Vietnam as a protectorate*

March 21 (2/13). Russian troops complete withdrawal from Yili.

30 (2/22). The Board of Rites sends in a memorial to say that it has received a formal request for help against France from the Vietnamese Emperor.

1882–3

December 14 (*11/5*). Weng Tonghe is appointed to the Grand Council.
15 (*11/6*). Pan Zuyin is appointed to the Grand Council.

C Cultural and Social

August. A workers' strike takes place at the Kaiping mines.

D Publications

Publication of Wang Xianqian's *Xu guwen ci leizuan* (*Continuation of the Classified Compendium of Literature in Guwen*) (preface dated March 19–April 17, 1882).
September 26 (*8/15*). Zhou Shouchang completes his *Hanshu zhu jiaobu* (*Collation and Supplement to the Commentary on the Han History*).

E Natural Disasters

December 2–8 (*10/22–8*). Disastrous earthquakes strike the Shenzhou region of Zhili; countless houses collapse and many people are crushed to death.

F Births and Deaths

March 11 (*1/22*). Scholar Chen Li d. aged 72.
April 5 (*2/18*). Song Jiaoren b. in Hunan (d. 1913).
15 (*2/28*). Ding Richang d. aged 59.
August 31 (*7/18*). Zhang Ji b. (d. 1947).
November 6 (*9/26*). Feng Yuxiang b. in Baoding (Zhili) (d. 1948).
December 9 (*10/29*). Mathematician Li Shanlan d. aged 72.
18 (*11/9*). Cai E. b. in Hunan (d. 1916).

1883 Birth of Wang Jingwei

A Economics

January 18 (*12/10*). Following Li Hongzhang's suggestion, the court orders that a telegraph line be laid overland along the coast from Shanghai to Guangdong.

1883

May 15 (4/9). France votes 5,500,000 francs for a military expedition to Tongking.

19 (4/13). Liu Yongfu's Black Flag Army attacks and defeats the French near Hanoi, killing their Commander, Henri Laurent Rivière.

June 8 (5/4). Li Hongzhang meets in Shanghai with A. Tricou, the French minister to Japan, sent as special envoy to China to negotiate over Vietnam. Li is told France's view that Vietnam is not a tributary state of China. Altogether Li and Tricou hold five conversations in Shanghai, their negotiations collapsing on July 1.

August 12 (7/10). James Logan, a British customs official, kills a Chinese boy; he is later sentenced under British law to seven years' penal servitude for manslaughter.

25 (7/23). At Hué, Vietnam signs a treaty with France recognizing Vietnam as a French protectorate; 'France shall control the relations of all foreign powers, including China', with the Vietnamese government.

September 1–3 (8/1–3). Liu Yongfu's and Vietnamese forces fight against the French in a bloody and costly battle near Hanoi.

10 (8/10). Liu Yongfu's and Vietnamese forces retreat and camp at Sontay. In protest at the lightness of Logan's punishment, people in Guangzhou attack the foreign settlement and burn and pillage thirteen foreign houses.

October 3 (9/3). China and Russia agree on their borders in the Tarbagatai area.

26 (9/26). Li Hongzhang writes to the *Zongli yamen* that China should avoid war with France, which it is not strong enough to win.

November 16 (10/17). The *Zongli yamen* informs the acting French Minister, de Semallé, that Vietnam is a tributary state of the Qing and that France, by refusing to recognize this, is not only behaving unjustly but also courting war.

29 (10/30). A *coup d'état* in Vietnam brings the infant Emperor Kienphuoc to the throne; his government renounces the Treaty of Hué.

30 (11/1). The Governor of Shanxi, Zhang Zhidong, sends in a memorial recommending an uncompromising war policy with France over Vietnam and suggesting concrete military and political strategies.

December 16 (11/17). French forces take Sontay near Hanoi. Liu Yongfu's troops retreat.

21 (11/22). The Viceroy of Yungui, Cen Yuying, is sent to lead troops into Vietnam.

1883

March 16 (*2/8*). Li Hongzhang sends Yuan Baoling and the German engineer Constantin Hannecken to construct naval defensive works at Lüshun.

April 8 (*3/2*). The laying of the telegraph line reaches Guangdong province (see January 18).

B OFFICIAL APPOINTMENTS, DISMISSALS, TRANSFERS ETC.

February 24 (*1/17*). Wu Tingfen is appointed to the *Zongli yamen*.
May 30 (*4/24*). Cen Yuying is confirmed as Viceroy of Yungui.
June 27 (*5/23*). Bianbaodi is appointed acting Viceroy of Huguang.
December 3 (*11/4*). Zhang Peilun is appointed to the *Zongli yamen*.

C CULTURAL AND SOCIAL

March 27 (*2/19*). In Langqiong (Yunnan), local people set a French church on fire, and kill a French missionary and some ten converts.

May 5 (*3/29*). Workers of the Jiangnan arsenal petitioning the management against increased workloads are beaten up.

July 18 (*6/15*). The court issues an edict banning the Observance Sect, a derivative of the White Lotus, found in the cities of the north.

August. A group of eunuchs set up an opium den in the Forbidden City and the court orders them to be severely punished.

E NATURAL DISASTERS

June 22–27 (*5/18–23*). The Yellow River floods in several places in Shandong.

August 25–27 (*7/23–5*). Three days' torrential rain causes the breach of dykes and flooding along the Yongding River (Zhili). (The dykes are closed up November 16.)

F BIRTHS AND DEATHS

May 4 (*3/28*). Wang Jingwei b. in Guangdong (d. 1944).
October 8 (*9/8*). Yan Xishan b. in Shanxi (d. 1960).

1884 The Sino-French War breaks out

March 12 (2/15). The French take Bacninh, north of Hanoi, defeating Chinese troops, some of whom retreat north to Thainguyen.

20 (2/23). The French take Thainguyen in Vietnam; the official Vietnamese soldiers surrender.

April 30 (4/6). The French government cables empowering Captain François Ernest Fournier to negotiate on its behalf with China over Vietnam.

May 4 (4/10). The court instructs Li Hongzhang to proceed with negotiations with Fournier but demands no compromise on four issues: the retention of Vietnam's dependent relationship with China, refusal to allow France to trade in Yunnan, the preservation of the Black Flag Army and refusal to pay France any indemnity.

11 (4/17). Li Hongzhang signs a Convention in Tianjin with Fournier over Vietnam. China agrees to recognize all past and future Franco-Vietnamese treaties, to open Yunnan and Guangxi to French trade, and 'to withdraw immediately to her frontiers the Chinese garrisons of Tongking'. France agrees not to invade China's southern provinces bordering on Tongking and demands no indemnity.

June 23 (int. 5/1). A battle breaks out between Chinese and French soldiers at Bacle. The Chinese had not received instructions to withdraw, while Alphonse Dugeune, commanding the French force, believed their presence was in contravention of the Li-Fournier Convention. After a three-day fight the French retreat, having failed to take Bacle.

July 1 (int. 5/9). The new French minister and negotiator, Jules Patenôtre, arrives in Shanghai.

12 (int. 5/20). Through its *chargé d'affaires* in China, de Semallé, France sends an ultimatum to China demanding, within seven days, observation of the Li-Fournier Convention and the payment of an indemnity of 250,000,000 francs.

13 (int. 5/21). The *Zongli yamen* refuses to pay an indemnity to France but agrees to the withdrawal of troops from Tongking.

16 (int. 5/24). The court orders the Chinese soldiers in Tongking to withdraw to the border.

19 (int. 5/27). The court sends Zeng Guoquan to Shanghai to negotiate with Patenôtre.

28 (6/7). Negotiations for a definitive Sino-French treaty begin in Shanghai between Zeng Guoquan and Patenôtre.

August 5 (6/15). French naval forces under Admiral Lespès bombard Jilong in Taiwan and destroy its gun emplacements, because of China's refusal to pay an indemnity.

The Tongwen Book Company publishes the **1884**
Twenty-Four Histories

B OFFICIAL APPOINTMENTS, DISMISSALS, TRANSFERS ETC.

February 16 (*1/20*). Zeng Guoquan is appointed acting Viceroy of Liangjiang and concurrently Superintendent of Trade for the southern ports.

April 8 (*3/13*). Because of the reverses in Vietnam, Prince Gong is dismissed from all his offices. All other members of the Grand Council, Weng Tonghe, Baoyun, Jinglian and Li Hongzao, are also dismissed and replaced the same day by Prince Li (Shiduo), Yan Jingming, Zhang Zhiwan, Sun Yuwen, Xu Gengshen and Elehebu. Baoyun, Jinglian, and Li Hongzao are dismissed from the *Zongli yamen*.

12 (*3/17*). Prince Qing (Yikuang) succeeds Prince Gong as head of the *Zongli yamen*.

19 (*3/24*). Yan Jingming and Xu Gengshen are appointed to the *Zongli yamen*.

May 22 (*4/28*). Zhang Zhidong is appointed acting Viceroy of Liangguang.

June 24 (*int. 5/2*). Fukun, Xizhen, Xu Yongyi and Liao Shouheng are appointed to the *Zongli yamen*.

September 7 (*7/18*). Zuo Zongtang is appointed Imperial Commissioner in charge of military affairs in Fujian; Zeng Guoquan is confirmed as Viceroy of Liangjiang.

16 (*7/27*). Yang Changxun is appointed Viceroy of Minzhe.

20 (*8/2*). Xu Gengshen is appointed to the Grand Council and Deng Chengxiu to the *Zongli yamen*.

23 (*8/5*). Li Hongzhang is appointed Grand Secretary, being confirmed as Viceroy of Zhili.

November 10 (*9/23*). Elehebu is appointed Grand Secretary and the following day Encheng assistant Grand Secretary.

19 (*10/2*). Liu Jintang is appointed Governor of the newly created Xinjiang province and Wei Guangtao the Financial Commissioner.

C CULTURAL AND SOCIAL

October 5 (*8/17*). Hongkong Chinese workers go on strike in protest against punishment by British officials for refusing to service French ships.

November. The celebrations for Cixi's fiftieth birthday (November 27) give rise to the practice of bringing actors from Peking city to court, some to take up residence as teachers and actors, others for isolated performances.

1884–5

6 (6/16). An attempt by Lespès to occupy the city of Jilong is repulsed.

19 (6/29). De Semallé presents China with an ultimatum to agree to an indemnity of 80,000,000 francs within forty-eight hours.

23 (7/3). French warships under Admiral Armédé Courbet attack Fuzhou and, within one hour, sink or disable all seven warships of the Chinese navy's Fujian fleet and destroy the Fuzhou dockyard.

26 (7/6). The court issues a decree declaring war on France.

October 1 (8/13). The French under Courbet bombard and occupy Jilong.

23 (9/5). Admiral Courbet declares a blockade of Taiwan.

November 17 (9/30). Xinjiang is made into a province.

December 6 (10/19). Following a *coup d'état* by pro-Japanese radicals two days before, Yuan Shikai leads some 2000 Qing forces stationed in Seoul and Korean forces in an attack on the royal palace defended by some 200 Japanese troops led by the Japanese minister to Korea, Takezoe Shinichirō. The Japanese are defeated and withdraw from Seoul the following day.

1885 Sino-French Treaty of Tianjin on Vietnam

January 10 (11/25). The head of the London office of the Chinese Maritime Customs, James Duncan Campbell, arrives in Paris to aid Sino-French peace talks. He had been sent by Sir Robert Hart, the Inspector-General of Maritime Customs.

13 (11/28). Cen Yuying's forces surround Tuyenquang, Vietnam.

24 (12/9). Campbell presents to the French Prime Minister, Jules Ferry, Hart's proposal to end the Sino-French war on the basis of the Li-Fournier Convention. Ferry rejects the proposal.

26 (12/11). Qing forces make a fierce attack on Tuyenquang.

February. Zhang Zhidong sets up the Guangdong Victorious Army.

13 (12/29). Pressed by the French under General François de Négrier, Qing troops under the Governor of Guangxi, Pan Dingxin, abandon Langson and retreat to Zhennanguan (Guangxi) on the border. Five Chinese warships going to relieve the blockade of Taiwan are defeated by Courbet's warships. Three of them retreat to Zhenhai (Zhejiang) and the other two to Shipu (Zhejiang), and sink there February 15.

14 (12/30). De Négrier's troops occupy Langson.

20 (1/6). France notifies England that as from February 26, it will regard rice destined for parts north of Guangzhou as contraband of war.

23 (1/9). The French take Zhennanguan. Pan Dingxin retreats. Two days later the French sack and burn Zhennanguan and return to Langson.

1884–5

D PUBLICATIONS

Printing of Wu Dacheng's *Shuowen guzhou bu* (*A Supplementary Work to the Shuowen*) on ancient characters (author's preface July 1883), and the same author's guide to artillery practice *Qianfa zhunsheng* (*Rules of Conduct in Gun Practice*).

April. The Tongwen Book Company publishes a lithographic version of the Palace edition of the twenty-four Standard Histories and a photolithographic edition of the *Gujin tushu jicheng* (*Compilation of Ancient and Modern Charts and Books*) and other works.

F BIRTHS AND DEATHS

March 15 (*2/18*). Wu Zhongxin b. (d. 1959).
October 18 (*8/30*). Li Jishen b. (d. 1959).
November–December. Scholar and bibliophile Zhao Zhiqian d. aged 55.

The death of Zuo Zongtang 1885

A ECONOMICS

The Kaiping Railway Company is set up.

January 21 (*12/6*). The court permits Zhang Zhidong to raise a loan from Germany to finance the war against France.
  23 (*12/8*). The court grants Zuo Zongtang permission to raise a foreign loan of 4,000,000 taels to be able to transport troops for the relief of the blockade of Taiwan.
February 4 (*12/20*). Zhang Zhidong is permitted to raise another loan for the war against France, this time £505,000 from the Hongkong and Shanghai Banking Corporation.
March 3 (*1/17*). The US Congress approves the return of $453,401 to China, part of the indemnity arising from injuries to US merchants at Guangzhou in 1856–57.
July 17 (*6/6*). China and Korea conclude a contract to lay an overland electric line between the two countries.
  18 (*6/7*). Zeng Jize and the British Foreign Secretary, Lord Salisbury, sign an additional article to the Chefoo Convention fixing import duty and *lijin* on opium, after the payment of which it is to be free of all taxation in China.
August 10 (*7/1*). The electric cable from Nanning (Guangxi) reaches Yunnan.

1885

28 (1/14). Hart cables China's views on solving the Sino-French conflict to Campbell, who passes them on to the French government the following day.

March 1–3 (1/15–17). The French attack Zhenhai (Zhejiang) but are repulsed.

3 (1/17). The French raise the siege of Tuyenquang.

14 (1/28). Itō Hirobumi arrives in Tianjin as Japanese plenipotentiary to negotiate with China over Korea.

23–24 (2/7–8). Qing forces under Feng Zicai beat off several attacks by the French against Zhennanguan; the latter finally retreat to Langson.

28 (2/12). Qing troops under Feng Zicai attack Langson. De Négrier is seriously wounded. Next day Feng takes Langson.

31 (2/15). Zeng Jize cables the *Zongli yamen* that the recapture of Langson has caused the resignation of Jules Ferry's cabinet in Paris (March 30) and that China should take the opportunity to talk peace. Courbet occupies the Penghu Islands (Pescadores).

April 3 (2/18). Li Hongzhang and Itō Hirobumi begin negotiations in Tianjin over Korea.

4 (2/19). Campbell signs for China an agreement with France to ratify the Li-Fournier Convention of Tianjin (1884) as a basis for a peace treaty between China and France; 'the two powers consent to a general cessation of hostilities as soon as the necessary orders can be given and received.'

6 (2/21). A timetable for ceasefire and withdrawal of troops is declared between China and France.

16 (3/2). The French raise their blockade of Taiwan and the northern ports.

18 (3/4). Li Hongzhang and Itō Hirobumi sign the Li-Itō Convention of Tianjin on Korea. Each agrees to withdraw troops from Korea within four months; neither China nor Japan is to train soldiers for Korea nor to send troops without first notifying the other.

June 9 (4/27). Patenôtre and Li Hongzhang sign the Sino-French Treaty on Vietnam in Tianjin; it reaffirms French protectorate over Vietnam, settles the border and trade regulations, and makes no mention of indemnity.

21 (5/9). The French withdraw from Jilong.

24 (5/12). Liu Yongfu's army withdraws into Yunnan.

28 (5/16). An uprising in Xianju (Zhejiang) by 2000 members of the Elder Brothers Society is put down.

July 21 (6/10). Chinese and Japanese troops stationed in Korea withdraw.

22 (6/11). The French withdraw from the Pescadores.

1885

B OFFICIAL APPOINTMENTS, DISMISSALS, TRANSFERS ETC.

March 24 (*2/8*). Pan Dingxin is dismissed because of the defeats he has suffered. Li Bingheng replaces him as Governor of Guangxi.
April 10 (*2/25*) Yulu is appointed acting Viceroy of Huguang.
July 27 (*6/16*). Sun Yuwen, Shen Bingcheng and Xuchang are appointed to the *Zongli yamen*.
August 7 (*6/27*). Sun Yuwen is confirmed as a member of the Grand Council.
October 13 (*9/6*). The court appoints the Emperor's father Yihuan to head the Board of Admiralty; other Board members include Li Hongzhang and Zeng Jize.
30 (*9/23*). Yuan Shikai is appointed Resident in Korea to deal with negotiations and trade matters.

C CULTURAL AND SOCIAL

June 17 (*5/5*). Li Hongzhang sends in a memorial suggesting the establishment of a military academy in Tianjin.
October. Founding of the Shanghai Polytechnic Institute by the British consul and missionary John Fryer and Xu Shou, Tang Jingxing, and others.

D PUBLICATIONS

Printing of the *Hunan tongzhi* (*General Gazetteer of Hunan*), compiled by Guo Songtao and others (preface of Yulu, Viceroy of Huguang, dated sixth month, July 12–August 9).

E NATURAL DISASTERS

August 8–11 (*6/28–7/2*). Rain causes serious flooding of the Yellow River in Shandong.

F BIRTHS AND DEATHS

February 23 (*1/9*). Commander-in-Chief Yang Yuke is killed in the battle for Zhennanguan.
March 22 (*2/6*). The British minister, Sir Harry Parkes, d. in Peking aged 57.
June 11 (*4/29*). Admiral Courbet d. in the Pescadores aged 58.
September 5 (*7/27*). Zuo Zongtang d. in Fuzhou aged 73.
October 12 (*9/5*). Zhu Zhixin b. (d. 1920).

1885-6

September 20 *(8/12)*. The court releases the *Taewongun* of Korea and orders him to be taken home (see also August 26, 1882).
October 5 *(8/27)*. Yuan Shikai brings the *Taewongun* into Seoul.
12 *(9/5)*. Taiwan is established as a separate province. The governorship of Fujian is transferred to the governorship of Taiwan. The functions of the Governor of Fujian are to be fulfilled by the Viceroy of Minzhe. The court sets up the Board of Admiralty.

1886 Sino-British Convention on Burma and Tibet

January 12 *(12/8)*. Britain having just proclaimed Burma as annexed to British India (January 1), the British Foreign Secretary, Lord Salisbury, promises Zeng Jize that Burma may still send tribute to China.
April 25 *(3/22)*. In Tianjin Li Hongzhang and the French minister, G. Gogordan, conclude an agreement settling the borders between China and Vietnam and regulations for trade between the two countries.
May 17 *(4/14)*. Yihuan, Li Hongzhang and others begin a tour of inspection of fortified areas, arsenals and military academies of Dagu, Lüshun, Weihaiwei and other places.
July 4 *(6/3)*. China and Russia agree on the border in the Hunchun area (Jilin).
24 *(6/23)*. Yihuang and N. O'Conor, the British *chargé d'affaires* in China, sign the 'Convention Relating to Burma and Thibet'. China recognizes British 'authority and rule' over Burma. Britain allows the continuation of tribute: 'England agrees that the highest authority in Burma shall send the customary decennial missions'. It also agrees not to push the opening of Tibet.
August 13 *(7/14)*. A unit of Chinese marines under naval Commander-in-Chief Ding Ruchang clashes with Japanese police in Nagasaki. Two days later the Japanese start a further clash; eight Chinese and two Japanese are killed.
September 2 *(8/5)*. The Empress Dowager, in theory persuaded by Yihuan and other courtiers, agrees to continue her regency for a few more years.
11 *(8/14)*. Sir Robert Hart, British minister in China, concludes an agreement with China that Hongkong should prohibit the possession, import or export of 'opium in quantities less than one chest' and should report all movements of opium, provided that China make a similar arrangement with Macao.
October 9 *(9/12)*. Zeng Jize leaves England for home.

Birth of Zhu De   **1886**

A   ECONOMICS

In this year silk replaces tea as China's single most important export item.

July 2 (*6/1*). The Jinling arsenal manufactures its first bullets, having been extended for the purpose.

August 6 (*7/7*). The court approves the establishment of an ammunition procurement bureau in Shanghai.

B   OFFICIAL APPOINTMENTS, DISMISSALS, TRANSFERS ETC.

June 8 (*5/7*). Liu Bingzhang is appointed Viceroy of Sichuan.

December 13 (*11/8*). Zeng Jize is appointed to the *Zongli yamen*.

C   CULTURAL AND SOCIAL

April 6 (*3/3*). A third group of students from the Fuzhou Dockyard Naval Academy sails for Europe.

May 29 (*4/26*). The French Bishop of Peking, Mgr A. Favier, agrees to remove a Catholic church which overlooked the Imperial Palace and thus offended the Chinese.

D   PUBLICATIONS

Printing of Wu Dacheng's *Hengxuan suojian suocang jijin lu* (*Catalogue of Ritual Objects which Hengxuan* [*Wu himself*] *Has Seen or Holds*).

April 28 (*3/25*). The *Shuntian fuzhi* (*The Gazetteer of Shuntian*), compiled by Zhang Zhidong and others, is presented to the throne.

June 24 (*5/23*). Kuang Qizhao inaugurates the *Guangbao* (*Guangdong News*) in Guangzhou.

October 2 (*9/5*). A new edition of the *Da Qing huidian* (*Qing Statutes*) is presented to the throne.

1886-7

29 *(10/3)*. In Zhongwei (Gansu) a rebellion breaks out, led by Zhao Shenxian, but it is quickly suppressed.

November 1 *(10/6)*. Feng Zicai inflicts a serious defeat on rebels in Qiongzhou, Hainan Island (Guangdong) and captures their leader, Chen Zhongming.

1887 Sino-Portuguese Treaty formally cedes Macao to Portugal

February 7 *(1/15)*. The Emperor is proclaimed to be of age but is not yet allowed to rule in his own right.

March 26 *(3/2)*. China and Portugal sign a protocol in Lisbon under which Macao and dependencies are for the first time formally ceded to Portugal, although not to be alienated by Portugal without agreement with China; Macao is to cooperate in opium work in the same way as Hongkong (see September 11, 1886).

29 *(3/5)*. China and France settle regulations covering the borders between Vietnam and Guangdong, Guangxi and Yunnan.

June 16 *(int. 4/25)*. The rebellion in Qiongzhou is suppressed.

26 *(5/6)*. Further Sino-French agreements are reached covering trade and the border with Vietnam. Under the series of agreements (see also April 25, 1886, and March 29), all possible points of entry for an invasion of Tongking are taken from China. Trade is regulated to ensure reciprocal treatment, except that China concedes a reduction of import and export duty.

October 8 *(8/22)*. The British protest over alleged intrusions by Tibetan soldiers into Sikkim, especially the occupation of Lingtu, near the border, and demand their immediate withdrawal.

17 *(9/1)*. The *Zongli yamen* receives a report from Lhasa saying that the Tibetans have built a fort at Lingtu 'with a view to protecting their country', and denying that the area was subject to India.

November 6 *(10/11)*. The *Tianjin shibao* (*Tianjin Times*) is inaugurated, edited by the missionary Timothy Richard.

E NATURAL DISASTERS

April 4–10 *(3/1–7)*. Serious flooding occurs along the Yellow River in Shandong. The dykes in several counties burst.

F BIRTHS AND DEATHS

May 24 *(4/21)*. The Viceroy of Sichuan, Ding Baozhen, d. aged 66.
October 7 *(9/10)*. Bao Chao d. aged 58.
December 1 *(11/6)*. Zhu De b. (d. 1976).

Birth of Chiang Kaishek **1887**

A ECONOMICS

March 1 *(2/7)*. The Sichuan–Yunnan electric line is completed.
16 *(2/22)*. The court gives approval for the construction of railway lines for commercial and military use, especially one from Dagu to Tianjin and then to connect with Tangshan.
July 26 *(6/6)*. Zhang Zhidong sends in a memorial saying that he has set up an arsenal in Guangzhou.
October 9 *(8/23)*. The underwater electric cable from Fuzhou to Taiwan is completed.

B OFFICIAL APPOINTMENTS, DISMISSALS, TRANSFERS ETC.

June 23 *(5/3)*. Hong Jun is appointed Imperial Commissioner to Russia, Germany, Austria and Holland; and Liu Ruifen to England, France, Italy and Belgium.
September 13 *(7/26)*. Li Shuchang is appointed Imperial Commissioner to Japan.

C CULTURAL AND SOCIAL

June 11 *(int. 4/20)*. Zhang Zhidong establishes the famous Guangya Academy.

1887–8

December 1 (*10/17*). In Peking, Yikuang and the special envoy Thomas de Souza Rosa sign Sino-Portuguese treaties confirming the protocol of March 26. The court orders that its Resident in Tibet, Wanyan, should arrange for the withdrawal of the Tibetan soldiers in Lingtu and not start a fight with the British. The order is repeated more forcefully December 23.
4 (*10/20*). Zhang Zhidong sends in a memorial suggesting the setting up of consulates in all the British, Dutch and Spanish colonies of South-east Asia to protect the Overseas Chinese there from ill-treatment and exploitation.

1888 The Beiyang Fleet is established

February 19 (*1/8*). British troops attack and destroy Tibetan barracks in Lingtu.
28 (*1/17*). Wenyan sends in a memorial saying that Tibetan troops have never crossed the border and that the British demand for their withdrawal from Sikkim is unreasonable.
March 13 (*2/1*). The minister to the United States, Zhang Yinhuan, signs with US Secretary of State Thomas Bayard a treaty prohibiting all immigration of Chinese labourers for twenty years and restricting return to the USA of Chinese who go back to China. The Peking government never ratified the treaty in this form.
20 (*2/8*). British troops again attack the camps and barracks of Tibetan soldiers in Lingtu, who retreat.
28 (*2/16*). The court censures the Tibetan soldiers' having clashed with the British.
May. Tibetan soldiers attempt a surprise attack on the British camp at Gnatong, Sikkim, but are repulsed with heavy losses.
September 22 (*8/17*). The British complete their occupation of Sikkim.
25 (*8/20*). The British defeat Tibetan troops and occupy Yadong and other places.

1887–8

D PUBLICATIONS

January. Zeng Jize's article 'China: the Sleep and the Awakening' is published in London's *Asiatic Quarterly Review*.
July. The *Yiwen yuebao* (*Progress Civilization Monthly*) is inaugurated in Hankou.

E NATURAL DISASTERS

Late September. The Yellow River bursts its southern banks at Zhengzhou (Henan), causing disastrous flooding over a vast area along its lower reaches.
December 16 (*11/2*). A series of earthquakes begins in Shiping (Yunnan), lasting about a fortnight and killing some 2000 people.

F BIRTHS AND DEATHS

September 30 (*8/14*). Liu Changyou d. aged 68.
October 31 (*9/15*). Chiang Kaishek b. in Zhejiang (d. 1975).
November 12 (*9/27*). The scholar and official Li Yuandu d. aged 66.

Birth of Li Dazhao   1888

A ECONOMICS

January 17 (*12/5*). Li Hongzhang sends in a memorial setting out the regulations for the gold mine in Mohe (Heilongjiang), which is to be made government-supervised and merchant-operated.
August. The Tianjin–Tangshan Railway is completed.
December 1 (*10/28*). Sino-French agreements are reached in Tianjin on regulations for electric cable connections between south China and north Vietnam.

B OFFICIAL APPOINTMENTS, DISMISSALS, TRANSFERS ETC.

March 3 (*1/21*). The Resident in Tibet, Wenyan, is dismissed, because of his reluctance to withdraw troops from Sikkim, and replaced by Changgeng.
April 6 (*2/25*). Yang Changxun is appointed Viceroy of Shan'gan, Kabaodi of Minzhe.
November 8 (*10/5*). The Empress Dowager appoints the daughter of Guixiang as Empress and the daughters of Changxu as *Jinpin* ('Gem Concubine') and *Zhenpin* ('Pearl Concubine').

1888–9

30 *(8/25)*. For the Board of Admiralty, Yihuan submits to the throne the regulations proposed by Li Hongzhang to govern the Beiyang Fleet.

November 19 *(10/16)*. Shengtai, assistant Resident in Tibet, goes to the border area from Lhasa to negotiate troop withdrawal and border demarcation with the British.

30 *(10/27)*. Acting on behalf of the Imperial College, Weng Tonghe refuses to hand Kang Youwei's first 'Ten-thousand-word letter' (*Wanyan shu*) on to the Emperor. It is thus rejected outright.

December 17 *(11/15)*. The Beiyang Fleet is set up on the basis of Li Hongzhang's regulations.

21 *(11/19)*. Shengtai meets with the British Political Officer A.W. Paul on the Tibet-Sikkim border. They are soon joined, for negotiations, by the Indian Foreign Secretary, H.M. Durand.

26 *(11/24)*. Li Hongzhang cables the *Zongli yamen* that the USA is banning totally the entry of Chinese labourers.

1889 *The Empress Dowager's regency ends*

January 10 *(12/9)*. The Durand-Shengtai talks break up without agreement.

February 5 *(1/6)*. Because Indian police in the British Concession in Zhenjiang (Jiangsu) had beaten and killed some Chinese, the masses angrily destroy foreign companies and the British and American consular offices.

26 *(1/27)*. The Emperor's wedding takes place.

March 4 *(2/3)*. The Emperor begins to rule in his own right. The Empress Dowager's regency ends.

12 *(2/11)*. The court issues a secret edict that Shengtai should permit Sikkim to be a British protectorate.

April. Sino-British talks on Sikkim reopen.

1888-9

December 17 (*11/15*). Ding Ruchang is appointed Commander-in-Chief of the Beiyang Fleet.

D PUBLICATIONS

Sun Yirang prints the *Guzhou shiyi* (*Epigraphical Notes*).

E NATURAL DISASTERS

Earthquakes in Zhili and Shandong, and floods in Henan, Shandong and Zhili result in the deaths of some 3,500,000 people.
June 13 (*5/4*). Disastrous earthquakes strike Zhili and Shandong.

F BIRTHS AND DEATHS

March 9 (*1/26*). Wu Tiecheng b. (d. 1953).
October 6 (*9/2*). Li Dazhao b. in Zhili (d. 1927).
29 (*9/25*). Zhu Peide b. (d. 1937).

China's first modern mint begins operations **1889**

A ECONOMICS

April 2 (*3/3*). Zhang Zhidong sends in a memorial proposing the construction of a railway from the Lugou (Marco Polo) Bridge outside Peking to Hankou.
May 25 (*4/26*). China's first modern mint starts operating in Guangzhou.
December 29 (*12/8*). The Shanghai cotton cloth mill formally starts work.

B OFFICIAL APPOINTMENTS, DISMISSALS, TRANSFERS ETC.

February 14 (*1/15*). Zhang Zhiwan becomes a Grand Secretary, and Xu Tong an assistant Grand Secretary.
March 29 (*int. 2/9*). Zhang Yinhuan is appointed to the *Zongli yamen*.
May 15 (*4/16*). Xue Fucheng is appointed Imperial Commissioner to Britain, France, Italy and Belgium.
June 30 (*6/3*). Wang Wenshao is appointed Viceroy of Yungui.
August 8 (*7/12*). Zhang Zhidong is appointed Viceroy of Huguang and Li Hanzhang of Liangguang.

D PUBLICATIONS

Wang Yirong's *Hanshi cunmu* (*Catalogue of Extant Han Stone Inscriptions*)

1890 Sikkim-Tibet Convention

January 6 (*12/16*). The court vetoes a suggestion from Heilongjiang to summon people there from the provinces of China proper to open wasteland. Disaster-affected people from Shandong are not allowed to be sent to north-east China.

March 17 (*2/27*). Shengtai and the Viceroy of India, Lord Lansdowne, sign the Sikkim-Tibet Convention in Darjeeling. The agreement defines the Sikkim-Tibet border, admits sole British control over Sikkim's internal and external affairs and provides for a joint Anglo-Chinese guarantee of the frontier as defined.

July 9 (*5/23*). In Sichuan, Lei Boyi rises in rebellion.

August 26 (*7/11*). The Sikkim-Tibet Convention is exchanged in London.

October 28 (*9/15*). Qing forces defeat Lei Boyi's troops.

November 7 (*9/25*). An uprising of the Elder Brothers Society breaks out in Shidai (Anhui) but it is quickly put down.

December 2 (*10/21*). Lei Poyi is decisively defeated by Qing troops.

12 (*11/1*). An edict is issued that the ministers of all countries should have an audience with the Emperor in the first month of every year beginning in 1891. The ministers receive the edict December 14.

is printed.
January 31 (*1/1*). The *Wanguo gongbao* recommences publication as a monthly. Until its first folding in 1883, it had been a weekly.
May 7 (*4/8*). Wu Dacheng completes his *Guyu tukao* (*Charts and Examination of Ancient Jades*).
June. The novel *Wu xiao yi* (*Five Younger Gallants*) is published in Peking.

F BIRTHS AND DEATHS

May 1 (*4/2*). Actor Ouyang Yuqian b. (d. 1962).
June 6 (*5/8*). Cen Yuying d. aged 60.
August 3 (*7/7*). Neo-Confucian scholar Wang Shiduo d. aged 87.

The Hanyang iron and steel works inaugurated **1890**

A ECONOMICS

Cotton replaces opium as China's chief import.
March 31 (*int. 2/11*). A supplement is signed to the Sino-British Chefoo Convention; under it Chongqing is opened to foreign trade.
May 19 (*4/1*). The telegraph lines between southern Guangxi and northern Vietnam are linked at Zhennanguan on the border.
November 9 (*9/27*). Work on the construction of the dock at Lüshun is completed.
December 1 (*10/20*). The electric line from Peking to Suzhou (Gansu) is completed.
4 (*10/23*). Zhang Zhidong inaugurates the Hanyang iron and steel works.

B OFFICIAL APPOINTMENTS, DISMISSALS, TRANSFERS ETC.

September 9 (*7/25*). The court appoints Xu Jingcheng minister to Russia, Germany, Holland and Austria, and Li Jingfang to Japan.
November 22 (*10/11*). Liu Kunyi is appointed Viceroy of Liangjiang.

C CULTURAL AND SOCIAL

August. Workers at the Jiangnan arsenal strike for half a day in protest over the extension of working hours.
8 (*6/23*). Anti-Christian riots occur in Dazu (Sichuan). Converts are killed and their houses damaged.

1891 Rebellion of the Golden Elixir Sect

January 16 (*12/7*). Lei Boyi's rebellion is totally suppressed.
February 20 (*1/12*). A secret society uprising breaks out, led by the Sichuanese Huang Zirong.
22 (*1/14*). Rebel troops under Huang Zirong seize Fumin (Yunnan).
24 (*1/16*). Huang Zirong's rebellion is suppressed.
March 5 (*1/25*). The ministers of all foreign countries are given audience with the Emperor.
May 23–June 9 (*4/16–5/3*). Li Hongzhang and others inspect the Chinese navy in Lüshun, headquarters of the Beiyang Fleet.
Mid-June. In Wanxian (Sichuan), Cui Yinghe, a secret society leader, and others cut the electric lines and are planning to rebel, when the matter leaks out and they are caught.
August. Russian troops move into the Pamir region, British troops into Hunza.
September 12 (*8/10*). Thirty-five boxes of foreign guns bought for

1890-1

D PUBLICATIONS

Printing of Huang Zunxian's *Riben guozhi* (*A History of Japan*); and Lu Xinyuan's *Wuxing jinshi ji* (*Records of the Epigraphy of Wuxing*); Wuxing (Zhejiang) is Lu's native district.

E NATURAL DISASTERS

July 14–27 (5/28–6/11). Owing to several days' torrential rain and heavy winds, several rivers in Zhili burst their banks, causing devastating floods.
29 (6/13). Torrential rain causes flooding in Peking.

F BIRTHS AND DEATHS

April 12 (int. 2/23). Zeng Jize d. aged 50.
24 (3/6). Peng Yulin d. aged 74.
August 12 (6/27). Yang Yuebin d. aged 68.
November 13 (10/2). Zeng Guoquan d. aged 66.
28 (10/17). Peking Opera actor Yu Shuyan b. (d. 1943).
December 11 (10/30). Pan Zuyin d. aged 60.
16 (11/5). Chen Bulei b. (d. 1948).
24 (11/13). Baoting d. aged 50.

Many incidents against Christian churches and missionaries **1891**

B OFFICIAL APPOINTMENTS, DISMISSALS, TRANSFERS ETC.

September 4 (8/2). Yikuang is put in charge of the Board of Admiralty.
December 15 (11/15). Chongli and Hong Jun are appointed to the *Zongli yamen*.

C CULTURAL AND SOCIAL

February 22 (1/14). The Jiangnan Naval Academy is established in Nanjing.
April. In the Kaiping coal mines the workers beat up foreign technicians and foremen in an outburst of resentment against foreign exploitation.
May 13 (4/6). In the belief that the missionaries were kidnapping children, the people destroy the Catholic mission premises in Wuhu (Anhui) and attack various Protestant missions.
June 5 (4/29). In Wuxue (Hubei), Christian mission premises are at-

167

1891–2

the Elder Brothers Society by Englishman Charles W. Mason, a former customs official at Zhenjiang (Jiangsu), and planned for use in an Elder Brothers Society rebellion, are seized by the authorities.

14 (*8/12*). A Miao rebellion breaks out in Xiajiang (Guizhou).

16 (*8/14*). Miao rebels fail in an attempt to take Xiajiang, and their uprising is soon suppressed.

November 11 (*10/10*). The uprising of the Golden Elixir Sect begins in Aohan Banner led by Yang Yuechun, Li Guozhen, and others. The rebels' slogans include 'annihilate the Qing, death to the foreigners'.

14 (*10/13*). The forces of the Golden Elixir Sect take the prefectural capital of Chaoyang (Zhili). Li Guozhen is declared 'the military sage who sweeps the north'. The Sect's troops reach several tens of thousands in number.

December 14 (*11/14*). Qing troops defeat forces of the Golden Elixir Sect, capturing and beheading more than 1400 of them.

15 (*11/15*). Qing troops defeat the army of Li Guozhen.

18 (*11/18*). Qing forces capture the major base areas of the Golden Elixir Sect and pacify Aohan Banner.

27 (*11/27*). The Golden Elixir Sect rebellion is put down; Yang Yuechun is captured, Chaoyang and other places are pacified.

1892 *Russian–British movements along China's western border*

July 10 (*6/17*). Xue Fucheng, the minister to Britain, France, Italy and Belgium, is sent to discuss the demarcation of the Yunnan–Burma border with Britain.

24 (*int. 6/1*). The Governor of Xinjiang, Tao Mo, sends in a memorial saying that Russian troops have entered the Pamir region and are

1891–2

tacked, missionaries' houses burned and two Englishmen killed.

8 (5/2). In Wuxi (Jiangsu) the Catholic mission is destroyed. There were several other similar incidents at this time.

13 (5/7). The court orders Liu Kunyi and Zhang Zhidong, Viceroys of Liangjiang and Huguang, to protect the Christian missions and punish those responsible for the incidents directed against them.

July 11 (6/6). An edict is issued to search for and arrest members of the Elder Brothers Society as responsible for the anti-missionary incidents.

September 2 (7/29). In Yichang (Hubei) the masses burn French and English-American churches.

November 18–20 (10/17–19). The Golden Elixir Sect, together with Observance Sect members, burn down Christian churches and pursue and kill converts.

D PUBLICATIONS

Printing of *Xinxue weijing kao* (*A Study of the Forged Classics of the Xin Period*) by Kang Youwei (the preface is dated May 8, 1898, by the author).

September. Printing of Lu Xinyuan's *Qianpi ting guzhuan tushi* (*Charts and Explanations of Ancient Bricks from the Qianpi Pavilion*).

10 (8/8). The court orders the republication of the *Quanshan yaoyan* (*Important Sayings Encouraging Good*) by the first Manchu emperor Shunzhi, first published in 1656.

E NATURAL DISASTERS

April 17 (3/9). An earthquake strikes the Fenzhou region (Shanxi).

F BIRTHS AND DEATHS

January 1 (11/21). The Emperor's father Yihuan d. aged 50.
July 18 (6/13). Guo Songtao d. aged 73.
December 17 (11/17). Hu Shi b. in Shanghai (d. 1962).

1892   *Birth of Guo Moruo*

A ECONOMICS

August 25 (7/4). China and Russia reach agreement in Tianjin on connecting their common border regions by electric power cable.

November 20 (10/2). The Wuchang cotton cloth mill, set up by Zhang Zhidong, begins work.

169

1892–3

advancing in the general direction of Yarkand (Xinjiang).

27 (*int. 6/4*). Following a memorial from the *Zongli yamen*, a court order forbids the private purchase of foreign munitions.

August 16 (*int. 6/24*). The Viceroy of Shan'gan, Yang Changxun, sends in a memorial asking for measures to be taken to defend the western borders because of the Russian advance into the Pamir region and the British takeover of Hunza, which China regarded as belonging to China.

September 15 (*7/25*). China and Britain jointly set up the chief of the Moslem people of Hunza.

18 (*7/28*). The Elder Brothers Society of Xiangtan (Hunan) rebels in Pingxiang (Jiangxi), and five days later attacks the county capital.

October 2 (*8/12*). Jiangxi official troops put down the rebellion of the Elder Brothers Society and capture its leaders.

10 (*8/20*). The forces of the Sichuan rebel Yu Dongchen of Dazu fight with government troops but are defeated.

1893

China's total population reaches about 386,700,000.

September 13 (*8/4*). Following Xue Fucheng's suggestion, the court relaxes the ban on Overseas Chinese merchants' returning home. They are now allowed to stay in China as long as they like, make a living and buy property.

1892–3

B Official Appointments, Dismissals, Transfers etc.

June 22 (5/28). Tan Zhongling is appointed Viceroy of Minzhe.
October 19 (8/29). Fukun is appointed Grand Secretary, Linshu assistant Grand Secretary.

C Cultural and Social

July 23 (6/30). Sun Yatsen graduates from the College of Medicine in Hongkong.
December 3 (10/15). The Governor of Xinjiang, Tao Mo, sends in a memorial that he has set up a school of Russian.

D Publications

Guo Songtao's collected works *Yangzhi shuwu yiji* (*Remaining Works from the Yangzhi Hall*) are printed (preface dated eighth month September 21–October 20, 1892).

E Natural Disasters

Locust plague afflicts Peking, Jiangsu, Anhui and Shanxi.
July 17 (6/24). The Yongding River dykes burst in several places, including Peking, Tianjin and Bazhou (Zhili), causing serious flooding. The dykes are closed up early in November.
August 21 (*int.* 6/29). The Yellow River dykes burst in Jiyang and other places in Shandong, causing serious flooding.

F Births and Deaths

March 7 (2/9). Yan Jingming d. aged 75.
October. Guo Moruo b. in Sichuan (d. 1978).
27 (9/7). Chen Guofu b. (d. 1951).

Birth of Mao Zedong   1893

C Cultural and Social

January. The rebuilt Summer Palace is completed.
July 1 (5/18). Two Swedish missionaries are beaten up and killed in Macheng (Hubei).
November. Zhang Zhidong sends in a memorial that the Self-

1893—4

December 5 *(10/28)*. China and British India sign at Darjeeling the Regulations regarding Trade, Communication and Pasturage to be appended to the Sikkim-Tibet Convention of 1890. A trade mart is to be established at Yadong (Tibet). China is to protect the lives and property of British subjects and provide a suitable residence for a British official to supervise the mart.

1894 Outbreak of the Sino-Japanese War

March 17 *(2/11)*. The nationalist *Tonghak* (Eastern Learning) rebellion breaks out in Korea.

The USA re-enacts the Chinese Exclusion Act of 1882 to extend the ban on immigration of Chinese for another ten years.

May 8 *(4/4)*. Yuan Shikai cables Li Hongzhang asking him to help the Korean court put down the *Tonghak* rebellion.

31 *(4/27)*. Korean King Kojong formally requests Yuan Shikai for Chinese military aid to put down the *Tonghak* rebellion.

June 2 *(4/29)*. The Japanese cabinet of Prime Minister Itō Hirobumi,

1893–4

Strengthening School has been opened in Wuchang with four departments: Western languages, natural sciences, mathematics and commercial affairs.

December 19 (*11/12*). A medical school organized by Li Hongzhang is opened in Tianjin.

D PUBLICATIONS

Printing of the *Xiku zhai huaxu* (*Paintings from the Xiku Studio*) edited by Huinian, a catalogue of most of the paintings of the famous painter Dai Xi between 1841 and 1856; *Zeng Huimin gong quanji* (*Zeng Jize's Complete Works*); and Zheng Guanying's *Shengshi weiyan* (*Warnings to the Seemingly Prosperous Age*), advocating reforms.

February 17 (*1/1*). The *Xinwen bao* newspaper begins publication in Shanghai.

E NATURAL DISASTERS

July 25 (*6/13*). The Yongding River floods at the Lugou Bridge outside Peking and other places.

August 29 (*7/18*). Several hundred people are killed or hurt in an earthquake in central-western Sichuan.

October 19 (*9/10*). The Shanghai cotton cloth mill is destroyed by fire.

F BIRTHS AND DEATHS

April. Chonghou d. aged 66.
October 2 (*8/23*). Hong Jun d. aged 53.
December 26 (*11/19*). Mao Zedong b. in Xiangtan (Hunan) (d. 1976).

Sun Yatsen sets up the Revive China Society 1894

A ECONOMICS

February 15 (*1/10*). In Hubei the Daye iron mines, opened by Zhang Zhidong, begin operations.

April 2 (*2/27*). The court grants a request to open a conservancy bureau at the Lugou Bridge outside Peking to protect the dykes of the Yongding River.

5 (*2/30*). Shao Youlian sends in a memorial announcing completion of work on the Taiwan railway from Taibei to Xinzhu.

August 4 (*7/4*). At the suggestion of the Englishman W.F. Tyler, the

1894

having just learned by cable from its legation in Seoul of Korea's request for help from China, decides to send troops to Korea.

5 (*5/2*). A Japanese army camp is set up at Seoul.

7 (*5/4*). Japan informs the Qing court that it has never recognized Korea as a tributary state of China.

8 (*5/5*). Chinese troops under Nie Shicheng arrive in Asan, Korea.

9 (*5/6*). Some 700 more Chinese troops under the Commander-in-Chief of Zhili, Ye Zhichao, leave Shanhaiguan (Zhili) for Asan.

10 (*5/7*). Ōtori Keisuke, the Japanese minister to Korea, leads more than 400 Japanese troops into Seoul.

14 (*5/11*). A Japanese cabinet meeting decides to reform Korea's domestic administration jointly with China and insists that, should China disagree, Japan will do so unilaterally.

15 (*5/12*). The Japanese cabinet decides not to withdraw troops from Korea.

25 (*5/22*). The legations of the USA, Russia, France and Britain in Seoul request simultaneous withdrawal of Chinese and Japanese troops from Korea.

26 (*5/23*). Ōtori demands that the Korean court expel all Chinese troops from Korea and accept Japanese participation in the reform of Korea's domestic administration.

28 (*5/25*). Ōtori demands that King Kojong should declare that Korea is an independent state and not a tributary state of China.

July 23 (*6/21*). Japanese troops take over the Korean imperial palace, install the Taewongun as regent, carry off Queen Min and her children to the Japanese legation, and attack the Chinese offices.

25 (*6/23*). In the Korean Bay Japanese troops on the cruiser *Naniwa* attack and sink the British steamer *Kowshing*, carrying Chinese reinforcements to Korea: the outbreak of the Sino-Japanese war.

27 (*6/25*). The Taewongun declares war on China.

29 (*6/27*). Japanese troops defeat a Qing force under Nie Shicheng near Asan, which they occupy the following day.

August 1 (*7/1*). China and Japan declare war against one another.

7 (*7/7*). Britain declares neutrality and non-intervention in the Sino-Japanese war. The following day Russia follows suit.

10 (*7/10*). Japanese warships bombard Weihaiwei.

29 (*7/29*). The Qing court renews treaties with foreign nations to protect Chinese labourers overseas.

September 15–16 (*8/16–17*). The Battle of Pyongyang results in a Chinese rout and the Japanese occupation of the city. Ye Zhichao and others retreat towards Manchuria.

17 (*8/18*). In a major naval battle off the mouth of the Yalu River,

court orders Li Hongzhang to purchase three destroyers from Great Britain.

September 6 *(8/7)*. China and Britain conclude an agreement on setting up an electric cable link between Yunnan and Burma.

19 *(8/20)*. The Huasheng cotton mill in Shanghai, the rebuilt Shanghai cotton cloth mill, begins work.

B OFFICIAL APPOINTMENTS, DISMISSALS, TRANSFERS ETC.

January 9 *(12/3)*. Xu Yongyi is appointed a probationary member of the Grand Council (confirmed July 28).

August 28 *(7/28)*. Jingxin and Wang Mingluan are appointed to the *Zongli yamen*.

September 29 *(9/1)*. Prince Gong, Yixin, is again appointed to head the *Zongli yamen* and join the Board of Admiralty.

November 3 *(10/6)*. Weng Tonghe, Li Hongzao and Gangyi are appointed to the Grand Council.

19 *(10/22)*. Tan Zhonglin is appointed Viceroy of Sichuan; Bianbaoquan of Minzhe.

December 15 *(11/19)*. Ronglu is appointed to the *Zongli yamen*.

28 *(12/2)*. Liu Kunyi is appointed Imperial Commissioner in charge of military affairs in the Shanhaiguan area.

C CULTURAL AND SOCIAL

June 30 *(5/27)*. Sun Yatsen sends a letter to Li Hongzhang suggesting the reform of Chinese administration and the development of China's talents through universal free education, vocational guidance, and the promotion of science and agriculture.

August 4 *(7/4)*. The Qing court orders Li Hanzhang to ban Kang Youwei's publication *Xinxue weijing kao* (*A Study of the Forged Classics of the Xin Period*).

D PUBLICATIONS

March. The *Peking and Tientsin Times* begins publication as a weekly (becoming a daily October 1, 1902).

E NATURAL DISASTERS

Drought and resultant famine reach a climax in north China, having begun in 1892. By 1894 some 1,000,000 people have died of starvation.

1894–5

the Beiyang Fleet under Admiral Ding Ruchang is totally defeated. Of twelve Chinese warships the four survivors retreat to Lüshun (Fengtian).

October 6 *(9/8)*. The British Foreign Office (unsuccessfully) submits a Chinese proposal for mediation to the US, French, German and Russian governments.

18 *(9/20)*. Ding Ruchang leads the remnants of the Beiyang Fleet from Lüshun to Weihaiwei.

24 *(9/26)*. The First Japanese Army crosses the Yalu River and moves into Chinese territory. The Second Japanese Army lands near Lüshun and proceeds towards it.

November 6 *(10/9)*. The Second Japanese Army takes Jinzhou (Fengtian).

12 *(10/15)*. The Qing sends the Financial Commissioner of Hubei, Wang Zhichun, to Russia to attend the funeral of Tsar Alexander III and the coronation of Nicholas II.

13 *(10/16)*. Ding Ruchang leads his fleet back into Lüshun; it leaves the same day.

21 *(10/24)*. The Second Japanese Army takes Lüshun.

24 *(10/27)*. Sun Yatsen organizes the Revive China Society in Honolulu.

December 13 *(11/17)*. The First Japanese Army seizes Haicheng (Fengtian).

22 *(11/26)*. The Qing court sends Zhang Yinhuan and Shao Youlian to Japan for peace negotiations.

1895 Treaty of Shimonoseki

January 7 *(12/12)*. A rebellion led by Meng Yuqi and Zhu Chengxiu in Jilin is put down and its leaders are captured.

18 *(12/23)*. Japanese warships bombard Dengzhou (Shandong).

20 *(12/25)*. The Japanese Second Division and Eleventh Brigade land at Rongcheng Bay and take Rongcheng (Shandong).

26 *(1/1)*. The Battle of Weihaiwei begins with attacks on the forts lining the south shore of its harbour.

February 1–2 *(1/7–8)*. Zhang Yiuhuan and Shao Youlian meet with the Japanese Prime Minister and Foreign Minister, respectively Itō Hirobumi and Mutsu Munemitsu, for peace talks, but the Japanese regard their powers as inadequate, and reject their credentials.

12 *(1/18)*. The Battle of Weihaiwei ends in a Japanese victory. The Qing's strongest naval point, Liugong Island off Weihaiwei (Shan-

May. Bubonic plague strikes Guangzhou.
31 (4/17). A cyclone strikes Hainan Island, causing great damage.

F BIRTHS AND DEATHS

March 28 (2/22). The Korean pro-Japanese radical Kim Okkyun is assassinated in Shanghai.
July 21 (6/19). Xue Fucheng d. aged 56.
September 15 (8/16). Zuo Baogui killed in the Battle of Pyongyang.
October 22 (9/24). Mei Lanfang, Peking Opera actor, b. in Jiangsu (d. 1961).
December 5 (11/9). The bibliophile, scholar and official Lu Xinyuan d. aged 60.
   20 (11/24). The official and scholar Li Ciming d. aged 64.

Establishment of the Russo-Chinese Bank **1895**

A ECONOMICS

June 20 (5/28). China and France sign in Peking a convention on frontier trade between China and Vietnam: it includes a provision that railways in Vietnam, existing or projected, may be extended into China.
July 6 (*int.* 5/14). China signs a contract in St Petersburg for a Franco-Russian loan of 400,000,000 francs to pay the indemnity to Japan.
November 30 (10/14). China concludes a secret agreement with Russia allowing it to build the Trans-Siberian Railway through Manchuria.
December 10 (10/24). The Russo-Chinese Bank is established.

B OFFICIAL APPOINTMENTS, DISMISSALS, TRANSFERS ETC.

February 13 (1/19). Wang Wenshao is appointed acting Viceroy of

1895

dong), is surrendered to the Japanese. The ships of the Beiyang Fleet which have survived the battle are handed over to the Japanese.

March 2 (2/6). The court cables the Chinese ministers in France, Germany, Britain and Russia to ask their respective nations for mediation.

4 (2/8). The Japanese Second Army captures Niuzhuang (Fengtian).

16 (2/20). Sun Yatsen and others settle on the double nine, i.e. the ninth day of the ninth month (October 26) as the day for revolt. They set out to raise 3000 men to capture Guangzhou and make it into a revolutionary base.

19 (2/23). Li Hongzhang arrives in Shimonoseki, Japan.

20 (2/24). Li Hongzhang meets Itō Hirobumi and Mutsu Munemitsu for peace talks. Credentials are accepted on both sides.

21 (2/25). Itō Hirobumi suggests an armistice on condition that Tianjin, Shanhaiguan, and Dagu (Zhili) are handed over to Japan, together with their armaments and railways. Li Hongzhang rejects the demand.

23 (2/27). Japanese troops begin attacking the Pescadores; they defeat the main forts and complete their occupation of the islands within a few days.

24 (2/28). Li Hongzhang is shot at by a Japanese. The bullet strikes his cheek near his left eye.

30 (3/5). China and Japan reach agreement that a ceasefire shall go into effect in Zhili, Shandong, and Manchuria for twenty-one days.

April 17 (3/23). The Treaty of Shimonoseki is signed by China and Japan. China recognizes the 'full and complete independence and autonomy of Korea'; cedes to Japan 'in perpetuity and full sovereignty' the Liaodong Peninsula, Taiwan, and the Pescadores; and agrees to pay an indemnity of 200,000,000 taels. Japanese are allowed into China for trade and commerce.

23 (3/29). The Russian, German and French ministers to Japan present notes to the Japanese Foreign Ministry urging the return of the Liaodong Peninsula to China.

May 8 (4/14). The Treaty of Shimonoseki is exchanged at Yantai (Shandong).

23 (4/29). A manifesto proclaims the Republic of Taiwan as an independent state.

29 (5/6). Japanese troops land on Taiwan near Jilong. Kang Youwei writes a letter seeking rejection of the Treaty of Shimonoseki, reform and modernization. The Emperor reads it June 3 and expresses approval.

June 2 (5/10). Taiwan is officially handed over by China to Japan.

3 (5/11). Jilong is captured by Japanese troops.

1895

Zhili. Li Hongzhang is appointed as plenipotentiary to negotiate peace with Japan.

April 16 (*3/22*). Tan Zhonglin replaces Li Hanzhang as Viceroy of Liangguang. Lu Zhuanlin is appointed Viceroy of Sichuan.

May 5 (*4/11*). Kang Youwei has audience with the Emperor and is given a minor appointment in the Board of Works.

July 26 (*6/5*). The Grand Councillor, *Zongli yamen* member, and President of the Board of War, Sun Yuwen, is dismissed.

August 6 (*6/16*). Xu Yongyi is dismissed from the Grand Council and the *Zongli yamen*. Weng Tonghe and Li Hongzao are appointed to the *Zongli yamen*. Qian Yingpu is appointed to the Grand Council; Linshu is appointed Grand Secretary and Kungang assistant Grand Secretary.

28 (*7/9*). Wang Wenshao is confirmed as Viceroy of Zhili.

30 (*7/11*). Songfan is appointed Viceroy of Yungui.

C CULTURAL AND SOCIAL

Early January. Sun Yatsen returns to Hongkong from Honolulu.

February 5 (*1/11*). The British missionary Timothy Richard calls on Zhang Zhidong and urges him to undertake social reforms.

April 20 (*3/26*). The workers of the Hanyang iron and steel works go on strike in protest against the ill-treatment of workers.

22 (*3/28*). The provincial graduates led by Kang Youwei and Liang Qichao send in a petition demanding the renunciation of the Treaty of Shimonoseki.

May 2 (*4/8*). Kang Youwei and others present a 'Ten-thousand-word Petition' signed by 603 graduates protesting against the Treaty of Shimonoseki and calling upon the government to implement social reforms. This occasion is known as *gongche shangshu* (petition presentation by examination candidates).

3 (*4/9*). Kang Youwei obtains the *jinshi* degree.

29 (*5/6*). The people of Chengdu (Sichuan) attack foreign churches. This anti-missionary movement spreads widely and lasts till the end of June. Many churches are destroyed.

August 1 (*6/11*). The people of Gutian (Fujian) destroy churches and kill over ten British and Australian missionaries.

September. Kang Youwei, Yuan Shikai, Liang Qichao and others organize the Society for the Study of National Strengthening.

8 (*7/20*). Sheng Xuanhuai inaugurates the Sino-Western Academy in Tianjin.

November 14 (*9/28*). Timothy Richard and William Muirhead, both members of the missionary Society for the Diffusion of Knowledge,

1895-6

7 (5/15). Japanese troops enter Taibei.

30 (int. 5/8). Kang Youwei submits a long memorial on reform to the throne, but it is blocked and does not reach the Emperor.

August 2 (6/12). Moslem rebels in Gansu defeat a Qing force under the Brigadier-General of Liangzhou, Liu Pu. The rebellion later spreads its influence over the whole province and over 100,000 of Han nationality are killed.

26 (7/7). The Japanese seize Taizhong (Taiwan).

27 (7/8). Sun Yatsen and his followers meet in Hongkong. A plot to attack Guangzhou is discussed.

October 3 (8/15). China and Germany sign a treaty under which concessions are yielded to Germany in Hankou.

9 (8/21). Moslem rebels under Ma Yonglin attack Hezhou (Gansu).

10 (8/22). Yang Quyun becomes the president of the Revive China Society as it prepares for revolt.

21 (9/4). The Japanese occupy Tainan, completing the suppression of the Republic of Taiwan.

26–28 (9/9–11). The Revive China Society attempts an uprising in Guangzhou, Sun Yatsen's 'first revolution', but it fails. Many of its members are captured.

29 (9/12). Sun Yatsen escapes from Guangzhou to Hongkong.

November 7 (9/21). Several leading members of the Revive China Society are executed.

8 (9/22). China and Japan sign an agreement by which Japan forgoes the cession of the Liaodong Peninsula in return for an increase of the indemnity from 200,000,000 to 230,000,000 taels.

29 (10/13). China and Japan exchange agreements on the return of the Liaodong Peninsula.

December 2 (10/16). The court orders the Viceroy of Liangguang, Tan Zhonglin, to arrest Sun Yatsen and Yang Quyun.

4 (10/18). Qing troops under the Commander-in-Chief of Kashgar, Dong Fuxiang, raise the Moslem rebel siege of Hezhou (Gansu). They capture several leaders of the rebellion.

21 (11/6). Japanese troops withdraw from Lüshun.

1896   *Sun Yatsen arrested in London*

March 14 (2/6). Qing troops relieve a Moslem rebel siege of Xining (Gansu).

20 (2/7). The court orders the establishment of an imperial postal system.

write to the *Zongli yamen* requesting support for the church and better treatment of missionaries.

D PUBLICATIONS

He Qiutao's *Yuan Shengwu qinzheng lu* (*Records of Yuan Imperial Expeditions*), an account of Genghiz Khan's campaigns.

July. Kang Youwei begins publication of *Zhongwai jiwen* (*The Chinese and Foreign News Record*), advocating reform. He sends many copies to court officials.

E NATURAL DISASTERS

April 28 (*4/4*). Floods hit Zhili province, causing severe damage and drowning many people.
August 2 (*6/12*). The Yellow River floods at Lijin (Shandong).

F BIRTHS AND DEATHS

February 12 (*1/18*). The Qing naval Commander-in-Chief Ding Ruchang d. through suicide.
March 19 (*2/23*). Scholar Dong Pei d. aged 67.
July 19 (*int. 5/27*). Xu Beihong b. (d. 1953).

National postal system established **1896**

A ECONOMICS

March 23 (*2/10*). China obtains a loan of £16,000,000 at 5 per cent interest from the Hongkong and Shanghai Banking Corporation and the German Deutsch-Asiatische Bank to pay the indemnity to Japan.

1896

27 *(2/14)*. Li Hongzhang leaves Shanghai on a goodwill tour of Russia, Germany, France, Britain and the United States. He is accompanied by a large retinue.

April 8 *(2/26)*. The *Zongli yamen* orders the Chinese minister to the USA, Yang Ru, to investigate and report on Sun Yatsen's activities in the USA.

24 *(3/12)*. Dong Fuxiang inflicts a serious defeat on Moslem rebels near Datong (Gansu); more than 3000 are killed.

27 *(3/15)*. Li Hongzhang arrives in Odessa on the first stage of his expedition and is given an imposing reception.

30 *(3/18)*. Li Hongzhang arrives in St Petersburg.

June 2 *(4/21)*. Li Hongzhang represents China at the coronation of Tsar Nicholas II.

3 *(4/22)*. Li Hongzhang signs, with the Russian Foreign Minister, Prince Lobanov-Rostovski, and the Minister of Finance, Count S. Witte, the secret Sino-Russian Treaty of Alliance in Moscow. Russia obtains the right to extend the Trans-Siberian railway through Manchuria; China and Russia agree to defend each other against any Japanese attack on China, Korea or the Russian Far East.

14 *(5/4)*. Li Hongzhang has an audience with Kaiser Wilhelm II in Berlin.

July 13 *(6/3)*. Li Hongzhang arrives in Paris.

August 5 *(6/26)*. In London Li Hongzhang has an audience with Queen Victoria.

18 *(7/10)*. The rebellion of the Gansu Moslems is totally defeated and its principal leader captured.

28 *(7/20)*. The court approves the secret Sino-Russian Treaty of Alliance.

31 *(7/23)*. Li Hongzhang meets US President Grover Cleveland in Washington.

October 1 *(8/25)*. Sun Yatsen arrives in London from the USA.

3 *(8/27)*. Li Hongzhang arrives back in Tianjin from his tour round the world.

11 *(9/5)*. Sun Yatsen is kidnapped and detained at the Chinese legation in London.

17 *(9/11)*. Sun Yatsen gets a message to his friend and teacher James Cantlie, seeking help.

21 *(9/15)*. China and Russia conclude a new treaty in Peking.

23 *(9/17)*. Following a request by Cantlie to the British Foreign Office and the latter's intervention with the Chinese legation, Sun Yatsen is released.

December 14 *(11/10)*. The German minister Baron von Heyking

June. A mechanized cotton mill is set up in Wuxi (Jiangsu).
5 *(4/24).* China signs a contract with France authorizing the building of a railway linking Longzhou (Guangxi) with Vietnam.
July 11 *(6/1).* China signs a contract with one Danish and one British telegraph company for the construction of electric lines.
21 *(6/11).* The Sino-Japanese Trade and Navigation Treaty is signed in Peking.
September 8 *(8/2).* China and the Russo-Chinese Bank sign in Berlin a contract setting up the Chinese Eastern Railway Company.
October. The Peking–Tianjin railway line is completed.
20 *(9/14).* The court sets up a general railway company.
November 12 *(10/8).* The court orders Sheng Xuanhuai to organize a Western-style bank.

B OFFICIAL APPOINTMENTS, DISMISSALS, TRANSFERS ETC.

March 4 *(1/21).* Sun Jia'nai is appointed to administer the official bookshop set up the same day.
20 *(2/7).* The court appoints Sir Robert Hart to direct its postal system.
June 4 *(4/23).* Kungang is appointed Grand Secretary and Ronglu assistant Grand Secretary.
October 20 *(9/14).* The court appoints Sheng Xuanhuai to administer the affairs of its general railway company.
24 *(9/18).* Li Hongzhang is appointed to the *Zongli yamen*.
November 9 *(10/5).* Tao Mo is confirmed as Viceroy of Shan'gan because of the suppression of the Moslem rebellion.
December 2 *(10/28).* Xu Tong is appointed Grand Secretary and Li Hongzao assistant Grand Secretary.

C CULTURAL AND SOCIAL

January 21 *(12/7).* The court orders the closure of the Society for the Study of National Strengthening.
February 26 *(1/14).* The court receives a memorial from Zhang Zhidong announcing the setting up of the School for Gathering Talent in Nanjing.
March 4 *(1/21).* The court sets up an official bookshop to publish selected foreign and Chinese works and to translate selected foreign newspapers.
May 13 *(3/21).* Yuan Shikai sets up a modern military institute at Tianjin, which teaches artillery, cavalry, infantry, and foreign languages.
June 15 *(5/5).* In Danxian (Shandong), the Big Sword Society attacks and sets fire to the houses of Christian converts and foreign institutions.

raises a demand with the *Zongli yamen* for a fifty-year lease of Jiaozhou Bay (Shandong).

1897 Germany occupies Jiaozhou Bay

February 4 (*1/3*). In Peking Li Hongzhang and the British minister, Sir Claude MacDonald, conclude a convention revising trade arrangements and ratifying the frontiers between China and Burma.
7 (*1/6*). French minister Gérard protests against the conclusion of the Anglo-Chinese treaty of February 4.
March 5 (*2/3*). A Japanese concession area is established in Suzhou (Jiangsu).
15 (*2/13*). The *Zongli yamen* makes to France a declaration on non-alienation of Hainan Island: it would not 'alienate or cede the island of Hainan to any other foreign power'.
Early April. Demonstrations organized by rickshaw drivers in the International Settlement of Shanghai, resisting tax increases, are suppressed by American and British troops and police.

1896–7

August 11 (7/3). Shanghai's first film programme is shown as part of a variety show.
21 (7/13). Sun Jia'nai recommends the opening of an Imperial University.

D   PUBLICATIONS

Publication of Wang Renjun's *Gezhi guwei* (*Scientific Traces of Ancient Times*); and Liang Qichao's *Xixue shumu biao* (*A Bibliography of Western Learning*); Yan Fu's translation of Thomas Huxley's *Evolution and Ethics* is completed under the title *Tianyan lun*.
January 12 (11/28). The *Qiangxue bao* (*Study for National Strengthening News*) begins publication in Shanghai as the mouthpiece of reformers.
August 9 (7/1). Huang Zunxian, Liang Qichao and others begin publication of the *Shiwu bao* (*Contemporary Affairs*) in Shanghai.

E   NATURAL DISASTERS

June 28 (5/18). The Yellow River floods in Lijin (Shandong), causing serious damage.

F   BIRTHS AND DEATHS

January 11 (11/27). Liu Mingchuan d. aged 59.
March 26 (2/13). Fu Sinian b. (d. 1950).

The Commercial Press set up in Shanghai   1897

A   ECONOMICS

January 17 (12/15). The American-owned International Cotton Manufacturing Company goes into production in Shanghai.
March 22 (2/20). The British-owned Laogongmao cotton mill begins production in Shanghai.
26 (2/24). The court orders provincial authorities to assist and encourage local enterprises by relying on local capital.
May. The British-owned Yihe mill begins operations.
27 (4/26). China's first modern-style bank, the Imperial Bank of China organized by Sheng Xuanhuai, is set up in Shanghai.
June 12 (5/13). The *Zongli yamen* allows France to construct a railway from Vietnam to Yunnan city (Yunnan) and grants France special mining rights in Yunnan, Guizhou and Guangdong.

1897

August 7 *(7/10)*. Kaiser Wilhelm II of Germany consults with Russian Tsar Nicholas II over his intention to take out a lease of Jiaozhou Bay.
October 30 *(10/5)*. German sailors are beaten up in Wuchang.
November 14 *(10/20)*. A German naval force expels the Chinese garrison of Qingdao (Shandong), seizes the forts and occupies Jiaozhou Bay.
20 *(10/26)*. The German minister, Baron von Heyking, makes six demands on the *Zongli yamen* because of the Caozhou Incident of November 1; they include an indemnity to compensate for the death of the two missionaries and the three chapels which require rebuilding, the lease of Jiaozhou Bay, mining and railway construction rights in Shandong, and the dismissal from the public service of the Governor of Shandong, Li Bingheng (who had been appointed Viceroy of Sichuan but had not yet taken up the post).
22 *(10/28)*. The *Zongli yamen* demands that Germany withdraw from Jiaozhou Bay.
December 4 *(11/11)*. German troops occupy Jiaozhou City.
5 *(11/12)*. German troops occupy Jihei City (Shandong).
15 *(11/22)*. Russian warships enter Lüshun, Russia explaining the occupation as protection for Chinese interests against German invasion.
16 *(11/23)*. Russian Minister of Finance Witte announces a loan to China under five conditions. Among them are that China accept Russian monopoly of the construction of the Manchuria–Mongolia railway; that a Russian be appointed as inspector-general of maritime customs; and that China agree to lease Russia a port on the Yellow Sea.
18 *(11/25)*. As German reinforcements are about to depart for China under his brother, Admiral Prince Heinrich of Prussia, Kaiser Wilhelm II expresses in a speech his determination that Germany should secure a hold on Chinese soil.

1897

August. The Chinese-owned Sulun cotton mill in Suzhou (Jiangsu) opens.

B OFFICIAL APPOINTMENTS, DISMISSALS, TRANSFERS ETC.

March 22 (*2/20*). Chongli and Xu Yingkui are appointed to the *Zongli yamen*.
August 6 (*7/9*). Liao Shouheng is again appointed to the *Zongli yamen*.
September 11 (*8/15*). Weng Tonghe is appointed as assistant Grand Secretary.
27 (*9/2*). Li Bingheng is appointed Viceroy of Sichuan.
December 11 (*11/18*). Li Bingheng is dismissed under pressure from Germany; Yulu is appointed Viceroy of Sichuan.

C CULTURAL AND SOCIAL

February. Xia Ruifang and others set up the Commercial Press in Shanghai.
March 1 (*1/28*). Zhang Zhidong sends in a memorial announcing that he has set up the Hubei Military Preparatory School in Wuchang.
November 1 (*10/7*). Two German Catholic missionaries are killed and churches damaged in Juye, Caozhou (Shandong).

D PUBLICATIONS

Kang Youwei's *Kongzi gaizhi kao* (*Confucius as a Reformer*) is published.
February 22 (*1/21*). The reformist *Zhixin bao* (*New Knowledge*) begins publication in Macao.
April 22 (*3/21*). Jiang Biao inaugurates the reformist *Xiangxue xinbao* (*New Hunan Journal*) in Changsha.
Summer. The radical *Subao* (*Jiangsu Tribune*) begins publication.
October 26 (*10/1*). Yan Fu and others begin publication of the daily *Guowen bao* (*National Review*) in Tianjin.
December 24–January 21, 1898 (*12*). Publication of Yang Shoujing's *Riben fangshu zhi* (*Notes on [Chinese] Books Found in Japan*).

E NATURAL DISASTERS

Spring. Severe drought afflicts northern Jiangsu.

1898 The Hundred Days' Reform

January 1 (12/9). Russia warns German troops not to enter Zhili or Manchuria.
4 (12/12). The court accepts the German demands of November 20, 1897.
24 (1/3). Kang Youwei discusses the reform programme with members of the *Zongli yamen*, including Li Hongzhang, Weng Tonghe, Ronglu and Liao Shouheng.
25 (1/4). Emperor Guangxu asks to see Kang Youwei; Prince Gong refuses. Guangxu asks to see Kang's publications dealing with reform.
February 11 (1/21). The *Zongli yamen* declares to Britain that 'China will never alienate any territory in the provinces adjoining the Yangzi to any other power.'
13 (1/23). The *Zongli yamen* declares that it will always appoint someone of British nationality to the post of inspector-general of maritime customs for as long as British trade with China is greater than that of any other nation.
March 3 (2/11). Through its acting minister in Peking, Pavlov, Russia demands a lease of Lüshun and Dalian.
6 (2/14). Li Hongzhang and the German minister, von Heyking, sign a convention under which China agrees to lease Jiaozhou Bay and all land within fifty kilometres of the Bay to Germany for ninety-nine years, allows the building of a railway from Jiaozhou Bay to Ji'nan, and grants Germany mining rights within thirty *li* on either side of the railway line.
13 (2/21). The French acting minister, M. Dubail, makes several demands on the *Zongli yamen*, including the right to build a railway between Yunnan and Vietnam and the lease of Guangzhou Bay.
27 (3/6). Li Hongzhang and the acting Russian minister Pavlov conclude a treaty, under which China leases Lüshun and Dalian to Russia for twenty-five years, with the possibility of an extension, and allows Russia to build a South Manchurian Railway.
April 9 (3/19). Dubail puts forward demands revising those of March 13, including the declaration of non-alienation of the provinces

F   BIRTHS AND DEATHS

January 15 (*12/13*). Poet Xu Zhimo b. (d. 1931).
June 14 (*5/15*). Zhang Zhiwan d. aged 86.
July 24 (*6/25*). Li Hongzao d. aged 77.

Death of Prince Gong; reformers executed   1898

A   ECONOMICS

April 14 (*3/24*). The American China Development Company concludes a contract with the Chinese minister to the USA, Wu Tingfang, to lend £4,000,000 at 5 per cent interest towards the construction of the Guangzhou–Hankou Railway.
June 26 (*5/8*). China and Belgium sign a contract for a loan to China of 112,500,000 francs at 5 per cent to build the Peking–Hankou Railway.

B   OFFICIAL APPOINTMENTS, DISMISSALS, TRANSFERS ETC.

March 2 (*2/10*). Liao Shouheng is appointed to the Grand Council.
June 10 (*4/22*). Ronglu is appointed as Grand Secretary.
   15 (*4/27*). Weng Tonghe is ordered to retire and return to his home town. Ronglu is appointed acting Viceroy of Zhili.
   16 (*4/28*). Kang Youwei is appointed secretary to the *Zongli yamen*.
   23 (*5/5*). Sun Jia'nai is appointed assistant Grand Secretary. Wang Wenshao is appointed to the Grand Council and the *Zongli yamen*. Ronglu is confirmed as Viceroy of Zhili.
July 11 (*5/23*). Yulu is appointed to the Grand Council.
   12 (*5/24*). Kuijun is appointed Viceroy of Sichuan.
September 5 (*7/20*). The reformers Yang Rui, Liu Guangdi, Lin Xu and Tan Sitong are appointed secretaries to the Grand Council.
   7 (*7/22*). Li Hongzhang and Jingxin are dismissed from the *Zongli yamen* and replaced by Yulu.
   21 (*8/6*). Kang Youwei is dismissed and his arrest ordered.
   24 (*8/9*). Zhang Yinhuan, Yang Rui, Liu Guangdi, Lin Xu and Tan Sitong are dismissed. Yang and Lin are arrested.
   25 (*8/10*). Tan Sitong and Liu Guangdi are arrested.
   28 (*8/13*). Ronglu is appointed to the Grand Council. Yulu is appointed Viceroy of Zhili.
October 2 (*8/17*). Yuan Chang is appointed to the *Zongli yamen*.
November 2 (*9/19*). Xu Jingcheng is appointed to the *Zongli yamen*.
December 4 (*10/21*). Weng Tonghe is dismissed and placed under

1898

bordering on Vietnam to any other country, but retaining the demand for the lease of Guangzhou Bay.

10 (*3/20*). The *Zongli yamen* agrees to France's demands of the previous day.

22 (*int. 3/2*). French troops occupy Guangzhou Bay.

24 (*int. 3/4*). The *Zongli yamen* declares to Japan that it will not alienate Fujian to any power.

May 7 (*int. 3/17*). A supplementary Sino-Russian treaty on the lease of Lüshun and Dalian is signed in St Petersburg.

18 (*int. 3/28*). The Emperor receives Prince Heinrich of Prussia at the Summer Palace near Peking.

23 (*4/4*). The court issues a decree that the Viceroys of Zhili and Liangjiang and Governors of Henan and Shandong should investigate the activities of an underground organization known as the Righteous People's Society (later known as the Righteous and Harmonious Militia, or Boxers).

27 (*4/8*). A draft convention for the lease of Guangzhou Bay to France is submitted to the *Zongli yamen*, but not yet signed.

June. A rebellion breaks out in Sichuan led by Yu Dongchen.

3 (*4/15*). The court approves a ninety-nine-year lease of Kowloon to the British.

9 (*4/21*). Li Hongzhang, Xu Yingkui and Sir Claude MacDonald conclude a convention under which China leases Kowloon to Britain for ninety-nine years.

11 (*4/23*). The Emperor issues a decree supporting reform and self-strengthening. The 'Hundred Days' Reform' begins.

16 (*4/28*). Kang Youwei is received in audience by the Emperor, who agrees to his reform proposals.

July 1 (*5/13*). Yikuang and Liao Shouheng sign with Sir Claude MacDonald a convention leasing Weihaiwei and Liugong Island to the British for as long as Lüshun remains leased to Russia.

10 (*5/22*). China signs a treaty of friendship and trade with the Congo Free State (not ratified).

August 2 (*6/15*). A decree orders that citizens and low-ranking officials should be allowed to send communications directly to the throne without censorship and obstruction.

30 (*7/14*). The Emperor issues an edict abolishing a number of central and provincial government agencies and posts, including the governorships of Hubei, Guangdong and Yunnan.

September 14 (*7/29*). Guangxu sends a secret decree to Kang Youwei and others saying he is in danger of being deposed and asking for help to save him.

house arrest because of his involvement with Kang Youwei.

16 (*11/4*). Guichun is appointed to the *Zongli yamen*.

17 (*11/5*). Zhao Shuhan and Lianyuan are appointed to the *Zongli yamen*; Qixiu is appointed to the Grand Council.

C CULTURAL AND SOCIAL

February 19 (*1/29*). The court decrees that military examinations should include tests in shooting and the use of artillery but drop the writing of military essays.

April 12 (*3/22*). Kang Youwei's Protect the Country Society is formally set up in Peking.

June 11 (*4/23*). The court orders the founding of the Imperial University.

23 (*5/5*). A decree is issued changing the examination system: the eight-legged essay is abolished and replaced by essays on current affairs.

28 (*5/10*). A court edict makes Liang Qichao's translation bureau in Shanghai government-supervised, merchant-operated and gives it 2000 taels per month for the translation of foreign works.

July 1 (*5/13*). In Dazu (Sichuan), Yu Dongchen leads the people to arrest French missionaries. This was one example of widespread anti-missionary disturbances at this time.

3 (*5/15*). The Emperor issues an edict sending Sun Jia'nai to administer the affairs of the Imperial University.

10 (*5/22*). The Emperor orders that all the traditional academies (*shuyuan*) be converted into modern institutions which provide both Chinese and Western studies.

26 (*6/8*). The *Shiwu bao* is made an official newspaper and Kang Youwei is appointed to direct its affairs. Press freedom is to be allowed.

August 13 (*6/26*). Kang Youwei asks for the prohibition of foot-binding and requests the court to encourage anti-foot-binding associations everywhere in China.

September 8 (*7/23*). The court orders a medical school to be set up, attached to the Imperial University, to teach both Chinese and Western medicine.

October 1 (*8/16*). The court orders the destruction of the publications of Kang Youwei and his associates.

9 (*8/24*). The court orders the revival of the traditional examination system, the closure of reformist newspapers in Tianjin, Shanghai and Hankou, and the arrest of their editors.

November 28 (*10/15*). In Changle (Hubei), the Elder Brothers Society leads attacks against Christians; churches are destroyed and a Belgian

1898-9

18 (*8/3*). Tan Sitong calls on Yuan Shikai and persuades him (*i*) to support the reform policies, (*ii*) to have Ronglu assassinated, and (*iii*) to send troops to surround the Summer Palace where the Empress Dowager is residing. Yuan appears to consent.

20 (*8/5*). Yuan Shikai secretly returns to Tianjin and informs Ronglu of Tan Sitong's conspiracy. Kang Youwei leaves Peking for the south.

21 (*8/6*). A *coup d'état* takes place, effectively ending the 'Hundred Days' Reform'. The Empress Dowager resumes the regency and places Emperor Guangxu under house arrest in the Summer Palace.

25 (*8/10*). Sun Yatsen's immediate arrest is ordered. Liang Qichao escapes from Peking for Japan.

26 (*8/11*). The court issues decrees prohibiting private citizens from sending in memorials on state affairs, and restoring the government agencies and posts abolished on August 30.

29 (*8/14*). Kang Youwei arrives in Hongkong.

October 1 (*8/16*). Troops of the powers are called by their respective ministers to protect the Peking legations.

December 19 (*11/7*). Yu Dongchen's rebellion makes trouble in Rongchang and Tongliang (Sichuan).

31 (*11/19*). Forces of the Elder Brothers Society seize Changle (Hubei).

1899   *The Boxers rebel in Shandong*

January 7 (*11/26*). A rebellion led by Liu Chaodong and Niu Shixiu breaks out in Woyang (Anhui) and is soon suppressed when Liu is captured (January 23).

14 (*12/3*). The rebellion of the Elder Brothers Society in Changle (Hubei) is suppressed.

22 (*12/11*). Yu Dongchen surrenders to the Qing.

February 5 (*12/25*). Peasants protesting against a Russian-imposed land tax in Lüshun are shot at by Russian Cossacks. The *North China Herald* (March 13) reports 94 Chinese killed and 123 wounded, including many women and children. Russia later agrees to pay compensation.

23 (*1/14*). Niu Shixiu is captured.

March 2 (*1/21*). Italy demands the cession of a naval station on Sanmen Bay (Zhejiang).

missionary is killed. Similar incidents at about this time occurred elsewhere in Hubei, and in Guizhou, Guangdong and Shandong.

D PUBLICATIONS

July 25 (*6/7*). The Emperor orders that Zhang Zhidong's *Quanxue pian* (*Exhortation to Study*), just printed, be widely distributed in all provinces.
December 23 (*11/1*). Liang Qichao begins publication of the *Qingyi bao* (*China Discussion*) in Japan.

E NATURAL DISASTERS

August 8 (*6/21*). A serious flood strikes Shandong. Over 400 villages south of the Yellow River are submerged, affecting more than 1,000,000 people. The harvest fails, causing famine.

F BIRTHS AND DEATHS

January 4 (*12/12*). Chen Cheng b. in Zhejiang (d. 1965).
March 5 (*2/13*). Zhou Enlai b. (d. 1976).
 13 (*2/21*). Dramatist Tian Han b. (d. 1968).
May 29 (*4/10*). Prince Gong, Yixin, d. aged 65.
September 28 (*8/13*). Six leading reformers, Yang Shenxiu (aged 49), Yang Rui (41), Lin Xu (23), Liu Guangdi (39), Kang Youwei's brother Guangren (31), and Tan Sitong (33), are executed.
November. Liu Shaoqi b. (d. 1969).

Major cultural discoveries in Dunhuang and Anyang **1899**

A ECONOMICS

April 17 (*3/8*). China and Germany agree on customs arrangements for Qingdao (Shandong).
May 21 (*4/12*). The court sends assistant Grand Secretary Gangyi to the Yangzi Valley provinces to investigate finances there with a view to increasing revenue for the court from that area.
 23 (*4/14*). Zhang Jian's Dasheng cotton mill in Nantong (Jiangsu) begins production.
June 1 (*4/23*). Russia is granted the right to build railways north from Peking, and in the north-east; Germany is allowed to build a railway from Ji'nan to Tianjin.
 14 (*5/7*). The German Schantung-Eisenbahn-Gesellschaft is set up.
August 15 (*7/10*). Russia and Germany respectively declare Dalian

1899

22 (2/11). Three German engineers are beaten up near Rizhao (Shandong) by some 100 villagers.

29 (2/18). German troops occupy Rizhao; they loot and burn to the ground two villages from which the crowd involved in the incident of March 22 had come. Britain and Russia agree to preserve the balance of interest in China. North of the Great Wall would remain Russia's preserve for building railways, the areas along the Yangzi River that of Britain. (Notes to this effect are exchanged April 28.)

April 15 (3/6). The people of Kowloon protest against its cession to the British. British troops and police suppress the struggle over the following three days.

May 8 (3/29). The International Settlement of Shanghai is extended.

15 (4/6). The court orders Liu Kunyi, Viceroy of Liangjiang, and Liu Shutang, Governor of Zhejiang, to prepare for war to defend Sanmen Bay against any attack by Italian forces.

31 (4/22). Italy withdraws its demand for a naval station in Sanmen Bay.

June 22 (5/15). The French consulate in Mengzi (Yunnan) is attacked and burned.

September 6 (8/2). John Hay, the US Secretary of State, sends a note to the American ambassadors in Britain, France, Germany and Russia to communicate America's approach to the 'China Open Door Policy' to the respective governments and to ask their support. Under the policy, all countries would be able to trade with China, irrespective of sphere of influence. (He sends the same note to the ambassadors in Japan and Italy on November 13 and 17 respectively.)

11 (8/7). China and Korea conclude a treaty of friendship and trade in Seoul.

October 9 (9/5). Boxer forces under Zhu Hongdeng defeat Qing troops near Pingyuan (Shandong).

15 (9/11). The Elder Brothers Society of Chen Yuchuan takes the county city of Renhuai (Guizhou).

18 (9/14). Qing forces defeat Boxer troops under Zhu Hongdeng in Pingyuan. The latter disperse.

25 (9/21). China leases a concession in Amoy (Fujian) to Japan.

November 7 (10/5). The Elder Brothers Society rebellion of Renhuai is suppressed.

16 (10/14). China signs a treaty leasing the Guangzhou Bay to France for ninety-nine years.

19 (10/17). Following a memorial from Sheng Xuanhuai, the court orders that telegraph companies should introduce telephones.

21 (10/19). The court issues a decree to all provincial viceroys and

1899

(Fengtian) and Jiaozhou (Shandong) as free ports.
17 (*7/12*). Qinhuangdao is opened as a trade port.
November 13 (*10/11*). Yuezhou (Hunan) opens as a trade port.

B Official Appointments, Dismissals, Transfers etc.

June 13 (*5/6*). Wu Tingfen is appointed to the *Zongli yamen*.
December 2 (*10/30*). Wei Guangtao is appointed acting Viceroy of Shan'gan.
6 (*11/4*). Under foreign pressure the court calls the Governor of Shandong, Yuxian, to the capital and appoints Yuan Shikai to act in his place.
12 (*11/10*). Zhao Shuqiao is appointed provisionally to the Grand Council to replace Liao Shouheng.
19 (*11/17*). Li Hongzhang is appointed acting Viceroy of Liangguang.
24 (*11/22*). Lu Zhuanlin is appointed acting Viceroy of Liangjiang.
27 (*11/25*). Wang Wenshao is appointed assistant Grand Secretary.

C Cultural and Social

Oracle bones first discovered in Anyang (Henan). These were to prove epoch-making in their impact on the reconstruction of ancient Chinese history.
March 15 (*2/4*). The court grants Catholic missionaries official status; bishops may deal with viceroys or governors as equals etc.
July 2 (*5/25*). A Taoist monk called Wang discovers an enormous deposit of manuscripts and paintings in a sealed chamber leading from a chapel at the Qianfo Caves just south of Dunhuang (Gansu). The discovery was to be of monumental importance for the study of Chinese history.
September 17 (*8/13*). The Boxer leader, Zhu Hongdeng, attacks Christian converts in Pingyuan (Shandong).
October 3 (*8/29*). In Renhuai (Guizhou) the Elder Brothers Society under Chen Yuchuan attacks and burns churches and twenty-six houses of converts.
December 31 (*11/29*). Members of the Big Sword Society kill the Anglican missionary S.M. Brooks near Ji'nan (Shandong).

D Publications

December. The *Zhongguo ribao* (*Chinese Daily*) begins publication in Hongkong as a revolutionary propaganda organ.

governors urging them to unite and prepare for foreign invasion.

December 5 (11/3). The American minister, E.H. Conger, demands the dismissal of Yuxian, the Governor of Shandong, because of his support for the anti-foreign and anti-missionary activities of the Boxers.

14 (11/12). In Washington the minister to the USA, Wu Tingfang, concludes a treaty of friendship and trade with Mexico.

31 (11/29). Liang Qichao arrives in Honolulu, where he engages in reformist activities.

1900 *Eight-Power allied invasion over the Boxers; Russia invades Manchuria*

January 27 (12/27). The ministers of Britain, France, America, Germany and Italy send a note to the *Zongli yamen* demanding the suppression of the Boxers and the Big Sword Society.

March 20 (2/20). The United States declares that its 'Open Door Policy' has been accepted by all other nations.

April 6 (3/7). The ministers of Britain, France, the USA and Germany again demand that the Boxers be eliminated. They warn the *Zongli yamen* that foreign troops will be called in to put down the Boxers unless the Qing has done so within two months.

May 27 (4/29). The main body of the Boxers, over 10,000 men, capture Zhuozhou (Zhili).

31 (5/4). Some 350 British, American, French, Italian, Russian and Japanese troops enter Peking. Some 80 German and Austro-Hungarian forces follow on June 3.

June 4 (5/8). The legations of the eight powers cable their home governments asking for urgent relief.

6 (5/10). The Boxers and foreign troops fight outside Tianjin.

11 (5/15). Sugiyama Akira, the chancellor of the Japanese legation, is killed in Peking by the Gansu soldiers of Dong Fuxiang.

13 (5/17). The Commander-in-Chief of Zhili, Nie Shicheng, is ordered to block the allied advance (of nearly 2000 men under Admiral Sir Edward Seymour) towards Peking. A large force of Boxers enters Peking.

16 (5/20). The court holds its first meeting, including princes and all senior officials, to discuss the emergency.

17 (5/21). The second court meeting is held. The Empress Dowager wishes to declare war. The allied troops of Britain, Russia, Germany,

1899–1900

E Natural Disasters

Famine continues in Anhui, Shandong, Henan and northern Jiangsu.

F Births and Deaths

January 29 *(12/18)*. Qu Qiubai b. (d. 1935).
April 18 *(3/9)* Bibliophile and publisher Ding Bing d. aged 67.
June. Huang Tifang d. aged 66.
November 6 *(10/4)*. Hu Zongnan b. (d. 1962).
December 24 *(11/22)*. The Boxer leader Zhu Hongdeng d.

The Boxers pursue anti-Christian and anti-foreign activities   1900

A Economics

May 28 *(5/1)*. Boxers attack railway stations and railways outside Peking, destroy machine shops at Fengtai, south-west of the city, and disrupt Peking–Tianjin and Peking–Baoding traffic.
June 9 *(5/13)*. The Boxers destroy the Peking–Tianjin railway line outside Peking.
10 *(5/14)*. The telegraph line from Peking to Tianjin is cut.
August 4 *(7/10)*. China, Denmark and Britain conclude a contract for a loan to construct an underwater electric cable linking Shanghai and Dagu.

B Official Appointments, Dismissals, Transfers etc.

January 24 *(12/24)*. Pujun, the son of Zaiyi, is appointed as son and successor to the Tongzhi Emperor.
March 14 *(2/14)*. Yuan Shikai is confirmed as Governor of Shandong.
May 24 *(4/26)*. Li Hongzhang is confirmed as Viceroy of Liangguang.
June 10 *(5/14)*. The pro-Boxer Prince Duan, Zaiyi, is appointed to head the *Zongli yamen*. Puxing, Qixiu and Natong are appointed to the *Zongli yamen*.
August 7 *(7/13)*. Li Hongzhang is appointed plenipotentiary to conduct peace negotiations with the Allied powers.
31 *(8/7)*. Zaiyi is appointed to the Grand Council.
September 25 *(int. 8/2)*. Pressed by the Allied powers to punish 'the principal culprits' of the Boxer uprising, the court reduces four members of the imperial clan, including Zaixun, to commoners. Zaiyi is dismissed from all offices and handed over for trial, and Gangyi is

1900

France, the USA, Italy, Austria and Japan capture the Dagu forts and kill or wound over 200 people. Sun Yatsen and Chen Shaobai arrive in Hongkong, planning an uprising in Guangdong.

18 (*5/22*). The third court meeting. Qing troops under Dong Fuxiang and Boxer forces defeat an allied army under Seymour at Langfang between Tianjin and Peking.

19 (*5/23*). The fourth court meeting decides in favour of declaring war and demands the withdrawal of the foreign legations within twenty-four hours.

20 (*5/24*). Baron Freiherr Klemens von Ketteler, the German minister, is killed in a Peking street. Dong Fuxiang's Gansu army and the Boxers begin their attack on the foreign legations and churches. The 'siege of the legations' begins.

21 (*5/25*). Liu Kunyi, Zhang Zhidong and others cable the court asking it to suppress the Boxers and apologize to the foreign nations. The court issues an edict declaring war on the powers.

22 (*5/26*). The court sends Zaiyi and Gangyi to take command of the Boxers.

25 (*5/29*). Zaiyi brings some Boxer troops into the Palace intending to kill the Emperor, 'the foreigners' friend', but the Empress Dowager prevents them.

July 3 (*6/7*). US Secretary of State Hay reiterates his 'Open Door Policy' and calls for the protection of China's territorial integrity and administrative independence.

14 (*6/16*). Some 10,000 Allied troops seize Tianjin; the city is looted and plundered.

16 (*6/18*). In response to a Chinese bombardment the previous day of the Russian town of Blagoveshchensk from the Chinese side of the Amur River, the Russians massacre several thousand Chinese and Manchus in Blagoveshchensk. The incident sparks off a Russian invasion of Manchuria.

26 (*7/1*). Tang Caichang and other reformers organize a congress in Shanghai, and declare non-recognition of the Qing government.

30 (*7/5*). The Tianjin Provisional Government, organized by the British, Japanese and Russians, is set up.

August 12 (*7/18*). The Allied troops occupy Tongzhou outside Peking; 3000 British reinforcements arrive in Shanghai.

14 (*7/20*). The Allied troops enter Peking; the siege of the legations is lifted. Savage and extended plunder, including massacre of civilians, begins.

15 (*7/21*). The Empress Dowager flees westward from Peking, taking the Emperor and Zaiyi with her.

1900

sent for trial. Lu Zhuanlin is appointed to the Grand Council.
26 (*int. 8/3*). Tao Mo is appointed Viceroy of Liangguang.
October 1 (*int. 8/8*). Li Hongzhang again takes over the position of Viceroy of Zhili.
November 13 (*9/22*). In response to demands by the Allied powers for heavy punishments for pro-Boxer officials, the court issues an edict that Zaixun and Zaiyi be deprived of all ranks and offices and imprisoned for life; others are in various degrees degraded or punished.
December 3 (*10/12*). Under pressure from the foreign powers, the Commander-in-Chief of Gansu, Dong Fuxiang, is disgraced, though kept in office.
5 (*10/14*). Songfan is appointed Viceroy of Shan'gan, Wei Guangtao of Yungui.
6 (*10/15*). Wang Wenshao is appointed Grand Secretary, Xu Fu and Chongli assistant Grand Secretaries.

C Cultural and Social

Allied occupation troops remove or destroy countless Chinese artefacts, including books, bronzes, paintings, scientific instruments and jade.
January 12 (*12/12*). The court orders provincial viceroys and governors to take severe measures to subdue the widespread anti-missionary activity.
February 23 (*1/24*). The court orders that the Tianjin *Guowen bao* be banned for spreading rumours and slandering the court.
May 12–14 (*4/14–16*). Boxers burn churches and the houses of Protestant converts in Laishui and attack Catholic villages near Baoding (Zhili), killing some sixty converts.
23 (*4/25*). Boxers fight with Catholic converts in Baoding (Zhili). Qing troops help the converts to suppress the Boxers.
25 (*4/27*). Boxers attack and destroy the houses of Christian converts of an American mission in Bazhou (Zhili) and kill nine Chinese Christians.
June 1–2 (*5/5–6*). Two English missionaries are killed near Baoding.
13 (*5/17*). The Boxers begin burning churches in Peking. They kill over 300 converts.
14–15 (*5/18–19*). Boxers destroy churches and the French Catholic cathedral in Tianjin.
27 (*6/1*). A mission hospital is destroyed by a crowd, and an English occupant is killed.
July 3 (*6/7*). In Shenyang (Fengtian), the Catholic bishop, several missionaries and a number of Chinese Christians are killed.

1900-1

21 (7/27). A plot by Tang Caichang to seize Hankou is discovered and Tang is arrested.

28-29 (8/4-5). Russian troops under General Rennenkampf capture and occupy Tsitsihar, capital of Heilongjiang.

September 21 (8/28). Russian troops under Rennenkampf take Jilin, capital of Jilin.

30 (*int.* 8/7). Russian troops take Shenyang, capital of Fengtian, virtually completing the occupation of Manchuria.

October 17 (*int.* 8/24). The Commander-in-Chief of Allied troops, Count Alfred von Waldersee, arrives in Peking and sets up headquarters in the Imperial Palace.

22 (*int.* 8/29). The 'second revolution' of Sun Yatsen fails when an uprising led by the Triad, Zheng Shiliang, in Huizhou (Guangdong) is defeated. Zheng flees to Hongkong.

26 (9/4). The Empress Dowager arrives in Xi'an (Shaanxi).

December 24 (11/3). The ministers of the foreign powers jointly propose twelve conditions for a peace settlement.

27 (11/6). The court issues an edict accepting all the conditions for peace proposed by the powers.

1901 The Boxer Protocol

January 12 (11/22). China signs an agreement leasing territory in Tianjin to Russia.

29 (12/10). The court issues a decree demanding reforms and soliciting advice on how to implement them.

February 1 (12/13). The court orders the local officials to protect

1900–1

October 2. The Hungarian-born Briton, Dr Mark Aurel Stein, arrives in Khotan (Xinjiang) at the beginning of his first major expedition in search of ancient cultural objects, manuscripts etc.

D Publications

Yan Fu completes his *Yuanfu*, a translation of Adam Smith's *The Wealth of Nations* (published 1902, translator's notes dated September 17, 1902). Publication of *Xushou tang wenji (Collected Literary Works of Wang Xianqian)* (prefaces dated intercalary eighth month, September 24–October 22, 1900).

E Natural Disasters

Severe drought afflicts most of north China; famine results.
February 21–22 *(1/22–23)*. The Yellow River bursts its banks at Binzhou (Shandong); serious flooding results in Binzhou, Lijin and other areas of Shandong near the mouth of the Yellow River. The dykes are closed up in April.

F Births and Deaths

January 5 *(12/5)*. Peking Opera actor Xun Huisheng b. (d. 1968).
7 *(12/7)*. Peking Opera actor Shang Xiaoyun b. (d. 1976).
July 9 *(6/13)*. Nie Shicheng is killed in battle with the allied force near Tianjin.
28 *(7/3)*. *Zongli yamen* members Xu Jingcheng (aged 54) and Yuan Chang (aged 53) are executed for being anti-Boxer and pro-foreign.
August 11 *(7/17)*. Xu Yongyi, Lishan (aged 62) and Lianyuan are executed for being pro-foreign. Li Bingheng commits suicide, aged 70.
20 *(7/26)*. Zhang Yinhuan d. aged 63.
22 *(7/28)*. Tang Caichang is executed aged 33.
October 18 *(int. 8/25)*. Gangyi d.

Death of Li Hongzhang   1901

A Economics

January. The Kaiping Mining Company is set up.
July 5 *(5/20)*. The Harbin–Lüshun railway starts carrying traffic.
November 11 *(10/1)*. Import duty is set at 5 per cent for all foreign goods.

1901

foreigners and bans membership in any anti-foreign society.

15 *(12/27)*. Von Waldersee issues an army order raising the possibility of resuming military operations.

16 *(12/28)*. The Russian Foreign Minister, Count Vladimir Lamsdorff, hands Yang Ru, Chinese minister at St Petersburg, twelve proposals for a settlement of the Manchurian question. They include that Russia should retain troops to protect the Chinese Eastern Railway and that no Chinese troops should be allowed in Manchuria pending the completion of the railway line.

27 *(1/9)*. The court orders that the foreign powers be asked to intervene with Russia in the Manchurian dispute.

March 1 *(1/11)*. The court issues a decree ordering Li Hongzhang and Yikuang to urge changes in the twelve Russian proposals.

12 *(1/22)*. Count Lamsdorff hands Yang Ru 'final' amendments to the twelve proposals.

24 *(2/5)*. Yang Ru declares to Russia that he will not sign the prepared agreement over Manchuria.

April 21 *(3/3)*. The court orders that a Bureau of Government Affairs be set up to formulate a reform programme.

May 5 *(3/17)*. American troops begin to withdraw from Peking.

25 *(4/8)*. Yikuang and Li Hongzhang send in a memorial suggesting that the *Zongli yamen* be reorganized and named the Ministry of Foreign Affairs.

June 3 *(4/17)*. Count von Waldersee leaves Peking for Germany.

July 24 *(6/9)*. An imperial edict transforms the *Zongli yamen* into the Ministry of Foreign Affairs giving it precedence over the six boards.

31 *(6/16)*. The allied troops begin withdrawing from Peking.

September 7 *(7/25)*. In Peking Yikuang and Li Hongzhang sign the Boxer Protocol with the eleven foreign nations: Germany, Austria, Belgium, Spain, USA, France, Britain, Italy, Japan, Holland and Russia. Among other concessions, China agrees (*i*) to pay a gigantic indemnity of 450,000,000 taels, (*ii*) to convey apologies for the deaths of von Ketteler and Sugiyama, (*iii*) to deny Chinese the right to reside in the legation quarter, (*iv*) to prohibit the importation of arms and ammunition, (*v*) to raze the Dagu forts, and (*vi*) to allow foreign occupation in Tangshan, Qinhuangdao, Shanhaiguan, Tianjin, Langfang and several other cities along the Peking–Shanhaiguan railway. The allies agree to withdraw troops from Peking on September 17 and from Zhili on September 22.

17 *(8/5)*. The allied troops complete their withdrawal from Peking.

October 6 *(8/24)*. The Emperor, Empress Cixi, and others leave

1901

B Official Appointments, Dismissals, Transfers etc.

February 13 (12/25). At foreign insistence, the court issues a decree ordering severe punishment for officials involved in the Boxer movement. They include exiling Zaiyi to Xinjiang for ever, compelling Zaixun to commit suicide and depriving Dong Fuxiang of office.

April 21 (3/3). Prince Qing, Yikuang, is appointed to head the newly set up Bureau of Government Affairs.

May 26 (4/9). Qu Hongji is appointed provisional Grand Councillor.

July 24 (6/9). Yikuang and Wang Wenshao are put in charge of the newly created Ministry of Foreign Affairs.

November 7 (9/27). Yuan Shikai is appointed as acting Viceroy of Zhili.

30 (10/20). Pujun is deposed as heir-apparent.

C Cultural and Social

March. Suzhou University, set up by American missionaries, starts teaching.

April 29 (3/11). The court punishes fifty-six local officials for failure to protect the Christian missionaries and converts.

June 11 (4/25). The court orders the suspension, for five years, of the official examinations in all places where foreigners have been harmed. (The edict is repeated August 19.)

August. The Japanese *Tōa dōbun shoin* (East Asia Common Culture Academy) is founded in Shanghai.

29 (7/16). The court changes the examination system. It abolishes military examinations and, in provincial and metropolitan examinations, replaces eight-legged essays with those on current topics.

September 14 (8/2). The court orders the reform of the *shuyuan* (academies); those in provincial capitals are to become universities, those in prefectures secondary schools, and those in districts or counties primary schools.

D Publications

May. Wang Guowei and others begin publishing in Shanghai the *Jiaoyu shijie* (*Education World*), initially a thrice-monthly, later a twice-monthly.

10 (3/23). Qin Lishan and others begin publishing *Guomin bao* (*The National News*) in Japan.

December 11–January 9, 1902 (11). Printing of Ye Dehui's *Guquan zayong* (*Songs on Ancient Coins*) is completed.

1901–2

Xi'an for Peking.
November 23 (*10/13*). In Jiayi (Taiwan) Huang Maosong and others lead troops in resistance against the Japanese.

1902 Russia agrees to withdraw troops from Manchuria

January 7 (*11/28*). The Emperor and Empress arrive back in Peking by rail.
18 (*12/9*). Sun Yatsen arrives in Hongkong from Japan.
30 (*12/21*). Japan and Britain conclude a five-year agreement that each might take any necessary action to protect its interests in China or Korea; and that if either power suffers attack in such action the other will try to prevent hostilities against it.
February 1 (*12/23*). US Secretary of State Hay announces that its 'Open door policy' has been extended to cover participation in mining, railway construction and other aspects, and in particular protests against Russian demands for sole economic rights in Manchuria.
24 (*1/17*). The court abolishes the office of Director-General of the Conservancy of the Yellow River and Grand Canal.
April 8 (*3/1*). Yikuang, Wang Wenshao and the Russian minister P.M. Lessar sign a convention under which Russian troops will be withdrawn from the three Manchurian provinces in three stages within eighteen months in return for China's ratification of all previous Sino-Russian agreements; Chinese troops are to reoccupy the Manchurian provinces only after agreement with the Russian authorities.
18 (*3/11*). Russia issues a statement agreeing to withdraw its troops from the Manchurian provinces according to the convention provided that other powers make no obstructions.
26 (*3/19*). Zhang Binglin and others call a meeting in Tokyo to commemorate the 242nd anniversary of China's fall to the foreign Manchus. The meeting is banned by the Japanese police, so it is held instead in Yokohama.

1901-2

E NATURAL DISASTERS

Mid-June. Serious flooding occurs in Fuzhou, Ji'an, Raozhou and other parts of Jiangxi due to heavy rainfall.
August 8 (*6/24*). The Yellow River floods in Shandong.

F BIRTHS AND DEATHS

January 10 (*11/20*). Yang Quyun is murdered in Hongkong.
February 21 (*1/3*). Zaixun commits suicide.
November 6 (*9/26*). Yang Kaihui b. (d. 1930).
  7 (*9/27*). Li Hongzhang d. aged 78.

Motor cars first seen in Shanghai **1902**

A ECONOMICS

Motor cars are seen in Shanghai for the first time.
April 16 (*3/9*). The Tartar General of Fengtian, Zengqi, and the Chinese Eastern Railway Company conclude an agreement to mine coal on both sides of the railway within the province.
September 5 (*8/4*). China and Britain conclude a trade and navigation treaty. Inland customs duty (*lijin*) is abolished and, to compensate, import tariff is increased to 7.5 per cent.
November 16 (*10/17*). The Beiyang General Minting Office starts minting.

B OFFICIAL APPOINTMENTS, DISMISSALS, TRANSFERS ETC.

January 10 (*12/1*). The court appoints Zhang Boxi as Superintendent of Educational Affairs of the Imperial University.
  31 (*12/22*). Qu Hongji is appointed a Grand Councillor, Sun Jia'nai a Grand Secretary.
February 13 (*1/6*). Wu Rulun is appointed to head the faculty of the Imperial University.
June 9 (*5/4*). Yuan Shikai is confirmed as Viceroy of Zhili.
July 3 (*5/28*). Deshou is appointed acting Viceroy of Liangguang.
August 5 (*7/2*). Cen Chunxuan is appointed acting Viceroy of Sichuan.
October 8 (*9/6*). Zhang Zhidong is appointed acting Viceroy of Liangjiang, Duanfang acting Viceroy of Huguang.
December 5 (*11/6*). Wei Guangtao is appointed Viceroy of Liangjiang.
  6 (*11/7*). Ding Zhenduo is appointed acting Viceroy of Yungui.

1902

May 25 (*4/18*). Huang Maosong's resistance to the Japanese in Taiwan is defeated.

June 25 (*5/20*). China and Britain conclude an agreement concerning procedure and regulations in the Mixed Court in Shanghai.

26 (*5/21*). Some 100 British troops, accompanied by J.C. White, Political Officer for Sikkim, expel about 40 Tibetans from Giaogong, a disputed tract of country on the Sikkim-Tibet border. The British feared Russian expansion in Tibet; to counter it Lord Curzon, British Viceroy of India, developed a policy of increasing pressure on the Sikkim-Tibet border.

July 12 (*6/8*). The ministers of Russia, Germany, Britain, Japan, France and Italy inform the Ministry of Foreign Affairs of the conditions under which they will hand back the administration of Tianjin to China and abolish the Tianjin Provisional Government (see July 30, 1900).

18 (*6/14*). The Ministry of Foreign Affairs accepts the conditions of the foreign ministers.

The *China Times* reports a secret Sino-Russian treaty, under which China cedes her rights and interests in Tibet to Russia.

August 4 (*7/1*). Tokyo police order two Chinese students, including Wu Zhihui, to leave Japan the following day.

15 (*7/12*). Yuan Shikai arrives in Tianjin and formally takes the administration of Tianjin back from the foreign powers.

16 (*7/13*). Cai Jun, the Chinese minister in Tokyo, refuses to see some Chinese students petitioning on behalf of the deportees (see August 4).

October 3 (*9/2*). A revolt breaks out in Guangxi, defeating an official army.

7 (*9/6*). More than 10,000 rebels from Guangxi take Xingyi (Guizhou).

8 (*9/7*). Russia hands back the territory west of the Liao to Chinese control.

13 (*9/12*). The Guangxi rebels withdraw from Xingyi.

November 20 (*10/21*). The Governor of Guangxi, Wang Zhichun, sends a cable to the Grand Council reporting that, apart from the capital Guilin and two other prefectures, there is nowhere in Guangxi that is free from rebels.

23 (*10/24*). Japanese troops withdraw from Shanghai.

December. German, French and British troops withdraw from Shanghai.

1902

C Cultural and Social

January 11 *(12/2)*. The court orders that Peking's College of Foreign Languages be incorporated into the Imperial University.
February 1 *(12/23)*. The court approves intermarriage between Han Chinese and Manchus and condemns the custom of foot binding.
24 *(1/17)*. The court orders every province to set up agricultural and technical institutes.
March 20 *(2/11)*. Yuan Shikai sends fifty-five military students from Tianjin to study in Japanese military institutes.
April 8 *(3/1)*. The court orders that Christian converts be treated identically before the law as other Chinese.
May 11 *(4/4)*. The carpenters of the Yesong shipyard in Shanghai go on strike for a wage increase.
August 15 *(7/12)*. The court orders the adoption of rules on education suggested by Zhang Boxi; these establish the hierarchy of institutions, standardize the syllabus etc.
October 5 *(9/4)*. The court orders all provinces to select students to be sent to the West to study with a view to becoming officials.
November 16 *(10/17)*. More than 200 students, including Cai Yuanpei, walk out of the Shanghai Nanyang Public Institute over the dismissal of three fellow students and organize the Patriotic School, which becomes operative within three days.
December 1 *(11/2)*. The court orders that specified categories of Hanlin compilers and graduates should study at the Imperial University.

D Publications

February 8 *(1/1)*. Liang Qichao's fortnightly *Xinmin congbao* (*New Citizen Journal*) begins publication in Yokohama.
May 8–June 5 *(4)*. Zhang Shouyong and others publish *Huangchao zhanggu huibian* (*Collected Historical Records of the Imperial Dynasty*).
June 17 *(5/12)*. The *Dagong bao* (*Impartial News*) begins publication in Tianjin.
September 2–October 1 *(8)*. The *Guangu tang suozhu shu* (*Books Written in the Guangu Hall*), a collection of Ye Dehui's works, is published.

E Natural Disasters

August 3 *(6/30)*. The Yellow River floods in Lijin (Shandong).

F Births and Deaths

March 6 *(1/27)*. Wu Dacheng d. aged 66.
October 6 *(9/5)*. Liu Kunyi d. aged 72.

1903 *The China Revival Society set up in Hunan*

April 8 (*3/11*). Russian troops remain in Shenyang, Niuzhuang (Fengtian), Jilin (Jilin) and other places, despite the arrival of the date agreed on for the withdrawal under the convention of April 8, 1902. Russian spokesmen in Peking, St Petersburg, London and other places assign various reasons for the failure to withdraw.

18 (*3/21*). The Russian acting minister, de Plançon, raises seven new demands as conditions for the withdrawal of Russian troops from Manchuria. They include: no new treaty ports or foreign consuls are to be allowed in Manchuria; no foreigners other than Russians are to be employed in the public service in north China; and no territory in Manchuria is to be alienated to any power but Russia.

21 (*3/24*). The Japanese Prime Minister Katsura Tarō, Foreign Minister Komura Jutarō and senior statesmen including Itō Hirobumi, meet and decide to protest to Russia over her refusal to withdraw from Manchuria, but to recognize Russia's superior rights in Manchuria in return for Russia's recognition of Japan's superior rights in Korea.

30 (*4/4*). Japan advises the Ministry of Foreign Affairs to reject Russia's new demands. The students of the Imperial University hold a big meeting opposing Russia's demands.

May 6 (*4/10*). China concludes a revised treaty with Portugal.

20 (*4/24*). The Viceroy of Yungui, Ding Zhenduo, cables a memorial that the people of Gejiu (Yunnan) have tried to prevent the French construction of the Yunnan–Vietnam railway, and official Qing troops have been sent to suppress them; a rebellion has broken out led by Zhou Yunxiang and more than 10,000 rebels have taken Lin'an and Shiping (Yunnan).

June 25 (*int. 5/1*). Guangxi rebels led by Lu Yafa take Donglan.

July 1 (*int. 5/7*). Yunnan official troops retake Lin'an, thus suppressing Zhou Yunxiang's rebellion.

3 (*int. 5/9*). Guangxi official troops retake Donglan and defeat Lu Yafa.

7 (*int. 5/13*). A British force led by Major Francis Younghusband arrives in Khambajong (Tibet) for talks with Tibetan authorities.

September 6 (*7/15*). Russia puts forward revised demands for withdrawal from Manchuria.

7 (*7/16*). The Ministry of Commerce is set up.

October 28 (*9/9*). Russian troops occupy the official offices of Shenyang, the capital of Fengtian, and capture the Tartar General Zengqi.

November 6 (*9/18*). The British India Office authorizes the temporary British occupation of Chumbi (Tibet) and the advance of a British force to Gyantse (Tibet).

December. Huang Xing, Song Jiaoren and others organize the China

A Economics

July 1 (*int. 5/7*). The Chinese Eastern Railway formally opens for traffic.
October 8 (*8/18*). China signs trade and navigation agreements with both Japan and the USA.

B Official Appointments, Dismissals, Transfers etc.

April 12 (*3/15*). Yikuang is appointed to the Grand Council.
  18 (*3/21*). Cen Chunxuan is appointed acting Viceroy of Liangguang, Xiliang of Sichuan and Li Xingrui of Minzhe.
May 23 (*4/27*). Chongli is appointed Grand Secretary and Jingxin assistant Grand Secretary.
September 7 (*7/16*). Zaizhen is appointed President of the Ministry of Commerce.
October 11 (*8/21*). Jingxin is appointed Grand Secretary, Yude assistant Grand Secretary.
November 4 (*9/16*). Rongqing is appointed a Grand Councillor, Natong President of the Ministry of Foreign Affairs.

C Cultural and Social

February 5 (*1/8*). Zhang Zhidong sends in a memorial that he has set up the Sanjiang Normal School in Nanjing.
April 27 (*4/1*). The Beiyang University in Tianjin formally starts classes under this name. Zhang Jian's Nantong Normal School begins classes.
June 30 (*int. 5/6*). Zhang Binglin and others are arrested because of their anti-Manchu newspaper *Subao*.
July 1 (*int. 5/7*). Revolutionary author Zou Rong is arrested.
  7 (*int. 5/13*). The office of the revolutionary anti-Manchu newspaper *Subao* is closed.

D Publications

Publication of *Huangchao fanshu yudi congshu* (*Collection of Geographical Works of the Dynasty's Outer Tribes and Dependencies*); and Liu E's *Tieyun canggui* (*Tieyun's Hidden Tortoise Shells*), the first work on the study of inscriptions on tortoise shells and animal bones.
January 29 (*1/1*). Hubei students in Japan begin publishing the monthly *Hubei xuesheng jie* (*Hubei Students' World*) in Tokyo.
May. Zou Rong publishes his revolutionary and anti-Manchu *Geming jun* (*The Revolutionary Army*).

1903–4

Revival Society in Changsha and plan a revolution. Huang becomes the head of the society.

4 (*10/16*). The court sets up a Bureau of Military Training.

11 (*10/23*). Russia informs Japan that it will not negotiate over Manchuria, and refuses to yield over its privileged position in either Manchuria or Korea.

13 (*10/25*). British troops led by Younghusband arrive in Yadong (Tibet): the beginning of the 'Younghusband Mission'.

25 (*11/7*). The Japanese Foreign Minister Komura Jutarō secretly informs the Chinese minister in Tokyo, Yang Shu, that Japan is already preparing for war with Russia, because of the failure of Russo-Japanese negotiations over Manchuria and Korea.

30 (*11/12*). The court orders all provinces to maintain neutrality should a Russo-Japanese war break out.

1904 *The Russo-Japanese War breaks out*

February 8 (*12/23*). Japan breaks off diplomatic relations with Russia while its fleet attacks Lüshun (Fengtian).

9 (*12/24*). Russia declares war on Japan. A Japanese fleet defeats a Russian fleet off Lüshun.

10 (*12/25*). Japan declares war on Russia.

12 (*12/27*). The Chinese court issues an edict of neutrality in the Russo-Japanese War.

March 31 (*2/15*). Near Tuna (Tibet) the troops of the Younghusband Mission have their first clash with Tibetans, who suffer some 800 casualties. Sun Yatsen arrives in San Francisco from Honolulu.

April 11 (*2/26*). The Younghusband Mission reaches Gyantse (Tibet).

29 (*3/14*). The Japanese First Army crosses the Yalu River from Korea into Manchuria and occupies Jiulian (Fengtian) on May 1; Russian troops retreat.

May 4 (*3/19*). The Japanese Second Army lands at Piziwo (Fengtian).

15 (*4/1*). Tibet declares war on the British.

19 (*4/5*). The Japanese Third Army lands at Dagushan (Fengtian).

22 (*4/8*). A Shanghai court revises the sentences of life imprisonment on the revolutionaries Zhang Binglin and Zou Rong to three and two years respectively.

26 (*4/12*). The Japanese Second Army occupies Jinzhou (Fengtian).

30 (*4/16*). The Japanese Third Army occupies Dalian (Fengtian).

June 13 (*4/30*). The Ministry of Foreign Affairs and the foreign diplomatic corps sign an agreement which expands and delineates the

August 7 (6/15). Zhang Shizhao, Zhang Ji and others begin publication of *Guomin ri ribao* (*The National Daily News*) in Shanghai.

E NATURAL DISASTERS

August 17 (6/25). The Yellow River floods at Lijin (Shandong).

F BIRTHS AND DEATHS

February 4 (1/7). Zhang Peilun d. aged 54.
April 11 (3/14). Ronglu d. aged 67.
May 4 (4/8). Hu Yepin b. (d. 1931).
September 18 (7/27). Feng Zicai d. aged 85.
October 5 (8/15). Liao Shouheng d. aged 64.
  12 (8/22). Ji Chaoding b. (d. 1963).

The Dongfang zazhi begins publication **1904**

A ECONOMICS

January 22 (12/6). Xiliang, the Viceroy of Sichuan, sends in a memorial that local shareholders have set up the Sichuan–Hankou Railway Company.
March 29 (2/13). Following a memorial from the Board of Revenue, the court sets up the Board of Revenue Bank.
June 29 (5/16). Work is completed on the Jiaozhou–Ji'nan railway.
July 1 (5/18). Changsha opens as a trade port.
October 26 (9/18). Work begins on the Shanghai–Ningbo railway.
November 11 (10/5). China and Portugal conclude a contract for a Guangdong–Macao railway, and also a trade treaty.

B OFFICIAL APPOINTMENTS, DISMISSALS, TRANSFERS ETC,

January 14 (11/27). Sun Jia'nai is appointed to the newly created post of Commissioner for Educational Affairs.
February 15 (12/30). Rongqing is appointed to the Grand Council.
September 1 (7/22). Wei Guangtao is appointed acting Viceroy of Minzhe.
October 31 (9/23). Zhou Fu is appointed acting Viceroy of Liangjiang.
November 4 (9/27). Tang Shaoyi is appointed plenipotentiary to negotiate with the British over Tibet.
  9 (10/3). Yude is appointed Grand Councillor and Shixu assistant Grand Councillor.

1904

Peking diplomatic quarter.

21 (5/8). The court grants a special pardon to all those involved in the 1898 reform, except for Kang Youwei, Liang Qichao, and Sun Yatsen.

24 (5/11). The Guangxi rebels, led by Lu Yafa of the Heaven and Earth Society, take Liucheng.

29 (5/16). China becomes a member of the International Committee of the Red Cross.

July 6 (5/23). British troops of the Younghusband Mission occupy Gyantse in Tibet.

31 (6/19). The Guangxi rebels having taken Qingyuan, the court orders the Viceroys and Governors of Guangdong, Guangxi, Yunnan, Guizhou and Hunan to unite to suppress them.

August 3 (6/22). British troops reach Lhasa, the capital of Tibet; they occupy the city the following day and the Dalai Lama flees.

24 (7/14). Qing troops defeat the Guangxi rebels in Qingyuan. The Russo-Japanese Battle of Liaoyang begins.

September 4 (7/2). The Battle of Liaoyang ends in a Japanese victory. The Japanese take Liaoyang.

7 (7/28). Younghusband signs the Lhasa convention with Tibetan representatives; under it the Tibetans agree to have no dealings with any foreign power without British consent. No Chinese representative ever signed this convention.

22 (8/13). The Younghusband Mission leaves Lhasa for India.

23 (8/14). The Guangxi Heaven and Earth Society rebels take Luocheng.

October 5 (8/26). Qing troops retake Luocheng (Guangxi).

23 (9/15). A planned uprising of the China Revival Society in Hunan under Huang Xing is discovered and defeated.

November. Cai Yuanpei and others organize the Restoration Society in Shanghai. The Guangxi rebel Lu Yafa is captured.

December 12 (10/6). The posts of Governor of Hubei and Yunnan are abolished and their affairs put respectively under the Viceroys of Huguang and Yungui.

14 (11/8). Sun Yatsen arrives in London from the United States.

December 13 *(11/7)*. Xiliang is confirmed as Viceroy of Sichuan, Wei Guangtao of Minzhe, and Ding Zhenduo of Yungui.

C CULTURAL AND SOCIAL

January 13 *(11/26)*. A joint memorial on education by Zhang Zhidong, Rongqing and Zhang Boxi is adopted by the court. It suggests that the number who might receive degrees in the traditional examinations should be cut by one-third, beginning in 1906, and that they should eventually be discontinued altogether. It includes many other suggestions for the modernization of education at all levels.
March 21 *(2/5)*. The Shanghai International Committee of the Red Cross is set up in response to the human misery caused by the Russo-Japanese war.
May 1 *(3/16)*. Shanxi University is established.
July 19 *(6/7)*. In Enshi (Hubei) many houses of Christian converts are destroyed; several French missionaries and converts are killed.
October 16 *(9/8)*. The Jingye Middle School is set up in Tianjin: the predecessor to Nankai University.
19 *(9/11)*. In Chongqing, a general strike is held to oppose heavy taxes and exploitation.
November 6 *(9/29)*. More than 10,000 Moslems go on strike in Xiangfu (Henan) and obstruct food and other supplies into Kaifeng, the provincial capital; they are soon suppressed by official troops.

D PUBLICATIONS

March 11 *(1/25)*. The *Dongfang zazhi* (*Eastern Magazine*) begins publication in Shanghai.

E NATURAL DISASTERS

February 19 *(1/4)*. The Yellow River dykes of Lijin (Shandong), closed January 30, again burst, causing serious flooding.
August 1–3 *(6/20–22)*. The Yongding River bursts its dykes, causing serious flooding. (The dykes are closed November 5.)

F BIRTHS AND DEATHS

April 30 *(3/15)*. Ren Bishi b. (d. 1950).
July 3 *(5/20)*. Weng Tonghe d. aged 74.

1905 *The Chinese United League is set up*

January 1 *(11/26)*. Japanese troops seize Lüshun after a long battle.
Late January. Qing troops complete the suppression of the Guangxi Heaven and Earth Society rebellion.
February 12 *(1/9)*. Central Asian Russian troops occupy Kashgar.
23 *(1/20)*. The Russo-Japanese Battle of Shenyang begins; Japanese troops number some 250,000, Russian some 300,000.
March 2 *(1/27)*. Tang Shaoyi begins discussions on Tibet with British representatives in Calcutta.
10 *(2/5)*. The Battle of Shenyang ends in a decisive Japanese victory. The Japanese occupy Shenyang. Some 90,000 Russian casualties, killed or wounded, result from the battle, and some 70,000 Japanese.
April 12 *(3/8)*. The Elder Brothers Society leader, Ma Fuyi, is arrested in Xiangtan (Hunan).
21 *(3/17)*. The American President Theodore Roosevelt urges Japan and Russia to hold direct peace talks and suggests that Japan return Manchuria to China.
May 10 *(4/7)*. The Chinese Chamber of Commerce and other commercial organizations meet in Shanghai and decide to boycott American goods unless the USA changes its discrimination against Chinese labourers within two months.
26 *(4/23)*. China's first modern boycott begins, against American products. Over the next few weeks it spreads to include Shanghai, Guangzhou, Swatow, Nanjing, Hangzhou, Amoy, Niuzhuang, and other cities.
July 2 *(5/30)*. Yuan Shikai, Zhou Fu and Zhang Zhidong send in a memorial calling for constitutional government to be introduced after twelve years.
6 *(6/4)*. The Ministry of Foreign Affairs issues a statement to the US, Russian and Japanese ministers that no peace provision affecting Chinese interests will be recognized as valid unless China has given its approval.
16 *(6/14)*. The court orders a mission of five, led by Zaize and including also Xu Shichang and Duanfang, to go abroad to study the political systems of other countries as a prelude to introducing a constitution.
18 *(6/16)*. The court abolishes the offices of vice-president of the Boards of Rites, Punishments, Works, War and Revenue.
23 *(6/21)*. The post of Governor of Guangdong is abolished.
30 *(6/28)*. Sun Yatsen and some seventy other revolutionaries representing seventeen provinces meet in Tokyo and discuss the formation of the Chinese United League.
August 9 *(7/9)*. Peace negotiations to end the Russo-Japanese war formally begin with a meeting in Portsmouth, New Hampshire, of

The traditional examination system abolished 1905

A Economics

January 25 (12/20). The court urges provincial governments to maintain or establish commercial steamship companies.
May 15 (4/12). Following a memorial from Ding Zhenduo, the court sets up a company to construct a railway from Yunnan to Sichuan.
23 (4/20). The court sets up a fishing company in Shanghai to implement new fishing techniques suggested by Zhang Jian.
June 11 (5/9). Work is finished on the Peking–Hankou railway's bridge over the Yellow River, completing the line itself.
August 22 (7/22). The Board of Revenue Mint (the Tianjin Mint) is set up.
September 27 (8/29). Peking's Board of Revenue Bank opens for business.
November 13 (10/17). A formal ceremony is held to signal the completion of the railway from the Lugou Bridge outside Peking to Hankou.
19 (10/23). The court adopts regulations for the minting and use of a silver currency.
December 28 (12/3). Work begins on the Guangzhou–Hankou railway.

B Official Appointments, Dismissals, Transfers etc.

February 24 (1/21). Shengyun is appointed Viceroy of Minzhe to replace Wei Guangtao.
April 8 (3/4). Shengyun is appointed Viceroy of Shan'gan, Songfan of Minzhe.
June 30 (5/28). Wang Wenshao retires from the Grand Council; Xu Shichang is appointed probationary Grand Councillor.
July 5 (6/3). Zhang Zhidong is ordered to supervise the construction of the Guangzhou–Hankou railway.
19 (6/17). Shixu is appointed Grand Secretary, Natong assistant Grand Secretary.
August 26 (7/26). Tieliang is appointed probationary Grand Councillor.
October 8 (9/10). Xu Shichang is appointed President of the newly created Ministry of Police.
December 6 (11/10). Rongqing is appointed to the newly created post of Minister of Education.

C Cultural and Social

April 24 (3/20). Following a request from Wu Tingfang and others, the court abolishes several categories of punishments, including the slow

215

1905

the Russian delegation, led by Count Sergius Witte, and the Japanese, led by Komura Jutarō.

20 (7/20). The Chinese United League is formally established in Tokyo. Sun Yatsen is elected as its president.

21 (7/21). The court orders provincial viceroys and governors to prevent boycotts of American goods.

27 (7/27). As the boycott of American goods reaches its height, the Ministry of Foreign Affairs informs the USA that 'the Chinese government assumes no responsibility for the boycott.'

September 5 (8/7). The Treaty of Portsmouth is signed, ending the Russo-Japanese War. China's sovereignty and administration in Manchuria are explicitly restored. Japan and Russia agree to evacuate Manchuria except that Japan obtains the previously Russian lease on the Liaodong Peninsula and the Chinese Eastern Railway as far north as Changchun.

24 (8/26). In an attempt to kill its members, the revolutionary, Wu Yue, bombs the mission sent to observe foreign forms of government (see July 16) as it boards a train in Peking to depart. Zaize is wounded. The mission postpones departure.

27 (8/29). The boycott against American goods ends.

October 8 (9/10). The Qing court sets up the Ministry of Police.

November 18 (10/22). The court orders the Bureau of Government Affairs to draft a constitution.

28 (11/2). China and Germany reach agreement that German troops stationed in Jiaozhou and Gaomi in 1900 should withdraw to Qingdao (Shandong).

December 6 (11/10). The court sets up the Ministry of Education.

11 (11/15). A reconstituted mission to examine foreign forms of government, still led by Zaize, and including Dai Hongci and Duanfang, leaves Peking.

22 (11/26). China and Japan sign in Peking a treaty on the three Manchurian provinces; China recognizes the Japanese rights ceded by Russia by the Treaty of Portsmouth and opens many new trading ports.

slicing of limbs, the public exposition of severed heads, and the beheading of corpses.

29 (3/25). Some 4600 workers of the Shanghai Jicheng cotton mill go on strike against wage reduction, and destroy machinery.

May 1 (3/27). The Grand Council cables all provinces to ban revolutionary publications.

August 17 (7/17). The people are forbidden to read the *Dagong bao* of Tianjin, because it has published articles on the boycotting of American goods.

September 2 (8/4). The court issues an edict ordering that the traditional examinations of all levels be discontinued, effective with the tests scheduled for 1906.

D Publications

Sun Yirang's *Zhouli zhengyi* (*Orthodox Interpretations of the Zhouli*) (completed 1899, author's preface dated the eighth month, September 5–October 4, 1899) and Liu E's edition of Liu Xihai's study of ancient bronzes found in Xi'an, the *Chang'an huogu bian* (*Catching Ancient Times from Chang'an*), are printed. Publication of Yan Fu's translation of John Stuart Mill's *The System of Logic* under the title *Mule mingxue*.

February 23 (1/20). The monthly *Guocui xuebao* (*Journal of National Quintessence*) begins publication in Shanghai.

June 25 (5/23). Huang Xing and other revolutionaries publish the periodical *Ershi shiji zhi Zhina* (*Twentieth-Century China*) in Tokyo.

November 26 (10/30). *Minbao* (*People's Tribune*), the organ of the United League, and successor to *Twentieth-Century China*, is inaugurated in Tokyo with Sun Yatsen's 'Three Principles of the People'.

E Natural Disasters

September 1 (8/3). A cyclone strikes the Jiangsu coast; it lasts five days, causes massive devastation and kills several thousand people.

F Births and Deaths

March 28 (2/23). Huang Zunxian d. aged 57.
April 3 (2/29). The revolutionary writer Zou Rong d. in prison aged 20.
16 (3/12). Ma Fuyi is executed.
June 13 (5/11). Xian Xinghai b. (d. 1945).
September 24 (8/26). The revolutionary Wu Yue is killed, aged 28.

1906 *Changes in China's administrative structure*

January 19 (*12/25*). The court sets up a General Police Office in the Inner and Outer Cities of Peking.

February 26 (*2/4*). British and French warships move into the Poyang Lake because of the incident in Nanchang (Jiangxi) the previous day (see *C*).

April 8 (*3/15*). The French minister makes five demands on the Ministry of Foreign Affairs because of the death of the French missionaries on February 25.

27 (*4/4*). In Peking, Tang Shaoyi and British minister Sir E.M. Satow sign a further convention on Tibet. Britain agrees not to occupy Tibet or interfere in its affairs.

May 9 (*4/16*). The court sets up the Bureau of Customs Affairs.

June 20 (*int. 4/29*). China agrees to pay an indemnity of 250,000 taels to France because of the Nanchang Incident.

July 4 (*5/13*). The people of Ruichang (Jiangxi) revolt against heavy taxation.

August 23 (*7/4*). Zaize's mission having returned from abroad, Zaize sends in a memorial recommending that a constitution be adopted.

28 (*7/9*). The court holds a conference to discuss constitutional reform.

September 1 (*7/13*). The court issues an edict announcing that a constitution is to be drafted but lays down no time limit.

October 22–25 (*9/5–8*). Important military manoeuvres are held in Zhangde (Henan) with 33,000 participants, inspected by Tieliang and Yuan Shikai.

November 6 (*9/20*). The court declares the entire government changed. The traditional Six Boards are expanded to make eleven ministries. Several major bodies, including the Grand Council, Ministry of Foreign Affairs, Hanlin Academy, and Ministry of Education, remain unchanged. New creations include the Ministry of Civil Affairs, the Ministry of Finance, the Ministry of Justice, the Ministry of Agriculture, Industry and Commerce, the Ministry of Posts and Communications, and the Ministry of the Army.

20 (*10/5*). The court approves a memorial from Yuan Shikai that the first, third, fifth and sixth divisions of the new-style Beiyang Army should be put under the direct command of the Ministry of the Army and so under the Manchu President of the Ministry, Tieliang; the second and fourth divisions should remain under Yuan's direct command. This move represented a considerable reduction of Yuan's power in favour of the Manchu nobles.

December 4 (*10/19*). In conjunction with Gong Chuntai and others of the Triad Hong River Society, the revolutionary Cai Shaonan begins a revolt in Pingxiang (Jiangxi) and Liling (Hunan). Several

A Economics

May 27 (*int. 4/5*). Zhang Zhidong concludes a loan of £1,100,000 from the Hongkong Government to redeem the Guangzhou–Hankou railway.

June 7 (*int. 4/16*). A Japanese Imperial order sets up the Southern Manchurian Railway Company.

B Official Appointments, Dismissals, Transfers etc.

January 7 (*12/13*). Natong is appointed Grand Secretary, Rongqing assistant Grand Secretary.

9 (*12/15*). Xu Shichang and Tieliang are appointed to the Grand Council.

April 15 (*3/22*). The Governor of Jiangxi, Hu Tinggan, is dismissed because of the Nanchang Incident of February 25 (see C).

September 2 (*7/14*). Duanfang is appointed Viceroy of Liangjiang.

11 (*7/23*). Cen Chunxuan is appointed Viceroy of Yungui, Zhou Fu of Liangguang, and Ding Zhenduo of Minzhe.

November 6 (*9/20*). Shixu is appointed Grand Councillor, Lin Shaonian provisional Grand Councillor.

C Cultural and Social

February 21 (*1/28*). The Empress Dowager orders the Ministry of Education to set up girls' schools.

25 (*2/3*). The people of Nanchang set fire to French churches and kill six French and three British missionaries.

March 25 (*3/1*). The court prohibits the buying and selling of people. It also lays down the five basic principles of national education as 'loyalty to the ruler, respect for Confucius, justice, militarism and honesty'.

April 14 (*3/21*). The workers of the Shanghai Huaxin cotton mill go on strike to protest against the Japanese takeover of the mill.

June 13 (*int. 4/22*). The Beiyang Women's Normal School in Tianjin begins classes.

17 (*int. 4/26*). Professor Paul Pelliot leaves Paris at the head of a French expedition to western China in search of cultural relics and manuscripts. Places visited included Kashgar, Kucha, Turfan (all in Xinjiang), and Dunhuang (Gansu).

29 (*5/8*). The revolutionary writer Zhang Binglin is set free from prison.

August 4 (*6/15*). The Ministry of Education lays down rules for female education.

thousand miners join it.

7 (*10/22*). Secret society elements in Liuyang (Hunan) join the revolt of Gong Chuntai and Cai Shaonan.

13 (*10/28*). The forces of the Hong River Society and others in Pingxiang and Liuyang are defeated by Qing troops. The revolt is completely suppressed within about one week.

24 (*11/9*). More than twenty persons are killed when the county magistrate orders the suppression of a revolt by starving people in Xuancheng (Anhui).

25 (*11/10*). Disturbances by starving people in Jiangsu, including in Kunshan, are put down with heavy casualties.

1907 *Further administrative reforms, as five revolutionary uprisings fail*

February 19 (*1/7*). Ordered by the United League, Xu Xueqiu and other revolutionaries attack Chaozhou (Guangdong), but are defeated.

March 4 (*1/20*). The Japanese authorities deport Sun Yatsen and other revolutionaries at the request of the Qing minister in Tokyo. Sun goes to Vietnam.

6 (*1/22*). In Gaoyou (Jiangsu), the starving masses plunder rice.

7 (*1/23*). In Yuyao (Zhejiang) hungry people ransack rice shops.

9 (*1/25*). In Shaoxing (Zhejiang), starving people ransack rice shops. In Dongguan (Guangdong) disturbances by the hungry masses are suppressed and over ten people are killed or wounded.

13 (*1/29*). Rice riots erupt in Hangzhou (Zhejiang).

16 (*2/3*). In Taiping (Anhui) the starving masses plunder rice.

April 20 (*3/8*). A programme for general reorganization of provincial level administration leads to abolition of traditional military government in the dynasty's homeland, Manchuria. The area is divided

September 20 (*8/3*). The court issues an edict banning opium and planning to eliminate all its evil effects within ten years.

October 27 (*9/10*). Following a memorial from Dai Hongci and others, the court orders every province to set up public libraries, museums, zoological gardens and parks.

December 30 (*11/15*). Confucius is deified in that he is raised to the status of Heaven and Earth to which only the Emperor could make ceremonial offerings.

D PUBLICATIONS

Liu E's novel *Lao Can youji* (*Adventures of Lao Can*) is published in book form.

October 15 (*8/28*). Yunnan students in Japan begin publication of the monthly *Yunnan zazhi* (*Yunnan Magazine*).

23 (*9/6*). Dai Hongci and Duanfang present to the Emperor their report on their trip to the West, *Oumei zhenghi yaoyi* (*Essentials of European and American Politics*) (see also December 11, 1905).

F BIRTHS AND DEATHS

February 7 (*1/14*). Puyi, the last Qing emperor b. (d. 1967).
March. Novelist Li Baojia d. aged 40.

The beginnings of the spoken play in China   1907

A ECONOMICS

January. A railway from Swatow to Chaozhou (Guangdong), built with Chinese capital, is completed.

1 (*11/17*). Nanning (Guangxi) is opened as a trade port.

February 3 (*12/21*). The court sets up the Jehol National Bank.

March 4 (*1/20*). The Chinese government regains control from the Russians of a number of mines in Heilongjiang and Jilin.

7 (*1/23*). A Sino-British contract is concluded for a loan of £1,500,000 to build the Guangzhou–Kowloon railway.

June 29 (*5/19*). The Peking–Shenyang railway begins taking traffic.

August 17 (*7/9*). The court adopts rules, proposed by the Ministry of Finance, for a new currency system. The *yuan* replaces the tael as the unit of currency.

December 8 (*11/4*). The court sets up the Bank of Communications.

into three provinces, Fengtian, Jilin and Heilongjiang, and placed under one viceroy and three governors.

May 22 (*4/11*). Yu Jicheng of the Heaven and Earth Society leads the revolution in Huanggang (Guangdong). The attempt is defeated May 27. (Sun Yatsen's third revolutionary failure). A hierarchy of officials and government offices is established in the three Manchurian provinces.

June 2 (*4/22*). The revolutionary Deng Ziyu leads an uprising in Huizhou (Guangdong). It is defeated June 12 (the 'fourth unsuccessful revolution').

10 (*4/30*). Japan and France sign a treaty under which they recognize Chinese independence and territorial integrity, and agree to support each other's situation and territorial rights on the continent.

25 (*5/15*). Further rice riots occur in Shaoxing (Zhejiang).

July 6 (*5/26*). Xu Xilin of the revolutionary Restoration Society leads an uprising in Anqing (Anhui). The Governor of Anhui is killed, but the revolt is put down, and Xu captured.

9 (*5/29*). A secret society uprising in Woyang (Anhui) fails.

13 (*6/4*). Qiu Jin, the famous woman revolutionary, is arrested in Shaoxing. She had plotted an uprising for July 19.

30 (*6/21*). Russia and Japan sign conventions under which they publicly support China's independence and territorial integrity, but secretly recognize each other's rights in China and Korea and agree to divide Manchuria into a northern sphere for Russian and a southern for Japanese exploitation.

August 13 (*7/5*). The Bureau of Constitutional Compilation is set up.

19 (*7/11*). Some seventy Japanese and Korean military and other police cross the frontier from Korea into the Yanji region of China's Jilin province.

31 (*7/23*). Britain and Russia sign a convention on Tibet. Each recognizes Chinese sovereignty in Tibet and agrees not to interfere in its affairs.

September 1 (*7/24*). The revolutionary leader and United League member Wang Heshun attacks and defeats Qing troops in Qinzhou (Guangdong).

9 (*8/2*). The court sends the Vice-President of the Ministry of Foreign Affairs, Wang Daxie, and two other senior officials to Britain, Germany and Japan to study constitutions.

17 (*8/10*). The Qinzhou uprising organized by the revolutionaries is defeated. The fifth attempt at revolution fails.

20 (*8/13*). An Imperial edict orders the establishment of a National Assembly.

1907

B OFFICIAL APPOINTMENTS, DISMISSALS, TRANSFERS ETC.

March 3 *(1/19)*. Xiliang is appointed Viceroy of Yungui.
4 *(1/20)*. Songshou replaces Ding Zhenduo as Viceroy of Minzhe.
April 20 *(3/8)*. Xu Shichang is appointed Viceroy of the Manchurian provinces.
May 16 *(4/5)*. The censor Zhao Qilin is dismissed because an accusation of bribery and corruption he made on May 7 against the head of the Grand Council Yikuang is held to be false.
June 19 *(5/9)*. Zaifeng is appointed probationary Grand Councillor and Lu Zhuanlin Grand Councillor.
July 23 *(6/14)*. Zhang Zhidong is appointed Grand Secretary and Lu Zhuanlin assistant Grand Secretary.
August 12 *(7/4)*. Zhang Renjun is appointed Viceroy of Liangguang.
September 4 *(7/27)*. Yuan Shikai is appointed President of the Ministry of Foreign Affairs, and concurrently Grand Councillor. Zhang Zhidong is appointed Grand Councillor.
5 *(7/28)*. Yang Shixiang is appointed acting Viceroy of Zhili; Zhao Ersun is appointed Viceroy of Huguang, Chen Kuilong of Sichuan.
20 *(8/13)*. Pulun and Sun Jia'nai are appointed to direct the inauguration of the National Assembly.

C CULTURAL AND SOCIAL

February 6 *(12/24)*. Japan announces that the number of Chinese students studying in Japan is more than 17,860.
May 28 *(4/17)*. Aurel Stein buys from the Taoist priest Wang some 7000 MSS from the library of the Qianfo Caves near Dunhuang (Gansu); they are later placed in the British Museum.
June 1–2 *(4/21–22)*. Ouyang Yuqian and others produce the play *Heinu yutian lu* (*The Black Slave's Cry to Heaven*) in Tokyo. This is the beginning of the Chinese spoken play.
August 10 *(7/2)*. The court issues an edict for equality between Manchus and Han Chinese and the elimination of discrimination; it orders government offices to find ways of putting the edict into effect.
September 25 *(8/18)*. In Nankang and Ganzhou (Jiangxi) the people ransack churches and the houses of converts, killing a French missionary and many converts.
December. The Frenchman Paul Pelliot obtains 5000 MSS from the library of the Qianfo Caves near Dunhuang (Gansu); 3000 are taken to Paris, 2000 transferred to the Chinese National Academy.
25 *(11/21)*. The court orders the Ministry of Education to forbid students to participate in politics or make public speeches.

25 (*8/18*). The clash with Christians in Nankang and Ganzhou (Jiangxi) leads on to a general siege and attack on Ganzhou.

October 19 (*9/13*). The court issues an edict that provincial assemblies be set up and that preparations be made for councils at prefecture, district and county levels.

Liang Qichao and others hold a meeting in Tokyo to inaugurate the Political Information Society; their aim is to promote responsible parliamentary government, legal reform and local self-government.

27 (*9/21*). The popular rebellion in Nankang and Ganzhou is put down.

November 30 (*10/25*). The revolutionaries led by Huang Mingtang attack three forts of Zhennanguan (Guangxi), from Vietnam.

December 2 (*10/27*). Sun Yatsen and Huang Xing arrive in Zhennanguan and themselves lead the fighting there.

8 (*11/4*). Qing troops defeat the revolutionary army at Zhennanguan; Sun Yatsen regards this as the sixth unsuccessful revolutionary attempt.

26 (*11/22*). The court prohibits all political gatherings and public speeches in Peking.

1908 *The Tatsu Maru Incident leads to a boycott of Japanese goods*

February 5 (*1/4*). The Japanese ship *Tatsu maru* is seized in Guangdong for smuggling arms.

14 (*1/13*). The Japanese minister, Hayashi Gonsuke, protests to the Ministry of Foreign Affairs over the seizure of the *Tatsu maru*.

March 13 (*2/11*). Because of the *Tatsu maru* Incident Hayashi Gonsuke makes five demands on the Chinese Ministry of Foreign Affairs, including the release of the seized ship, an indemnity and an apology. The demands are accepted on March 15.

17 (*2/15*). The merchants of Guangzhou boycott Japanese goods because of Japan's reaction to the *Tatsu maru* Incident.

19 (*2/17*). Several tens of thousands of people in Guangdong hold mass meetings and set down this day to commemorate national shame because of the *Tatsu maru* Incident. About this time mass boycott of Japanese goods spreads to other parts of China.

D Publications

Completion of Ye Dehui's collection of erotic literature *Shuangmei ying'an congshu* (*Collectanea of Veiled Works on the Double Plum*).
February. Pi Xirui's *Jingxue tonglun* (*Comprehensive Discussions on the Study of Classics*) completed.
April 2 (*2/20*). *Shenzhou ribao* (*The China Daily News*) begins publication in Shanghai.
June 22 (*5/12*). The weekly *Xin shiji* (*The New Century*) begins publication in Paris.
August 20 (*7/12*). The United League's *Zhongxing ribao* (*China Revival Daily*) begins publication in Singapore.

E Natural Disasters

Winter–Spring. Serious famine, especially in northern Anhui, Jiangsu, Shandong and Henan.

F Births and Deaths

February 5 (*12/23*). Scholar Yu Yue d. aged 86.
March 30 (*2/17*). Zhang Boxi d. aged 60.
July 7 (*5/27*). The revolutionary Xu Xilin d. aged 34.
  15 (*6/6*). Qiu Jin is beheaded, aged 28.

Death of the Empress Dowager Cixi 1908

A Economics

January 13 (*12/10*). The Ministry of Foreign Affairs concludes a contract with the Deutsch-Asiatische Bank and the London-based Chinese Central Railways Company for a loan of £5,000,000 to build a railway from Tianjin (Zhili) to Pukou (Jiangsu).
February 17 (*1/16*). The court accepts a memorial from the Ministry of Finance on the banking system. Four types of banks are recognized: central, ordinary, current and savings.
March 5 (*2/3*). A tram (street car) system begins operating in Shanghai's International Settlement.
  6 (*2/4*). A Sino-British contract is concluded for a loan of £1,500,000 to cover the construction of the Shanghai–Hangzhou–Ningbo railway.
  13 (*2/11*). The Hanyang arsenal, Daye (Hubei) iron mines and Pingxiang (Jiangxi) coal mines amalgamate under the management of

1908

21 (2/19). At Japanese insistence the Ministry of Foreign Affairs cables the Viceroy of Liangjiang, Duanfang, to prohibit the boycott against Japanese goods.

22 (2/20). The court cables the Viceroy of Liangguang to prohibit the boycott against Japanese goods.

27 (2/25). The revolutionaries led by Huang Xing again attack Qinzhou (Guangdong) from Vietnam.

April 2 (3/2). Huang Xing's revolutionary troops defeat Qing forces in Qinzhou. However, they are eventually beaten and withdraw back to Vietnam on May 3. Sun Yatsen calls this defeat the seventh unsuccessful revolutionary attempt.

5 (3/5). The women of Guangzhou hold a national shame memorial meeting over the *Tatsu maru* Incident.

29 (3/29). The revolutionaries led by Huang Mingtang and Wang Heshun attack and occupy Hekou (Yunnan).

May 26 (4/27). Qing troops retake Hekou and defeat the revolutionary army, which retreats back into Vietnam. This is Sun Yatsen's eighth unsuccessful attempt at revolution.

June 23 (5/25). The US Congress passes a bill to return part of the Boxer indemnity to China.

July 22 (6/24). The court promulgates regulations for the elections for the provincial assemblies and prefectural, district and county councils.

August 11 (7/15). Representatives of the constitutional reform societies from all provinces submit a petition to the Bureau of Constitutional Compilation urging the convening of a parliament.

13 (7/17). A decree orders the banning of the Political Information Society and the arrest of its members.

27 (8/1). The court accepts a Draft Constitution submitted by Yikuang, the Bureau of Constitutional Compilation and others. It declares that the Qing dynasty will rule for ever, and defines the powers of the Emperor, the duties of his ministers, the rights and obligations of the citizen, and the rights and limitations of parliament. The court lays down a period of nine years of progressive constitutional reform, at the end of which the constitution will be promulgated and parliament convened.

November 18 (10/25). The beginning of a new reign-period: Xuantong.

19 (10/26). The revolutionary Xiong Chengji revolts in Anqing (Anhui) and attacks the city.

20 (10/27). Xiong Chengji is defeated: he flees north towards Tongcheng (Anhui) and later to Japan.

30 (11/7). The American Secretary of State, Elihu Root, and the

1908

Sheng Xuanhuai to form the Hanyeping Coal and Iron Company.
April 1 *(3/1)*. The Shanghai–Ningbo railway begins taking traffic.
20 *(3/20)*. China and Britain conclude a revised Tibet-India trade treaty.
July 1 *(6/3)*. The Board of Revenue Bank alters its name to The Great Qing Bank.
2 *(6/4)*. China and Sweden conclude a trade treaty.
October 12 *(9/18)*. Japan and China conclude an agreement under which electric cables in southern Manchuria are redeemed and Japan is allowed to set up a submarine cable from Lüshun (Fengtian) to Yantai (Shandong).
December 28 *(12/6)*. Through an Anglo-French loan raised in October 1908, China completes repayment of the Belgian loan (see *A*, June 26, 1898) to construct the Peking–Hankou railway.

B Official Appointments, Dismissals, Transfers etc.

February 2 *(1/1)*. Zaifeng is confirmed as Grand Councillor.
March 6 *(2/4)*. Zhao Ersun is appointed Viceroy of Sichuan, Chen Kuilong of Huguang. Zhao Erfeng is appointed Resident in Tibet.
July 23 *(6/25)*. Yang Shixiang is confirmed as Viceroy of Zhili.
November 14 *(10/21)*. Zaifeng is appointed Regent and his son Puyi Heir Apparent.
December 2 *(11/9)*. Puyi ascends the throne as Emperor.

C Cultural and Social

July 4 *(6/6)*. The court approves a memorial from the Ministry of Education to set up the Girls' Normal School in Peking.
20 *(6/22)*. The Ministry of Education sends in a memorial proposing that the money returned by the USA from the Boxer Indemnity be used to send Chinese students to the USA.
October 19 *(9/25)*. The Japanese police suppress the *Minbao*.
25 *(10/1)*. The *Xin shiji* is banned because of its revolutionary stance.

D Publications

Duanfang publishes the catalogue of his collection of artefacts *Taozhai jijin lu* (*Records of Taozhai's Ritual Vessels*); Zaize his *Kaocha zhengzhi riji* (*My Diary of Political Studies Abroad*).
November. The Japanese begin publishing the *Taidong ribao* (*Japan Daily*) in Dalian.

1908–9

Japanese minister in Washington, Takahira Kogorō, exchange notes on a variety of subjects. On China these 'Root-Takahira notes' express both parties' respect for China's territorial integrity, their support for equality of opportunity, for China's independence and for the maintenance of the *status quo*.

December 3 (*11/10*). The court proclaims that the constitution will be promulgated and the parliamentary system put into operation in 1916.

25 (*12/3*). The court sets up a new palace guard.

1909 *The provincial assemblies meet*

January 1 (*12/10*). China regains from Belgium the right of control over the Peking–Hankou railway.

February 1 (*1/11*). The second International Opium Conference convenes in Shanghai.

5 (*1/15*). Preliminary local elections begin to choose delegates for the provincial assemblies.

17 (*1/27*). The court orders that all provincial assemblies be established by the end of the year.

19 (*1/29*). The court reorganizes the navy.

March 6 (*2/15*). The court issues an edict to confirm that constitutional reform will be implemented.

July 15 (*5/28*). In the name of the Emperor, the Regent Zaifeng takes personal command over the army and navy.

18 (*6/2*). In Fengcheng (Jiangxi), violence flares up when an official census is misunderstood as conscription; similar disturbances erupt in other parts of Jiangxi.

27 (*6/11*). Japanese troops stationed in Korea cross the border into Chinese territory towards Yanji (Jilin). Zhao Erfeng puts down a disturbance in Dege (Sichuan).

August 4 (*6/19*). The Ministry of Foreign Affairs protests against movement of Japanese troops and armaments over the Korean border into Jilin, and cables the minister to Japan, Hu Weide, to discuss their withdrawal with the Japanese Foreign Ministry.

6 (*6/21*). A Japanese announcement, made the same day, that it intends to take over full control of the construction of a railway from Shenyang

1908–9

E NATURAL DISASTERS

April 24 (*3/24*). A strong typhoon strikes Hankou.
Mid-June. Heavy rainfall over several days causes devastating flooding in Nanhai, Sihui and other counties of Guangdong, the province's worst disaster for several decades.

F BIRTHS AND DEATHS

February 10 (*1/9*). Dong Fuxiang d. aged 69.
March 6 (*2/4*). Pi Xirui d. aged 57.
June 20 (*5/22*). Sun Yirang d. aged 59.
November 14 (*10/21*). Emperor Guangxu d. aged 37.
  15 (*10/22*). Empress Dowager Cixi d. aged 73.

Death of Zhang Zhidong 1909

A ECONOMICS

May 24 (*4/6*). The court orders the provinces to reorganize their financial administration and to set up bureaux to examine the currency system.
  30 (*4/12*). The privately-owned railway from Shanghai to Jiaxing (Zhejiang) begins taking traffic.
September 25 (*8/12*). The Ministry of Posts and Communications announces the completion of the Peking–Zhangjiakou (Zhili) railway.

B OFFICIAL APPOINTMENTS, DISMISSALS, TRANSFERS ETC.

January 2 (*12/11*). Yuan Shikai is ordered to resign all his official posts and to return to his native place.
  23 (*1/2*). Natong is appointed to the Grand Council.
February 9 (*1/19*). Xiliang is appointed Viceroy of the Manchurian provinces, Li Jingxi of Yungui.
June 23 (*5/6*). Shengyun is replaced by Changgeng as Viceroy of Shan'-gan.
  28 (*5/11*). Duanfang is appointed Viceroy of Zhili, Zhang Renjun of Liangjiang and Yuan Shuxun of Liangguang.
October 6 (*8/23*). Dai Hongci is appointed to the Grand Council.
November 2 (*9/20*). Lu Zhuanlin is appointed Grand Secretary.
  23 (*10/11*). Chen Kuilong is appointed Viceroy of Zhili, Ruizheng of Huguang.

1909–10

to Andong (Fengtian) on the Korean border, on the grounds of procrastination from China, sparks off a boycott of Japanese goods in Peking, Tianjin, the Manchurian provinces and elsewhere.

22 (7/7). Japanese troops provoke hostilities with Qing forces in Yanji (Jilin), causing casualties on both sides.

September 4 (7/20). At the Tumen River, which itself forms part of the border, China and Japan conclude an agreement concerning the Sino-Korean border.

October 14 (9/1). The provincial assemblies of every province convene.

November 6 (9/24). The US Secretary of State, P.C. Knox, suggests the neutralization of the Manchurian railways.

8 (9/26). Sun Yatsen arrives in New York from London.

December 7 (10/25). On behalf of the Dalai Lama, cables are sent from Gyantse (Tibet) to the Japanese, Russian and British Ministers in Peking asking them to protest against China's despatch of Sichuanese troops into Tibet.

10 (10/28). Zhao Erfeng arrives in Changdu (Tibet) to assist the Sichuanese troops moving into Tibet.

1910 *The National Assembly meets*

January 21 (12/11). Japan and Russia oppose the US suggestion (November 6, 1909) to neutralize the railways of Manchuria.

26 (12/16). Representatives of the provincial assemblies petition in Peking for the immediate convening of parliament.

30 (12/20). The petition of January 26 for the immediate convening

1909–10

C CULTURAL AND SOCIAL

February 6 (1/16). An Imperial edict prohibits the buying and selling of female slaves.
March 15 (2/24). The court issues an edict on methods of fighting opium.
August 6 (6/21). In Shanghai, over 100 female workers of Qinchang silk mill go on strike in protest over increased hours of work.
September 28 (8/15). The court sets up a school to prepare students destined for US colleges: the predecessor of Qinghua University.

D PUBLICATIONS

Duanfang publishes his *Taozhai cangshi ji* (*Records of Taozhai's Rubbings on Stone*). Wu Woyao completes his satirical novel *Ershi nian mudu zhi guai xianzhuang* (*Strange Events of the Last Twevty Years*).
February 15 (1/25). *Jiaoyu zazhi* (*The Chinese Educational Review*) begins publication.
   21 (2/2). Grand Secretary Shixu is ordered to supervise the compilation of the *Dezong huangdi shilu* (*The Veritable Records of the Guangxu Reign*).

E NATURAL DISASTERS

September 15 (8/2). A great fire in Fuzhou (Fujian), fanned by strong winds, causes several thousand casualties.
October 19 (9/6). A cyclone strikes Guangzhou, causing many casualties.

F BIRTHS AND DEATHS

August 23 (7/8). Liu E, scholar and writer, d. aged 51.
October 4 (8/21). Zhang Zhidong d. aged 72.
   26 (9/13). The Japanese statesman Itō Hirobumi is assassinated in Harbin (Heilongjiang).
November 29 (10/17). Sun Jia'nai d. aged 82.

A plague epidemic in Manchuria 1910

A ECONOMICS

April. The Yunnan–Vietnam railway is completed.
May 23 (4/15). In Paris, the British Hongkong and Shanghai Bank, the German Deutsch-Asiatische Bank, the French Banque de l'Indo-Chine and four American New York banks, including the First National Bank

of parliament is rejected.

February 9 (*12/30*). A clash breaks out between the New Army and the police in Guangzhou. The revolutionary Ni Yingdian becomes involved.

12 (*1/3*). Ni Yingdian leads the New Army in a revolt but is put down. Sun Yatsen regards this as the ninth unsuccessful attempt at revolution. Qing troops occupy Lhasa, and the Dalai Lama escapes towards Darjeeling.

26 (*1/17*). The British minister, Sir John Jordan, protests to the Ministry of Foreign Affairs over the Chinese invasion of western Tibet.

April 10 (*3/1*). In Wukang county (Zhejiang), the local people revolt against exorbitant taxes; they attack the county offices and beat up the magistrate.

16 (*3/7*). Wang Jingwei and other revolutionaries are arrested: they had plotted to assassinate the Regent Zaifeng.

18 (*3/9*). The Ministry of Foreign Affairs issues a formal statement of its claim to sovereign rights in Tibet.

Food riots erupt in Qingjiang (Jiangsu).

May 2 (*3/23*). In Wuxue (Hubei), the hungry masses plunder rice shops, continuing for several days.

9 (*4/1*). The court proclaims that the National Assembly will be officially opened on October 3 (9/1); half of the 200 members are to be elected by provincial assemblies and half selected from among the royal family, the nobles, ministries, officials and scholars.

June 6 (*4/29*). The people of Haiyang (Shandong) attack the county capital in resistance against excessive tax. The disturbance is pacified two days later when the magistrate agrees to their demands.

12 (*5/6*). The people of Laiyang (Shandong) set fire to the residences of village leaders and surround the county offices. The disturbance lasts till June 16, when the county magistrate accepts the people's demands.

22 (*5/16*). Representatives of the provincial assemblies present a second petition for the immediate opening of parliament, signed by some 300,000 people.

27 (*5/21*). The second request for the immediate opening of a parliament is turned down by the court.

July 4 (*5/28*). Japan and Russia sign a second secret treaty to maintain the *status quo* in Manchuria and recognize each other's rights there.

7 (*6/1*). Hungry people plunder rice in Xuancheng (Anhui).

14 (*6/8*). Qing troops in Laiyang attack the people, killing several hundred.

and the National City Bank, set up the Four-power Consortium to provide loans to the Chinese government and to divide the railways of Huguang among its members.

24 (*4/16*). The court lays down a currency system based on silver with the *yuan* as basic unit.

June. The Russo-Asiatic Bank is set up with joint Chinese and Russian capital.

September 28 (*8/25*). The Chinese government concludes a second loan of £4,800,000 from a German and an Anglo-French concern for the construction of the Tianjin–Pukou railway.

October 22 (*9/20*). The court orders the Ministry of Finance to prepare a national budget (China's first) for approval by the National Assembly.

B   OFFICIAL APPOINTMENTS, DISMISSALS, TRANSFERS ETC.

January 1 (*11/20*). Lu Runxiang is appointed Grand Secretary.
June 12 (*5/6*). Ruizheng is confirmed as Viceroy of Huguang.
August 17 (*7/13*). Yulang and Xu Shichang are appointed Grand Councillors.
September 28 (*8/25*). Xu Shichang is appointed Grand Secretary.

C   CULTURAL AND SOCIAL

Some 9000 MSS are collected from the Qianfo Caves near Dunhuang (Gansu) by the Chinese government.

January 10 (*11/29*). The Ministry of Education sends in a memorial that the Imperial University has set up several preparatory faculties, including economics, law, agriculture, industry, natural sciences and medicine.

31 (*12/21*). The court issues regulations prohibiting the buying and selling of people.

April 14–15 (*3/4–5*). In Changsha (Hunan) the hungry masses burn schools and churches; official troops open fire on them and many are killed.

19–25 (*3/10–16*). The people of Cixi (Zhejiang) burn down schools.
May 15 (*4/7*). A new legal code is issued.
July 27 (*6/21*). In Yizhou (Zhili), the people set fire to schools.
September 15 (*8/12*). In Lianzhou (Guangdong), the villagers enter the city and set fire to schools. The disturbances last some two months.
October 18–24 (*9/16–22*). China's first National Games take place.

1910–11

October 3 *(9/1)*. The national assembly convenes; the Regent Zaifeng makes the opening speech. Representatives of the provincial assemblies present a third petition for the immediate convening of a parliament, purportedly signed by some 25,000,000 people, and supported by high provincial officials.
26 *(9/24)*. The National Assembly urges that a genuine parliament be convened quickly.
November 4 *(10/3)*. The court issues an edict that parliament be convened in 1913, reducing the constitutional preparation period by three years. It also orders the petitioners for the immediate opening of parliament to dissolve their organization.
December 4 *(11/3)*. The court sets up the Ministry of the Navy.
18 *(11/17)*. Through a memorial, the national assembly criticizes the Grand Councillors as ignoring the interests of the public, and urges the organization of a cabinet responsible to the national assembly. The court rejects the memorial.

1911 *The Wuchang uprising succeeds*

January 21 *(12/21)*. In the British concession of Hankou a policeman kills a rickshaw driver. The next day British soldiers open fire on striking rickshaw drivers, killing more than ten of them.
30 *(1/1)*. The Literary Society, consisting largely of members of the Hubei New Army, is set up in Wuchang as a revolutionary organization; its name aims to disguise its nature.
April 27 *(3/29)*. Huang Xing leads an uprising in Guangzhou, attacking the offices of the Viceroy, but is defeated, with 86 revolutionaries killed, by Qing troops under the naval Commander-in-Chief, Li Zhun. This is the well-known uprising which Sun Yatsen calls the tenth unsuccessful revolutionary attempt.
May 8 *(4/10)*. The system of cabinet government is set up. The Grand Council and Grand Secretariat are abolished.
22 *(4/24)*. Following strong protests in Hunan against the nationalization of the railways, the court orders the provincial Governor, Yang Wending, to take strong measures to stop the disturbances.

1910-11

D PUBLICATIONS

February 19 *(1/10)*. The *Guofeng bao* (*National Spirit*) begins publication in Shanghai as the major publication of the constitutionalists.
April 7 *(2/28)*. Liu Jinzao completes his *Huangchao xu wenxian tongkao* (*Supplement to the Imperial Dynasty's Complete Examination of Documents*).

E NATURAL DISASTERS

June 14 *(5/8)*. Heavy flooding strikes Changde (Hunan) and nearby regions, and southern Anhui.
July 3 *(5/27)*. Flooding strikes Wuhu and Ningguo (Anhui).
Autumn. A bubonic plague epidemic breaks out in Manchuria. Serious famine in Jiangsu and northern Anhui.

F BIRTHS AND DEATHS

February 12 *(1/3)*. The revolutionary Ni Yingdian d. in the 'ninth unsuccessful revolutionary attempt'.
22 *(1/13)*. Dai Hongci d. aged 57.

Sun Yatsen becomes provisional President of the Republic of China — 1911

A ECONOMICS

March 24 *(2/24)*. Sheng Xuanhuai signs a contract with a Japanese bank for a loan of 10,000,000 *yuan* to help pay off debts incurred in railway construction.
April 15 *(3/17)*. The Ministry of Finance raises a loan of £10,000,000 from the Four-power Consortium to support monetary reform and the development of Manchuria.
May 9 *(4/11)*. Following a memorial from Sheng Xuanhuai, the Minister of Posts and Communications, the court issues an edict to nationalize all China's main railways; only the branch lines are allowed to be owned privately.
20 *(4/22)*. Sheng Xuanhuai concludes a contract with the Four-Power Consortium for a loan of £10,000,000 repayable in forty years at 5 per cent to build the Sichuan–Hankou and Hankou–Guangzhou railways.
July 24 *(6/29)*. Germany signs a contract with Shandong province

1911

28 (5/1). The Chinese postal system is severed from the customs and placed under the Ministry of Posts and Communications.

June 17 (5/21). The Railway Protection League is established in Sichuan in protest against the nationalization of the railways.

July 31 (*int. 6/6*). Tan Renfeng, Song Jiaoren, Chen Qimei and others set up the Central China United League in Shanghai.

August 13 (*int. 6/19*). Two revolutionaries attempt, unsuccessfully, to assassinate Li Zhun.

24 (7/1). The Railway Protection League and others hold a meeting of over 10,000 people in Chengdu, which decides on student and commercial strikes, refusal to pay taxes, and other measures against the nationalization of the railways.

September 2 (7/10). The court sends Duanfang with units of the Hubei New Army to suppress the people's movement in Sichuan.

7 (7/15). The Viceroy of Sichuan, Zhao Erfeng, orders the arrest of the leaders of the Railway Protection League. A large demonstration demands their release; over thirty demonstrators are killed.

8 (7/16). Several tens of thousands of people gather outside Chengdu and, together with leaders of the Elder Brothers Society, form themselves into the Railway Protection League Army.

24 (8/3). The Literary Society and the Progressive Society hold a meeting in Wuchang and set a date for a revolutionary uprising against the Qing dynasty.

October 9 (8/18). The revolutionaries in the office of the Progressive Society in the Russian Concession of Hankou accidentally let off a bomb from among those intended for use in the anti-Qing uprising. The Qing police are thus alerted and arrest several scores of revolutionaries.

10 (8/19). The Wuchang uprising begins when elements of the New Army mutiny in the evening.

11 (8/20). The revolutionaries take the offices of the Viceroy of Huguang, Ruizheng, who escapes. Wuchang joins the revolution and becomes independent of the Qing. The revolutionaries seize Hanyang and set up a military government in Wuchang.

12 (8/21). The revolutionaries take Hankou.

15 (8/24). The revolutionaries take Huangzhou (Hubei).

18 (8/27). The consuls of the foreign powers in Hankou proclaim neutrality.

22 (9/1). In Changsha (Hunan), the New Army revolts; Hunan becomes independent of the Qing.

29 (9/8). Shanxi proclaims itself independent of the Qing.

30 (9/9). The court issues an edict of self-criticism and offers numerous

1911

agreeing to return railways and mining rights there.
August 12 (*int. 6/18*). The Russo-Chinese Bank and the Banque du Nord amalgamate into the Russo-Asiatic Bank.
October 4 (*8/13*). The Guangzhou–Kowloon railway starts taking traffic.

B OFFICIAL APPOINTMENTS, DISMISSALS, TRANSFERS ETC.

April 20 (*3/22*). Zhao Ersun is appointed Viceroy of the Manchurian provinces.
21 (*3/23*). Zhao Erfeng is appointed acting Viceroy of Sichuan.
May 8 (*4/10*). Yikuang is appointed Prime Minister of the newly created cabinet dominated by Manchu appointees.
October 11 (*8/20*). The revolutionaries appoint Li Yuanhong as military governor of the Hubei military government. He accepts two days later.
14 (*8/23*). The Qing appoints Yuan Shikai Viceroy of Huguang, Cen Chunxuan of Sichuan.
23 (*9/2*). Jiao Dafeng becomes military governor of Hunan.
29 (*9/8*). Yan Xishan becomes military governor of Shanxi.
31 (*9/10*). Cai E is elected military governor of Yunnan.
November 1 (*9/11*). Yikuang resigns as the Qing Prime Minister and is replaced by Yuan Shikai.
2 (*9/12*). Wu Jiezhang becomes military governor of Jiangxi.
4 (*9/14*). Tang Shouqian is elected military governor of Zhejiang.
5 (*9/15*). Cheng Dequan becomes military governor of Jiangsu.
7 (*9/17*). Shen Bingkun becomes military governor of Guangxi, Chen Qimei of Shanghai.
9 (*9/19*). Hu Hanmin becomes military governor of Guangdong, Sun Daoren of Fujian.
December 6 (*10/16*). The Qing Regent Zaifeng resigns.
26 (*11/7*). Sun Yatsen is elected provisional President of the Republic of China.

C CULTURAL AND SOCIAL

January 2 (*12/2*). Following student strikes in Fengtian, Sichuan, Zhili and other provinces, demanding the convening of parliament, the court strictly forbids all students to take part in politics.
26 (*12/26*). The Ministry of Education reports to the court that there are 47,995 schools and 1,300,739 students in China.
February 8 (*1/10*). At the Xiehe silk mill in Shanghai some 300 women workers go on strike to oppose a wage reduction.

1911

concessions to the revolutionaries. Yunnan joins the revolution. The Viceroy of Yungui, Li Jingxi, escapes.

31 (*9/10*). The New Army in Nanchang (Jiangxi), turns against the Qing and sets up a military government two days later.

November 2 (*9/12*). Qing troops under Feng Guozhang retake Hankou.

3 (*9/13*). The Qing court issues a constitution with nineteen articles. The New Army revolts in Shanghai and the following day the whole city falls to the revolutionaries.

4 (*9/14*). The New Army revolts in Guizhou, which becomes independent of the Qing. The New Army revolts in Hangzhou; the revolutionaries' capture of the city is completed two days later.

5 (*9/15*). Jiangsu joins the revolution.

7 (*9/17*). Guangxi proclaims independence of the Qing.

8 (*9/18*). Anhui proclaims independence of the Qing.

9 (*9/19*). The New Army revolts in Fujian. Guangdong proclaims independence of the Qing. Li Yuanhong invites representatives of all provinces to Wuchang to discuss the establishment of a provisional central government.

13 (*9/23*). Shandong proclaims independence of the Qing.

16 (*9/26*). Yuan Shikai organizes a cabinet for the Qing.

27 (*10/7*). Sichuan's capital city, Chengdu, proclaims independence of the Qing. Qing troops retake Hanyang.

29 (*10/9*). On behalf of the Qing, Yuan Shikai cables Wuchang agreeing to a ceasefire.

30 (*10/10*). In Hankou, the representatives from all provinces hold a conference under the chairmanship of Tan Renfeng and declare the Hubei military government as the central military government.

December 2 (*10/12*). The revolutionary army takes Nanjing. The Hankou conference decides to set up a provisional government and draft a constitution; and to reserve the presidency for Yuan Shikai should he change sides.

4 (*10/14*). The Hankou conference decides on Nanjing as the capital of the provisional government.

25 (*11/6*). Sun Yatsen arrives in Shanghai from overseas.

24 *(1/26)*. A decree is issued that the use of torture in cross-examining people in courtrooms be ended immediately.

March 30 *(3/1)*. Wu Zonglian, China's minister in Italy, sends in a memorial suggesting that all schools set up Mandarin (*Guoyu*) faculties in order to unify the country's language.

April 29 *(4/1)*. Qinghua school in Peking begins classes with 460 students.

29–May 12 *(4/1–14)*. The National Education Union holds a conference in Shanghai.

May 8 *(4/10)*. The Ministry of Foreign Affairs and Britain sign a convention providing for continuing decrease in opium imports, and complete cessation at the end of 1917.

August 5 *(int. 6/11)*. In Shanghai, some 2000 women workers of the Xiehe and three other silk mills go on strike to oppose a wage reduction.

September 18 *(7/26)*. The carpenters of Shanghai's dockyards go on strike as a body for higher wages; they go back to work on September 22.

E Natural Disasters

March 1 *(2/1)*. The last plague case of the five-month epidemic in Manchuria is registered; it has killed some 60,000 people.

July 10 *(6/15)*. Rain and wind cause serious flooding in Changde (Hunan) and neighbouring areas.

August 26 *(7/3)*. Serious floods strike Fujian province.

30 *(7/7)*. In Zhili the Yongding River bursts its banks. In Shandong, Ji'nan and other areas are struck by floods.

September 4 *(7/12)*. Serious flooding occurs in Chaozhou and neighbouring areas of Guangdong.

12 *(7/20)*. In Wuhu (Anhui) the Yangzi watermark stands at 9.27 metres, the highest ever recorded, reflecting unprecedented flooding.

F Births and Deaths

March 4 *(2/4)*. The eunuch Li Lianying d. aged 63.

April 8 *(3/10)*. The acting Tartar General of Guangzhou, Fuqi, is assassinated by the revolutionary Wen Shengcai.

September 22 *(8/1)*. Prominent Buddhist layman Yang Wenhui d. aged 74.

November 9 *(9/19)*. The Viceroy of Minzhe Songshou commits suicide.

27 *(10/7)*. Duanfang is killed by his own men in Sichuan, aged 50.

1912 The Republic of China proclaimed

January 1. The Republic of China (ROC) is officially proclaimed.

3. The provisional government of the ROC is established.

5. President Sun announces his foreign policy: he recognizes the treaties signed by the Qing court with foreign nations, and agrees to protect foreign interests in China.

7. The New Army revolts in Yili (Xinjiang) which declares itself independent from the Qing.

16. An attempt to assassinate Yuan Shikai in Peking fails.

26. Directed by Yuan Shikai, Duan Qirui and over forty other Qing military leaders cable the Emperor demanding his abdication and declaring their allegiance to the ROC.

28. The provisional Senate holds its inaugural meeting in Nanjing with 38 senators from 17 provinces.

February 13. Yuan Shikai cables the ROC provisional government declaring his support for a republic. Sun Yatsen declares to the Senate his willingness to resign as President in favour of Yuan Shikai.

15. The Senate decides on Nanjing as China's capital.

29. The Third Division, led by Cao Kun, mutinies in Peking, looting and burning property in the city.

March 2. The military mutiny spreads to Baoding (Zhili).

3. Military mutiny breaks out in Tianjin (Zhili).

About 2000 British, US, French, German and Japanese troops arrive in Peking as the foreign powers become alarmed at the military mutinies.

10. The Senate adopts the revised provisional constitution of the ROC, which Sun Yatsen proclaims the following day.

15. Yuan Shikai orders that the previous titles *zongdu* (viceroy) and *xunfu* (governor) be changed to *dudu* (military governor).

April 2. The Senate decides to transfer the provisional government to Peking.

6. A clash occurs between Chinese troops in Lhasa and local Tibetan troops.

29. The Senate is formally inaugurated in Peking by Yuan Shikai. The United League transfers its headquarters to Peking.

May 5. At a meeting in Shanghai, several political parties amalgamate to form the pro-Yuan Shikai Republican Party.

10. British troops move into Tibet and take Yadong and Gyantse.

12. Yuan Shikai prohibits private organizations from participation in politics.

June 1. Russian troops invade Yili (Xinjiang).

8. The Senate adopts the five-coloured flag as the national flag.

Sun Yatsen resigns as provisional President in **1912**
favour of Yuan Shikai

A Economics

February 5. The Great Qing Bank is renamed the Bank of China.
March 15. Yuan Shikai signs a contract with a syndicate of Russian, French, Belgian and British financiers for a loan of £10,000,000 for government administration and the relief of the people.
   24. The Bank of Guangzhou begins operating.
May 17. The Ministry of Finance concludes a contract for the loan of 76,000,000 taels from the Four-power Consortium (UK, France, Germany, and USA).
June 1. A substantially reduced internal telegraph tariff comes into force.
   7–20. Representatives of banks from six powers, UK, USA, France, Germany, Russia, and Japan (the International Group), meet in Paris and arrange terms for a gigantic loan to China.
   21. The whole of the railway from Tianjin to Pukou (Jiangsu) opens for traffic, apart from the bridge over the Yellow River.
August 1. The Bank of China begins operations.
   30. In London the Chinese government signs a contract with C. Brich Crisp and Co. of London for a loan of £10,000,000.
September 24. China concludes a contract with a Belgian syndicate for a loan of 250,000,000 francs to build a railway from Luoyang (Henan) to Xi'an (Shaanxi).
October 1. The Jilin–Changchun railway in Jilin province begins taking traffic.
   21. A new scale of stamp duties is proclaimed.
November 16. Work is completed on the bridge over the Yellow River near Ji'nan on the Tianjin–Pukou railway.

B Official Appointments, Dismissals, Resignations etc.

January 1. In Nanjing Sun Yatsen takes up the position of provisional President of the ROC.
   3. The provincial representatives select Li Yuanhong as provisional Vice-President of the ROC.
February 12. The Emperor issues an edict of abdication and appoints Yuan Shikai as plenipotentiary to form a republican government.
   14. The Senate accepts Sun Yatsen's resignation as provisional President of the ROC.
   15. The Senate appoints Yuan Shikai as provisional President of the ROC.
   20. The Senate appoints Li Yuanhong as provisional Vice-President of the ROC.

1912

13. A military mutiny breaks out in Ji'nan (Shandong), but is soon suppressed.

July 10. At the head of some 2500 men the Governor of Sichuan, Yin Changheng, departs on a military expedition to Tibet to suppress the disorders there.

20. A military mutiny erupts in the Anhui provincial capital, Anqing.

August 10. General elections of China's first regular parliament and of new provincial assemblies begin with the promulgation of the organic laws of the Senate and House of Representatives, and of electoral laws and regulations.

17. The British minister in Peking, Sir John Jordan, sends a note to the Ministry of Foreign Affairs, asking that Yin Changheng's military expedition be stopped from entering Tibet, and calling for Tibetan self-determination.

19. 'Rules for the Treatment of Mongolia' are promulgated, under which Mongolia is to be placed on an equal footing with other Chinese provinces.

24–25. A serious mutiny takes place in Tongzhou (Zhili).

25. The United League and other bodies hold a Party congress in Peking to mark their amalgamation and reformation into the Nationalist Party (NP) to campaign in the general elections.

September 28. October 10 (Double Ten) is promulgated as the ROC's National Day.

October 10. The first National Day celebrations are held.

November 3. In Urga, Russia and Mongolia sign a trade and friendship agreement under which Russia will 'give its aid to Mongolia in order that Mongolia may maintain its independence'.

7. The Ministry of Foreign Affairs informs the Russian minister of its view that Mongolia is part of China and thus has no right to sign treaties with another country.

9. The Russian minister, M.B. Kroupensky, notifies China of the contents of the Russo-Mongolian agreement. The Chinese government protests against the conclusion of the treaty as an infringement of China's sovereignty.

December 9. The British minister protests to the Ministry of Foreign Affairs over the ban on opium.

10. A military mutiny breaks out in Nanchang, the capital of Jiangxi.

23. The Ministry of Foreign Affairs replies to Britain's August 17 communication over Tibet. It affirms China's right to send troops to Tibet, but denies any intention to make Tibet a province of China.

1912

March 10. Yuan Shikai is inaugurated as the new provisional President of the ROC in Peking.
    13. Yuan Shikai appoints Tang Shaoyi as Premier.
    29. The Senate approves the cabinet list submitted by Tang Shaoyi.
April 1. Sun Yatsen formally resigns as provisional President.
June 15. Tang Shaoyi resigns as Premier by suddenly leaving Peking.
    27. Yuan Shikai announces his acceptance of Tang Shaoyi's resignation.
    29. The Senate appoints Lu Zhengxiang as Premier.
July 14. The resignations of five cabinet ministers are announced. They include four members of the United League, Cai Yuanpei, Song Jiaoren, Wang Zhengting and Wang Chonghui.
    26. The Senate yields to pressure from Yuan Shikai and appoints his nominees to several cabinet vacancies.
August 1. Yuan Shikai appoints the Australian G.E. Morrison as his political adviser.
    25. Sun Yatsen is elected first Chairman of the NP at the Party's congress.
September 7. Yuan Shikai appoints Li Yuanhong, Huang Xing and Duan Qirui as Generals.
    25. Zhao Bingjun is appointed Premier (Lu Zhengxiang having resigned because of illness).

C Cultural and Social

January 23. Twelve countries, including China, sign the International Opium Convention in The Hague.
February 24. The Nanjing government abolishes the traditional appellations like *daren* and replaces them with Mr (*xiansheng*) or Sir (*jun*).
    25. China's first boy scout group is set up at the Wenhua School in Wuchang (Hubei).
March 2. Sun Yatsen orders bans on opium and the buying and selling of people.
    11. Sun Yatsen issues an order to ban the binding of women's feet and corporal punishment.
    19. Datong Academy is set up in Shanghai. In the Senate, women demand the right to take part in politics equally with men.
April 13. Yuan Shikai issues a statement encouraging intermarriage between the different nationalities, Han, Mongolians, Tibetans, Moslems and Manchus.
May. The Ministry of Education transmits orders to all provinces to revise the curricula in primary schools. The study of classics is to be

1913 The 'Second Revolution' fails

January 10. Mongolia and Tibet conclude an alliance under which each recognizes the other's independence.

March 20. The NP leader Song Jiaoren is shot at the Shanghai railway station.

25. Sun Yatsen, Huang Xing and others meet in Shanghai to decide on action against Yuan Shikai for Song Jiaoren's murder.

April 8. The National Assembly, including the Senate and House of Representatives, holds its inaugural meeting, with nearly half the constituents being NP members. The provisional Senate disbands. Brazil formally recognizes the ROC.

28. Premier Zhao Bingjun sends a telegram to Vice-President Li Yuanhong and others defending himself against documentary evidence implicating him in the murder of Song Jiaoren.

29. The Senate declares the £25,000,000 loan of April 26 as null and void.

May 2. The US and Mexican governments officially recognize the ROC.

abolished and military training, handicrafts and technical education to be increased.

June 11. The secret planting of the opium poppy is banned in China.

July 10–August 10. The Ministry of Education holds a Provisional Education Conference in Peking.

September 2. The Ministry of Education proclaims that the moral, technical and military aspects of education should take precedence.

3. The Ministry of Education issues guidelines on the education system. It stipulates that the new system should include four years' compulsory primary schooling.

October 8. A presidential mandate repeats the Qing ban on gambling.

October–December. The China Bookshop opens in Shanghai.

D PUBLICATIONS

Wang Guowei completes his *Song Yuan xiqu shi* (*History of Drama in the Song and Yuan*).

F BIRTHS AND DEATHS

January 29. The monarchist Liangbi d. aged 35.
February 15. Musician Nie Er b. (d. 1935).

Song Jiaoren assassinated   1913

A ECONOMICS

April 10. The Ministries of the Navy and Finance sign contracts to cover a total loan of £3,200,000 to purchase eighteen torpedo-boat destroyers from the Austrian firm Arnhold, Karberg and Co. of Peking.

27. Premier Zhao Bingjun and others, representing the ROC government, sign a contract for a loan of £25,000,000 with five banks, the Hongkong and Shanghai Banking Corporation (British), Deutsch-Asiatische Bank (German), Banque de l'Indo-Chine (French), Russo-Asiatic Bank (Russian) and Yokohama Specie Bank (Japanese). The contract is dated April 26 but the signing actually took place in the early hours of April 27.

June 8. The Hunan section of the Guangzhou–Hankou railway is nationalized.

12. The Shanghai–Hangzhou–Ningbo railway is nationalized.

November 7. An order is issued to all provinces against flooding the market with paper money.

1913

4. Cuba recognizes the ROC.
5. Acting Premier Duan Qirui appears before the House of Representatives to defend the £25,000,000 loan, in response to which the House votes to reject the government's notification of the loan. Disturbance continues through the month in the National Assembly over the loan.
7. Yuan Shikai orders all provinces to prevent revolutionary movements.
29. In order to oppose the NP effectively the Republican and two other Parties unite to form the Progressive Party, led by Li Yuanhong.
31. Under government pressure the NP organization in Nanjing is closed down.

July 10. Yuan Shikai issues an order prohibiting army men from joining any political party.
12. Li Liejun organizes a revolutionary army in Hukou (Jiangxi), and declares himself independent of Yuan Shikai. The 'Second Revolution' begins.
15. Huang Xing arrives in Nanjing to organize an anti-Yuan army. The military governor of Jiangsu, Cheng Dequan, is forced to declare independence from Yuan.
17. Anhui declares independence from Yuan Shikai's government.
18. The Governor of Guangdong, Chen Jiongmin, declares his opposition to Yuan and his province's independence.
23. Anti-Yuan troops attack the Jiangnan arsenal in Shanghai but fail to take it.
25. Tan Yankai, the military governor of Hunan, declares independence. Northern troops under Duan Zhigui take Hukou (Jiangxi); the anti-Yuan army retreats towards Nanchang, capital of Jiangxi.
29. Cheng Dequan retracts his declaration of independence from Yuan Shikai; Huang Xing retreats to Shanghai.

August 3. Military mutiny breaks out in Guangzhou; Chen Jiongming escapes, arriving in Hongkong the following day.
7. The anti-Yuan army of Anhui is defeated, Bo Wenwei flees, Anhui's independence is retracted.
10. Yuan Shikai has several members of both houses of the National Assembly arrested for stirring up rebellion.
11. In Nanjing He Haiming declares himself Commander-in-Chief of the anti-Yuan forces and announces independence. General Long Jiguang's pro-Yuan troops enter Guangzhou.
13. The anti-Yuan army in Shanghai is defeated. Tan Yankai declares his retraction of Hunan's independence.
18. Pro-Yuan troops peacefully reoccupy Nanchang.

8. The Chinese government signs a contract with the Banque Industrielle de Chine for a loan of 150,000,000 francs to be spent on harbour works in Pukou, a bridge over the Yangzi from Wuchang to Hankou, and other things.
14. The Ministries of Finance and Communications conclude a contract with the British and Chinese Corporation for a loan of £3,000,000 to build a railway from Xinyang (Henan) to Pukou (Jiangsu).
December 24. Yuan Shikai promulgates a law governing the collection of salt duty.

B OFFICIAL APPOINTMENTS, DISMISSALS, RESIGNATIONS ETC.

May 1. Premier Zhao Bingjun, suspected of having Song Jiaoren assassinated, temporarily resigns for 'health' reasons. Duan Qirui, the Minister of the Army, replaces him as acting Premier.
June 9. Yuan Shikai dismisses the military governor of Jiangxi, Li Liejun, an NP member; Li Yuanhong replaces him.
14. Yuan Shikai dismisses the military governor of Guangdong and NP member Hu Hanmin, and replaces him with Chen Jiongming.
30. Yuan Shikai dismisses the military governor of Anhui, Bo Wenwei, a member of the NP.
July 13. The Jiangxi provincial assembly declares Ouyang Wu military governor and Li Liejun as Commander-in-Chief of the anti-Yuan army.
16. Yuan Shikai appoints Duan Zhigui as General and Pacification Commissioner of Jiangxi with orders to suppress the rebellion in that province.
31. Yuan Shikai appoints Xiong Xiling as Premier.
August 3. Long Jiguang is appointed military governor of Guangdong.
September 3. Zhang Xun replaces Cheng Dequan as Governor of Jiangsu.
11. Xiong Xiling's 'first-class' cabinet is appointed and announced.
October 6. The National Assembly, under pressure, elects Yuan Shikai as President on the third ballot.
10. Yuan Shikai and Li Yuanhong are formally inaugurated as President and Vice-President respectively.

C CULTURAL AND SOCIAL

February 1–9. China takes part in the first Far Eastern Games, held in Manila.
15. Some 80 phoneticians gather from all over China for a three-week

1913

27. Yuan Shikai has eight members of the House of Representatives and the Senate arrested.

September 1. Pro-Yuan troops under Zhang Xun retake Nanjing after strong resistance; the 'Second Revolution' ends. The city is looted for three days and many are killed, including three Japanese.

28. Zhang Xun goes to the Japanese consulate in Nanjing to apologize for the death of the three Japanese on September 1.

October 6. The ministers of the UK, Russia, France, Italy, Japan and eight other countries notify the Ministry of Foreign Affairs of recognition of Yuan Shikai's new government.

9. US President Woodrow Wilson congratulates Yuan Shikai on being elected President.

13. Yuan Shikai issues an order to the military governor of Jiangxi to arrest those members of the provincial assembly who had joined the anti-Yuan army. The Simla conference on Tibet opens under the chairmanship of Sir A.H. McMahon. The UK, China and Tibet are represented.

25. Yuan Shikai cables every province's senior officials opposing the draft constitution just drawn up by the Constitutional Drafting Committee.

November 4. Yuan Shikai orders the dissolution of the NP and the cancellation of its parliamentary membership. This measure was carried efficiently into effect, resulting in the National Assembly's inability to meet through lack of a quorum.

In Peking, Russia and China sign an agreement under which China recognizes the autonomy of Outer Mongolia, and Russia that Outer Mongolia is 'part of Chinese territory'.

10. The Constitutional Drafting Committee is automatically dissolved, following the dismissal of the NP members of the National Assembly.

12. Yuan Shikai orders the dismissal of all NP provincial assemblymen.

26. Yuan Shikai issues an order to convene a Political Council to replace the National Assembly.

December 15. The Political Council holds its inaugural meeting.

meeting, sponsored by the Ministry of Education, to standardize the Chinese phonetic script.

April. Wuchang's Zhonghua Academy is changed into Zhonghua University.

May 29. In Hanyang the workers of the arsenal go on strike for higher wages, resuming normal work on June 4.

D PUBLICATIONS

January. Luo Zhenyu completes his *Yinxu shuqi qianbian* (*Anyang Inscriptions, First Part*).

February. The monthlies *Buren* (*We Can't Bear It*) and *Kongjiao hui zazhi* (*Magazine of the Confucianism Society*) begin publication.

April 15. NP branches in Tokyo begin publishing *Guomin zazhi* (*Nationalist Magazine*).

May 20. The NP begins publication of the *Guomin yuekan* (*The Nationalist Monthly*) in Shanghai.

E NATURAL DISASTERS

January 26. An explosion at the Tangshan (Zhili) coal mines kills several tens of people.

June 17. News is cabled of serious flooding in Lingchuan and several other places in north-east Guangxi.

27. News of severe flooding in Tongling and several other parts of southern Anhui is cabled.

29. News is cabled of severe flooding in several parts of northern Hunan in June; many people are drowned.

September 2. The military governor of Shanxi, Yan Xishan, cables asking for relief to fight serious flooding which has struck Yangqu and other places in central Shanxi.

December 21. An earthquake strikes the provincial capital of Yunnan, Kunming. Some three-quarters of residences collapse and many people are crushed to death.

F BIRTHS AND DEATHS

February 22. The Qing Empress Longyu d. aged 44.
March 22. Song Jiaoren d. aged 31.
April 24. Wu Shiying, Song Jiaoren's assassin, d. in a Shanghai prison.
July 12. Historian and scholar Shen Jiaben d. aged 72.

1914 Japan invades Shandong as World War I breaks out

January 10. Yuan Shikai orders the formal suspension of both houses of the National Assembly.

11. Rebels led by Bai Lang seize Guangshan (Henan).

February 3. Yuan Shikai orders the dissolution of local self-government bodies.

28. Yuan Shikai issues an order to dissolve the provincial assemblies.

March 1. China formally joins the Universal Postal Union.

2. Yuan Shikai promulgates the Security Police Acts.

6. Disturbances break out in Yuxian (Shanxi); they are suppressed and over forty people are killed.

15. Li Zhengpin revolts with over 2000 men in Dongchuan (Yunnan), but is soon suppressed.

29. A rebel force in Dingyuan (Anhui) seizes the county capital, but is defeated and ejected on March 31.

May 1. Yuan Shikai annuls the provisional constitution of March 11, 1912, and promulgates the Constitutional Compact which provides for an elected House of Legislature and a Council of State. He abolishes the cabinet and the post of Premier, replacing them with the Board of Political Affairs and Secretary of State respectively.

4. The Bai Lang rebels, having moved from Henan to Gansu, through Shaanxi, seize Qinzhou (Gansu).

23. Yuan Shikai promulgates a new system of provincial government under which civil power is vested in a Governor.

June 2. Bai Lang's rebel troops are defeated in Fuqiang (Gansu).

30. Yuan Shikai abolishes the post of provincial military governor, replacing it with that of General-in-Chief.

July 3. At the Simla Conference Britain and Tibet conclude a treaty, the Simla Convention, never ratified by China. Britain recognizes the autonomy of Tibet.

8. The Chinese Revolutionary Party holds its founding congress in Tokyo, with Sun Yatsen as Premier (*zongli*).

28. World War I breaks out in Europe.

August 6. China declares its neutrality in the European war.

12. China's neutrality in the world war is accepted by all nations.

15. Japan issues an ultimatum to Germany demanding the withdrawal of all German fleets from Chinese seas and the handing over to Japan, by September 15, of the leased territory of Qingdao (Shandong), with a view to its return to China.

23. Japan declares war on Germany.

September 1. Sun Yatsen proclaims the manifesto of the Chinese Revolutionary Party and pledges its unity to achieve the third revolution. The Universal Postal Convention and Parcel Post Convention

The National Currency Law promulgated 1914

A ECONOMICS

January 8. Guihua (now Huhehot), Zhangjiakou (Zhili), Chifeng (now in Liaoning) and four other cities are ordered open to international trade.
21. The Peking government settles a contract with the Banque Industrielle de Chine for a loan of 600,000,000 francs to build a 1000-mile railway from Qinzhou (Guangxi) to Chongqing (Sichuan).
February 7. The National Currency Law is promulgated, restricting the right of minting and issuing of national currency to the government alone, naming the unit of national coin *yuan*, and fixing silver as the standard.
12. The Chinese government concludes a contract with the US Standard Oil Company for the joint exploitation of petroleum in Yanchang (Shaanxi), and other places in Shaanxi and Zhili.
March 3. The railways of Anhui province are nationalized.
9. The Chinese government signs a contract with the British and Chinese Corporation for £8,000,000 to be spent on a railway from Nanjing to Zhuzhou (Hunan).
April 11. The railways of Zhejiang are nationalized.
July 3. China begins payment of compensation to six European nations and the USA for losses sustained during the Revolution of 1911.
October 4. China and Russia conclude a contract to build a railway from Tsitsihar (Heilongjiang) to Aigun with Russian capital.
November 11. The oil wells at Yanchang (Shaanxi) start operations.

B OFFICIAL APPOINTMENTS, DISMISSALS, RESIGNATIONS ETC.

February 12. Yuan Shikai accepts the resignation of Premier Xiong Xiling and appoints Sun Baoqi in his place.
May 1. Yuan Shikai appoints Xu Shichang as Secretary of State.

C CULTURAL AND SOCIAL

February 7. Regulations are promulgated for ceremonies of sacrifice to Heaven and to commemorate Confucius.
8. Yuan Shikai orders all provinces to intensify the protection of Christian churches and missionaries as the suppression of Bai Lang's rebel movement proceeds.
March 11. The Nanyuan Aviation School in Peking conducts its first experimental flights.
June 9. Peking's first Western-style theatre, *Diyi wutai* (First Stage) is established.

1914

come into operation in China.

2. Japanese troops land at Longkou and other places in Shandong.

9. Representatives of China, Russia and Outer Mongolia begin a meeting in Kiakhta, Outer Mongolia, to negotiate Outer Mongolia's status *vis-à-vis* China, their mutual border and other problems.

25. Some 400 Japanese troops occupy the railway station of Weixian (Shandong), and arrest several Chinese; one person is killed.

October 6. Japanese troops occupy Ji'nan railway station, Shandong. The Ministry of Foreign Affairs protests against Japan's westward invasion.

22. The organization of the Chinese Revolutionary Party in Hangzhou is raided; over twenty people are arrested and shot on suspicion of plotting against the government.

November 7. Japanese troops occupy Qingdao, 2300 German troops are captured, and the German garrison surrenders.

10. Germany formally hands Qingdao over to the Japanese.

December 3. The Japanese minister to Peking, Hioki Eki, receives from his government the text of Twenty-one Demands on China with instructions that they be handed to the Chinese government.

24. The Tianjin mint produces a new coin, depicting Yuan Shikai's head.

29. Yuan Shikai promulgates a revised Presidential Election Law, under which the President's term of office is ten years, but he is eligible for re-election.

1914

12. A religious society, called the Republican Society of the Ten Thousand Buddhas, is discovered in the Shandong-Henan-Jiangsu border areas. It is somewhat similar to the Righteous and Harmonious Militia and the government orders the arrest of its members.

September 1. The Institute of Chinese History opens.

December 4. Publication laws are promulgated.

23. Yuan Shikai performs a ceremony of sacrifice to Heaven at the Temple of Heaven in Peking.

D Publications

Kang Liang shichao (*Transcribed Poems of Kang Youwei and Liang Qichao*) and *Linyi xiaoshuo congshu* (*Collection of Lin's Novel Translations*) by Lin Shu are published in Shanghai.

January. The monthly *Zhengyi* (*Justice*) begins publication in Shanghai, expressing disappointment over Yuan Shikai.

May 10. The monthly *Jiayin zazhi* (*1914 Magazine*) begins publication in Tokyo under the editorship of Zhang Shizhao; it advocates liberal constitutional government.

E Natural Disasters

May–June. Owing to serious drought, a locust plague strikes Jiangsu, Anhui, Shandong and other provinces, especially in the regions north of the Yangzi River.

June–July. About 1400 square miles of Guangdong, Guangxi, Hunan, Jiangxi and other provinces are struck by severe floods. Many people are drowned, much property is destroyed.

August 3. The Governor of Henan reports that drought has reached disaster proportions in his province, covering over forty-five counties.

November 18. The Yellow River floods at Puyang (Henan).

F Births and Deaths

February 27. Zhao Bingjun d.

March 3. Taiwan anti-Japanese revolutionary Luo Fuxing d.

August 5. Bai Lang d. in Henan of a serious wound, signalling the total defeat of his rebellion.

1915   The Twenty-one Demands

January 18. The Japanese minister to Peking, Hioki Eki, presents the 'Twenty-one Demands' to Yuan Shikai, asking him to keep them secret.

20. Hioki Eki formally presents the Twenty-one Demands to the Ministry of Foreign Affairs.

27. Japan publicly denies having made the Twenty-one Demands to China.

February 2. The Chinese Minister of Foreign Affairs, Lu Zhengxiang, and Hioki Eki hold their first negotiation conference on the Twenty-one Demands.

March 10. The Chinese Revolutionary Party denounces the Twenty-one Demands and calls on its members to try to overthrow Yuan Shikai.

18. At an anti-Japanese mass rally in Shanghai, a resolution is adopted to boycott Japanese goods. Some 360 Japanese troops enter Shenyang (Fengtian).

25. Yuan Shikai prohibits the boycott against Japanese goods.

April 17. At the twenty-fourth negotiation conference, Sino-Japanese talks on the Twenty-one Demands break up without full agreement.

26. Japan proposes amendments to the Twenty-one Demands, enabling negotiations to proceed; among the changes is the withdrawal of the demand for the appointment of Japanese police advisers.

May 7. Hioki Eki sends an ultimatum on the amended Twenty-one Demands to China, demanding a reply by 6 p.m. on May 9.

8. A ministerial meeting held by Yuan Shikai decides to accept Japan's amended Twenty-one Demands.

9. The Ministry of Foreign Affairs acknowledges the ultimatum sent by Japan.

13. In Hankou, Chinese businessmen clash with Japanese celebrating China's surrender; several Japanese shops are ransacked.

25. The Sino-Japanese Treaties, based on the Twenty-one Demands, are signed by Lu Zhengxiang and Hioki Eki.

June 7. At Kiakhta, China, Russia and Outer Mongolia sign an agreement under which Outer Mongolia recognizes itself as part of Chinese territory, but China and Russia recognize the autonomy of Outer Mongolia.

8. Japan and China exchange and ratify the Sino-Japanese Treaties.

29. Yuan Shikai prohibits boycotts against foreign goods.

July 17. An assassination attempt against the General-in-chief of Guangdong, Long Jiguang, in Guangzhou fails.

August 23. The Society for Planning Peace announces its establishment. It aims to promote the monarchical system.

Youth Magazine begins publication · 1915

A ECONOMICS

February 3. The Nanchang–Jiujiang (Jiangxi) railway starts taking traffic.
  21. The Xinhua Savings Bank starts operations.
March 17. China and Japan sign a contract for an underwater telegraphic cable from Wusong near Shanghai to Nagasaki.
June. The Fuzhong Corporation in Henan is founded through a merger of two coal-mining companies, one of them British, the other Chinese.
  1. Pukou (Jiangsu) opens as a trading port.
  8. The Kaifeng (Henan)–Xuzhou (Jiangsu) railway begins taking traffic.
September 1. The railway from Zhangjiakou (Zhili) to Fengzhen (Inner Mongolia) opens to traffic.
November 1. Longkou (Shandong) opens to international trade.
December 1. In accordance with one of the Twenty-one Demands the administration of the Jilin–Changchun railway is transferred to the Japanese.

B OFFICIAL APPOINTMENTS, DISMISSALS, RESIGNATIONS ETC.

December 15. Yuan Shikai enfeoffs Li Yuanhong as a Prince.

C CULTURAL AND SOCIAL

January 1. Wireless telegraph stations are set up in Guangzhou and Wusong.
March 17. Yuan Shikai holds a ceremony in honour of Confucius.
April 23–May 12. The National Union of Educational Associations holds its first congress in Tianjin.
May 15–22. The second Far Eastern Games are held in Shanghai.
September. The Nanjing Women's Union College formally begins work.
  10. The Nanjing Higher Normal College holds its opening ceremony.
December 20. The Ministry of Education opens a training school in Peking for the trial of the phonetic script and invites the provinces to send students to take part.
  22. Yuan Shikai institutes a system of female palace attendants in place of the eunuchs of the past.

1915

September 1. The Council of State meets, representing the House of Legislature; it hears calls for a change in the structure of the state, specifically the re-establishment of the system of monarchy.

11. Chinese and Russian troops clash in Harbin.

October 8. Yuan Shikai promulgates the Law on the Organization of the Convention of Citizens' Representatives, the body which is to vote on whether or not to re-establish the monarchy.

25. In Ji'nan (Shandong), some Japanese shoot and wound seven Chinese policemen.

28. The British, Japanese and Russian envoys urge the Ministry of Foreign Affairs to postpone the re-establishment of the monarchy.

December 5. Chen Qimei and other revolutionaries in Shanghai attack the Jiangnan arsenal and revolt against the Peking government, but are soon put down.

11. The House of Legislature scrutinizes the votes of the members of the Convention of Citizens' Representatives on the subject of the re-establishment of the monarchy. The result is 1993 in favour, none against.

15. Japan, Russia, Britain, France and Italy again urge the Ministry of Foreign Affairs to postpone the re-establishment of the monarchy in China.

22. The General-in-chief of Yunnan, Tang Jiyao, the Governor of Yunnan, Ren Kechen, the former military governor of Yunnan, Cae E, and others hold a meeting in Kunming and decide to oppose Yuan Shikai's monarchical plan and defend the republic.

23. Tang Jiyao and Ren Kechen cable the Peking government issuing an ultimatum that unless they have heard by December 25 that Yuan has abandoned his monarchical plans Yunnan will declare independence.

25. Cai E, Tang Jiyao, Ren Kecheng, Li Liejun and others declare the independence of Yunnan. They organize the National Protection Army to fight the monarchists.

31. Yuan Shikai orders that the following year be 'the first year of Hongxian'.

1915

D Publications

Linsu Laoren nianpu (*Chronology of Yang Shoujing's Life*) by Yang Shoujing and others is published.

January 1. *Kexue zazhi* (*Science Magazine*) begins publication.

  20. Liang Qichao's monthly *Da Zhonghua* (*Great China*) begins publication in Shanghai.

August 3. The American F.J. Goodnow, Yuan Shikai's constitutional adviser, publishes his essay 'Republic or Monarchy?' advocating the monarchical system for China.

  26. Yang Du, head of the Society for Planning Peace, publishes his 'Junxian jiuguo lun' ('On Constitutional Monarchy and National Salvation') in defence of monarchy.

September 3. Liang Qichao publishes his 'Yizai suowei guoti wenti zhe' ('This Strange So-called Problem of State Structure') against the re-establishment of monarchy.

  15. *Qingnian zazhi* (*Youth Magazine*), the predecessor of *Xin Qingnian* (*New Youth*), begins publication in Shanghai under the editorship of Chen Duxiu.

October 10. The *Zhonghua xinbao* (*New China Daily*) begins publication in Shanghai.

E Natural Disasters

February 1. An explosion and fire at the Zhongxing coal mines near Yanzhou (Shandong) kill some 500 miners.

May 26. The Yellow River bursts its dykes at Puyang (Henan).

June 23. Severe floods strike parts of Anhui, Jiangxi, Hunan and Hubei.

July–September. A locust plague afflicts Hubei.

July 27–28. A typhoon strikes the coastal provinces of Jiangsu and Zhejiang, causing tidal waves. Several tens of thousands are killed or injured. Torrential rains also cause flooding in parts of Shandong and the Manchurian provinces.

F Births and Deaths

January 9. Calligrapher, geographer and bibliographer Yang Shoujing d. aged 75.

February 11. Sun Yatsen's elder brother, Dezhang, d. aged 60.

November 10. Men sent by Chen Qimei assassinate Zheng Rucheng, Garrison Commander of Shanghai.

1916 *Yuan Shikai's plan to restore the monarchy is defeated*

January 6. Chen Jiongming begins a rebellion against Yuan Shikai's supporter Long Jiguang, the General-in-chief of Guangdong, by attacking Huizhou (Guangdong).
20. The First Army of the National Protection Army moves into Sichuan and enters Xuzhou, occupying it the following day.
27. Liu Xianshi proclaims Guizhou's independence.
February 6. The National Protection Army takes Luzhou (Sichuan).
18. A revolt by the Chinese Revolutionary Party in Wuchang is put down.
March 1. Troops under Feng Yuxiang defeat the National Protection Army at Xuzhou (Sichuan), reoccupying the city.
15. Lu Rongting declares Guangxi independent of the Peking government.
18. The First Army of the National Protection Army, having mounted a counterattack, takes Jiang'an and Nanchuan (Sichuan).
22. Yuan Shikai declares the abandonment of his plan to become Emperor.
30. The General-in-chief of Sichuan, Chen Yi, a close friend of Yuan's, cables Cai E supporting Cai's demand for Yuan Shikai's overthrow.
April 6. Long Jiguang declares Guangdong's independence.
12. Zhejiang declares independence.
14. Negotiations take place in Haizhu, near Guangzhou, between the representatives of the pro-Yuan Long Jiguang and those of Lu Rongting and Liang Qichao. Long has Liang's and Lu's representatives killed. This is known as the Haizhu Incident.
21. Yuan Shikai proclaims the re-establishment of a cabinet system, headed by a Secretary of State. This indicates a further retreat of Yuan's power.
May 4. Ju Zheng of the Chinese Revolutionary Party leads an anti-Yuan Shikai rising in Shandong by occupying positions beside the Ji'nan–Qingdao railway and attacking Weixian.
8. Leaders of the National Protection Army formally set up the Military Affairs Council in Zhaoqing (Guangdong), to act as the government of China as long as Yuan Shikai remains in office.
9. Chen Shufan, the Garrison Commander of Southern Shaanxi, declares his province's independence.
14. The Huimin Corporation, organized by Liang Shiyi to recruit Chinese labourers to assist in the European war, signs a contract with France under which about 200,000 Chinese served in France and elsewhere during the war.
15. Some 600 men of the Chinese Revolutionary Party enter Ji'nan

A Economics

March. The Anshan iron works are established with Sino-Japanese capital.

28. The Chinese government signs a contract with the Russo-Asiatic Bank for a loan of £5,000,000 to build a railway from Harbin to Aigun (Heilongjiang).

August. The half-brothers Zhou Xuexi and Zhou Xuehui set up the Huaxin cotton mill in Tianjin.

September 30. The Minister of Communications, Cao Rulin, signs a contract with the American Siems Carey Railway and Canal Co. for a loan of US $10,000,000 for five railway lines with a total of some 1100 miles (a revision of a contract originally signed May 17).

November 16. Because of opposition from Britain, France and Russia to the September 30 loan from the USA, a revised Sino-US contract is signed, reducing the sum and changing the proposed railway lines.

B Official Appointments, Dismissals, Resignations etc.

January 1. Tang Jiyao becomes military governor of the independent Yunnan military government.

27. Liu Xianshi takes over as military governor of independent Guizhou.

February 1. Liu Cunhou takes over as Sichuan Commander-in-Chief of the National Protection Army.

March 15. Lu Rongting becomes military governor of Guangxi and Commander-in-Chief of the National Protection Army of Guangdong and Guangxi.

22. Yuan Shikai appoints Xu Shichang as Secretary of State.

April 23. Yuan Shikai appoints the cabinet, with Duan Qirui as Secretary of State.

June 7. Li Yuanhong succeeds Yuan Shikai as President.

29. Duan Qirui is appointed Premier.

30. Li Yuanhong appoints his various ministers.

July 6. Li Yuanhong appoints the provincial military governors and governors.

October 30. The National Assembly elects Feng Guozhang as Vice-President.

December 26. Li Yuanhong appoints Cai Yuanpei as Vice-Chancellor of Peking University.

1916

and attack the offices of the General-in-chief of Shandong, but are defeated.

22. Chen Yi declares Sichuan's independence of Yuan Shikai's government.

26. In the face of attacks from Chen Shufan's forces, the General-in-chief of Shaanxi, Lu Jianzhang, withdraws from the capital, Xi'an.

29. Hunan declares independence.

June 4. Several hundred men under Chinese Revolutionary Party leadership again launch an attack on Ji'nan but are defeated.

7. Chen Shufan retracts the independence of Shaanxi.

8. Chen Yi retracts the independence of Sichuan.

9. Long Jiguang retracts the independence of Guangdong. Zhang Xun holds his first interprovincial conference at Xuzhou (Jiangsu) with the aim of securing solidarity among the Beiyang group against the southern military leaders.

29. Li Yuanhong orders the restoration of the ROC provisional constitution of March 11, 1912, and abolishes the Council of State.

July 6. Li Yuanhong orders that the title of the senior civil provincial official be changed from *xun'an shi* to *shengzhang* (governor) and military official from *jiangjun* (general-in-chief) to *dujun* (military governor).

14. Li Yuanhong orders the arrest of the leading monarchist advocates: Yang Du, Liang Shiyi and others. (Both Yang and Liang fled and escaped.) Tang Jiyao and others announce the dissolution of the Military Affairs Council set up on May 8.

August 1. The National Assembly dissolved in 1914 reconvenes.

13. Chinese and Japanese troops clash in Zhengjiatun, Liaoyuan (Fengtian), with casualties on both sides.

September 21. The military governor of Anhui, Zhang Xun, holds his second Xuzhou conference.

October 1. The provincial assemblies dissolved in 1914 reconvene.

20. Germany protests to the Ministry of Foreign Affairs over France's hiring of 30,000 Chinese labourers for service in the European war.

December 19. Military personnel are forbidden to join any political party.

C CULTURAL AND SOCIAL

February 7–12. In Shanghai the Chinese National Medical Association holds its first annual conference.
March. Workers in the printing office of the Ministry of Finance in Peking go on strike.
October 10–25. The National Union of Educational Associations holds its second congress in Peking.
November 1–20. The Ministry of Education holds an education administration conference.
　26. More than 1000 Chinese shipbuilders in the Jiangnan dockyard go on strike in protest against police brutality.

D PUBLICATIONS

June. *Kang Nanhai wenchao* (*Prose Works of Kang Youwei*) is published in Shanghai.
September 1. 'Qingchun' ('Spring') by Li Dazhao published in Vol. II, No. 1 of *Xin qingnian*, appearing for the first time under that title.

E NATURAL DISASTERS

August 12. Many parts of Jiangsu north of the Yangzi are reported seriously affected by flood.

F BIRTHS AND DEATHS

April 27. Sheng Xuanhuai d. aged 71.
May 18. Chen Qimei assassinated in Shanghai, aged 38.
June 6. Yuan Shikai d. aged 56.
August. Zhang Bishi d. aged 76.
October 6. Jiang Weiguo, Chiang Kaishek's son, b.
　20. Wang Kaiyun, former director of the Institute of Chinese History, d. aged 83.
　31. Huang Xing d. in Shanghai aged 42.
November 8. Cai E d. in Japan aged 33.

1917 *China declares war on Germany; the Guangzhou military government is established; civil war breaks out*

January 11. Zhang Xun concludes his third Xuzhou conference.

27. In Tokyo Japan informs Britain of her demands for succession to Germany's rights in Shandong and requests Britain's assurances of support.

February 9. The Ministry of Foreign Affairs protests to the German minister in Peking, Admiral Paul von Hintze, against Germany's new policy (communicated to the Ministry February 1) of using submarines to blockade the allies.

16. Britain gives Japan the assurances requested on January 27.

March 4. Duan Qirui asks President Li Yuanhong to sever diplomatic relations with Germany, but the latter disagrees, demanding that the issue be put to parliament.

10. The House of Representatives votes to break diplomatic relations with Germany. Cables of support for a policy of neutrality in the European war are sent by many influential men, including the military governors of Hubei, Anhui, and other provinces, Sun Yatsen, Kang Youwei and Tang Shaoyi.

11. The Senate votes to break diplomatic relations with Germany.

14. The Peking government announces its formal breach of diplomatic relations with Germany.

16. Zhili and Hubei respectively take over the administration of the German Concessions in Tianjin and Hankou.

30. China recognizes the new government of Russia, where on March 15 the last Tsar, Nicholas II, had been forced to abdicate.

April 13. Japanese troops withdraw from Zhengjiatun (Fengtian).

25. The various provincial military governors meet in Peking to discuss foreign policy. They agree that China should declare war against Germany.

May 10. In Peking a 'citizens' petition group' organized by Duan Qirui surrounds the National Assembly in an attempt to force its members to declare war with Germany; a riot breaks out.

22. Zhang Xun holds the fourth Xuzhou conference, using it as part of his plan to restore the monarchy.

29. In response to Premier Duan Qirui's dismissal, the Governor of Anhui, Ni Sichong (though not the military governor Zhang Xun), and the military governor of Shaanxi, Chen Shufan, break relations with the Peking government.

June 7. Zhang Xun leads some 5000 men north towards Peking.

12. On the demand of Zhang Xun and other military governors, Li Yuanhong dissolves both houses of the National Assembly.

14. Zhang Xun arrives in Peking, in theory to mediate in the dispute

The Literary Revolution gathers momentum; 1917
Puyi again briefly ascends the throne

A ECONOMICS

January 20. Cao Rulin, the managing director of the Bank of Communications, concludes a loan agreement of 5,000,000 *yen* with a consortium of three Japanese banks, the Bank of Taiwan, the Bank of Chosen, and the Industrial Bank of Japan.
March 18. The Ministry of Finance announces the termination of payments to Germany (indemnities, interest on loan repayments etc.). The Jincheng Banking Corporation is set up in Tianjin.
August 28. The Ministry of Finance signs a contract with the Yokohama Specie Bank and other Japanese banks for a loan of 10,000,000 *yen*.
September 5. The Wuchang (Hubei)–Yueyang (Hunan) section of the Wuhan–Guangzhou railway opens to traffic.
  29. The Bank of Communications signs a contract with the Industrial Bank of Japan, the Bank of Chosen and the Bank of Taiwan for a loan of 20,000,000 *yen* (the first Nishihara loan).
October 12. The Peking government and the Japanese South Manchurian Railway sign a revised contract on the Jilin–Changchun railway: China raises a further loan of 6,500,000 *yen*.
  15. The Peking government raises a loan of 700,000 taels from a Four-power Banking Consortium (the UK, France, Japan and Russia), and other banks, for flood relief.
November 20. The Chinese government and the American International Corporation sign an agreement for a loan of US$6,000,000 for the restoration of the Grand Canal in Shandong and Zhili.
December 25. The Peking government promulgates national customs regulations.

B OFFICIAL APPOINTMENTS, RESIGNATIONS, DISMISSALS ETC.

May 11. Wu Tingfang, the Minister of Foreign Affairs, Cheng Biguang, the Minister of the Navy, and several other ministers resign in protest over the assault on the National Assembly.
  23. President Li Yuanhong dismisses Premier Duan Qirui and appoints Wu Tingfang to replace him.
June 12. Li Yuanhong accepts Premier Wu Tingfang's resignation and replaces him with Jiang Zhaozong.
  24. Li Jingxi takes over as Premier.
July 1. Zhang Xun, Kang Youwei and others restore the former Qing Emperor Puyi to the throne in Peking.
  2. Li Yuanhong appoints Feng Guozhang as acting President and Duan Qirui as Premier.

1917

between Li Yuanhong and the military governors, in fact planning to restore the monarchy. He is accompanied by Li Jingxi.

19–22. Ni Sichong and the break-away military governors retract their independence of the Peking government.

20. The military governors of Guangdong and Guangxi, respectively Chen Bingkun and Tan Haoming, declare their provinces' temporary autonomy.

July 2. Li Yuanhong takes refuge in the Japanese embassy.

7. Duan Qirui's troops defeat Zhang Xun's at Langfang (Zhili). An aeroplane from the Nanyuan Aviation School outside Peking bombs the Imperial Palaces, the first air raid in China's history.

12. Duan Qirui's troops capture Peking. Zhang Xun takes refuge in the Dutch embassy.

14. Duan Qirui arrives in Peking.

21. Former Navy Minister Cheng Biguang declares his refusal to recognize the Peking government.

22. Cheng Biguang leads his fleet from Wusong towards Guangzhou.

August 14. A presidential mandate is issued declaring war on Germany and Austria-Hungary.

September 10. Sun Yatsen sets up the ROC military government in Guangzhou.

22. The Guangzhou National Assembly resolves to declare war on Germany.

October 6. Clashes take place between the forces of the Guangzhou and Peking governments in the region of Hengshan (Hunan), marking the outbreak of the north-south civil war.

November 2. The USA and Japan conclude the Lansing-Ishii Agreement under which the USA recognizes Japan's special relationship with China owing to its geographical propinquity.

14. The military governor of Hunan, Fu Liangzuo, retreats from Changsha as the southern forces take Baoqing.

16. The southern forces take Hengshan.

December 1. Jingzhou (Hubei) declares autonomy.

3. The various military governors hold a conference in Tianjin and decide to try to force Feng Guozhang to order an attack against the military government of the ROC in the south.

12. Following the accession of the Bolsheviks in Russia on November 7 (the October Revolution), the workers' delegates in Harbin assume control of the Chinese Eastern Railway.

16. Jilin and Heilongjiang provinces are ordered to send troops to Harbin to intervene against the Bolshevik workers' delegates. Xiangyang (Hubei) declares autonomy.

12. Puyi prepares an edict of abdication.
17. Duan Qirui appoints his new cabinet.
September 1. Meeting in Guangzhou, ex-members of the National Assembly appoint Sun Yatsen as the Generalissimo of the Navy and Army of the ROC military government.
2. The Guangzhou National Assembly appoints Tang Jiyao and Lu Rongting as Marshals of the ROC military government.
10. Sun Yatsen, Generalissimo of the ROC military government, and his ministers are inaugurated in their posts.
November 15. Duan Qirui resigns as Premier.
22. Feng Guozhang approves Duan's resignation.
30. Feng Guozhang appoints Wang Shizhen acting Premier.

C Cultural and Social

May 6. The China Vocational Education Society is formally established at a meeting of several hundred in Shanghai.
June 26. The Ministry of Education approves the absorption of the Institute of Chinese History into the Arts Faculty of Peking University.

D Publications

January 1. Hu Shi publishes 'Wenxue gailiang chuyi' ('My View on Literary Reform') in *New Youth*, advocating the use of *baihua* vernacular Chinese.
February 1. Chen Duxiu publishes 'Wenxue geming lun' ('On Literary Revolution') in *New Youth*.
6. The English newspaper *Chefoo Daily News* begins publication.
October. The China Vocational Education Society begins publication of its magazine *Jiaoyu yu zhiye* (*Education and Vocation*).

E Natural Disasters

January 16. A big fire in Sixian (Guizhou) destroys most of the people's houses within the city.
Summer–Autumn. Serious flooding, among the worst ever recorded, affects wide areas of northern China, being especially severe in Zhili.
August 23. A severe earthquake strikes the region of Daguan (Yunnan). Many houses are destroyed and many people killed.

1917–18

25. Feng Guozhang announces his intention to attempt a truce in the north-south civil war.
26. Chinese troops begin disarming Russian troops in Harbin, sending them home, and taking over control of the Chinese Eastern Railway.

1918 *World War I ends; the Siberian intervention*

January 10. The Peking government sends troops under Cao Kun and Wu Peifu to attack Jingzhou and Xiangyang (Hubei), to defeat their declarations of autonomy.
20. The autonomous provinces of the south-west form an alliance in Guangzhou, with the overt aim of protecting the constitution.
22. Northern troops occupy Jingzhou.
27. Northern troops occupy Xiangyang. Southern (Guangxi and Hunan) troops take Yuezhou (Hunan).
30. President Feng Guozhang orders an attack into Hubei and Hunan to unify the country.
February 17. The Peking government proclaims the ROC National Assembly Organization Law and Election Laws for Members of the Senate and House of Representatives, which lead to new elections in all but the south-western provinces.
March 7. The Anfu Club, nominally headed by Wang Yitang, is set up to promote the political power of Duan Qirui and his Anhui clique.
13. Enraged at the arrest of two Tibetans in Changdu the previous July, more than 10,000 Tibetan troops cross the Sichuanese border and advance into Changdu. The troops soon occupied several counties in the area, including Changdu and Dege.
17. Northern troops under Wu Peifu retake Yuezhou.
25. The Hunan and Guangxi allied troops are defeated in Changsha and withdraw; northern troops under Wu Peifu complete the occupation of the city the following day.
April 23. Wu Peifu's northern army takes Hengyang (Hunan).
May 4. In Guangzhou the National Assembly, dissolved in 1914, reconvenes and adopts the Law to Amend the Organization of the Military Government, under which the Generalissimo is to be replaced by a seven-man committee, thus depriving Sun Yatsen of authority in favour of the warlords.
15. Wu Tingfang, Tang Jiyao, Lu Rongting, Chen Jiongming and others cable Feng Guozhang urging a peace conference to settle all

1917–18

F DEATHS

January 28. Prince Yikuang d. in Qingdao aged 80.
February 3. Liu Yongfu d. aged 80.
May 10. Peking Opera actor Tan Xinpei d. aged 70.

Japanese loans to China reach a peak **1918**

A ECONOMICS

January 6. Peking's Ministry of Finance concludes a contract with the Japanese Specie Bank for a loan of 10,000,000 *yen*.
12. The Peking government and Japan conclude a loan contract of 40,000,000 *yen* for the purchase of armaments.
February 1. The Exchange Bank of China, a joint Sino-Japanese enterprise, opens for business.
April 30. The Minister of Communications, Cao Rulin, concludes a loan agreement with the Exchange Bank of China for 20,000,000 *yen* to build telegraph lines.
May 1. Peking's Ministry of Communications concludes with the Industrial Bank of Japan a loan agreement for 20,000,000 *yen* to build a railway from Shunde (Zhili) to Ji'nan (Shandong).
June 18. Peking's Ministries of Finance and Communication sign a contract with the Industrial Bank of Japan for a loan of 10,000,000 *yen* for a railway from Jilin (Jilin) to Huining on the Korean border.
July 3. The Ministries of Agriculture and Commerce and of Finance conclude with the Exchange Bank of China a loan agreement of 30,000,000 *yen* for the development of forestry and gold mining in Jilin and Heilongjiang provinces.
11. The Siping–Zhengjiatun railway in Fengtian begins taking traffic.
September 16. The Changsha–Wuchang section of the Guangzhou–Hankou railway begins taking traffic.
28. The Chinese minister in Tokyo, Zhang Zongxiang, signs three contracts with a syndicate composed of the Industrial Bank of Japan, the Bank of Taiwan and the Bank of Chosen, each of 20,000,000 *yen*, one for four railways in Shandong, and one for China's participation in the European war. (These are the last 'Nishihara loans'.)

B APPOINTMENTS, RESIGNATIONS, DISMISSALS ETC.

March 23. On the demand of the northern warlords, Feng Guozhang reappoints Duan Qirui as Premier of the Peking government.

1918

issues and opposing the signing of any pact with Japan to send troops to Siberia.

16. The Peking government signs the Military Mutual Assistance Convention with Japan, covering joint military action in Siberia and providing that the troops of both countries should be subject to Japanese commanders.

19. The Sino-Japanese Naval Mutual Assistance Convention is signed.

21. More than 2000 students from Peking University and other institutions hold a rally outside the presidential palace demanding the abolition of the Sino-Japanese Military Mutual Assistance Conventions. Sun Yatsen leaves Guangzhou in disgust at the warlord takeover of the military government.

July 5. Tang Jiyao and others formally declare the establishment of the reorganized military government in Guangdong.

August 3. British troops land in Vladivostok, the first in the allied Siberian intervention; the same day the US government states the aims of the intervention as being the defence of Czechoslovak troops who had fled east after fighting against the Germans, and the promotion of self-government or self-defence by the Russians.

12. Japanese troops land in Vladivostok for the Siberian intervention. Peking's new National Assembly holds its inaugural meeting, dominated by the Anfu clique.

15. Japanese troops begin to move north from Liaoyang, very quickly occupying the Harbin–Manzhouli (Heilongjiang) section of the Chinese Eastern Railway and taking over the Chinese barracks. These troops were part of the Siberian intervention.

18. The first Chinese troops leave Peking for Vladivostok to take part in the Siberian intervention.

21. Wu Peifu, largely responsible for the northern victories in Hunan, and others send out a circular cable requesting an end to the still continuing north-south civil war.

September 6. A further Sino-Japanese military agreement is signed to supplement that of May 16.

24. The Japanese Minister of Foreign Affairs, Goto Shimpei, sends a note to the Chinese minister in Tokyo, Zhang Zongxiang, suggesting extensions of Japanese political and economic influence in Shandong; Zhang agrees to them the same day in a return note.

29. Sun Yatsen cables congratulating the USSR on the success of its Revolution.

October 10. A peace agreement is reached with Tibet to settle the disturbances along the border with Sichuan.

23. Following the resignation of the pro-war Duan Qirui, acting

1918

May 4. Sun Yatsen resigns as Generalissimo of the military government.

20. The Guangzhou National Assembly elects Sun Yatsen, Tang Jiyao, Wu Tingfang, Tang Shaoyi, Lin Baoyi, Lu Rongting, and Cen Chunxuan to the governing seven-man committee of the military government, with Cen Chunxuan as chairman.

August 21. Cen Chunxuan assumes the chairmanship of the military government governing committee.

September 4. Peking's newly elected National Assembly elects Xu Shichang as China's President.

October 10. Xu Shichang is inaugurated as President. He accepts Duan Qirui's resignation as Premier and replaces him with Qian Nengxun.

C Cultural and Social

April 18. Mao Zedong, Cai Hesen, He Shuheng, and other revolutionaries formally set up the New People's Study Society in Changsha.

May 1. The workers of the British-American Tobacco Company in Shanghai go on strike.

5. Chinese students at a meeting in Tokyo decide to return to China before May 20 to protest against the proposed Sino-Japanese Military Mutual Assistance Conventions; they also set up the National Salvation Corps of Chinese Students in Japan.

July 20. The Peking government's Ministry of Education issues statistics for the period from August 1915 to July 1916: 129,739 schools, 4,294,251 students and an education budget of 37,406,212 *yuan*.

August 20. The China Vocational Education Society sets up the China Vocational School in Shanghai.

September. Mao Zedong goes to Peking for the first time and soon takes up work as Li Dazhao's assistant at the Peking University Library.

Early October. Mao Zedong joins the Young China Study Society, initiated the previous July by Li Dazhao and others, although not yet formally established.

November 23. Peking's Ministry of Education issues its official table of phonetic script.

D Publications

April 15. Li Dazhao publishes the article 'Jin' ('Now') in *New Youth*.

May 15. Lu Xun's short novel *Kuangren riji* (*Diary of a Madman*) is published in *New Youth*.

July 1. Li Dazhao publishes the article 'Fa E geming zhi bijiao guan' ('A View on a comparison between the French and Russian Revolutions')

1918–19

Premier Qian Nengxun and others cable Cen Chunxuan and others of the Guangzhou military government suggesting peace negotiations to end the north-south civil war.

Twenty-four influential men, including Xiong Xiling, Cai Yuanpei, Wang Chonghui and Zhang Jian, send out a circular telegram calling for peace in the civil war and announcing their intention to establish an association to that end.

November 11. World War I ends.

16. The Peking government orders a truce and the withdrawal of troops from all fronts in the north-south civil war.

22. The military government of Guangzhou orders a ceasefire.

December 1. Peking's Minister of Foreign Affairs, Lu Zhengxiang, leaves Peking for Paris to attend the international Peace Conference.

2. The ministers of the USA, UK, France, Italy and Japan present President Xu Shichang with a formal document calling for an end to the civil war and for the reunification of China.

1919 *China refuses to sign the Treaty of Versailles; the May Fourth Movement*

January 28. At the Paris Peace Conference (first plenary session January 18), Gu Weijun puts forward reasons why Germany's rights in Shandong should be transferred to China, not to Japan.

February 20. Peace talks are held in Shanghai to end the north-south civil war. Tang Shaoyi heads the delegation of the Guangzhou government and Zhu Qiqian that of the Peking government.

25–March 26. In Chita, Siberia, Grigorii Semenov, an anti-Bolshevik leader in Siberia, organizes a conference to set up a Mongol state.

March 2. The peace talks in Shanghai terminate, following military attacks on Shaanxi by northern forces.

6. Lenin sets up the Third International (Communist International or Comintern) in Moscow at the end of its first Congress (March 2–6).

in the journal *Yanzhi jikan* (*Words and Politics*).

October 15. Li Dazhao publishes 'Shumin de shengli' ('The Victory of the People') and 'Bolshevism de shengli' ('The Victory of Bolshevism') in *New Youth*.

December 22. Chen Duxiu, Li Dazhao and others begin publishing the *Meizhou pinglun* (*Weekly Critic*) in Peking.

30. Sun Yatsen prefaces his work *Sun Wen xueshuo* (*The Philosophy of Sun Wen*) in Shanghai, thus completing it.

E NATURAL DISASTERS

July 7. The area along the Yellow River in Shandong is struck by severe floods.

F DEATHS

January 8. Wang Xianqian d. aged 75.

February 26. Cheng Biquang, Minister of the Navy in the military government, is assassinated in Haizhu, near Guangzhou.

March 15. Qu Hongji d. in Shanghai aged 68.

June 14. Lu Jianzhang, a senior member of the Beiyang clique, anti-Duan Qirui and an opponent of the policy of war against the south, is assassinated in Tianjin aged 39.

September 12. Tang Hualong d. in Canada aged 43.

The May Fourth Movement promotes progressive societies and journals — 1919

A ECONOMICS

May 26. China concludes a further contract with the Belgian Compagnie Générale Bruxelles de Chemins de Fer et de Tramways en Chine and the Netherlands Syndicate for a loan of 20,000,000 French francs on the Longhai railway from Gansu to Haizhou (Jiangsu).

August 27. Liang Shiyi and others establish the Zhonghua Savings Bank.

B OFFICIAL APPOINTMENTS, DISMISSALS, RESIGNATIONS ETC.

May 9. Cai Yuanpei, Vice-Chancellor of Peking University, resigns and leaves Peking because of the government suppression of students.

1919

30. Xu Shichang orders an end to the civil war in Shaanxi.

April 8. North-south peace talks resume in Shanghai.

20. The people of Shandong hold a mass rally of some 100,000 in Ji'nan demanding the abolition of all secret treaties with Japan and all mining and railway rights, and also the return of Qingdao to China.

30. At the Paris Peace Conference, the powers decide to accept Japan's demands for the transfer of all previously German interests in Shandong, and to reject China's position.

May 4. Some 3000 students from Peking University and twelve other educational institutions in Peking hold a demonstration to protest against the treatment of China at the Paris Conference. The demonstrators surround and set fire to the residence of Cao Rulin, the Minister of Communications, and beat up Zhang Zongxiang, the Chinese minister to Japan. Thirty-two students are arrested (released May 7) and a general strike is called to protest against the arrests. The May Fourth Movement begins.

At the Paris Peace Conference Lu Zhengxiang protests against the decision of April 30 on the Shandong question.

7. Citizens' rallies in Shanghai and in various provinces protest against the Paris decision on Shandong, call for the release of arrested students and the punishment of Cao Rulin and others. In Tokyo, Chinese students clash with Japanese police as they demand the return of German rights in Shandong to China; over twenty students are wounded and many are arrested.

13. The delegates of both sides of the north-south peace conference in Shanghai resign; negotiations break down without agreement May 15.

14. The Peking government prohibits student participation in politics and orders the police to prevent public meetings.

19. A general strike by tertiary students begins in Peking, and soon spreads to secondary students and to other cities. The strikers demand the return of Qingdao to China and a boycott on Japanese goods.

June 3. Several hundred students, out of about 1000 attending a patriotic Peking rally, are arrested by military policemen.

4. Several hundred students giving patriotic street lectures in Peking are arrested.

5. A series of strikes of businessmen and workers in support of the demands made by the students begins in Shanghai, then over the next days spreads to Wuhan, Tianjin, Ji'nan, Amoy and other cities.

8. The Peking government sends two representatives to apologize to the arrested students in Peking, who leave prison the same day.

12. Following the dismissals of June 10, a mass demonstration is

1919

June 10. Under public pressure the Peking government dismisses the Minister of Communications, Cao Rulin, Zhang Zongxiang, minister to Japan, and the managing director of the Bureau of Currency, Lu Zongyu.

13. Premier Qian Nengxun's resignation is accepted.

September 20. Cai Yuanpei resumes his post as Vice-Chancellor of Peking University.

24. Jin Yunpeng is appointed as acting Prime Minister (confirmed November 5).

C Cultural and Social

January. Cai Yuanpei and others organize the Chinese New Education Promotion Society.

17. The International Anti-Opium Association meets in Shanghai.

29. The Ministry of Education notifies all provinces that foreign languages besides English should be taught in secondary schools.

February 11. Wang Daxie and others set up the League of Nations Association at Peking University.

18. The Peking government bans opium cultivation in China.

March 7. In Shanghai some 20,000 rickshaw drivers go on strike.

15. Some 2000 printing workers in Shanghai go on strike.

26. Peking's Ministry of Education lays down that foreign-run higher educational institutions in the interior shall not include the teaching of religion among their aims.

April 21–25. The Preparatory Committee for the Unification of the Chinese Official Language holds its foundation meeting in Peking.

May 1–July 11. US philosopher Professor John Dewey visits China and lectures there.

6. The Peking Union of Students of Secondary Schools and Above (Peking Students Union) is set up at a conference.

16. The National Union of Student Associations is established at a conference in Shanghai.

June 16. The National Student Union is established in Shanghai.

August 31. The Peking government suppresses the *Weekly Critic*.

December. The Society for the Study of Socialism is founded at Peking University.

1. Students in Fuzhou go on strike to protest against a ban on a student weekly by the military governor of Fujian, Li Houji.

10. Students in Jiangxi go on strike to protest against the ban on their student union by the provincial military governor, Chen Guangyuan.

held in Shanghai to celebrate the victory, and all workers' and business strikes are called off; strikes in other cities quickly end.

27. The Urga government decides to ask China for more troops to oppose Semenov's pan-Mongolists.

28. The Treaty of Versailles is signed. The Chinese delegation issues a press statement declaring its refusal to sign.

July 19. Chinese and Japanese troops clash in Changchun (Jilin), causing casualties on both sides.

22. The National Student Union declares an end to the national student strike.

25. The USSR assistant People's Commissar for Foreign Affairs, Leo Karakhan, issues a manifesto to both the Peking and Guangzhou governments renouncing all territory seized by Russia from China under the Tsars, extraterritoriality, Boxer indemnity payments and Russia's unequal treaties with China, and promising to return the Chinese Eastern Railway to China (the first Karakhan Manifesto).

August 15. Semenov sends Russian troops to Outer Mongolia.

September 15. President Xu Shichang issues a mandate declaring the restoration of peace with Germany.

October 10. Sun Yatsen announces the reorganization of the Chinese Revolutionary Party as the Chinese Nationalist Party (NP).

November 15. The Outer Mongolian princes and lamas agree, under Chinese pressure, to revoke the autonomy of Outer Mongolia and temporarily accept Chinese control.

16. In Fuzhou (Fujian), Chinese students helping the boycott of Japanese goods clash with Japanese; police intervention leads to further casualties, including one death, and the arrest of three Japanese.

22. President Xu Shichang formally declares the abolition of the June 1915 Sino-Russo-Mongolian Kiakhta Agreement and of the autonomy of Outer Mongolia.

25. Following the incident of November 16, the Japanese government sends a warship to Fuzhou to make a show of strength.

27. The Peking government demands an apology from Japan for the November 16 incident and other things.

December 7. In Peking, the students and commercial circles hold an anti-Japanese rally demanding an apology from Japan over the November 16 incident, the withdrawal of the warship from Fuzhou and other things.

30. Japan announces the withdrawal of the warship from Fuzhou.

1919

D PUBLICATIONS

Ke Shaomin's *Xin Yuanshi* (*New Yuan History*) is published.

January 1. Students of Peking University begin publication of *Xinchao* (*New Tide*) and *Guomin zazhi* (*Citizens' Magazine*).

February. Hu Shi's *Zhongguo zhexue shi dagang* (*Outline History of Chinese Philosophy*) is published in Shanghai.

1. The Chinese New Education Promotion Society begins publishing the monthly *Xin jiaoyu* (*New Education*) in Shanghai.

20–23. The Peking *Morning Post Supplement* publishes Li Dazhao's article, 'Qingnian yu nongcun' ('Youth and the Villages').

April 6. The 'Gongchan dang de xuanyan' ('Communist Manifesto') is published in the *Weekly Critic*.

15. Lu Xun's 'Kong Yiji' is published in *New Youth*.

Early May. Li Dazhao publishes the first part of 'Wo de Makesizhuyi guan' ('My Marxist Views') in an issue of *New Youth* devoted entirely to Marxism (the article being completed in the following issue, November 1, 1919).

9–June 1. 'Laodong yu ziben' ('Labour and Capital') is published in *Chenbao* (*Morning Post*), a translation of Marx's *Wage, Labour and Capital*; this was the first time a major work by Marx was published in translation in China.

July 14. The weekly *Xiangjiang pinglun* (*Xiang River Review*), edited by Mao Zedong in Hunan, begins publication. (It is banned after five issues.)

15. The Chinese Revolutionary Party begins publishing the monthly *Jianshe* (*Construction*) in Shanghai.

September 1. Liang Qichao and others initiate in Peking the magazine *Jiefang yu gaizao* (*Emancipation and Reform*), later (September 15, 1920) renamed *Gaizao* (*Reform*).

December 1. Publication of *Xinwen xue* (*Journalism*) by Xu Baohuang, the first Chinese specialist work on the subject.

F DEATHS

April 5. Hong Shuzi, involved in the assassination of Song Jiaoren (see March 1913), is executed.

24. Zhan Tianyou, engineer, d. aged 58.

November 20. Liu Shipei d. in Peking aged 35.

December 28. Feng Guozhang d. in Peking aged 60.

1920 Sun Yatsen re-establishes authority in Guangzhou

January 16. The League of Nations holds its first meeting in Paris; Gu Weijun attends as observer for China.

29. Following claims of authority in the area by the anti-Bolshevik Russians Grigorii Semenov and Dmitri Horvath, Peking's Ministry of Foreign Affairs declares to the foreign powers that the Chinese Eastern Railway is on China's territory and therefore China alone may administer it as sovereign power.

March 18. Wu Peifu begins to move his troops north from southern Hunan to evacuate the province.

April 1. All allied troops of the Siberian intervention, except Japanese and Chinese, complete their withdrawal from Siberia.

11. The National Student Union cables the Soviet government calling for the resumption of relations with the USSR and applauding the Karakhan Manifesto.

30. The Peking government withdraws its troops from Siberia.

May. Influenced by G. Voitinsky, the Comintern representative who has just arrived in Shanghai, Chen Duxiu and others secretly initiate the Chinese Communist Party (CCP) and adopt a draft constitution.

21. The Ministry of Foreign Affairs protests against the occupation by Japanese troops of several railway stations on the Chinese Eastern Railway.

26. The military governor of Hunan, Zhang Jingyao, cables Peking that the north-south civil war has again broken out in Hunan in the wake of Wu Peifu's evacuation and that the southern army has taken Baoqing and other places.

27. In Yining the military governor of Xinjiang, Yang Zengxin, signs the Yili Protocol with the Soviet government of Tashkent; the latter formally abandons Russia's rights of extraterritorial jurisdiction in Xinjiang.

June 1. China and Persia sign a Treaty of Friendship in Rome.

3. Sun Yatsen, Wu Tingfang, Tang Jiyao and Tang Shaoyi issue a joint cable declaring the Guangzhou military government no longer legally in existence.

7. The Hunan and other southern armies, led by Zhao Hengti and others, take Hengshan (Hunan).

12. Southern armies under Zhao Hengti occupy Changsha, the capital of Hunan, Zhang Jingyao having set fire to the city and then retreated to Yuezhou (Hunan).

26. Zhao Hengti's Hunan Army takes Yuezhou.

29. China joins the League of Nations.

July 12. Members of the Zhili clique, led by Cao Kun, and the Fengtian clique, led by Zhang Zuolin, issue a telegram condemning Duan

Disastrous earthquakes strike China **1920**

A Economics

May 25. The Peking government signs a contract with Britain for a loan of £1,803,200 to purchase aeroplanes.
October 2. The Chinese government signs an agreement with the Russo-Asiatic Bank under which China takes over the supreme administration of the Chinese Eastern Railway.
15. Representatives of each of the four banking groups sign the New Consortium Agreement to set up an International Consortium, consisting of numerous banks from each of the USA, UK, France and Japan, to lend money to China.

B Official Appointments, Dismissals, Resignations etc.

May 4. In view of the departure from the Guangzhou military government's seven-man governing committee of Tang Shaoyi, Wu Tingfang and Tang Jiyao, following serious internal divisions, the Guangzhou National Assembly elects Liu Xianshi and others to replace them.
14. In view of Jin Yunpeng's wish to resign as Premier, the Peking government appoints Sa Zhenbing as acting Premier.
July 19. Duan Qirui resigns from all posts.
28. The Peking government accepts Duan Qirui's resignation from all posts.
August 9. The Peking government appoints Jin Yunpeng as acting Premier.
October 23. Cen Chunxuan announces his resignation as head of the governing committee of the Guangzhou military government.
November 1. Chen Jiongming is appointed Governor of Guangdong.

C Cultural and Social

January 1. Police intervene in drama performances put on by the Shandong Student Union, a clash develops and over ten students are hurt. Teachers go on strike in sympathy the following day.
12. Peking's Ministry of Education orders all primary schools, from autumn 1920, to start using vernacular instead of classical language in grades 1 and 2 of Chinese language teaching.
February. Peking University enrols two female students, one from Hunan, the other from Jiangsu: the beginning of coeducation in government institutions in China.
15. Peking police announce their intention to disband the Peking Students Union.
March. The Ministry of Education notifies all primary schools that they

1920

Qirui and his Anfu clique and announcing their intention to fight him.
14. Civil war breaks out between the Anfu and Zhili cliques at Liulihe (Zhili).
18. The Zhili army takes Liulihe; the Fengtian army takes Zhuozhou.
19. With the total defeat of Duan Qirui's Anfu forces, Xu Shichang announces a ceasefire.
22. The Governor of Hunan, Tan Yankai, declares the autonomy of Hunan, planning this action as the beginning of a system of federal government in China.

August 3. President Xu Shichang orders that the Anfu Club be disbanded; the action shows that the Zhili and Fengtian cliques have gained control of the Peking government.
16. Chen Jiongming, acting under a request from Sun Yatsen, leads troops from Zhangzhou (Fujian) to attack Guangdong province and oust the Guangxi warlords from their political power there.
19. Chen Jiongming's Guangdong Army takes Meixian and Swatow (Guangdong).

September. Mao Zedong and Li Dazhao initiate socialist groups in Changsha and Peking respectively, among a number of such groups throughout China set up at about this time.
23. A presidential mandate suspends recognition by China of the Tsarist Russian minister and consuls and declares neutrality towards the civil war in Russia.
27. The second Karakhan Manifesto is issued by the USSR. It renounces extraterritoriality, all rights, concessions and treaties forced on China by the Tsars; in return for China's resuming trade and formal diplomatic relations with the new government in Moscow, it also asks for a special treaty on the Chinese Eastern Railway.

October 22. After a long battle the Guangdong Army seizes Huizhou (Guangdong) and ousts the Guangxi Army.
29. Chen Jiongming's forces take Guangzhou.

November 4. Tan Haoming, the military governor of Guangxi, retracts the autonomy of Guangxi.
5. Sun Yatsen cables Jin Yunpeng, the Peking Premier, calling for the continuation of the peace conference to reach a final reunification of north and south.
12. The Fuzhou incident of November 16, 1919, is resolved; the Japanese government gives compensation money to the wounded and apologizes.
29. Sun Yatsen, Wu Tingfang and Tang Shaoyi return to Guangzhou, intending to revive the military government and use it as a base to reunify the whole country.

1920

must stop using textbooks with classical language and change to those in the vernacular. Li Dazhao and other staff of Peking University initiate, though not yet formally, the Society for the Study of Marxist Theory.

April 2. The Ministry of Education establishes a plan for compulsory education to be implemented throughout China within eight years.

May 1. China's first May Day celebrations are held in Shanghai, Peking, Guangzhou and other places.

6. At a meeting in Shanghai, women's groups organize the Chinese Women's League for Participation in Politics.

June 6. More than 10,000 workers of the Kailuan coal mines in Tangshan (Zhili) go on strike for higher wages; the authorities agree to increases.

August. The Chinese Socialist Youth Corps is established in Shanghai.

September 1. The *New Youth* editorial board moves from Peking to Shanghai. From this point on the magazine's viewpoint becomes more radical. The Ministry of Education sends to all provinces directions to reform the traditional drama and rules on the popularization of the reformed theatre.

October 12. The British philosopher Bertrand Russell arrives in Shanghai to give lectures in China, staying in China a year.

D Publications

March. Hu Shi publishes his *Changshi ji* (*A Collection of Experiments*), China's first collection of poems written in the vernacular.

25. *Shuntian shibao* (*Peking Times*) publishes the first Karakhan Manifesto.

May 5. Shao Piaoping begins publishing the *Jingbao* (*Peking Report*).

August 15. The CCP begins publishing the weekly *Laodong jie* (*Labour Circles*).

November 7. The CCP begins publishing the monthly *Gongchan dang* (*The Communist Party*) in Shanghai.

December 24. The Ministry of Education publishes its *Guoyin zidian* (*Dictionary of National Phonetic Symbols*).

E Natural Disasters

In the northern provinces of Zhili, Shandong, Shanxi, Shaanxi and Henan, severe drought results in serious famine.

December 16. Earthquakes and landslides strike north China, especially Gansu, causing several hundred thousand casualties.

1920-1

1921 *The First Congress of the Chinese Communist Party*

February 3. The White Guards of the anti-Bolshevik Russian Roman Nikolaus von Ungern-Sternberg take Urga, the capital of Outer Mongolia.

6. Chiang Kaishek arrives in Guangzhou for talks with Sun Yatsen and others. The meeting decides on military action to extend the Guangzhou government's control to Guangxi.

March 13. The Revolutionary Mongol People's Party proclaims the Provisional Revolutionary Mongol People's government at Kiakhta.

April 7. A special session of the Guangzhou National Assembly adopts the organizational outline of the ROC government, determining to confront the northern regime led by Xu Shichang.

25. In Tianjin several key warlords confer on the situation, including Cao Kun and Wu Peifu of the Zhili clique and Zhang Zuolin of the Fengtian clique: the Tianjin Conference.

May 20. President Xu Shichang orders the northern troops to wage war against Sun Yatsen's ROC government, and the Guangxi warlord Lu Rongting to join forces against Guangzhou. China and Germany sign an agreement restoring diplomatic relations; Germany renounces all rights obtained under the convention of March 6, 1898.

June 13. Lu Rongting orders an attack on Guangdong.

18. Chen Jiongming, the Commander-in-Chief of the Guangdong Army, orders a full-scale attack on Guangxi.

25. The Guangdong Army launches a fierce attack on Wuzhou (Guangxi), taking it the following day.

July 6. Soviet troops take Urga, defeating the remnants of Ungern's White Guards.

13. In the Guangdong–Guangxi war, the Guangdong Army takes Beiliu (Guangxi).

15. The Guangdong Army takes Nanning (Guangxi).

23–31. The First Congress of the CCP is held in Shanghai and, on July 31, in Jiaxing (Zhejiang). Thirteen delegates from various provinces represent over 50 members. Mao Zedong represents Hunan. In addition G. Maring (pseudonym of H. Sneevliet) and Voitinsky

1920–1

F DEATHS

September 21. Zhu Zhixin d. aged 34.
October 12. Li Chun d. aged 49.

Sun Yatsen is appointed President of the *Guangzhou government* 1921

A ECONOMICS

March 3. A presidential mandate approves the establishment of a National Consolidated Loan Service to consolidate domestic credit for the Peking government.
October 13. The Peking Ministry of Finance signs the Wine and Tobacco Loan agreement with the Savings Bank of Chicago for a loan of US$16,000,000, wine and tobacco taxes being security.

B OFFICIAL APPOINTMENTS, DISMISSALS, RESIGNATIONS ETC.

May 5. Sun Yatsen is inaugurated as Extraordinary President of the Guangzhou government; he issues a list of his ministers.
July 31. The First Congress of the CCP elects a Central Committee (CC) including Chen Duxiu, Zhou Fohai and Zhang Guotao.
August 9. The Peking government appoints Wu Peifu as Inspector-General of Hubei and Hunan and Xiao Yaonan as military governor of Hubei.
October. Mao Zedong becomes secretary of the newly formed Hunan branch of the CCP.
December 24. With the support of Zhang Zuolin, President Xu Shichang appoints Liang Shiyi as Premier of the Peking government; Liang organizes a new cabinet.

C CULTURAL AND SOCIAL

January 4. Zhou Zuoren and others formally establish the Literary Association in Peking.
February 8. Cai Hesen and others organize Chinese students in Paris, whose money had just been cut off and who thus had to support themselves, to demonstrate outside the Chinese legation.
28. Self-supporting Chinese students in Paris surround the Chinese legation in Paris, demanding student allowances. French policemen are called to suppress the students and many of them are wounded.

1921

represent the Comintern. Zhang Guotao chairs the meeting. The Party Constitution is adopted on the last day. (July 1 is still celebrated as the birthday of the CCP, because that is the traditional, though incorrect, date for the Congress's opening.)

29. Civil war breaks out between Hunan and Hubei with an armed clash on their mutual border. The Peking government decides to assist Hubei and the same day sends reinforcements to aid the province.

August 1. The National Assembly reconvenes in Peking.

26. The Far Eastern Republic and Japan begin a conference at Dalian (Fengtian).

27. In the Hunan-Hubei war, Zhili troops under Wu Peifu take Yuezhou (Hunan).

September 1. A truce to end the Hunan-Hubei war is agreed on in Yuezhou, Wu Peifu leaving much of Hunan under the control of its own leaders.

26. China and Mexico conclude an agreement under which each prohibits its 'citizens of the labouring classes' to enter the other's territory.

30. The Guangdong Army captures Longzhou (Guangxi), completing its conquest of the province.

October. The Hunan branch of the CCP is set up.

11. China signs the Universal Postal Agreement.

November 5. The Soviet Union signs a treaty in Moscow with the Mongolian national government recognizing it as the legal government of Outer Mongolia, and making no reference to China.

12. The Washington Conference holds its first plenary session. The conference aims to deal with the limitation of armaments and the questions of the Pacific and Far East; participating powers include Great Britain, France, Japan, Italy, China, Portugal, the Netherlands, Belgium and the USA.

16. At the first meeting of the Washington Conference's Committee on Pacific and Far Eastern Questions, the chief Chinese delegate Dr Shi Zhaoji (Alfred Sze) puts forward ten points, including a request that the powers 'respect and observe the territorial integrity and political and administrative independence' of the ROC.

21. Mr Elihu Root of the US delegation at the Washington Conference endorses most of Dr Shi's ten points, including respect for China's territorial integrity.

December 4. Sun Yatsen arrives in Guilin (Guangxi) where he makes arrangements for the forthcoming Northern Expedition which he plans to reunify the entire country.

10. The Washington Conference agrees to set up a commission to

1921

March 10. A ministerial order formalizes the amalgamation of four colleges, one in Shanghai, one in Tangshan and two in Peking, to found the Communications University with Ye Gongzhuo, the Minister of Communications, as Vice-Chancellor.

14. Teachers of all government universities and institutes in Peking begin a strike because of government failure for over three months to finance their schools.

April 6. A ceremony marks the beginning of teaching at Amoy University, established by Chen Jiageng, the Singapore entrepreneur known as Tan Kah Kee.

May 30–June 4. The Fifth Far Eastern Games are held in Shanghai.

June 3. Teachers of eight government schools in Peking, followed by thousands of students, go to the presidential palace to petition against the suspension of government finance, and clash with guards; many teachers and students are wounded. This is known as the June 3 Incident.

July. The CCP sets up the China Labour Union Secretariat in Shanghai, with Zhang Guotao as its head.

28. The teachers' strike ends, following the government's establishment of a special fund for Peking's schools.

August 29. Mao Zedong initiates the Self-Study University of Hunan in Changsha.

September 19. The Peking Union Medical College is formally opened.

October 12. Some 800 workers and staff of the Hankou–Changsha section of the Guangzhou–Hankou railway go on strike for higher wages and better conditions, among fifteen demands. The strike is resolved October 17, the workers winning their demands.

24–26. More than 10,000 workers of the British-American Tobacco Company in Shanghai go on strike.

December 7. In Guilin, where his forces were preparing the Northern Expedition, Sun Yatsen gives his lecture 'The Three Principles of the People are the Tool for Creating a New World' ('*Sanminzhuyi wei zaocheng xin shijie zhi gongju*').

D Publications

Publication of the sixteen-volume *Foxue da cidian* (*Dictionary of Buddhist Studies*), compiled by Ding Fubao (compiler's preface dated June 1921).

January. *Xiaoshuo yuebao* (*Short Story Monthly*) is taken over as the official organ of the Literary Association under the editorship of Shen Yanbing.

August 5. Guo Moruo publishes his first collection of poetry, *Nüshen* (*The Goddesses*).

look into 'the present practice of extraterritorial jurisdiction in China', with a view to the Chinese government's bringing about such reforms 'as would warrant the several powers in relinquishing ... their respective rights of extraterritoriality'.

23. The Comintern representative Maring meets Sun Yatsen in Guilin. They discuss, among other matters, the question of a united front between the CCP and NP. Maring stays several days in Guilin.

1922 Chen Jiongming and Sun Yatsen split; Sun withdraws from Guangzhou

January 1. Hunan proclaims a provincial constitution as part of a national federalist movement calling for provincial self-government.

5. Wu Peifu issues the first of several demands for the dismissal of the newly appointed Premier, Liang Shiyi, as a traitor for the Japanese.

30. Sun Yatsen moves his military headquarters from Guilin (Guangxi) to Shaoguan (Guangdong), ready for the Northern Expedition.

February 3. Sun Yatsen issues the order for the launching of the Northern Expedition, towards Hunan and Jiangxi.

4. As a result of the Washington Conference, China and Japan sign a treaty in Washington on the Shandong question; former German leases in Jiaozhou are to be returned to China, Japanese troops are to withdraw from Qingdao and the Qingdao–Ji'nan Railway, and China is to open Jiaozhou to foreign trade.

6. The Washington Conference concludes; the Nine Power Treaty is signed. The powers agree to respect China's sovereignty, and territorial and administrative integrity, and 'China's rights as a neutral in time of war to which China is not a party'. China agrees that 'throughout the whole of the railways in China, she will not exercise or permit unfair discrimination of any kind'.

13. The Northern Expedition army moves into southern Hunan.

March 21. Deng Keng, a supporter of Sun Yatsen, arriving in Guangzhou to negotiate with Chen Jiongming following a rift between

October. The pro-Confucian Liang Shuming publishes his *Dongxi wenhua ji qi zhexue (The Cultures of East and West and their Philosophies).*
December 4–February 12, 1922. Lu Xun publishes his story *A Q zhengzhuan (The True Story of A Q)* in a supplement of *Chenbao (Morning Post).*

E   NATURAL DISASTERS

According to 'conservative estimates' the drought-famine of 1920–21 in north China results in not less than 500,000 deaths.

F   DEATHS

June 14. Chiang Kaishek's mother d. aged 57.
October 27. Yan Fu d. aged 67.

Workers at Anyuan and Kailuan coal mines go on strike   **1922**

A   ECONOMICS

February 4. The Washington Conference adopts a treaty on Chinese customs tariff. The Nine Powers recognize the 'principle of uniformity in the rates of customs duties levied' in China, and agree to hold a special conference on Chinese tariffs.
September 25. The eleven member nations of the Tariff Revision Commission set up as a result of the Washington Conference resolve to recommend to their governments that new Chinese tariff rates come into force on December 1, 1922.
November 5. The Peking government orders that Xuzhou (Jiangsu) open as a trade port.

B   OFFICIAL APPOINTMENTS, DISMISSALS, RESIGNATIONS ETC.

January 25. Owing to the opposition of Wu Peifu and others, Liang Shiyi begs leave to step down as Premier and is replaced by Yan Huiqing (W.W. Yen) in an acting capacity.
April 8. Zhou Ziqi replaces Yan Huiqing as acting Premier of the Peking government.
  20. Sun Yatsen accepts Chen Jiongming's resignation as Governor of Guangdong and Commander-in-Chief of the Guangdong Army. He appoints Wu Tingfang Governor of Guangdong.

1922

Chen and Sun, is shot at the railway station (see *F*).

April 28. The first Zhili-Fengtian war, fought over the issue of Liang Shiyi's cabinet, erupts with major engagements near Peking.

30. The most serious battle of the Zhili-Fengtian war breaks out at Changxindian near Peking, between troops loyal to Zhang Zuolin and those loyal to Wu Peifu.

May. CCP member Peng Pai begins to organize the peasants for revolution in Haifeng (Guangdong).

1. Zhang Zuolin proclaims the independence of the three Manchurian provinces and united action with the south-west (i.e. Sun Yatsen's forces).

4. The Zhili-Fengtian war ends with the total defeat of Zhang Zuolin's army.

5. The defeated Fengtian Army is ordered to withdraw beyond the Great Wall at Shanhaiguan towards Manchuria, the Zhili Army to its original place.

June 1. Sun Yatsen returns to Guangzhou to settle the trouble with Chen Jiongming in person.

2. Cao Kun, Wu Peifu and others invite Li Yuanhong to resume the presidency of the Peking government.

10. The CCP completes its First Manifesto on the Current Situation, proposing a united front with the NP and other democratic parties which oppose imperialism and feudalism.

11. The Fengtian and Zhili Armies clash near Shanhaiguan following the breakdown of peace negotiations.

13. Northern Expedition forces take Ganzhou (Jiangxi).

16. Chen Jiongming demands Sun Yatsen's resignation as President and orders his troops to prepare an attack on the Guangzhou presidential palace. Sun Yatsen escapes to a warship in the Pearl River.

29. In response to an emergency cable from Sun, Chiang Kaishek arrives to join Sun Yatsen on his warship.

July. The Second CCP Congress takes place in Shanghai with twelve participants. The Congress resolves to join the Comintern and to form a united front with the NP.

1. Chen Jiongming sends an envoy to seek peace with Sun Yatsen. Sun refuses to negotiate.

2. Northern Expedition troops arrive at the Guangdong border on their way back to Guangzhou to assist Sun Yatsen and fight Chen Jiongming.

11. Northern Expedition troops engage in battle with Chen's troops in Shaoguan.

15. In Peking, disturbances break out among 800 personnel of the

June 2. Xu Shichang resigns as President of the Peking government.
11. Li Yuanhong resumes the Presidency of the Peking government.
August 5. The Peking government appoints a new cabinet with Tang Shaoyi as Premier and Gu Weijun as Minister of Foreign Affairs.
September 19. The Peking government appoints a new cabinet with Wang Chonghui as acting Premier. He and his entire cabinet resign November 21.
November 29. The Peking government appoints a new cabinet, with Wang Daxie as Premier.
December 11. Wang Zhengting replaces Wang Daxie as acting Premier of the Peking government.

C CULTURAL AND SOCIAL

January 13. The Hongkong Chinese Seamen's Union begins a strike after its claim for a wage increase has been finally turned down the preceding day. The strike spreads in the following days to Shanghai, Swatow and other places.
17. The Governor of Hunan, Zhao Hengti, has two workers' representatives killed at one of Changsha's city gates just after they have negotiated with him over a strike at one of the city's cotton mills. At the same time Zhao grants most of the workers' demands causing the strike and closes down the labour union.
February 1. The Hongkong government orders the closure of the Seamen's Union and the transport union which supported its strike, and the arrest of the strike leaders and other workers.
7. The Hongkong seamen's strike spreads with several other unions striking in sympathy.
24. The Guangzhou government prohibits the keeping of female household slaves.
26. General strike begins in Hongkong, involving some 120,000 workers by the beginning of March.
March 3. British soldiers open fire on workers in Shatin, Hongkong, killing four and wounding several hundred.
5. The Hongkong strike terminates; the Hongkong government increases the seamen's wages and releases the arrested workers.
April 4–9. The World's Student Christian Federation holds its conference at Qinghua College, Peking, attended by over 500 people.
May 1. Liu Shaoqi and others set up a workers' club at the Anyuan coal mines on the Jiangxi-Hunan border.
1–6. The All-China Labour Federation holds its first congress in Guangzhou.

1922

Ministries of Army, Finance and others demanding their salaries. The Minister of Finance, Dong Kang, is wounded.

August 9. Realizing his forces cannot defeat Chen Jiongming's, Sun Yatsen abandons Guangzhou for Hongkong accompanied by Chiang Kaishek.

14. Sun Yatsen arrives in Shanghai from Hongkong.

22. The Second Plenum of the Second Central Committee of the Chinese Communist Party (CCPCC) in Hangzhou accepts a proposal by the Comintern representative G. Maring to allow members of the CCP to join the NP.

September 4. In Shanghai Sun Yatsen convenes a meeting of the NP in order to plan its reorganization following the failure of his attempt to reunify the country.

6. Sun Yatsen sets up a committee, including the CCP head, Chen Duxiu, to draft a plan for the reorganization of the NP.

October 1. Northern Expedition troops retake Guilin (Guangxi).

12. Northern Expedition troops take Fuzhou (Fujian).

26. Japanese troops are withdrawn from Siberia and the Chinese Eastern Railway. The evacuation is completed by November 1.

November 11. The Chinese Minister of Foreign Affairs, Gu Weijun, demands that the Soviet authorities return the Chinese Eastern Railway to China unconditionally as promised in the first Karakhan Manifesto.

14. Adolf Joffe, sent by the Soviet Union to China, denies that the first Karakhan Manifesto promised to return the Chinese Eastern Railway to China: the 'Third Manifesto'.

30. Britain completes the closure of its twelve post offices in China.

December 5. China and Japan agree on detailed arrangements to put the treaty of February 4 on Shandong into effect.

10. Japan hands over the administration of Qingdao to China.

31. Except those in the South Manchurian Railway Zone, France, the USA and Japan complete the closure of their eighty post offices in China.

5. The first Congress of the Chinese Socialist Youth Corps is held in Guangzhou.

August 5. In Shanghai several thousand female workers in silk factories, as well as several thousand seamen of the China Merchants' Steam Navigation Company and other shipping companies, go on strike for higher wages and better conditions.

23. The Women's Rights League holds its foundation meeting at the Peking Women's Higher Normal College.

24–25. More than 3000 workers of the Peking–Hankou railway at Changxindian near Peking go on strike. The management makes several concessions, including recognition of the workers' clubs and a rise in salaries.

September 13. Led by Liu Shaoqi and others, some 17,000 miners of the Anyuan coal mines begin a five-day strike; they put forward seventeen demands, including higher wages, better conditions and the right of the workers' club to represent the workers. The miners win their demands.

October 23. Workers in four of the five Kailuan coal mines go on strike for higher wages, better conditions and recognition of the workers' clubs and other demands.

25. Several miners are killed and some fifty wounded in clashes with military police at the Kailuan mines. Leading workers are arrested.

26. Workers in the fifth Kailuan mine join the strike, bringing the entire mining complex to a halt.

November 1. A presidential mandate promulgates a new education system, including six years of primary school (four lower, two upper) and six of middle school (usually three lower and three upper) and providing for four years' compulsory education.

16. Miners at the Kailuan mines resume work, having failed to win most of their demands.

D PUBLICATIONS

May 1. The Creation Society begins publishing the *Chuangzao jikan* (*Creation Quarterly*).

September. Chen Duxiu begins publication of a new CCP organ, *Xiangdao* (*Guide Weekly*).

E NATURAL DISASTERS

August 2–3. A typhoon and tidal waves strike Swatow (Guangdong). Many houses are washed away and several tens of thousands of people are killed.

1923 The CCP and USSR befriend Sun Yatsen

January 1. Sun Yatsen proclaims the manifesto of the NP, including the Three Principles of the People and the restoration of China's free and equal international status.

15. Forces loyal to Sun Yatsen take Zhaoqing (Guangdong).

16. Forces loyal to Sun Yatsen take Guangzhou.

26. Sun Yatsen and the Soviet representative Adolf Joffe issue a joint communiqué in Shanghai. Its points include (*i*) the USSR will assist in the reunification of China; (*ii*) both parties agree that China should be allowed to choose its own political system and that communism cannot be applied to China; and (*iii*) the USSR will not encourage the independence of Outer Mongolia.

February 21. Sun Yatsen arrives back in Guangzhou.

March 10. The Ministry of Foreign Affairs of the Peking government informs the Japanese Foreign Ministry in Tokyo and the Japanese legation in Peking that China is demanding the return of the concessions of Lüshun and Dalian and the abrogation of the agreements connected with the Twenty-one Demands of 1915. (The original lease to Russia was due to expire on March 27, see March 27, 1898.)

14. The Japanese Foreign Ministry rejects the Chinese demands of March 10.

25. A demonstration takes place in Shanghai demanding the abrogation of the Twenty-one Demands and the return of Lüshun and Dalian to China.

May 6. Before dawn, bandits seize and wreck an express train near Lincheng (Shandong) on the Pukou–Tianjin railway. The bandits take most of the 300 or so passengers prisoner. Of the thirty-five foreigners, one was killed. The incident raised doubt among the foreign powers of China's ability to maintain order.

June. The Third Congress of the CCP is held in Guangzhou. Thirty delegates from all provinces represent some 430 members. The Congress criticizes Chen Duxiu's 'right' opportunism and decides to maintain the united front with the NP.

1. In Changsha, disturbances erupt as Japanese marines supervise the disembarcation of some Japanese from a steamship. Japanese marines shoot at the crowd and kill several Chinese, seriously wounding others.

1922–3

F DEATHS

March 23. Deng Keng d. aged 37.

The strike of the Peking–Hankou railway workers 1923

A ECONOMICS

January 1. The Qingdao–Ji'nan railway is transferred from Japan to China with all its branch lines and attendant properties.
17. New tariff rates, as agreed by the Tariff Revision Commission, come into force.

B OFFICIAL APPOINTMENTS, DISMISSALS, RESIGNATIONS ETC.

January 4. President Li Yuanhong approves Wang Zhengting's resignation and appoints a new cabinet with Zhang Shaoceng as Premier.
15. Chen Jiongming announces retirement from public office.
March 2. Sun Yatsen becomes Generalissimo of a new government in Guangzhou. He appoints Tan Yankai as Minister of the Interior and four other ministers.
17. Sun Yatsen appoints Chiang Kaishek as the Chief-of-Staff of the Guangzhou government.
May 7. Sun Yatsen appoints Liao Zhongkai as Governor of Guangdong.
June. Mao Zedong is elected to the CCPCC.
6. Zhang Shaoceng's cabinet resigns as a body.
13. Harassed by Cao Kun and his Zhili clique, Li Yuanhong is forced to resign the Presidency.
July 16. Sun Yatsen appoints Tan Yankai as the Governor of Hunan and Commander-in-Chief of the Hunan Army.
October 5. The National Assembly, its members bribed by Cao Kun, elects Cao as President of the Peking government.
10. Cao Kun is inaugurated as President of the Peking government.

C CULTURAL AND SOCIAL

January 1. The Haifeng Federation of Peasant Unions is formally inaugurated by Peng Pai with a membership of about 20,000.
February. The Agricultural University is established in Peking.
2. The meeting in Zhengzhou (Henan) to establish the Peking–Hankou Railway General Trade Union is harassed by Wu Peifu's military police and some delegates arrested.

1923

The incident leads to complicated government negotiations which yield no result.

2. Mass demonstrations and a general strike are held in Changsha to protest against the behaviour of the Japanese on the previous day.

July 7. In Peking more than thirty political groupings participate in a forum which calls for a peace conference between Cao Kun and Sun Yatsen.

August 23. The Governor and Commander-in-Chief of Hunan, Zhao Hengti, orders a general attack against Sun Yatsen's appointee as Governor, Tan Yankai. A war breaks out over control of Hunan.

September 1. Tan Yankai's troops take Changsha, capital of Hunan; Zhao Hengti retreats.

2. Chiang Kaishek arrives in Moscow to study the Soviet political and military system and party organization. The Soviet plenipotentiary Leo Karakhan arrives in Peking for talks with the government on formal recognition, the Chinese Eastern Railway and other issues of Sino-Soviet relations.

13. Zhao Hengti, having invited Wu Peifu to intervene in the Hunan civil war, re-enters Changsha.

24. Sun Yatsen leads an attack on Huizhou (Guangdong), Chen Jiongming's headquarters, but it fails.

26. A bomb attack on Cao Kun's life in a Baoding (Zhili) theatre fails.

27. Sun Yatsen returns to Guangzhou.

October 5. Representatives of Tan Yankai and Zhao Hengti hold (unsuccessful) peace talks in Xiangtan (Hunan) to resolve the Hunan civil war.

6. The Soviet representative Michael Borodin arrives in Guangzhou to act as adviser to Sun Yatsen and the NP.

9. Sun Yatsen cables Duan Qirui, Zhang Zuolin and others, asking them for joint action against Cao.

10. A new Constitution is proclaimed in Peking. Demonstrations against Cao Kun's October 5 election as President (see *B*) take place in Shanghai, Wuhu (Anhui), Hangzhou and other places.

November 14. Tan Yankai's armies, defeated by Zhao Hengti with help from Wu Peifu's forces, retreat back to the Guangdong border.

18–19. Chen Jiongming's forces launch fierce attacks on Guangzhou, reaching to the city's outskirts, but are beaten back by Sun Yatsen's troops under Tan Yankai and others.

December 2. The Chinese Youth Party is established.

15. Chiang Kaishek arrives in Shanghai from the USSR.

4. The great Peking–Hankou railway strike begins. The workers protest against the incident of February 2.
7. In Hankou troops loyal to Wu Peifu clash with the workers of the Peking–Hankou railway. Over thirty are shot dead, several heads being displayed as warning, and over 200 wounded. Workers are also killed in the strike in Zhengzhou, and Changxindian near Peking.
9. Peking students and workers hold a mass demonstration to support the workers of the Peking–Hankou railway. However, the strike is put down by the army and communications resume.
March 29. The Ministry of Agriculture and Commerce issues its Provisional Factory General Regulations.
August 2. The wireless station at Shuangqiao, between Peking and Tongzhou, begins communications with the world.
September 15. The North-eastern University in Shenyang (Fengtian) holds its formal opening ceremony.
November 3. In Anhui, the head of the Education Bureau, Jiang Wei, and the local school principals and teachers resign in a body, and students go on strike demanding that the provincial Governor, Lü Tiaoyuan, be disciplined, because the latter, in response to a request for their salaries by teachers, had called out troops and had many of them beaten.

D Publications

Publication of Xie Wuliang's *Gudai zhengzhi sixiang yanjiu* (*Research on Ancient Chinese Political Thought*) in Shanghai.
January 29. Sun Yatsen completes his *Zhongguo geming shi* (*The History of the Chinese Revolution*).
April. The *Guangzhou Minguo ribao* (*Guangzhou Republic Daily*) begins publication.
July 1. The CCP journal *Qianfeng* (*Vanguard*) begins publication in Guangzhou.
October 20. *Zhongguo qingnian* (*Chinese Youth*), the organ of the Chinese Socialist Youth Corps, begins publication.
December. Publication of volume I of Lu Xun's *Zhongguo xiaoshuo shilüe* (*A Brief History of Chinese Fiction*) (volume II follows, June 1924).

E Natural Disasters

Twelve provinces suffer from floods and droughts, the affected areas covering 10,000 square miles and the death figure exceeding 100,000.
April 8. The Sungari River floods, drowning more than 3000 people.

1924 *The first Congress of the NP;*
Feng Yuxiang wins a civil war against the Zhili clique

January 20. The First National Congress of the NP opens in Guangzhou, attended by 165 representatives and 198 participants. Sun Yatsen takes the chair and makes the opening speech.

23. The First National Congress of the NP adopts its Party Manifesto.

28. The First National Congress of the NP adopts the Party Constitution.

30. The First National Congress of the NP closes.

May 31. The Soviet representative, Leo Karakhan, and the Chinese Minister of Foreign Affairs, Gu Weijun, sign the Sino-Soviet Agreements. Among other matters, (*i*) China recognizes the USSR diplomatically, (*ii*) the USSR renounces extraterritoriality and the remainder of the Boxer Indemnity, (*iii*) both sides recognize China's sovereignty in Outer Mongolia; (*iv*) the future of the Chinese Eastern Railway is to be determined by the Soviet and Chinese governments 'to the exclusion of any third party'.

June 7. The Japanese, French, American and other ministers in Peking declare to the Ministry of Foreign Affairs that their right to speak on the Chinese Eastern Railway will not be restricted by the Sino-Soviet Agreement of May 31.

16. Peking's Ministry of Foreign Affairs responds to the declarations by the foreign powers of June 7 by reaffirming that the Chinese Eastern Railway is an issue concerning only China and the USSR and that no third country should interfere.

August 7. Following the terms of the Sino-Soviet Agreement the Russian Concession in Tianjin is formally returned to China.

9. Sun Yatsen orders Chiang Kaishek to deal with the problem of the private transportation of armaments by the Guangzhou Merchants' Corps. This organization had been in touch with Chen Jiongming against the Guangzhou government.

27. The British consul in Guangzhou warns the government that if it attacks the Guangzhou Merchants' Corps, it can expect opposition from British naval forces.

F Deaths

February 7. CCP member and leader of the Peking–Hankou Railway Workers' Union, Lin Xiangqian, killed in the Peking–Hankou railway strike.
August 27. Zhang Jizhi d. aged 68.

Duan Qirui takes over the Peking government again 1924

A Economics

June 6–7. The Peking Ministry of Foreign Affairs and the German minister exchange notes reaching agreement resolving Chinese indemnities and debts to Germany. The Chinese minister in London announces the signing of a Sino-Chilean trade treaty in London.
August 15. The Central Bank of the Guangzhou government formally begins operations in Guangzhou.

B Official Appointments, Resignations, Dismissals etc.

January 10. President Cao Kun appoints Sun Baoqi as Premier of the Peking government.
30. The First National Congress of the NP elects a Central Executive Committee (CEC) of seventeen: Hu Hanmin, Wang Jingwei, three members of the CCP, including Li Dazhao, and others, with Mao Zedong among the alternates; and a Central Supervisory Committee (CSC) of five, including Deng Zeru.
February 3. Sun Yatsen appoints Chiang Kaishek as a member of the NP's Military Affairs Committee.
May 3. Sun Yatsen's appointment of Chiang Kaishek to head the Whampoa Military Academy and concurrently as Chief-of-Staff of the Guangdong Army is proclaimed.
August 2. Sun Yatsen appoints Song Ziwen (usually known outside China as T.V. Soong) as manager of the Central Bank.
September 14. President Cao Kun sets up a new cabinet, headed by Yan Huiqing as Premier, for the Peking government.
17. Cao Kun appoints Wu Peifu as Commander-in-Chief of all troops in the war against Zhang Zuolin, and Feng Yuxiang as Commander-in-Chief of the First, Second and Third Armies.
October 3. Hu Hanmin is formally inaugurated as Governor of Guangdong.

1924

September 1. Sun Yatsen issues a statement condemning the British consul's threat of August 27 and declares his determination to oppose imperialist intervention in China. Troops of the military governor of Jiangsu, Qi Xieyuan, of the Zhili clique, clash with those of the military governor of Zhejiang, Lu Yongxiang, of the Anhui clique, along the Shanghai–Nanjing railway. The Jiangsu-Zhejiang war begins.

5. Sun Yatsen calls a military conference which decides on and plans a northern expedition to reunify China.

17. President Cao Kun orders war against Zhang Zuolin; the declaration of the second Zhili-Fengtian war.

20. In Shenyang Zhang Zuolin's representatives conclude an agreement with the USSR on the Chinese Eastern Railway similar to that of May 31.

October 6. In Yunnan, Tang Jiyao cables Sun Yatsen his willingness to cooperate in the planned northern expedition.

13. The Jiangsu-Zhejiang war ends in a victory for Jiangsu; Lu Yongxiang leaves Shanghai for Japan.

15. In a sharp battle in Guangzhou, troops of the Sun Yatsen government, including cadets of the Whampoa Military Academy, defeat and disarm the militia of the Guangzhou Merchants' Corps.

23. Having turned against Cao Kun and Wu Peifu, the troops of Feng Yuxiang occupy Peking and surround the President's palace.

24. Cao Kun is forced to order an end to the fighting.

27. Sun Yatsen cables agreeing to requests from Feng Yuxiang, Duan Qirui and others to come north. Allied foreign troops arrive in Peking to protect the legations.

30. Feng Yuxiang and others launch a general attack on Wu Peifu's Zhili army near Peking.

November 3. Wu Peifu retreats from Tianjin; Feng Yuxiang's troops occupy the city. The Zhili-Fengtian war ends in victory for Feng Yuxiang.

5. Feng Yuxiang forces Puyi to leave the Imperial palaces.

10. Sun Yatsen issues a declaration that he will go to Peking 'to plan China's unification and construction'. Zhang Zuolin, Lu Yongxiang, Feng Yuxiang and others begin a series of meetings in Tianjin.

13. Qi Xieyuan convenes a military-naval conference in Nanjing, attended by representatives from Jiangsu, Zhejiang, Henan, Hubei, Jiangxi, Anhui, Fujian and Shaanxi; it declares it will not recognize orders from Peking.

21. Duan Qirui announces that he will convene an 'Aftermath Conference'.

13. Because of his defeat in the Jiangsu-Zhejiang war, Lu Yongxiang, the military governor of Zhejiang, cables his resignation.

24. The cabinet of Yan Huiqing resigns. Feng Yuxiang forces President Cao Kun to dismiss Wu Peifu from his posts and exile him to Qinghai.

November 2. Under pressure from Feng Yuxiang, Cao Kun resigns the Presidency and Huang Fu takes over as acting President of the Peking government.

24. Duan Qirui is inaugurated as provisional Chief Executive of the Peking government. He appoints his cabinet.

December 11. Duan Qirui orders the dismissal of Qi Xieyuan as military governor of Jiangsu and appoints Lu Yongxiang as Pacification Commissioner of Jiangsu and Anhui.

C CULTURAL AND SOCIAL

February 7. The All-China Railway Workers' General Union is formally set up at a meeting in Peking; among its stated aims are improvement of livelihood, unity and mutual help, and the raising of consciousness.

23. Peking's Ministry of Education proclaims the National Universities Regulations.

March 31. The Peking government decides that all foreign church property in China should be regarded as on permanent lease.

April 1. The Central News Agency is set up in Guangzhou to provide news for local as well as overseas NP newspapers.

May 1. The Peking Women's Higher Normal College becomes the Women's Normal University.

June 1. To commemorate the anniversary of the Changsha incident of the previous year (see June 1, 1923), nearly 100,000 people in Changsha go on strike and demonstrate.

16. A ceremony marks the formal opening of the Whampoa Military Academy.

July 13–15. Taixu and others hold the First Conference of the World Buddhist Federation on Lushan (Jiangxi).

August 13. Sun Yatsen promulgates his University Regulations.

September 17. The Peking government's Ministries of Foreign Affairs and Education approve the setting up of a management committee for the China Foundation for the Promotion of Education and Culture to take charge of the remainder of the US Boxer Indemnity, which is to be devoted to the development of Chinese science and education.

October 1. Sun Yatsen promulgates trade union regulations which recognize unions, and give the right of collective bargaining and strikes.

22. Duan Qirui arrives in Peking to organize a provisional government.

26. The Great People's Assembly of the Mongolian People's Republic adopts a constitution proclaiming Mongolia as 'an independent People's Republic'.

29. Puyi takes refuge in the Japanese legation in Peking.

December 9. The ministers of the USA, Belgium, Britain, France, Italy, Japan and Holland declare that they recognize the provisional Executive Government of Duan Qirui (see *B*, November 24) on condition that it respects all existing treaties.

30. Duan Qirui sends out cables convening the Aftermath Conference in Peking before February 1, 1925.

31. Sun Yatsen arrives on his sickbed in Peking and is warmly welcomed.

1925 *The May Thirtieth Incident*

January 7. Chen Jiongming mobilizes his troops from Swatow, again planning to attack Guangzhou.

10. Attempting to regain his influence in the south the Pacification Commissioner of Jiangsu and Anhui, Lu Yongxiang, arrives with his ally Zhang Zongchang in Nanjing to make war against Qi Xieyuan.

15. Duan Qirui orders the demilitarization of Shanghai.

20. The Soviet minister in Peking, Leo Karakhan, and the Japanese

10. Peking Opera actor Mei Lanfang visits Japan, returning to Peking November 29.

November. The National Wuchang Normal University is renamed National Wuchang University.

11. The National Guangdong University holds its opening ceremony.

D PUBLICATIONS

Publication of Wu Zongci's *Zhonghua minguo xianfa shi* (*History of the ROC Constitution*).

February 20. The *Minguo ribao* (*Republic Daily*) begins publication in Peking.

April. The *Shijie wanbao* (*World Evening News*) begins publication in Peking.

October. Zhang Guotao and others begin publishing the weekly *Zhongguo gongren* (*Chinese Worker*).

E NATURAL DISASTERS

June 28. Hunan is struck by devastating floods affecting the whole province. Among areas particularly badly hit are Changsha, Xiangtan and Hengshan.

July 4. Serious flooding strikes the three provinces of Guangdong, Guangxi and Jiangxi.

15. The Yongding River bursts its banks in Zhili province, flooding the area near Peking and Tianjin.

November 30. A large fire in Wuzhou (Guangxi) causes damage estimated at about 30,000,000 *yuan*.

F DEATHS

August 15. Prose-writer and poet Zhang Xigong d. aged 66.

Sun Yatsen dies **1925**

A ECONOMICS

January 15. Duan Qirui orders that the Jiangnan arsenal in Shanghai cease to be used for military purposes and henceforth only as a commercial and industrial plant.

February 1. China redeems from Japan the undersea cable linking Sasebo in Japan with Qingdao (Shandong).

April 12. China agrees to a French demand to make Boxer Indemnity

1925

minister in Peking, Yoshizawa Kenkichi, sign a convention establishing diplomatic relations.

22. The Fourth Congress of the CCP convenes in Shanghai and adopts a Party Constitution.

25. Karakhan and Yoshizawa both state that their convention of January 20 preserves Chinese interests and sovereign rights.

28. Troops loyal to Qi Xieyuan and his ally Sun Chuanfang abandon Suzhou in the face of the advancing Fengtian troops led by Zhang Zongchang. Qi retreats to Shanghai and later takes refuge in Japan.

29. Zhang Zongchang leads over 10,000 troops into Shanghai.

February 1–April 21. The Aftermath Conference takes place in Peking, chaired by Duan Qirui (see November 21, 1924).

1. Chiang Kaishek leads cadets from the Whampoa Military Academy, together with sections of the Guangdong, Guangxi and Yunnan armies, in an attack on Huizhou (Guangdong). The first Eastern Expedition, aimed at defeating Chen Jiongming, begins.

2. The NP's CEC issues a statement opposing the Aftermath Conference: the NP will not participate.

3. Sun Chuanfang and Zhang Zongchang sign a peace agreement as all troops prepare to leave Shanghai.

24. Puyi, the last Manchu Emperor, secretly arrives in the Japanese Concession in Tianjin.

27. The Eastern Expedition takes Haifeng (Guangdong), supported by the CCP peasant leader Peng Pai.

March 7. The Eastern Expedition takes Swatow (Guangdong).

April 2. The funeral of Sun Yatsen takes place (see *F*). More than 100,000 people mourn him as his corpse is taken to the Biyun Temple in the Western Hills outside Peking.

16. The government of Guangdong renames Xiangshan as Zhongshan in honour of Sun Yatsen.

May 30. In Shanghai's International Settlement, several thousand university and high school students and workers hold a demonstration to mourn Gu Zhenghong, killed on May 15. A clash develops and a British police inspector gives the order to open fire; at least nine students are killed and many seriously injured or arrested. This is known as the May Thirtieth Incident.

June 1. In Shanghai the May Thirtieth Incident provokes demonstrations and strikes and a call for a general strike, in answer to which strikes spread in the following days. British police open fire, killing four more people.

2. In a note to the leader of the diplomatic corps in Peking (the Italian minister, V. Cerruti), the Peking Ministry of Foreign Affairs protests payments in gold: the 'gold franc controversy' is settled.

October 26. The Special Conference on the Chinese Tariff Customs, envisaged by the Washington Conference (see A, February 4, 1922), opens in Peking; thirteen countries are represented: China, USA, Belgium, Britain, France, Italy, Japan, the Netherlands, Portugal, Denmark, Norway, Spain and Sweden. A student demonstration outside the meeting place for Chinese tariff independence results in clashes with police and many arrests.

B Official Appointments, Dismissals, Resignations etc.

April 24. Duan Qirui appoints Zhang Zongchang military governor of Shandong.

May 12. Zhang Shizhao, Peking Minister of Education, resigns.

July 1. Wang Jingwei is inaugurated as Chairman of the NG Committee, Hu Hanmin as Minister of Foreign Affairs, Liao Zhongkai as Minister of Finance, among other ministers and NG Committee members.
3. The NG sets up its Military Affairs Committee; Wang Jingwei is the Chairman, Chiang Kaishek and others are members.

August 26. Chiang Kaishek is appointed Commander of the First Army of the NRA.

September 28. The NG's Military Affairs Committee appoints Chiang Kaishek to command the second Eastern Expedition.

October 15. Sun Chuanfang proclaims himself Commander-in-Chief of the allied armies of five provinces: Zhejiang, Jiangsu, Anhui, Fujian and Jiangxi.

November 25. Duan Qirui appoints Sun Chuanfang military governor of Jiangsu.

December 26. Duan Qirui appoints Xu Shiying as Premier of the Peking government.

C Cultural and Social

February. The Chinese Socialist Youth Corps holds its third congress and changes its name to the Communist Youth League of China.
10. Strikes begin in Japanese-owned cotton mills in Shanghai; workers demand pay increases, reinstatement of dismissed workers and other things.
27. The strikes at the cotton mills in Shanghai are resolved through a settlement, largely on the Japanese owners' terms.

March 11. Sun Yatsen signs his will, a document calling for continuation of the revolution and friendly relations with the USSR.

April 19. Chinese workers in the Japanese-owned cotton mills in Qing-

1925

over the May Thirtieth Incident and demands the release of those arrested. (The note is presented June 3.) In Shanghai, foreign warships and volunteers patrol the International Settlement, and the New World amusement centre is occupied. Several Chinese are killed in clashes.

3. In Peking at least 30,000 students go on strike and demonstrate, among other matters to protest against the May Thirtieth Incident and to demand that the Peking government take back British and Japanese Concessions throughout China.

4. In a common note the Peking legations of all nations reject the Chinese charges over the behaviour of the British police and lay responsibility on 'the demonstrators and not on the Authorities of the Concessions'.

11. In Hankou anti-foreign disturbances result in the deaths of at least eight Chinese, through British machine-gun fire, and one Japanese. This was only one of many incidents, strikes and demonstrations following the May Thirtieth Incident.

13. Despite Duan Qirui's order (see January 15) Zhang Xueliang, son of the Fengtian warlord Zhang Zuolin, leads an army of 2000 into Shanghai to help the foreign volunteers keep order in the Concessions.

19. General strike aimed against the British begins among Chinese workers in Hongkong; it quickly spreads to Guangzhou (June 21) and to include boycott of British goods.

23. British and French troops fire into a crowd of demonstrators in Guangzhou, killing fifty-two people. The incident provokes expansion of strike action and disturbances.

24. Peking's Ministry of Foreign Affairs sends a note to the US, British, French, Japanese, Italian, Dutch, Portuguese and Belgian legations requesting that China's treaty relations be changed and placed 'on an equitable basis'.

25. A national general strike of one day takes place to commemorate the May Thirtieth Incident. In Peking 100,000 people demonstrate demanding that the government send troops into the British Concessions and attack the British legation.

July 1. The National Government (NG) of the ROC is formally set up in Guangzhou.

August 26. The Military Affairs Committee of the NG resolves to divide the National Revolutionary Army (NRA) into five armies.

September 4. The legations of the eight powers reply to the note of June 24. They inform the Ministry of Foreign Affairs that China may amend the unequal treaties if she can guarantee to protect foreign

dao (Shandong) begin a strike for higher wages and improved dormitories. Eventually the strike involves well over 10,000 textile workers.

23. The Chinese Library Association is founded in Shanghai.

24. The anti-communist Society for the Study of Sun Yatsen's Principles is founded in Guangzhou.

May 1–7. The All-China Labour Federation holds its Second Congress in Guangzhou.

7. Because of an attempt by the Ministry of Education to stop a student demonstration to commemorate 'national shame' (the Twenty-one Demands of 1915), students damage the residence of the Minister of Education, Zhang Shizhao; as a result of clashes with police three students are killed and many wounded and arrested.

9. Thousands of students in Peking go on strike and demonstrate, demanding the release of the students arrested on May 7, the dismissal of the Minister of Education and the repeal of several laws they regard as offensive, such as the publication (i.e. censorship) laws.

10. The workers in the Qingdao cotton mills resume work after winning most of their demands (see April 19).

25. Chinese authorities, under Japanese pressure, arrest the leaders of the cotton mill strike in Qingdao; a new strike begins.

29. Fengtian troops sent by Zhang Zongchang suppress the Qingdao strike; they shoot at workers, killing at least two and wounding many.

31. The Shanghai General Trade Union is established, with Li Lisan as its head.

June 4. The authorities close down the CCP Shanghai University because of its role in the May Thirtieth Movement.

8. In Nanjing, workers of the British International Export Company begin a successful month-long strike in demand for higher wages, guarantee of work stability and recognition of their trade union. This was one of many strikes showing the growth of the labour movement after May 30.

July 28. In Ji'nan a general trade union is set up, one of many regional unions spawned by the May Thirtieth Movement.

August 11. In Tianjin cotton mill workers go on strike for higher wages. This results in a clash with military police to suppress the strike; many workers are killed or wounded.

23. The Nationalist University is formally established.

September 19. Following instructions from the Duan Qirui and Jiangsu provincial governments the Shanghai authorities issue an order disbanding the General Trade Union and a warrant for the arrest of two of its leaders, including Li Lisan.

20. The workers at the Anyuan coal mines on the Hunan-Jiangxi

interests in China, and may control her own customs if she reforms her finances.

October 14. In a second Eastern Expedition, troops under Chiang Kaishek seize Chen Jiongming's stronghold, Huizhou (Guangdong).

16. Sun Chuanfang's troops attack and seize Shanghai; the occupying Fengtian army (see June 13) retreats to Suzhou.

November 4. The Eastern Expedition troops enter Swatow (Guangdong). Within a few days, Chen Jiongming's military power is obliterated.

22. Guo Songling of the Fengtian clique demands that Zhang Zuolin, leader of the Fengtian clique, step down and thus signals revolt against him.

23. Ten right-wing members of the NP's CEC, including Lin Sen, Zou Lu and Ju Zheng, begin a meeting at the Biyun Temple in the Western Hills outside Peking. They decide to eliminate all communist influence within the party by expelling all CCP members and demand punishment for Wang Jingwei. This later becomes known as the Western Hills Conference and its participants as the Western Hills Clique.

December 1. Sun Chuanfang refuses to recognize the authority of the Peking government in the provinces under his control (Jiangsu, Anhui, Zhejiang, Fujian and Jiangxi) and starts making his own appointments.

2. The Zhili-Shandong Allied Army is formed by an agreement between the military governors of the two provinces, Li Jinglin, a member of the Fengtian clique, and Zhang Zongchang.

5. Shandong, under Zhang Zongchang, declares it does not recognize the orders of the Peking government and will allow no armies from other provinces on its soil.

23. Troops under Guo Songling are defeated in a decisive battle at Juliuhe (Fengtian).

24. Feng Yuxiang's Nationalist Army occupies Tianjin, the headquarters of the military governor of Zhili, Li Jinglin. The latter flees to the Concessions; some of his troops are disarmed, the remainder move to Shandong to join Zhang Zongchang.

border go on strike in demand for their salaries, which had not been paid for several months.

21. With military force, the Hanyeping Company authorities close down the workers' club in the Anyuan coal mines together with all its dependent organizations, spare-time schools etc. Many workers are killed or wounded.

October. The Imperial Palace Museum is formally established in Peking.

November 10. The Peking General Trade Union proclaims its establishment.

D PUBLICATIONS

January. Jiang Guangci publishes his first volume of poetry, *Xinmeng* (*New Dream*), in Shanghai.

February 10. The *Shijie ribao* (*World Daily News*) begins publication in Peking.

June 5. The *Huaqiao ribao* (*The Overseas Chinese Daily*) begins publication in Hongkong.

E NATURAL DISASTERS

Over eighty counties of Sichuan province are affected by famine, some 3,000,000 people starve to death, and countless numbers are rendered destitute.

March 16. The city of Dali in Yunnan is destroyed by an earthquake and resultant fires. Many buildings collapse and are burned; over 10,000 people are crushed to death, another several thousand dying of famine or other causes resulting from the earthquake.

F DEATHS

March 12. Sun Yatsen d. in Peking aged 58.

May 15. The CCP trade union leader Gu Zhenghong d. aged 19 when Japanese fire on cotton mill strikers in Shanghai.

   23. Actor Tian Jiyun d. aged 60.

August 20. Liao Zhongkai, the ROC NG's Minister of Finance, is assassinated in Guangzhou, aged 48.

October 16. Huang Jingyuan, leader of the Anyuan Workers' Club, is executed.

December 17. Liu Hua, CCP member and one of the leaders of the May Thirtieth Movement, is executed, aged 22.

   24. Guo Songling is executed on orders of Zhang Zuolin, aged 41.

   30. Xu Shuzheng is assassinated at Langfang (Zhili), aged 45.

1926 The Northern Expedition begins

January 1–19. The Second Congress of the NP is held in Guangzhou.
5. Zhang Zuolin cables Wu Peifu suggesting reconciliation between the two. This action signals the beginning of the alliance between the Fengtian and Zhili cliques, against Feng Yuxiang's Nationalist Army under Zhang Zhijiang and, in the Tianjin sector, Lu Zhonglin.
13. The NP's Second Congress rejects the Western Hills Conference as invalid (see November 23, 1925).
19. War breaks out between the forces of Feng Yuxiang's successor Zhang Zhijiang and those of the Fengtian clique, when the Fengtian Army occupies Shanhaiguan (Zhili).
March 8. The Nationalist Army blockades and mines Dagu harbour (Zhili).
12. Two Japanese warships exchange fire with the Nationalist Army at Dagu.
16. The ministers in Peking of the eight Boxer Protocol powers issue an ultimatum to the Peking Ministry of Foreign Affairs demanding that, by midday on March 18, all mines be removed from Dagu harbour, and free access to Dagu be allowed to foreign vessels.
18. Peking's Ministry of Foreign Affairs accepts the foreign demands of March 16. Several thousand students and others demonstrate against the ultimatum and its acceptance. Outside Duan Qirui's residence they clash with Duan's guards. Several tens of demonstrators are killed, and many more wounded.
20. In Guangzhou, Chiang Kaishek orders the arrest of Li Zhilong, a member of the CCP and captain of the S.S. *Zhongshan*, and some 50 other Communists, accusing them of mutiny. He declares military law in Guangzhou city and captures the *Zhongshan*. This is later known as the '*Zhongshan* Incident' and represents the beginning of Chiang's campaign against the CCP.
24. On Chiang Kaishek's orders the Soviet advisers begin to leave Guangzhou for home.
April 3. The allied Fengtian, Zhili and Shandong Armies bomb Peking from the air in an attempt to seize the city from the Nationalist Army under Lu Zhonglin.
9. Lu Zhonglin's Nationalist Army surrounds Duan Qirui's offices to force him to resign; Duan flees to the Legation Quarter.
18. The Nationalist Army having evacuated Peking shortly before, the allied troops of Fengtian, Zhili and Shandong enter Peking.
23. Shandong troops destroy many villages as part of Zhang Zongchang's ruthless campaign to uproot the Red Spears Society, a secret peasant society active in Shandong for several years.
May 11. Wang Jingwei secretly leaves Guangdong for France. He had

B   Official Appointments, Dismissals, Resignations etc.

January 1. Feng Yuxiang cables Duan Qirui resigning all his posts.
4. Feng Yuxiang hands over his powers and duties to his subordinate Zhang Zhijiang.
16. The NP's Second Congress elects a CEC of thirty-six, including Wang Jingwei, Tan Yankai, Hu Hanmin, Chiang Kaishek, and Li Dazhao, and a CSC of twelve, including Wu Zhihui and Cai Yuanpei. Mao Zedong is again elected among the alternates to the CEC.
February 15. Premier Xu Shiying submits his resignation because of Duan Qirui's refusal to hand over any power to his cabinet.
March 4. Duan Qirui appoints a new cabinet, including Jia Deyao as Premier.
21. Sun Yue resigns as military governor of Zhili over the March 18 massacre, among other reasons.
22. Wang Jingwei, Chairman of the NG and of the NP's CEC, is granted leave of absence. In fact, as head of the left faction of the NP he was under suspicion after the *Zhongshan* Incident of March 20.
April 20. Jia Deyao's resignation is accepted. Duan Qirui resigns all posts and moves to the Japanese Concession in Tianjin.
May 13. In Peking a new cabinet, with Yan Huiqing as Premier.
19. The Second Plenum of the NPCEC elects Zhang Renjie as Chairman of the CEC's Standing Committee.
June 5. The NG appoints Chiang Kaishek Commander-in-Chief of the NRA.
22. Yan Huiqing resigns and Du Xigui is appointed as acting Premier.
July 6. The CEC of the NP elects Chiang Kaishek as chairman of its Standing Committee to replace Zhang Renjie.
8. The Vice-Chancellor of Peking University, Cai Yuanpei, resigns.
August 21. Du Xigui and his cabinet resign.
23. In response to the arrival in Guangzhou of two emissaries sent by Feng Yuxiang, the NG appoints Feng a member of its Military Affairs Committee and of the NG Committee, and as the NP representative in the Nationalist Army.
September 17. Having arrived in Wuyuan (Suiyuan) the preceding day from the Soviet Union, Feng Yuxiang again takes over as Commander-in-Chief of the Nationalist Army and accepts the post given him by the NG on August 23. He swears an oath of allegiance to the NP.
December 1. In Tianjin, Zhang Zuolin is inaugurated as Commander-in-Chief of the National Pacification Army set up to oppose the Northern Expedition. He appoints Sun Chuanfang and Zhang Zongchang as his deputies.

1926

gone into hiding soon after being granted leave of absence (see *B*, March 22).

17. The Second Plenary Session (Plenum) of the Second NPCEC passes restrictions on CCP membership and influence in the upper echelons of the NP.

June 5. The Guangzhou government sends Song Ziwen and others to Hongkong to negotiate with the authorities there and resolve the year-old strike.

7–11. Representatives of Wu Peifu and Zhang Zuolin confer in Tianjin. On the last day they agree to be allies to the end and to oppose the new cabinet of Yan Huiqing, among other matters.

July 1. Chiang Kaishek orders the Northern Expedition to begin.

11. The NRA takes Changsha, the capital of Hunan.

12. The CCPCC issues a statement calling on revolutionaries of all classes to unite, support the Northern Expedition and overthrow warlords and imperialists.

August 9. Chiang Kaishek arrives in Hengyang and prepares for an attack on Wuhan.

22. The NRA takes Yuezhou (Hunan).

25. Wu Peifu arrives in Hankou at the head of a large force to take personal command of the defence of Wuhan against the oncoming Northern Expedition. At a military conference in Nanjing Sun Chuanfang decides to send 100,000 troops to Jiangxi to fight the NRA.

September 5. In retaliation against the Sichuan warlord Yang Sen for detaining two British ships, British marines and sailors shell the town of Wanxian (Sichuan); they destroy Yang Sen's local headquarters and many other buildings, and, according to the Peking government, kill or wound some thousand people.

6. The NRA's Eighth Army takes Hanyang (Hubei), its Fourteenth takes Ganzhou (Jiangxi).

7. The NRA takes Hankou (Hubei).

October 10. The NRA takes the walled city of Wuchang. Following settlement of the sixteen-month-old Hongkong-Guangzhou strike, the boycott against British goods is lifted.

24. A small workers' uprising in Shanghai, led by the CCP, is suppressed by Sun Chuanfang's troops, the 'first Shanghai workers' uprising'.

November 5. The NRA takes Jiujiang (Jiangxi).

8. The NRA takes Nanchang, the capital of Jiangxi, Chiang Kaishek entering the city the following day.

15. In Tianjin, Zhang Zuolin convenes a joint meeting of military officers of Fengtian, Zhili and Shandong and representatives from all

1926

C CULTURAL AND SOCIAL

January. Led jointly by the CCP and NP, the peasants of Hunan begin to organize themselves into associations.
  16. The Second Congress of the NP adopts resolutions on the youth, women's and workers' movements.
  31. The Hunan University is formally set up as a combination of the three Colleges of Technology, Law and Commerce.
March 1. The NG sets up a committee on educational administration. The Peking Library (now the National Library), built by the China Foundation for the Promotion of Education and Culture, is formally opened.
April 26. The police close down the left-wing newspaper *Jingbao* and arrest its editor, Shao Piaoping. (The takeover of Peking on April 18 by the Fengtian-Zhili-Shandong coalition led by Zhang Zuolin resulted in a fierce anti-Communist campaign; many other arrests took place at about this time and many newspaper reporters and university teachers left Peking.)
May 1–12. The Third Congress of the All-China Labour Federation is held in Guangzhou.
  3. The Eastern Library, set up by the Shanghai Commercial Press, opens.
July 24. Printing workers of all newspapers in Guangzhou go on strike for higher wages and other demands.
August 1. The Guangdong University is renamed as the National Sun Yatsen University. Guangzhou postal workers go on strike for higher wages.
  6. Lin Wanli, in charge of Peking's *Shehui ribao* (*Society Daily*) is arrested on orders of Zhang Zongchang for using the newspaper to attack the warlord.
  8. The demands of the printing workers in Guangzhou having been met, they return to work.
  20. Workers in Japanese cotton mills in Shanghai go on strike for a 20 per cent pay rise and better conditions, among other matters.
September 1. The National Association for the Promotion of the Teaching of the National Language holds its inaugural meeting in Shanghai.
November. According to a calculation in *Xiangdao*, the total membership of Hunan's peasant associations in this month is 1,367,727.
  25. In the British Concession in Tianjin, police arrest fourteen NP members on a charge of preparing a strike in a cotton mill and hand them over to Zhang Zuolin's police.

provinces to decide on tactics of alliance with Sun Chuanfang and Wu Peifu to resist the Northern Expeditionary NRA.

20. Zhang Zuolin, Sun Chuanfang, Du Xigui and other military leaders hold a meeting in Tianjin to discuss the sending of troops to the south against the NRA.

21. The First Army of the NRA takes Quanzhou (Fujian).

28. The NG decides to transfer its capital from Guangzhou to Wuhan.

30. At the Seventh Enlarged Plenum of the Executive Committee of the Comintern, meeting in Moscow (November 29-December 16), Stalin urges the CCP to rely on the NP's NRA and to consolidate the united front with the NP.

December 10. The foreign legations in Peking discuss the possibility of recognizing the NG and despatch representatives to Wuhan to investigate the matter; the British minister in Peking, Sir Miles Lampson, visits NG representatives in Wuhan the same month.

1927 *The NP turns against the CCP; the Nanchang Uprising; Chiang Kaishek establishes the NG at Nanjing*

January 1. The NG's capital is formally transferred to Wuhan.

3. British marines in Hankou clash with Chinese crowds attempting to move into the British Concession; the marines withdraw.

4. Chinese crowds move into the British Concession in Hankou.

December 3. In Hankou the Chamber of Commerce stages a demonstration of several thousand demanding that working hours not be shortened, rights for shop owners to dismiss workers, and other conditions. This demonstration was in response to demands and strikes by the unions in Hankou, especially since its fall to the NRA.

D PUBLICATIONS

January. Jiang Guangci's novel *Shaonian piaobozhe* (*The Young Tramp*) is published.

November 10. The Ministry of Education publishes the *Guoyin luomazi pinyin fashi* (*Romanization Models for Chinese Sounds*), completed by the Preparatory Committee for the Unification of the Chinese Official Language.

E NATURAL DISASTERS

July 1. Following a severe drought, floods strike Shaoxing and other places in Zhejiang near the Qiantang River.
5. Serious flooding strikes the parts of Hubei and Anhui along the Yangzi River; the Gan and several other rivers in Jiangxi also flood.
14. A cyclone strikes northern China, among other damage cutting off telecommunications between the Tianjin-Peking area and Shanghai.
August 14. The Ministry of Finance is ordered to send relief to Xianxian and other parts of Zhili, where a cyclone has caused dykes to burst, resulting in disaster affecting more than twenty counties.

F DEATHS

February 14. Xiao Yaonan d. in Wuchang aged 50.
April 26. Shao Piaoping is executed in Peking, aged 37.
August 6. Lin Wanli is executed, aged 53.
  24. Zhang Jian d. aged 73.

The Shanghai Massacre 1927

A ECONOMICS

January 12. The Peking government imposes a $2\frac{1}{2}$ per cent surtax on imported goods and 5 per cent on luxuries, to come into effect on February 1.

1927

7. In Wuchang 100,000 people demonstrate against British imperialism.

February 5. In Yunnan, Long Yun, Hu Ruoyu and other military leaders carry out a *coup d'état* against Tang Jiyao, demanding reform of the government.

19. Owen O'Malley, representing the British minister, and Chen Youren, the NG's Minister of Foreign Affairs, sign an agreement under which the British Concession in Hankou (Hubei) will be returned to China.

20. Owen O'Malley and Chen Youren sign an agreement that the British Concession in Jiujiang (Jiangxi) will be returned to China.

22. The All-China General Trade Union orders an uprising in Shanghai; the masses set up a workers' government.

24. Troops loyal to Sun Chuanfang suppress the second Shanghai uprising.

25. In Guangzhou more than 300,000 people take part in an 'international rally to oppose intervention in China by the imperialists'.

March 15. The British Concessions in Hankou and Jiujiang are formally handed over to the Chinese.

21. The workers of Shanghai begin armed revolution; they begin a general strike, clash with police and attack allied Zhili and Shandong troops: the third Shanghai uprising.

22. The NRA enters Shanghai.

24. The NRA enters Nanjing city. British and US gunboats bombard the city.

April 5. In Shanghai Wang Jingwei (just returned from Europe on April 1) and Chen Duxiu issue a joint statement of their continuing support for the united front between the CCP and the NP.

6. In Peking armed police surround and raid the Soviet legation and arrest Li Dazhao and many other Communists; they obtain many important documents.

8. The Shanxi warlord Yan Xishan issues an order for the suppression of the Communists.

12. Chiang Kaishek carries out an anti-CCP *coup* in Shanghai and begins a massive purge against the CCP in the south-east provinces.

18. Chiang Kaishek sets up his NG in Nanjing; the NG in the former capital Wuhan continues in existence under Wang Jingwei.

27-May 5. The Fifth Congress of the CCP is held in Hankou, some eighty delegates representing nearly 58,000 members. Chen Duxiu's policy of continuing the united front with the Wuhan left-wing NP government led by Wang Jingwei but opposing Chiang Kaishek is adopted.

1927

February 7. The ministers in Peking of Britain, the Netherlands, Japan, the USA, France and Italy formally protest against the surtaxes on imported goods.

July 20. The Nanjing NG proclaims that, as from September 1, it will abolish *lijin* of all description, all native customs duties, all transit duties and all coast trade duty. It proclaims, also to come into effect on September 1, $7\frac{1}{2}$ per cent duty on ordinary goods in addition to the existing 5 per cent, an additional duty of 15 or 25 per cent for luxuries and an additional duty of $57\frac{1}{2}$ per cent for alcoholic liquor or tobacco.

B Official Appointments, Dismissals, Resignations etc.

March 8. Tang Jiyao becomes managing director of a committee which is to govern Yunnan province; Hu Ruoyu and other leaders of the *coup* of February 5 become committee members.

22. A committee of nineteen people, including the chairman of the All-China General Trade Union and CCP member Wang Shouhua, takes office as the Provisional Municipal Government of Shanghai.

April 17. The Wuhan NP's CEC expels Chiang Kaishek from the Party.

27–May 5. The Fifth Congress of the CCP appoints a Political Bureau (Politburo), including Chen Duxiu, Zhou Enlai, Zhang Guotao, Qu Qiubai and Li Lisan.

June 6. Yan Xishan takes over as Commander-in-Chief of the NRA in north China; this signals his allegiance to the NG.

18. Zhang Zuolin assumes the office of Generalissimo in Peking.

August 1. In Nanchang the CCP sets up a central revolutionary committee, including Guo Moruo, Zhou Enlai, Song Qingling, Li Lisan, He Long and Zhu De.

7. The August 7 Conference dismisses Chen Duxiu as head of the CCP and replaces him with Qu Qiubai.

13. Chiang Kaishek announces his retirement from office.

November 14. Holding him responsible for the defeat of the Autumn Harvest Uprising, the CCPCC's provisional Politburo dismisses Mao Zedong from his positions as alternate member of the Politburo and member of the Hunan Provincial CCP Committee.

20. The Preparatory Committee of the Central Research Institute (Academia Sinica) appoints Cai Yuanpei as President of the Institute.

C Cultural and Social

January 1. The Jiangsu provincial government establishes the Shanghai Provisional Court to replace the Mixed Court in the Shanghai International Settlement; all judges in the new court are appointees of the

1927

May 13. The Nanjing NG announces that it will launch a general attack on Wuhan to eliminate the rival NG.

24. At the Eighth Plenum of the Executive Committee of the Comintern, held in Moscow, Stalin makes a speech opposing the creation of peasant soviets in China and advocating the continuation of the united front with Wang Jingwei's branch of the NP.

30. Led by the Hunan CCP, peasant troops from Xiangtan (Hunan) and elsewhere surround Changsha. They were part of a peasant army of nearly 100,000 which had been gathering in preparation for a counter-attack on Changsha following the massacre of May 20–21 (see C).

31. Chen Duxiu orders the peasant armies to lift the siege of Changsha. Some 2000 Japanese troops land in Qingdao (Shandong) to preserve Japanese interests in Shandong in the face of the Northern Expedition.

June 1. Feng Yuxiang's Nationalist Army occupies Kaifeng (Henan).

10–13. In Zhengzhou (Henan) Feng Yuxiang holds a conference with a delegation from the Wuhan government, including Wang Jingwei. They agree to leave Henan in Feng's control and to try to restrict CCP influence.

16. A conference of cadres of Zhang Zuolin's National Pacification Army concludes in Peking with a decision to organize a military government in Peking in opposition to Chiang Kaishek.

19–21. Feng Yuxiang and Chiang Kaishek confer in Xuzhou (Jiangsu). At the end they issue a joint statement proclaiming their determination to complete the Northern Expedition.

21. Feng cables the Wuhan government urging opposition to the Communists and unity with Chiang Kaishek's Nanjing government.

July 13. The CCPCC issues a statement saying it has decided to withdraw CCP members from the Wuhan government, but does not intend to break with the NP.

15. In Wuhan, the NP's CEC orders all CCP members of the NP to renounce CCP membership. This is the final break of the Wuhan government with the Communists and the beginning of fierce suppression of the CCP in Hubei.

27. Borodin and other Soviet advisers of the Wuhan government leave Wuhan for home.

August 1. Ye Ting, He Long and others lead a Communist uprising in Nanchang, and take the city. This 'Nanchang Uprising' is regarded by the CCP as the birthday of the Red Army.

5. He Long's and Ye Ting's forces withdraw from Nanchang and retreat towards the coast.

7. In Jiujiang (Jiangxi) the CCP holds an emergency conference.

1927

Jiangsu provincial government.

4–February 5. Mao Zedong undertakes his investigation into the peasant movement in several counties in Hunan, including Liling, Hengshan, and Xiangtan.

16. At the Yong'an [Wing On] Co. Ltd. in Shanghai over 4000 workers go on strike for increased wages, reduced working hours and better conditions. The strike ends on January 25 after partial agreement to the demands. This was one of many strikes in Shanghai at about this time. The New York Trustees of the missionary Lingnan University in Guangzhou decide to hand over its administration to a predominantly Chinese Board of Managers: a first success in the movement by the Chinese to win back authority in educational institutions.

February 19. The All-China General Trade Union calls a general strike in Shanghai; it puts forward seventeen demands, including higher workers' wages, recognition of unions, better working conditions, civil liberties, and support for the NRA and its Northern Expedition.

24. Following considerable bloodshed, the Shanghai strike is broken and the workers resume work.

March 27. The All-China General Trade Union holds a ceremony in Shanghai to mark the official resumption of legal activities in the new political climate in Shanghai. Labour activities and union membership expand rapidly about this time.

April 12. The 'Shanghai Massacre' begins. Chiang Kaishek orders a general attack against the trade unions of Shanghai. His army disarms workers, and suppresses labour organizations. Workers' demonstrations are attacked and many workers are killed, wounded or arrested. This action places Chiang Kaishek in the right wing of the NP.

13. Some 100,000 workers take part in a general strike in Shanghai. A similar number attends a mass meeting demanding punishment for the destroyers of the unions, and protection for the All-China General Trade Union. Troops fire at the demonstrators, killing over 100 and wounding many more.

14. Shanghai authorities order the closure of the All-China General Trade Union.

15. In Guangzhou, troops are sent to attack trade unions, peasant associations, students' and women's organizations. More than 100 leftist organizations are closed, some 100 people are killed, over 2000 are arrested, and many leftist workers are dismissed. This action was but one of many similar against the labour movement and the Communists at about this time.

May 21–22. In Changsha a wave of terror begins against the Hunan General Trade Union, and other revolutionary groups. Troops move

1927

Chen Duxiu is denounced as a right opportunist. The policy of agrarian revolution against the NP 'white terror' is adopted. This is called the August 7 Conference.

13. Chiang Kaishek issues a statement in Shanghai calling for unity between the Wuhan and Nanjing factions of the NG and the completion of the Northern Expedition.

20. On Lushan (Jiangxi), Wang Jingwei and others of the Wuhan government confer with Li Zongren and other Nanjing representatives on ways to effect a merger of the two governments.

September 8. Mao Zedong and the Workers' and Peasants' Revolutionary Army (WPRA) formally launch the Autumn Harvest Uprising in eastern Hunan.

12. The WPRA takes Liling (Hunan).

15. A joint meeting of the NP's CEC and CSC in Nanjing decides to set up the Central Special Committee of the Chinese NP. It is composed of members of the three major NP factions, the Nanjing and Wuhan governments and the Western Hills clique, and thus represents the merger of the three groups. The Committee holds its first meeting the following day. The WPRA takes Liuyang (Hunan).

19. The WPRA is seriously defeated on the Jiangxi-Hunan border.

25. Ye Ting, He Long, Zhou Enlai and their troops occupy Swatow (Guangdong), but are forced to retreat September 30.

October. Mao Zedong moves to the Jinggang Mountains (Jiangxi) and sets up the first revolutionary base there.

November 1. In Guangdong, a peasant army led by Peng Pai occupies Haifeng. They took several other towns, including Lufeng, at about the same time.

13. A General Conference of Workers, Peasants and Soldiers in Lufeng (Guangdong) sets up a soviet government, China's first soviet political power.

18. Troops under Mao seize Chaling (Hunan) and hold it for over forty days, after which they return to the Jinggang Mountains.

18–21. A public General Conference of Workers, Peasants and Soldiers is held in Haifeng (Guangdong). It results in the establishment of the Haifeng soviet government.

December 1. Chiang Kaishek marries Song Meiling (the sister of Sun Yatsen's widow Song Qingling) in Shanghai.

11. Ye Ting, Zhang Tailei and other CCP members lead some 50,000 workers in an armed uprising in Guangzhou; they seize control of the city and set up a soviet government: the Canton [Guangzhou] Commune.

13. The Canton Commune is suppressed; several thousand workers

into the quarters of workers', peasants' and students' organizations, shooting or arresting the occupants. Executions, often preceded by torture, continue through the following days; many flee to the countryside.

June 6. Zhu Peide, the Wuhan-appointed Governor of Jiangxi, exiles all Communists from the province; he orders the suspension of the peasant, worker and student movements in Jiangxi, and the closure of the peasant associations, student unions, and the General Trade Union. All CCP newspaper offices are closed down. Zhu sends in troops to enforce these orders.

23. Wang Jingwei appears before, and is cheered by, the Fourth Congress of the All-China Labour Federation (opened in Wuhan on June 19).

28. Troops move in to suppress the General Trade Union in Wuhan.

July 14–19. Soldiers are sent to the premises of twenty-five trade unions in Hubei, confiscating their archives and property. This action was part of the systematic destruction of the labour movement in Hubei.

September 23. The Nanjing Shortwave Wireless Station is completed; it is capable of direct communication with many parts of China and the Philippines.

25. Military police in Peking raid nine government schools and the private universities; they arrest some thirty students and execute ten.

October 4. Some 8000 workers from the British-American Tobacco Company in Shanghai go on strike.

16. The first tooth of Peking Man (*Sinanthropus pekinensis*) is discovered at Zhoukoudian, near Peking.

November 15. The National Conservatory of Music in Shanghai begins classes. The opening ceremony takes place November 27.

20. The Preparatory Committee of the Central Research Institute (Academia Sinica) holds its inaugural meeting and adopts guidelines for the organization of the Central Research Institute.

D PUBLICATIONS

In Shanghai the thirty-two-volumed *Xiangqi lou riji* (*Diary of Wang Kaiyun*).

March. Mao Zedong's 'Hunan nongmin yundong kaocha baogao' ('Report on an Investigation of the Peasant Movement in Hunan').

March–November. The *Xiaoshuo yuebao* serializes the comic novel *Zhao Ziyue* by Lao She (pen-name of Shu Qingchun).

October. The *Minsheng bao* (*People's Livelihood*) begins publication in Nanjing.

and peasants are killed. The Soviet consulate is closed down.

14. The NG breaks off diplomatic relations with the USSR and orders all Soviet diplomats and citizens to leave.

16. The NRA takes Xuzhou (Jiangsu), the headquarters of the warlord Zhang Zongchang, who retreats towards Shandong.

17. Wang Jingwei leaves Shanghai by ship for France.

1928 *Completion of the Northern Expedition*

January 12. The CCP forces surviving from the Nanchang Uprising (see August 1, 1927) and the occupation of Swatow (see September 25, 1927), led by Zhu De and Chen Yi, occupy Yizhang (Hunan), the beginning of the South Hunan Uprising. At the end of January a soviet government is set up in Yizhang, one of several in southern Hunan at about this time.

February 28. Anti-CCP troops assault the soviets of Haifeng and Lufeng, destroying them within a few days.

April. Zhu De and Chen Yi lead their troops out of southern Hunan and towards the Jinggang Mountains to join forces with Mao Zedong, arriving late April.

20. Japanese naval forces land in Qingdao (Shandong).

26. The NG's Ministry of Foreign Affairs protests against the sending of Japanese troops to Shandong.

Winter. Publication of Lao Naixuan's miscellaneous writings *Tongxiang Lao xiansheng yigao* (*Posthumous Manuscripts of Mr Lao of Tongxiang*).

E   NATURAL DISASTERS

May 23. A severe earthquake strikes Gansu, killing some 37,000 people. In the Liangzhou region many villages and towns are totally destroyed; in Liangzhou itself some 70 per cent of the population is killed.

F   DEATHS

March 31. Kang Youwei d. in Qingdao (Shandong) aged 69.
April 11. Ye Dehui d. aged 63.
  28. Li Dazhao is executed in Peking, aged 37.
May 23. The Yunnan warlord Tang Jiyao d. aged 44.
June 2. The eminent scholar Wang Guowei drowns himself at the Summer Palace outside Peking, aged 49.
July 5. Chen Yannian, son of Chen Duxiu, is killed during an anti-CCP purge in Shanghai, aged 27.
September 3. Zhao Ersun d. aged 83.
  19. Lu Deming, one of the main leaders of the WPRA, is killed in battle.
December 12. Zhang Tailei, leader of the Canton Commune, is killed, aged 28.

Death of Zhang Zuolin   1928

A   ECONOMICS

June 20–30. The NG's Ministry of Finance holds a National Economic Conference in Shanghai. It adopts resolutions to disband surplus troops, to liquidate national debts, to reform taxation, and others.
July 1–10. A National Financial Conference is held in Nanjing. It adopts a general programme of financial unification and plans for the administration of the proposals put forward by the Shanghai Economic Conference.
July 25. The Treaty Regulating Tariff Relations between the ROC and the USA is signed in Beiping.
August 17. The Treaty Regulating Tariff Relations between China and Germany is signed in Nanjing.
November 1. The NG's Central Bank of China formally opens for business in Shanghai.

1928

29\. The warlord Zhang Zongchang flees from Ji'nan in the face of the continuing advance of the Northern Expedition.

30\. NRA troops under He Yaozu and others occupy Ji'nan.

May 3. Japanese and NRA troops clash in Ji'nan causing considerable destruction and loss of life: the May Third Incident. Chiang Kaishek orders the Northern Expedition forces to withdraw from Ji'nan.

4\. The NG's Minister of Foreign Affairs, Huang Fu, telegraphs the Japanese Prime Minister Tanaka Giichi protesting strongly against the May Third Incident.

7\. The Japanese in Ji'nan put forward five demands on China, including that all Chinese troops should withdraw to a limit of twenty *li* from Ji'nan and from either side of the Ji'nan–Qingdao railway; they demand a reply within twelve hours.

8\. Japanese troops begin driving Chinese to positions at least twenty *li* from Ji'nan, completing the process by May 11.

9\. Japanese troops bombard Ji'nan.

18\. In identical notes the Japanese government informs Zhang Zuolin and the NG that if disorders persist in north China Japan will need 'to take appropriate and effective steps' for the maintenance of peace and order in Manchuria.

June 4. Zhang Zuolin's special train is blown up as he is returning to Shenyang; the incident is directed by a staff officer of the Japanese Kwantung Army.

6\. Peking falls to the NRA.

8\. Yan Xishan's Third Army Group of the NRA formally occupies Peking.

12\. The NRA takes Tianjin.

18–**July 11.** The Sixth Congress of the CCP is held in Moscow. It denounces Qu Qiubai's putschism and advocates the overthrow of the NG.

23\. Red Army troops defeat Jiangxi forces at Longyuankou (Jiangxi). This leads to a peak of CCP control in the Jinggang Mountains, embracing Ninggang and other counties, and to the establishment of a border government.

28\. The name of Peking is changed to Beiping, and of Zhili Province to Hebei.

July 7. The NG's Ministry of Foreign Affairs declares its wish to revise all unexpired unequal treaties.

9\. Jin Shuren carries out a *coup d'état* in Xinjiang and seizes power.

21\. Huang Gonglüe revolts in Jiayi (Hunan). A day later, Peng Dehuai seizes Pingjiang (Hunan), and joins forces with Huang Gonglüe.

August 6. Hayashi Gonsuke delivers to Zhang Xueliang, the new

December 7. The NG promulgates detailed customs import tariff rates, to come into effect on February 1, 1929.
19. The Treaty Regulating Tariff Relations between the ROC and the Kingdom of the Netherlands is signed in Nanjing.
20. The Tariff Autonomy Treaty between China and Great Britain and the Treaty Regulating Tariff Relations between China and Sweden are signed in Nanjing.
22. The Treaty Regulating Customs Relations between the ROC and the French Republic is signed in Nanjing.

B OFFICIAL APPOINTMENTS, RESIGNATIONS, DISMISSALS ETC.

January 4. Chiang Kaishek, arriving in Nanjing, resumes his position as Commander-in-Chief and other offices.
February 27. The NG's Military Affairs Committee appoints Chiang Kaishek Commander-in-Chief of the NRA's First Army Group, and Feng Yuxiang and Yan Xishan Commanders-in-Chief of the Second and Third Army Groups respectively.
April 23. The NG formally confirms Cai Yuanpei as President of the Academia Sinica.
30. Zhu De becomes the Commander and Mao Zedong the Party Representative of the Fourth Workers' and Peasants' Red Army, formed the same day through a merger of Zhu's and Mao's troops.
June 18–July 11. The Sixth Congress of the CCP elects Xiang Zhongfa as Secretary-General, and Zhou Enlai to head the Organization Department, Li Lisan the Propaganda Department and Liu Shaoqi the Labour Department.
July 4. Zhang Xueliang assumes office as Commander-in-Chief Preserving Peace in the Three Manchurian Provinces, symbolizing his control of Manchuria in succession to his father Zhang Zuolin.
9. Jin Shuren takes over as Chairman of the Xinjiang provincial government and Commander-in-Chief of Xinjiang.
23. Peng Dehuai becomes Commander of the Workers' and Peasants' Fifth Red Army, set up the same day.
October 10. Chiang Kaishek is formally inaugurated as Chairman of the NG; Tan Yankai as President of the Executive Yuan, Hu Hanmin of the Legislative Yuan, Wang Chonghui of the Judicial Yuan, Dai Jitao of the Examination Yuan and Cai Yuanpei of the Control Yuan.

C CULTURAL AND SOCIAL

February 6. The Third Sun Yatsen University, in Hangzhou, is renamed

1928

ruler of Manchuria, a message from the Japanese Prime Minister, Tanaka Giichi, informing Zhang of Japan's opposition to the union of Manchuria with China.

October 3. The NP's CEC adopts the Organic Law of the NG of the ROC. It stipulates that the NG will be led by a Chairman and consist of five *yuan*: the Executive Yuan, the Legislative Yuan, the Judicial Yuan, the Examination Yuan, and the Control Yuan.

20. The NG promulgates the Organic Laws of the Five Yuan of the NG.

November 22. In Nanjing the Chinese Minister of Foreign Affairs, Wang Zhengting, and the Belgian *chargé d'affaires*, J. Guillaume, sign the Preliminary Treaty of Amity and Commerce between the ROC and the Union of Belgium and Luxembourg.

December. The CCP of the Jinggang Mountains convenes a conference to decide on strategy to deal with the encirclement campaign of the NP Jiangxi and Hunan forces against the Jinggang Mountains. It is attended by the special committee of Jinggangshan, the representatives of the Fourth and Fifth Red Armies and others. It decides that Mao Zedong and Zhu De should lead the Fourth Red Army to attack southern Jiangxi and western Fujian and link up with other soviet areas to create a new revolutionary base, while Peng Dehuai's Fifth Red Army should remain to defend the Jinggang Mountains.

11. The main force of Peng Dehuai's Fifth Red Army and Zhu De's Fourth Red Army meet at Ninggang (Jiangxi).

19. China and Portugal sign the Preliminary Treaty of Amity and Commerce in Nanjing.

27. China and Spain sign the Preliminary Treaty of Amity and Commerce.

29. Zhang Xueliang formally pledges the loyalty of the Manchurian provinces to the NG. The unification of China is thus more or less achieved.

1928

the University of Zhejiang.

10. The Fourth Sun Yatsen University, in Nanjing, is renamed the National University of Jiangsu.

21. The NG orders the abolition of the spring and autumn ceremonies in commemoration of Confucius.

March 9. In Shanghai 6000 men and 111,600 women workers of 93 textile mills go on strike demanding redress and compensation for the family of a worker killed by police during a demonstration. The strike terminates on March 13 when the workers are given an assurance that their demands will be met.

10. The NG promulgates the Provisional Criminal Code; it goes into force April 1.

May 15–28. The National Education Conference is held in Nanjing; it resolves, through education, to promote nationalism, democracy and social justice, and to reorganize China's school system.

June 7. After the judgment goes against them (see March 9), 5000 male, 50,000 female and 10,000 juvenile filature workers in Shanghai go on strike. Part of the compensation requested and a portion of other demands is granted and almost all workers return to work on June 25.

October 28. Ma Fuxiang and others set up the Chinese Islamic Society in Nanjing.

November 1–10. The National Opium Prohibition Conference is held in Nanjing.

D   PUBLICATIONS

Publication of *Xiying xianhua* (*The Causeries of Xiying*), a selection of essays by Chen Yuan (Xiying) (March), and *Hua zhi si* (*Temple of Flowers*), a collection of stories by his wife Ling Shuhua.

March 10. *Xinyue* (*Crescent Moon*) begins publication.

June 22. Date of the 'explanation of compilation and printing', which follows the preface, in the *Qingshi gao* (*Draft History of the Qing*), published in Peking in some 130 volumes.

August 5. The *Xin chenbao* (*New Morning Post*) begins publication in Beiping.

October. Zhu Ziqing's collection of essays *Beiying* (*The Back View*) is published in Shanghai.

December. The Institute of History and Philology of Academia Sinica publishes the first *Anyang fajue baogao* (*Report on the Anyang Excavations*) by Li Ji and others.

1929 *The Gutian Conference; the Khabarovsk Protocol*

January 1–25. China's major military men, NG and NP leaders, meet in Nanjing to discuss ways of reducing China's armed forces.
14. The Fourth Red Army under Zhu De and Mao Zedong leaves the Jinggang Mountains base.
27. He Jian orders a general attack on the Jinggang Mountains.
30. He Jian's troops retake the Jinggang Mountains base; Peng Dehuai and his Fifth Red Army withdraw to join Mao and Zhu.
February 9. The CCPCC, dominated by Li Lisan, writes a letter criticizing Mao Zedong's tactics and advises him to disperse his troops in small groups over the countryside.
10. Though suffering very heavy casualties, Mao Zedong's Fourth Red Army defeats an NP force at Dabaidi, north of Ruijin (Jiangxi), establishing the basis for developing a central soviet.
16. The NG promulgates a new system of weights and measures, to be standard throughout China. The system is two-pronged: the standard metric units, envisaged as permanent, and a temporary one

E Natural Disasters

Drought and resultant famine reach serious proportions in Gansu, Henan, Chahar, Suiyuan, Shaanxi, Shanxi, Shandong, and Hebei.

August 19. Two rivers in Shandong flood and drown more than 1800 people and leave some 30,000 homeless.

F Deaths

March 28. Guo Liang, Hunan trade union leader and CCP activist, is executed in Changsha, aged 28.

April 21. Luo Yinong, leading CCP figure, is executed in Shanghai, aged 27.

May 1. Xiang Jingyu, the wife of Cai Hesen and a prominent CCP leader, is executed, aged 33.

4. Late at night, Japanese soldiers kill Cai Gongshi, the Commissioner for Foreign Affairs for Shandong, in Ji'nan aged 40.

June 4. Zhang Zuolin d. aged 53.

July 7. The Governor of Xinjiang, Yang Zengxin, is assassinated, aged 63.

9. Fan Yaonan is executed on orders of Jin Shuren for the assassination of Yang Zengxin.

Significant archaeological discoveries are made 1929

A Economics

February 1. The NG's import tariff rates come into effect (see also A, December 7, 1928).

26. The Ministry of Finance announces the results of its research on China's foreign indebtedness: (*i*) long-term debts 1,046,700,000 *yuan*; (*ii*) short-term debts 100,070,000 *yuan*.

April. The Commission of Financial Experts, presided over by Dr E.W. Kemmerer, makes an estimate of China's total indebtedness, domestic and foreign, as at December 31, 1928: 2,530,286,000 *yuan* (principal only).

B Official Appointments, Resignations, Dismissals etc.

January 1. Lu Diping, the Chairman of Hunan, is appointed General Commander of Bandit Suppression in Hunan and Jiangxi provinces, and He Jian his deputy.

1929

closer to the old system, for market use only.

March 15–28. The NP holds its Third National Congress in Nanjing.

26. The NG orders a punitive military action against the Guangxi warlords Li Zongren and Bai Chongxi (see also B, February 21).

28. The Chinese Minister of Foreign Affairs, Wang Zhengting, and the Japanese minister in Nanjing, Yoshizawa Kenkichi, sign an agreement on the May Third Incident in Ji'nan: China guarantees to protect Japanese lives and property in China; Japan agrees to withdraw all troops within two months.

April 5. Mao Zedong answers the letter of February 9, rebutting the criticisms. Chiang Kaishek arrives with troops in Wuhan during the military campaign against the Guangxi warlords. By the end of April the campaign breaks their power in Hunan and Hubei.

May 20. Japanese troops complete their withdrawal from Shandong.

23. As Feng Yuxiang prepares to fight Chiang Kaishek one of his key subordinates, Han Fuju, declares in favour of Chiang. Han's defection included several other generals and over 100,000 troops and rendered Feng's position temporarily impossible.

27. Chinese police raid and search the Soviet consulate in Harbin (Heilongjiang) and arrest nearly forty Soviet citizens there.

June. Peng Dehuai's Fifth Red Army returns to Jinggang Mountains; it restores the Hunan-Jiangxi soviet area and soviet political power.

1. The ceremony by which Sun Yatsen's body is laid to rest in a mausoleum outside Nanjing is completed.

17. The USSR increases its military strength near Manzhouli (Heilongjiang) on the border with the Soviet Union.

July 10. Chinese authorities in Heilongjiang seize the Chinese Eastern Railway by force from the USSR.

13. The USSR sends an ultimatum to the NG: the Soviet government demands return to the *status quo ante* on the Chinese Eastern Railway within three days or it will 'resort to other means for the protection of the lawful rights of the USSR'.

18. The Chinese *chargé d'affaires* in Moscow is handed a note saying that the USSR is breaking all diplomatic relations with China and suspending all railway communications between the two countries.

August 11. Military clashes between Soviet and Chinese troops occur near Manzhouli (Heilongjiang).

15. Zhang Xueliang sends out 60,000 men to reinforce the border.

18. Soviet troops occupy Dongning (Heilongjiang).

October 10. Song Zheyuan and twenty-six other leading officers of Feng Yuxiang's Nationalist Army cable Feng and Yan Xishan denouncing the NG and calling for a military campaign against it.

16. The Ministry of Education appoints Cai Yuanpei, Wu Zhihui and thirty others to the Preparatory Committee for the Unification of the Chinese Official Language.

February 21. The Wuhan branch of the high NP organ, the Political Council, orders the dismissal of the Chairman of Hunan, Lu Diping. (The Wuhan branch of the Political Council had continued to exist after the dissolution of the Wuhan regime in 1927, and was dominated by the Guangxi warlords Li Zongren and Bai Chongxi.)

March 2. He Jian takes over as Chairman of Hunan to replace Lu Diping.

26. The NG dismisses Li Zongren and Bai Chongxi from all their posts for plotting against the NG.

27. The Third National Congress of the NP elects a CEC of thirty-six, including Chiang Kaishek, Tan Yankai, Hu Hanmin, Feng Yuxiang, and Wang Jingwei; and a CSC of twelve, including Wu Zhihui, Zhang Renjie and Cai Yuanpei. It also expels Li Zongren and Bai Chongxi from the Party.

May 16. Feng Yuxiang accepts appointment by his generals as Commander-in-Chief of 'the north-western army to protect the Party and save the nation', independent of Chiang Kaishek. This action was tantamount to rebellion against the NG.

23. The Standing Committee of the NP's CEC decides to expel Feng Yuxiang from the NP and to dismiss him from all NG posts.

July 11. The Soviet general manager of the Chinese Eastern Railway, F. Emshanov, is dismissed and replaced by Fan Qiguang.

November 15. The CCPCC resolves to expel Chen Duxiu from the Party, among other reasons for failing to side with the USSR against China in the conflict over the Chinese Eastern Railway.

C CULTURAL AND SOCIAL

March 7–May 10. Excavations directed by Li Ji are carried out at Anyang (Henan) and result in the discovery of numerous inscribed oracle bones and tortoise shells.

April 18. The Ministry of Communications orders all postal organizations to adopt Chinese in place of English as the language for official documents.

July 25. The NG promulgates the Anti-Opium Law.

October 7–December 12. Further excavations at Anyang result in the discovery of numerous inscribed oracle bones, vessels, and a fragment of painted pottery.

November 1. The NG's Trade Union Act comes into force; the func-

1929

27. Feng Yuxiang's Nationalist Army launches a general attack in the direction of Luoyang and Zhengzhou (Henan).

November 17. Soviet troops with aircraft and tanks launch a fierce attack in the Manzhouli area.

20. Soviet troops seize Manzhouli.

22. After much fighting in the war between Feng Yuxiang's and Chiang Kaishek's troops and a decisive victory by the latter in the Luoyang area, Feng's Nationalist Army retreats towards Shanzhou (Henan).

27. Chiang's troops occupy Shanzhou.

December. The Ninth CCP Congress of the Fourth Red Army (the 'Gutian Conference') is held in Gutian (Fujian). Following Mao Zedong it attacks adventurism and stresses the political and non-combatant nature of the Red Army.

22. Representatives of China and the USSR sign the Khabarovsk Protocol: the *status quo* of the Chinese Eastern Railway before July 10 is to be restored; the Chinese are to release all arrested Soviet citizens; Soviet consulates in Manchuria are to be restored.

23. The Soviet government orders the withdrawal of its troops in China.

tions of unions include the social and cultural well-being of members and 'the settlement of disputes between workers and employers'.

7–11. The Fifth Congress of the All-China Labour Federation is held secretly in Shanghai.

December 2. Pei Wenzhong unearths the first Peking Man skull at Zhoukoudian (Hebei).

30. The NG promulgates the Factories Act; among many other provisions on working conditions in factories it lays down that no child under fourteen may be employed and that 'the regular working day for adults is eight hours'. The date set for the Act to come into force is February 1, 1931.

D PUBLICATIONS

February 1. The Nanjing *Zhongyang ribao* (*Central Daily*) begins publication.

March. The *Baoxue yuekan* (*The Journalism Monthly*) begins publication in Shanghai.

May. The *Nanguo yuekan* (*South China Monthly*) begins publication, edited by Tian Han.

June 16. The *Wuhan ribao* (*Wuhan Daily News*) begins publication in Hankou.

October. Li Feigan (penname Ba Jin) publishes his first novel *Miewang* (*Destruction*) in Shanghai.

December 1. The *Huabei ribao* (*North China Daily*) begins publication in Beiping, the *Xinjing ribao* (*New Capital Daily*) in Nanjing.

E NATURAL DISASTERS

Severe drought-famine continues in Gansu, Henan, Shaanxi, Shanxi, Chahar, Suiyuan, Shandong and Hebei, severely affecting some 20,000,000 people.

August. The Yongding River (Hebei) floods seriously. Parts of the Beiping–Shenyang railway are submerged by flooding on the Grand Canal and Liao River.

F DEATHS

January 19. Liang Qichao d. aged 55.

August 30. The CCP peasant leader Peng Pai is executed near Shanghai, aged 32.

1930 *Chiang Kaishek wins a civil war against Feng Yuxiang and Yan Xishan; the CCP briefly takes Changsha*

February 3. Mao Zedong's Fourth Red Army returns from Fujian to Jiangxi and takes Huichang, and several other counties.
7. A CCP conference in southern Jiangxi decides to establish the Jiangxi provincial soviet government.
10. Yan Xishan cables Chiang Kaishek suggesting they should both retire from politics.
26. The CCPCC issues a circular calling on the Party to organize workers' strikes, local uprisings and army mutinies; and on the Red Army to move towards key cities and join in the workers' struggle. This is 'the Li Lisan line'.
March 18. Mao Zedong's forces seize Ganzhou (Jiangxi). Yan Xishan has all NP and NG offices in the areas under his control seized.
23. Mao Zedong's forces take Nankang (Jiangxi).
April 18. The British minister to China, Sir Miles Lampson, and the NG's Minister of Foreign Affairs, Wang Zhengting, sign an agreement under which Weihaiwei (Shandong) is to be returned to China.
May 1. Chiang Kaishek makes a speech declaring war against Feng Yuxiang and Yan Xishan.
16. The French minister to China, D. de Martel, and Wang Zhengting sign the Convention Regulating the Relations between China and France Concerning French Indo-China and the Chinese Provinces Adjoining.
20. A National Congress of delegates from the soviet areas meets outside Shanghai and decides to set up a central soviet government.
June 11. The CCP Politburo adopts a resolution repeating the ideas in the February 26 circular and calling on the Party to 'plan for an initial victory in Wuhan and the adjoining provinces'.
26. Yan Xishan's forces occupy Ji'nan (Shandong) in the civil war against Chiang Kaishek.
July 13. In Beiping, Wang Jingwei, Yan Xishan, Feng Yuxiang, and others begin an 'enlarged conference' to try to organize an alternative government to Chiang Kaishek's NG.
15. Peng Dehuai's troops occupy Pingjiang (Hunan).
27. CCP troops under Peng Dehuai seize Changsha, capital of Hunan.
August 1. Japanese, US and other foreign warships open fire on Changsha.
1–2. The CCP forces of Zhu De and Mao Zedong attempt unsuccessfully to take Nanchang.
5. Troops of the NG's Chairman of Hunan, He Jian, protected by the foreign warships, recapture Changsha. Peng Dehuai's troops retreat to Liuyang.

League of Left-Wing Writers set up **1930**

A ECONOMICS

January 15. Song Ziwen, the Minister of Finance, issues an order that from February 1, 1930, 'customs duties on imports from abroad will be collected on a gold basis'. The unit of calculation of duties is to be equal to 60.1866 centigrammes of pure gold.

May 6. The Japanese *chargé d'affaires*, Shigemitsu Mamoru, and the Chinese Minister of Foreign Affairs, Wang Zhengting, sign the Sino-Japanese Tariff Agreement in Nanjing.

September 22. The British minister, Sir Miles Lampson, informs Wang Zhengting of the British government's agreement that the British share of the Boxer Indemnity should return to Chinese government control as from December 1, 1922. It is to be used for building railways and educational purposes.

October 20. China National Aviation Corporation inaugurates an air service from Shanghai to Hankou, stopping at Nanjing, Anqing (Anhui), and Jiujiang (Jiangxi).

B OFFICIAL APPOINTMENTS, RESIGNATIONS, DISMISSALS ETC,

March 1. The Third Plenum of the NP's Third CEC expels Wang Jingwei from the Party.

8. Zhang Qilong is appointed Chairman of the county soviet government of Liuyang (Hunan), set up simultaneously by a conference of workers, peasants and soldiers of the county.

April 1. Yan Xishan sends a circular cable from Taiyuan that he has assumed the office of Commander-in-Chief of land, naval and air forces opposed to Chiang Kaishek. Feng Yuxiang and Li Zongren send out circular cables that they are the deputy Commanders-in-Chief.

5. The NG issues an order dismissing Feng Yuxiang from all his posts.

June 21. The NG appoints Zhang Xueliang as deputy Commander-in-Chief of land, naval and air forces.

July 15. A conference of workers, peasants and soldiers in Pingjiang (Hunan) appoints Zhang Huaiyi as Chairman of the Pingjiang county soviet executive committee.

30. Li Lisan is appointed Chairman of the soviet government of Hunan, set up the same day with the CCP capture of Changsha.

September 1. The 'enlarged conference' in Beiping forms Yan Xishan, Feng Yuxiang, Wang Jingwei, Li Zongren and others into a seven-man National Government Committee with Yan as Chairman.

1930

15. Against strong resistance, Chiang Kaishek troops retake Ji'nan; Yan Xishan's retreat in disorder.

30. The combined CCP forces of Zhu De and Peng Dehuai begin a second attack on Changsha, which lasts about a fortnight.

September 15. The CCP forces of Zhu De and Peng Dehuai split up and begin returning to southern Jiangxi. This action results from a decision taken by Mao Zedong, without the CCPCC's permission, to abandon the attempt to take large cities.

23. Zhang Xueliang's troops, intervening in the civil war, arrive in Beiping from the north-east and take over full control of the city on behalf of Chiang Kaishek's NG.

24–28. At the Third Plenum of the CCP's Sixth CC, held on Lushan (Jiangxi), Qu Qiubai and Chen Shaoyu attack Li Lisan's policy. Zhou Enlai defends its 'spirit' as 'correct'. (Chen Shaoyu, also called Wang Ming, was the leader of the 'Twenty-eight Bolsheviks', or 'Returned Students', who had come back to China from Moscow in mid-1930.) Xiang Zhongfa's report which opens the plenum places current CCP membership at 122,318.

October 1. The British return Weihaiwei to China.

3. Chiang Kaishek's troops take Kaifeng (Henan) from Feng Yuxiang's Nationalist Army.

5. CCP troops under Zhu De and Mao Zedong take Ji'an (Jiangxi).

6. Chiang Kaishek's troops recover Zhengzhou (Henan).

9. Chiang Kaishek's forces recapture Luoyang (Henan); this action in effect concluded the civil war against Yan Xishan and Feng Yuxiang.

11. Chinese and Soviet representatives Mo Dehui and Leo Karakhan hold their first meeting in Moscow to negotiate on the Chinese Eastern Railway, trade, and diplomatic relations.

November 5. Chiang Kaishek's troops begin a general attack against the soviet areas of Hunan, Hubei and Jiangxi for the 'First Encirclement Campaign'.

16. The Comintern issues an attack on the Li Lisan line.

18. Chiang Kaishek's troops retake Ji'an (Jiangxi) from the CCP forces.

25. The CCP Politburo passes a resolution denouncing the Li Lisan line.

December 8. Soldiers, claimed by Mao to be supporters of Li Lisan, mutiny against Mao Zedong and, in Futian (Jiangxi), release prisoners Mao had earlier had arrested. Mao takes about two months to suppress the rebellion, and 2000–3000 people are killed. This is known as the Futian Incident.

27. Encirclement Campaign troops commanded by Zhang Huizan

1930

9. Yan Xishan formally assumes office as Chairman of the Beiping NG, set up the same day.

October 31. Following the collapse of their war against Chiang Kaishek and mutual consultations in Taiyuan, Feng Yuxiang and Yan Xishan both retire from politics.

November 25. Li Lisan resigns from the CCP's Politburo.

C   CULTURAL AND SOCIAL

February 17. Representatives of China, Brazil, Great Britain, the USA, the Netherlands, and Norway sign the Agreement Relating to the Chinese Courts in the International Settlement at Shanghai, under which the NG will set up a District Court and Branch High Court, both to be subject to Chinese law, in the International Settlement at Shanghai; an important step in the abolition of extraterritoriality. The French representative signs the agreement February 22.

March 2. The League of Left-Wing Writers is set up in Shanghai.

April 1–11. The Fourth National Games are held in Hangzhou (Zhejiang).

15–25. The Second National Educational Congress is held in Nanjing, under the chairmanship of the Minister of Education, Jiang Menglin. It adopts several important concepts, including compulsory education, with a plan to train 14,000,000 primary school teachers within twenty years, and mass education for adults.

16. The National Meteorological Conference, convened by Academia Sinica, is held in Nanjing.

21. The NP's CEC resolves to name the phonetic script *zhuyin fuhao* (phonetic alphabet).

29. The Society of Arts and Drama, founded the previous autumn, is closed down by the NG's police; it is among several left-wing cultural organizations suspended at about this time.

July 2. A branch office of the International Labour Organization is formally set up in Nanjing.

15. A conference of workers, peasants and soldiers in Pingjiang (Hunan) passes land, marriage and labour laws for the county.

30. The soviet government of Hunan promulgates land and labour laws.

D   PUBLICATIONS

Publication of Ma Xulun's *Zhuangzi yizheng* (*Commentary on the Zhuangzi*), Guo Moruo's *Zhongguo gudai shehui yanjiu* (*Research on Ancient*

launch an attack against the CCP's central base area in the Huangpi (Jiangxi) region, but are defeated in battle by Mao's forces.
30. Britain formally returns its Concession in Amoy to China. Zhang Huizan is taken prisoner by Mao's forces.

1931 *The Shenyang Incident; Japan occupies Manchuria*

January 1. CCP troops completely defeat Zhang Huizan's in the Huangpi (Jiangxi) area, after which the NP forces withdraw, thus ending the First Encirclement Campaign.
7 or 8. The CCP's Sixth CC holds its Fourth Plenum in Shanghai, and formally abandons the Li Lisan line. It decides to hold a congress of soviets in Jiangxi.
15. Belgium formally hands its Concession in Tianjin back to China.
February 28. Chiang Kaishek and Hu Hanmin disagree violently over the question of the constitution during discussion outside Nanjing. Almost immediately Chiang Kaishek has Hu Hanmin placed under house arrest.
March 19. He Yingqin gives the order for a general attack against the Jiangxi soviet: the Second Encirclement Campaign begins.
29. The Executive Yuan orders that the militia groups and *baojia* organizations be set up before August 1 in the provinces of Hunan,

1930–1

Chinese Society) and translations by Tian Han of Shakespeare's *Hamlet* and *Romeo and Juliet*, under the titles *Hamengleite* and *Luomiou yu Zhuliye*.

July 29. The *Hongjun ribao* (*Red Army Daily*) begins publication in Changsha.

E Natural Disasters

January 28. Writing in the *North China Herald* (p. 136) John Dorrock claims that 'two million people have already perished of hunger' in the Gansu famine, and 'that two million are starving' and most will probably die.

July. A writer in the *Shishi yuebao* (*Times Monthly*) claims that, in Shaanxi alone, 3,000,000 people have died of starvation and resultant disease owing to the famine of 1928–30. (Shaanxi and Gansu were the two provinces worst hit by the famine.)

F Deaths

July 1. Wang Shizhen d. aged 69.
September 22. Tan Yankai d. in Nanjing aged 54.
November 14. Mao Zedong's wife Yang Kaihui is executed on orders of He Jian, aged 29.

Disastrous flooding along the Yangzi River 1931

A Economics

January 1. All provinces put into effect the abolition of the *lijin* tax.
April 1. The China National Aviation Corporation extends its Shanghai–Hankou service to Yichang (Hubei), through Shashi (Hubei).
  15. The China National Aviation Corporation formally begins commercial flights between Nanjing and Beiping.
  19. The first aircraft of the Sino-German Eurasia Aviation Corporation flies from Shanghai to Manzhouli (Heilongjiang). (The Corporation aimed to establish a through airmail service to Europe, but did not succeed.)
June 1. Wireless telecommunications formally open between Germany and China.
October 21. The China National Aviation Corporation extends its Shanghai–Yichang service to Chongqing (Sichuan) through Wanxian (Sichuan).

1931

Hubei, Anhui, Henan, Jiangxi, Zhejiang and Fujian, as an anti-CCP measure.

May 5–17. The National Convention is held in Nanjing.

12. The National Convention adopts the Provisional Constitution of the Political Tutelage Period.

13. The National Convention issues a manifesto abrogating the unequal treaties.

16–30. The Red Army wins five battles against He Yingqin's troops and takes territory over some 400 kilometres near the Jiangxi-Fujian border. This effectively ends the Second Encirclement Campaign.

June 22. Chiang Kaishek arrives in Nanchang and holds a military conference to decide on plans for a Third Encirclement Campaign.

July 1. Chiang Kaishek personally orders the launching of the Third Encirclement Campaign.

2. Chinese peasants in Wanbaoshan (Jilin) clash with some Korean immigrants over the occupation of land; Japanese police intervene. Many Chinese and Koreans are killed or injured. This is known as the Wanbaoshan Incident.

3. In response to the Wanbaoshan Incident, riots directed against Chinese people and property erupt in Chemulpo (now called Inch'on) and Seoul; they spread to other Korean cities in following days.

15. Chiang Kaishek's troops retake Guangchang (Jiangxi) in the Third Encirclement Campaign. Several other towns fall at about this time.

September 3. Troops of the Third Encirclement Campaign advance to Nankang (Jiangxi) and other places, completing their encirclement of the central soviet area. However, owing to the September 18 Shenyang Incident and other causes, the campaign was shelved.

18. Japanese troops occupy a Chinese camp outside Shenyang, the capital of Fengtian.

19. The Japanese Kwantung Army occupies Shenyang.

21. Japanese troops take the capital of Jilin province, Jilin.

22. After heated debate on the Manchurian situation between the Chinese and Japanese delegates Shi Zhaoji and Yoshizawa Kenkichi, the Council of the League of Nations adopts a resolution urging China and Japan 'to proceed immediately with the withdrawal of their respective troops'. The CCPCC issues a statement calling for guerrilla warfare against the Japanese in Manchuria and general resistance against Japanese imperialism.

26. In Shanghai an enormous demonstration against the Japanese resolves to request the NG to declare war and break off diplomatic relations with Japan unless it withdraws from Manchuria.

1931

November 15. The National Economic Council, set up by the NG to coordinate and plan economic reconstruction, holds its inaugural meeting.

B OFFICIAL APPOINTMENTS, RESIGNATIONS, DISMISSALS ETC.

January 8. The Fourth Plenum of the Sixth CCPCC dismisses Li Lisan, Qu Qiubai and others from the CC and Politburo and replaces them with Chen Shaoyu, Qin Bangxian (both among the returned students) and others.

March 2. The NP's CEC resolves to replace Hu Hanmin by Lin Sen as President of the Legislative Yuan.

May 28. In Guangzhou Wang Jingwei, Li Zongren, Tang Shaoyi and others assume office as committee members of a government rival to Chiang Kaishek's. (Their action was sparked off by Chiang's arrest of Hu Hanmin.)

Late June. Chen Shaoyu succeeds Xiang Zhongfa as Secretary-General of the CCP.

November 7. Zhu De is appointed as Commander-in-Chief of the Red Army. Mao Zedong, Zhu De and Zhou Enlai, Liu Shaoqi, Qu Qiubai, Chen Shaoyu, Lin Biao, Fang Zhimin, He Long, Peng Dehuai, Xiang Ying and over fifty others become members of the CEC of the CSR.

9. The CEC of the NP resolves to restore Party membership to Wang Jingwei and others.

27. The CEC appoints Mao Zedong as its Chairman, in effect the CSR's Chairman, and Zhang Guotao and Xiang Ying as deputy Chairmen.

December 16. Chiang Kaishek resigns all his posts in the NG in accordance with the agreement made with the Guangzhou government.

28. The First Plenum of the NP's Fourth CEC (meeting in Nanjing December 22–29) appoints Lin Sen as Chairman of the NG and Chiang Kaishek, Hu Hanmin and Wang Jingwei as the three members of the Standing Committee of the NP's Central Political Council.

C CULTURAL AND SOCIAL

March 15. The first Chinese sound feature film, *Genü Hong mudan* (*Singing Girl Red Peony*) has its public première showing.

April 29. The Ministry of Education promulgates regulations for the establishment of a commission to study health education for primary and secondary schools.

1931

October 27. A conference of delegates of the Guangzhou and Nanjing governments opens in Shanghai to negotiate reunification.

November 1–7. The First All-China Soviet Congress is held in Ruijin (Jiangxi) with over 600 delegates.

7. The Chinese Soviet Republic (CSR) is established with Ruijin as its capital; the CSR constitution is promulgated.

The Shanghai conference concludes. It issues a circular telegram of its results, which include agreement of the Guangzhou government to dissolve itself upon reorganization of the Nanjing NG and resignation of Chiang Kaishek from all posts in the NG.

10. The last Qing Emperor, Puyi, secretly leaves Tianjin on board a Japanese launch.

12–23. The NP holds its Fourth National Congress in Nanjing.

19. The Japanese Kwantung Army takes the Heilongjiang capital city, Tsitsihar.

December 1. The CSR government is formally proclaimed.

10. The Council of the League of Nations sets up a commission of enquiry, chaired by the Earl of Lytton, to report on 'any circumstance which ... threatens to disturb peace between China and Japan'.

14. The 73rd and 74th Brigades of the NP's 26th Route Army, some 10,000 men, mutiny in Ningdu (Jiangxi), and go over to the CCP; Zhu De immediately reorganizes them into the Fifth Red Army Corps.

17. Students from Beiping and other parts of China demonstrate in Nanjing for declaration of war against Japan. They seriously damage the *Central Daily* printing plant. Police intervene; many students are wounded or arrested and at least one is killed.

29. Chinese troops abandon Jinzhou (Fengtian), their last major stronghold in Manchuria.

1931

June. The Central Field Health Station, designed to 'study various medico-social problems, including medical relief' begins work.

August. The Ministry of Education releases statistics for university students in China: altogether 20,925, of whom 18,764 are male, 2,161 female.

October 24. The Ministry of Education approves the amalgamation of three universities in Chengdu (Sichuan) and renames them the National Sichuan University.

November 7. The First All-China Soviet Congress adopts the Labour and Land Laws of the CSR; these provide that all the lands of the landlords 'shall be subject to confiscation' and distributed 'among the poor and middle peasants'.

December 5. The NG enacts a law forbidding student groups to come to Nanjing to petition the government.

D Publications

January 1. *Shijie zazhi* (*World Magazine*) begins publication.

July 9. The *Jiaoji ribao* (*Qingdao-Ji'nan Daily*) begins publication in Qingdao.

December 11. *Hongse Zhongguo* (*Red China*), CSR newspaper, begins publication.

E Natural Disasters

July 17. The provinces of Anhui, Henan and Guangdong are struck by disastrous floods.

28. The Yangzi River bursts its banks at Hankou, causing disastrous floods.

August–September. Flooding reaches a peak along the Yangzi River from Shashi (Hubei) to the mouth, a distance of some 1500 km.

August 19. Flood waters in Hankou reach a height of 18.15 metres, the highest since the beginning of records in the 1860s.

26. The Legislative Yuan receives a report that flooding has spread to seventeen provinces and that the number of people affected now stands at 80,000,000 to 100,000,000.

October 17. The NG orders relief action against a serious plague epidemic in Shanxi and Shaanxi.

F Deaths

January 28. Zhang Huizan is killed by the Communists.

February 7. He Mengxiong, leading CCP trade unionist, is executed,

1932 *The Japanese briefly seize Shanghai*

January 2. Japanese troops move into Jinzhou (Fengtian), completing its occupation the next day.
3. The Red Army takes Ganzhou (Jiangxi).
28. Late at night Japanese troops and naval forces begin to attack Shanghai, and clash with the Chinese 19th Route Army, sparking off the Battle of Shanghai.
30. The NG declares the removal of its capital to Luoyang (Henan).
February 6. Japanese troops take Harbin (Heilongjiang).
18. A Japanese-constituted administrative council declares the independence of Manchuria and announces the forthcoming establishment of the Manchurian state Manzhouguo.
21. The NG's Ministry of Foreign Affairs announces it will never recognize Manchurian independence or any Japanese puppet state there.
March 3. Chinese troops abandon Wusong near Shanghai; the Japanese declare they will cease fire in Shanghai because they have fulfilled their aim of protecting their own nationals.
4. The Assembly of the League of Nations adopts a resolution urging a ceasefire and negotiations between China and Japan over Shanghai.
9. The state of Manzhouguo is formally set up in Manchuria, with its capital in Changchun (Jilin).
April 7–12. The NG holds a National Emergency Conference in Luoyang.
15. The CSR government formally declares war on Japan.
May 5. The Sino-Japanese Shanghai Ceasefire Agreement is formally signed.
6. Japanese troops begin to withdraw from Shanghai.
23. The Military Affairs Committee orders the 19th Route Army, which had resisted the Japanese in Shanghai, to move to Fujian to fight the Communists.

aged 28. Hu Yepin is executed, aged 27, together with three other members of the League of Left-Wing Writers.

June 24. Xiang Zhongfa, CCP Secretary-General, is executed in Shanghai.

July 29. Actor Sun Juxian d. aged 90.

November 19. Poet Xu Zhimo d. aged 34.

December 16. Deng Yanda, leader of a political party opposed to Chiang Kaishek, is executed for treason near Nanjing, aged 36.

Puyi becomes Chief Executive of Manzhouguo 1932

A ECONOMICS

June 29. The Japanese forcibly seize control of customs houses in Manchuria on behalf of Manzhouguo.

November 5. A highway conference in Hankou, with representatives from Henan, Hubei, Anhui, Jiangxi, Jiangsu, Zhejiang and Hunan, draws up detailed plans for a network of highways in the relevant provinces.

B OFFICIAL APPOINTMENTS, RESIGNATIONS, DISMISSALS ETC,

January 28. The Central Political Council appoints Wang Jingwei as President of the Executive Yuan to replace Sun Fo, who had resigned January 25.

29. The Central Political Council appoints Chiang Kaishek, Feng Yuxiang, Zhang Xueliang and Yan Xishan as members of the Military Affairs Committee.

March 9. Puyi is inaugurated as Chief Executive of Manzhouguo and Zheng Xiaoxu as Premier.

18. Chiang Kaishek assumes office as Chairman of the Military Affairs Committee.

June 28. The Executive Yuan resolves to appoint the deputy Minister of Education, Duan Xipeng, as acting Vice-Chancellor of the National Central University in Nanjing.

August 26. The NG appoints Luo Jialun as Vice-Chancellor of the National Central University.

C CULTURAL AND SOCIAL

May 22. Postal workers in Shanghai go on strike, being followed in later days by those of many other cities, including Beiping and Tianjin.

1932

31. The Japanese complete withdrawal of those troops which had taken part in the Battle of Shanghai.

June 28. Chiang Kaishek arrives in Hankou and sets up headquarters for the Fourth Encirclement Campaign against the CCP in Henan, Hubei and Anhui.

July 18. The coastal city of Yingkou (Fengtian) is attacked by the Righteous and Courageous Army, an anti-Japanese underground force.

25. The NG's Ministry of Communications announces a total ban on postal services to or through Manchuria.

August. In preparation for an attack by Chiang Kaishek's forces on the central soviet the CSR holds a conference in Ningdu (Jiangxi) to discuss strategy. Mao Zedong is criticized at the conference and as a result his influence shrinks temporarily. The conference decides to expand the Red Army and the central soviet area and rejects Mao's policy of 'luring the enemy in deep'.

13. NP troops complete their encirclement of He Long's Second Red Army Corps at the Honghu (Hubei).

September. The NP's Hankou headquarters for the Encirclement Campaign orders that in the soviet areas all able-bodied men be killed, all houses burned down, and all grain, except that used by NP troops, be destroyed.

1. The Righteous and Courageous Army makes attacks into Shenyang.

8. Encirclement Campaign troops seize control of the Honghu area.

15. The Japan-Manzhouguo Protocol is signed, under which Japan formally recognizes Manzhouguo.

16. Japan and Manzhouguo sign a military agreement.

October 10. Civil war breaks out with clashes near Chengdu in Sichuan where the warlords Liu Wenhui and his nephew Liu Xiang, both in effect independent of Nanjing, tussle for power.

11. The main force of Zhang Guotao's Fourth Front Red Army crosses the Beiping–Hankou railway as it retreats from the Henan-Hubei-Anhui soviet area, under pressure from the Fourth Encirclement Campaign troops, and prepares to enter Sichuan.

15. The former CCP leader Chen Duxiu is arrested in Shanghai.

18. The Red Army takes Lichuan (Jiangxi). This was one of several towns occupied at about this time; the action was part of the strategy of expanding the central soviet areas to resist the Fourth Encirclement Campaign.

November 19. The NP launches a general attack against the main force of the Red Army in the Jiangxi-Fujian border area.

December 1. The NG holds a ceremony to mark the return of the

Demands include better working conditions and the use of postal revenue for no other purpose than the maintenance and improvement of the postal service.

26. Postal workers resume work after the NG agrees to consider their demands. The Ministry of Education promulgates regulations for holding official examinations for primary and secondary school graduating students.

June. The Chinese Social Education Association holds its first conference and draws up plans for spreading popular education in the villages.

14. The National Bureau of Compilation and Translation is set up.

29. The newly appointed Vice-Chancellor of the National Central University, Duan Xipeng, arrives at the campus to take up his post. Students assault and insult him. As a result the Executive Yuan orders the University to be closed down.

July 6. The Executive Yuan sets up a committee to reorganize the National Central University.

October 15. Workers of the Belgian Tram Company in Tianjin strike for better working conditions, including an educational subsidy for their children. They resume work October 28 after winning most demands.

November 1. The Ministry of Education lays down standard curricula for kindergartens, primary schools and secondary schools throughout China. Junior secondary curricula are to include physical culture, hygiene, national language, English, mathematics, botany, geology, history, geography and music.

12. The Central Broadcasting Station formally starts broadcasting.

December 24. The NG promulgates laws on secondary, vocational and normal schools, under which the last two categories must be established independently and separately from the first.

D PUBLICATIONS

Yu Dafu's novel *Ta shi yige ruo nüzi* (*She was a Weak Woman*) and Zheng Zhenduo's *Chatu ben Zhongguo wenxue shi* (*Illustrated History of Chinese Literature*) published.

April 11. The *Zhonghua ribao* (*China Daily*) begins publication in Shanghai.

30. Jiang Guangci's last novel *Tianye de feng* (*Wind in the Fields*) is published posthumously.

June 7. The English-language *Peiping Chronicle* begins publication in Beiping.

July. The National Bureau of Compilation and Translation begins the

1932–3

capital to Nanjing.

12. In Geneva China's delegate to the League of Nations, Yan Huiqing, and the Soviet Foreign Minister, M. Litvinov, simultaneously announce resumption of diplomatic relations between the two countries.

25. Zhang Guotao's Fourth Front Army takes Tongjiang (Sichuan), which becomes the centre of a new soviet.

30. In Sichuan Liu Xiang's and Liu Wenhui's armies send delegates to Neijiang to hold a peace conference; the civil war stops.

1933 *The Japanese occupy Jehol; the League of Nations refuses to recognize Manzhouguo*

January. The CCP headquarters are moved from Shanghai to the CSR in Jiangxi.

3. Japanese air, sea and land troops take Shanhaiguan.

17. The CSR government issues a declaration urging the formation of a united front of all Chinese armies to resist the Japanese, on three conditions, including 'immediate cessation of attacks against the soviet areas'.

February 7. A military conference convened by Chiang Kaishek decides to set up the headquarters for the military campaigns against the Communists in Nanchang.

15. The Central Bureau of the soviet areas begins a campaign against Luo Ming, Secretary of the Fujian CCP Committee, for pessimism in the face of the Fourth Encirclement Campaign.

24. The Assembly of the League of Nations adopts a resolution that its members will not recognize Manzhouguo.

27. The Japanese begin a general military offensive to take over Jehol province.

27–28. NP troops of the Fourth Encirclement Campaign are ambushed by CCP forces south of Yihuang (Jiangxi) and wiped out in an overnight battle. Actions such as this one defeat the Campaign by the end of March.

March 3. Chengde, the capital of Jehol, falls to the Japanese without resistance.

12. Overcoming fierce Chinese resistance, the Japanese seize Gubeikou,

monthly *Tushu pinglun* (*Review of Charts and Books*).

October 2. The Lytton Commission's *The Report of the Commission of Enquiry of the League of Nations into the Sino-Japanese Dispute*, signed at Beiping on September 4, is released in Geneva, Nanjing and Tokyo.

E NATURAL DISASTERS

December 26. An earthquake strikes Gansu province, killing some 70,000 people.

F DEATHS

September 3. The warlord Zhang Zongchang is assassinated at Ji'nan railway station, aged 50.

A new standard silver dollar comes into circulation **1933**

A ECONOMICS

March 1. The Central Political Council adopts the Regulations Governing Coinage of the New Standard Silver Dollar; under them only the Central Mint in Shanghai may mint the standard silver dollar which is to be called the *yuan* and to be 88 per cent silver. The Central Mint begins operations the same day.

July 1. The Central Mint's new currency comes into circulation.

August 20. Mao Zedong gives a report at an economic construction conference of seventeen CCP-held counties in southern Jiangxi, held in Ruijin to devise economic strategy against the NP blockade of the soviet areas.

B OFFICIAL APPOINTMENTS, RESIGNATIONS, DISMISSALS ETC.

March 10. A conference convened by Chiang Kaishek in Baoding (Hebei) accepts Zhang Xueliang's retirement from office.

12. The NG appoints He Yingqin as acting Chairman of the Beiping branch of the Military Affairs Committee.

May 26. Feng Yuxiang assumes the office of Commander-in-Chief of the People's Anti-Japanese Allied Army.

August 6. Feng Yuxiang resigns from his post of Commander-in-Chief of the People's Anti-Japanese Allied Army by issuing a cable handing over all political and military authority in Chahar to the Chairman of Chahar, Song Zheyuan.

1933

a strategic pass on the Great Wall north-east of Beiping.

27. Japan formally announces its withdrawal from the League of Nations over the latter's refusal to recognize Manzhouguo.

April 7. In Fuzhou (Jiangxi) Chiang Kaishek declares that 'the state's greatest worry is not so much the dwarf-pirates [Japanese] as Jiangxi's local bandits [the CCP]'.

26. Chen Duxiu is sentenced to thirteen years' imprisonment.

29. Japanese troops take Duolun (Chahar) near the Chahar-Jehol border and move on to take other Chahar towns at about the same time.

May 31. NG and Japanese representatives sign the Tanggu Truce Agreement: withdrawal points of Chinese and Japanese troops are stipulated to end the fighting in north China, and the Japanese agree to withdraw voluntarily and completely to the Great Wall. The NG thus cedes Heilongjiang, Jilin, Fengtian and Jehol to Japan.

June 1. The CSR government denounces the Tanggu Truce.

July 12. Feng Yuxiang's People's Anti-Japanese Allied Army retakes Duolun (Chahar) thus bringing back all Chahar to Chinese hands.

24. The CCPCC adopts a resolution laying down strategy to defeat the coming Fifth Encirclement Campaign. It stresses expanding the Red Army and the soviet areas and waging guerrilla warfare on the edges of the soviet areas.

October 6. The Nanchang headquarters of the Fifth Encirclement Campaign orders a total blockade of the soviet areas, including all mail and provisions.

9–24. Demchukdonggrub (known to the Chinese as Prince De) and other Mongolian leaders hold a conference in Bailingmiao (Suiyuan) and organize an autonomous Inner Mongolian government.

26. The CSR government and Red Army conclude a 'preliminary anti-Japanese and anti-Chiang agreement' with the Fujian Provincial Government and the NRA's Nineteenth Route Army which were about to revolt against Nanjing. Under the agreement neither side would attack the other militarily and trade relations would resume.

November 10. Troops of the Fifth Encirclement Campaign seize Yihuang (Jiangxi) as bitter fighting begins with the Red Army.

20. Chen Mingshu and others proclaim the ROC People's Government in Fuzhou (Fujian).

21. The CSR and ROC People's Government sign their Anti-Japanese Armistice Agreement.

December 15. Hu Hanmin issues a statement denouncing both Chiang Kaishek's and the Fujian rebel governments.

16. Fighting breaks out in northern Fujian between the troops of the Nanjing and Fujian governments.

17. The NG appoints Wang Jingwei as the Minister of Foreign Affairs (concurrently with his post as President of the Executive Yuan).

October 29. The NP's CEC approves Song Ziwen's resignation as Minister of Finance and replaces him with Kong Xiangxi.

November 21. Li Jishen assumes office as Chairman of the ROC People's Government in Fujian.

23. The NP CEC's Standing Committee expels Chen Mingshu, Li Jishen and other leaders of the Fujian ROC People's Government from the Party.

December 13. The NP's Central Political Council issues a cable dismissing Chen Mingshu, Li Jishen and other leaders of the ROC People's Government from all their posts.

C Cultural and Social

January 17. The NP's CEC decides to remove the important treasures of the Imperial Palaces in Beiping to the south in order to guarantee their safety.

February 1–3. The Ministry of Education holds a conference of specialists in adult mass education.

June 2. The Central Bureau of the soviet areas adopts a resolution to begin a movement 'to check on land distribution' to eradicate the influence of landlords and rich peasants in the land reform process.

July 5. In Shanghai silk mill workers go on strike for a restoration of former wages, which had been reduced. The strike spreads in later days and eventually involves some 20,000 workers in nearly 40 silk mills in Shanghai.

13–14. The silk mill workers return to work after their demands are mainly met.

D Publications

January. The novel *Ziye* (*Twilight*) by Mao Dun, penname of Shen Yanbing, is published (dated December 1932 at its conclusion by the author). The Kaiming Book Company publishes Ba Jin's novel *Jia* (*Family*) as a book (preface on publication dated April 1932).

June 20. Ding Ling's novel *Muqin* (*Mother*) is published (author's preface dated June 11, 1932).

August. Lao She's novel *Lihun* (*Divorce*) is published.

November. The *Jiuguo ribao* (*National Salvation Daily*) begins publication in Nanjing.

1934 *The Communists abandon their central soviet and begin the Long March*

January 10. NG naval forces retake Amoy (Fujian).
13. NG naval forces retake Fuzhou, capital of the ROC People's Government.
21. NG troops recapture Zhangzhou (Fujian): the end of the Fujian rebellion.
22–February 1. The Second National Soviet Congress is held in Ruijin, the CSR capital.
February 28. The NP's Central Political Council adopts principles on Mongolian autonomy, accepting the idea of autonomous government in Inner Mongolia.
April 4. China and Turkey sign a Treaty of Amity establishing diplomatic relations.
10. With the central soviet completely surrounded, including by numerous blockhouses, a critical battle begins over the strategic city of Guangchang (Jiangxi) between troops of the Fifth Encirclement Campaign and the Red Army.
The CCPCC issues a declaration calling for a united front against Japanese imperialism, and denouncing the Tanggu Agreement (see May 31, 1933), direct negotiations with Japan, and the NG's policy of not resisting Japan.
17. Amau Eiji, a spokesman for the Japanese Ministry of Foreign Affairs, declares that Japan opposes all foreign technical, financial or military assistance to China except its own: the April 17 Declaration.
In Xinjiang Sheng Shicai proclaims the 'Six Great Principles' of his rule, which include friendship with the Soviet Union and anti-imperialism.

E   NATURAL DISASTERS

August 23. The Yellow River bursts its dykes in western Shandong; flooding devastates 5000 villages with a total population of 2,000,000.

F   DEATHS

May 7. Zhang Jingyao, the Hunan warlord, is assassinated in Beiping, aged 53.
September 22. Chen Jiongming d. aged 55.
December 17. The thirteenth Dalai Lama d. in Lhasa aged 63.

Devastating floods and drought strike China; the New Life Movement **1934**

A   ECONOMICS

March 20. The Executive Yuan adopts regulations on minimum wages in all government enterprises.
May 1. The Eurasia Aviation Corporation inaugurates an air service between Beiping and Guangzhou.
21–27. The Second National Financial Conference, convened by the Minister of Finance, Kong Xiangxi, takes place in Nanjing. Among its resolutions are those for reduction of farm taxes, abolition of certain taxes and reform of the local taxation system.
29. The NG orders a ban on foreign loans to government organizations.
June 5. The Executive Yuan approves the resolutions of the Second National Financial Conference.
25. China and Japan reach agreement on the resumption of traffic along the Beiping–Shenyang Railway; and decide to set up the jointly managed Oriental Travel Bureau in Shanhaiguan to handle the through traffic.

B   OFFICIAL APPOINTMENTS, RESIGNATIONS, DISMISSALS ETC.

January 12. Chen Yi is appointed Chairman of the Fujian provincial government.
February 1. The Second National Soviet Congress elects a CEC as the CSR's supreme organ of power, including Mao Zedong, Qin Bangxian, Chen Shaoyu, Liu Shaoqi and Zhou Enlai.
3. The CSR's CEC elects a Praesidium to exercise power when the CEC is in recess: Mao Zedong as Chairman, Xiang Ying and Zhang

1934

28. Fifth Encirclement Campaign troops take Guangchang. Ruijin is threatened.

May 8. The Ministry of Foreign Affairs protests against the Japanese occupation of inhabited land in Tianjin for the construction of an airfield.

9. Ignoring the Chinese protest, Japan continues the airfield construction under the guard of armed police.

10. In Xinjiang Ma Zhongying, a Moslem military leader and fighter against Chinese rule and Sheng Shicai, proclaims the organization of an independent Islamic state.

June 11. Xinjiang government troops retake the capital of Ma Zhongying's Islamic state, Aksu.

July 1. As rail traffic resumes between Beiping and Shenyang a bomb explosion on the first express train near Tanggu kills several passengers and wounds many more.

10. Ma Zhongying crosses the border into the Soviet Union.

15. The CSR and Red Army announce that a Red Army vanguard is being sent north to fight the Japanese.

Late July. The Sixth Red Army Corps under Ren Bishi breaks out of the Fifth Encirclement Campaign blockade from the Hunan-Jiangxi border area. It prepares to march from the Shatian area of eastern Guangxi on August 1.

October 11. NP troops take Xingguo (Jiangxi), as the Fifth Encirclement Campaign closes in on Ruijin.

16. The First Front Red Army, led by Mao Zedong and Zhu De, starts to move west, abandoning Ruijin and the central soviet area, and begins the historic Long March.

22. In Songtao (Guizhou) the Sixth Red Army Corps under Ren Bishi joins forces with the Second Red Army Corps under He Long. They immediately merge to form the Second Front Red Army.

26. Troops of the Fifth Encirclement Campaign take Ningdu (Jiangxi).

November 10. Troops of the Fifth Encirclement Campaign enter Ruijin, the CSR capital.

15. The First Front Red Army under Mao Zedong and Zhu De takes Yizhang (Hunan), having earlier broken through the NP forces' blockade.

17. The Second Front Red Army under Ren Bishi and He Long takes Yongshun (Hunan) and there immediately establishes the Hunan-Hubei-Sichuan-Guizhou Border Soviet Government.

27. Chiang Kaishek tells Japanese newsmen that he believes the Sino-Japanese dispute can be resolved on the basis of morality, righteousness and truthfulness.

1934

Guotao as deputy Chairmen.

March 1. Puyi ascends the throne as Emperor of Manzhouguo in Changchun.

C Cultural and Social

February 19. Chiang Kaishek launches the 'New Life Movement' with a speech to a mass meeting in Nanchang. He calls for the revival of Confucian virtues and urges simple living, cleanliness, honesty, courage, patriotism etc.

August 27. On government orders elaborate ceremonies are held to celebrate Confucius' birthday: part of Chiang Kaishek's New Life Movement and consequent Confucian revival.

November 15. The Standing Committee of the NP's CEC adopts a resolution to honour the contribution of Confucius to culture and to give special privileges to his descendants.

30. Chiang Kaishek and Wang Jingwei issue a joint circular telegram urging preservation of China's cultural antiquities.

D Publications

The Commercial Press publishes the first 881 volumes of its edition of the rare books of the *Siku quanshu* (*Complete Works of the Four Treasuries*); the Zhonghua Book Company the first 60 volumes of its edition of the *Gujin tushu jicheng* (*Compilation of Ancient and Modern Charts and Books*); and the Kaiming Book Company the first volume of its edition of the *Ershiwu shi* (*Twenty-five Dynastic Histories*).

August. Pan Guangdan publishes a translation of Havelock Ellis's *Sex Education* under the title *Xing de jiaoyu*.

September. Feng Youlan's *Zhongguo zhexue shi* (*A History of Chinese Philosophy*) is published by the Commercial Press in Shanghai; Wang Guangqi's *Zhongguo yinyue shi* (*History of Chinese Music*) by the Zhonghua Book Company in Shanghai.

November. Wang Shunu's *Zhongguo changji shi* (*History of Chinese Prostitution*) is published in Shanghai.

E Natural Disasters

January. Flooding along the Yellow River ravages many counties and drowns many thousands of people.

August 12. The Yellow River bursts its dykes in Changyuan county (Hebei), causing serious flooding.

1934–5

December 14. Mao Zedong's First Front Red Army takes Liping (Guizhou). There the Politburo leaders hold a conference on strategy, deciding to march to Zunyi (Guizhou).
31. The advance guard of the First Front Red Army reaches the Wu River and prepares to cross it.

1935 The Long March brings the communists to northern Shaanxi

January 1–2. Mao Zedong's First Front Red Army crosses the Wu River in Guizhou.
5. The First Front Red Army occupies Zunyi (Guizhou).
6–8. The CCP's Politburo holds its Zunyi Conference. On the last day it adopts Mao Zedong's resolutions attacking the mistakes which had resulted in the fall of the CSR.
19. NP troops retake Zunyi.
23. The Japanese Minister of Foreign Affairs, Hirota Kōki, calls on China to meet Japan's 'genuine aspirations' and expresses hope for an end to 'anti-Japanese agitation' in China.
27. Chiang Kaishek bans foreigners from any trade or travel contact with the CCP areas.
February 9. Liu Xiang's Sichuan Army retakes Tongjiang (Sichuan), one of the major actions in destroying Zhang Guotao's north Sichuan soviet and forcing Zhang Guotao's Fourth Front Army to retreat west.
11. The First Front Red Army takes Weixin (Yunnan), giving it contact with the Miao national minority, some of whose youths join the Red Army.
20. The NG's Minister of Foreign Affairs, Wang Jingwei, comments on Hirota's statement of January 23 by calling for 'close friendship' between China and Japan.

21. The Ministry of the Interior unofficially reports that in the last three months two-thirds of the whole country has suffered from drought and flood, causing total damage valued at more than 1,000,000,000 *yuan*: fourteen provinces have been affected by drought and thirteen by flood. This reflects the worst combination of floods and drought for several decades.

F DEATHS

January 2. Wu Chaoshu, former Minister of Foreign Affairs under Chiang Kaishek, d. in Hongkong aged 46.
July 14. Linguist Liu Fu d. aged 43.
November 13. Shi Liangcai, the editor of *Shenbao* (*Shanghai News*), is assassinated, aged 55.
December 19. Tin-miner Deng Zeru d. aged 65.
  23. Chen Shaobai d. aged 65.

Mao Zedong becomes Chairman of the CCP Politburo at the Zunyi Conference — 1935

A ECONOMICS

May 16. Sheng Shicai concludes an agreement with the Soviet Union under which his Xinjiang government is to receive financial and technical aid.
July 15. Japan and Manzhouguo sign an economic agreement and agree to set up a joint economic committee.
November 3. The Ministry of Finance promulgates regulations to reform the monetary system, under which silver is abandoned in favour of paper currency. 'As from November 4, 1935, the bank-notes issued by the Central Bank of China, the Bank of China and the Bank of Communications shall be full legal tender.' Holders of silver 'are required to exchange their silver for legal tender notes' from the same day.

B OFFICIAL APPOINTMENTS, DISMISSALS, RESIGNATIONS ETC,

January 8. The Zunyi Conference of the CCP Politburo elects Mao Zedong Chairman of the Politburo.
March 28. The NG appoints Kong Xiangxi (H.H. Kung) as managing director of the Central Bank of China.
April 1. Song Ziwen becomes director-general of the Bank of China.

1935

27. The First Front Red Army retakes Zunyi.

March 11. The Soviet Union, Japan and Manzhouguo initial an agreement in Tokyo under which the Soviet Union sells all its interests in the Chinese Eastern Railway.

18. The NG's Ministry of Foreign Affairs issues a statement protesting against the agreement of March 11 on the Chinese Eastern Railway.

19. Zhang Guotao crosses the Jialing River at Cangxi (Sichuan) as he moves west from his former soviet area.

May 1–9. The First Front Red Army works eight days and nights to cross the Jinsha River and its vanguard reaches Huili (Xikang).

17. Japan, the UK and the USA announce that their missions in China will henceforth be embassies, not legations, in grade.

30. The First Front Red Army captures Luding Bridge, made only of iron chains; it thus crosses the Dadu River, perhaps the most difficult obstacle in the whole epic of the Long March, and captures Luding city (Sichuan).

June 10. The NG issues its Goodwill Mandate demanding 'proper amenities towards friendly countries' (i.e. mainly Japan).

The He-Umezu Agreement is concluded by China's Minister of War, He Yingqin, and Umezu Yoshijirō, Commander of the Japanese North China Garrison; under it China agrees to withdraw its armies and NP organizations from Hebei. The agreement is formally signed July 6.

11. In accordance with the He-Umezu Agreement the NP's Hebei, Beiping and Tianjin branches are ordered to close down.

16. Mao Zedong's First and Zhang Guotao's Fourth Front Red Armies meet at Mougong (Sichuan).

July 8. The editor and publisher of *Xinsheng zhoukan* (*New Life Weekly*), Du Zhongyuan, is sentenced to fourteen months' imprisonment for publishing in his paper an article derogatory to the Japanese Emperor.

August 1. From a Buddhist monastery near Maoergai (Sichuan), the CCP Politburo issues its 'Appeal to Fellow-countrymen to Resist Japan and for National Salvation', advocating a united front policy.

5. The Maoergai Conference of the CCP Politburo ends without agreement between Zhang Guotao and Mao Zedong on strategy. Part of the First Front and Fourth Front Armies prepare to move northward with Mao Zedong, the other part of each army to turn back to Xikang under Zhu De and Zhang Guotao.

October 20. Mao Zedong and his Red Army followers meet with Xu Haidong, Commander of the Fifteenth Red Army Corps, in Wuqizhen (northern Shaanxi) in the Shaanxi-Gansu-Ningxia Soviet. The meeting ends the Long March.

1935

October 2. The NG appoints Chiang Kaishek as Commander-in-Chief of North-west Bandit Suppression and Zhang Xueliang as his deputy, with headquarters in Xi'an (Shaanxi).

December 1. Wang Jingwei resigns from his posts as President of the Executive Yuan and Minister of Foreign Affairs because of ill health following the attempt on his life.

7. The First Plenum of the NP's Fifth CEC elects Hu Hanmin as the Chairman of the CEC Standing Committee, and the Presidents of the five Yuan as follows: Executive, Chiang Kaishek; Legislative, Sun Fo; Judicial, Ju Zheng; Examination, Dai Jitao; Control, Yu Youren.

11. The NG appoints Song Zheyuan as Chairman of the Hebei-Chahar Political Affairs Committee and sixteen others to the committee.

C CULTURAL AND SOCIAL

February 20. The Executive Yuan promulgates regulations on film censorship under which all films, foreign or Chinese, must be censored before being shown.

October 5. The NG orders all its organizations to adopt simplified Chinese characters in official documents and announcements.

November 5. The students of Qinghua and other institutions in Beiping and Tianjin cable the NP's CEC, at the time holding a Plenum, accusing the NG of having killed over 300,000 youths, imprisoned countless numbers, and banned their associations and publications. The students demand freedom of speech and assembly and the prohibition of illegal arrest and killing.

December 20. A Women's National Salvation Society is established to protest against Japanese encroachments in China; it is among a number of national salvation societies set up at about this time.

23. All educational institutions in Beiping and Tianjin receive an order from Song Zheyuan to close down before the usual winter vacation.

D PUBLICATIONS

The Kaiming Book Company completes publication of its edition of the *Ershiwu shi* (*Twenty-five Dynastic Histories*); the Commercial Press republishes the Bona edition of the *Ershisi shi* (*Twenty-four Dynastic Histories*) and issues the first series, first collection, of the *Congshu jicheng* (*Collected Collectanea*). Ba Jin's *Dian* (*Thunder*) is published, the last novel of his *Aiqing sanbuqu* (*Love Trilogy*). The first two *Wu* (*Mist*) and *Yu* (*Rain*) appeared in 1934 and 1933 respectively. Wu Zuxiang publishes his collection of short stories *Fanyu ji* (*After-dinner Collection*)

1935

November 1. Wang Jingwei is wounded in an assassination attempt.

12–23. The NP's Fifth National Congress is held in Nanjing.

19. The Second Front Red Army of He Long and Ren Bishi begins its Long March from Sangzhi (Hunan), abandoning its base in the Hunan-Hubei-Sichuan-Guizhou border area.

25. In Tongxian (Hebei) Yin Rugeng, instigated by the Japanese, sets up the Anti-Communist Autonomous Committee of Eastern Hebei, based on twenty-two counties of Eastern Hebei, and declares independence of the NG.

27. Japanese troops seize Tianjin and Fengtai railway stations, the latter just outside Beiping.

29. The Ministry of Foreign Affairs protests to Japan against 'the autonomy campaign in northern China' and the Japanese seizure of Fengtai railway station.

December 5. Japanese planes scatter leaflets over Beiping city, advocating autonomy activities.

9. Students in Beiping demonstrate against Japanese imperialism, the autonomy campaign and the proposed Hebei-Chahar Political Affairs Committee as sellouts to Japan. Song Zheyuan has the demonstration suppressed; many students are arrested or wounded and one woman killed. This is the beginning of the December 9 Movement. In the following days demonstrations in sympathy take place in various cities.

16. Another enormous student demonstration takes place in Beiping to oppose the establishment of the Hebei-Chahar Political Affairs Committee and Japanese imperialism. Song Zheyuan orders his military police to suppress the demonstrators, and many are wounded or arrested.

25. At Wayaobao (Shaanxi), the CCP Politburo adopts a policy of national united front against the Japanese.

1935

and Xiao Jun his novel *Bayue de xiangcun* (*Village in August*) (dated by the author June 6, 1935 at the conclusion).

January. The Commercial Press publishes Ma Yinchu's *Zhongguo jingji gaizao* (*Chinese Economic Reform*). The drama *Leiyu* (*Thunderstorm*) by Cao Yu (pen-name of Wan Jiabao) is published as a book. In 1934 it had appeared in the *Wenxue jikan* (*Literary Quarterly*).

August 15. The English-language literary journal *T'ien Hsia Monthly* begins publication.

November. The Commercial Press publishes Xie Xingyao's *Taiping tianguo shishi luncong* (*Discussions on the Taiping Heavenly Kingdom's History*).

December. The Commercial Press publishes *Yinyue cidian* (*Dictionary of Music*).

E Natural Disasters

March 11. The Yellow River floods at Changyuan (Hebei), devastating nearly 450 villages.

April 21. Taiwan is shaken by a severe earthquake, which kills over 3000 people.

Early July. Devastating flooding occurs along the middle reaches of the Yangzi River, affecting Hubei, Jiangxi and other provinces.

10. The Yellow River floods seriously through a wide breach in the dykes near Heze (Shandong), destroying an area of over 25,000 sq. km., and the houses and crops of several million people.

August 8. A report by Xu Shiying, Chairman of the National Flood Relief Commission, on the floods in Anhui, Hubei, Hunan and Jiangxi puts the area affected at some 100,000 sq. km., of people at some 14,000,000, the number of drowned at more than 100,000 and the value of property losses, public and private, at some 500,000,000 *yuan*.

24. A further report by Xu Shiying claims that flooding in Hebei, Shandong and Henan has affected 5,500,000 people and 40,000 sq. km. of land, and caused property damage valued at over 300,000,000 *yuan*.

F Deaths

January 31. Lu Diping, recently retired Chairman of Hunan, d. aged 47.

February. He Shuheng, one of the founders of the CCP, d. aged 61.

March. Mao Zetan, Mao Zedong's brother, killed in action by NP troops, aged 30.

8. Film-star Ruan Lingyu commits suicide, aged 25.

June 18. Qu Qiubai, former CCP head, is executed at Nanchang, aged 36.

1935-6

1936 The Xi'an Incident

January 21. The Japanese Foreign Minister, Hirota Kōki, makes a speech to the Diet outlining his three-point policy towards China: (*i*) mutual good-will and assistance; (*ii*) economic cooperation among Japan, Manzhouguo and China; and (*iii*) unity against communism.

February 14. The Soviet Union closes down its consulate-general in Shenyang (Fengtian).

15. Radio-telephone service between Shanghai and Tokyo is formally inaugurated.

March 12. The USSR and People's Republic of Mongolia sign a Protocol at Ulan Bator under which each side guarantees to render the other all assistance, including military, should it be attacked.

April 7. The NG's Ministry of Foreign Affairs sends a note to the Soviet ambassador in China, Dmitri Bogomoloff, protesting against the signing of the Soviet-Mongolian Protocol, on the grounds that Outer Mongolia is part of China and not an independent country.

23. On its Long March the Second Front Red Army under He Long and Ren Bishi crosses the Jinsha River in Yunnan north-west of Kunming and marches north towards Xikang.

May 5. The NG promulgates the May 5 Constitution of the ROC. The Chinese Soviet Government and the Revolutionary Military Affairs Committee of the Red Army cable the NG calling for peace talks to end the CCP-NP civil war and for national unity to fight Japan.

6. The Hebei-Chahar Political Affairs Committee and the Japanese authorities secretly conclude the North China Anti-Communist Agreement.

June 23. Chiang Kaishek's troops, attempting to seize the CCP's base area in northern Shaanxi, retake its centre Wayaobao, forcing the CCP leadership to move headquarters to Baoan (Shaanxi).

July 10. Japanese troops clash with the NG's Twenty-ninth Army in Dagu (Hebei).

16–17. At his residence in Baoan Mao Zedong gives an evening–night interview to the American journalist Edgar Snow (one of many at

July 6. Fang Zhimin, a CCP leader, is executed, aged 34.

16. Film artist Zheng Zhengqiu d. in Shanghai aged 46.

17. Nie Er, famous song composer, d. in Japan aged 23.

October 22. Well-known journalist Ge Gongzhen d. in Shanghai aged 45.

Income tax introduced; death of Lu Xun — 1936

A ECONOMICS

February 1. Through its Ministry of Finance the NG issues the 1936 Consolidation Loan of 1,460,000,000 *yuan* 'with a view to the unification and refunding of all existing internal loan bonds, treasury notes and treasury certificates'. The period of redemption depends on the class of loan, with a maximum of twenty-four years.

8. The NG promulgates Regulations Governing the 1936 Consolidation Loan.

25. The Ministries of Finance and Railways announce terms for the resumption of repayments of the loans for the Tianjin–Pukou railway (see A, January 13, 1908, and September 28, 1910). These had been in default since 1925. The announcement was one of several similar made in 1936.

July 21. The NG promulgates the Provisional Regulations Governing Income Tax, thus introducing income tax for the first time.

August 22. The Executive Yuan promulgates the Rules Concerning the Enforcement of the Provisional Regulations Governing Income Tax under which enforcement is to come into effect from October 1, 1936.

September 1. The whole of the Guangzhou–Hankou railway opens to traffic.

October 1. The NG begins to collect income tax.

B OFFICIAL APPOINTMENTS, DISMISSALS, RESIGNATIONS ETC.

June 28. Prince De is inaugurated as head of the Inner Mongolian military government, set up the same day independent of the NG and subservient to Japan.

July 30. Li Zongren and Bai Chongxi appoint Li Jishen as Chairman of the military government in Guangxi, set up the same day in rebellion against the NG.

August 19. Li Zongren takes over as Chairman of the independent Guangxi government, Bai Chongxi as one of his deputies.

1936

about this time); he discusses patriotic collaboration of all patriotic forces to fight the national enemy, Japan, and advocates a united front.

August 24. Two Japanese newspaper men are killed during a demonstration in Chengdu (Sichuan) in protest against a Japanese intention to set up a consulate-general in the city.

September 3. A Japanese merchant is killed during an anti-Japanese demonstration in Beihai (Guangdong).

9. Two Japanese warships leave Shanghai for Guangdong because of the Beihai incident of September 3.

17. The CCPCC Politburo adopts a resolution calling for a united front with the NP and the establishment of a democratic republic to fight Japan, but 'the independence of the soviet and Red Army in their organization and leadership shall not be abolished'.

18. Japanese and Chinese troops clash in Fengtai, near Beiping.

19. A Japanese policeman is attacked and killed in the Japanese Concession in Hankou.

23. In Shanghai a Japanese marine is killed and two wounded.

October 8. In Huining (Gansu), Zhu De's and Zhang Guotao's section of the First and Fourth Front Red Armies completes its Long March and meets the Central Red Army, i.e. the section of the First and Fourth Front Red Armies which had earlier followed Mao Zedong to north Shaanxi (see August 5, 1935).

22. The Second Front Red Army, under He Long and Ren Bishi, also completes its Long March. A reunion of all three Red Armies takes place in Huining (Gansu).

November 4. Japanese planes reconnoitre over Suiyuan province as Prince De's Mongolians and Manzhouguo troops, helped by the Japanese, prepare to invade Suiyuan.

10. Mongolian forces attack northern Suiyuan from Bailingmiao (Suiyuan) but are defeated by the troops of Fu Zuoyi, Chairman of Suiyuan.

21–22. Troops of Hu Zongnan's First Army of the NG are seriously defeated by the Red Army at Shanchengbao (Gansu), one regiment defecting intact to the Red Army. Hu Zongnan's troops had been moving east in an attempt to retake Baoan, the CCP's north Shaanxi headquarters.

24. Fu Zuoyi's forces take Bailingmiao from the Japan-supported Mongolian troops of Prince De.

25. Germany and Japan sign the Anti-Comintern Protocol.

29. The Italian government announces Italy's recognition of Manzhouguo.

December 3. Japanese marines land in Qingdao; they raid NG and NP

1936

September 6. The NG appoints Li Zongren as Pacification Commissioner of Guangxi province and Bai Chongxi as a member of the Standing Committee of the Military Affairs Committee. This signals the end of the independent Guangxi government and Li Zongren's and Bai Chongxi's submission to Chiang Kaishek.

December 29. The NPCEC's Standing Committee resolves to dismiss Zhang Xueliang from all official posts. Chiang Kaishek submits his resignation from all posts but is requested by the NPCEC's Standing Committee to retain them.

C   CULTURAL AND SOCIAL

January 9. Student leaders in Beiping and Tianjin decide to send out teams to the villages to spread propaganda against tax collectors, landlords and the Japanese.

13. A large-scale anti-Japanese student demonstration in Guangzhou results in the proclamation, by the authorities, of martial law, a ban on all student and other strikes, and the suspension of freedom of assembly.

February 20. The NG promulgates its Urgent Means for the Maintenance of Public Security, giving military police extensive powers over student and other political activists, including that of shooting at demonstrators, closing down anti-Japanese associations etc.

21. Chiang Kaishek and others cable the Beiping and Tianjin authorities ordering them to suppress the student movement there because 'it is secretly managed by the CCP'. As a result secret police are sent out to various educational institutions to arrest student activists.

March 31. Students in Beiping hold a rally to commemorate a comrade killed in the December 9 student movement. The meeting is suppressed by military police, who arrest many students.

April 1. The Beiping Student Union is closed down, being replaced April 25 by the Beiping Student National Salvation Union.

June. The Anti-Japanese University is set up at Wayaobao headed by Lin Biao. (It is transferred to Yan'an early in 1937.)

3. The NG promulgates the revised Provisional Regulations on Penal Offences Relating to Opium Suppression, imposing a maximum of the death penalty for cultivating the poppy to manufacture opium, and prison terms of six months to two years for smoking opium. This is one of a number of anti-narcotic laws promulgated the same day and in August 1936.

7. The Chinese Writers Association is founded.

Early October. Twenty-one authors, including Lu Xun, Ba Jin, Zhou Yang and Guo Moruo, issue their 'Manifesto for Consolidation

offices, and other organizations.

10. At a military meeting in Xi'an Chiang Kaishek finalizes plans for a Sixth Encirclement Campaign to suppress the Communists.

12. The Xi'an Incident. Zhang Xueliang and Yang Hucheng, Pacification Commissioner of Shaanxi, place Chiang Kaishek under house arrest and demand that he agree to eight points, the main one being to end all civil war immediately and adopt a policy of armed resistance to Japan.

15. Zhou Enlai arrives in Xi'an from Baoan to negotiate a united CCP-NP front against Japan with the imprisoned Chiang Kaishek; Zhou is among a number of people who converge on Xi'an to negotiate over Chiang's imprisonment.

Mid-late December. The CCP moves its headquarters to Yan'an (Shaanxi).

21. Prince De announces a ceasefire, in effect conceding the failure of the Japanese-sponsored attempt to invade Suiyuan.

25. Zhang Xueliang releases Chiang Kaishek, who has accepted the need to resist Japan, although he signed no formal acceptance of Zhang Xueliang's demands at any time. Zhang and Chiang go together to Nanjing.

30. The NG's Minister of Foreign Affairs, Zhang Qun, writes to the Japanese ambassador, Kawagoe Shigeru, apologizing over the Chengdu and Beihai Incidents (see August 24 and September 3) and sends an indemnity for the injured and relatives of those killed. Kawagoe replies the same day that the incidents are regarded as settled.

31. Zhang Xueliang is court-martialled and sentenced to ten years' imprisonment.

1937 *The Sino-Japanese War breaks out*

February 1. Radio telephone services begin between Guangzhou and Hongkong.

10. The CCPCC cables the NPCEC putting forward a five-point

1936-7

of the Literary and Art World to Resist the Foreign Enemy and for Freedom of Speech'. This ended a long-standing and bitter controversy over 'national defence literature'.

November 9. In Shanghai workers of seven Japan-owned textile mills go on strike. In following days the strike spreads to other mills and involves some 45,000 workers; Qingdao textile workers join the strike on November 19. The strike ends in early December, after (*i*) the Shanghai employers agree to raise wages and reduce working hours, and not to dismiss workers without cause, or beat them; and (*ii*) Japanese troops suppress strikers in Qingdao (see December 3).

D Publications

Ba Jin publishes his collection of essays *Yi* (*Memoirs*); the feminist Xie Bingying her autobiography *Yige nübing de zizhuan* (*Autobiography of a Woman Soldier*); Cao Yu his play *Richu* (*Sunrise*).

January. The Commercial Press publishes the *Falü da cishu* (*Dictionary of Chinese Legal Terminology*) in three volumes.

December. Mao Zedong completes his 'Zhongguo geming zhanzheng de zhanlüe wenti' ('Problems of Strategy in China's Revolutionary War'); the Zhonghua Book Company publishes the *Cihai* (*Sea of Terms*) in two volumes.

E Natural Disasters

August 17. A typhoon strikes the Guangdong coast, causing extensive damage.

F Deaths

January 5. The geologist Ding Wenjiang d. aged 48.
May 12. Hu Hanming d. in Guangzhou, aged 56.
June 14. Zhang Binglin d. aged 67.
October 19. Lu Xun d. in Shanghai aged 55.
November 2. Duan Qirui d. in Shanghai aged 71.
December 6. Huang Fu d. aged 56.

Mao Zedong writes 'On Contradiction'   1937

A Economics

January 15. A ceremony is held to mark the opening of the Sichuan–Hunan highway to traffic.

1937

proposal, in particular an end to civil war to form a united front against Japan. It agrees 'to abandon its policy of armed uprising' against the NG, to discontinue confiscation of land, and to place its soviet and army under the command of the NG and its Military Affairs Committee.

21. The NPCEC adopts a resolution to 'uproot the Red menace' but does not reject the CCP's alliance proposals.

March 1. In an interview with the American journalist Agnes Smedley, Mao Zedong makes it clear that the united front policy does not mean giving up communism.

China and the Soviet Union conclude an agreement on the exchange of parcel post.

May 19. Radio telephone services begin operating between North America and Shanghai.

July 7. The Lugou Bridge (Marco Polo Bridge) Incident. Japanese soldiers in night manoeuvres near the Lugou Bridge outside Beiping attack Wanping at the southern end of the bridge. This action sparks off the Sino-Japanese War.

8. Mao Zedong, Zhu De and others cable Chiang Kaishek that the Red Army is prepared to fight the Japanese invaders under Chiang's leadership.

15. The CCPCC hands over to the NP its manifesto on the united front, repeating the points of the February 10 cable.

25. Japanese troops and aircraft attack Langfang (Hebei) near Beiping.

27. Japanese troops besiege Beiping.

28. Japanese troops launch a general attack on Beiping. Song Zheyuan, Chairman of the Hebei-Chahar Political Affairs Committee, retreats to Baoding and evacuates the NG's Twenty-ninth Army from Beiping during the night.

29. Full-scale fighting breaks out in Tianjin; the Japanese bomb the city.

30. Chinese forces abandon Tianjin. The Japanese occupy Dagu (Hebei).

August 6. Japan orders its nationals to leave Hankou.

7. The Japanese Concession in Hankou is handed back to China.

13. Full-scale warfare breaks out in Shanghai as Chinese troops resist Japanese attacks.

14. The Chinese air force bombards Japanese warships in Shanghai.

15. A declaration by the NG's Ministry of Foreign Affairs, dated this day, denounces Japan as responsible for the war, states China's duty to defend her territory and national existence and in effect declares war on Japan.

1937

June 29. During a US visit, the Finance Minister Kong Xiangxi holds talks with President Franklin D. Roosevelt on China's financial requirements; he informs the President that China welcomes foreign investment.

July 5. The NG issues an order prohibiting the export of wheat.

August 15. The NG promulgates regulations aimed at preventing wholesale withdrawal of funds from banks in Shanghai; they include a prohibition, as from August 16, on depositors from drawing more than 5 per cent of the balance of current accounts in any one week.

September 1. The NG's Ministry of Finance issues its Liberty Bonds, a total sum of 500,000,000 *yuan* to be lent 'for the purpose of encouraging the people to consolidate their financial resources for national salvation'.

November 1. The Soviet Union extends to China a loan of US $50,000,000.

December 16. The China National Aviation Corporation formally inaugurates an air service between Chongqing and Honkong, through Guiyang (Guizhou), Liuzhou (Guangxi) and Wuzhou (Guangxi), connecting with other countries.

December 20. Eurasia Aviation Corporation begins an air service between Kunming (Yunnan) and Hanoi.

B OFFICIAL APPOINTMENTS, DISMISSALS, RESIGNATIONS ETC.

January 18. Prince De proclaims himself Chairman of the Japanese-sponsored Inner Mongolian military government.

February 23. The Executive Yuan appoints Li Zongren as Commander-in-Chief of its Fifth Route Army and Bai Chongxi as his deputy.

March 3. The Central Political Council appoints Wang Chonghui as Minister of Foreign Affairs.

August 22. The NG's Military Affairs Committee appoints Zhu De as Commander-in-Chief of the Eighth Route Army of the NRA and Peng Dehuai as his deputy.

September 6. Lin Boqu and Zhang Guotao are inaugurated as Chairman and deputy Chairman respectively of the Shaanxi-Gansu-Ningxia Border Region government.

October 12. The NG's Military Affairs Committee appoints Ye Ting as Commander-in-Chief of the NRA's New Fourth Army and Xiang Ying as his deputy.

15. Xia Gong is inaugurated as Chairman of the North Shanxi autonomous government, set up the same day in Datong by the Japanese.

29. Princes Yun and De are inaugurated Chairman and deputy Chair-

1937

The British authorities in Shanghai decide to begin evacuating British nationals to Hongkong.

21. China and the USSR sign a Non-Aggression Pact in Nanjing.

22. The Red Army is formally reorganized into the NRA's Eighth Route Army.

25. The CCPCC's Politburo issues its principles for resistance to Japan from its Luochuan (Shaanxi) Conference.

27. Chinese troops evacuate Zhangjiakou, capital of Chahar.

30. China makes its first statement appealing to the League of Nations against Japanese aggression.

September 1. Japanese troops take Wusong, near Shanghai.

5. The Japanese Second and Third Fleets declare a blockade of the Chinese coast from Qinhuangdao (Hebei) in the north to Beihai (Guangdong) in the south.

6. The Shaanxi-Gansu-Ningxia Soviet is renamed the Shaanxi-Gansu-Ningxia Border Region.

13. The Japanese take Datong (Shanxi).

20. Numerous Japanese planes bomb Nanjing; almost daily bombardment follows until the city's fall.

22. The NG's Central News Agency releases the CCP's manifesto of July 15, thus confirming the united front policy.

24. Baoding falls to the Japanese.

25. The Eighth Route Army's 115th Division, under Lin Biao, defeats Japanese forces at Pingxingguan (Shanxi). This is the first major Chinese victory of the war.

October 6. The US State Department issues a statement denouncing Japan's invasion of China. The Assembly of the League of Nations resolves on moral support for China against Japan's invasion and lays responsibility for the war on Japan.

12. The NG's Military Affairs Committee formally reorganizes the Red Army south of the Yangzi into the NRA's New Fourth Army.

14. Guisui, the capital of Suiyuan, falls to the Japanese.

19. In Shanghai, Chinese forces launch a counterattack against the Japanese, who also increase attacks; bitter fighting continues over control of Shanghai.

27. The Japanese government issues a statement formally refusing to take part in the forthcoming Brussels Conference of the signatories of the Nine Power Treaty (see February 6, 1922).

November 3. The Brussels Conference opens without Japanese representation. Gu Weijun, the Chinese representative, denounces Japanese aggression.

5. Japanese troops land at Hangzhou Bay.

man respectively of the autonomous government of the Mongol Alliance, set up the same day in Guisui (Suiyuan) by the Japanese.

December 9–13. At a meeting of the CCPCC's Politburo in Yan'an (Shaanxi), Chen Shaoyu and Kang Sheng are appointed Secretaries, along with reappointments such as Mao Zedong, Zhang Guotao and Zhou Enlai.

14. Wang Kemin is inaugurated as Chairman of the Japanese-sponsored ROC provisional government, set up in Beiping the same day.

C   CULTURAL AND SOCIAL

April 1. The New China News Agency (NCNA) is founded in Yan'an

May 18. Several hundred students of North-eastern University in Beiping hold a demonstration and occupy the Beiping railway station to oppose the appointment of the University's new Vice-Chancellor and to demand the release of Zhang Xueliang.

June 3. The Standing Committee of the NP's CEC resolves to adopt the NP's song as the national anthem.

July 28. In Shanghai the Cultural Circles' National Salvation Association is set up to assist the war effort against Japan through cultural activities.

August 1. Song Meiling and others set up the Chinese National Women's Association for War Relief in Nanjing to mobilize women to contribute in every possible way to the war effort against Japan.

20. In Shanghai theatrical circles establish thirteen national salvation troupes to spread anti-Japanese propaganda.

September 1. Japanese planes bomb and destroy Tongji University in Shanghai; it is one among several Chinese universities to suffer the same fate at about this time.

2. The NG's Ministry of Education orders the coastal schools of all provinces to move inland.

October 13. The Japanese occupy Qinghua University in Beiping and take it over for military purposes. Several other universities were similarly treated at about this time.

30. Beiping's Yanjing University is forced to suspend operations.

Late December. Many of China's distinguished actors and dramatists, including Mei Lanfang, Cao Yu and Tian Han, meet in Hankou and set up the National Chinese Theatre World Association to Resist the Enemy. They aim to use the theatre for propaganda against the Japanese everywhere in China.

1937–8

6. In Rome, Japan, Germany and Italy sign a joint Protocol against the Comintern.
9. The Japanese take Songjiang near Shanghai; Chiang Kaishek orders the evacuation of Shanghai. The Japanese complete their occupation of Taiyuan, the capital of Shanxi.
12. Japanese forces complete their occupation and takeover of the Shanghai area.
15. The Brussels Conference adopts a declaration calling for a ceasefire in China and condemning Japan for breaking the Nine Power Treaty of February 6, 1922. The Chinese destroy the Yellow River bridge on the Tianjin–Pukou railway at Ji'nan (Shandong) to prevent the advance of Japanese troops to the south.
20. The NG formally declares the removal of its capital from Nanjing to Chongqing (Sichuan). Japan formally announces the establishment of its Imperial Headquarters to direct the military campaign in China.
22. Representatives of the Japanese-sponsored autonomous Mongolian governments sign an agreement in Zhangjiakou setting up the Mongolian Joint Committee to coordinate the three governments.
25. Wuxi (Jiangsu) falls to the Japanese.
December 2. The German ambassador, Dr Oskar Trautmann, visits Chiang Kaishek in Nanjing and transmits to him Japan's terms for peace; these include recognition of Manzhouguo, China's cooperation with the anti-Comintern powers and China's economic cooperation with Japan and Manzhouguo.
7. The Japanese launch a general attack on Nanjing; bitter fighting follows.
10. Wuhu (Anhui) falls to the Japanese.
12. Japanese planes strike and sink the US warship *Panay* on the Yangzi River above Nanjing.
13. Japanese forces occupy Nanjing, and begin looting, sacking and burning the city. Many thousands are slaughtered in the 'rape of Nanjing'.
24. Hangzhou, the capital of Zhejiang, falls to the Japanese.
27. Japanese troops occupy Ji'nan, capital of Shandong.
31. The Chinese evacuate Qingdao (Shandong).

1938 *The Japanese seize Guangzhou and Wuhan*

January 11. The Japanese occupy Jining (Shandong).
16. Following China's refusal of its peace terms (see December 2, 1937), the Japanese government issues a formal statement that it will

D Publications

The Commercial Press publishes the first collection of the *Zhongguo wenhua shi congshu* (*Collectanea on the History of Chinese Culture*); the Zhonghua Book Company *Waijiao da cidian* (*Dictionary of Diplomacy*) (Wang Chonghui's preface dated June 25, 1937). Zhang Tianyi publishes his novel *Zai chengshi li* (*In the City*); Guo Moruo his five-volumed *Yinqi cuibian* (*Fragments of Inscribed Bones and Tortoise Shells of the Yin*) in Tokyo (author's preface dated April 15, 1937); and Hollington K. Tong his *Chiang Kaishek, Soldier and Statesman: Authorized Biography* in Shanghai (author's preface June). *The shilu* (veritable records) of all the Manchu Emperors are reprinted in Shenyang as *Daqing lichao shilu* (*The Veritable Records of Successive Reigns of the Qing*).

August. Mao Zedong completes his 'Maodun lun' ('On Contradiction') in Yan'an.

24. *Jiuwang ribao* (*Salvation Daily*) begins publication.

December 11. The *Jinchaji ribao* (*The Shanxi-Chahar-Hebei Daily*) begins publication.

E Natural Disasters

April 13. Uncontrollable fires in Wanxian (Sichuan) seriously affect over 3000 families.

F Deaths

February 17. Zhu Peide d. aged 48.
March 20. Huang Musong, Chairman of Guangdong, d. aged 52.
September 15. The scholar Chen Sanli d. aged 85.

The Yellow River floods and changes course **1938**

A Economics

March 1. The Soviet Union extends to China credit of US$50,000,000 as aid for its war effort.

1938

have no further dealings with the NG and looks forward 'to the establishment and growth of a new Chinese regime'.

18. The Japanese government recalls its ambassador in China, Kawagoe Shigeru.

20. Xu Shiying, Chinese ambassador to Japan, leaves Japan for home.

February 2. The Council of the League of Nations recommends that League members individually send aid to China.

3. Japanese forces take Yantai (Shandong).

4. Japanese aeroplanes bomb Guangzhou.

20. Hitler announces Germany's recognition of Manzhouguo.

23. The Chinese air force bombs the Japanese airfield in Taibei (Taiwan), the first time foreign military aircraft had bombed any area under Japanese control.

March 23. The Japanese Tenth Division begins attacking Taierzhuang (Shandong), planning to use it as a base to seize Xuzhou.

29–April 1. The NP holds a Provisional National Congress in Wuhan.

April 1. The Provisional National Congress of the NP adopts its Programme of Armed Resistance and National Construction and decides to set up a National Political Council.

3. Bitter fighting intensifies for control of Taierzhuang.

7. The Chinese claim victory in the Battle of Taierzhuang, in which Li Zongren's Fifth Route Army inflicts very heavy casualties on Japanese troops.

29. A fierce air battle develops when Japanese planes raid Wuhan; both sides lose many aircraft. NP and CCP guerrillas clash at Xingtai (Hebei), the first known time since the beginning of the United Front.

May. The Eighth Route Army and guerrilla groups establish the Hebei-Henan-Shandong base.

12. The Japanese capture Amoy (Fujian). In Berlin, Germany concludes a Treaty of Amity with Manzhouguo.

19. Li Zongren's Fifth Route Army evacuates Xuzhou (Jiangsu) and the Japanese occupy the city after a long and bitterly fought military campaign.

20. Chinese aeroplanes scatter leaflets over western Japan, the first time hostile foreign military aircraft visited Japan proper.

21. Germany recalls its military advisers in the Chinese army.

June 6. Japanese troops complete their occupation of Kaifeng, the capital of Henan.

7. NP troops burst the dykes of the Yellow River at Huayuankou near Zhengzhou (Henan) to prevent the southward movement of Japanese forces.

12. Japanese land and naval forces open fire on Anqing (Anhui), and

10. The Japanese-sponsored ROC provisional government in Beiping formally opens the Federal Reserve Bank in Beiping.

13. The Ministry of Finance issues a mandate controlling the sale of foreign exchange, which 'shall be centralized through the Central Bank of China at the seat of the Government' as from March 14.

May 1. The Ministry of Finance issues the 1938 National Defence Loan of 500,000,000 *yuan* for the purpose of raising and replenishing funds for national defence.

3. A communiqué of a Japan-UK Agreement on the Chinese Maritime Customs is published in Tokyo and London, under which revenues collected by customs at ports under Japanese occupation will be deposited in the Yokohama Specie Bank.

6. The Ministry of Foreign Affairs issues a statement that 'China is in no way bound' by the Japan-UK agreement on the Chinese customs.

June 1–3. The Ministry of Finance holds a conference of Chinese bankers in Hankou to discuss ways of strengthening China's wartime financial system.

July 1. The Soviet Union extends a further US$50,000,000 credit to China for its war effort against Japan. The NG issues the first instalment of 30,000,000 *yuan* of a 100,000,000 *yuan* War Relief Loan 'for the purpose of relieving war refugees and promoting productive enterprises'.

November 15. Through the Export-Import Bank the US government agrees to grant a loan of US$25,000,000 to China to purchase trucks and gasoline for the war effort; the loan is to be repaid through the export of Chinese tung oil to the USA.

December 2. The Xiaguan–Wanding (Yunnan) section of the Yunnan–Burma highway or 'Burma road' is completed; this means the road is trafficable from Kunming to the Burmese border.

B OFFICIAL APPOINTMENTS, DISMISSALS, RESIGNATIONS ETC.

January 1. In a reorganization of the NG, Kong Xiangxi replaces Chiang Kaishek as the President of the Executive Yuan.

10. A congress of CCP military and political groups elects Song Shaowen as Chairman of the provisional Executive Committee of the Shanxi–Chahar–Hebei Border Region, set up the same day to govern the Border Region.

The Supreme National Defence Council appoints He Yingqing as Chief of the General Staff of the Military Affairs Committee and Bai Chongxi as his deputy.

1938

Chinese troops evacuate the city. The major aim of the Japanese was to take Wuhan, Chiang Kaishek's centre. The Battle of Wuhan thus begins this day.

July 5. Hukou (Jiangxi) falls to the Japanese as they proceed along the Yangzi River towards Wuhan.

6–15. The National Political Council holds its inaugural meeting in Wuhan.

7. To mark the anniversary of the War of Resistance against Japan, the CCP mobilizes its forces in the Shanxi–Chahar–Hebei military area, making attacks along the Beiping–Hankou and Beiping–Guisui railway lines and north of Beiping city.

26. Jiujiang (Jiangxi) falls to the Japanese.

August 12. The Soviet Union and Japan conclude a truce ending a war of only about a fortnight but involving several thousand casualties. The Japanese Kwantung Army had advanced a few kilometres into Soviet territory near the point where the Soviet, Manzhouguo and Korean borders met; the truce left all borders as before the war.

23. Japanese troops employ poison gas in attacking Ruichang (Jiangxi), and occupy it the following day.

September 24. The Japanese mobilize some 60,000 men with tanks and aircraft to surround and attack the Shanxi–Chahar–Hebei Border Region. The battle lasts till the end of November; the Japanese drive the CCP forces from the cities but fail to annihilate its administration.

October 15. Japanese forces take Huizhou (Guangdong) and press on Guangzhou, capital of Guangdong.

21. Guangzhou falls to the Japanese; fire spreads through the whole city.

24. Chiang Kaishek decides to abandon Wuhan. He leaves the city for Hunan.

25. Chinese troops abandon Wuhan after setting fire to the city. Japanese troops occupy Hankou.

26. Japanese troops occupy Wuchang and complete their occupation of Hanyang and hence of the triple city of Wuhan.

November 7. The British, American and French ambassadors in Tokyo present the Ministry of Foreign Affairs with a demand to reopen the Yangzi River.

12. Japanese forces take Yuezhou (Hunan). Believing (wrongly) that the Japanese had arrived, Changsha authorities send people to set the city on fire.

14. Japan replies to the demand from the UK, France and USA on the Yangzi River. It refuses to reopen the river, among other reasons because 'areas along the Yangzi still are infested with Chinese guerrillas'.

1938

March 28. Liang Hongzhi is inaugurated as President of the Executive Yuan of the Japanese-sponsored reformed government set up in Nanjing the same day.

April 1. The NP's Provisional National Congress elects Chiang Kaishek as the Party's managing director.

18. The CCPCC expels Zhang Guotao from the Party for engaging in struggle against the CCP's central leadership, among other causes; it claims he formally deserted the Party in Wuhan on April 17.

June 16. The NP's CEC Standing Committee resolves to appoint Wang Jingwei as President of the National Political Council. It also appoints Mao Zedong, Chen Shaoyu and five other Communists as members of the council.

July 9. Chiang Kaishek is formally inaugurated as President of the Three People's Principles Youth Corps, set up the same day.

November 20. The military tribunal set up to investigate the Changsha fire implicates Zhang Zhizhong, the Chairman of Hunan, and demotes him while retaining him in office.

C Cultural and Social

March 27. The Chinese National Anti-Japanese Association of Literature and Art Circles is formally founded in Hankou with the aim of using literature and art as weapons against the Japanese.

April 1. The NP's Provisional National Congress resolves to revise the education system and teaching material to suit wartime needs; to train youths 'to work in the war areas or rural districts'; and to train women 'so that they may be of service to social enterprises'.

Early April. Mao Zedong meets the Canadian doctor Norman Bethune.

October 28. The NG promulgates the Provisional Regulations for Special Examinations in the period of National Emergency, allowing the Examination Yuan to hold examinations as practical need arises.

D Publications

Xu Shichang's compilation in 208 chapters, *Qingru xuean* (*Studies of the Qing Confucianists*), and Ding Fubao's *Guqian da cidian* (*Dictionary of Ancient Coins*) in twelve volumes (Ding's preface dated mid-May) are published.

January 1. *Kang daodi* (*Resist to the End*), a semi-monthly periodical of anti-Japanese *quyi* (ballads), begins publication in Wuhan.

11. The CCP's *Xinhua ribao* (*New China Daily*) formally begins publication in Hankou.

1938

20. A military tribunal set up to investigate the Changsha fire sentences three senior Changsha officials to death for causing the disaster.

December 2. Japanese planes strike the area of Guilin (Guangxi), causing heavy civilian casualties.

18. Having decided to come to terms with Japan, Wang Jingwei leaves Chongqing, arriving in Hanoi on December 21.

22. The Japanese Prime Minister, Prince Konoye Fumimaro, issues a statement putting forward three principles for the settlement of the Sino-Japanese war and the establishment of a 'new order in East Asia'.

26. In Chongqing, Chiang Kaishek denounces Japanese Prime Minister Konoye's statement of December 22 as showing that Japan intends the 'annexation and total extinction' of China.

29. In Hanoi, Wang Jingwei issues a statement urging acceptance of Konoye's three principles for peaceful settlement of the war.

1938

February 28. Date of the preface to Ba Jin's novel *Chun* (*Spring*), published the same year.

May 4. *Kangzhan wenyi* (*War of Resistance Literature and Art*), the journal of the Chinese National Anti-Japanese Association of Literature and Art Circles, begins publication in Wuhan. (It moved to Chongqing when Wuhan fell to the Japanese.)

June 15. *Lu Xun quanji* (*The Complete Works of Lu Xun*) is published in twenty volumes in Shanghai.

July 1. Mao Zedong's 'Lun chijiu zhan' ('On Protracted War') is published in *Jiefang*.

August. The Commercial Press publishes Zheng Zhenduo's *Zhongguo suwenxue shi* (*History of Chinese Vernacular Literature*) in Changsha.

October 1. The *Saodang bao* (*Sweep Clean*), a mouthpiece of NG military circles, begins publication in Chongqing.

Immediately before October 21. Lao She's novel *Luotuo Xiangzi* (*Camel Xiangzi*) is printed in Guangzhou as a book. (It was completed early summer 1937; an English translation, *Rickshaw Boy*, was published in New York in 1945.)

E NATURAL DISASTERS

June 7 and thereafter. Owing to the destruction of the Yellow River dykes at Huayuankou, the river floods disastrously, covering numerous counties, drowning many people and causing incalculable damage to crops, houses and property. The river changes course to empty itself into the Huai River and part of the flood waters later enter the Yangzi. The dykes remained unrepaired owing to the war.

November 13. An enormous fire breaks out early in the morning in Changsha (see also November 12). It lasts several days and causes innumerable deaths and immense property destruction throughout the whole city.

F DEATHS

January 20. Liu Xiang d. aged 48.

    24. Han Fuju, Chairman of Shandong, is executed, aged 48, among other crimes for disobeying military orders in yielding Shandong to the Japanese.

February 14. Peking Opera actor Yang Xiaolou d. aged 60.

May 17. Cao Kun d. in Tianjin, aged 75.

August 24. Banker Xu Xinliu is killed in an aeroplane shot down by the Japanese, aged 48.

1939 *War breaks out in Europe*

January 1. Xikang becomes a separate province.
   17–February 4. The first Council of the Shaanxi-Gansu-Ningxia Border Region meets in Yan'an.
February 10. Japanese forces land in Hainan Island (Guangdong).
March 21. Assassins attempt to kill Wang Jingwei in Hanoi, but fail; they shoot and wound fatally his associate Zeng Zhongming.
   28. Nanchang, capital of Jiangxi, falls to Japanese troops.
April 15. Kunming and Rangoon are formally linked through radio-telephone.
   26. Chinese troops arrive on the outskirts of Nanchang in an attempt to retake the city.
May. The CCP's New Fourth Army sets up a liberated area in Jiangsu, centred on the Suzhou, Changshu and Taicang region.
   3–4. Japanese aeroplanes begin their bombing of Chongqing, causing several thousand civilian casualties and enormous property damage.
   9. Chinese troops attempting to retake Nanchang are ordered to withdraw because of heavy casualties and other reasons.
   11. The Battle of Nomonhan begins between Japanese troops, who had encroached into Outer Mongolia from Manzhouguo, and Soviet troops.
   27. The Council of the League of Nations calls on member states to aid China and condemns the aerial bombing of open towns in China by Japanese aircraft.
June 1. Wang Jingwei arrives in Tokyo to discuss the creation of another Japanese-sponsored regime in China.
   Wireless telegraph services begin between Chengdu (Sichuan) and Urumchi (Xinjiang).
   8. The NG orders the arrest of Wang Jingwei for collaboration with Japan.
   11. Zhang Yinwu leads a large NP force in an attack on the rear of Eighth Route Army troops in Shenxian (Hebei).
   12. NP troops raid the liaison office of the New Fourth Army in Pingjiang (Hunan), killing six men.
   14. Japanese forces blockade the British and French Concessions in Tianjin.

September 30. Tang Shaoyi is assassinated in Shanghai, aged 77.
November 4. NG military official Jiang Fangzhen d. aged 56.

Mao Zedong makes his speech 'In Memory of Norman Bethune' **1939**

A ECONOMICS

January 9. The Eurasia Aviation Corporation begins an airline between Chongqing (Sichuan) and Xi'an (Shaanxi).

February 24. The Eurasia Aviation Corporation opens a new air route from Chongqing to Hami (Xinjiang).

March 8. Sir John Simon, the British Chancellor of the Exchequer, announces a grant to China under which British banks, guaranteed by the British government, will lend China £5,000,000 to stabilize its currency.

15. China National Aviation Corporation's Chongqing–Hanoi air route formally opens to traffic. Great Britain grants its first Export Credit Loan, of £188,000, to China.

April 14. The NG issues regulations for the 1939 Reconstruction Loan of 600,000,000 *yuan*, aimed at financing reconstruction projects.

June 1. The NG issues its 1939 War Supplies Loan of 600,000,000 *yuan*, aimed at meeting war expenditure.

10. The Soviet Union concludes its third Credit Loan, of US$150,000,000, to China.

16. In Moscow, Sun Fo, Chairman of the NG's Legislative Yuan, and A.I. Mikoyan, Soviet Commissar of Foreign Trade, conclude the Sino-Soviet Commercial Treaty.

August 18. Great Britain grants the second Export Credit Loan, of £2,859,000 to China.

December 5. The Sino-Soviet Aviation Corporation formally inaugurates an air route linking Hami, Urumchi (Dihua), Yining and Alma-Ata, the first three in Xinjiang, the last in the Soviet Union.

17. The Hunan–Guangxi railway opens to traffic from Hengyang (Hunan) to Liuzhou (Guangxi) with the completion of the Guilin–Liuzhou section.

B OFFICIAL APPOINTMENTS, RESIGNATIONS, DISMISSALS ETC.

January 1. Liu Wenhui is inaugurated as Chairman of the Xikang provincial government, set up the same day.

1939

21. Japanese forces land at Swatow (Guangdong).

21–22. He Long's Eighth Route Army troops attack Zhang Yinwu's NP forces at Mazhuang, north of Shenxian (Hebei). The Eighth Route Army troops suffer serious casualties, and Zhang Yinwu's troops are virtually wiped out.

30. The NG promulgates the Measures for Restricting the Activities of Alien Parties, aimed against the Communists. Mao Zedong makes a speech calling for continuation of the united front and opposing any thought of capitulation.

July 15. Anglo-Japanese negotiations on the Tianjin Concessions issue begin in Tokyo.

24. The British Prime Minister, Neville Chamberlain, announces preliminary agreement with Japan on the Tianjin issue: the British government understands that 'the Japanese forces in China have special requirements for the purpose of safeguarding their own security', and will not oppose them.

26. The US government notifies the Japanese government that the US-Japanese Treaty of Commerce and Navigation (February 21, 1911) will be terminated as from January 26, 1940. (The treaty was a major obstacle to retaliatory action by the US against Japan.)

August 1. In Yan'an, Mao Zedong denounces the Measures for Restricting the Activities of Alien Parties (see June 30).

16. Japanese forces move into Shenzhen (Guangdong) to blockade Hongkong.

20. In the Battle of Nomonhan, Soviet and Mongolian troops, led by General G. Zhukov, win a decisive victory over the Japanese.

23. Pandit Jawaharlal Nehru, Indian National Congress leader, arrives in Chongqing and meets Chiang Kaishek on August 28.

September 1. Mao Zedong interprets the Treaty of Non-Aggression between the Soviet Union and Germany (signed August 23, 1939), as 'the result of the growing socialist strength of the Soviet Union and the policy of peace persistently followed by the Soviet government'.

3. The UK and France declare war on Germany; the European War begins.

5. Nehru leaves Chongqing for India.

15. The Soviet Union and Japan sign the Nomonhan Ceasefire Agreement.

20. Wang Jingwei arrives in Nanjing and at the 'Nanjing Conference' holds discussions with Wang Kemin and Liang Hongzhi, respectively heads of the Japanese-sponsored provisional government in Beiping and reformed government in Nanjing, on the formation of a new 'central government' of China.

28. The Fifth Plenum of the NP's CEC (held January 21–30) appoints Chiang Kaishek as Chairman of the Supreme National Defence Council, which the same day it resolves to set up.
September 1. Prince De is inaugurated as Chairman of the Japanese-sponsored autonomous government of the Mongol alliance, now moved to Zhangjiakou (Hebei).
8. The NG appoints Chiang Kaishek as Chairman of the joint board of directors (set up the same day) of the four government banks (i.e. the Central Bank of China, the Bank of China, the Bank of Communications, and the Farmers' Bank of China).
November 20. The Sixth Plenum of the NP's CEC (held November 12–20) appoints Chiang Kaishek as President of the Executive Yuan and Kong Xiangxi as his deputy.

C CULTURAL AND SOCIAL

March 1–9. The Ministry of Education holds the Third National Educational Conference in Chongqing.
31. Xian Xinghai completes his *Huanghe da hechang* (*Yellow River Cantata*).
May 1. Chiang Kaishek presides over a ceremony and makes a broadcast speech to mark the beginning of a national spiritual mobilization movement aimed at instilling patriotism, determination and other moral virtues into the people to win the war against Japan.
July 23. The Chinese Border Studies Society is set up in Chongqing.
September 1. The New China Bookshop is formally established in Yan'an.
December 1. On behalf of the CCPCC, Mao Zedong calls for the recruiting of more intellectuals (i.e. those with secondary school or higher education) to join the CCP, so that they can 'organize the millions of peasants, develop the revolutionary cultural movement and expand the revolutionary united front'.
8. Pope Pius XII issues a decree lifting the ban (imposed in 1704 and 1715) which forbade Chinese Catholics to take part in ceremonies revering Confucius and to observe ancestral rites.
11. The NG's Military Affairs Committee approves the Wartime Press Censorship Regulations, under which a wide variety of reports are forbidden, including military mobilization or other plans, anything which 'alienates ... the different sections of the nation', or 'other reports derogatory to the prestige of the Government'.
21. Mao Zedong makes his speech 'In Memory of Norman Bethune'.

1939–40

29. As some 100,000 Japanese troops converge on Changsha, the capital of Hunan, from three routes, they reach Yongan and other places on the outskirts of the city; bitter fighting breaks out with Chinese troops.

October 1. The Headquarters of the Japanese China Expeditionary Army are set up in Nanjing with General Nishio Juzō as Commander-in-Chief.

2. Chinese troops counterattack at Changsha, forcing the Japanese to retreat.

6. Chinese forces complete regaining all positions lost around Changsha, including Pingjiang, and win the first Battle of Changsha.

November 11. NP troops and secret agents attack the New Fourth Army liaison offices in a town in Queshan (Henan). More than 200 invalids of the New Fourth Army and their dependants are killed. CCP sources call this the Queshan massacre.

13. Japanese forces land at Beihai (Guangdong).

17. Japanese forces take Qinzhou (Guangxi).

24. Nanning, the Guangxi capital, falls to Japanese forces.

December 10–14. NP and CCP forces clash in Ningxian (Gansu) and the former occupy the town. This is but one example of several incidents at about this time involving struggle for control of areas on the periphery of the Shaanxi-Gansu-Ningxia Border Region.

14. The Assembly of the League of Nations re-elects China to its Council.

30. Wang Jingwei and Japan finalize and initial secretly the Principles of Readjustment to the New Relationship Between Japan and China; these are the terms on which Wang Jingwei's 'central government' will be set up.

1940 The Hundred Regiments Offensive

January 21. In Hongkong, two former associates of Wang Jingwei, Gao Zongwu and Tao Xisheng, reveal the contents of Wang's secret agreement of December 30, 1939.

February 1. At a mass rally in Yan'an to denounce Wang Jingwei, Mao Zedong calls for a strengthening of the united front against Japan.

3. The Japanese seize Wuyuan (Suiyuan).

1939-40

D PUBLICATIONS

January. Liberation Press publishes *Sidalin xuanji* (*Selected Works of Stalin*) in Yan'an.

May 6-August 12. Ten Chongqing newspapers of varying political shades, including the NP's *Zhongyang ribao* and the CCP's *Xinhua ribao* publish a joint edition, owing to the destruction of their offices by the intensive Japanese bombing on May 3 and 4.

August 20, 30, September 20. The magazine *Jiefang* publishes Liu Shaoqi's *Lun Gongchan dangyuan de xiuyang* (*How to be a Good Communist*) in three instalments.

October 4. Mao Zedong formally inaugurates the inner-CCP journal *Gongchan dangren* (*The Communist*).

December. Mao Zedong and others write the textbook *Zhongguo geming he Zhongguo gongchan dang* (*The Chinese Revolution and the CCP*) in Yan'an.

F DEATHS

February 19. The Minister of Foreign Affairs in the Japanese-sponsored reformed government, Chen Lu, is assassinated in Shanghai, aged 62.

March 17. Dramatist and drama specialist Wu Mei d. aged 56.

22. Zeng Zhongming d. in Hanoi aged 43.

April 16. Xie Chi d. aged 63.

June 6. Xu Shichang d. aged 83.

November 4. Ma Liang, Jesuit priest, government official and educator, d. aged 99.

12. Dr Norman Bethune, a Canadian doctor who worked in the Shanxi-Chahar-Hebei Border Region, d. in Hebei aged 49.

15. Protestant leader Cheng Jingyi d. aged 58.

December 4. Wu Peifu d. in Beiping aged 65.

Wang Jingwei becomes the head of a Japanese client regime **1940**

A ECONOMICS

January 20. The NG promulgates the County Bank Law, under which county governments are to establish a system of county banks 'with the public funds of the county and towns and the voluntary contributions of the people'.

March 1. The NG's Ministry of Finance issues the first instalment of the 1940 War Supplies Loan of 1,200,000,000 *yuan*.

1940

28. CCP forces occupy Anding (Shaanxi), one of several places in the Yan'an area retaken at about this time. A force led by the Elder Brothers Society counterattacks but is defeated on March 1.

March 30. The Japanese-sponsored NG of the ROC is formally inaugurated in Nanjing.

The Chongqing NG's Ministry of Foreign Affairs denounces the new Nanjing regime as illegal. Cordell Hull, US Secretary of State, declares his government will not recognize the new Nanjing government but continues to recognize Chiang Kaishek's government as the government of China.

April 1. After a strong counterattack against the Japanese in western Suiyuan, Chinese troops under Fu Zuoyi recapture Wuyuan.

May 1. Japanese troops begin moving from Xinyang (Henan) and other places, intending to seize Yichang, Zaoyang and Xiangyang, all in Hubei. This is the beginning of a large-scale campaign against Chinese troops in Hubei and southern Henan aimed at securing the Japanese position in Wuhan.

8. The Japanese seize Zaoyang (Hubei).

June 1. Xiangyang (Hubei) falls to the Japanese.

3. In a counterattack Chinese troops retake Zaoyang and Xiangyang.

6. Jingmen (Hubei) falls to the Japanese.

7. Japanese troops begin a forty-five-day 'mopping up campaign' against the CCP's north-west Shanxi base area.

9. Shashi (Hubei) falls to the Japanese.

12. Yichang (Hubei), gateway to the Yangzi gorges, falls to the Japanese. This concludes the Battle of Zaoyang-Yichang; the Japanese being in control of the southern Hubei-Yichang-Shashi area, the Chinese of the northern Xiangyang-Zaoyang region. Direct telecommunications open between Chengdu (Sichuan) and Geneva, Switzerland.

19. The Anglo-Japanese Tianjin Agreement is signed in Tokyo. Under it, Japan and Britain will cooperate to suppress 'all terrorist activities prejudicial to ... the security of the Japanese forces', and in other ways.

20. Under pressure from Japan the French agree not to allow the transport of any war materials through French Indochina to China.

24. Japan formally demands that Britain close the Burma road and prevent any war materials moving through Hongkong to Chongqing.

26–July 2. Puyi, the Emperor of Manzhouguo, visits Japan.

July 16. Following negotiations between Zhou Enlai for the CCP and He Yingqin and Bai Chongxi, respectively Chief and deputy Chief of the General Staff of the NG's Military Affairs Committee, Chiang

1940

April 20. China and the USA sign an agreement for the Tin Loan of US$20,000,000, under which the loan will be repaid through tin exports from Yunnan to the USA.

May 1. The NG's Ministry of Finance issues the first instalment of the £10,000,000 and US$50,000,000 Reconstruction Loan of 1940 for carrying out reconstruction projects in the interior.

July 1. Inheritance taxes come into operation.

30. The Executive Yuan decides to set up the National Food Administration to control the production, marketing, storage and transportation of food and to stabilize its prices.

September 1. The NG issues the second instalment and remainder of the 1940 War Supplies Loan.

25. The USA and China conclude the Tungsten Loan agreement, under which a loan of US$25,000,000 to China will be repaid through the export of Chinese tungsten to the USA.

October 18. The Burma Road reopens.

November 1. The NG's Ministry of Finance issues the remainder of the 1940 Reconstruction Loan.

12–28. A food conference is held in Chongqing.

26. In Urumchi, Sheng Shicai signs with the Soviet Union an agreement to grant it, among other economic privileges in Xinjiang, 'exclusive rights to prospect for, investigate and exploit tin mines and its ancillary minerals'.

B Official Appointments, Resignations, Dismissals etc.

February 22. A ceremony marks the formal enthronement of the 14th Reincarnation of the Dalai Lama in Lhasa (Tibet).

March 30. Wang Jingwei is formally inaugurated as head of the Japanese-sponsored NG of the ROC.

April 2. The Executive Yuan appoints Sheng Shicai as Chairman of Xinjiang.

November 13. The Executive Yuan appoints Zhang Qun as Chairman of Sichuan.

C Cultural and Social

February 22. The Cooperative League of China is founded in Chongqing to encourage cooperative economic and other development and the establishment of cooperative societies throughout China.

28. The Sichuan Provincial National Library opens to readers.

March 11–13. A National People's Education Conference is held in

1940

Kaishek approves instructions limiting the areas under CCP control and transferring the New Fourth Army 'to the area under the command of ... Zhu De, i.e. Hebei and Chahar provinces, northern Shandong and northern Shanxi'.

18. The British Prime Minister, Winston Churchill, announces in the House of Commons that Britain has agreed to close the Burma road to arms, ammunition, petrol, lorries and railway material; he states that no war materials are transmitted through Hongkong.

August 9. The British government informs the Japanese government of its intention to withdraw all its forces from Shanghai and North China.

19–20. Japanese aerial bombing of Chongqing reaches a climax with raids which destroy the major part of the city and cause enormous fires.

20. Some 400,000 Eighth Route Army men in 115 regiments launch a large-scale campaign in five northern provinces against the Japanese, the 'Hundred Regiments Offensive'. In the first phase of the battle the Eighth Route Army concentrates on attacking major railways.

27. Britain completes withdrawal of its troops from Shanghai.

September 6. The NG formally designates Chongqing as the wartime capital.

20. The second phase of the Hundred Regiments Offensive begins; during it the Eighth Route Army concentrates on attacking Japanese strongpoints, including blockhouses.

22. Under strong Japanese pressure, Admiral Jean Decoux, Governor of French Indochina, signs an agreement with Japan to allow Japanese troops to land in Haiphong.

23. The NG's Ministry of Foreign Affairs issues a strong protest against the French-Japanese agreement of the preceding day.

27. In Berlin, Japan, Germany and Italy sign the Tripartite Economic and Military Pact, to be effective for ten years.

October 1. The NG's Eighty-Ninth Army attacks the New Fourth Army under Chen Yi in the area of Taixing (Jiangsu). This leads on to extensive engagements for about a fortnight.

6–December 5. The third and final phase of the Hundred Regiments Offensive; the Eighth Route Army concentrates on counterattacks against Japanese mopping-up operations. The Offensive causes serious damage to Japanese power in North China.

19. He Yingqin and Bai Chongxi cable Zhu De and Ye Ting, the Commanders-in-Chief respectively of the Eighth Route and New Fourth Armies, criticizing them and ordering them to move those of their forces south of the Yellow River to the north of the river.

1940

Chongqing; it draws up a five-year plan, in the final year of which at least 90 per cent of school-age children should receive education.

21. The NP's CEC decides to honour Sun Yatsen with the title 'father of the country'.

April 16. The Zhonghua Police Research Society is set up in Chongqing to study matters relating to police theory and practice.

June 3. A National Opium-Suppression Conference convenes in Chongqing.

September 15. The CCPCC's Secretariat issues a directive on cadres: (*i*) their functions are to include participation in the labour and student movements, setting up radio stations and becoming teachers; (*ii*) they must be carefully screened and recruited, and secret training classes must be set up; once assigned they should work in the same place for a long time.

October 10. The CCPCC's propaganda department issues a call for greater emphasis on propaganda, not organization, in Party work and calls on CCP members to take the lead in agitation and propaganda, promote cultural activities in literature and the arts, and organize the Party press for propaganda purposes.

31. The National Chiang Kaishek University is set up in Taihe (Jiangxi).

D PUBLICATIONS

Cao Yu publishes his plays *Shuibian* (*Metamorphosis*) and *Beijing ren* (*Peking Man*). The Commercial Press publishes Guo Tingyi's *Zhongguo jindai shi* (*Modern Chinese History*) in two volumes.

January. The monthly *Xin yinyue* (*New Music*) begins publication in Chongqing.

15. Mao Zedong publishes 'Xin minzhuzhuyi lun' ('On New Democracy') in the inaugural issue of the magazine *Zhongguo wenhua* (*Chinese Culture*) in Yan'an.

February 7. The monthly *Zhongguo gongren* (*The Chinese Worker*) begins publication.

May. Ba Jin completes his novel *Qiu* (*Autumn*), published the same year. (With *Jia*, 1933, and *Chun*, 1938, this novel makes up the *Jiliu sanbuqu* (*Torrent, a Trilogy*).

July. The Commercial Press publishes Qian Mu's two-volumed history textbook *Guoshi dagang* (*Outline of National History*) in Changsha.

E NATURAL DISASTERS

July. Flood waters caused by the breaching of the Yellow River dykes

29. Japanese troops withdraw from Nanning, capital of Guangxi, and Chinese troops complete its reoccupation the following day. (This is the climax of a long military campaign which cleared the whole of southern Guangxi of Japanese forces.)

November 9. Zhu De and others cable He Yingqin and Bai Chongxi that they are following the instructions of the NG but pointing out that a split in the united front is threatening to turn the war of resistance into civil war.

30. Japan formally recognizes Wang Jingwei's regime. Wang Jingwei signs with Japan the Treaty Adjusting Sino-Japanese Relations, the clauses of which include friendship, anti-communism and joint economic cooperation, and leave all the major power with Japan. The Chongqing NG's Ministry of Foreign Affairs declares that the treaty signed between Wang Jingwei and Japan is illegal. The NG issues a reward of 100,000 *yuan* for the arrest of Wang Jingwei.

1941 The Pacific War breaks out

January 4. Some 9000 New Fourth Army troops move to Maolin, in Jingxian (Anhui). A large NP force attacks them the following day and clashes continue until January 15. As a result, virtually the whole New Fourth Army contingent is killed or captured, and Ye Ting is taken prisoner. This is called the Southern Anhui Incident.

17. The Military Affairs Committee issues an order disbanding the New Fourth Army as rebellious.

18. The CCPCC issues a statement on the Southern Anhui Incident, describing it as 'a move planned by pro-Japanese conspirators and anti-CCP diehards'. It calls for the elimination of He Yingqin and the release of Ye Ting.

29. The new headquarters of the New Fourth Army are set up in Yancheng (Jiangsu).

February 5. A Japanese navy aeroplane is shot down over Zhongshan (Guangdong); over ten Japanese high-ranking naval officers are killed.

15. Mao Zedong and other CCP members of the National Political Council issue a telegram putting forward twelve demands as conditions for their participation in the forthcoming first session of the Second National Political Council; they include rescinding the order of January 17 and punishing He Yingqin.

18. The New Fourth Army is reorganized into seven divisions.

March 1. The first session of the Second National Political Council

in 1938 swell and breach further dykes in Taikang (Henan) and other places; the waters merge with the Wo River, worsening the floods.

F DEATHS

March 5. Cai Yuanpei d. in Hongkong aged 72.
April 5. Song Zheyuan d. in Sichuan aged 54.
May 16. General Zhang Zizhong, Commander-in-Chief of the NG's Thirty-third Army Group, is killed in battle in Xiangyang (Hubei), aged 48.
June 19. Classical scholar Luo Zhenyu d. aged 74.
September 26. Legal specialist Xu Qian d. in Hongkong aged 69.

Continuing disastrous flooding occurs along the Yellow River **1941**

A ECONOMICS

February 1. The NG issues the first instalment of the 1941 War Supplies Loan of 1,200,000,000 *yuan* (second and third instalments are issued June 1 and October 1).
4. China and the USA conclude an agreement for a US loan of $50,000,000 to China, to be repaid through metal exports: the Metal Loan.
March 1. The NG issues the first instalment of the 1,200,000,000 *yuan* 1941 Reconstruction Loan (second and third instalments issued July 1 and November 1).
April 25. The Sino-US and Anglo-Chinese Currency Stabilization Agreements are signed separately in Washington, USA. The Sino-US Agreement provides US$50,000,000 while the Anglo-Chinese provides £5,000,000. Chinese banks contribute US$20,000,000.
May 1. The CCPCC adopts a decision calling on Party members to take part in economic and technical work, and to learn from experts, both in and outside the CCP.
20. The Executive Yuan orders the establishment of the Ministry of Food to replace the National Food Administration.
21. The NG issues regulations for the Yunnan–Burma Railway Fund Loan of US$10,000,000.
25. The US government approves a further US$50,000,000 in military aid for China.

1941

opens in Chongqing, boycotted by CCP members.

6. The first session of the Second National Political Council rejects the twelve demands put forward by the CCP members.

10. The first session of the Second National Political Council closes.

April 13. The Soviet-Japanese Neutrality Pact is signed in Moscow; Japan agrees to respect the territorial integrity of the People's Republic of Mongolia, the Soviet Union that of Manzhouguo.

14. The Chinese Minister of Foreign Affairs, Wang Chonghui, declares that Outer Mongolia and the north-eastern provinces are Chinese territory and that China is not bound by the Soviet-Japanese Pact of the previous day.

20. Japanese troops take Ningbo (Zhejiang).

22. Japanese forces occupy Fuzhou, capital of Fujian.

May 7. Japanese troops begin an assault in the region of the Zhongtiao Mountains (Shanxi), aiming to occupy the mountains, thus strengthening their military position in southern Shanxi. Bitter fighting continues till late May; at the end Chinese forces remain in control of the Zhongtiao Mountains. This is the Battle of Southern Shanxi.

13. The NG's Ministry of Foreign Affairs announces that China and Australia have decided to establish diplomatic relations.

June 18. In exchanges of notes in Chongqing the Chinese Minister of Foreign Affairs, Wang Chonghui, and the British ambassador, Sir Archibald Clark Kerr, agree on the delimitation of the Sino-Burmese border.

22. German troops invade the Soviet Union.

23. In an inner-Party directive commenting on the German invasion of the Soviet Union, Mao Zedong calls for an international united front against fascism.

July 1. Germany and Italy officially recognize Wang Jingwei's government.

2. The NG's Ministry of Foreign Affairs declares the severance of diplomatic relations with Germany and Italy.

18. Over 10,000 Japanese forces and some 25,000 Chinese troops allied to them attack the New Fourth Army anti-Japanese base in northern Jiangsu. Despite a bitter onslaught lasting till August 20, they fail to destroy the base.

August. A large Japanese force attacks the CCP Shanxi-Chahar-Hebei Border Region, among other reasons, to retaliate against the CCP for its Hundred Regiments Offensive of 1940. Over a two-month battle the Japanese burn down a great many villages. They succeed in reducing, but not destroying, the base area.

1. Chiang Kaishek orders that the American Volunteer Group under

1941

June 5. China and Britain sign agreement on the third Sino-British Export Credit Loan of £5,000,000.
16–24. The Third National Financial Conference is held in Chongqing. Its decisions include the collection of land tax in kind, not in money.
July 1. The NG takes over the land tax from the provincial governments.
25. Britain freezes all Chinese and Japanese assets in the British empire, the USA all Chinese and Japanese assets in the USA.
29. The previously Sino-German Eurasia Aviation Corporation is handed over to become entirely Chinese-owned and operated. Japan freezes all British and American assets in Manchuria.
September 5. The NG promulgates regulations on the Farmers' Bank of China, under which a department is to be set up 'to handle land finance for the purpose of assisting the government in the enforcement of the policy of equalization of land ownership'; the department will issue loans for the purchase of land.
October 8. The NG promulgates regulations dividing China's finance into national and local, and laying down which kinds are national (e.g. land tax, income tax, inheritance tax) and which local (e.g. butchery tax).
16. The Anglo-American Economic Mission, headed by the Bank of England's Sir Otto Niemeyer, arrives in Chongqing. Its aims include making recommendations to the British and US governments on effective ways of giving economic assistance to China.

B OFFICIAL APPOINTMENTS, RESIGNATIONS, DISMISSALS ETC.

January 20. Following the Southern Anhui Incident, the CCPCC's Revolutionary Military Affairs Committee appoints Chen Yi as the Commander-in-Chief of the New Fourth Army and Liu Shaoqi as political commissar.
April 2. The Eighth Plenum of the NP's Fifth CEC (held March 24 to April 2) appoints Guo Taiqi as Minister of Foreign Affairs.
June 29. Chiang Kaishek appoints the American Owen Lattimore as his personal political adviser.
July 7. Yang Xiufeng and Bo Yibo are elected Chairman and deputy Chairman of the government of the CCP's Shanxi-Hebei-Shandong-Henan Border Region, set up the same day.
December 23. The Ninth Plenum of the NP's Fifth CEC (held December 15 to 23) appoints Song Ziwen as Minister of Foreign Affairs.

1941

Claire Chennault should be absorbed into the Chinese armed services. The government of Thailand recognizes Manzhouguo.

7–13. Japanese planes carry out day-and-night 'exhaustion' bombing raids on Chongqing.

14. US President Roosevelt and British Prime Minister Churchill issue the Atlantic Charter; this lays down eight points, including the right of self-determination and self-government for all peoples.

17. The NG's Ministry of Foreign Affairs announces endorsement of the Atlantic Charter.

29. The NG's Ministry of Foreign Affairs announces that China and Canada have agreed to establish diplomatic relations.

September 3. Chinese forces retake Fuzhou (Fujian).

7. In northern Hunan, a large Japanese force attacks a Chinese force near Yuezhou, beginning the second Battle of Changsha.

26–28. Japanese forces press on the outskirts of Changsha and begin to encircle the city. Small squads of Japanese penetrate into the city but are annihilated.

29–30. Chinese relief forces arrive in Changsha; bitter fighting breaks out, resulting in a general Japanese retreat to the north and heavy Japanese casualties.

October 8. Chinese troops arrive outside Yuezhou, ending the second Battle of Changsha.

9. The American Military Mission to China, headed by Brigadier-General John Magruder, arrives in Chongqing from Hongkong.

November 14. US President Roosevelt formally declares that he has ordered withdrawal of US marines from Beiping, Tianjin and Shanghai.

December 7. Some 360 Japanese aircraft attack the US Pacific Fleet in Pearl Harbour, Hawaii. Since the attack took place at dawn it was already December 8 in the West Pacific.

8. Japanese aircraft bomb Hongkong. Japan declares war on Britain and the USA. Britain, Australia, and other countries declare war on Japan. The Pacific War breaks out. Japanese troops occupy the International Settlements in Shanghai, and Gulang Island, Amoy, and the British Concession in Tianjin.

9. The NG formally declares war against Japan, Germany and Italy, and the USA declares war on Japan.

20. The American Volunteer Group of the Chinese air force engages its first air battle with the Japanese over Kunming (Yunnan).

24. A large Japanese force launches the third Battle of Changsha by fighting its way across the Xinqiang River, south of Yueyang, in a southerly direction.

25. The Japanese complete their occupation of Hongkong.

1941

C CULTURAL AND SOCIAL

March 16. The Chinese National Press Association is inaugurated in Chongqing. Its constitution lays down its object as 'the study of journalistic science and advancement of the Chinese press'.

April 1. The Eighth Plenum of the NP's Fifth CEC adopts a resolution calling for the popularization of the phonetic system to combat illiteracy.

May. In a speech given at Yan'an ('Reform our Study') Mao Zedong calls for more highly organized and more thoroughly Marxist-Leninist study of present conditions and of Chinese history.

June 1. The Chinese Society of Border Problems is founded in Chongqing to research China's border cultures and problems.

August 1. The CCPCC calls for better education and greater objectivity in the study of 'history, the environment and events inside and outside the country'; it decides to 'set up an investigation and research organ' to deal with the problem.

September 21. Chinese astronomers observe the total solar eclipse visible in China.

D PUBLICATIONS

May 16. *Jiefang ribao* (*Liberation Daily*) begins publication in Yan'an as the organ of the CCP.

May 17–September 27. Mao Dun's novel *Fushi* (*Putrefaction*) is published serially in the first twenty issues of the new series of the journal *Dazhong shenghuo* (*Life of the Masses*) (it is published as a book in October).

June. The last volume is published of the seven of *Gushi bian* (*Analyses of Ancient History*), compiled by Gu Jiegang and others (the first six appeared respectively in June 1926, September 1930, November 1931, March 1933, January 1935, and September 1938).

E NATURAL DISASTERS

January. The Yellow River, which changed course in 1938, again bursts its dykes at Taikang (Henan). The waters spread eastwards, expanding the flood area to some 80,000 sq. km. in Henan, Anhui and Jiangxi and affecting several million people.

F DEATHS

September 6. Zhang Jiluan, the editor of *Dagong bao*, d in Chongqing aged 53.

31. Bitter fighting breaks out outside Changsha. The Chinese Expeditionary Force enters Burma to help in the war against the Japanese there.

1942 China wins the third Battle of Changsha

January 1. Along with representatives of twenty-five other nations, the Chinese Minister of Foreign Affairs, Song Ziwen, signs the Declaration of the United Nations (UN) in Washington, pledging to carry the war against the Axis Powers to a successful conclusion.
1–3. Japanese forces launch severe attacks against Changsha.
4–5. Chinese relief forces arrive at Changsha and inflict heavy casualties on the attacking Japanese, forcing them to begin a retreat.
15. The third Battle of Changsha ends in a victory for the Chinese; the Japanese forces retreat northwards across the Xinqiang River.
21. As a result of cooperation between the NG's Radio Administration and the Australian Wireless Corporation, direct radio services are inaugurated between Chengdu (Sichuan) and Sydney.
February. The Japanese launch a large-scale spring mopping-up campaign against the CCP bases in North China.
5. Chiang Kaishek arrives in Calcutta for a visit to India.
15. Singapore falls to the Japanese.
21. Chiang Kaishek returns to Kunming (Yunnan).
24. The Ministry of Foreign Affairs announces that China and Poland have agreed to resume diplomatic relations.
March 1. Chiang Kaishek leaves Kunming for Lashio, Burma.
5. Chiang Kaishek arrives back in Chongqing from his Burmese trip.
7. Japanese forces take Rangoon, Burma.
The international radio station in Chengdu opens services to India.
16. China and Iraq sign a Treaty of Amity in Baghdad.
29. After a fierce ten-day battle, Japanese troops seize the Burmese town of Toungoo from the Chinese Expeditionary Force defending it. The NG promulgates the National General Mobilization Act, to come into force on May 5; it lists the very great wartime powers of the government.
30. President Roosevelt announces the establishment of the Pacific War Council in Washington, to include China.
April 19. The Chinese Expeditionary Force takes Yenangyaung, Burma, from a Japanese occupying force and rescues over 7000 British, Indian and Burmese troops from Japanese encirclement.

1942 Mao Zedong gives his 'Talks at the Yan'an Forum on Literature and Art'

A ECONOMICS

February 1. The Ministry of Finance allocates 450,000,000 *yuan* to a Price Stabilization Fund.
12. US President Roosevelt approves a credit loan of US$500,000,000 aid to China.
March 27. Chiang Kaishek and the British ambassador, Sir Horace James Seymour, exchange notes agreeing that China National Aviation Corporation shall establish an air service between Chongqing and Calcutta.
May 1. The NG Ministry of Finance issues its Allied Victory American Gold Loan of US$100,000,000 to be used, among other aims, to stabilize prices, and to strengthen the monetary system.
13. The NG promulgates regulations laying down the mechanisms of the government monopolies in sugar, matches and tobacco.
26. The NG promulgates its 'Regulations Governing the Monopoly of Salt in Wartime', laying down the mechanisms of the government salt monopoly.
July 1. The NG's Ministry of Finance issues the 1942 Allied Victory Loan of 1,000,000,000 *yuan* with the same aims as the Allied Victory American Gold Loan. The Ministry of Finance's 'Methods to Unify the Issue of Banknotes' comes into effect; under them the right to issue bank notes is vested with the Central Bank of China alone.
August 22. China National Aviation Corporation opens an air route between Chongqing and Lanzhou (Gansu).
December. The CCPCC issues a call for a campaign to increase production. At a conference of senior cadres of the Shaanxi-Gansu-Ningxia Border Region Mao Zedong calls on those engaged in economic and financial work to 'develop the economy and ensure supplies', that is to find a balance between public and private interests, and to overcome surviving bureaucratic practices such as graft and red tape.
17. The NG promulgates regulations by which 'provincial and municipal governments shall enforce the restriction of commodity

1942

23. Sun Liangcheng, deputy Commander-in-Chief of the NP's Thirty-ninth Army Group and former Chairman of Shandong, surrenders to the Japanese with several other senior NP officers.

24. Through the British ambassador, Sir Horace Seymour, Chiang Kaishek receives the high British honour, the Grand Cross of the Order of the Bath, from King George VI.

28. Chinese troops engage in bitter fighting with Japanese forces in Lashio, Burma. Japanese forces take the city the following day.

May 1. As Japanese troops press on Mandalay, Burma, the Chinese Expeditionary Force evacuates the city and retreats to the north.

3. A Japanese force advancing along the Burma road takes Wanding (Yunnan).

29. In the early stages of a large-scale offensive in Zhejiang and Jiangxi (the Battle of Zhejiang-Jiangxi) the Japanese seize Jinhua, the wartime capital of Zhejiang.

June. The Japanese attempt to destroy the CCP base in south-east Shanxi but are defeated.

2. Song Ziwen, the NG's Minister of Foreign Affairs, and Cordell Hull, the US Secretary of State, conclude the Sino-American Lend-Lease Agreement in Washington, under which each side agrees to provide the other with defence articles, service and information, to be returned, as far as possible, after the war.

3. Chinese troops abandon Quxian (Zhejiang), the site of an important air base from which US forces had bombed Japan.

11. Wenzhou (Zhejiang) falls to the Japanese.

15. Shangrao (Jiangxi) falls to Japanese troops.

25. Mao Zedong's younger brother, Mao Zemin, arrested earlier in Xinjiang, signs a confession of implication in a plot to overthrow the government of Sheng Shicai in Xinjiang.

July 4. The American Volunteer Group ('Flying Tigers') of the Chinese air force is formally inaugurated as the China Air Task Force of the US Army Air Force, remaining under the command of General Claire Chennault.

7. Thailand recognizes Wang Jingwei's Nanjing regime.

August 15. In the Battle of Zhejiang-Jiangxi Chinese troops retake Wenzhou (Zhejiang).

19. Chinese troops retake Shangrao (Jiangxi).

28. Chinese troops retake Quxian (Zhejiang). This action basically concludes the Battle of Zhejiang-Jiangxi with Chinese and Japanese positions very similar to those at the beginning of the battle in May.

September 1. The CCPCC's Politburo issues a resolution calling for centralized leadership in the Party and the correction of current faults

1942

prices at important markets, transportation charges, and wages under their jurisdiction as from January 15, 1943'.

B Official Appointments, Resignations, Dismissals etc.

January 2. Chiang Kaishek cables President Roosevelt, accepting Supreme Command of the Allied Nations in the China theatre.

March 4. US General Joseph Stilwell assumes command as Chief-of-Staff of the China theatre of war.

C Cultural and Social

January 28. The CCPCC issues its 'Decision on Land Policy in the Anti-Japanese Base Areas'. This encourages cuts in land rent and interest rates, but also protects landlords since most are anti-Japanese.

February 1. At the opening of the CCPCC's Party school in Yan'an, Mao Zedong makes his speech, 'Rectify the Party's Style of Work' to reinforce his previous report 'Reform Our Study' (see C, May 1941). He calls on the whole Party to rectify its style of study and denounces sectarianism and subjectivism. This is the beginning of the Rectification Campaign.

April. Guo Moruo's play *Qu Yuan* is premiered in Chongqing.

May 2 and 23. Mao Zedong addresses the Yan'an Forum on Literature and Art, held as part of the Rectification Campaign. He puts forward the view that art should reflect the interests of the workers, peasants and soldiers and rejects the theory of art for art's sake.

27–June 11. A series of meetings takes place in Yan'an to discredit the writer Wang Shiwei.

July 6. The National Association for the Welfare of the Blind is founded in Chongqing.

September 9. Chongqing holds its first Sports Day.

October 14. A woodcut exhibition opens in Chongqing.

December 29. The Executive Yuan resolves to make several private universities national, including Shanxi University and Yingshi University in Zhejiang; and to incorporate several of the tertiary institutions which had remained in Shanghai after the Pacific War's outbreak into the National Yingshi University in Zhejiang and the National Ji'nan University in Fujian.

D Publications

January 11. Guo Moruo completes the historical play *Qu Yuan*.

1942–3

such as disunity and disharmony among the Party, government, army and masses.

October 2–7. US President Roosevelt's special envoy Wendell Willkie visits Chongqing.

4. Chiang Kaishek meets Wendell Willkie and they discuss post-war issues.

5. Sheng Shicai writes to the Soviet consul-general in Dihua (Urumchi) (Xinjiang) demanding that 'all Russians in Xinjiang, including military advisers,... and the tin miners and explorers in the Altai and Yili regions, should leave the province within three months'.

10. USA and Great Britain announce their intention to begin immediate negotiations with China to relinquish their extraterritorial rights and other privileges in China.

12. In an editorial in Yan'an's *Liberation Daily* Mao Zedong describes the Battle of Stalingrad, where Soviet troops were defeating the German invasion, as 'decisive for the whole world war' and 'the turning point in the history of all mankind'.

22–31. The First Session of the Third National Political Council takes place in Chongqing, boycotted by the CCP members.

November. Japanese forces mobilize some 40,000 men to attack CCP military base areas in Shandong and some 50,000 to mop up the CCP northern Jiangsu base. Neither move succeeds in destroying the bases.

12. China and Cuba sign a Treaty of Amity in Havana. Under it the nationals of each country 'shall be at liberty to enter or leave the territory of the other' in the same way as those of other countries.

December 15. Radio photo service is officially inaugurated between Chongqing and the USA.

1943 *The Cairo Conference; the Battle of Changde*

January 9. Wang Jingwei's Nanjing regime declares war against the USA and Britain.

11. In Washington the Chinese ambassador, Wei Daoming, and the US Secretary of State, Cordell Hull, sign the New Sino-American Treaty; in Chongqing the Chinese Minister of Foreign Affairs, Song Ziwen, and the British ambassador, Sir Horace Seymour, sign the New Sino-British Treaty. Both treaties provide, among other things, for the abolition of extraterritorality, the handing over of the Concessions to the NG, and the abrogation of the Boxer Protocol (see September 7, 1901).

16. Following Sheng Shicai's break with the Soviet Union, a branch

February 11. Guo Moruo completes the historical play *Hu Fu* (published the same month).
March 13 and 23. Yan'an's *Liberation Daily* publishes Wang Shiwei's essay 'Ye baihehua' ('Wild Lily'), satirizing life in Yan'an.
October, December. Tao Xisheng's two-volumed *Zhongguo zhengzhi sixiang shi* (*A History of Chinese Political Thought*) is published in Chongqing.

E   NATURAL DISASTERS

Drought in western Henan province results in serious famine and mass migration to Hubei, Gansu and other provinces. Famine afflicts Guangdong; many migrate to Fujian in search of food.
September 8. As a result of torrential rains the Yellow River breaches its dykes in five places in the region of Daolinggang (Henan), causing flooding in nearby areas.

F   DEATHS

May 27. Chen Duxiu, former CCP leader, d. aged 62.
June 3. Zuo Quan, deputy Chief-of-Staff of the Eighth Route Army, d. in battle against the Japanese in south-east Shanxi, aged 36.

The Great Henan Famine; China's Destiny *is published*   **1943**

A   ECONOMICS

March. The CCP initiates production competitions in the liberated areas to stimulate the 'increase production' campaign.
1. The Highway Administration is formally set up under the Ministry of Communications.
15. The Sichuan–Shaanxi highway linking Chongqing and Baoji (Shaanxi) is opened to traffic.
April 20–29. The Ministries of Economics and Education hold an Industrial Construction Plans Conference to discuss post-war industry.
June 1. The Ministry of Finance issues the 1943 Allied Victory Loan of 3,000,000,000 *yuan*, among other purposes to stabilize prices.

1943

of the NP is formally established in Xinjiang.

February. Japanese forces launch a spring mopping-up campaign against the CCP areas in north-western Shanxi; it is defeated after eighty-four days of battles of varying scale.

15. The NG's Ministry of Foreign Affairs announces that China and the Netherlands have agreed to raise the status of their respective envoys to that of ambassador.

March 19. Direct radio communications are inaugurated between Chengdu and Teheran.

28. In Chongqing Zhou Enlai and Lin Biao negotiate with He Yingqin over the worsening relations between the NP and CCP. Zhou puts forward four demands, including NP recognition of the CCP as a legal party. The demands are refused.

April 10. Radio photo and radio facsimile services begin operating between Chongqing and Kunming.

May 5. Japanese forces launch a two-pronged attack against Chinese strategic points along the upper Yangzi River in western Hubei; this action marks the beginning of the Battle of Western Hubei.

8. In the Battle of Western Hubei, Japanese forces take Nanxian (Hunan) after a day-long battle.

13. Chinese troops evacuate Gongan (Hubei).

20. Ratification of the New Sino-American and Sino-British Treaties is exchanged in Washington and Chongqing respectively.

24. Changyang (Hubei) falls to the Japanese.

30. Chinese troops launch a general counter-attack in the Battle of Western Hubei.

June 2. Chinese and American aircraft bomb Japanese troops in the Yichang region (Hubei). Chinese troops retake Changyang (Hubei).

3. Chinese troops retake Nanxian (Hunan).

14. Chinese troops retake Gongan (Hubei), and in the next days restore the *status quo* in western Hubei as of May 5. The Battle of Western Hubei ends.

July 7. On behalf of President Roosevelt, Joseph Stilwell confers on Chiang Kaishek the Legion of Merit, the highest US decoration available to foreigners.

August 1. The NG issues a declaration breaking off diplomatic relations with the Vichy French Government, among other reasons because it 'concluded recently certain agreements with that [Wang Jingwei's Nanjing] regime for the relinquishment of extraterritorial rights and for the rendition of the French Concessions in China'. Japan hands over its Concessions in China to the Wang Jingwei regime.

7. A serious military clash takes place at Juxian (Shandong) between

August 1. The NG takes over from France the administration of that part of the Yunnan–Vietnam railway within Chinese territory.

September 11. The Eleventh Plenum of the NP's Fifth CEC adopts resolutions on (*i*) foreign investment and (*ii*) post-war industrial reconstruction. The first lays down that 'hereafter no fixed restriction shall be placed on the ratio of foreign capital investment in joint enterprises. In the organization of a Chinese-foreign joint enterprise ... the general manager need not necessarily be a Chinese'. The second emphasizes simultaneous development of state and private industry and welcomes foreign capital and technical co-operation.

October 1. The Sichuan–Hunan highway begins taking traffic.

November 9. Forty-four nations sign an agreement in Washington setting up the United Nations Relief and Rehabilitation Administration (UNRRA).

29. In a speech to model workers in the Shaanxi-Gansu-Ningxia Border Region Mao Zedong attributes the success of the 1943 production campaign to the mobilization of the masses, including the people, the army, the government and the schools; he calls for collectivization of the economy through cooperatives.

B OFFICIAL APPOINTMENTS, RESIGNATIONS, DISMISSALS ETC.

September 13. The Eleventh Plenum of the NP's Fifth CEC appoints Chiang Kaishek as Chairman of the NG, and reappoints the Presidents of the Executive, Legislative, Judicial, Examination and Control Yuan, respectively Chiang Kaishek, Sun Fo, Ju Zheng, Dai Jitao and Yu Youren.

October 10. Chiang Kaishek is formally inaugurated as Chairman of the NG.

19. The Supreme National Defence Council appoints Chiang Kaishek as Chairman of the Committee for the Establishment of Constitutional Government, which it sets up the same day with fifty-two members.

C CULTURAL AND SOCIAL

February 5. The first Spring Festival since the Rectification Campaign is celebrated in Yan'an through mass performances of new *yangge* dramas.

March 15. The Council for the Promotion of Science and Technology is founded, promoted by Chen Lifu, Minister of Education, and others.

1943

NP and CCP troops as civil war threatens again.

September 8. The Italian armistice is signed, with Italy surrendering unconditionally to the Allies.

13. The Eleventh Plenum of the NP's Fifth CEC (held September 6–13) resolves to maintain cooperation with the CCP, based on the negotiations of 1937 (see February 10, July 15 and September 22, 1937) but accuses it of sabotaging the War of Resistance against Japan.

October 16. Lord Mountbatten, Supreme Allied Commander, Southeast Asia Command, arrives in Chongqing for talks with Chinese military leaders.

18–19. A joint military conference, attended by Chiang Kaishek, He Yingqin, Mountbatten, Stilwell, Chennault and others, is held in Chongqing to formulate strategy against Japan.

20. The NG's Minister of Foreign Affairs, Song Ziwen, and the Belgian ambassador, Jules Guillaume, sign in Chongqing a treaty under which Belgium and Luxembourg relinquish extraterritoriality and all their Concessions in the International Settlements in Shanghai and Amoy.

30. The Declaration on General Security is signed in Moscow between China (Fu Bingchang, ambassador to USSR), USA (Cordell Hull, Secretary of State), USSR (V.M. Molotov, Foreign Commissar) and Great Britain (Anthony Eden, Foreign Secretary): the Moscow Declaration. They declare, among other things, 'that their united action will be pledged for the prosecution of the war against their respective enemies and will be continued for the organization and maintenance of peace and security', the latter section to be effected through the UN.

November 2. A large Japanese force of some 100,000 men launches a two-pronged attack on Gongan (Hubei) from Shashi (Hubei), and on Nanxian (Hunan) from Huarong (Hunan); this marks the beginning of the Battle of Changde (Hunan), through which the Japanese aim to cut off Hunan from Hubei.

3. Nanxian again falls to the Japanese.

4. The Japanese again occupy Gongan.

21. Chiang Kaishek, accompanied by Madame Chiang, arrives in Cairo to take part in the Cairo Conference, with US President Roosevelt and British Prime Minister Churchill, on the war.

24. The Japanese reach the outskirts of Changde (Hunan); fierce fighting breaks out for control of the city.

December 1. Chiang Kaishek and Madame Chiang arrive back in Chongqing from Cairo. The Cairo Declaration, the result of the Cairo Conference, is issued. It declares that Manchuria, Taiwan and

1943

24. The Chinese Society of History is founded in Chongqing by Gu Jiegang and others.

August 15. The CCPCC cables to all CCP organs its decision on the screening of cadres as part of the Rectification Campaign. Under it the masses are to be involved in examining cadres to stamp out espionage and corruption of all kinds.

October 5. In an editorial in Yan'an's *Liberation Daily*, Mao Zedong describes Chiang Kaishek's recent book *China's Destiny* as 'a diatribe against communism and against the people' and perfectly acceptable to the Japanese.

23. The NG's Central Commission for the Censorship of Books and Periodicals issues its 'Table of Banned Plays'; the table lists some 120 banned plays, including some by Cao Yu, Guo Moruo, Ouyang Yuqian, Hong Shen, Tian Han, Zhou Yibai, Lao She and others.

November 7. The CCP's Propaganda Department adopts the 'Decision on the Implementation of Party Policy on Literature and Art'. It calls on artists to follow the principles of Mao Zedong's 'Talks at the Yan'an Forum' and lays emphasis, among the arts, mainly on drama and news reporting.

20. The NG promulgates a Revised Trade Union Act (see also C, November 1, 1929).

D PUBLICATIONS

Mao Dun publishes his novel *Shuangye hong si eryue hua* (*Maple Leaves Red as the Flowers of February*); and Xie Wanying her collection of essays *Guanyu nüren* (*On Women*).

January. Zhang Tianyi's collection of short stories *Suxie sanpian* (*Three Sketches*) is published in Chongqing.

30. Chiang Kaishek completes his book *Zhongguo zhi mingyun* (*China's Destiny*).

March 10. Chiang Kaishek's *China's Destiny* is formally published in Chongqing.

May. Zhao Shuli writes his short story *Xiao Erhei jiehun* (*The Marriage of Little Blacky*) (published in 1946).

October. Zhao Shuli writes his short story *Li Youcai banhua* (*The Rhymes of Li Youcai*) (published as a book in 1947).

19. Yan'an's *Liberation Daily* publishes Mao Zedong's 'Zai Yan'an wenyi zuotanhui shang de jianghua' ('Talks at the Yan'an Forum on Literature and Art').

December. The Kaiming Book Company publishes *Congwen zizhuan* (*Autobiography of Shen Congwen*).

1943–4

the Pescadores will be restored to the ROC and that 'in due course Korea shall become free and independent'.
3. The Chinese forces defending Changde are annihilated and the Japanese break into the city.
9. Chinese reinforcements recapture Changde. The Japanese forces retreat in a north-easterly direction.
17. US President Roosevelt signs legislation laying down an annual quota of Chinese allowed to migrate to the USA.
25. Chinese troops retake Gongan, restoring the *status quo* in northern Hunan as of November 2. This represented the effective end of the Battle of Changde, which cost both sides and civilians heavy casualties and totally destroyed the city of Changde.

1944 *The Japanese carry out their Trans-Continental Offensive from Henan to Guangxi*

January 15–February 16. Anti-war Japanese hold a conference in Yan'an (Shaanxi) and decide to set up the Japanese People's Liberation League.
30. The Chinese Expeditionary Force takes Taro, northern Burma.
February 6. The Eighth Route Army takes Ningcheng (Jehol).
17. Eighth Route Army troops launch a night attack into Shijiazhuang (Hebei), and capture eleven policemen of the Japanese authority.
21. The Eighth Route Army takes Taigu (Shanxi).
March 2. The Sino-Afghan Treaty of Amity is signed in Ankara.
14. The Eighth Route Army takes Jinxian (Hebei).
22. The Sino-Canadian Mutual Aid Agreement is signed in Ottawa.
April 6. The Eighth Route Army takes Boye (Hebei); it also takes several other towns in the Shijiazhuang area at about the same time.
14. A new Sino-Canadian Treaty is signed in Ottawa, under which Canada renounces extraterritoriality and all special privileges in China.
18. The Japanese attack the defences of the Yellow River near Zhengzhou. This action marks the beginning of a general offensive in central Henan and of the Trans-Continental Offensive.
22. Zhengzhou (Henan) falls to the Japanese.
May 2. Japanese troops begin moving north from Xinyang (Henan) to link up with those coming south along the Beiping–Hankou railway.

E NATURAL DISASTERS

Catastrophic drought-famine continues in Henan; the number of dead and refugees to other provinces each reaches 2,000,000 to 3,000,000 since the beginning of the famine in 1942. Serious famine also afflicts Shaanxi, Hubei, Guangdong, Shandong, Sichuan and other provinces.

F DEATHS

May 19. Peking Opera actor Yu Shuyan d. aged 42.
August 1. Lin Sen, Chairman of the ROC's NG, d. in Chongqing aged 75.
September 27. Mao Zemin, younger brother of Mao Zedong, and Chen Tanqiu, a founder of the CCP, are executed in Xinjiang on orders of Sheng Shicai, for trying to overthrow him, aged respectively 48 and 54.

Mao Zedong makes his speech 'Serve the People'; **1944**
death of Wang Jingwei

A ECONOMICS

February 16. China and the Soviet Union sign a contract for the Chinese purchase of equipment for the oilfield in Wusu (Xinjiang).
May 2. China and Great Britain sign agreement in London on the Fourth Sino-British Export Credit Loan of £50,000,000 for the provision of military equipment on lend-lease terms by Britain to China.
July 1. The NG's Ministry of Finance issues the 1944 Allied Victory Loan of 5,000,000,000 *yuan*.
   1–23. The UN Monetary and Financial Conference is held in Bretton Woods, New Hampshire, USA; China participates, Minister of Finance Kong Xiangxi heading its delegation.
   19. The UN Monetary and Financial Conference names China as one of the twelve executive directors of the proposed International Bank for Reconstruction and Development (World Bank).
   22. The UN Monetary and Financial Conference closes with the signing of the Final Act, annexed to which are the Agreements on the International Monetary Fund and on the International Bank for Reconstruction and Development.
September 15. The Central Bank of China, the Bank of China, the Farmers' Bank of China, the Bank of Communications and other bodies put into effect a new gold savings deposit system, under which

1944

Negotiations begin in Xi'an between the NG, represented by Zhang Zhizhong and Wang Shijie, and the CCP, represented by Lin Boqu, on recognition by the NG of the local administrations in the Shaanxi-Gansu-Ningxia Border Region and other CCP areas, the organization of the CCP armed forces, and a coalition government. The negotiations last over a week, but yield no major agreement.

5. The Sino-Costa Rican Treaty of Amity is signed in San Jose.

13. The Eighth Route Army enters the city of Baoding (Hebei), but is soon forced to retreat.

17. Chinese and US forces under Stilwell take the airfield at Myitkyina, northern Burma. The Eighth Route Army briefly enters the city of Shijiazhuang (Hebei).

21. The Eighth Route Army takes the city of Gaoyang (Hebei).

25. In their Trans-Continental Offensive the Japanese seize Luoyang (Henan) after overcoming strong resistance.

June 1. Pingjiang (Hunan) falls to Japanese troops as over a wide front they attack south from the Wuhan area in a fourth attempt to seize Changsha. This is the second major prong in the Trans-Continental Offensive.

6. The Allied landing on the coast of Normandy begins: the D-Day invasion.

9. The New Fourth Army attacks a newly built airfield in Japanese-occupied Nanjing, causing considerable destruction.

15. From a base in Chengdu US B29 Superfortresses make their first air raid on Japan, striking steel mills in Yahata.

17. Japanese troops moving north along the Beiping–Hankou railway from Xinyang join forces with those moving south, giving the Japanese control of the entire railway.

18. Changsha falls to the Japanese. US Vice-President Henry Agard Wallace arrives in Dihua, capital of Xinjiang, at the beginning of a visit to China.

20. US Vice-President Henry Wallace arrives in Chongqing. In a report dated this day on 'The Situation in China and Suggestions Regarding American Policy', John S. Service, a political adviser in Stilwell's Chongqing headquarters, draws attention to the disintegration of the NP and expansion of the CCP. He calls for friendly US relations with 'the liberal elements' in the NP and with the CCP.

26. The Chinese Expeditionary Force takes Mogaung, site of a Japanese base in northern Burma.

July 2. US Vice-President Wallace leaves Lanzhou (Gansu) for home.

22. The first batch of the US Military Observers (DIXIE) Mission, including John Service, arrives in Yan'an; it aims to evaluate potential

1944

they may enter deposit in gold, or in legal tender currency for gold.

November 13. The successful completion of a trial run marks the opening to traffic of the Xining (Qinghai) to Yushu (Qinghai) section of the Qinghai–Tibet highway, overall the world's most elevated highway.

B   OFFICIAL APPOINTMENTS, RESIGNATIONS, DISMISSALS ETC.

February 8. The Tenth Reincarnation of the Panchen Lama is formally enthroned.

August 18. The NG appoints Gu Weijun, Chinese ambassador to Great Britain, as chief delegate to the Dumbarton Oaks Conference on the organization of post-war world security.

September 26. The Executive Yuan resolves to appoint Wu Zhongxin as Chairman of Xinjiang, to replace Sheng Shicai, as part of a reorganization of the Xinjiang government.

October 19. Chiang Kaishek receives a cable from Roosevelt saying that he has recalled Joseph Stilwell from China and replaced him as Chief-of-Staff in the China theatre by General Albert Wedemeyer (Stilwell leaves Chongqing October 21).

November 14. US ambassador Clarence Gauss leaves Chongqing in resignation of his post over Stilwell's recall. (His decision to resign had been taken earlier and revealed in the US press on October 31.)

20. The NG appoints Yu Hongjun (known in the West as O.K. Yui) as Minister of Finance in succession to Kong Xiangxi, Chen Cheng as Minister of War to replace He Yingqin (whose removal from the post had been demanded by the USA), and Zhu Jiahua as Minister of Education to replace Chen Lifu. Chen Gongbo assumes leadership of the Japanese-sponsored Nanjing NG in succession to the deceased Wang Jingwei.

C   CULTURAL AND SOCIAL

January 9. Mao Zedong writes to the Yan'an Beiping Opera Troupe commending them for taking dominance of the stage away from 'lords and ladies' and giving it to the people, 'the creators of history'; he is commenting on a performance of the historical Peking Opera *Bishang Liangshan* (*Driven Up Mount Liang*), newly adapted in Yan'an from a story in the novel *Shuihu zhuan* and premiered there in December 1943.

February 2. Chen Lifu, the NG's Minister of Education, promulgates regulations governing the ideology of professors and lecturers who go abroad.

1944

for military collaboration with the CCP against the Japanese, including the possibility of US aid.

29. US B29 Superfortresses strike the Shenyang area in Manchuria.

August. The Eighth Route Army defeats a Japanese encirclement campaign against the CCP's Shandong base areas and also captures several cities in the province.

1. The Sino-Mexican Treaty of Amity is signed in Mexico City; under it Chinese enjoy access to Mexican territory and Mexicans to Chinese 'under the same conditions as the nationals of any third country'.

3. After a very long siege and fierce resistance from the Japanese, Chinese and US forces capture Myitkyina, northern Burma, one of Stilwell's principal objectives in the Burma campaign.

7. The second group of the US DIXIE Mission arrives in Yan'an.

8. In their Trans-Continental Offensive the Japanese occupy Hengyang, strategic railway junction in southern Hunan, after a siege and extremely bitter fighting lasting nearly seven weeks.

19. US President Roosevelt announces that Brigadier-General Patrick Hurley will visit China as his personal representative to discuss military and economic issues with Chiang Kaishek.

September. The Chinese Democratic League is established from a combination of various minor political parties as a 'third force' between the NP and CCP.

14. The Chinese Expeditionary Force and other Chinese units retake Tengchong (Yunnan) after a two-month siege.

15. Zhang Zhizhong and Lin Boqu, representing the NP and CCP respectively, report to the third session of the Third National Political Council (held September 5 to 18) on their negotiations. Lin Boqu suggests the reorganization of the NG and its military arm into a democratic coalition government and joint command.

20. Wuzhou (Guangxi) falls to the Japanese.

25. Chiang Kaishek presents Patrick Hurley with a demand that Stilwell be recalled from China.

29–October 7. China, represented by Gu Weijun and others, takes part in the second session of the conference on the organization of post-war world security, held in Dumbarton Oaks, USA.

October 5. Fuzhou, the capital of Fujian, again falls to the Japanese.

9. The Chinese, Soviet, British and US governments simultaneously issue the Dumbarton Oaks Proposal for the Establishment of a General International Organization, under which an organization called the United Nations is to be set up, and the ROC is to hold a permanent seat on its Security Council.

April 12. Following lengthy discussions on CCP history among senior cadres and the central Party organ, Mao Zedong makes a speech on the subject to senior cadres in Yan'an called 'Our Study and the Current Situation', summarizing the CCPCC Politburo's views. In it he urges the cadres to be clear ideologically, to treat those who have made mistakes leniently, to treat all questions analytically etc.

June 20. The NG promulgates its Regulations Governing the Censorship of Wartime Books and Periodicals, under which newspapers, maps, charts, books, periodicals, films, dramas etc. must undergo censorship by the Central Commission for the Censorship of Books and Periodicals or local organs, except 'books and periodicals that do not concern military, political and foreign affairs', which authors and publishers are to censor.

July 15. The NG promulgates the Regulations for Safeguarding the Freedom of the Human Person (sometimes called the Habeas Corpus Act) to come into effect on August 1. Under these 'no agency, unless authorized to exercise prosecution ..., shall arrest, detain, fine or subject anybody to trial'; they allow cases of arrests concerning military affairs to be held in secrecy.

18. The NG issues its Regulations Governing the Enforcement of Compulsory Education, under which all parents must send their school-age children to school under pain of a fine.

September 8. Mao Zedong makes the speech 'Serve the People' at a memorial meeting for a dead CCP soldier, Zhang Side.

October 3. The Foreign Trade Association of China is set up in Chongqing to promote import and export trade.

11. The Ministry of Education promulgates Regulations Governing Students Going Abroad, under which all such students, both government and private, must first pass examinations in various subjects, including the Three People's Principles and Chinese history.

22. The Economic Research Society of China is organized in Chongqing to advance the study of economics and to inaugurate economic enterprises.

November 5. The Association of Chinese Authors is formally inaugurated in Chongqing to unite literary minds for the advancement of learning.

24. The Chinese National Press Association issues a declaration in support of the freedom to gather, transmit, receive and publish news.

D PUBLICATIONS

The Commercial Press publishes Zou Lu's four-volumed *Zhongguo*

1944–5

23. China, together with the USA, USSR and Britain formally recognize Charles de Gaulle's provisional government of the Republic of France.

November 3. Chinese forces retake Longling (Yunnan).

7. Patrick Hurley flies to Yan'an for talks with Mao Zedong.

10. Hurley and Mao sign an agreement under which the NG, NP and CCP are to work together for Japan's defeat and all forces will obey a coalition NG.

11. After pressing their Trans-Continental Offensive south from Hengyang, the Japanese overcome fierce resistance at Guilin (Guangxi) and complete their occupation of the city. They also seize Liuzhou (Guangxi).

22. Nanning (Guangxi) falls to the Japanese; shortly after this action they win effective control over a continuous railway from Vietnam to Korea.

December 15. The Chinese Expeditionary Force recaptures Bhamo, northern Burma, the site of a strategic Japanese base.

1945 *Japan surrenders: the end of World War II*

January 15. The Chinese Expeditionary Force takes Namkham, Burma.

20. Chinese forces retake Wanding (Yunnan), on the border with Burma.

28. Shaoguan (Guangdong) falls to the Japanese. Japanese forces thus take full control of the Guangzhou–Hankou railway to link up with the Japanese-controlled Beiping–Hankou railway.

The first convoy for nearly three years enters Wanding (Yunnan) along the Sino-Indian road through Ledo, Assam. A ceremony in Wanding marks the reopening of the road and the defeat of Japanese troops in the area. The same day Chiang Kaishek publicly renames the Sino-Indian Road the Stilwell Road.

31. Uighur-Kazakh rebels seize Yining (Xinjiang), which becomes the capital of their East Turkestan Republic.

February 4–11. Roosevelt, Churchill and Stalin meet in Yalta, USSR, to discuss the world situation. They reach secret agreement that Russian troops will be sent to Manchuria after the end of the European war on condition that the *status quo* is preserved in Outer Mongolia, that the port of Dalian is internationalized and Port Arthur (Lüshun) leased to the USSR for use as a naval base.

April 5. Song Ziwen and the Swedish minister to China, Sven Allard,

1944–5

Guomin dang shigao (*Draft History of the Chinese NP*) in Chongqing (a smaller version was published in 1941).

F DEATHS

March 24. Painter Tang Yihe d. aged 39.
May 20. Chen Youren d. aged 66.
July 5. Historian Zhu Xizu d. aged 65.
September 5. Zhang Side d. aged 29. (See also C, September 8.)
November 10. Wang Jingwei d. in Japan aged 61.

The police raid South-west Associated University in Kunming, killing four people **1945**

A ECONOMICS

January 1. The War Transport Board is formally set up to replace the Highway Administration and various other bodies. Its functions are to administer centrally all operations of highways, railways, inland navigation and air transport.
23. The Executive Yuan resolves on various tax reform measures, including the abolition of a number of taxes such as those on tea, chinaware and cement. The Chinese National Relief and Rehabilitation Administration is formally inaugurated.
March 29. As inflation gathers momentum, the Ministry of Finance announces that the price of gold has risen to 35,000 *yuan* per tael (from 20,000 *yuan* per tael on November 13, 1944).
May 19. The NP's Sixth National Congress adopts its Industrial Reconstruction Programme; it envisages the nationalization of capital and a system of state enterprise, especially in key industries such as steel, iron, coal and oil, as well as private enterprise, and 'gives the fullest protection to foreign capital in China',
June 8. The Central Bank of China raises the official price of gold to 50,000 *yuan* per tael.
25. The Ministry of Finance orders the suspension of gold savings

1945

sign the New Sino-Swedish Equal Treaty in Chongqing, under which Sweden renounces extraterritorial and related rights in China. The USSR declares its abrogation of the Soviet-Japanese Neutrality Pact of April 13, 1941.

15. In Moscow, Hurley discusses the situation in China with Stalin. They agree that Hurley will not tell Chiang Kaishek about the agreements reached at Yalta without first consulting Stalin.

23. The Seventh National Congress of the CCP opens in Yan'an. In his opening speech Mao Zedong reports membership of the CCP at 1,210,000 and the population of the liberated areas at 95,500,000.

24. In his political report to the CCP's Seventh National Congress, entitled 'On Coalition Government', Mao Zedong lays down the general programme and policies of the CCP and calls for the formation of a coalition government.

25. The UN Conference on International Organization, attended by forty-six nations, opens in San Francisco; Song Ziwen heads the ROC delegation.

May 5–21. The Sixth National Congress of the NP is held in Chongqing. It adopts a new political programme on May 18.

7. Germany surrenders unconditionally to the Allies; the European war concludes.

27. Chinese troops retake Nanning (Guangxi).

29. The New Sino-Dutch Treaty is signed in London, under which the Netherlands agrees to renounce extraterritorial and related rights in China.

30. The NG's Ministry of Foreign Affairs announces that China and Argentina have decided to establish diplomatic relations.

June 6. On President Truman's orders, the US Federal Bureau of Investigation arrests John S. Service and five other people, for disclosing secret US documents, criticizing the US China policy and giving their support to the CCP. (Truman had succeeded as US President following Roosevelt's death on April 12.)

8. The Chinese retake Longzhou (Guangxi) near the border with Vietnam.

9. President Truman informs Song Ziwen in Washington about the Yalta decisions.

11. The Seventh National Congress of the CCP concludes with Mao Zedong's speech 'The Foolish Old Man Who Removed the Mountains'.

25. NP troops in Chunhua (Shaanxi) mutiny, according to Hu Zongnan instigated by the CCP, and seize the city and surroundings.

26. The nations at the UN Conference on International Organization

1945

because of the tense situation in the financial market.

July 25. The National Relief Commission is abolished.

August 14. Wang Shijie and Molotov sign an agreement on the Chinese Changchun railway, the name given to the combination of the Chinese Eastern railway from Manzhouli to Suifenhe (both in Heilongjiang) and the South Manchurian railway from Harbin (Heilongjiang) to Dalian (Liaoning). Under the agreement the '"Chinese Changchun Railway" shall be in joint ownership of the USSR and the ROC and shall be operated by them jointly'. They sign a separate agreement declaring Dalian 'a free port open to the commerce and shipping of all nations'.

November 7. In an inner-Party directive Mao Zedong calls for urgent economic measures to defend the liberated areas against attack by the NP forces; they include increased production and improvement of the people's livelihood; he urges CCP members to see that 'the peasants generally get the benefits of wage reduction and that the workers ... benefit by appropriate wage increases'.

24. Marshal Malinovsky's economic adviser presents Zhang Jia'ao, Director of the Economic Committee of the North-east Headquarters, with a proposal for joint Sino-Soviet operation of four-fifths of Manchuria's heavy industry.

26. The Executive Yuan resolves to establish the Supreme Economic Council to direct and promote economic reconstruction, to coordinate economic activities and to bring about a steady rise in the people's standard of living.

December 7. Malinovsky's economic adviser informs Zhang Jia'ao that the Soviet Union regards Manchuria's industry as its 'war booty'.

25. A successful trial run marks the completion of the railway from Baoji (Shaanxi) to Tianshui (Gansu), a particularly difficult stretch from an engineering point of view. This line was actually an extension from Baoji of the proposed Longhai line to run from Haizhou (Jiangsu) to Lanzhou (Gansu).

B   OFFICIAL APPOINTMENTS, RESIGNATIONS, DISMISSALS ETC.

January 8. Patrick Hurley presents his credentials to Chiang Kaishek, thus formally assuming office as US ambassador to China.

March 26. The NG announces the list of the Chinese delegation to the San Francisco Conference on International Organization: Song Ziwen is the chief delegate, and others include Gu Weijun, Wang Chonghui, Wei Daoming, Hu Shi and Dong Biwu (the CCP representative).

1945

sign the UN Charter in San Francisco; Gu Weijun signs for China.

29. Chinese forces retake Liuzhou (Guangxi).

July 17. Truman, Churchill, Stalin and others begin a conference in Potsdam, Germany.

21. A large NG force under Hu Zongnan attacks Yetaishan, a CCP base area in Chunhua (Shaanxi).

26. Truman, Churchill and Chiang Kaishek (who had assented by radio) issue the Potsdam Declaration, an ultimatum to Japan to surrender unconditionally or face 'prompt and utter destruction'.

(The same day Churchill resigns as British Prime Minister in favour of Clement Attlee following the electoral victory of the British Labour Party the preceding day.)

27. CCP troops withdraw from Yetaishan.

29. The Japanese Prime Minister, Admiral Suzuki Kantarō, declares that Japan will ignore the Potsdam surrender ultimatum.

August 6. A US atomic bomb, the first ever used, destroys the Japanese city of Hiroshima.

8. The USSR declares war against Japan. CCP troops counterattack in the Yetaishan area of Chunhua (Shaanxi) and retake the base.

9. A second US atomic bomb destroys Nagasaki, Japan. A gigantic Soviet force enters Manchuria under the command of Marshal R. Malinovsky and others.

10. The Japanese government declares it accepts the Potsdam ultimatum, provided the prerogatives of the Emperor are not affected. Commander-in-Chief Zhu De of the CCP forces orders the armies of the liberated areas to disarm the Japanese forces there.

11. US Secretary of State James Byrnes declares that when Japan surrenders the authority of the Emperor 'shall be subject to the Supreme Commander of the Allied Powers'. General Headquarters in Yan'an orders CCP troops to march on Inner Mongolia and the north-eastern provinces to force the Japanese to surrender.

14. The NG's Minister of Foreign Affairs, Wang Shijie, and the People's Foreign Commissar of the USSR, V.M. Molotov, sign the Sino-Soviet Treaty of Friendship and Alliance in Moscow. In addition they exchange notes recognizing the independence of Outer Mongolia 'should a plebiscite of the Outer Mongolian people confirm this desire' and sign a separate agreement on Port Arthur (Lüshun) under which the two countries may use it jointly as a naval base 'against further aggression by Japan'.

The Japanese Emperor issues an Imperial Rescript that he has 'ordered the acceptance of the provisions of the joint declaration of the powers' (i.e. unconditional surrender).

1945

May 31. The First Plenum of the NP's Sixth CEC appoints Song Ziwen as the President of the Executive Yuan to succeed Chiang Kaishek.

June 9–10. The Seventh National Congress of the CCP elects a new CC of forty-four regular and thirty-three alternate members, the former including Mao Zedong, Zhu De, Liu Shaoqi, Ren Bishi, Lin Boqu, Lin Biao, Dong Biwu, Zhou Enlai and Chen Tanqiu (not realizing that he was already dead, see F, September 27, 1943).

July 6. General Claire Chennault resigns his command of the US Fourteenth Air Force.

25. The NG appoints Yu Hongjun as managing director of the Central Bank of China in succession to Kong Xiangxi.

30. The NG appoints Wang Shijie as Minister of Foreign Affairs in succession to Song Ziwen.

August 31. The NG appoints Xiong Shihui as Director of the North-east Headquarters of the Military Affairs Committee, with his seat at Changchun.

September 4. The NG appoints Xiong Shihui as Director of the Political Committee of the North-east Headquarters; this makes him the supreme official in Manchuria, where the NG is trying to reassert control with the fall of Manzhouguo. The same day the NG also appoints Zhang Jia'ao as Director of the Economic Committee of the North-east Headquarters; and the various Chairmen of the nine provinces of the north-east (set up on August 31 to replace the original three provinces).

November 26. The Executive Yuan appoints Song Ziwen as President of the Supreme Economic Council.

27. The US government receives from Hurley a letter of resignation as US ambassador to China, which criticizes diplomats in the embassy and the State Department, and US policy in China. President Truman appoints General George C. Marshall as special envoy with the rank of ambassador to succeed Hurley.

December 9. Chiang Kaishek orders the dismissal of garrison commander Guan Linzheng as responsible for the massacre of students (see C, December 1).

C CULTURAL AND SOCIAL

January 6–17. A Study Conference is held by the Institute of Pacific Relations at Hot Springs, Virginia, USA, to discuss security; a Chinese delegation of twelve takes part, headed by Jiang Menglin.

1945

15. Zhu De cables the British, US and Soviet ambassadors saying that Chiang Kaishek does not represent the liberated areas and demanding that the CCP share in the Japanese surrender and post-war settlement.
16. The Japanese Emperor issues orders to all Japanese forces to cease hostilities.
18. China and France sign a pact under which France agrees to return the lease in Guangzhou Bay to China.
20. The Soviet Red Army occupies Harbin, Changchun, and Shenyang. Radio Moscow announces the arrest of Puyi, former Emperor of Manzhouguo.
25. China and the USSR ratify the Sino-Soviet Treaty of Friendship and Alliance.
28. Mao Zedong and Zhou Enlai, accompanied by US ambassador Patrick Hurley, fly to Chongqing to discuss with Chiang Kaishek and his representatives the problems of peace, democracy and unity: the Chongqing negotiations.
29. Chiang Kaishek and Mao Zedong meet in Chongqing.

September 2. World War II ends formally as representatives of the Japanese government and army sign the surrender documents on the USS *Missouri* in Tokyo Bay.
9. In Nanjing He Yingqin formally accepts the Japanese surrender in the China theatre.
20. US warships arrive in Qingdao (Shandong) to assist in the disarming and evacuation of Japanese troops.
30. US marines land in Tanggu, near Tianjin, to assist in the disarming and evacuation of Japanese troops. (They are among some 50,000 US marines who land in several Chinese ports at about this time for the same purpose.)

October 1. The Democratic League adopts a manifesto of neutrality and freedom at its national congress.
10. As a result of the Chongqing negotiations, representatives of the NG, including Zhang Qun, and of the CCP, including Zhou Enlai, sign and issue the 'Summary of Conversations'. Both sides resolve to avoid a civil war and to build an independent, free and strong new China. Many questions remain unresolved: the NG refuses to recognize the CCP liberated areas; a committee is set up to consider further the nationalization of troops.
11. Mao Zedong returns to Yan'an.
18. The CCP forces of southern Jiangsu, southern Anhui, eastern Zhejiang and western Zhejiang begin to move to the north of the Yangzi River.

1945

April. The revolutionary opera *Baimao nü* (*The White-Haired Girl*) is premiered in Yan'an.

8. The Foreign Policy Association of China is founded in Chongqing to study foreign policy, sponsor lectures and forums etc.

May 17. The Sixth National Congress of the NP adopts the National Health and Labour Programmes. Under the first, marriage is forbidden for men under the age of twenty or women under eighteen, monogamy is to be enforced, sex education and advice on rational birth control are to be encouraged. Under the Labour Programme, the contractor system is to be abolished, housing projects for labourers are to be launched, and all workmen are to join trade unions.

June 26–28. Guo Moruo attends the 220th anniversary celebrations of the Russian Academy of Sciences in Leningrad (the celebrations ran June 16–28).

September 5. The Yan'an Xinhua Broadcasting Station, the first radio station set up by the CCP and the forerunner of the Central People's Broadcasting Station, goes on the air for the first time.

23. Francis Spellman, Catholic Archbishop of New York, arrives in Chongqing for a visit at the invitation of Chiang Kaishek and Song Meiling.

October 1. Wartime press censorship is abolished.

November 1–16. The UN Educational, Scientific and Cultural Conference is held in London; the Chinese delegation is headed by Hu Shi.
16. The delegates of forty-four nations at the UN Educational, Scientific and Cultural Conference sign documents bringing into existence the United Nations Educational, Scientific and Cultural Organization (UNESCO).
25. The Executive Yuan resolves to establish the National Taiwan University.

December 1. Under orders from the garrison commander of Yunnan, Guan Linzheng, some 400 armed agents and military police raid the South-west Associated University in Kunming (the wartime amalgamation of Peking, Qinghua and Nankai Universities) to suppress students and teachers who had demonstrated against civil war on November 25 and subsequently held a strike. The raiders kill four students and wound over ten. As a result the strike continues with prolonged mourning for the four as martyrs to freedom.
7. Chiang Kaishek issues a statement on the student strike in Kunming, saying that the killing of the four must be handled in accordance with proper procedures and calling for classes to be resumed.
11. Two ringleaders of the December 1 massacre at the South-west Associated University are executed.

25. Japanese forces in Taiwan formally surrender; a ceremony and the arrival of Chen Yi to administer the government mark the island's official restoration to China.

31. Some 70,000 NG troops moving along the Beiping–Hankou railway to attack the Shanxi-Hebei-Shandong-Henan CCP-held areas are defeated by CCP troops in the Handan region (Hebei).

November 15. Chiang Kaishek orders the evacuation of the NG's headquarters from Changchun (Jilin), the political centre of Manchuria, leaving CCP and Soviet troops in control.

26. NG troops move into Jinzhou, the first major city to be occupied by them in Manchuria, where already CCP troops were in control of many regions.

30. China and the USSR agree that all Soviet troops should withdraw from the north-eastern provinces by January 3, 1946.

December 5. In talks with Chiang Kaishek's son, Jiang [Chiang] Jingguo, Marshal Malinovsky agrees to guarantee the security of a division of NG troops in Changchun and two divisions in Shenyang.

16. The CCP delegation, consisting of Zhou Enlai, his wife Deng Yingchao, Ye Jianying, Lu Dingyi, and others arrives in Chongqing to attend the Political Consultative Conference aimed at paving the way for constitutional government. (Before the end of the month Zhou Enlai also holds negotiations over a ceasefire in the already expanding civil war.)

28. On behalf of the CCPCC, Mao Zedong issues a directive to the CCP's North-east Bureau to build stable military and political base areas in Manchuria, avoiding big cities and main communication lines, and concentrating on small cities and rural areas.

1946 *Full-scale civil war breaks out; ROC Constitution promulgated*

January 2. Zhang Zhizhong concludes a peace agreement with Akhmedjan Kasimov and other representatives of the East Turkestan Republic. (See January 31, 1945); under it the NG grants self-government to

D Publications

Mao Dun's play *Qingming qianhou* (*Around the Qingming Festival*) is published in Chongqing. Guo Moruo publishes two works on ancient Chinese history, *Qingtong shidai* (*The Bronze Age*) (author's preface dated February 11, 1945) and *Shi pipan shu* (*Ten Critiques*) (final postface dated September 28, 1945), both in Chongqing.

May. Liberation News Agency in Yan'an publishes Mao Zedong's *Lun lianhe zhengfu* (*On Coalition Government*) as a book. He Qifang's poetry collection *Yege* (*Night Songs*) is published in Chongqing.

18. During the Conference on International Organization the *Memorandum on China's Liberated Areas*, written by Dong Biwu and others, is published in San Francisco, discussing conditions in the CCP areas of China.

June. Liberation News Agency publishes *Zhongguo Gongchan dang diqici quanguo daibiao dahui wenxian* (*Documents of the Seventh National Congress of the CCP*).

July. The third and last volume of Ba Jin's novel *Huo* (*Fire*) is published by the Kaiming Book Company. (The first two were published in December 1940 and January 1941, the third was completed in October 1943.)

December. The New China Bookshop publishes *Sun Zhongshan xiansheng xuanji* (*Selected Works of Mr Sun Yatsen*) in Yan'an.

E Natural Disasters

Summer. Famine afflicts Shaanxi province (an Executive Yuan allocation of 20,000,000 *yuan* to relieve the famine being announced on July 16).

F Deaths

February 15. Traditional scholar Zhang Ertian d. aged 70.
September 17. Author Yu Dafu is killed by Japanese police, aged 49.
October 30. Revolutionary musical composer Xian Xinghai d. in Moscow aged 40.

Severe famine in Hunan **1946**

A Economics

January 21. The Soviet Ambassador, A. Petrov, informs the Ministry of Foreign Affairs formally of the Soviet demand for economic

1946

Yining.

3. The NG begins to airlift troops to Changchun, capital of Jilin.

5. The NG issues a statement formally recognizing the independence of Outer Mongolia.

10. Zhang Qun, representing the NG, Zhou Enlai the CCP, and George Marshall as mediator (the Committee of Three) reach agreement on a ceasefire between NP and CCP troops to come into effect January 13. The Political Consultative Conference opens in Chongqing; the NP, CCP and other political parties, and independents take part.

23. CCP forces enter Changchun after the withdrawal of Soviet troops.

26. NG troops move into Shenyang, capital of Liaoning.

31. The Political Consultative Conference passes resolutions to reorganize the NG on the basis of coalition of political parties but not convoke a National Assembly without discussion with the Political Consultative Conference; nationalize the armed forces; and others. The conference closes the same day.

February 25. Zhang Zhizhong, for the NG, Zhou Enlai, for the CCP, and Marshall as adviser, sign the Agreement for Military Reorganization and for the Integration of the Communist Forces into the National Army.

28. The French ambassador, Jacques Meyrier, and the NG's Minister of Foreign Affairs, Wang Shijie, sign the Treaty for the Relinquishment by France of Extraterritorial and Related Rights in China.

March 13. NG forces complete their takeover of Shenyang following the withdrawal of Soviet troops.

17. CCP troops under Lin Biao occupy Sipingjie, a strategic rail centre and the capital of Liaobei, one of the nine provinces of Manchuria (see B, September 4, 1945).

21. CCP forces enter Harbin, capital of Songjiang in Manchuria.

23. The Chinese Foreign Ministry receives a note from the Soviet ambassador, A. Petrov, that Soviet troops will completely withdraw from Manchuria by the end of April.

31. NG troops launch an offensive against CCP forces in Sipingjie and other places.

April 18. CCP forces complete their takeover of Changchun after a battle with NG troops.

26. CCP forces occupy Harbin and Tsitsihar as Soviet troops withdraw.

May 1. The CCP adopts the name People's Liberation Army (PLA) to designate its armed forces.

3. Soviet troops complete their withdrawal from Manchuria, except for Lüda.

cooperation in Manchuria and of the Soviet belief that industry in Manchuria is their war booty. At about this time Soviet troops loot very large quantities of industrial goods and machinery for transport to the Soviet Union.

April 17. The Ministry of Finance promulgates a new set of banking regulations, under which 'no more banks are allowed to be established' except for county banks and those already granted licences.

May 20. The provincial Taiwan government takes over the Bank of Taiwan and issues a new Taiwan currency.

June 28. The Chinese and US governments conclude a military aid agreement under which lend-lease aid is extended. (It was planned to continue only to the end of the war, see June 2, 1942.)

August 30. The US government signs an agreement with the NG that it will transfer to China all the surplus property stockpiled in the western Pacific, except for combat materials, ships and aircraft.

B OFFICIAL APPOINTMENTS, RESIGNATIONS, DISMISSALS ETC.

March 29. The Executive Yuan appoints Zhang Zhizhong as Chairman of Xinjiang to replace Wu Zhongxin.

June 1. Bai Chongxi is inaugurated as Minister of National Defence and Chen Cheng Chief of the General Staff in the Ministry of National Defence set up the same day to replace the wartime Military Affairs Committee.

July 11. The US government appoints John Leighton Stuart as ambassador to China.

C CULTURAL AND SOCIAL

February 14. An exhibition is held in Chongqing of the works of such famous modern painters as Qi Baishi and Xu Beihong.

April 3. The NG authorities arrest thirty-nine staff members of the CCP's *Jiefang bao* (*Liberation Newspaper*) in Beiping.

May 4. The CCPCC issues its Directive on the Land Question, changing its policy from rent reduction to encouraging confiscation of landlords' land and distribution among the peasants.

29. The NG closes down the *Jiefang bao* and a number of other newspapers, periodicals and news agencies in Beiping.

June 23. Leading philosopher and academic Ma Xulun is assaulted and beaten up by NP agents at Nanjing railway station, forcing him to remain in bed for about a month. Ma was on his way from an enormous demonstration in Shanghai against the civil war, which had

1946

5. A ceremony marks the formal return of the nation's capital from Chongqing to Nanjing.
19. US-equipped and transported NG troops retake Sipingjie after a long battle, completing their occupation the following day.
23. Changchun falls to NG forces.
June 6. Zhang Zhizhong reaches a further peace agreement with Akhmedjan Kasimov, under which the non-Han peoples in Xinjiang are to enjoy cultural autonomy and rights of representation in the Xinjiang government.
22. Mao Zedong issues a statement opposing US military aid to the NG and calling for the withdrawal of US troops from China.
26. NG troops launch a large-scale offensive by encircling the CCP-held areas in eastern Hubei and southern Henan. CCP sources describe this action as 'the signal for the launching of an all-round civil war by the NP'.
July 4. The NG orders the convening of the National Assembly on November 12. (This action was in contravention of the agreement made at the Political Consultative Conference.)
12. A large NG force attacks the CCP-held areas of Jiangsu and Anhui, leading to full-scale civil war.
15. The PLA inflicts a serious defeat on an NG brigade in the Taixing (Jiangsu) area; the first in a series of encounters lasting until August 27 through which the NG troops retake some cities in central Jiangsu but fail to destroy the CCP base areas there.
29. A temporary embargo, arranged by Marshall, on the export of arms and munitions to China becomes effective in the USA. It is aimed at stopping the civil war.
August. In an interview with Anna Louise Strong, Mao Zedong claims the US government is helping Chiang Kaishek fight the civil war. He also describes 'all reactionaries', including the USA and Chiang Kaishek, as 'paper tigers'.
September 16. NG forces recapture Jining (Shandong) from the PLA.
19. Zhou Enlai sees Marshall in Nanjing to protest about the sale of US surplus to the NG (see A, August 30). Marshall claims 'there is absolutely no United States military intervention in China'.
22. NG troops recapture Heze (Shandong), among a number of formerly CCP-held medium and small towns in various parts of China retaken by NG troops at about this time.
30. The NG announces the beginning of its military operations for the recapture of Zhangjiakou, a principal CCP centre in Inner Mongolia. Zhou Enlai informs Marshall that 'if the NP does not immediately halt all military actions against Zhangjiakou and surrounding areas,

elected him to lead a delegation to petition the NG.

November 30. Because the authorities have forbidden them to ply their trade in certain parts of the city, 3000 street vendors demonstrate to petition a change in policy. A clash develops between them and military police; seven street vendors are killed and many wounded or arrested.

December 1. As shop vendors strike in sympathy, 5000 street vendors in Shanghai surround the municipal police station to protest against the November 30 incident. A riot breaks out as military police move in; ten street vendors are killed and over 100 wounded.

24. In Beiping, Shen Chong, a female student from Peking University, is raped, according to her own claim, by a group of US soldiers. This incident leads to a large-scale anti-US movement.

25. The ROC Constitution lays down, among other matters, that all children aged six to twelve shall receive free primary education, and that the state shall assist the education, culture, etc. of the 'various nationalities in the border regions'.

D   PUBLICATIONS

Qian Zhongshu's collection of stories *Ren, shou, gui* (*Men, Beasts, Ghosts*) is published (preface dated April 1, 1944, table of contents January 3, 1946).

April. Guo Tingyi's *Taiping tianguo shishi rizhi* (*Day-by-day Chronology of Historical Events in the Taiping Heavenly Kingdom*) is published (the compiler's *fanli* are dated May 13, 1937).

August. The third and fourth (final) volumes of Feng Ziyou's *Zhonghua minguo kaiguo qian geming shi* (*The History of the Revolution before the Establishment of the ROC*) are published (the first two had appeared in 1928 and 1930).

E   NATURAL DISASTERS

April 15. An UNRRA report, urging immediate relief, estimates that over 30,000,000 Chinese in nineteen provinces are seriously affected by famine.

May 20. The Hunan delegation to the National Assembly reports that a critical famine situation is afflicting Hunan, with two-thirds of the counties and over 20,000,000 people seriously affected.

September 11. *Liberation Daily* reports the number of people killed by starvation or resultant disease in the Hunan famine as 4,000,000.

the CCP representatives cannot but consider the NG publicly to have proclaimed a total split'.

October 11. NG forces take Zhangjiakou.

November 4. Chinese and US representatives sign the Treaty of Friendship, Commerce and Navigation.

15. The National Assembly opens in Nanjing, boycotted by the CCP and the Democratic League.

19. Zhou Enlai flies back to Yan'an; this signals the collapse of negotiations to end the civil war. Dong Biwu remains as CCP representative in Nanjing.

December 25. The National Assembly adopts and promulgates the Constitution of the ROC, under which the five-Yuan system of government is retained, and universal suffrage, secret ballot and equality for all are laid down. The Assembly adjourns the same day.

30. Large-scale student demonstrations begin following the rape of Shen Chong (see C, December 24). Over the next month, students in Beiping, Tianjin, Chongqing, Shanghai, Wuhan, Kunming and other cities demonstrate and strike in demand of the withdrawal of US troops and other things.

1947 *The civil war turns decisively in favour of the Communists; uprising in Taiwan*

January 8. Marshall leaves China for the USA to become Secretary of State, having failed to bring about peace in China.

29. US ambassador Leighton Stuart announces the US government's decision to withdraw from the Committee of Three and other mechanisms of mediation in China.

February 1. The CCPCC declares that all loan contracts, agreements and treaties made between the NG and foreign nations after January 10, 1946 (the date of the ceasefire agreement) are invalid.

20–23. The PLA inflicts a serious defeat on a large NP force near Laiwu (Shandong). They capture two senior NP commanders and take thirteen towns in the area.

28. The NG authorities in Nanjing, Shanghai and Chongqing order all CCP representatives to leave their offices and return to the CCP area before March 5.

A demonstration against the NP in Taibei (Taiwan) is fired on by Chen Yi's troops; several people are killed. In the following days activities mount throughout Taiwan, demanding the reform of Chen Yi's administration.

1946–7

F DEATHS

February 20. Li Liejun d. aged 64.
March 9. Li Zhaolin, a CCP military leader, is stabbed to death in Harbin, aged 38.
17. Dai Li, the head of intelligence services, d. in an aeroplane crash, aged 51.
April 8. CCP peace delegates Wang Ruofei aged 50, Qin Bangxian aged 39, and prominent CCP companions Ye Ting aged 49, and Deng Fa aged 40 are killed in an aeroplane accident on the way to Yan'an from Chongqing.
June 3. Chen Gongbo, former head of the Nanjing pro-Japanese government, is executed for collaboration with the Japanese, aged 53.
July 12. The Democratic League leader Li Gongpu is assassinated in Kunming, aged 45.
15. The writer and Democratic League leader Wen Yiduo is assassinated in Kunming, aged 46, after attending Li Gongpu's funeral.
25. Tao Xingzhi, educational theorist, d. aged 54.

The student movement gathers momentum 1947

A ECONOMICS

February 16. The NG promulgates its emergency economic measures, under which it forbids all sale and purchase of gold and circulation of foreign currency inside China.
March 15. Repair work is completed on the dykes of the Yellow River at Huayuankou (Henan) where they had been burst on June 7, 1938. As a result the Yellow River changes back to its pre-1938 course.
May 2–9. Rice riots break out in Hangzhou (Zhejiang), Wuhu (Anhui), Hefei (Anhui), Chengdu (Sichuan), Wuxi (Jiangsu), Shanghai, Nanjing and other cities, galloping inflation having caused serious food shortages.
4. A ceremony is held to mark the completion of work to seal the dykes at Huayuankou on the Yellow River.
June 4. The NG's committee considering war reparations from Japan issues an estimate that direct losses to China in the War of Resistance against Japan amounted to US$31,000,000,000.
July 23. Chinese and British representatives sign an aviation agreement in Nanjing.

1947

March 7. Dong Biwu and all other representatives of the CCP in Shanghai, Chongqing and Nanjing arrive back in Yan'an.

9. Indiscriminate and widespread killing begins in Taiwan to suppress reformist activities.

12. NG planes begin bombing raids on Yan'an.

14. NG troops led by Hu Zongnan launch an attack on the Shaanxi-Gansu-Ningxia Border Region as they resume the offensive in the area.

15. At the Third Plenary Session of the NP's Sixth CEC (held March 15–24) Chiang Kaishek proclaims the NP's break with the CCP and its determination to fight the civil war through to the end.

18. Mao Zedong, Zhou Enlai and others leave Yan'an.

19. NG forces capture Yan'an, the headquarters of the CCP.

23. The PLA launches an offensive in northern Henan, capturing several counties by May 28.

April 4–May 4. PLA forces launch a large-scale offensive in southern Shanxi, capturing practically the whole region, including twenty-two county towns.

18. China and the Philippines sign a Treaty of Friendship in Manila.

May 6–16. PLA forces under Chen Yi win the Battle of Menglianggu (Shandong), annihilating the NG's 74th Division and killing its commander.

13. PLA forces under Lin Biao launch a large-scale summer offensive in Manchuria.

20–June 2. The National Political Council convenes in Nanjing.

24. PLA forces attack Sipingjie.

26. The USA lifts the embargo on the export of arms and ammunition to China (see July 29, 1946).

June 30. A large PLA force under Liu Bocheng forces a southward crossing over the Yellow River in south-western Shandong. This action marks the beginning of a large-scale nationwide offensive by the PLA, a major turning-point in the War of Liberation. The long battle over Sipingjie ends with the PLA withdrawing.

July 1. The PLA's summer offensive in Manchuria ends, the CCP claiming to have taken more than forty county towns.

4. The NG declares the CCP to be in open rebellion and calls for total national mobilization to suppress it.

14. The Ministry of the Interior issues an estimate of China's population: 461,000,000.

22. US President Truman announces he is sending Albert C. Wedemeyer as special representative on a fact-finding mission to China.

August 7–8. Chiang Kaishek visits Yan'an on an inspection tour.

October 27. The Sino-US Relief Agreement is signed in Nanjing, under which the US government grants US$27,700,000 economic aid to China.
December 30. According to the Central Bank of China the exchange rate of the *yuan* to the pound sterling reaches 290,000 *yuan* to the pound, as compared with 124,800 on August 19.

B OFFICIAL APPOINTMENTS, RESIGNATIONS, DISMISSALS ETC.

March 1. The Supreme National Defence Council approves Song Ziwen's resignation as the President of the Executive Yuan and replaces him with Chiang Kaishek. Zhang Jia'ao assumes office as managing director of the Central Bank of China.
April 17. A joint sitting of the NPCEC Standing Committee and the Supreme National Defence Council appoints Sun Fo to the newly created post of Vice-President of the NG.
18. The NG appoints Zhang Qun as President of the Executive Yuan, and Sun Fo as President of the Legislative Yuan in a governmental reorganization. It also appoints Sun Fo, Ju Zheng, Zhang Qun, Dai Jitao and others, including several non-NP members, to the NG Committee.
22. The Executive Yuan appoints Wei Daoming as Chairman of Taiwan, thus replacing Chen Yi's disastrous temporary administration with a formal provincial government.
May 1. Appointed by an Inner Mongolian People's Congress, Ulanfu assumes office as leader of the People's Government of the Inner Mongolian Autonomous Region, set up the same day.
19. The Executive Yuan appoints the Uighur Masud Sabri as Chairman of Xinjiang, the first non-Han to hold the post.
August 6. The Standing Committee of the NP's CEC resolves to expel Li Jishen, a member of the NP's CSC, from the Party for making unwarranted statements and inciting the people. (On March 8 he had issued a statement in Hongkong urging an end to the civil war.)
29. The NG appoints Chen Cheng to replace Xiong Shihui as Director of the North-east Headquarters (see B, August 31 and September 4, 1945).

C CULTURAL AND SOCIAL

February 28. The NG Chongqing authorities order the closure of the offices of the CCP's *Xinhua ribao* and have its staff arrested, forcing it to cease publication.
May 4. In Shanghai, a new student-worker movement begins against

1947

11. PLA forces led by Liu Bocheng cross the Longhai railway heading southward for the Dabie mountains region, where they arrive by the end of August.

24. At the end of his visit to China Wedemeyer issues a public statement in Nanjing condemning the NG and calling on it 'to effect immediately drastic, far-reaching political and economic reforms'.

September 1. In an inner-Party directive Mao Zedong puts forward his 'Strategy for the Second Year of the War of Liberation' which is 'to launch a country-wide counter-offensive' and carry the war into the NP-held areas.

19. Wedemeyer presents his 'Report on China-Korea' to President Truman; in it he advocates giving the NG 'sufficient and prompt assistance', supervised by US advisers, and economic aid over at least five years.

27. NG forces take Longkou (Shandong).

October 1. NG forces complete the occupation of Yantai (Shandong). This action represents part of a large-scale NG offensive to seize cities in eastern Shandong from the PLA.

1–13. PLA forces launch attacks around Luoyang (Henan) and seize eight towns in the area.

5. NG forces take Weihaiwei (Shandong).

10. The Manifesto of the Chinese PLA is issued. Drafted by Mao Zedong in Jiaxian (Shaanxi), it calls for a united front of 'workers, peasants, soldiers, intellectuals and businessmen, all oppressed classes, all people's organizations, democratic parties, minority nationalities, overseas Chinese and other patriots' to overthrow Chiang Kaishek.

27. The NG outlaws the Chinese Democratic League.

November 9–19. PLA forces under Chen Yi and Liu Bocheng seize control of the Longhai railway between Xuzhou (Jiangsu) and Zhengzhou (Henan).

12. As part of a general offensive along the Beiping–Hankou railway, the PLA captures Shijiazhuang (Hebei) the first major city to fall to CCP troops in the North China area.

21–23. General elections are held for membership of the National Assembly.

December 8. China and the USA conclude a naval agreement under which the USA obtains rights to use naval bases in China, and gives 140 warships to the NG.

13–16. The PLA forces in Central China attack NG positions along the Beiping–Hankou and Longhai railways, destroy a large NG force and seize control of Xuchang (Henan) and more than twenty other cities.

high prices, hunger, persecution, bureaucrat capital, and civil war with a demonstration by students from all over the city. The movement spreads quickly to Nanjing, Hangzhou, Beiping, Shenyang, Qingdao and other big cities. At about the same time 5000 cotton-mill workers demonstrate against hunger, and similar events take place in other cities.

12. In Nanjing, special drama students and those of the Central University boycott classes to protest against hunger.

18. The NG issues its Provisional Measures for the Maintenance of Public Order, banning all strikes and demonstrations, and prohibiting petitions by groups of more than ten people; they also give wide powers to local NG authorities to suppress movements threatening the NG.

20. In Nanjing, several thousand students from institutions in the Nanjing, Shanghai and Hangzhou area hold a 'demonstration to solve the critical state of education', and petition the National Political Council opening the same day. Military police are called in to suppress the demonstration and over 100 students are injured (some 20 seriously). About 50 are wounded in a student demonstration in Tianjin the same day.

June 1. In Wuhan over ten students from Wuhan University are wounded and three are killed in a clash with military police. This is only one of many similar cases at about this time.

19. The Chinese Student Union is founded in Shanghai, to direct the student movement against hunger, civil war etc.

September 13. Liu Shaoqi presides over a national land conference which adopts the Outline Land Law (promulgated by the CCPCC on October 10). Under it all land ownership and debts owed to landlords are abolished and land in the villages is to be redistributed according to population.

D PUBLICATIONS

The Commercial Press completes publication of Feng Ziyou's five-volumed *Geming yishi* (*Unauthorized History of the Revolution*) (earlier volumes published June 1939, February 1943, September 1945, and August 1946).

January. The literary journal *Wenyi fuxing* (*Literary Renaissance*) completes serializing Ba Jin's novel *Hanye* (*Cold Nights*), published as a book in March.

February. The New China Bookshop publishes the first volume of Fan Wenlan's *Zhongguo jindai shi* (*The Modern History of China*) in Yan'an.

1947-8

15. The PLA's winter offensive begins in Manchuria.

25. At a CCPCC meeting of December 25–28, Mao Zedong presents his report on 'The Present Situation and Our Tasks' in which he claims that the Chinese people's war of liberation has reached a turning-point and gone over to the offensive everywhere.

1948 *The Liaoxi-Shenyang campaign ends in the liberation of all Manchuria*

January 1. In Hongkong, the Revolutionary Committee of the NP announces itself established; it calls for the uniting of all parties, including the CCP, the overthrow of Chiang Kaishek's dictatorial regime and the elimination of US interference in Chinese internal affairs.

5. At a meeting in Hongkong, Shen Junru and other leaders of the outlawed Chinese Democratic League decide to set up the League's headquarters in Hongkong and to revive its activities. A declaration is issued calling for unity with the CCP and other democratic parties and for the overthrow of Chiang Kaishek's dictatorship.

February 19. The PLA takes Anshan (Liaoning).

28–March 3. The North-west PLA wins its first major victory in the north-west theatre by defeating several brigades of Hu Zongnan's NG troops, inflicting extremely heavy casualties, including killing two senior commanders, and taking the town of Yichuan (Shaanxi) on March 3.

March 11. The PLA begins its spring offensive against NG positions along the Jiaozhou–Ji'nan railway in Shandong.

13. The PLA enters Sipingjie, capital of Liaobei.

14. The PLA takes Luoyang (Henan).

15. The PLA completes the occupation of Sipingjie and its winter

August. The Commercial Press publishes Li Jiannong's *Zhongguo jin bainian zhengzhi shi (Political History of China in the Past Century)*.

E NATURAL DISASTERS

August 17. The Yellow River overflows its dykes in two places in north-eastern Henan, flooding Changyuan (Henan) and other nearby counties. (CCP sources claim the dykes were deliberately broken by NP authorities because the affected counties were held by CCP forces.)

F DEATHS

March 17. Taixu, leading Buddhist reformer, d. aged 57.
April 18. Tan Zhen, senior NP member, d. in Shanghai aged 62.
September 26. Zhou Xuexi, industrialist, d. aged 81.
December 15. NPCSC member Zhang Ji d. in Nanjing aged 65.

Inflation reaches catastrophic proportions **1948**

A ECONOMICS

February 18. US President Truman asks Congress for an appropriation of US$570,000,000 for 'essential imports into China'.
April 2. The US Congress passes the China Aid Act, which provides for US$338,000,000 in economic aid to China, and in addition a special fund of $125,000,000. It is approved by President Truman April 3. (Only $275,000,000 of the $338,000,000 were subsequently appropriated by Congress.)
May 17. According to the records of the Central Bank of China, the exchange rate of the *yuan* to the US dollar reaches 474,000 *yuan* to the US dollar (as compared with 113,500 on January 12, 1948).
July 3. In Nanjing, the Chinese Minister of Foreign Affairs, Wang Shijie, and the US ambassador, Leighton Stuart, sign the Economic Aid Agreement, providing joint supervision of the aid goods purchased under the China Aid Act.
August 19. Chiang Kaishek issues a presidential mandate promulgating the Financial and Economic Emergency Discipline Regulations. Under them a new currency, the gold *yuan* note, is to be issued; the people are to hand in all private holdings of silver, gold and foreign currency by September 30; wages and prices are to be controlled. The regulations aim to control inflation.

1948

north-east offensive; Shenyang, Changchun and other major cities are now isolated.

29–May 1. The National Assembly holds its first session in Nanjing.

30. The PLA takes Weihaiwei (Shandong).

April 5. The PLA recaptures Luoyang after a brief evacuation.

22. PLA troops under Peng Dehuai recapture Yan'an (Shaanxi).

23. The PLA takes Duolun (Chahar).

26. The PLA takes Baoji (Shaanxi).

27. The PLA takes Weixian (Shandong).

May 1. To commemorate May Day the CCPCC issues a statement calling for the convening of the Political Consultative Conference, in which the democratic parties, people's organizations and prominent individuals should take part, with the aim of establishing a coalition government.

5. The Revolutionary Committee of the NP, the Chinese Democratic League, and various other organizations cable their support for the convening of a new Political Consultative Conference.

8. The PLA's spring offensive along the Jiaozhou–Ji'nan railway ends; its result has been the capture of seventeen towns and, apart from Qingdao, Yantai and a few other strategic points, the whole of Shandong province east of the Tianjin–Pukou railway.

22. Several thousand students hold a demonstration in Shanghai to protest against US support for the revival of Japanese militarism. This anti-US movement spreads to Beiping, Wuhan, Chengdu, Kunming and other big cities.

29. The PLA launches a general attack on the Xuzhou–Ji'nan section of the Tianjin–Pukou railway.

July 21. A thirty-five-day campaign by the PLA in central Shanxi ends; fourteen cities have been captured, and the capital of Shanxi, Taiyuan, is isolated.

22. Chiang Kaishek arrives in Taiyuan and meets Yan Xishan to discuss Taiyuan's defence.

August 13. US Secretary of State Marshall informs Leighton Stuart, US ambassador to China, that the US government 'must preserve a maximum freedom of action' in its policy towards China.

22–September 17. The NG air force launches a series of air raids on Shijiazhuang, the capital of the newly formed North China People's Government, killing or wounding some 160 people.

September 12. The North-east PLA launches its autumn offensive in Manchuria, the Liaoxi-Shenyang campaign, under Lin Biao. This was the first of the three greatest campaigns of the War of Liberation.

24. PLA troops seize Ji'nan, capital of Shandong, after eight days and

23. The gold *yuan* notes begin to be issued.
September 20. The wholesale price index for Nanjing, measured by the University of Nanjing, reaches 8,740,600, as compared with 1,335,303 in June 1948 and 5485 in August 1946. Inflation continues to accelerate in the following months.
October 31. The Executive Yuan adopts the Supplementary Measures to Improve Economic Control, an abandonment of wage and price control. (The adoption of the Supplementary Measures was a recognition of the total failure of the Emergency Economic Regulations of August 19 and the utter collapse of the new gold *yuan* note.)
December 1. Various CCP-held areas jointly set up the Chinese People's Bank.
10. Song Meiling, Chiang Kaishek's wife, visits US President Truman and asks him (unsuccessfully) for US$3,000,000,000 aid over three years.

B OFFICIAL APPOINTMENTS, RESIGNATIONS, DISMISSALS ETC.

April 19. The National Assembly elects Chiang Kaishek as President of the ROC.
29. The National Assembly elects Li Zongren as Vice-President of the ROC against Chiang Kaishek's nominee Sun Fo.
May 20. Chiang Kaishek and Li Zongren are inaugurated as President and Vice-President, respectively, of the ROC.
24. Chiang Kaishek appoints Weng Wenhao as President of the Executive Yuan.
August 19. The North China People's Representative Congress (held August 7–19) appoints Bo Yibo and Dong Biwu as Chairman and deputy Chairman respectively of the North China People's Government, which it sets up the same day with the capital in Shijiazhuang (Hebei).
21. Chiang Kaishek appoints Yu Hongjun, Song Ziwen, Jiang Jingguo and others to enforce his Financial and Economic Emergency Discipline Regulations in various parts of the country. In effect this means giving his son Jiang Jingguo very great power to carry out the anti-inflation campaign in Shanghai.
November 1. Jiang Jingguo, having carried out the Emergency Economic Regulations of August 19 with great severity, including executions of black marketeers and speculators, resigns with a statement of his 'deepest apology to the citizens of Shanghai' and an admission that in certain respects his measures 'have rather deepened the sufferings of the people'.

1948

nights of fighting and the defection of an entire NG division; they also capture the Provincial Chairman of Shandong, Wang Yaowu.

October 10. Mao Zedong sends out an inner-Party circular reporting that a meeting of the Politburo, the largest since the Japanese surrender, has taken place in September. He claims CCP membership is 3,000,000 and the population of the liberated areas is 168,000,000.

15. The PLA seizes Jinzhou in Manchuria, after a day's fierce fighting, capturing over 100,000 NG troops; mass surrenders by NG troops in Manchuria follow this action.

19. The PLA takes Changchun, capital of Jilin province.

23. The PLA captures Zhengzhou (Henan).

24. PLA forces retake Kaifeng (Henan).

November 1. In accordance with a decision of the September Politburo meeting (see October 10), the CCPCC's Revolutionary Military Affairs Committee classifies the PLA troops, including the division of the field forces into five field armies according to area.

2. The PLA takes Shenyang. The action represents the final victory for the PLA's fifty-day Liaoxi-Shenyang campaign and the completion of the capture of the north-eastern provinces.

6. The PLA under Chen Yi launches the Huaihai campaign, the second of the three major campaigns of the War of Liberation.

12. The PLA captures Chengde, capital of Jehol province.

14. Mao Zedong declares that 'only another year or so may be needed to overthrow it [the NG] completely'.

22. The PLA captures Baoding (Hebei).

27. The PLA captures Shanhaiguan and Qinhuangdao (Hebei).

Early December. The Beiping-Tianjin campaign, the third of the War of Liberation's three most important campaigns, begins under the command of Lin Biao and others.

December 1. The PLA seizes Xuzhou (Jiangsu) after a very long battle: a decisive step in the Huaihai campaign (the NP had thrown nearly 500,000 men into the defence of Xuzhou).

12. PLA forces take Tangshan (Hebei).

25. CCP authorities proclaim a list of the forty-three worst war criminals. It is headed by Chiang Kaishek, Li Zongren, Chen Cheng, Bai Chongxi and He Yingqin. Li Zongren and others suggest peace talks with the CCP and demand the resignation of Chiang Kaishek.

26. Chiang Kaishek accepts Weng Wenhao's resignation as President of the Executive Yuan and replaces him with Sun Fo.
December 31. The NG appoints Burhan as Chairman of Xinjiang, to replace Masud Sabri.

C CULTURAL AND SOCIAL

January 31. Some 3000 dance girls and night club managers and workers in Shanghai demonstrate against the banning of night clubs in the city by the Bureau of Social Affairs. They ransack the bureau's offices.
February 2. NG military police suppress striking cotton-mill workers in Shanghai, killing three and wounding over sixty. Gu Zhenggang, the Minister of Social Affairs, declares that all dancing parties on a business basis must be thoroughly banned. The Bureau of Social Affairs in Shanghai orders that all night clubs cease activities.
11. In an inner-Party directive, Mao Zedong warns against 'left' errors in land reform propaganda, including that of placing too much emphasis on the role of the poor peasants, not enough on that of the middle peasants and intellectuals.
April. Students' and teachers' strikes take place in Beiping, Tianjin, Shanghai, Chengdu, Nanjing and other cities to support the anti-hunger and anti-oppression movements.
July 5. In Beiping, a clash takes place between students from Manchuria and NG police; eighteen students are killed, twenty-four seriously wounded and over 100 slightly. (Similar incidents took place elsewhere at about the same time.)
August 1–22. The Sixth Congress of the All-China Labour Federation is held in Harbin, the first since 1929 (see C, November 7–11, 1929). The Congress decides to revive the All-China General Trade Union.

D PUBLICATIONS

Ding Ling's novel *Taiyang zhaozai Sanggan he shang* (*The Sun Shines on the Sanggan River*) (author's preface dated June 15, 1948); Shi Tuo's (penname of Wang Changjian) *Ma Lan* (completed in 1942, preface October 12, 1942) and Zhou Libo's novel *Baofeng zouyu* (*The Hurricane*) (dated by the author December 2, 1948 at its completion) are published.
June 15. *Renmin ribao* (*People's Daily*) begins publication in Shijiazhuang (Hebei).

1949 *The People's Republic of China is established*

January 10. PLA troops annihilate a large NG force near Yongcheng (Henan) and capture Du Yuming, now the senior commander of NG troops in the Huaihai campaign. This concludes the campaign and leaves the way open for PLA advance to South China.
14. Mao Zedong announces eight conditions under which the CCP is willing to open peace talks with the NG. They include abolition of the 1946 Constitution, the reorganization of all the reactionary armies on democratic principles, and the convening of the Political Consultative Conference without reactionary participation.
15. Tianjin falls to the PLA after a sharp fight.
19. The Executive Yuan declares the NG's willingness to begin talks with the CCP.
22. Fu Zuoyi reaches agreement with CCP representatives to surrender, including the handover of Beiping to the PLA.
25. The PLA captures Yangzhou (Jiangsu).
31. The PLA peacefully moves into Beiping, concluding the Beiping-Tianjin campaign.

1948–9

E Natural Disasters

May 7. A cyclone in the Dongting Lake area of northern Hunan causes great damage to property and results in many deaths, over 200 in Yueyang alone. Later in the month torrential rain leads to serious flooding in the same region.
July. Flooding worsens in north-eastern Hunan as the Yangzi River rises. In the counties beside the Dongting Lake over 20,000 houses are washed away, over 8300 people drowned, and 1,800,000 rendered destitute.

F Deaths

February 28. Zhou Fohai d. in Nanjing aged 51.
August 12. Zhu Ziqing, essayist, poet and educationalist, d. aged 49.
 30. Educationalist Zhou Yichun d. aged 65.
September 1. Feng Yuxiang d. at sea near Odessa, USSR, aged 67.
October 4. Chen Shuren d. aged 64.
November 13. Chen Bulei, Chiang Kaishek's private secretary, commits suicide, aged 57.
December 26. Duan Xipeng d. in Shanghai aged 51.

1949 Mao Zedong becomes Chairman of the Central People's Government

A Economics

February 20. The transfer of the Central Bank of China's entire gold reserve to Taibei is completed.
September 29. The Common Programme lays down the various sectors of the economy, including state-owned, cooperative, individual peasant, private capitalist and state capitalist.
December 2. The CPG Council adopts the state budget for 1950.
 8–20. A National Agricultural Production Conference is held in Peking to make plans for 1950.

B Official Appointments, Resignations, Dismissals etc.

January 21. Chiang Kaishek retires from office and hands the presidency of the ROC over to Li Zongren.
March 12. Li Zongren appoints He Yingqin President of the Executive Yuan, Sun Fo having resigned March 8.

1949

March 26. The CCPCC announces it will open peace talks in Beiping with NG representatives on April 1.

April 1. An NG delegation headed by Zhang Zhizhong arrives in Beiping for peace talks with the CCP. At the Beiping peace talks Zhou Enlai, the CCP delegation's head, puts forward an ultimatum that the NG must accept the CCP's terms, the original eight points of January 14 plus twenty-four others, by April 20.

21. Mao Zedong and Zhu De issue an order to the PLA for a country-wide advance, the NP's CEC having issued a declaration the previous day refusing the ultimatum. The PLA's Second Field Army under Liu Bocheng and Deng Xiaoping, and Third Field Army under Chen Yi force a crossing of the Yangzi River over a wide span.

23. The PLA captures Nanjing; NG troops and remaining senior officials evacuate the city, planning to move their capital to Guangzhou.

24. The PLA captures the Shanxi capital Taiyuan after a long siege.

May 3. The PLA captures Hangzhou, the capital of Zhejiang.

16–17. The PLA's Fourth Field Army under Lin Biao captures Wuhan, capital of Hubei.

20. Xi'an, the capital of Shaanxi, falls to the PLA.

22. Nanchang, the capital of Jiangxi, falls to the PLA.

27. The PLA completes the capture of Shanghai, which NP troops had surrendered with barely a fight.

June 2. The PLA captures Qingdao, thus completing the liberation of Shandong.

August 4. The Chairman of Hunan province, Cheng Qian, surrenders to the PLA.

17. Fuzhou, capital of Fujian, is captured by the PLA.

24. Chiang Kaishek flies to Chongqing (Sichuan), planning a last stand in the south-west.

26. The PLA captures Lanzhou, capital of Gansu.

September 5. The PLA captures Xining, capital of Qinghai.

21. The Chinese People's Political Consultative Conference (CPPCC) opens in Beiping. Mao Zedong makes the opening speech.

26. Burhan, Chairman of Xinjiang, cables his surrender and allegiance to the CCP.

27. The CPPCC adopts the Organic Law of the CPPCC, and of the Central People's Government (CPG) of the People's Republic of China (PRC); reverts Beiping's name to Peking and declares it China's capital; adopts a national flag, emblem and anthem.

29. The CPPCC adopts the Common Programme, an interim constitution setting out the CPG's policies.

30. The CPPCC closes in Peking.

June 3. Li Zongren appoints Yan Xishan as the President of the NG's Executive Yuan, He Yingqin having resigned on May 30.

August 27. Gao Gang is formally inaugurated as Chairman and Li Fuchun and others as deputy Chairmen of the North-east People's Government set up the same day.

September 30. The CPPCC elects Mao Zedong as the Chairman of the CPG and Zhu De, Liu Shaoqi, Song Qingling, Li Jishen, Gao Gang and Zhang Lan as deputy Chairmen. It also elects Chen Yi and others to the CPG Council.

October 1. The first meeting of the CPG Council appoints Zhou Enlai as Premier of the Government Administrative Council (GAC) and Minister of Foreign Affairs of the CPG; Mao Zedong as Chairman of the CPG's Revolutionary Military Affairs Committee; Zhu De as Commander-in-Chief of the PLA; Shen Junru as President of the Supreme People's Court; and Luo Ronghuan as Chief Procurator of the Supreme People's Procuratorate.

5. The CPG appoints Wang Jiaxiang as the PRC's first ambassador to the USSR.

December 17. Burhan, the Chairman of the Xinjiang Provincial Government, is inaugurated as Chairman of the Xinjiang Provincial People's Government, set up the same day.

C Cultural and Social

February 27. The PLA's Beiping military command orders foreign news agencies and journalists in Beiping to suspend activities owing to the military situation.

March 1–6. The National Student Congress is held in Beiping. On its last day it resolves to establish the Chinese National Student Federation.

24. The first National Women's Congress opens in Beiping.

April 1. Students at a rally of several thousand in Nanjing, bidding farewell to the NG's delegation to the Beiping peace talks and petitioning acceptance of Mao Zedong's January 14 terms, are beaten up by military police; two are killed and over 100 injured.

11–18. The First Congress of the Chinese New Democratic Youth League is held in Beiping, adopting its programme and constitution on the last day.

May 4–11. The First National Youth Congress is held in Beiping. On its last day it adopts a constitution and lays down the direction of the youth movement, and declares established the Chinese National Federation of Democratic Youth.

July 2–19. The First National Congress of Literature and Art Workers

1949

October 1. At a large-scale ceremony in Tiananmen Square, Peking, Mao Zedong officially proclaims the establishment of the PRC.
2. The USSR formally announces its recognition of the CPG of the PRC.
3. The CPG's Minister of Foreign Affairs, Zhou Enlai, cables the Soviet government welcoming diplomatic relations and the exchange of ambassadors. The Guangzhou (NP's) Ministry of Foreign Affairs announces the rupture of diplomatic relations with the Soviet Union.
4. Zhou Enlai cables Bulgaria welcoming its notification of willingness on the previous day to establish diplomatic relations. The US State Department issues a statement reaffirming its recognition of the NP government.
5. Zhou Enlai cables Rumania agreeing to diplomatic relations.
6. Zhou Enlai cables Hungary, Czechoslovakia and the Democratic People's Republic of Korea (DPRK) agreeing to diplomatic relations.
7. Zhou Enlai cables Poland agreeing to diplomatic relations.
14. The PLA captures Guangzhou, ending the NP's hope to establish a government in South China.
16. Zhou Enlai cables the People's Republic of Mongolia agreeing to diplomatic relations.
17. The PLA captures Amoy (Fujian).
27. The German Democratic Republic and the PRC agree to establish diplomatic relations.
November 15. Zhou Enlai cables the United Nations rejecting the NP's claim to represent China, and declaring that only the CPG of the PRC can do so. The PLA captures the capital of Guizhou Province, Guiyang.
23. Zhou Enlai cables Albania agreeing to establish diplomatic relations.
30. The PLA takes Chongqing. Chiang Kaishek flies to Chengdu (Sichuan).
December 2. The CPG Council decides to celebrate October 1 as National Day.
4. The Government Administrative Council (GAC) decides to set up six Regional Military and Political Committees: North-east, East China, Central South, North-west, South-west and Suiyuan.
9. The NP Chairmen of Yunnan and Xikang, respectively Lu Han and Liu Wenhui, both surrender to the CPG. The NP's Executive Yuan meets for the first time in Taibei (Taiwan) as its capital.
10. Chiang Kaishek leaves Chengdu by air for Taibei on his last departure from the Chinese mainland.
16. Mao Zedong arrives in Moscow and meets Stalin.

1949

is held in Beiping. The Federation of Literary and Art Circles of China is established.

September 29. The Common Programme lays down that all nationalities in China 'shall have equal rights and duties', and guarantees freedom of thought, speech, publication, religious belief, assembly, and the right to elect and be elected.

October 5. The Sino-Soviet Friendship Association is formally established in Peking with Liu Shaoqi as President.

6. The National Moslem Institute is established in Peking.

10. The Chinese Character Reform Association holds its inaugural meeting in Peking.

12. The Supreme People's Court and Supreme People's Procuratorate hold inaugural sessions.

November 16–December 1. The Asian and Australasian Trade Union Conference is held in Peking; Liu Shaoqi presides.

December 10–16. Peking hosts the Asian Women's Conference.

D Publications

March 15. *People's Daily* formally moves to Beiping.

June 16. The newspaper *Guangming ribao* (*Guangming Daily*) begins publication.

July. *Shouchang wenji* (*Collected Works of Li Dazhao*) is published in Beiping.

1. Mao Zedong publishes his 'Lun renmin minzhu zhuanzheng' ('On the People's Democratic Dictatorship') in which, among many other things, he declares that China will 'lean to one side' (that of the USSR) in foreign affairs. (The article was completed and dated June 30.)

August 5. The US State Department publishes its *United States Relations with China* (the China White Paper) in Washington.

September 1. The *Gansu ribao* (*Gansu Daily*) begins publication in Lanzhou (Gansu).

25. The periodical *Wenyi bao* (*Literature and Art*) begins publication.

November 1. The monthly *Zhongsu youhao* (*Sino-Soviet Friendship*) begins publication.

15. *Xinhua yuebao* (*New China Monthly*) begins publication in Peking.

28. *Xin Qian ribao* (*The New Guizhou Daily*) begins publication in Guiyang.

December 3. *Guangxi ribao* (*Guangxi Daily*) begins publication.

10. *Xinhua ribao* (*New China Daily*) and *Qingdao ribao* (*Qingdao Daily*) begin publication in Chongqing and Qingdao respectively.

1949–50

17. The former NG's ambassador to Burma, Xu Yuntan, cables Zhou Enlai that from this day on he and his embassy accept the CPG's leadership.
25. The PRC and DPRK sign agreements in Peking to establish postal and telephone services between the two countries.
27. The PLA captures Chengdu.
30. India notifies China of its willingness to establish diplomatic relations.

1950 China intervenes in the Korean War

January 6. Great Britain notifies Peking of its intention to establish diplomatic relations.
7. Norway and Ceylon cable Zhou Enlai their willingness to establish diplomatic relations with China.
13. The UN Security Council votes, by six to three, against a Soviet resolution to expel the ROC. This results in a USSR boycott of the Security Council.
14. The CPG takes over the US compounds in Peking; the US State Department orders all its official personnel in China to leave, and the closure of its establishments there.
18. Zhou Enlai cables the Democratic Republic of Vietnam (DRVN) of Ho Chi Minh agreeing to establish diplomatic relations.
31. The Panchen Lama, in Qinghai, cables Mao Zedong and Zhu De denouncing the Lhasa authorities and requesting that the PLA intervene in Tibet.
February 6. NP aeroplanes bomb Shanghai, killing or wounding some 1000 people.
14. Zhou Enlai for China and A. Vyshinsky for the USSR sign the Sino-Soviet Treaty of Friendship, Alliance and Mutual Assistance in Moscow. It provides for mutual consultation on all international

1949–50

E Natural Disasters

July 15. Hunan's *Central Daily* claims that 57,877 people have been killed, 15,350,000 *mou* of arable land destroyed, and 1520 bridges washed away by disastrous floods which have afflicted the province since early June.

September 2–3. A large fire burns through Chongqing, burning several thousand people to death and causing uncountable property damage.

F Deaths

January 10. The NP commander Qiu Qingquan d. in the Huaihai campaign, aged 46.

31. Sa Bendong, physicist, d. in San Francisco aged 46.

February 12. Dai Jitao is found dead through an overdose of sleeping tablets, aged 58.

August 18. Zeng Dao, senior NP official, d. aged 67.

September 17. Yang Hucheng is executed in Chongqing by NP authorities, aged 66.

The Marriage and Agrarian Reform Laws are promulgated 1950

A Economics

January 1. The Peking–Hankou and Wuchang–Guangzhou railways formally resume traffic after the disruption caused by war. The following day the New China News Agency (NCNA) quotes the Ministry of Railways as claiming that China's railway network was basically restored.

February 14. Zhou Enlai and A. Vyshinsky sign in Moscow an agreement under which the Soviet Union grants the PRC's CPG, over five years, credits of US$300,000,000 at 1 per cent annual interest.

March 22. The GAC orders the reorganization of the Bank of China to bring it under the control of the People's Bank.

27. China and the USSR sign agreements for the formation of Sino-Soviet joint stock companies for oil, non-ferrous and rare metals and civil aviation, the last being to operate flights between Peking and Irkutsk, Chita and Alma-Ata.

April 25. China and the Soviet Union formally establish the joint Chinese Changchun Railway Company.

June 6. At the Third Plenum of the Seventh CCPCC Mao Zedong makes his speech 'Fight for a Fundamental Turn for the Better in the Financial and Economic Situation in China', in which he calls for the

1950

issues affecting both parties and lays down that should either side be attacked by 'Japan or States allied with it', the other 'will immediately render military and other assistance'. The two also sign an agreement under which the USSR hands the entire administration of the Chinese Changchun railway to China and promises to withdraw its troops from the Lüshun area by the end of 1952.

March 4. Mao Zedong and Zhou Enlai arrive back in Peking from Moscow.

27. The Netherlands government informs the PRC of its willingness to establish diplomatic relations.

April 1. China and India formally establish diplomatic relations.

17. The PLA lands on Hainan Island (Guangdong).

30. The PLA completes its capture of Hainan Island.

May 9. China and Sweden formally establish diplomatic relations.

11. China and Denmark formally establish diplomatic relations.

17. The Chinese Ministry of Foreign Affairs protests strongly against the detention of 70 Chinese aeroplanes by the British Hongkong authorities (May 10).

The PLA occupies Dinghai City in the Zhoushan Archipelago off Zhejiang.

18. The PLA completes the capture of the Zhoushan Archipelago.

June 6–9. The Third Plenum of the Seventh CCPCC is held in Peking.

8. Burma and China formally establish diplomatic relations.

9. Indonesia and China formally establish diplomatic relations.

28. Zhou Enlai issues a statement commenting on President Truman's statement of June 27 in which he announces his order to 'the Seventh Fleet to prevent any attack on Formosa'. Zhou denounces the move as aggression and claims 'the fact that Taiwan is part of China will remain unchanged for ever'. At a meeting of the CPG Council the same day Mao Zedong denounces US aggression in Korea (where the Korean War had broken out on June 25) and Taiwan.

July 6. Zhou Enlai sends a message to the UN denouncing the Security Council's resolution of June 27 calling on UN members to assist the Republic of Korea as illegal.

August 9. The PLA captures the islands outside the mouth of the Pearl River (Guangdong).

27. Zhou Enlai cables Dean Acheson, US Secretary of State, protesting against repeated intrusions by US military aircraft into China's air space and bombing in China's territory near the border with Korea, and demanding that the US government compensate for all losses.

September 14. Switzerland and China formally establish diplomatic relations.

completion of agrarian reform, tax reduction and other things.

August 28. The USSR and China sign an agreement in Shenyang (Liaoning) under which the USSR will hand back to China all former Japanese properties in Manchuria.

October 10. In Peking the CPG's Ministry of Trade signs with the Democratic Republic of Germany the 1951 Sino-German Trade Agreement.

November 23–December 7. A national water conservation conference is held; it lays down the water control tasks for 1951 to reduce the danger of flooding.

December 16. The US government freezes all Chinese assets under its jurisdiction and bans US ships or aircraft from trading with China or loading any goods believed to be destined for China.
28. The GAC orders the takeover of all US property and the freezing of all US assets in China.

B   OFFICIAL APPOINTMENTS, RESIGNATIONS, DISMISSALS ETC.

January 19. Peng Dehuai is formally inaugurated as Chairman of the North-west Military and Political Committee, set up the same day.
27. A rally in Shanghai marks the formal inauguration of the East China Military and Political Committee, with Rao Shushi as Chairman.
February 5. Lin Biao is formally inaugurated as Chairman of the Central South Military and Political Committee, set up the same day.

C   CULTURAL AND SOCIAL

January 1. The Southern University formally opens in Guangzhou, with Ye Jianying as Vice-Chancellor.
4. The Chinese New Law Studies Research Institute is set up in Peking.
April 2. The Central Drama Institute is set up with Ouyang Yuqian as President.
4. The Central Music Institute is formally set up.
May 1. By an order issued by Mao Zedong the previous day, the CPG promulgates the Marriage Law of the PRC, which bans arranged marriages, concubinage, polygamy and interference in the remarriage of widows, and lays down equal rights for both sexes.
June 1. The GAC issues a directive on spare-time education, to aim at the ability of staff and workers of all organizations to read simple books and newspapers within three to five years.
29. The CPG promulgates the Trade Union Law of the PRC;

1950

19. The UN General Assembly votes by 33 to 16, with 10 abstentions, to defeat an Indian motion to seat the PRC in China's UN seat.

October 19. According to Chinese claims, four French aircraft bomb Tianbao (Guangxi), killing or wounding some forty people. PLA troops capture Changdu (Xikang) after a fierce battle, as they advance towards Tibet.

25. The Chinese People's Volunteers publicly enter Korea to support DPRK forces. (Some Chinese troops had moved into Korea secretly between October 14 and 16.)

28. Finland and China formally establish diplomatic relations.

30. The PRC's Ministry of Foreign Affairs replies to notes delivered to it by the Indian embassy on October 21 and 28 on Tibet. It states that 'Tibet is an integral part of Chinese territory. The problem of Tibet is entirely the domestic problem of China'.

November 2. Chinese and US troops clash in Korea for the first time.

4. The democratic parties issue a joint declaration of their support for the movement to resist America and aid Korea.

23. The Chinese Ministry of Foreign Affairs issues a statement accusing French land and air forces in Indochina of numerous violations of China's southern border since December 1949, including the killing of many civilians and soldiers.

25–26. In the night the Chinese People's Volunteers launch a full-scale offensive to drive the UN and allied Korean forces south of the 38th parallel.

28. The PRC Delegate Wu Xiuquan addresses the UN Security Council and accuses the US of 'the unlawful and criminal act of armed aggression' against Taiwan.

December 5. The CPG's General Postal Bureau cables the Universal Postal Union accepting the provisions of the Universal Postal Convention of 1947.

12. Telephone connections are inaugurated between Peking and Moscow, using the world's longest overland telephone wire (12,000 km.)

31. According to Chinese claims, US planes bomb China's Andong (Liaoning), killing or wounding fifty-eight people.

defining 'the legal status, functions and duties of trade union organizations'.

30. The CPG promulgates the Agrarian Reform Law of the PRC; under it 'the system of peasant land ownership shall be introduced', the land of landlords is to be confiscated, that of religious bodies to be requisitioned and given to peasants' associations for 'distribution to poverty-stricken peasants'.

July 10. The Ministry of Culture organizes the Drama Reform Committee to develop the work of drama reform.

12. The GAC orders people's governments at all levels 'everywhere to collect revolutionary cultural objects' and 'to protect ancient cultural objects and buildings'.

August 7–18. The first National Public Health Work Conference is held in Peking. It adopts the principles of emphasizing the workers, peasants and soldiers, preventive medicine and combining Chinese and Western medicine.

September 15–25. The first National Publishing Conference is held.

October 3. A formal ceremony attended by Vice-Presidents Liu Shaoqi and Zhu De, and Ma Xulun, the Minister of Education, marks the beginning of classes at the Chinese People's University in Peking.

November 24. The GAC decides to set up the Central Nationalities Institute.

30. A group of Catholics in Guangyuan (Sichuan) issue a manifesto calling for the Church in China to be self-governing, self-supporting and self-propagating: the beginning of the Three Autonomies Movement.

December 29. The GAC issues regulations on US-subsidized educational, cultural, charitable and religious organizations in China, bringing them under total Chinese control. Under them also 'Chinese Christian churches and other organizations should immediately sever all relations with US mission boards', but could continue service projects.

D PUBLICATIONS

January 1. The English-language fortnightly *People's China* begins publication in Peking.

19. The fortnightly *Zhongyang zhengfa gongbao* (*Central Political and Legal Gazette*) begins publication.

September 5. The periodical *Renmin yinyue* (*People's Music*) begins publication.

1950–1

1951 *The Three-Antis campaign begins*

January 4. DPRK troops and Chinese People's Volunteers take Seoul, capital of the Republic of Korea.

23. The US Senate resolves 'that the UN should immediately declare Communist China an aggressor in Korea'.

29. Chinese and Polish representatives sign in Peking seven agreements, including on trade, postage, telecommunications, shipping and aviation.

February 1. The UN General Assembly adopts a US resolution condemning China as an aggressor in Korea.

2. Zhou Enlai issues a statement denouncing the UN condemnation of China as an aggressor in Korea.

5. The GAC issues the Several Decisions Concerning National Minority Affairs. Under it the regional autonomy of the minorities is to be promoted and cadres trained from among them.

18. Mao Zedong issues an inner-Party circular summarizing a resolution of a mid-February meeting of the CCPCC Politburo. It includes guidelines on the 'suppression of counter-revolutionaries', such as 'before passing a death sentence, refer the case to the masses and consult democratic personages'.

21. Mao Zedong promulgates the PRC Statute on Punishment of Counter-revolutionary Activity; it lays down which crimes are counter-revolutionary and the punishments for them.

March 7. Twenty-two ringleaders of a pro-NP and pro-US spy ring are executed, their main specific crime being arson in Lingling (Hunan) on February 22. Executions of counter-revolutionaries were common at about this time.

14–15. In Korea, Chinese People's Volunteers and DPRK troops evacuate Seoul in the face of strong pressure from UN forces.

April 22. The delegation on the local government of Tibet arrives in Peking for negotiations on the future of Tibet. It is headed by Ngapo

F   DEATHS

February 28. Poet Dai Wangshu d. aged 45.
June 17. Chen Yi, former ruler of Taiwan, is executed in Taiwan as a Communist conspirator, aged 70.
October 27. Ren Bishi d. aged 46.
December 20. Fu Sinian, historian and May Fourth leader, d. in Taibei aged 54.

The Labour Insurance Regulations are promulgated   **1951**

A   ECONOMICS

February 14–26. A National Agricultural Work Conference is held in Peking; it summarizes 1950's achievements, discusses methods for expanding production and lays down targets for 1951.
April 18. The GAC promulgates the PRC Provisional Customs Law to take effect on May 1.
30. The GAC orders the properties in China of the British-owned Asiatic Petroleum Company, a subsidiary of Shell Oil Company, to be taken over and its oil stocks to be requisitioned.
July 18. The Shanghai Municipal Military Affairs Control Committee takes over the properties of the US-owned Standard Vacuum, Texas Co. (China) and Cathay Oil Co. and requisitions their oil stocks.
September 4. The Shanghai Municipal Military Affairs Control Committee issues orders to take over fourteen public properties of the former French Concession in the city.

B   OFFICIAL APPOINTMENTS, RESIGNATIONS, DISMISSALS ETC.

February 28. The Peking Municipal People's Representative Conference (held February 26–28) elects Peng Zhen as Mayor of Peking.

C   CULTURAL AND SOCIAL

January 1. The CCPCC issues its decision 'to establish in the whole Party a propaganda network for the masses of the people'.
8. The Lu Xun Memorial Hall is set up in Shanghai. The Central Literary Institute begins operations.
17. Zhou Enlai and other CPG leaders hold a meeting with Catholic leaders. Zhou calls for support for the three autonomies (see C, November 30, 1950); and states that relations with the Vatican must be limited to ideology, not practice.

1951

Ngawang Jigme. They begin negotiations on April 29 with a CPG delegation headed by Li Weihan.

May 16. The GAC issues a directive against names, monuments, etc. discriminatory against or offensive to the national minorities.

18. The UN General Assembly approves a world-wide embargo on the transportation of arms and war materials to the Chinese.

21. China and Pakistan formally establish diplomatic relations.

22. The Chinese Ministry of Foreign Affairs denounces the UN resolution of May 18. Zhou Enlai notifies the Soviet ambassador, N.V. Roshchin, of Chinese support for a Soviet proposal of May 9 for an overall peace treaty with Japan.

23. In Peking, Li Weihan and others for the CPG and Ngapo Ngawang Jigme and others for the local government of Tibet sign the Agreement of the CPG and the Local Government of Tibet on Measures for the Liberation of Tibet. Under it, Tibet is part of the PRC; the local government of Tibet 'shall actively assist the PLA to enter Tibet'; 'the Tibetan people have the right to exercise national regional autonomy' and freedom of religion; and 'the CPG will handle the external affairs of the region of Tibet'.

June 23. Soviet UN delegate J.A. Malik proposes ceasefire negotiations to end the Korean War.

July 1. The Commander-in-Chief of the Korean People's Army, Kim Il Sung, and Peng Dehuai, Commander-in-Chief of the Chinese People's Volunteers, notify UN Commander Matthew B. Ridgway of their agreement to hold talks on a ceasefire in Korea.

10. Armistice negotiations on Korea begin in Kaesong in Korea, just south of the 38th parallel (but break down on August 23).

August 15. Zhou Enlai declares that China regards any peace treaty with Japan as null and void unless there is PRC participation in its preparation. (From September 4 to 8 representatives of forty-nine countries, not including any from China or Taiwan, held a peace conference in San Francisco and on the last day a peace treaty with Japan was signed.)

September 9. The first PLA units arrive in Lhasa in accordance with the agreement of May 23.

October 24. The Dalai Lama cables Mao Zedong his support for the agreement of May 23.

25. Armistice negotiations on Korea resume at Panmunjom in neutral ground between the DPRK and the Republic of Korea.

November 29. NCNA reports the entry of a PLA unit into the important Tibetan city of Gyantse.

December 7. The GAC adopts a directive by Zhou Enlai 'to begin a

1951

February 12. The Ministry of Education takes over the Christian private Yanjing University in Peking. (Almost all the Christian universities had been taken over by the end of 1951.)

26. The GAC promulgates the Labour Insurance Regulations of the PRC ' to protect the health of workers and staff members and alleviate difficulties in their livelihood'. Among many other provisions the Regulations provide women workers and staff members a total of fifty-six days' leave on full pay before and after confinement.

March 8–April 2. A film festival of twenty-six full-length feature and many other films takes place in sixty cinemas in twenty cities.

March 19–31. The First National Conference on Secondary Education formulates policies and tasks in secondary education.

April 3. The Chinese Drama Research Institute is set up in Peking.

May 20. A *People's Daily* editorial condemns the film *Wu Xun zhuan* (*The Story of Wu Xun*) for the first time, and begins a campaign against the film, its hero the beggar Wu Xun, and 'ideological confusion in cultural circles'. (The film was premiered in December 1950.)

June 16–29. A National Work Conference of Cultural Troupes is held by the Ministry of Culture. It lays down the tasks of such troupes as educating the people through developing new spoken plays, new operas, new music and new dances.

July 13. The Tianjin Municipal Military Affairs Control Committee issues a notice banning the Legion of Mary as an imperialist-controlled reactionary secret organization.

September 3. The CPG Council adopts the Provisional Organic Regulations of the PRC Law Courts and the Provisional Organic Regulations of the CPG's Supreme People's Procuratorate.

October 1. The GAC issues its Decision on the Reform of the Education System, laying down a greater stress on political and ideological training.

12. A committee is set up under the GAC to study the languages of the national minorities.

December 26. The GAC's Culture and Education Committee decides to set up the Chinese Character Reform Research Committee.

D Publications

April 27. The *Zhongguo qingnian bao* (*China Youth*) begins publication.

August. *Quanguo xinshu mu* (*National Catalogue of New Books*) begins publication in Peking.

October 12. The first volume of *Mao Zedong xuanji* (*The Selected Works of Mao Zedong*) is published.

campaign on a nationwide scale for simplicity and economy, to increase production, to oppose corruption, to oppose waste, and to oppose bureaucratism': the Three-Antis Movement. The resolution formalizes a movement which had started in August in the north-east.

1952 The Three- and Five-Antis Movements are completed

January 1. At the New Year's celebration of the CPG Mao Zedong calls for struggle against corruption, waste and bureaucratism.

9. The Minister of Finance, Bo Yibo, delivers a report proposing that the Three-Antis Movement be extended to launch a struggle in industrial and business circles against bribery, evasion of taxes, stealing state property, cheating on government contracts and stealing economic information for private speculation: the Five-Antis Movement.

February 1. The CPG launches the Five-Antis Movement with a public trial in Peking of those accused of various types of corruption; a number are sentenced to death or imprisonment. Bo Yibo makes a speech.

24. Zhou Enlai announces China's support for the protest against germ warfare made on February 22 by the DPRK Foreign Minister Bak Hun Yung, both bringing accusations against the USA.

March 8. Zhou Enlai protests against intrusions by US aircraft into China's air space and the US use of germ warfare in Manchuria.

15. Li Dequan, President of the Chinese Red Cross Society and widow of Feng Yuxiang, leaves Peking bound for the North-east as the head of a PRC commission which plans to make an on-the-spot investigation on US germ warfare there.

April 1. Li Dequan's commission issues its findings that the USA has spread germs and poisonous insects in China's North-east.

28. A Sino-Japanese peace treaty is signed in Taibei.

June 13. The GAC issues a 'directive on a few problems in concluding the Five-Antis Movement'.

November 5. The *Zhongguo shaonian bao* (*Chinese Youth*) begins publication in Peking.
Autumn. The English-language *Chinese Literature* begins publication in Peking.

F DEATHS

February 23. Christian educator Zhang Boling d. in Tianjin aged 74.
May. Mao Anying, the son of Mao Zedong and Yang Kaihui, d. in the Korean War aged 29.
August 16. Industrialist Du Yuesheng d. in Hongkong aged 63.
25. Chen Guofu, banker and NP official, d. in Taibei aged 58.
October 20. PLA martyr Huang Jiguang d. in Korea aged 21.

Economic restoration and land reform are basically completed **1952**

A ECONOMICS

May 26. Chinese and Indian representatives sign a contract in Peking to export 100,000 tons of rice from the PRC to India.
June 1. A Sino-Japanese trade agreement is signed in Peking; under it 'the value of the commodities to be bought or sold by each party is £30,000,000 sterling'.
20. The Jingjiang Flood Dispersion Project on the Yangzi River in Hubei is completed, after seventy-five days' work.
July 1. The Chengdu–Chongqing (Sichuan) railway opens for traffic.
August 6. The CPG Council approves a report from Finance Minister Bo Yibo in which he claims that the budget is balanced and commodity prices stable, reflecting a decisive improvement in China's economic situation.
September 15. A Sino-Soviet joint communiqué in Moscow announces that the Chinese Changchun railway will be transferred to the PRC. China, the USSR and Mongolia sign an agreement to build a railway from Jining (Chahar) to Ulan Bator.
29. The Tianshui–Lanzhou (Gansu) railway opens to traffic. This marks the completion of the long-projected Longhai railway from Haizhou (Jiangsu) to Lanzhou.
October 17. A ceremony marks the opening of a new port at Tanggu (Hebei).
23. Chinese and Chilean representatives sign a trade agreement in Peking.
November 20. The Kangding–Changdu section of the Xikang–Tibet

1952

15. A *People's Daily* editorial announces the 'victorious completion' of the Five-Antis Movement.

July 4. The GAC receives a report 'on the concluding work of the Three-Antis Movement', a formalization of its completion.

13. Zhou Enlai announces the PRC's recognition of the four Geneva Conventions for the protection of various types of war victims, signed on August 12, 1949; and of the Protocol for the Prohibition of the Use of Asphyxiating, Poisonous and Other Gases, and of Bacteriological Methods of Warfare (June 1925).

25, 26, 29, 30. Border clashes occur along the frontier between Macao and Zhongshan (Guangdong).

August 9. The CPG issues an order promulgating the PRC General Programme for the Implementation of Regional Autonomy for the National Minorities; it allows for one or more national minority to belong to any single autonomous region, county or district, but repeats that all autonomous areas are part of the PRC.

17. A PRC delegation led by Zhou Enlai arrives in Moscow for a conference with Soviet leaders.

20. Stalin and Zhou Enlai hold a meeting.

23. China and Portugal sign an agreement in Hongkong settling the border disputes between China and Macao.

September 15. In Moscow Zhou Enlai and the Soviet Commissar of Foreign Affairs, A. Ya. Vyshinsky, exchange notes under which the USSR agrees to a Chinese request to extend the period for the withdrawal of its troops from Lüshun 'pending the conclusion of peace treaties between the PRC and Japan, and the USSR and Japan'.

24. Peking–Moscow radio facsimile services formally open.

28. A Mongolian People's Republic government delegation arrives in Peking; it is led by the Prime Minister, Y. Tsedenbal.

October 2. A CCP delegation headed by Liu Shaoqi arrives in Moscow to attend the Nineteenth Congress of the Communist Party of the Soviet Union (CPSU), which takes place October 5–14. Liu stays in the USSR for over three months.

2–13. The Peace Conference of the Asian and Pacific Regions is held in Peking. It is attended by delegates and observers from thirty-seven countries. Among other matters it decides to set up a Peace Liaison Committee of the Asian and Pacific Regions, and demands an end to the remilitarization of Japan.

4. The Sino-Mongolian Agreement on Economic and Cultural Cooperation is signed in Peking, to cover the period 1952 to 1962.

November 15. The CPG Council adopts a resolution to adjust the boundaries of some provinces.

highway opens to traffic. The PLA's Shanghai Municipal Military Affairs Control Committee orders that all British properties of the Shanghai Electric Construction Co. Ltd., Shanghai Water Works Co. Ltd., Shanghai Gas Co. Ltd., and Mackenzie and Co. Ltd. be requisitioned. With respect to the last company the PLA's Tianjin and Wuhan counterparts take the same action the same day.

December 18. CPG and Ceylonese government representatives sign an agreement under which China will sell rice to Ceylon in exchange for rubber over 1953 to 1957.

24. At a meeting of the Standing Committee of the CPPCC's National Committee Zhou Enlai announces that a Five-Year Plan will begin in 1953.

31. A formal ceremony marks the completion of the transfer of the Chinese Changchun railway by the USSR to the PRC.

B OFFICIAL APPOINTMENTS, RESIGNATIONS, DISMISSALS ETC.

February 10. Zhang Guohua is inaugurated as Commander of the PLA's Tibetan military region, set up the same day, and Ngapo Ngawang Jigme as his first deputy.

September 1. Li Jingquan is formally inaugurated as Chairman of the Sichuan Provincial People's Government, set up the same day.

October 10. The CPG Council approves the appointment of Gao Gang to chair the State Planning Commission, and the formation of the Commission the same day.

C CULTURAL AND SOCIAL

May 16. The China-India Friendship Association is founded.

June 19. The Soviet Red Cross Hospital formally opens in Peking.

July 5. NCNA announces that the overwhelming majority of regions have completed land reform.

October 6–November 14. The Ministry of Culture holds the First National Festival of Classical and Folk Drama in Peking. Some 1600 'theatre workers' take part and perform nearly 100 individual pieces, representing twenty-three different styles of local theatre.

D PUBLICATIONS

April 10. The second volume of *Mao Zedong xuanji* (*Selected Works of Mao Zedong*) is published.

June. Hu Feng's collection of essays *Cong yuantou dao hongliu* (*From the Source to the Flood*) is published in Shanghai.

1953 End of the Korean War

January 5. Mao Zedong issues an inner-Party directive to 'combat bureaucracy, commandism and violations of the law and of discipline' in the Party and government.
11. Liu Shaoqi returns to Peking from the USSR.
12. A US aircraft is shot down in China's North-east. Eleven of the fourteen men survive and are taken prisoner.
13. The CPG Council adopts resolutions 'to convene the National People's Congress and local people's congresses at all levels'; and to set up a committee, chaired by Mao Zedong, to draft a constitution.
16. Postal and telecommunications agreements between the PRC and the Mongolian People's Republic are signed in Peking.
February 2. In his first State of the Union Message, US President Dwight Eisenhower announces a reversal of the policy 'that Formosa should not be used as a base of operations against the Chinese Communist mainland', on the grounds that 'we certainly have no obligation to protect a nation fighting us in Korea'.
7. At the close of a Conference of the National Committee of the CPPCC (held February 4 to 7), Mao Zedong calls for more intense struggle against the USA in Korea, study of Marxism and the Soviet Union, and opposition to bureaucratism.
15. The Chinese air force shoots down five US planes over the North-east.
22. In a speech made at Lüda in celebration of Soviet Army Day (the thirty-fifth anniversary of the founding of the Soviet Red Army), Zhou Enlai accuses the USA of sponsoring raids by the NP on the

July. The monthly *Zhongguo yuwen* (*Chinese Language*) begins publication under the editorship of Luo Changpei. The *Taiping tianguo* (*Taiping Heavenly Kingdom*), a compilation in eight volumes by Xiang Da and others of source materials on the Taipings, is published in Shanghai.

September. Yu Pingbo publishes *Honglou meng yanjiu* (*Studies on A Dream of Red Mansions*), a re-edition under a different title of research originally published in April 1923 (author's preface December 1950).

F DEATHS

February 11. Writer Tao Jingsun d. aged 55.
29. Guo Taiqi d. in the USA, aged 63.

Beginning of the First Five-Year Plan 1953

A ECONOMICS

January 1. The *People's Daily* editorial includes among its list of 'the great tasks for 1953' 'the beginning of implementation of the First Five-Year Plan of national construction'.
February 24. The Guangzhou Municipal Military Affairs Control Committee orders the requisition of the British property of Butterfield and Swire in the city.
March 21. In Moscow Chinese and Soviet representatives sign agreements on a Soviet loan to the PRC and Soviet assistance in the expansion and construction of power stations.
July 1. China's first modernized giant open-cut coal mine formally moves into production in Fuxin (Liaoxi).
6. The China National Import and Export Company signs a business arrangement with a British trade delegation in Peking.
August. Mao Zedong lays down the CCP's 'general line' for the period of transition to socialism as 'basically to accomplish the country's industrialization and the socialist transformation of agriculture, handicrafts and capitalist industry and commerce over a fairly long period of time'.
October 16. China's first large-scale electric machinery plant is completed in Harbin (Heilongjiang).
23–November 12. The foundation conference of the Chinese National Industrial and Commercial Association is held in Peking; it discusses how private industrialists and merchants can apply the 'general line'.

1953

PRC and of turning Japan into a military base.

25. Chiang Kaishek orders the abrogation of the Sino-Soviet Treaty of Friendship and Alliance of August 14, 1945, and its related documents.

March 1. Mao Zedong promulgates the Electoral Law of the PRC for the National People's Congress (NPC) and the Local People's Congresses of All Levels, adopted by the CPG Council on February 11. Under it 'all citizens of the PRC who have reached the age of eighteen shall have the right to elect and be elected irrespective of race, sex, occupation, social origin, religion, education, property status, or residence'.

9. Zhou Enlai attends Stalin's funeral in Moscow. (Stalin had died on March 5.) Some 600,000 people attended a memorial meeting in his honour in Peking.

April 11. In Panmunjom, Korea, representatives of the Chinese People's Volunteers, Korean People's Army and UN Command sign the Agreement for the Repatriation of Sick and Injured Captured Personnel.

17. The GAC issues a 'directive on dissuading peasants from blindly moving into the cities'.

20. The conflicting parties in the Korean War begin the exchange of sick and wounded prisoners of war at Panmunjom.

June 8. Delegates of the Chinese People's Volunteers, Korean People's Army and UN Command sign the Agreement on the Repatriation of Prisoners of War from the Korean War in Panmunjom, Korea.

9. Experimental work for basic-level elections in Peking formally begins.

30–July 1. China's first census is taken and the results published November 1, 1954. They show China's population at 601,938,035 including 11,743,320 Overseas Chinese, 7,591,298 in Taiwan and 582,603,417 in the PRC; 51.82 per cent are male and 48.18 female; nearly 94 per cent are Han, 6 per cent National Minorities numbering 35,320,360 (excluding Taiwan). The largest province is Sichuan with 62,303,999; Peking's population is 2,768,149 and Shanghai's 6,204,417.

July 27. Delegates of the Chinese People's Volunteers, Korean People's Army and UN Command sign the Korean armistice at Panmunjom in the morning. The same afternoon Kim Il Sung and Peng Dehuai respectively issue ceasefire orders to the Korean People's Army and the Chinese People's Volunteers.

August 11. Peng Dehuai arrives back in Peking from the Korean War; a large welcome is held.

September 28. In an interview Zhou Enlai tells Professor Ōyama Ikuo, Chairman of the Japanese National Peace Committee, that

1953

26–November 5. The CCPCC holds a Conference on Mutual Aid and Cooperation in Agriculture. It decides on the 'steady development' of mutual aid teams and agricultural producers' cooperatives through 'active leadership'.
29. A new Sino-Japanese Trade Agreement is signed in Peking for the exchange of goods of £30,000,000 sterling value.
November 2. The Shanghai Municipal People's Government orders the requisitioning of the properties of the last remaining French company in Shanghai; this is the end of foreign ownership of public utilities in Shanghai.
30. Chinese and Indonesian representatives sign a trade agreement in Peking.
December 16. The CCPCC adopts the Resolution to Develop Agricultural Producers' Cooperatives (APC's).
26. At the Anshan iron and steel works, China's first large-scale mechanized automatic steel-rolling mill, a large iron-smelting furnace, and a seamless tubing mill start work; a ceremony marks the occasion.
31. China's first modernized textile machine plant is completed in Yuci (Shanxi).

B OFFICIAL APPOINTMENTS, RESIGNATIONS, DISMISSALS ETC.

January 14. The CPG Council appoints Gao Gang, Rao Shushi, Peng Dehuai, Lin Biao and Liu Bocheng as Chairmen respectively of the North-east, East China, North-west, Central South, and South-west Administrative Committees (which replace the Military and Political Committees).

C CULTURAL AND SOCIAL

January 15. The Nationalities Publishing House is set up in Peking to publish material in the languages of the National Minorities.
April 15–23. The Second National Women's Congress is held in Peking.
May 2–11. The Seventh All-China Labour Congress is held in Peking.
11. The Chinese Islamic Association is formally established with Burhan as its director.
30–June 3. The Chinese Buddhist Association holds its inaugural conference in Peking, being established formally on the last day.
June 10–15. The Second National Youth Congress is held in Peking.
23–July 2. The Second National Congress of the Chinese New Democratic Youth League is held in Peking.
July 16. A *People's Daily* editorial, 'Wipe Out Imperialist Elements

China wants diplomatic relations with Japan but is blocked because the Japanese government 'continues to maintain so-called diplomatic relations with the remnant Chiang Kaishek gang'; he adds that trade and cultural exchange between China and Japan should be encouraged even without diplomatic relations.

October 8. Zhou Enlai issues a statement supporting a Soviet proposal (September 28) to call a five-power conference of foreign ministers (USA, UK, France, USSR, China) to discuss measures to ease international tension.

November 12. A government delegation of the DPRK arrives in Peking, led by Kim Il Sung.

23. The Sino-Korean Agreement on Economic and Cultural Cooperation is signed in Peking to cover the years 1954 to 1964. The Korean delegation leaves Peking for home November 25.

December 8. Mao Zedong casts his vote in the elections for the National People's Congress as these proceed in Peking and throughout the country.

1954 *The First National People's Congress adopts the Constitution*

February 6–10. The Fourth Plenum of the Seventh CCPCC is held in Peking. In his formal report Liu Shaoqi calls for Party unity and attacks those who regard the region they lead as 'their individual inheritance or independent kingdom', a reference to Gao Gang and Rao Shushi.

March 6. Suiyuan province is formally abolished and its territories absorbed into the Inner Mongolian Autonomous Region.

April 20. Zhou Enlai leaves Peking to head the Chinese delegation to

Hiding in the Catholic Church', reports that the Shanghai Municipal Security Bureau on March 25 and June 15 broke two spy cases in which imperialism made use of the Catholic Church to undertake sabotage activity, and arrested 20 ringleaders. A number of other arrests of Catholics on similar grounds were made at about this time.

August 21. The CC of the Chinese New Democratic Youth League announces the renaming of the Chinese Youth and Children Corps as the Chinese Young Pioneers.

September 23–October 6. The Second National Congress of Literature and Art Workers is held in Peking. On its last day it adopts a new constitution of the Federation of Literary and Art Circles of China and calls on writers and artists to serve the workers, peasants and soldiers.

D PUBLICATIONS

March. The Zhonghua Book Company publishes Zhou Yibai's three-volumed *Zhongguo xiju shi* (*History of Chinese Drama*) in Shanghai (author's preface dated November 10, 1950). The Kaiming Book Company publishes the *Zhu Ziqing wenji* (*Zhu Ziqing's Collected Works*) in four volumes.

March–April. The six-volumed *Nianjun* (*The Nian Army*), compiled by Fan Wenlan and others, is published in Shanghai.

April 10. The third volume of *Mao Zedong xuanji* (*Selected Works of Mao Zedong*) is published.

December. The Writers' Publishing House puts out its first publication, a three-volume modern edition of the classical novel *Honglou meng* (*A Dream of Red Mansions*).

F DEATHS

September 26. Painter Xu Beihong d. aged 58.
November 19. Senior NP official Wu Tiecheng d. in Taibei aged 65.

Gao Gang is dismissed and commits suicide   1954

A ECONOMICS

January 1. In Moscow, representatives of China, the Soviet Union, DPRK, Mongolia, the Democratic Republic of Germany, Poland, Czechoslovakia, Rumania, Hungary, Bulgaria and Albania sign an agreement for passenger and freight through railway services.

31. A ceremony at Peking railway station marks the inauguration of direct Peking–Moscow passenger rail service.

1954

the Geneva conference on Korea and Indochina.

25. Guisui, the capital of the Inner Mongolian Autonomous Region, is renamed Huhehot.

26. The Geneva Conference opens.

29. Chinese and Indian representatives sign in Peking the Agreement on Trade and Intercourse between the Tibet Region of China and India; the first PRC agreement to invoke the five principles of peaceful coexistence (mutual respect for sovereignty and territorial integrity; mutual non-aggression; non-interference in each other's internal affairs; equality and mutual benefit; and peaceful coexistence). Under the agreement free travel is allowed to religious pilgrims on both sides of the border. The two sides also exchange notes providing for the withdrawal of Indian 'military escorts' from Tibet and the handover 'at a reasonable price' of India's 'postal, telegraph and public telephone services' in Tibet.

May 11. China and Albania agree to establish diplomatic relations.

June 4. Chinese and US representatives begin meeting in Geneva 'for preliminary talks on problems relating to residents of the two countries'.

14. The CPG Council adopts the Draft Constitution of the PRC.

17. NCNA reports that the Chinese and British governments have agreed that a Chinese *chargé d'affaires* should be sent to London.

19. The CPG Council decides on several major administrative changes, including (*i*) the abolition of the major administrative regions and their administrative committees; (*ii*) the merging of Liaodong and Liaoxi provinces to form Liaoning, and (*iii*) the amalgamation of Songjiang province into Heilongjiang and Ningxia into Gansu.

24. Zhou Enlai arrives in India from Geneva.

28. Zhou Enlai and Indian Prime Minister Jawaharlal Nehru issue a joint communiqué reaffirming the five principles of peaceful coexistence.

29. In Rangoon Zhou Enlai and Burmese Prime Minister U Nu issue a joint communiqué affirming the five principles of peaceful coexistence.

July 3–5. Zhou Enlai and Ho Chi Minh hold talks on the Sino-Vietnamese border discussing the problems relating to the Geneva Conference.

12. Zhou Enlai arrives back in Geneva.

21. China and six other countries agree to the Final Declaration of the Geneva Conference which lays down a ceasefire in Indochina, and the division of Vietnam along the 17th parallel.

26. Zhou Enlai arrives in Warsaw for a visit.

28. Zhou Enlai arrives in Moscow for a visit.

1954

May 13. NCNA reports completion, earlier in May, of the Guanting reservoir on the Yongding River north-west of Peking; China's first large gorge-type reservoir.

June 3. Direct passenger rail service begins from Peking to Pyongyang, capital of the DPRK.

July 26. A ceremony, including experimental flights, marks the completion of China's first group of locally made aeroplanes.

September 2. The GAC adopts the Provisional Regulations on Joint State-Private Industrial Enterprises, which give the CPG some control over such enterprises, while protecting the interests of shareholders.

14. The GAC issues an order for the rationing of cotton.

October 1. The Chinese People's Bank of Construction formally begins operations.

December 3. Chinese and Albanian representatives sign several economic agreements in Tirana, including on long-term credits to Albania and technical cooperation.

24. China and the DRVN sign several agreements and protocols covering Chinese aid in Vietnamese economic reconstruction and other matters.

25. Ceremonies at Lhasa, Yaan and Xining mark the formal opening to traffic of the Qinghai–Tibet and Xikang–Tibet highways, respectively running from Xining to Lhasa and Yaan to Lhasa.

30. China and the Soviet Union sign an air service agreement in Peking.

B OFFICIAL APPOINTMENTS, RESIGNATIONS, DISMISSALS ETC.

March 31. A national conference of the CCP resolves to expel Gao Gang and Rao Shushi from the Party and dismiss them from all posts held for trying to split the Party and set up an independent kingdom.

June 19. The CPG Council makes a number of new appointments, including Li Xiannian as Minister of Finance.

August 4–23. Provincial, autonomous regional, and municipal people's congresses meet and elect representatives to the NPC.

September 27. The NPC elects Mao Zedong as Chairman of the PRC and Zhu De as deputy Chairman, and elects Liu Shaoqi as Chairman of the Standing Committee of the NPC, Dong Biwu as President of the Supreme People's Court, and Zhang Dingcheng as Chief Procurator of the Supreme People's Procuratorate. It also approves Mao Zedong's nomination of Zhou Enlai as Premier of the State Council which, under the September 20 Constitution, replaces the GAC as 'the highest administrative organ of state'.

1954

31. Zhou Enlai arrives in Ulan Bator for a visit.
August 1. Zhou Enlai arrives back in Peking.
2. Vice-Premier Pham Van Dong of the DRVN arrives in Peking for a visit.
14. Clement Attlee arrives in Peking at the head of a British Labour Party delegation. They see Mao Zedong August 24 and leave Peking the following day.
September 3–6. Chinese artillery shells Quemoy and Little Quemoy Islands (Fujian), still occupied by NP troops.
15–28. The First Session of the NPC is held in Peking with 1141 delegates.
20. The NPC adopts the Constitution of the PRC.
23. Zhou Enlai makes the Report on Government Work at the NPC. Among other points he denounces the South-east Asia Collective Defence Treaty (signed in Manila September 8) as showing that the USA aims to destroy the Geneva Conference agreement.
29. A high-level Soviet government delegation led by Nikita Khrushchev, First Secretary of the CPSU, arrives in Peking to take part in the celebrations marking the fifth anniversary of the founding of the PRC.
October 12. The Soviet delegation and CPG leaders issue joint communiqués on a number of issues, including (*i*) Soviet military withdrawal from Lüshun before May 31, 1955; (*ii*) transfer to the PRC of Soviet shares in four joint-stock companies; and (*iii*) granting of long-term credit of 520,000,000 roubles by the USSR to the PRC.
19–30. Indian Prime Minister Nehru visits China.
30. The capital city of Henan Province is transferred from Kaifeng to Zhengzhou.
November 1. The State Statistical Bureau issues the results of the 1953 census (see June 30–July 1, 1953).
19. China and the Netherlands agree to establish diplomatic relations at *chargé d'affaires* level.
December 1–16. Burmese Prime Minister U Nu visits China.
2. In Washington US Secretary of State John Foster Dulles and the NP's Minister of Foreign Affairs, Ye Gongchao (George Yeh), sign the Sino-American Mutual Defence Treaty.
8. Zhou Enlai issues a statement denouncing the Mutual Defence Treaty of December 2, and demands US withdrawal from Taiwan.
12. Zhou Enlai and U Nu issue a joint communiqué on border questions, postal services and other matters.

1954

C Cultural and Social

January 14–27. The Second National Conference on Secondary Education is held by the Ministry of Education in Peking; it drafts policies and tasks according to the 'general line'.

May 3. The Chinese People's Association for Cultural Relations with Foreign Countries is formally set up in Peking.

August 9–15. The Council of the World Federation of Democratic Youth meets in Peking; some 50 countries are represented by some 200 delegates.

October 7. Pope Pius XII issues his encyclical *Ad sinarum gentem*, in which he condemns the 'three autonomies' and lays down that 'a "national" church ... would not be Catholic'.

16. Mao Zedong writes to the CCPCC Politburo in support of a movement 'against the Hu Shi school of bourgeois idealism in the field of classical literature' and in particular against Yu Pingbo's interpretations of *A Dream of Red Mansions*.

31–December 8. The Praesidiums of the Federation of Literary and Art Circles of China and the Chinese Writers Union hold eight meetings to oppose the bourgeois idealism of the Hu Shi school of thought in their research on the novel *A Dream of Red Mansions*, and to criticize Feng Xuefeng, the editor of *Literature and Art*.

November 25. The Asian Students' Sanatorium opens in Peking.

December 31. Mao Zedong orders the proclamation of regulations under which urban residents' committees and street offices can be set up. According to an NCNA report of the same day, these have already been established in Peking, Shanghai, Tianjin, Shenyang and other cities.

D Publications

February. The journal *Lishi yanjiu* (*Historical Research*) begins publication. The People's Literary Publishing House in Peking publishes the last of the four volumes of *Qu Qiubai wenji* (*Collected Works of Qu Qiubai*) (the first three appeared respectively in October, December and November, 1953).

May 5. A Mongolian-language edition of the first volume of the *Selected Works of Mao Zedong* is released in Huhehot and other cities of the Inner Mongolian Autonomous Region.

E Natural Disasters

July. Flooding occurs in the Gyantse and Shigatse regions of Tibet.

1955 *Cooperativization of agriculture is endorsed by the CCPCC Plenum*

January 1. Sino-DRVN post and telegraph services commence.
5. Dag Hammarskjöld, Secretary-General of the UN, arrives in Peking for talks with Zhou Enlai.
10. China and Yugoslavia issue a joint communiqué agreeing to the exchange of ambassadors. PLA air force units bombard the Dachen Islands off the coast of Zhejiang. Zhou Enlai and Dag Hammarskjöld issue a joint communiqué on 'questions pertinent to the relaxation of world tension'.
18. PLA naval and air force units attack and, after a sharp battle, capture the small island of Yijiangshan, off the coast of Zhejiang, from occupying NP troops.
20. China and Afghanistan agree to establish diplomatic relations and exchange ambassadors.
29. The US House of Representatives and Senate jointly resolve to authorize President Eisenhower to use the US armed forces to protect Taiwan and the Penghu Islands (Pescadores) and related territories insofar as he judges their protection 'to be required or appropriate in assuring the defense of Formosa and the Pescadores'.
February 5. US President Eisenhower orders US forces to assist NP troops in the evacuation of the Dachen Islands.
13. PLA forces occupy the Dachen and a number of other islands off the Zhejiang coast.
26. The PLA captures the Nanjishan Islands, thus completing the liberation of all the islands off the coast of Zhejiang.
April 6–10. The Asian Countries Conference is held in New Delhi. Guo Moruo heads the Chinese delegation.
7. Mao Zedong issues an order ending the state of war between the

August 4. NCNA reports that the level of the Yangzi River at Wuhan has surpassed the 1931 level by 0.71 metres; this reflects unprecedentedly heavy rains and severe flooding, mitigated in its effects by efficiently organized dykes and flood fighting, along the Yangzi and Huai Rivers, affecting many areas in Hubei, Hunan, Anhui, Jiangxi, Jiangsu and Henan.

F   DEATHS

Spring. Gao Gang commits suicide, aged 49.

Campaign against Hu Feng   **1955**

A   ECONOMICS

March 1. According to a State Council order of February 21, the People's Bank begins to issue a new people's currency at the rate of 10,000 old *yuan* to 1 new.
25. The Chinese Agricultural Bank formally opens for business; its aims include to promote village credit cooperatives and agricultural production.
28. Chinese and Burmese representatives sign three trade contracts under which China is to exchange steel and other things for rice.
June 10. The Chinese People's Bank announces the completion of the changeover from the old to the new currency.
July 1. The railway from Litang (Guangxi) to Zhanjiang (Guangdong) formally opens to traffic.
5. Vice-Premier Li Fuchun, Director of the State Planning Commission, gives a report to the NPC on the First Five-Year Plan, emphasizing the importance of industrial construction and the assistance of the Soviet Union.
30. The NPC adopts the First Five-Year Plan for the Development of the National Economy.
August 2. A ceremony in Peking marks the opening of through rail traffic between Peking and Hanoi (a similar ceremony took place in Hanoi August 1).
October 20. Ceremonies mark the formal opening to traffic of the Lhasa–Shigatse and Shigatse–Gyantse highways in Tibet.
November 27. The first entirely Chinese-designed and made new-style passenger and freight coastal steamship is launched at a ceremony in Shanghai.

1955

PRC and Germany.

11. An Indian aeroplane carrying Chinese and others on their way from Hongkong to Djakarta for the Afro-Asian Conference in Bandung explodes near Borneo, killing all eleven passengers.

12. The Chinese Ministry of Foreign Affairs issues a statement accusing US and NP agents of deliberately planting a bomb in the Indian aeroplane and thus causing the explosion of the previous day; it demands that the British Hongkong authorities investigate the matter. (An Indonesian government investigation later found that a bomb had been planted in the aeroplane's wheel well.)

18–24. The Afro-Asian Conference is held in Bandung, Indonesia, twenty-nine countries attending. Zhou Enlai heads the Chinese delegation and addresses the plenary session on April 19.

22. The Sino-Indonesian Treaty Concerning the Question of Dual Nationality is signed in Bandung. It requires, among other matters, that all Chinese in Indonesia of eighteen or over must choose between Chinese and Indonesian citizenship within two years.

23. In Bandung, Zhou Enlai declares that the PRC is willing to negotiate with the USA on 'relaxing tension in the Far East'.

May 24. A joint Sino-Soviet communiqué announces that the USSR has withdrawn all its forces from the Lüshan naval base and transferred it to the PRC without compensation.

26–June 3. The Indonesian Prime Minister, Ali Sastroamidjojo, visits Peking. On the last day he and Zhou Enlai exchange notes on the implementation of the Treaty on Dual Nationality.

June 22–29. The World Peace Assembly meets in Helsinki. Shen Yanbing, the Minister of Culture, heads the Chinese delegation and Guo Moruo attends as Vice-President of the World Peace Council.

25. DRVN President Ho Chi Minh arrives in Peking at the head of a delegation.

July 5–30. The Second Session of the First NPC is held in Peking. On its last day it resolves to abolish Xikang and Jehol provinces, absorbing the territory of the former into Sichuan and of the latter into the Inner Mongolian Autonomous Region, Hebei and Liaoning. (The former takes effect October 1, 1955, the latter January 1, 1956.)

7. The DRVN delegation and CPG leaders issue a joint communiqué calling for thorough implementation of the Geneva Agreements and announcing PRC economic and technical aid to the DRVN, including a gift of 800,000,000 *yuan*.

25. Announcements from Washington and Peking report that talks at ambassadorial level will begin in Geneva on August 1.

31. Mao Zedong delivers his report 'On the Cooperative Transforma-

1955

December 1. The railway from Jining (Inner Mongolia) to Erenhot (Inner Mongolia) on the border with the People's Republic of Mongolia opens formally to domestic business.
27. The Guanting reservoir hydroelectric station, north-west of Peking, the first entirely Chinese-made of its kind, begins generating.
31. A ceremony marks the opening to traffic of the railway linking Ulan Bator, capital of Mongolia, and Peking.

B OFFICIAL APPOINTMENTS, RESIGNATIONS, DISMISSALS ETC.

March 9. The State Council sets up the Preparatory Committee for the Tibetan Autonomous Region; it appoints the Dalai Lama as Chairman and the Panchen Lama and Zhang Guohua as deputy Chairmen of the Committee.
September 27. Mao Zedong confers the title of Marshal of the PRC on Zhu De, Peng Dehuai, Lin Biao, Liu Bocheng, He Long and five others.
October 1. A large-scale ceremony in Urumchi marks the inauguration of the Xinjiang Uighur Autonomous Region, to replace Xinjiang Province, and of Saifudin as its Chairman.

C CULTURAL AND SOCIAL

January 10. The Peking Opera Company of China is established.
February 5, 7. The Chinese Writers Union decides on all-out criticism of the writer and poet Hu Feng for his bourgeois and idealist ideas on literature and art.
April 1–10. The Ministry of Culture holds its first puppet and shadow play festival in Peking.
May 1. Newspapers and magazines in Peking and Tianjin begin using the first batch of fifty-seven simplified characters according to the draft plan announced on January 31 by the Chinese Character Reform Committee.
25. A joint meeting of the Praesidiums of the Federation of Literary and Art Circles of China and Chinese Writers Union resolves to expel Hu Feng from all posts held in literary and art circles and to expand the campaign against him to include all Hu Feng elements throughout the country.
June 1. A China-Indonesia Friendship Association is formed at a meeting in Peking.
6. The State Council issues a directive calling for the 'planned eradication of illiteracy in the rural areas'.

tion of Agriculture' at a CCPCC-convened conference of Party secretaries in Peking. He calls for 'active, enthusiastic and systematic' Party leadership in the setting up of agricultural producers' cooperatives (APCs) and claims 'the high tide of cooperation has already swept a number of places and will soon sweep the whole country'.

August 1. China and Nepal issue a joint communiqué establishing diplomatic relations. Ambassadorial talks between China and the USA begin in Geneva; Wang Bingnan represents China, U. Alexis Johnson the USA.

September 10. Wang Bingnan and U. Alexis Johnson announce agreement in Geneva on the return of civilians to their respective countries.

October 4–11. The Sixth Plenum of the Seventh CCPCC is held in Peking. On its last day it adopts the 'Resolution on the Question of Agricultural Cooperativization' in accordance with Mao's report of July 31 and decides to hold the Eighth National Party Congress in the second half of 1956.

26. According to a spokesman for the Chinese People's Volunteers Headquarters, nineteen divisions of its troops have completed withdrawal from Korea by this day.

December 8. The Prime Minister of the German Democratic Republic, Otto Grotewohl, arrives in Peking for a visit.

25. A Treaty of Friendship and Cooperation between the PRC and the German Democratic Republic is signed in Peking.

1955

July 13. The Ministry of Education issues a directive calling for the promotion of a common Chinese language based on the Peking dialect.
18. Hu Feng is arrested as a counter-revolutionary. (At about this time many mass meetings against Hu's ideas took place throughout China.)
August 15. Some forty newspapers and magazines in Peking and Tianjin begin using the second batch of eighty-four simplified characters.
September 18. The CC of the Chinese New Democratic Youth League decides to change the name to Communist Youth League of China.
20–28. The first National Conference of Young Activists in Socialist Construction is held in Peking. Mao Zedong, Liu Shaoqi, Zhou Enlai and other leaders attend the final session.
October 15–23. A National Conference on Character Reform is held in Peking.
December 19. The Research Institute of Chinese Medicine opens in Peking.

D PUBLICATIONS

January–April. Zhao Shuli's novel *Sanli wan* is serialized in *Renmin wenxue* (*People's Literature*) and published as a book next year.
April 22. The journal *Jingji yanjiu* (*Economic Research*) begins publication in Peking.
May 13, 24. *People's Daily* publishes in two batches 'Guanyu Hu Feng fandang jituan de yixie, dierpi, cailiao' ('A Few, A Second Batch of Materials on the Hu Feng Anti-Party Clique') as part of the campaign against him.
June 10. *People's Daily* concludes the foregoing materials under the title 'Guanyu Hu Feng fangeming jituan de disanpi cailiao' ('Third Batch of Materials on the Hu Feng Counter-revolutionary Clique').
December. The first volume of Lenin's complete works is published in Chinese under the title *Liening quanji* (by 1959 all thirty-eight volumes appeared).

F DEATHS

February 9. Zhang Lan d. aged 83.
August 29. Hong Shen, dramatist, d. aged 62.

January 4. Zhou Enlai issues a cable declaring the PRC's recognition of the new Republic of the Sudan (proclaimed independent on January 1).

25. The Supreme State Conference adopts the Draft National Programme for Agricultural Development (1956–67), Mao Zedong's grand design to transform all aspects of the countryside in twelve years.

February 14. The Cambodian Prime Minister, Norodom Sihanouk, arrives in Peking for a visit at the head of a Cambodian delegation.

15. Zhu De addresses the Twentieth Congress of the CPSU, meeting in Moscow, as head of the CCPCC delegation. The previous day, the first of the Congress, CPSU First Secretary N. Khrushchev had given a report stating 'peaceful coexistence of states with different social systems' as 'the general line' of Soviet foreign policy and declaring that 'war is not fatalistically inevitable'.

18. Zhou Enlai and Norodom Sihanouk issue a joint communiqué in Peking on Sino-Cambodian relations and affirming the five principles of peaceful coexistence.

25. At a closed session of the Twentieth Congress of the CPSU Khrushchev criticizes Stalin and denounces the personality cult.

March 17. Mao orders the promulgation of the Model Regulations for an APC; it divides the development of APCs into two stages; elementary, in which the means of production are privately owned, and advanced, in which they are common property.

April 4. Zhou Enlai hails the independence of Morocco and Tunisia.

25. At a meeting of the CCPCC's Politburo, Mao Zedong makes his speech 'On The Ten Major Relationships', including those 'between heavy industry on the one hand and light industry and agriculture on the other', 'between Party and non-Party', and 'between China and other countries'.

May 12. The NPC Standing Committee decides to reorganize the State Council; twelve ministries and commissions are to be added and three ministries abolished.

29. The CPG's Ministry of Foreign Affairs issues a statement that China's sovereignty over the Nansha Islands in the South China Sea must not be violated.

30. China and Egypt issue a joint communiqué announcing the establishment of diplomatic relations and the exchange of ambassadors.

June 28. In a speech to the NPC, Zhou Enlai expresses the PRC's willingness to negotiate with the Taiwan authorities on the peaceful liberation of Taiwan.

30. Mao Zedong orders the proclamation of the Model Regulations for Advanced APCs, which lay down distribution of income, political

Mao Zedong makes his 'Hundred Flowers' speech 1956

A ECONOMICS

January 15. A rally in Peking celebrates the changeover of the city's industrial and commercial enterprises to joint state-private ownership earlier the same month. Other major cities proclaim the completion of their socialist transformation at about the same time, including Tianjin on January 18 and Shanghai on January 20.
March 13. A *People's Daily* editorial for the first time gives official sanction to the slogan, attributed to Mao Zedong and later used constantly, to undertake socialist construction 'more, faster, better and more economically'.
April 7. A Soviet delegation led by deputy Prime Minister A. Mikoyan, and CPG leaders issue a joint communiqué in Peking. The Soviet Union agrees to assist in the construction of fifty-five further factories and of a railway from Lanzhou (Gansu) to Aktogai, north of Alma-Ata in the Soviet Union.
11. A ceremony in Kunming marks the inauguration of air services from Kunming (Yunnan) to Rangoon, through Mandalay.
24. A ceremony in Guangzhou marks the inauguration of air services between China and the DRVN.
May 26. The first plane lands in Lhasa from Peking, signalling the beginning of air services between the two cities.
June 21. A Sino-Cambodian agreement is signed in Peking under which China is to give Cambodia 800,000,000 riels of aid.
July 13. A ceremony marks the completion of the 668-km. railway from Baoji (Shaanxi) to Chengdu (Sichuan), linking north-west to south-west China.
August 18. China and the Soviet Union sign in Peking an agreement on the joint exploration and development of natural resources in the basin of the Amur (Heilong) River, part of which forms part of the boundary between Heilongjiang and the Soviet Union.
September 27. The Eighth National Congress of the CCP adopts the Proposals for the Second Five-Year Plan for Development of the National Economy (1958–1962).

B OFFICIAL APPOINTMENTS, RESIGNATIONS, DISMISSALS ETC.

April 22. The Preparatory Committee for the Autonomous Region of Tibet is inaugurated in Lhasa with the Dalai Lama as Chairman.
September 26. The CCP Eighth National Congress elects the Eighth Central Committee, including Mao Zedong as Chairman, Chen Yun, Zhou Enlai, Zhu De, and Lin Biao.
28. The First Plenum of the Eighth CCPCC re-elects Mao Zedong

1956

work, cultural and welfare services and other things.

August 4. Zhou Enlai tells foreign journalists in Peking of China's support for the Egyptian government declaration of July 26 nationalizing the assets in Egypt of the Suez Canal Company.

6. The PRC offers visas to fifteen US journalists. The following day the US State Department issues a statement that 'it continues to be the policy of the State Department not to issue such passports', i.e. those 'validated for travel to Communist China'.

10. China and Syria issue a joint communiqué announcing their decision to establish diplomatic relations and exchange ambassadors.

20. The Laotian Prime Minister, Prince Souvanna Phouma, arrives in Peking for a visit at the head of a delegation.

25. Zhou Enlai and Souvanna Phouma issue a joint statement supporting the five principles of coexistence, and the development of bilateral economic and cultural relations.

September 14. China and Ceylon issue a joint communiqué in Peking agreeing to establish diplomatic relations and to develop economic and cultural ties.

15–27. The Eighth National Congress of the CCP, the first since liberation, is held in Peking, with 1021 delegates representing some 10,730,000 CCP members. Mao Zedong makes the opening speech and Liu Shaoqi the political report.

20. China and Nepal sign in Katmandu an agreement on the maintenance of friendly relations, trade between Nepal and Tibet, Nepalese military withdrawal from Tibet, and other matters.

24. China and Yemen issue a joint communiqué establishing diplomatic relations.

26. The Eighth National Congress of the CCP adopts a revised Party Constitution. It states that 'the CCP takes Marxism-Leninism as its guide to action' but makes no reference to Mao Zedong's thought.

30–October 14. Indonesian President Sukarno visits the PRC, the first non-Communist head of state to do so. On the last day a joint press communiqué is issued in Peking on the UN, West Irian, mutual trade and other matters.

November 1. The Chinese government issues a statement denouncing British and French aggression against Egypt. (On October 31, British and French planes began bombarding targets in Egypt; their forces landed in the Port Said region November 5.) The Chinese government issues a statement the same day supporting a Soviet declaration of October 30 on cooperation between the Soviet Union and other socialist countries. (October 30 was the day Soviet reinforcements entered Hungary against the government of Imre Nagy.)

as Chairman, Liu Shaoqi, Zhou Enlai, Zhu De and Chen Yun as deputy Chairmen, and Deng Xiaoping as Secretary-General.

C CULTURAL AND SOCIAL

January. Fifteen of Tianjin's drama troupes and sixty-nine of Shanghai's are nationalized.
1. China's newspapers appear with characters printed horizontally, reading from left to right, not, as previously, vertically from right to left.
14–20. The CCPCC convenes a meeting attended by 1279 CCP officials on the problems of intellectuals. Zhou Enlai gives the report on January 14; he calls for better use to be made of them in development, and claims that 80 per cent of them are either active or general supporters of the CCP.
28. The State Council resolves (*i*) to issue the Scheme for the Simplification of Chinese Characters; and (*ii*) to promote the standard common speech (*putonghua*).
February 10. The Character Reform Committee issues a draft Chinese phonetic alphabet (*Hanyu pinyin*).
March 1–April 4. A festival of spoken plays (*huaju*) is held in Peking; some fifty plays are performed.
26. The Soviet Union, China and nine other socialist countries sign in Moscow an agreement on the establishment of the Joint Institute for Nuclear Research in Moscow.
May 2. In a speech to the Supreme State Conference, Mao Zedong calls for greater intellectual and artistic freedom with the slogan 'let a hundred flowers bloom, let a hundred schools of thought contend'.
3. The Peking Hospital of Chinese Traditonal Medicine is formally set up, the largest and best-equipped of its kind in China.
June 1. China's first children's theatre opens in Peking with a performance of the children's play *Ma Lanhua*.
1–15. The Ministry of Culture holds a National Drama Work Conference in Peking; it decides to rearrange more classical operas, and liberalize theatre policy generally.
8. The Sino-Pakistan Friendship Association is set up in Peking.
12. China, the Soviet Union, the DPRK and DRVN sign in Peking an agreement to cooperate in fishery, limnological and oceanographic research in the Western Pacific.
August 12–16. The First National Youth Games are held in Qingdao (Shandong).

6. Zhou Enlai cables Janos Kadar congratulating him on the establishment of his Hungarian Worker-Peasant Revolutionary Government and announcing that China will send him material aid. (Soviet troops entered Budapest in support of Kadar on November 4.)

15. Mao Zedong closes the Second Plenum of the Eighth CCPCC (which had begun November 10) with a speech urging all officials to combat subjectivism, sectarianism, and bureaucratism.

18. Zhou Enlai arrives in Hanoi at the head of a delegation.

22. Zhou Enlai and Pham Van Dong of the DRVN issue a joint communiqué in Hanoi on the Suez and Hungarian crises and other matters. Zhou Enlai arrives in Phnom Penh.

28. Zhou Enlai and his delegation arrive in New Delhi.

December 10. Zhou Enlai and his delegation arrive in Rangoon for a visit.

20. Zhou Enlai and his delegation arrive in Karachi.

24. Mao Zedong gives a talk to music workers. (See D, September 9, 1979.)

September 28. A ceremony marks the opening of the Chinese Buddhist Academy in Peking.

D PUBLICATIONS

January 1. *Jiefang jun bao* (*Liberation Army Daily*) begins publication.
April 22. *Xizang ribao* (*Tibet Daily*) begins publication, using both Chinese and Tibetan.
June. A modern fully punctuated edition of Sima Guang's *Zizhi tongjian* (*Comprehensive Mirror of Aid to Government*) of 1085 is published in Peking.
July. Fu Yiling's *Ming Qing shidai shangren ji shangye ziben* (*Merchants and Commercial Capital in the Ming and Qing Periods*) is published.
October. *Zhongguo dianying* (*Chinese Cinema*) begins publication. (In July 1959 it combines with another periodical and is renamed *Dianying yishu* [*Cinema Art*].)
November. The People's Publishing House publishes *Sun Zhongshan xuanji* (*Selected Works of Sun Yatsen*) in two volumes to mark the ninetieth anniversary of Sun's birth (November 12, 1866).
December. The People's Publishing House publishes the first volume of *Makesi Engesi quanji* (*The Complete Works of Marx and Engels*) (and later volumes in subsequent years, vol. XXXIX in November 1974).

E NATURAL DISASTERS

Late May–early June. Flooding strikes Anhui, Henan and Jiangsu, inflicting severe damage on early summer crops, especially wheat.
August 25. As a result of disastrous typhoons in Zhejiang, Jiangsu, and Anhui early in August and severe flooding in Hebei, Henan, Jilin and Heilongjiang at the same time, the State Council decides to allocate 170,000,000 *yuan* to relief of the people in the afflicted areas.

F DEATHS

March 8. Banker Zhou Zuomin d. aged 72.
April 2. Tan Pingshan, CCP and CPG leader, d. aged 69.
   25. He Jian d. in Taibei aged 69.

1957 *Mao revisits Moscow; the Hundred Flowers and Anti-Rightist Campaigns*

January 7. Zhou Enlai arrives in Moscow at the head of the Chinese government delegation.

11. In Moscow, a Hungarian government delegation, led by Janos Kadar, the Chinese, led by Zhou Enlai, and Soviet leaders issue a joint communiqué on their intention to expand ties among the socialist countries. Zhou Enlai proceeds to Warsaw.

16. Zhou Enlai arrives in Budapest.

17. Zhou Enlai returns to Moscow, where, the following day, he and Soviet Prime Minister N. Bulganin issue a joint statement covering foreign affairs in general.

19. Zhou Enlai and his delegation arrive in Kabul, Afghanistan.

24. Zhou Enlai arrives in New Delhi and holds talks with Indian Prime Minister Nehru.

25. Zhou Enlai arrives in Katmandu, Nepal.

31. Zhou Enlai arrives in Colombo.

February 12. Zhou Enlai returns home to Peking.

27. At the meeting of the Supreme State Conference (held from February 27 to March 1) Mao Zedong makes his speech 'On the Correct Handling of Contradictions among the People'; he divides contradictions into antagonistic, 'between ourselves and the enemy', and non-antagonistic, 'those among the people'; he also discusses 'the question of eliminating counter-revolutionaries' and other matters.

March 9. A Czechoslovakian government delegation led by Prime Minister V. Siroky arrives in Peking.

27. China and Czechoslovakia sign a Treaty of Friendship and Cooperation in Peking.

April 11. A joint Sino-Polish statement is issued, signed by Zhou Enlai and Jozef Cyrankiewicz, Polish Chairman of the Council of Ministers (arrived in Peking April 7); it covers friendly relations between the two countries, implementation of the Geneva Agreements on Indochina, and other matters.

27. The CCPCC issues a directive to launch a rectification campaign against bureaucratism, sectarianism and subjectivism throughout the CCP, based on Mao Zedong's speech of February 27. NCNA releases the directive on April 30.

May 1–June 7. The period of 'the Hundred Flowers' reaches its climax with many open criticisms of the CCP from non-members; they come from all sectors of society and vary greatly in topic and intensity, some attacking the socialist system itself.

May 11. The Ministry of Foreign Affairs issues a statement protesting against the installation of US guided-missile units in Taiwan.

The Hundred Flowers and Anti-Rightist Campaigns 1957

A ECONOMICS

April 12. The 690-km. railway from Amoy (Fujian) to Yingtan (Jiangxi) formally opens to traffic. (In Yingtan it links with the Shanghai–Hangzhou–Nanchang–Zhuzhou line.)
24. The Yongding canal linking Peking with the Yongding River is opened; a hydroelectric power plant on the canal goes into operation.
July 1. Modern coal mines in Tongchuan (Shaanxi) and Baotou (Inner Mongolia) formally move into production.
31. In Hanoi, Chinese and DRVN representatives sign a trade agreement and a protocol under which China is to provide aid to the DRVN.
October 5. NCNA announces the completion of the 1179-km. highway from Kargilik (Xinjiang) to Gartok (Tibet).
15. A ceremony marks the formal opening of the road-railway Yangzi River bridge at Wuhan to traffic. The bridge links the two great railways from Wuhan north to Peking and south to Guangzhou; on November 10 these are renamed the Peking–Guangzhou railway.
November 6. China's biggest newsprint paper mill, the Guangzhou paper mill, begins production.
16. The Lanzhou (Gansu) thermopower station, the largest in China's north-west, formally starts generating.
December 12. A National Economic Planning Conference adopts the draft plan for 1958 on the principles of giving priority to heavy industry, catching up with Britain within fifteen years in steel output, and following the idea in the National Programme for Agricultural Development.
24. NCNA reports the completion of the first Chinese-made civil N-2 aircraft.
29. A ceremony marks the opening to traffic of the railway-road bridge over the Xiang River at Hengyang (Hunan).

B OFFICIAL APPOINTMENTS, RESIGNATIONS, DISMISSALS ETC.

June 17. The CCPCC and State Council announce the dismissal of several senior officials of Guangxi province, including the Chairman of the Guangxi Provincial People's Government, He Zhongshi, for failing to deal with a combination of flooding and drought in 1955, as a result of which 550 people starved to death in 1956.
September 4. The Guangxi Provincial People's Congress sets up the Preparatory Committee of the Guangxi Zhuang Autonomous Region, with Wei Guoqing, a Zhuang, as director.
December 13. The CCP Zhejiang Provincial Congress expels the

1957

June 7. The State Council decides to establish the Ningxia Hui and Guangxi Zhuang Autonomous Regions.

8. A *People's Daily* editorial argues that the rectification campaign is being used by rightists to try to overthrow the CCP. This and similar editorials on the following days signal the end of 'blooming and contending' and the beginning of the Anti-Rightist Campaign.

26–July 15. The Fourth Session of the First NPC is held in Peking. During it, Zhang Bojun, the Minister of Communications and a leader of the Chinese Democratic League, is criticized as a rightist along with two other ministers belonging to the League. Zhang makes a self-criticism on July 15 in the NPC.

July 11. Lu Dingyi, head of the CCP's Central Propaganda Department, makes a speech to the NPC called 'Our Essential Disagreement with the Bourgeois Rightists'; he calls for rightists to be 'mercilessly criticized'.

August 2. Zhou Enlai cables Tunisia, formally extending recognition to the Republic of Tunisia (where President Habib Bourguiba had replaced the monarch as head of state on July 25).

22. The US State Department issues a statement allowing twenty-four journalists to go to China, but adding that the US 'will not accord reciprocal visas to Chinese bearing passports issued by the Chinese Communist regime'. On August 25 *People's Daily* describes this arrangement as 'completely unacceptable to the Chinese people'.

28. DRVN President Ho Chi Minh arrives in Peking for a visit on his way home from Moscow.

30. Zhou Enlai and Mao Zedong cable congratulations to the Federation of Malaya on its independence (formally granted by Britain the following day) and their declaration of recognition of the new state.

September 20–October 9. The Third Plenum of the Eighth CCPCC is held in Peking. On September 23 Deng Xiaoping delivers his 'Report on the Rectification Campaign'; he divides the campaign into four stages: (*i*) 'frank and full discussion', (*ii*) 'counterattacking the rightists', (*iii*) 'emphasis on rectification and improvement', and (*iv*) the stage 'when each person must study documents, undertake criticism and self-review'.

27. Hungarian Prime Minister Janos Kadar arrives in Peking to take part in China's National Day celebrations (among several foreign dignitaries to participate). On October 4 a Sino-Hungarian joint statement is issued on international tensions and Sino-Hungarian friendship.

October 13. At a meeting of the Supreme State Conference Mao Zedong makes the speech 'Have Firm Faith in the Majority of the

Provincial Governor, Sha Wenhan, from the Party as a rightist, together with several other senior provincial officials.

29. The Hunan Provincial People's Congress dismisses the Provincial deputy Governor, Cheng Xingling, as a rightist.

C CULTURAL AND SOCIAL

February 5–9. The foundation congress of the Chinese Geophysical Association in Peking lays down work plans for seismologists, meteorologists and other geophysicists.

March 7. The Minister of Public Health, Li Dequan, makes a speech on 'Birth Control and Planned Families' to the CPPCC National Committee. She calls on public health personnel 'to regard the giving of guidance in planned childbirth' as their duty and condemns the attitude 'that contraception is only women's business'.

26–31. The Chinese Buddhist Association holds its Second National Congress in Peking.

April 12. The Chinese Taoist Association is formally founded at a conference in Peking.

May 10. The CCPCC issues a directive that leading personnel at all levels should take part in physical labour.

15. The Ministry of Public Health issues directives to promote contraception, and relax the limitations on sterilization and abortion operations.

15–25. The Third National Congress of the Chinese New Democratic Youth League is held in Peking; 1494 delegates attend, representing some 23,000,000 members. On May 24 the Congress confirms the change of name to the Communist Youth League of China. On May 25 Mao Zedong calls on the delegates to unite and adds that 'any word or deed at variance with socialism is completely wrong'.

19. As part of the 'Hundred Flowers' campaign, students at Peking University begin placing posters on a wall, soon known as the 'Democracy Wall', on the campus. The posters take many forms – essays, cartoons, poems etc – and cover many topics, including attacks on CCP policy towards intellectuals, on adherence to Soviet educational models, and on over-emphasis on politics in university courses.

June 6–September 17. During twenty-seven meetings the CCP nucleus of the Chinese Writers Union criticizes Ding Ling and other writers as rightists and an anti-Party clique.

July 15–August 2. A conference in Peking organizes the Chinese Catholic Patriotic Association with Pi Shushi, Archbishop of Shenyang, as Chairman. It resolves to recognize the religious authority of the

People'; he endorses Deng Xiaoping's four stages of the rectification campaign, predicting that the second, anti-rightist, stage will soon be over.

15. China and the Soviet Union conclude the Agreement on New Technology for National Defence, under which, according to a Chinese government statement of August 15, 1963, the USSR promised China a sample atomic bomb.

22. The NPC and CPPCC Standing Committees adopt a revised draft of Mao's National Programme for Agricultural Development (1956–67).

23. The Afghan Prime Minister Sardar Mohammed Daud arrives in Peking; he and Zhou Enlai issue a joint communiqué on Sino-Afghan relations and other matters on October 26.

November 2–21. Mao Zedong heads a Chinese delegation to the Soviet Union (mainly Moscow, November 2–20) to participate in celebrations for the fortieth anniversary of the October Socialist Revolution. The delegation includes Song Qingling, Deng Xiaoping, Peng Dehuai and Guo Moruo.

November 17. In Moscow Mao Zedong tells the Chinese students and trainees studying in the Soviet Union that the current international situation is one in which 'the east wind prevails over the west wind'; his confidence in the socialist camp is due in part to the launching of Sputnik I, the world's first artificial satellite, by the USSR on October 4, 1957.

December 30. The NPC Standing Committee ratifies the Sino-Indonesian Treaty Concerning the Question of Dual Nationality (see April 22, 1955).

Pope, but not his right to issue counter-revolutionary orders.

21. An announcement of several famous actors, including Mei Lanfang, Cheng Yanqiu and Zhou Xinfang, urging a halt to the indiscriminate revival of old dramas signals the end of the liberal phase of theatre.

September 9–20. The third National Women's Congress is held in Peking.

26. The Standing Committees of the NPC and CPPCC jointly resolve that all death sentences in future should be confirmed by the Supreme People's Court.

29. China's first planetarium, the Peking Planetarium, is formally opened.

October 14. The Inner Mongolian University in Huhehot formally starts classes, with 330 students.

December 2–12. The Eighth All-China Labour Congress is held in Peking.

18. The CCPCC and State Council jointly issue a directive to prevent the flow of peasants to the cities through ideological education and through control points along the main lines of communication.

D PUBLICATIONS

January 25. The journal *Shikan* (*Poetry*) begins publication.

February. The People's Literary Publishing House publishes *Yang Hansheng juzuo xuan* (*A Selection of Yang Hansheng's Dramas*) (the dates of completion of the four dramas range from August 2, 1937 to March 19, 1943). The Science Publishing House publishes *Putong yuyinxue gangyao* (*Outline of General Linguistics*) by Luo Changpei and Wang Jun.

June 19. *People's Daily* publishes Mao Zedong's 'Guanyu zhengque chuli renmin neibu maodun de wenti' ('On the Correct Handling of Contradictions among the People'). (NCNA had released the article the day before.)

July. Shanghai People's Publishing House publishes *Xinhai geming* (*The 1911 Revolution*), compiled by Chai Degeng and others, in eight volumes (compilers' preface dated December 1956).

December. Liang Bin's novel *Hongqi pu* (*Keep the Red Flag Flying*) is published in Peking.

E NATURAL DISASTERS

June 15. Zhou Enlai reports to the NPC Standing Committee that in 1956 some people had starved to death in Pingle (Guangxi), because

1958 The commune system is established

February 14. Zhou Enlai arrives in Pyongyang at the head of a Chinese government delegation.
19. Zhou Enlai, Chen Yi and Kim Il Sung issue a joint Chinese-DPRK statement in Pyongyang that all the Chinese People's Volunteers will withdraw from Korea by the end of 1958.
22. Zhou Enlai and his delegation return to Peking from the DPRK.
23. Zhou Enlai declares China's formal recognition of the United Arab Republic (proclaimed in Cairo on February 1).
March 5. The Guangxi Zhuang Autonomous Region is formally set up.
20. A Polish government delegation arrives in Peking, led by the deputy Chairman of the Council of Ministers, Piotr Jaroszewicz. Mao Zedong addresses the Chengdu Conference of the CCPCC (held from February 28 to about March 22). He discusses mass mobilization, agricultural development and various aspects of the Great Leap Forward. This was one of several speeches Mao made at the Chengdu Conference, which resulted in greater radicalization of the Great Leap Forward.
April 2–10. A Rumanian government delegation, led by the Chairman of the Council of Ministers, Chivu Stoica, visits China.
7. Zhou Enlai, Premier of the State Council, and Rumanian Chairman Chivu Stoica sign a joint statement on international tensions, socialist solidarity, disarmament and other matters.
29. China's first people's commune, the Sputnik Federated Cooperative, is set up in Henan.
May 5–23. The Second Session of the Eighth Congress of the CCP is held in Peking. On its last day it adopts the Draft National Programme for Agricultural Development (1956–67) and affirms the 'general line for building socialism' ('going all out, aiming high and achieving greater, faster, better and more economic results to build socialism'), an endorsement of the Great Leap Forward.

1957–8

of natural calamities (see also B, June 17).

July 21. Disastrous floods strike Shandong and Jiangsu provinces, submerging 1,100,000 hectares of land, affecting some 1,000,000 people, and drowning 557.

F DEATHS

September 16. Painter Qi Baishi d. in Peking aged 93.

The Great Leap Forward 1958

A ECONOMICS

January 1. The Second Five-Year Plan (Great Leap Forward) moves into operation.
March 5. Several Japanese and Chinese organizations sign the Fourth Civil Trade Agreement to the value of £35,000,000 either way.
10. China's biggest meat-packing plant goes into production in Wuhan.
April 7. China and Poland sign two trade agreements in Peking.
16. The 1958 Spring Export Commodities Fair opens in Guangzhou.
May 12. The first entirely Chinese-made motor car is produced in Changchun (Jilin).
July 1. The Ming Tombs reservoir near Peking is completed.
August 1. The 1000-km. Baotou–Lanzhou railway opens to traffic.
September 5. The Dahuofang reservoir near Fushun (Liaoning) is completed.
October 15–November 30. The Autumn Export Commodities Fair is held in Guangzhou.
November 25. The engineering for the Sanmen Gorge reservoir at the bend of the Yellow River near Xi'an is completed.
27. The first Chinese-built ocean-going freighter, the *Yuejin* (*Leap Forward*) of 15,930 tons dwt is launched in Lüda (Liaoning). (She foundered on rocks off South Korea on May 1, 1963 and sank.)
December 5. Trial flights are held of the first Chinese-made multi-purpose helicopter, manufactured in Harbin.

B OFFICIAL APPOINTMENTS, RESIGNATIONS, DISMISSALS ETC.

January 15. The Zhejiang Provincial People's Congress dismisses the provincial governor, Sha Wenhan, as a rightist and elects Zhou Jianren to replace him.

1958

18. Elections take place in Peking for the Municipal People's Congress, Mao Zedong, Zhou Enlai, Zhu De and other leaders voting together. NCNA reports the completion of elections in 22 provinces and municipalities.

June 13. China's first experimental atomic reactor goes into operation.

25. *Guangming Daily* reports that the students of Peking University have criticized the Vice-Chancellor of the University, Ma Yinchu, for his 'new population theory' which favoured strict population control: part of a campaign against the new population theory at this time.

July 16. The Minister of Foreign Affairs, Chen Yi, cables recognizing the Republic of Iraq government (declared July 14 following the overthrow of the monarchy). The CPG issues a statement denouncing US intervention in Lebanon; US troops had landed the day before.

24. China and Cambodia issue a joint communiqué in Phnom Penh announcing the establishment of diplomatic relations and exchange of ambassadors.

31. N. Khrushchev, First Secretary of the CPSU and Chairman of the USSR Council of Ministers, arrives in Peking.

August 3. Khrushchev and Mao Zedong sign a joint communiqué expressing unity of views on all matters, including the situation in the Middle East, international tension, disarmament and the need 'to end the tests and ban the use of atomic and hydrogen weapons'; however, the communiqué makes no mention of Taiwan, a currently pressing issue for China. Khrushchev returns home.

6. Mao Zedong visits a people's commune in Henan and declares his approval of communes.

15–25. Cambodian Prime Minister Prince Sihanouk visits Peking at the head of a government delegation.

17–30. The CCPCC's Politburo holds an enlarged meeting at Beidaihe (Hebei): the Beidaihe Conference.

23. The Chinese begin firing on the NP-held island of Quemoy, harassing shipping around the Mazu Islands.

24. Zhou Enlai and Norodom Sihanouk issue a joint statement declaring their desire to develop relations on the basis of the five principles of peaceful coexistence, among other matters.

25. China and Iraq issue a joint communiqué announcing the establishment of diplomatic relations and exchange of ambassadors.

27. Chinese coastal radio stations threaten to move into Quemoy and call on the NP troops there to surrender.

29. The Beidaihe Conference adopts the Decision of the Party Centre on the Question of Establishing People's Communes in the Rural Areas.

31. The NPC Standing Committee dismisses the Minister of Communications, Zhang Bojun, and two other ministers as rightists. Mao Zedong confirms the dismissals.
February 11. Mao Zedong appoints Chen Yi to succeed Zhou Enlai as Minister of Foreign Affairs.
May 25. The Fifth Plenum of the CCPCC elects Lin Biao as deputy Chairman of the CCPCC, and member of the standing committee of the Politburo. It also elects Ke Qingshi, Li Jingquan and Tan Zhenlin to the Politburo.
October 12. The appointment of the deputy Minister of National Defence Huang Kecheng as Chief of the General Staff of the PLA to replace Su Yu is announced in Peking.
December 10. The Sixth Plenum of the Eighth CCPCC approves 'Comrade Mao Zedong's proposal that he will not stand as candidate for Chairman of the PRC for the next term of office'.

C CULTURAL AND SOCIAL

January 15. A large meeting in Peking begins a hygiene campaign in the city to get rid of the four pests (*sihai*) flies, mosquitoes, rodents, and sparrows.
  18. Chinese and Soviet representatives sign in Moscow protocols providing for joint research and Soviet help to China in studying major scientific and technological subjects, and for cooperation between the agricultural science academies and the Ministries of Higher Education of the two countries.
March 13. The Ministry of Education issues a directive to all schools to teach the *Hanyu pinyin*.
April 1. China's first museum on a neolithic site opens at Banpo, a village near Xi'an (Shaanxi).
  9–14. The Third National Youth Congress is held in Peking. On its last day it resolves to mobilize young people to take a more active role in socialist construction.
June 13–July 15. The Ministry of Culture holds a forum on drama in Peking; in accordance with general Great Leap Forward policy it introduces the idea of 'walking on two legs' in theatre: i.e. emphasizing both traditional and modern drama.
  23. The Nationalities Research Institute of Academia Sinica is set up in Peking.
  29. Pope Pius XII issues the encyclical *Ad Apostolorum Principis* (*To the Leaders of the Apostles*), condemning the Church of the Catholic Patriotic Association and declaring its bishops invalid.

1958

September 4. The CPG declares that the breadth of the territorial sea of the PRC is twelve nautical miles. This was a threat to US ships bringing supplies to Quemoy Island. Dulles issues a statement of the US intention to help defend Quemoy and Mazu Islands against any attack by China.

6. Zhou Enlai issues a statement reaffirming China's right to liberate its own territory, including Taiwan and the offshore islands; and suggests resumption of the Sino-US ambassadorial talks.

22. The Chinese government recognizes the provisional government of the Algerian Republic (set up on September 19).

30. Dulles declares at a news conference that 'if there were a ceasefire in the area which seemed to be reasonably dependable, I think it would be foolish to keep these large [NP] forces on these [offshore] islands'.

October 6. An announcement by the PRC Minister of National Defence, Peng Dehuai, of a seven-day suspension of the bombardment of Quemoy effectively ends the offshore islands crisis.

7. Chen Yi cables China's recognition of the Republic of Guinea (proclaimed as a republic independent of France on October 2).

13. Peng Dehuai issues an order to Fujian PLA troops to suspend the shelling of Quemoy for two further weeks.

23. Chiang Kaishek and Dulles issue a joint communiqué in Taibei in which the former states that 'the principal means' of restoring 'freedom to its people on the mainland' is 'the implementation of Dr Sun Yatsen's three people's principles ... and not the use of force'.

25. The Ningxia Hui Autonomous Region is formally established.

26. The Chinese People's Volunteers complete their withdrawal from Korea.

November 1. China and Morocco issue a joint communiqué announcing the establishment of diplomatic relations.

22–December 9. Kim Il Sung leads a DPRK delegation to China.

28–December 10. The Sixth Plenum of the Eighth CCPCC is held in Wuchang; it reverses some of the more radical innovations of the Great Leap Forward.

December 1. The CPG decides to establish diplomatic relations with the Republic of the Sudan.

3–21. A delegation of the Algerian Republic's provisional government visits China. A joint communiqué is signed December 20.

8. Zhou Enlai and Kim Il Sung sign a joint communiqué promising the development of mutual friendship and demanding withdrawal of UN troops from Korea.

10. The Wuchang CCPCC Plenum adopts the Resolution on Some Questions Concerning the People's Communes.

1958

September 2. Peking Television formally begins broadcasting.
25, 28. NCNA reports claim illiteracy as 'basically eliminated' in Heilongjiang, Jilin, Gansu, Guizhou, Zhejiang, Henan, Fujian, Guangdong and Shanxi provinces.
October 22–26. An 'assembly of protest' is held in the Changsha cathedral against the Pope's encyclical of June 29.

D Publications

January. Yang Mo's novel *Qingchun zhi ge* (*The Song of Youth*) is published.
February. *Zhongguo huaju yundong wushi nian shiliao ji 1907–1957* (*Collection of Historical Material on the Chinese Spoken Play Movement over the Fifty Years 1907 to 1957*) by Tian Han and others is published by the Chinese Drama Publishing House in Peking (further volumes follow in April 1959 and April 1963). Ma Yinchu's *Wo de jingji lilun zhexue sixiang he zhengshi lichang* (*My Economic Theory, Philosophical Thought and Political Stand*) is published.
15. *Yinyue yanjiu* (*Musical Research*) begins publication.
March 4. The English-language weekly *Peking Review* begins publication in Peking.
May 3. Tian Han's play *Guan Hanqing* is published in *Juben* (*Play Scripts*).
June. Tao Juyin's five-volumed *Beiyang junfa tongzhi shiqi shihua* (*On the Period of Northern Warlord Rule*) is published in Peking.
1. *Hongqi* (*Red Flag*), the organ of the CCPCC, begins publication in Peking.
September. The People's Literary Publishing House publishes Gao Yubao's novel *Gao Yubao* and Peking University Chinese Department's *Zhongguo wenxue shi* (*History of Chinese Literature*); Liu Liu's novel *Liehuo jingang* (*Steel in the Raging Flames*) is published in Peking.
4. The monthly *Minzu yanjiu* (*Nationalities Research*) begins publication.
November 25. The bimonthly *Qianxian* (*Front Line*) begins publication, under the auspices of the Peking Municipal CCP Committee.

F Deaths

January 4. Shi Zhaoji d. in USA, aged 80.
March 9. Peking Opera actor Cheng Yanqiu d. aged 54.
15. Wang Chonghui d. aged 76.
May 20. CCPCC member Lai Ruoyu d. in Peking aged 48.
October 17. Zheng Zhenduo d. in a plane crash aged 60.
December 13. Luo Changpei d. aged 59.

1959 Revolt in Tibet suppressed

January 22–29. A German Democratic Republic delegation led by Prime Minister Otto Grotewohl visits Peking. Chen Yi and Grotewohl sign a joint statement on January 27 on the German question and other matters.

24–February 9. Zhou Enlai visits Moscow to attend the Twenty-first Congress of the CPSU, held January 27 to February 5, which he addresses January 28.

February 9–12. The DRVN's President, Ho Chi Minh, visits Peking.

March 10. Armed rebellion against the Peking government starts in Tibet; the rebels surround the PLA headquarters and CPG offices in Lhasa.

17. The Dalai Lama leaves Lhasa.

19. The Tibetan local government directs the Tibetan local army and others to launch a general offensive against the PLA garrison in Lhasa.

20–23. The Chinese PLA puts down the Tibetan revolt in Lhasa, and continues its suppression in other places in the following period.

28. The State Council orders the dissolution of the Tibetan local government and the transfer of its functions and powers to the Preparatory Committee for the Tibetan Autonomous Region.

31. The Dalai Lama enters India.

April 14. The Panchen Lama arrives in Peking to attend the NPC session.

18–28. The First Session of the Second NPC takes place in Peking. On the last day it adopts the Resolution on the Question of Tibet which directs the Preparatory Committee for the Tibetan Autonomous Region 'to carry out democratic reforms in Tibet step by step'.

29. The Wuhan *Changjiang ribao* (*Yangzi Daily*) reports the breakup of a counter-revolutionary group in the city which had been 'plotting against the people' since mid-March.

29–May 7. The Hungarian Prime Minister, Dr Ferenc Muennich, visits China. On May 6, Zhou Enlai and Muennich sign the Treaty of Friendship and Cooperation.

May 18. The Ministry of Foreign Affairs issues a statement accusing the Laotian government of 'repudiating the Geneva agreements and endangering peace in Indochina'. (On May 11 the Royal Lao government had ordered some former Pathet Lao units to surrender their arms, and when they refused they were surrounded by Royal Lao forces on May 14.)

June 5. The International Commission of Jurists issues a statement in Geneva saying there has been a 'deliberate violation of fundamental human rights in Tibet'.

The Lushan Plenum results in Peng Dehuai's dismissal 1959

A ECONOMICS

January 15. China's first oil pipeline goes into operation; 147 km. long, it links the Karamai oilfields (Xinjiang) with the refinery at Dushanzi (Xinjiang).
16. A Sino-Albanian trade agreement for 1961–65 and an agreement for a PRC loan are signed in Peking.
February 6. Lauching of the 5,100-ton *Jiangsu*, China's biggest ferry-boat, to be used to connect the Tianjin–Pukou and Nanjing–Shanghai railways across the Yangzi at Nanjing.
7. The 605-km. Guizhou–Guangxi railway, from Guiyang to Liuzhou, opens to traffic. Zhou Enlai and Khrushchev sign an agreement in Moscow on Soviet economic and technical aid in the period 1959 to 1967.
18. The DRVN and China sign in Peking six agreements and protocols on trade and PRC aid to the DRVN, and exchange notes on a gift of 100,000,000 *yuan* to the DRVN.
April 9. The Ministry of Railways announces the completion of double tracking of the Peking–Hankou railway.
June 6. A hydro-electric station of 32,000 kW begins operating east of Shenyang.
October 2. The Xining–Lanzhou railway formally opens to traffic.
30. A large open-hearth furnace goes into operation at the Wuhan iron and steel works.
November 1. A ceremony marks the completion of the Luoyang tractor plant, China's first.
December 16. *Jane's All the World's Aircraft* devotes a section to the PRC for the first time and says that China's state aircraft factory near Shenyang is producing MIG-17 jet fighters at the rate of 20–25 per month.

B OFFICIAL APPOINTMENTS, RESIGNATIONS, DISMISSALS ETC.

March 28. The State Council appoints the Panchen Lama Chairman of the Preparatory Committee for the Tibetan Autonomous Region for as long as the Dalai Lama 'is under duress by the rebels'.
April 27. The NPC appoints Liu Shaoqi as Chairman of the PRC to succeed Mao Zedong, Mme Song Qingling and Dong Biwu as deputy Chairmen of the PRC, and Zhu De as Chairman of the Standing Committee of the NPC.
28. The NPC approves the composition of Zhou Enlai's new State Council; new appointments among the sixteen Vice-Premiers include Tan Zhenlin, Lu Dingyi and Luo Ruiqing.

25. The State Council issues an order adopting the international metric system as China's basic system of weights and measures.

July 17. The Preparatory Committee for the Tibetan Autonomous Region adopts the Resolution Concerning the Carrying out of Democratic Reforms.

August 2–16. The Eighth Plenum of the Eighth CCPCC is held in Lushan (Jiangxi): the Lushan Plenum.

25. An armed clash on the Sino-Indian border results in the withdrawal of an Indian garrison from Longju to a position south of the McMahon line in the North-east Frontier Agency (NEFA).

26. NCNA releases the communiqué of the Lushan Plenum. According to the communiqué, the Plenum reduces targets for 1959, and concludes that 'the principal danger now facing the achievement of a continued leap forward this year is the emergence of right opportunist ideas among some cadres'; they oppose the Great Leap Forward and people's communes, and must be criticized.

September 8. Zhou Enlai writes to Nehru, Prime Minister of India, setting forth China's position on the Sino-Indian border; he argues that the Sino-Indian border has never been delineated and that China does not recognize the McMahon Line.

26. Nehru writes to Zhou Enlai setting forth India's position on the Sino-Indian border; he argues that the McMahon Line must 'be regarded as binding on both China and Tibet'.

Kim Il Sung and Ho Chi Minh arrive in Peking to take part in the celebrations for the PRC's tenth anniversary (Kim leaves October 2; Ho, October 4).

30. N.S. Khrushchev arrives in Peking and makes a speech at a banquet in Peking celebrating the tenth anniversary of the PRC. (From September 25 to 27, Khrushchev had held talks with US President D. Eisenhower at Camp David, USA, thus beginning a period of Soviet-US detente.)

October 4. Khrushchev ends his visit to Peking. China and Guinea issue a joint communiqué announcing their intention to establish diplomatic relations and exchange ambassadors.

7–11. The Indonesian Minister of Foreign Affairs, Subandrio, visits Peking. On the last day he and Chen Yi sign a joint communiqué on various international issues and on the Chinese in Indonesia; they agree that 'the economic resources of those Chinese nationals will still play a useful role in the economic development of Asia'. (A series of Indonesian government regulations had created difficulties for Chinese businessmen in Indonesia.)

21. An armed clash in Ladakh on the Sino-Indian border results in

August 16. The Lushan Plenum adopts the Resolution of the CCPCC Concerning the Anti-Party Clique headed by Peng Dehuai, which dismisses Peng Dehuai, Huang Kecheng, and others from all posts except membership of the CCPCC and Politburo.

September 17. Chairman Liu Shaoqi proclaims the appointment of Lin Biao as Minister of National Defence (to replace Peng Dehuai), Luo Ruiqing as Chief of the General Staff of the PLA (to replace Huang Kecheng) and Xie Fuzhi as Minister of Public Security (to replace Luo Ruiqing).

C CULTURAL AND SOCIAL

March 14. China's Second National Central Library is opened in Shanghai on the basis of a number of university and other libraries, the first being in Peking.

July 7. Thirty-three members of a mixed men's and women's expedition reach the peak of Muztagh Ata (Xinjiang) in the Pamirs, 7546 metres above sea level.

17. The Quanzhou (Fujian) Museum is opened, showing the history of China's contacts with foreign countries.

September 5. A nationwide survey of dialects conducted by the Ministry of Education is completed.

9–October 3. The PRC's First National Games are held in the Peking Workers' Stadium.

17. Liu Shaoqi issues an amnesty order for certain reformed war criminals, common criminals and counter-revolutionaries.

21–October 10. A large-scale drama festival takes place in Peking to mark the tenth anniversary of the founding of the PRC.

D PUBLICATIONS

The Foreign Languages Press publishes the English translation, by Yang Hsien-yi and Gladys Yang, of Lu Hsun's *A Brief History of Chinese Fiction*.

March. Chen Jing's novel *Jinsha jiang pan* (*Beside the Jinsha River*) is published.

April. *Qi Baishi yanjiu* (*Research on Qi Baishi*) by Wang Zhaowen and others is published in Shanghai.

September. Ouyang Shan's novel *Sanjia xiang* (*Three Family Lane*) is published by the Guangdong People's Publishing House (completed July 1, 1959). The Zhonghua Book Company publishes a modern edition of the *Shiji* (*Records of a Historian*).*Weida de shinian, Zhonghua renmin gongheguo jingji he wenhua jianshe chengjiu de tongji* (*Ten Great*

casualties on both sides, including the deaths of nine Indian border police.

The UN General Assembly adopts a resolution calling for 'respect for the fundamental human rights of the Tibetan people'. The CPG on October 23 issues a statement describing the resolution as unlawful.

November 7. Zhou Enlai writes to Nehru proposing mutual withdrawal of Chinese and Indian troops twenty kilometres from the McMahon Line in the eastern sector, and the line of 'actual control' in the western sector; and a meeting with Nehru.

16. Nehru writes to Zhou Enlai replying to his suggestions of November 7 with 'alternative proposals'.

1960 *Soviet withdrawal of experts; Sino-Soviet dispute takes decisive turn for the worse*

January 20. China and Indonesia exchange ratifications of their Dual Nationality Treaty (see April 22, 1955).

24–29. General Ne Win, Prime Minister of Burma, visits China. On January 28 he and Zhou Enlai sign in Peking the Agreement on the Question of the Boundary between the Two Countries and Treaty of Friendship and Mutual Non-aggression.

February 12. The Indian ambassador to China, G. Parthasarathi, hands Zhou Enlai a letter from Nehru inviting him to New Delhi for talks.

March 21. In Peking, the Nepalese Prime Minister, Shri Bishweshwar Prasad Koirala, and Zhou Enlai sign the Sino-Nepalese Agreements on the Question of the Boundary between the Two Countries and on Economic Aid; they also issue a joint communiqué on bilateral relations and other matters.

30–April 10. The Second Session of the Second NPC is held in Peking.

April 15. Zhou Enlai arrives in Rangoon.

16. *Red Flag* warns against changing Lenin's notion of the nature

1959–60

Years, Statistics on the Success of the PRC's Economic and Cultural Construction) is published in Peking by the People's Publishing House.
December. The Shanghai People's Publishing House publishes *Zhongguo jindai shishi ji* (*Chronology of Events in China's Modern History*). The Zhonghua Book Company publishes a modern edition of the *Sanguo zhi* (*Records of the Three Kingdoms*).

E Natural Disasters

June 11. Torrential rains begin in Guangdong. Until the end of the month widespread serious flooding occurs in the province.
July–August. Serious drought reaches a climax in huge areas of China. Some 30 per cent of China's land under cultivation is affected in seventeen provinces and autonomous regions, including Henan, Shandong, Anhui, Jiangsu, Hubei, Hunan, Shaanxi, Shanxi and Sichuan.
August 14. NCNA reports that locusts are afflicting the crops in Henan, Hebei, Shandong, Jiangsu and Anhui. (Collectively these were the worst natural calamities China had experienced for several decades.)

F Deaths

October 9. Li Jishen d. in Peking aged 75.
December 16. Wu Zhongxin d. in Taibei aged 75.

Serious national calamities affect agricultural production; famine results   1960

A Economics

January 3. China and Ceylon sign an agreement in Colombo for the exchange of Chinese rice for Ceylonese rubber.
11. The Changchun tractor plant goes into production.
30. The Soviet-equipped Nanjing heat and power plant begins operation.
March 5. A ceremony marks the completion of the Shenzhen reservoir in Baoan (Guangdong).
22. Mao Zedong's note on industrial development dated this day. (See A, March 22, 1970.)
April 1. A ceremony marks the formal opening of the 256-km. Peking–Chengde (Hebei) railway.
19. Lhasa's Ngajim hydroelectric plant, the largest on the Tibet plateau, formally begins generating.
21. A ceremony marks the formal opening to traffic of the new double-track railway bridge over the Yellow River at Zhengzhou (Henan).

1960

of imperialism, and indirectly but clearly takes issue with Soviet attitudes. This represents the beginning of polemics between China and the Soviet Union.

19. Zhou Enlai arrives in New Delhi.

25. Zhou Enlai and Nehru sign a joint communiqué that representatives of both governments should jointly study problems relating to the joint border and submit reports to their governments.

26. Zhou Enlai arrives in Katmandu.

28. Zhou Enlai and Koirala sign the Sino-Nepalese Treaty of Peace and Friendship in Katmandu.

29. Zhou Enlai arrives back in Peking.

May 5. Zhou Enlai arrives in Phnom Penh.

9. Zhou Enlai arrives in Hanoi.

14. Zhou Enlai returns to China.

27–June 1. Zhou Enlai visits the People's Republic of Mongolia.

31. Zhou Enlai and the Mongolian Prime Minister, Y. Tsedenbal, sign the Sino-Mongolian Treaty of Friendship and Mutual Assistance in Ulan Bator, as well as agreements on economic and technical aid and cooperation.

June 21. At the Third Congress of the Rumanian Workers' Party in Bucharest, Khrushchev attacks the Chinese notions of Leninism, imperialism and war.

28. Chinese troops kill a Nepalese officer and capture other Nepalese on the joint border.

July 2. Zhou Enlai writes to Nepalese Prime Minister Koirala apologizing for the June 28 incident on the Sino-Nepalese border.

4. China returns the Nepalese personnel captured and killed from the June 28 incident.

5. NCNA announces that China and Ghana have decided to establish diplomatic relations.

16. The Soviet Union notifies China of its decision to withdraw all its experts within a month (according to *People's Daily* of July 20, 1963).

18. China pays Nepal 50,000 rupees as compensation for the June 28 incident.

23. Sino-Cuban trade, technical and cultural cooperation agreements are signed in Havana.

August 13. Agence France Presse reports from Peking that the departure of Soviet technicians and their families from Peking and from the industrial provinces has 'increased at such a rate since the end of July that they are now coming to be spoken of openly in diplomatic circles in the Chinese capital as a veritable exodus'.

26. The Sino-Afghan Treaty of Friendship and Mutual Non-Aggres-

22. The *Dongfeng* (*East Wind*), claimed by NCNA as the first entirely Chinese-designed and made 10,000-ton ocean-going freighter, is launched at Shanghai's Jiangnan dockyard.

May 23. The Sino-DPRK Border River Navigation Cooperation Agreement is signed in Peking.

October 13. China and the DPRK sign two agreements in Peking under which China grants a long-term loan of 420,000,000 roubles, equipment and technical aid.

November 15. Representatives of Baoan (Guangdong) and Hongkong sign an agreement whereby the Shenzhen reservoir will supply 5,000,000,000 gallons of water per year to Hongkong.

B OFFICIAL APPOINTMENTS, RESIGNATIONS, DISMISSALS ETC.

April 17. The appointment of Lu Ping to replace Ma Yinchu as Vice-Chancellor of Peking University is announced.

May 6. NCNA announces the election, by the Shanghai Catholic Conference (see C, April 23–26), of Zhang Jiashu as Bishop of Shanghai.

C CULTURAL AND SOCIAL

February 10. *People's Daily* announces the 'recent' approval by the Xinjiang Uighur Autonomous Region's People's Council of a new Uighur and Kazakh script.

March 6–20. A national conference on 'cultural work in the peasant villages' is held in Taiyuan (Shanxi). It calls for greater 'popularization' of culture in the villages.

16. The China-Latin American Friendship Association is founded in Peking.

17. The Shanghai Intermediate People's Court sentences the Catholic Bishop of Shanghai, Gong Pinmei, to life imprisonment for a variety of crimes, including 'setting up counter-revolutionary organizations and training special agents'. The next day it sentences the American Bishop James Walsh to twenty years' imprisonment for spying and other crimes.

April 9. In a speech to the NPC, Lu Dingyi, head of the CCPCC's Propaganda Department, outlines proposed reforms in primary and secondary education. The plans are to 'shorten the schooling period, appropriately raise the educational level, control the study hours and increase participation in physical labour'.

12. The Sino-African People's Friendship Association is founded in Peking.

23–26. The Shanghai Municipal Catholic Patriotic Association is

1960

sion is signed in Kabul.

September. The CCPCC writes to the CPSU calling for 'comradely and unhurried discussion' and 'full preparation' for the coming Moscow Conference, in order to settle the Sino-Soviet dispute.

10–15. President Sekou Touré of Guinea visits China. On September 13 he and Zhou Enlai sign the Sino-Guinean Treaty of Friendship and two agreements on trade and aid.

28. NCNA announces that China and Cuba have decided to establish diplomatic relations.

28–October. Burmese Prime Minister U Nu visits Peking. On October 1, he and Zhou Enlai sign the Sino-Burmese Boundary Treaty.

October 17. Zhou Enlai and Chen Yi cable Mali expressing a wish for diplomatic relations; Mali answers, agreeing, October 19.

25–26. A meeting of the Standing Committee of the Preparatory Committee for the Tibetan Autonomous Region decides to issue title deeds to the emancipated peasants of Tibet, because 'the democratic reform has been mainly completed in the agricultural districts'.

November 2–4. DRVN's President, Ho Chi Minh, visits Peking on his way to the Moscow Conference.

5. Liu Shaoqi and Deng Xiaoping arrive in Moscow at the head of a CCP and Chinese government delegation to Moscow to celebrate the forty-third anniversary of the Socialist Revolution and to attend the Moscow Conference of Representatives of Communist and Workers' Parties.

December 1. The Moscow Conference unanimously adopts a 'Statement' (published December 6), the result of three weeks' bitter ideological debate.

2. Liu Shaoqi begins a series of goodwill engagements in the Soviet Union. He and his delegation arrive back in Peking December 9.

3–6. Ho Chi Minh visits Peking on his way home from Moscow.

14. The Panchen Lama reports to the NPC Standing Committee on progress in Tibet; he claims land reform is nearly complete and that the development of democratic reform is 'normal and healthy'. The Somali Republic agrees to a suggestion from Zhou Enlai (November 28) to establish diplomatic relations.

14–26. Cambodian Prince Norodom Sihanouk visits China.

15. China and Indonesia sign in Jakarta the Agreement for the Implementation of the Dual Nationality Treaty (see April 22, 1955).

19. The Sino-Cambodian Treaty of Friendship and Mutual Non-Aggression is signed in Peking, together with other documents concerning aid, navigation and other matters.

set up at a conference of Catholics in Shanghai.

May 25. For the first time, Chinese mountaineers reach the summit of Jomo Lungma (Mt Everest).

June 1–11. A national conference of 'advanced units and workers in socialist construction in the cultural, hygiene, physical education and journalism fields' is held in Peking, jointly sponsored by the CCPCC and State Council.

5–9. The World Federation of Trade Unions holds its eleventh session in Peking.

10. China and the Soviet Union sign an agreement in Peking on cooperation between the two countries' medical science academies.

July 22–August 13. The Third Congress of the Federation of Literary and Art Circles of China is held in Peking.

October 6. Xinjiang University, the Autonomous Region's first, formally opens in Urumchi with some 1000 students.

November 24. Qinghai University formally opens in Xining with some 2800 students.

D PUBLICATIONS

January. *Zhongguo gudian xiqu lunzhu jicheng* (*Collection of Works on Chinese Classical Theatre*), vol. VIII, is published in Peking. (The other nine volumes were published July–December 1959.)

April. The People's Literary Publishing House publishes *Tangshi xuan* (*Selection of Tang Poems*) edited by Ma Mouyuan in two volumes.

October 1. The fourth volume of *Mao Zedong xuanji* (*Mao Zedong's Selected Works*) is published.

E NATURAL DISASTERS

June 9. A typhoon strikes Guangdong and Fujian. This was one of a number of factors causing disastrous flooding in these two provinces in May and June.

December 29. NCNA reveals for the first time the extent of the natural disasters of 1960, claimed as the worst in a century. A combination of drought, floods, typhoons and insect pests has ravaged '60,000,000 hectares of land, or over half of China's total farm land . . . . Of this, 20,000,000 to 26,000,000 hectares were seriously affected, with some land producing nothing'. Only Tibet and Xinjiang escaped the disasters. Widespread and serious famine results.

F DEATHS

May 23. Yan Xishan, former Shanxi warlord, d. aged 76.
   29. Politburo member Lin Boqu d. in Peking aged 75.

1961 Zhou Enlai and Khrushchev clash in Moscow

January 2–9. Zhou Enlai heads a delegation to Burma to celebrate independence day (January 4); in his and Burmese President U Win Maung's presence the instruments of ratification of the Boundary Treaty (see October 1, 1960) are exchanged January 4.

14–18. The Ninth Plenum of the Eighth CCPCC is held in Peking.

20. NCNA releases the communiqué of the Ninth Plenum of the CCPCC. The decisions of the Plenum mentioned in it include (*i*) concentration on agriculture and light industry, and reduction in emphasis on heavy industry, (*ii*) implementation of a nationwide rectification campaign, and (*iii*) the establishment of six regional CCP bureaus, North-east, North, East, Central-south, South-west and North-west.

February 20. NCNA releases the text of the joint communiqué that China and the Republic of the Congo (Stanleyville) have decided to establish diplomatic relations and exchange ambassadors.

March 1–22. A central work conference takes place in Guangzhou, the Guangzhou Conference. It discusses the communes and other matters. Deng Xiaoping asserts that the communes are developing too quickly and without enough preparatory investigation.

April 1. In Jakarta the PRC and Indonesian Ministers of Foreign Affairs, Chen Yi and Subandrio, sign a Treaty of Friendship and an Agreement on Cultural Cooperation.

6–16. The Burmese Prime Minister, U Nu, takes a holiday in Yunnan province. Zhou Enlai holds talks with him and a joint communiqué is issued April 16 on technical aid, NP troops in Burma and other matters.

22–25. Prime Minister Prince Souvanna Phouma of Laos and Prince Souphanouvong, Chairman of the Neo Lao Hak Xat (Pathet Lao) visit China. On April 25, Zhou Enlai and Souvanna Phouma issue a joint communiqué in Hangzhou, announcing the establishment of diplomatic relations.

May 16. The fourteen-nation Geneva Conference on Laos opens; Chen Yi heads the Chinese delegation and makes his first speech. Among other points, he demands the abolition of the South-east Asia Treaty Organization which he describes as 'the root of tension . . . in the whole of South-east Asia'.

June 13–15. Indonesian President Sukarno visits China. Instruments of ratification of the Sino-Indonesian Treaty of Friendship are exchanged June 14.

July 10–15. A DPRK delegation, led by Kim Il Sung, visits China.

11. Zhou Enlai and Kim Il Sung sign in Peking the Sino-Korean Treaty of Friendship, Cooperation and Mutual Assistance.

A Economics

January 9. In Rangoon Zhou Enlai and Burmese Prime Minister U Nu sign an Agreement on Economic and Technical Cooperation.
   21. China and Cuba sign two contracts in Havana on the purchase of Cuban sugar and export of Cuban copper ore to the PRC.
   31. The PRC and DRVN sign an agreement under which China will provide loans of 141,750,000 roubles, and five other documents on economic matters.
February 2. China and Albania sign a Treaty of Commerce and Navigation in Peking. They also sign four protocols and one agreement covering PRC aid to Albania. The Canadian Minister of Agriculture, Alvin Hamilton, announces the sale of 28,000,000 bushels of wheat and 12,000,000 of barley to the PRC.
   6. The Australian Wheat Board announces the sale of 1,050,000 tons of wheat and 40,000 tons of flour to the PRC.
April 25. China and Albania sign three protocols and other documents in Peking concerning PRC aid to Albania and related economic matters.
May 2. The Canadian Minister of Agriculture, Alvin Hamilton, announces the signing of an agreement to sell 5,000,000 tons of wheat and flour and 1,000,000 tons of barley to China.
   11. The Australian Wheat Board announces that China has ordered from Australia 2,250,000 tons of wheat, barley, oats, flour and milk powder.
December 26. China and Albania sign in Peking an agreement to establish a joint-stock shipping company.

C Cultural and Social

March 1. A *Red Flag* editorial calls for 'the hundred flowers to bloom in academic research', i.e. for greater liberalism.
April 4–14. The Twenty-sixth World Table Tennis Championships are held in Peking with over 200 players participating. Chinese players win both the men's and women's singles titles (respectively Zhuang Zedong and Qiu Zhonghui) as well as the men's team event.
May 11. NCNA reports that the house, temple and tomb of Confucius in Qufu (Shandong) have been restored.
June 19. Zhou Enlai addresses a conference on literature and art. (See D, February 4, 1979.)
July 1. The Museums of Chinese History and of the Chinese Revolution are formally opened simultaneously in the same building in Peking.
September 14. NCNA reports the discovery of 138 stone tools and

1961

August 14–19. Ghana's President, Kwame Nkrumah, visits China.

18. China and Ghana sign a Treaty of Friendship and three other agreements on economic and cultural cooperation and trade.

September 18. The Stanleyville Congolese government announces the termination of diplomatic relations with the PRC.

28–October 15. King Mahendra Bir Bikram Shah Deva of Nepal and his Queen visit China.

October 5. Liu Shaoqi and King Mahendra sign the Sino-Nepalese Boundary Treaty in Peking.

15. Zhou Enlai leaves Peking for Moscow at the head of a Chinese delegation to attend the Twenty-second Congress of the CPSU, held October 17–31.

18–November 4. The General Political Department of the PLA holds an important army-wide political work conference in Peking; it calls for better work in company-building and for consolidation of the revolutionary and modern construction of the PLA.

19. Zhou Enlai addresses the CPSU Congress. He strongly defends Albania and criticizes 'any public, one-sided censure of any fraternal party' (Khrushchev had publicly censured the Albanian Party of Labour in his political report to the Congress on October 17).

23. Zhou Enlai leaves Moscow for Peking, without waiting for the end of the CPSU Congress.

December 6. The Ministry of Foreign Affairs issues a statement on the Sino-Indian boundary problem. It counters Indian charges of Chinese intrusion into its territory.

7. China and Tanganyika announce their decision to establish diplomatic relations on the latter's independence from Britain, proclaimed December 9.

15. The UN General Assembly adopts a resolution, sponsored by the USA and four other countries, designating the PRC's admission as an important question requiring a two-thirds majority.

18. The Geneva Conference, with Chinese participation, adopts the Draft Declaration on the Neutrality of Laos, the Protocol of the Declaration and several other documents on Laos.

21. The Ministry of Foreign Affairs issues a statement denouncing the UN General Assembly resolution of December 15.

13 kinds of mammal fossils, perhaps 500,000 years old, in Ruicheng (Shanxi).
November 1. The Chinese Taoist Association holds its second conference in Peking.
December 11. NCNA reports that a team from Academia Sinica has been excavating the site of the Tang dynasty capital Chang'an for over four years and has found a great deal; among other conclusions it has established the length of the Tang city wall as over five times that of the current wall around Xi'an on the same site.
23. Tibet's first primary teachers' training school, the Lhasa Normal School, formally opens classes.

D PUBLICATIONS

February. Wu Yuanzhi's novel *Jinse de qunshan* (*The Golden Mountain Range*) is published in Peking.
April. The Shanghai People's Publishing House publishes *Yangwu yundong* (*The Foreign Things Movement*) in eight volumes.
July. The Zhonghua Book Company publishes volume II of *Zhongguo congshu zonglu* (*Catalogue of Chinese Collectanea*) (volume I had appeared December 1959).
July–August. Tian Han's play *Xie Yaohuan* is published in the journal *Juben* (*Play Scripts*).
October 10. The column 'Sanjia cun zhaji' ('Notes from the Three-Family Village') by Deng Tuo, Wu Han and Liao Mosha, begins publication in the magazine *Qianxian* (*Front Line*).
November. Wu Han's play *Hai Rui baguan* (*The Dismissal of Hai Rui*) is published in Peking as a book (author's preface dated August 8, 1961). (The play appeared originally on January 9, 1961 in the journal *Beijing wenyi*, *Peking Literature and Art*.)
December. The novel *Hongyan* (*Red Crag*) by Luo Guangbin and Yang Yiyan, is published in Peking.

E NATURAL DISASTERS

March 6. A spokesman for the Central Meteorological Bureau states that the 1959–60 drought ranked with those of 1640 and 1877 as the most severe in over 300 years.
April 2. Zhengzhou radio reports serious drought in Henan resulting in 'tremendous difficulties in production'. This was one of many reports of natural calamities affecting agricultural production in many parts of China at about this time; drought in Shandong, Henan, Hebei, Shanxi and Shaanxi, floods in Guangdong, Fujian, Zhejiang and

1961—2

1962 Sino-Indian Border War

January 1. Direct telecommunications services open formally between Shanghai and Havana.
March 25. Radio-photo service opens between Guiyang (Guizhou) and Peking and Shanghai.
April–May. See September 6, 1963.
April 30. The Ministry of Foreign Affairs sends a note to the Indian government protesting against numerous alleged intrusions of Indian troops into China's Xinjiang region in the second half of April.
May 11. China protests against Indian intrusion and provocation in western Tibet and expresses regret that the Indian Ministry of External Affairs has, on April 11, refused a Chinese proposal to negotiate.
19. The CPG issues a strong protest to India concerning a 'grave violation of Chinese territory' by Indian troops 'at Longju in the Tibet region of China'. (Numerous charges of aggression were made by each side against the other at about this time.)
25. A flood of refugees from the PRC into Hongkong, which started at the beginning of May, ends abruptly, with negligible numbers after this day. (The Hongkong government had taken various measures to stop the influx, including a barbed wire barricade on the border.)
June 4. Indian troops set up the Dhola Post just north of the McMahon Line.
23. NCNA reports that the NP on Taiwan are planning a landing on the coast of China 'with the support and encouragement of US imperialism'.
26. Through the ambassadorial talks in Warsaw, the USA informs the PRC it will not support any NP attempt to attack the Chinese mainland.
July 2. Khrushchev declares that the 'whole socialist camp' would be

Jiangxi. Resultant serious and widespread famine continues, enormous numbers of people dying of starvation.

F DEATHS

March 16. CCPCC member Chen Geng d. aged 58.
May 21. Wang Zhengting d. in Hongkong aged 78.
August 8. Mei Lanfang, Peking Opera actor, d. aged 66.
12. The Overseas Chinese leader Chen Jiageng (Tan Kah Kee) d. in Peking aged 86.

The Liao-Takasaki memorandum on Sino-Japanese trade 1962

A ECONOMICS

January 13. China and Albania sign an agreement for a PRC loan, and in addition three protocols and one exchange of notes on technical cooperation, trade and other economic matters. China and Laos sign an agreement under which the PRC will build a highway from Yunnan to Phong Saly in Laos.
March 20. China and the DRVN sign in Hanoi a protocol on trade and two note exchanges on matters concerned with trading in border areas.
April 22–27. The International Railway Transport Conference on Through Freight Traffic is held in Peking. Representatives attend from the USSR, China, the DRVN, DPRK and Mongolia. A protocol is signed.
May 10. The Preparatory Committee for the Tibetan Autonomous Region declares the formal inauguration of the Tibetan Customs House as well as eight 'provisional measures' on trade, customs, the circulation of foreign currency and other economic matters, all to take effect the same day.
October 3. In Peking, China and Ceylon sign two agreements and a protocol on trade and economic and technical cooperation, and two contracts on the exchange of rubber and rice in 1963.
November 5. In Peking, China and the DPRK sign the Treaty of Commerce and Navigation, and an agreement and protocol on trade over the period 1963–67.
9. Liao Chengzhi and Takasaki Tatsunosuke sign a memorandum in Peking for a 'long-term, comprehensive trade by exchange of goods' between China and Japan.
December 4. In Peking, China and Laos issue a joint press communiqué

1962

on China's side if NP forces invaded the Chinese mainland.

10. India protests to China over the surrounding of a small Indian outpost by Chinese troops. The PRC Ministry of Foreign Affairs sends a note to the Indian government protesting against the 'recent setting up of four new military strongpoints by Indian troops in China's Xinjiang' and other similar matters.

17–25. Chen Yi visits Geneva at the head of the Chinese delegation to the Conference on Laos, reconvened on July 2.

23. In Geneva, representatives of China, USSR, USA, UK and other states sign the Declaration on the Neutrality of Laos and the protocol on the withdrawal of foreign troops from Laos.

August 1–6. The World Conference for the Prohibition of Atomic and Hydrogen Bombs and the Prevention of Nuclear War takes place in Tokyo attended by a Chinese delegation, led by Ba Jin.

September 6. NCNA claims that since mid-July Indian troops have taken over seventeen additional strongpoints on Chinese soil in the western sector.

7. The governments of the PRC and the Kingdom of Laos issue a joint communiqué agreeing to establish diplomatic relations and exchange ambassadors.

8. Chinese troops occupy positions near the Dhola Post.

9. The PLA's air force shoots down an NP U-2 aeroplane in the East China area.

20. A clash occurs near the Dhola Post on the Sino-Indian border, resulting in casualties on both sides.

24–27. The Tenth Plenum of the Eighth CCPCC is held in Peking. Mao Zedong makes a speech on September 24 calling for greater emphasis on class struggle. Several resolutions are adopted including one on September 27, 'on the further strengthening of the collective economy of the people's communes and expansion of agricultural production'. The plenum is most famous for Mao's call 'never forget class struggle'; it is also the origin of the Socialist Education Movement.

October 6. A series of Sino-Indian exchanges of diplomatic notes on negotiations over the border issue results in an Indian note, this day, that India would 'not enter into any talks and discussions under duress' and would talk only after China had withdrawn all its forces north of the Thagla Ridge.

11. A serious clash occurs between Chinese and Indian troops at Tseng Jong on the Sino-Indian border.

12. Indian Prime Minister Nehru informs a news conference in New Delhi that he has instructed the army, at a time of its choosing, 'to free our territory' of Chinese troops.

1962

under which China agrees to provide a long-term loan and technical aid.

5. In Peking, China and the DRVN sign a Treaty of Commerce and Navigation and other documents on trade.

27. Chinese and Japanese representatives sign in Peking a protocol and memorandum on economic and trade relations, and technical exchanges.

B Official Appointments, Resignations, Dismissals etc.

September 24–27. The Tenth Plenum of the Eighth CCPCC elects Lu Dingyi, Kang Sheng and Luo Ruiqing to the CCP secretariat and dismisses two members from it, including Huang Kecheng.

C Cultural and Social

January 6–19. The Chinese Catholic Patriotic Association holds its Second National Conference. In its final resolution the conference expresses determination 'to shake off the control of the Vatican'.

10. A report from Tibet claims that a 1300-year-old trading monastery has been reopened and is functioning with fifty lamas.

21. In Peking, Archbishop Pi Shushi consecrates seven new bishops for Kaifeng, Taiyuan, Fuzhou and four other dioceses.

February 12–15. The Afro-Asian Writers Conference is held in Cairo. Mao Dun, Minister of Culture, heads the Chinese delegation.

12–27. The Chinese Buddhist Association holds its Third National Congress with representatives from the Han, Tibetan, Mongolian, and other nationalities.

March 3–26. In Guangzhou over 200 playwrights, opera composers and others hold the National Conference for the Creation of Spoken Plays and Operas. It encourages the policies of 'letting a hundred flowers bloom' and less rigid Party control over literature and the arts.

April 19. Afro-Asian Society of China is founded in Peking with Zhou Yang as chairman.

21–May 29. A Nationalities Work Conference is held in Peking; it decides to strengthen their unity and improve their standard of living and economic development.

June. China's first coloured, stereoscopic, narrow-screen sound film *Moshushi de qiyu (The Adventures of the Magician)* is completed.

October 8. The State Council issues a directive urging strenuous efforts towards the protection and care of wild animals.

November 6–12. A national forum of Confucius' ideas is held in Ji'nan (Shandong), attended by some 150 historians and philosophers.

1962

18. A Sino-Ugandan joint communiqué is issued in Kampala announcing the establishment of diplomatic relations.

20. China launches a major offensive in NEFA and Ladakh. A spokesman for China's Ministry of National Defence states that Indian troops have launched all-out attacks on Chinese frontier guards on both the eastern and western sectors. The Sino-Indian Border War begins.

24. Zhou Enlai writes to Nehru putting forward proposals for ending the border conflict, including that each side should respect the 'line of actual control' as of November 1959.

November 16. Chinese troops, having defeated Indian attempts to halt their advance, take the key town of Walong (eastern NEFA) and two days later Bomdi La (western NEFA). By early November 20, Indian resistance both in NEFA and the western sector (Ladakh) has collapsed.

20. Just before midnight China announces a unilateral ceasefire in the Sino-Indian war to be effective from midnight November 21–22, and that its troops will withdraw 20 km. 'behind the line of actual control which existed between China and India on November 7, 1959'.

December 1. Chinese troops begin their voluntary withdrawal from NEFA.

6. The Indian External Affairs Ministry announces that it will close the Indian consulates-general in Shanghai and Lhasa as from December 15.

8. At the Twelfth Congress of the Czechoslovak Communist Party (held in Prague December 4–8), the Chinese delegate, Wu Xiuquan, hands the First Secretary, Antonin Novotny, a statement criticizing the Congress for attacking the Albanian Party of Labour and CCP.

10–12. Representatives of Ceylon, Cambodia, Burma, Indonesia, the United Arab Republic and Ghana meet in Colombo to discuss the Sino-Indian border problem with a view to offering their good offices in finding a solution.

15. Staff members of the Chinese consulates-general in Calcutta and Bombay complete withdrawal. A long *People's Daily* editorial on various international issues implies that the Russians were guilty of 'adventurism' in putting missile bases into Cuba and 'capitulationism' in withdrawing them under pressure. (In the Cuban crisis US President Kennedy ordered the naval blockade of Cuba October 22, and on October 28 Khrushchev agreed to dismantle Soviet missiles there.)

25–27. Mongolian Prime Minister Tsedenbal visits China.

26. The Sino-Mongolian Boundary Treaty is signed in Peking.

28. A Sino-Pakistani joint communiqué, issued in Peking, announces 'agreement in principle' on the location of the border between the two countries.

1962

D Publications

June. The Zhonghua Book Company publishes a modern punctuated edition of the *Hanshu* (*Han History*). Shanghai People's Publishing House publishes Feng Youlan's *Zhongguo zhexue shi lunwen* (*Theses on the History of Chinese Philosophy*).

July. The Zhonghua Book Company publishes *Tang Xianzu ji* (*Collection of Tang Xianzu*), compiled by Xu Shuofang, in two volumes.

August. The last of fourteen volumes of *Ba Jin wenji* (*Collected Works of Ba Jin*) is published by the People's Literary Publishing House (the first in March 1958). A revised edition of Liu Shaoqi's *Lun Gongchan dangyuan de xiuyang* (*How to be a Good Communist*) is published. (On September 27, NCNA reports that Mongolian, Tibetan, Uighur, Kazakh and Korean versions have also appeared.) The Zhonghua Book Company publishes *Pu Songling ji* (*Collection of Pu Songling*), compiled by Lu Dahuang, in two volumes. Deng Tuo's *Yanshan yehua* (*Evening Talks at Yanshan*) is published in Peking in four volumes (vol. I appeared in August 1961). This is a collection of essays originally published as a column in three Peking newspapers from March 1961 to September 2, 1962.

November. The Zhonghua Book Company publishes *Zhongguo gudai yinyue shiliao jiyao (diyi ji)* (*Compendium of Historical Materials on Ancient Chinese Music, First Collection*) and Wang Li's *Gudai Hanyu* (*Ancient Chinese*).

E Natural Disasters

May 31. Flooding is reported from Fujian, Hunan, Zhejiang, Jiangxi and Guangdong, and drought from Qinghai, Gansu, Shaanxi, Shanxi and Jilin. (Rainfall beginning June 18 alleviates serious drought in many areas of China.)

F Deaths

February 9. CCPCC member Li Kenong d. in Peking aged 55.
   14. Hu Zongnan d. in Taibei aged 62.
   24. Hu Shi d. in Taibei aged 70.
April 15. Lei Feng, young PLA martyr later held up for emulation, d. aged 22.
June 27. Long Yun d. in Peking aged 74.
September 21. Ouyang Yuqian d. aged 73.

1963 *Liu Shaoqi visits several Asian countries, Zhou Enlai several African countries*

January 8. In Peking Ceylonese Prime Minister Mrs Bandaranaike (who visits China December 31 1962–January 9) and Zhou Enlai issue a joint communiqué on the Sino-Indian border dispute. The PRC and Indonesian governments issue a joint communiqué in Peking on the Sino-Indian border dispute and other matters, following the visit of Indonesian Minister of Foreign Affairs Subandrio to China (January 2–7).

February 2–27. The General Political Department of the PLA holds a PLA political work conference. The Conference adopts the Draft Regulations Governing Political Work in the PLA.

27. Liu Shaoqi and Cambodian Prince Norodom Sihanouk issue a joint communiqué on the Sino-Indian border dispute, Cambodian and Laotian neutrality and other matters. (Sihanouk visited China February 8–28.)

March 2. The PRC Ministry of Foreign Affairs informs the Indian embassy that the Chinese guards had completed their withdrawal along the entire border. The Chinese and Pakistani Ministers of Foreign Affairs, Chen Yi and Z.A. Bhutto, sign in Peking an agreement on the boundary between 'China's Xinjiang and the contiguous areas, the defence of which is under the actual control of Pakistan'.

6–10. Laotian King, Sri Savang Vatthana, and Prime Minister Souvanna Phouma visit China.

27. The CCPCC promulgates the Regulations Governing Political Work in the PLA, designed to ensure Party leadership over the PLA.

30. The Standing Committee of the NPC ratifies the Regulations for Elections for the People's Congresses at all Levels in the Tibetan Autonomous Region.

April 12–20. Liu Shaoqi, his wife Wang Guangmei, Chen Yi and others visit Indonesia. (This is the first time a PRC head of state has gone to a non-socialist country.)

20–26. Liu Shaoqi and his party visit Burma.

27. A spokesman for the CPG's Overseas Chinese Affairs Commission issues a protest against the bad treatment of Chinese nationals in India.

May 1–6. Liu Shaoqi and his party visit Cambodia.

10–16. Liu Shaoqi visits the DRVN, declaring in Hanoi on May 15 that it is not possible 'to act as onlookers or to follow the middle course' in the Sino-Soviet dispute. The following day Liu Shaoqi and Ho Chi Minh sign a joint statement in Hanoi, including an attack on revisionism and calling for 'indefatigable struggle against imperialism headed by the USA'.

20. A Central Work Conference in Hangzhou issues the Draft Resolu-

China's economy turns decisively for the better 1963

A ECONOMICS

January 1. The *People's Daily* editorial declares that 'China's economic situation has been changing for the better with each passing day. The harvest of 1962 was normal to good ... better than in 1961'.
13. In Katmandu China and Nepal sign a protocol on the building of the Lhasa–Katmandu highway.
24. Zhou Enlai declares in Shanghai that 'China's socialist construction is in the first year of its Third Five-Year Plan'.
February 1–16. A major conference of East China's advanced agricultural units and a conference on agricultural scientific and technical work are held jointly in Shanghai.
8–March 31. A National Conference of Agricultural, Scientific and Technological Work, jointly convened by the State Council and CCPCC, takes place in Peking. It lays down a programme to develop agricultural science and technology with some 3000 topics for research.
22. In Peking, China and Cuba sign an agreement for a PRC loan to Cuba and two other trade protocols.
March 30. The State Council adopts tentative provisions to adjust industrial and commercial taxes and improve the methods of collection, and tentative provisions for price control.
April 1. The 2495-km. stretch along the Yangzi from Chongqing to Shanghai, China's longest inland route, is opened to navigation.
May 25. The completed Chinese-built road from the Yunnan border to Phong Saly in Laos is formally handed over to the Laotian government.
August 9. In Peking, Zhou Enlai and Somali Prime Minister Shermarke sign an Agreement on Economic and Technical Cooperation.
October 11. China and Algeria sign in Algiers a communiqué by which the PRC grants Algeria a long-term interest-free loan of 250,000,000 French francs.

B OFFICIAL APPOINTMENTS, RESIGNATIONS, DISMISSALS ETC.

March 8. Tibet's first elected county government, the People's Congress of Naidong County, elects Trashi Geltseng, a former Tibetan serf, as county head.
December 12. Liu Shaoqi appoints Deng Xiaoping as acting Premier during Zhou Enlai's forthcoming trip abroad.

C CULTURAL AND SOCIAL

January 26. Liu Shaoqi and Deng Xiaoping receive over 100 leading

1963

tion of the CCPCC on Some Problems in Current Rural Work, usually called the First Ten Points. Drafted by Mao Zedong, and emphasizing class struggle, this gives momentum to the Socialist Education Movement in the countryside.

26. The CPG's Ministry of National Defence issues a statement declaring the repatriation of Indian prisoners of war complete as of May 25.

June 14. The CCP writes a long letter to the CPSU on 'the general line of the international Communist movement'.

19. The PLA air force shoots down a US-made NP plane over east China.

23. In Peking DPRK President Choi Yong Kun and Liu Shaoqi sign a joint statement denouncing the modern revisionists because they 'do not themselves oppose imperialism and forbid others to do so'.

27. Display windows in front of the PRC embassy in Moscow are smashed by several Russian youths.

28. The Mongolian Ministry of Foreign Affairs delivers a note to the Chinese embassy in Ulan Bator denouncing China for interference in Mongolia's domestic affairs.

29. The Ministry of Public Security issues a communiqué reporting that six groups of armed US-NP agents, having landed secretly in Guangdong, Fujian and Zhejiang, were put out of action from June 21 to 28.

30. Three Chinese diplomats and two Chinese students, expelled from Moscow (through a Soviet note to the Chinese embassy of June 27) for distributing Russian translations of the CCP letter of June 14, arrive in Peking.

July 5. Bilateral Sino-Soviet talks open in Moscow to try to resolve the dispute between the two. The Chinese delegation is led by Deng Xiaoping and Peng Zhen, the Soviet by Mikhail Suslov. The talks fail to resolve the differences. Deng Xiaoping and Peng Zhen depart for home July 20 without arranging a definite time for the resumption of the talks.

31. The CPG issues a statement advocating the total destruction of nuclear weapons and denouncing the Partial Nuclear Test Ban Treaty (initialled July 25, and signed, August 5, by US, USSR and UK representatives in Moscow).

August 2. Zhou Enlai writes to the heads of government of all countries proposing a world conference to discuss the total destruction of nuclear weapons.

4–10. Somali Prime Minister Abdirashid Ali Shermarke visits China.

26. The PRC Ministry of Foreign Affairs hands the Indian embassy

1963

scientists, including the physicist Wu Youxun, the mathematician Hua Luogeng, the nuclear physicist Qian Sanqiang, and the dynamics expert Qian Xuesen.

February 22–March 10. A National Medical Science Work Conference, convened by the Ministry of Public Health, takes place in Peking. It summarizes experience in the field of medical science and lays down a long-term programme for the future.

March 2. *Chinese Youth* carries an instruction from Mao Zedong: 'Learn from Comrade Lei Feng'. This begins a movement among China's youth to copy the selfless proletarian virtues of a young soldier, Lei Feng.

April 3–26. The heads of the CCP Cultural Bureaux meet to discuss the content of dramas and literary works. At the meeting the 'Circular on Suspending the Performance of Ghost Plays' is distributed, instigated by Jiang Qing.

27. A meeting of the National Committee of the Chinese Federation of Literary and Art Circles opens in Peking. It launches a campaign to eliminate harmful and bourgeois influence from literature and the arts.

May 3–21. The First Congress of the Tibetan Autonomous Region's Communist Youth League of China is held in Lhasa.

6. The State Council adopts regulations on the establishment and operation of radio stations.

June 19. Zhou Enlai gives his support to family planning. In a northeast Chinese factory a 32-year-old woman told him she and her husband practised family planning and he replied: 'It is indeed a good thing; you and your husband might well be called examples to be followed'.

September. A central work conference discusses drama reform. Mao Zedong calls for the development of new drama from the traditional.

October 4. The China-Japan Friendship Association is set up in Peking with Liao Chengzhi as President.

11. A television films exchange accord is signed in Peking between the Peking Television Station and the British Commonwealth International News Film Agency.

17–19. The Buddhist Conference of Eleven Asian Countries and Regions is held in Peking. Its closing session appeals to Buddhists everywhere to join forces to bring about an end to the persecution of Buddhists in southern Vietnam.

21–November 8. The Third National Conference of the Chinese Islamic Association is held in Peking.

24–29. A conference to organize the exchange of scientific research materials is held in Peking. Zhou Yang calls on intellectuals to 'refute

1963

a note protesting against an intrusion by Indian troops into Chinese territory on August 10, one of several such notes about this time.

28–September 7. D.N. Aidit, Chairman of the Indonesian Communist Party, visits China. After a visit to the DPRK he revisits China September 16–27.

September. The CCPCC issues the Later Ten Points, called Some Concrete Policy Formulations of the CCPCC in the Rural Socialist Education Movement, drafted by Peng Zhen.

6. *Red Flag* and *People's Daily* claim that, in April and May 1962, the Soviet Union carried out 'large-scale subversive activities in the Yili region [of Xinjiang] and enticed and coerced several tens of thousands of Chinese citizens into going to the Soviet Union'.

15–27. Liu Shaoqi visits the DPRK.

21. A Soviet government statement accuses China of having 'systematically violated the Soviet frontier since 1960, including over 5000 violations in 1962'.

November 1. The PLA air force shoots down a US reconnaissance U-2 plane of the NP air force.

4. The Ministry of Public Security issues a communiqué that nine groups of armed US-NP agents have recently been put out of action in Guangdong, Fujian, Zhejiang, Jiangsu and Shandong.

17–December 3. The Fourth Session of the Second NPC is held in Peking.

22. In Peking, Chen Yi and Abdul Kayeum, Afghan Minister of the Interior, sign the Sino-Afghan Boundary Treaty.

28. Tang Mingzhao, PRC delegate at the World Peace Council in Warsaw, comments on US President Kennedy's assassination on November 22, saying that 'instead of paying tribute to the US President we should pay tribute to all men and women who heroically fought for peace against US aggression and against racial discrimination'.

December 11. China and Zanzibar issue a joint communiqué in Zanzibar establishing diplomatic relations at ambassadorial level.

14. China and Kenya issue a joint communiqué of their decision to establish diplomatic relations at ambassadorial level.

14–21. Zhou Enlai and Chen Yi visit the United Arab Republic.

20. In Cairo, Zhou Enlai states that the annual rate of increase of the PRC's population is about 2 per cent.

21–27. Zhou Enlai and Chen Yi visit Algeria.

23. China and Burundi issue a joint communiqué establishing diplomatic relations at ambassadorial level.

27–31. Zhou Enlai and Chen Yi visit Morocco.

31. Zhou Enlai and Chen Yi leave Morocco for Albania.

modern revisionism' and to compile 'a world history from the Marxist-Leninist point of view'.
November 10–22. The Games of the Newly Emerging Forces, of which China was a main participant and sponsor, are held in Jakarta.
December 25. The East China Drama Festival of twenty revolutionary plays opens (closing January 22, 1964). In his opening speech the Mayor of Shanghai, Ke Qingshi, criticizes the lack of modern plays in the repertory of some troupes.

D PUBLICATIONS

February. The last of five volumes of *Xinhai geming huiyi lu* (*Reminiscences of the 1911 Revolution*) is published in Peking (first volume October 1961).
June. The Zhonghua Book Company publishes a new edition in four volumes of *Zhushi suoyan* (*Trifling Comments on All the Histories*) by the Qing scholar Shen Jiaben.
July. Liang Shangquan's poetry collection *Shanquan ji* (*Mountain Stream*) is published in Peking.
August. Ruan Zhangjing's poetry *Kantanzhe zhi ge* (*Songs of the Surveyors*) is published in Peking.
September. The People's Literary Publishing House publishes *Zhu De shixuan ji* (*Selection of Zhu De's Poems*). *Qi Baishi zuopin ji* (*Collection of Qi Baishi's Works*) is published.
December. Xiao San's *Fuli ji* (*In the Stable*) is published in Peking. The People's Literary Publishing House publishes *Mao zhuxi shici* (*Poems of Chairman Mao*); the Zhonghua Book Company *Xu Guangqi ji* (*Collection of Xu Guangqi*), compiled by Wang Zhongmin.

E NATURAL DISASTERS

August 7. Reuter reports the Peking–Guangzhou railway cut by floods about 300 km. south of Peking. This reflects very serious inundation in the area at about this time.

F DEATHS

January 3. Zhu Jiahua, NP official, d. in Taibei aged 69.
June 11. Shen Junru, Vice-chairman of the NPC Standing Committee, d. aged 89.
August 9. Economist Ji Chaoding, d. aged 59.
December 16. Marshal Luo Ronghuan, member of the CCP's Politburo, d. in Peking aged 57.

1964 China's first nuclear explosion

January 1. Direct radio telegraph services begin between Shanghai and Colombo.
9. Zhou Enlai and Chen Yi arrive in Tunis from Albania to continue their African tour. They visit Tunisia (9–10), Ghana (11–16), Mali (16–21), Guinea (21–27), Sudan (27–30), Ethiopia (30–February 1), and Somalia (February 1–4).
10. China and Tunisia issue a joint communiqué establishing diplomatic relations.
27. China and France issue a joint communiqué in Peking and Paris, establishing diplomatic relations, and agreeing to exchange ambassadors within three months.
February 1. A *People's Daily* editorial launches an important campaign to 'learn from the PLA'.
5. Zhou Enlai and Chen Yi arrive in Kunming (Yunnan) after their African tour.
10. The NP regime announces the rupture of diplomatic relations with France.
14. Zhou Enlai and Chen Yi arrive in Rangoon at the start of visits to Burma (14–18), Pakistan (18–26) and Ceylon (26–29).
22. China and the Congo (Brazzaville) issue a joint communiqué establishing diplomatic relations at ambassadorial level.
25. Sino-Soviet boundary talks begin in Peking.
29. A CCPCC letter to the CPSU expresses China's willingness to respect the 'old treaties', i.e. those of Aigun (see May 28, 1858), Peking (see November 14, 1860) and others, and 'take them as the basis for a reasonable settlement of the Sino-Soviet boundary question'.
March 1. Zhou Enlai and his party arrive at Kunming (Yunnan) at the end of their trip to Burma, Pakistan and Ceylon.
2–12. A Rumanian delegation, led by Politburo member I. Maurer, visits China. It attempts to mediate in the Sino-Soviet dispute but fails.
7. The CPSUCC writes to the CCPCC calling for bilateral talks with China to continue in May and for a world conference of communist parties in the autumn.
14–26. The Xinjiang Uighur Autonomous Region People's Congress is held in Urumchi. It reaffirms accusations of subversion against Xinjiang by the USSR.
April 3. Nine PRC trade workers and journalists are arrested in Rio de Janeiro.
4–8. Prime Minister Souvanna Phouma of Laos visits China.
10–15. The preparatory meeting for the second Afro-Asian Conference is held in Jakarta. Chen Yi succeeds in preventing agreement on and hence blocking an Indian proposal to invite the Soviet Union.

A Economics

January 1. *People's Daily* advocates concentrating agricultural investment in areas with better conditions.

7. A National Conference on Industrial and Communications Work in Peking, presided over by Bo Yibo, closes after three weeks' meetings. It emphasizes learning from the PLA and ideological work.

March 23. Peking–Kunming air services are inaugurated.

26. Peking–Changsha–Guangzhou air services are inaugurated.

28. The *Jianshe* (*Construction*), an entirely Chinese-designed and made ocean-going freighter, is launched in Shanghai.

April 11. NCNA reports the opening of five new air routes: Shanghai–Chengdu, Shanghai–Kunming, Shanghai–Shenyang, Shanghai–Lanzhou, and Guangzhou–Chengdu.

20. Chinese newspapers report the discovery of oil at Daqing and the building of a big modern refinery there over the past few years. (The first well was sunk there September, 1959.)

29. Pakistan International Airline's inaugural flight to China lands at Shanghai International Airport.

May 19. Air services are inaugurated between Phnom Penh and Guangzhou.

August 6. The Peking–Hangzhou–Guangzhou air service is formally inaugurated.

November 6. At a meeting of the Railway Cooperation Organization of Socialist Countries, held in Peking (October 15–November 6) and attended by representatives of China, the USSR and nine other countries, a multilateral protocol is signed on 'through freight railway service'. (A protocol on 'through passenger railway service' is signed October 27.)

9–27. A Conference of Experts on Economics of Posts and Telecommunications of Socialist Countries is held in Peking, attended by representatives of the USSR, China and ten other countries. It signs a multilateral protocol on November 27.

B Official Appointments, Resignations, Dismissals etc.

April 27. NCNA reports Chairman Liu Shaoqi's appointment of Huang Zhen as Chinese ambassador to France.

June 9. Liu Shaoqi appoints Fang Yi as director of the Commission for Economic Relations with Foreign Countries, which the NPC Standing Committee decides to set up the same day.

September 21. NCNA reports Liu Shaoqi's appointment of Xiao Hua as director of the General Political Department of the PLA.

1964

24. NCNA reports that the Mongolian government is repatriating the 6100 Chinese workers remaining in Mongolia; this reflects decisive deterioration in Sino-Mongolian relations.

May 3. At a news conference for journalists from the UK, France, Switzerland, West Germany, Italy and Pakistan, Chen Yi states that the new Pakistani air service will result in much more tourism; he warns that in view of the anti-China bias of sections of the foreign press there will be restrictions on unfriendly journalists and visitors.

June 1–11. Abdullah Al Sallal, President of the Arab Republic of Yemen, visits China. On June 9 a Treaty of Friendship, and two agreements, one on cultural cooperation, the other' on economic and technical cooperation, are signed.

10. Zhou Enlai sends a message of goodwill to the new Indian Prime Minister, Lal Bahadur Shastri (Nehru had died May 27), expressing the hope that friendly relations can be restored.

11. The PLA air force shoots down an NP US-made P2V aircraft over north China. NP sources report the safe return to Taiwan of a guerrilla mission which attacked Shandong June 2, killing at least thirty PLA soldiers.

13. The CPG issues a protest against the US bombing of the Chinese Economic and Cultural Mission at Khang Khay in Laos on June 11. Mongolia accuses China of discriminating against its minorities, including the Mongolians, and reiterates support for the USSR in the Sino-Soviet dispute.

15. The CPSUCC writes to the CCPCC again, suggesting a world conference of communist and workers' parties (see March 7).

16. At a CCPCC Work Conference in Peking Mao Zedong makes a speech on the militia, the need to train revolutionary successors and other matters.

29. The Ministry of Public Security announces the putting out of action of nine groups of armed US-NP agents, totalling 74 men, between November 1963 and June 1964.

30. In Ulan Bator China and Mongolia sign a protocol on the demarcation of their boundary.

July 7. The PLA's air force shoots down a U-2 reconnaissance aircraft over east China.

10–11. Zhou Enlai and Chen Yi visit Burma.

Mid-month. At a conference in Shanghai Wang Guangmei, wife of Liu Shaoqi, reports that she spent from late November to April 1964 incognita in the Taoyuan production brigade in Funing (Hebei), investigating the situation there. This is called 'the Taoyuan Experience'.

1964

December 17. The State Council formally deprives the Dalai Lama of his positions as Chairman and member of the Preparatory Committee for the Tibetan Autonomous Region.

C CULTURAL AND SOCIAL

January 1. The Peking Hall of Sciences is formally opened.
February 20–29. The Chinese Society of Aeronautics is set up at a meeting in Peking.
April 1. *People's Daily* applauds the regrowth of theatre on contemporary revolutionary themes and calls for more such operas and plays which 'uphold proletarian ideology and stamp out bourgeois ideology'.
May 2. Tibet's 8012-m. Mt Gosainthan is conquered for the first time by a PRC mountaineering expedition.
June 5–July 31. The Festival of Peking Operas on Contemporary Themes is held in Peking. In the opening speech Lu Dingyi, director of the CCPCC's Propaganda Department, argues that in order to prevent the victory of modern revisionism in China 'Peking Opera needs a new revolutionary flower'. Twenty-nine drama troupes take part and perform thirty-five items, including *Hongdeng ji* (*The Red Lantern*). The festival heralds the virtually total temporary disappearance of traditional operas, apart from during the Spring, National Day and May Day festivals.
11–29. The Ninth Congress of the Communist Youth League of China is held in Peking, attended by 2396 delegates. The Congress revises the League's constitution, to include an exhortation to be guided by Mao Zedong's thought.
August 3. A *People's Daily* editorial calls for a nationwide campaign 'to train and educate thousands of millions of successors to the proletarian revolution'.
18. At a conference in Peking, Mao Zedong gives a 'Talk on Problems of Philosophy'. He argues that intellectuals must go to the countryside to gain experience of class struggle there, and attacks Yang Xianzhen, member of the CCPCC and former President of its Higher Party School and veteran philosopher, for wrong dialectical thinking in saying 'two combine into one' instead of 'one divides into two'.
21–31. A symposium of 367 scientists from 44 countries in Asia, Africa, Latin America and Oceania is held in Peking.
September 23. Peng Zhen convenes a meeting to discuss rectification in literature, the arts, philosophy and the social sciences.
30. Shanghai's *Wenyi bao* (*Literature and Art*) attacks the idea of 'writing about middle characters' (i.e. those midway between positive and

1964

20. A rally in Peking to mark the tenth anniversary of the signing of the Geneva Accords pledges China's support to the DRVN and the National Liberation Front (NLF) of southern Vietnam.

28. The Chinese reply to the CPSUCC June 15 letter: 'We will never take part in any international meeting ... which you call for the purpose of splitting the international communist movement.'

August 6. The CPG issues a statement, protesting against the US air strikes on the DRVN of August 5, denouncing the USA for fabricating the alleged Tongking Gulf incidents of August 2 and 4 to extend the war in Indochina, and declaring that aggression against the DRVN is aggression against China.

September 10. The CCPCC adopts 'Some Concrete Policy Formulations of the CCPCC in the Rural Socialist Education Movement', known as the 'Revised Later Ten Points'. This ushers in a new phase in the movement in attacking certain basic-level rural cadres, among whom it sees serious problems.

26–October 7. Prince Norodom Sihanouk visits China for the National Day celebrations.

28–October 3. President A. Massamba-Debat of the Congo (Brazzaville) visits China. On October 2 a Treaty of Friendship, and agreements on maritime transport and economic, technical and cultural cooperation are signed.

29. China and the Central African Republic issue a joint communiqué in Bangui announcing diplomatic relations and sign agreements on economic, technical and cultural cooperation.

29–October 4. President Mobido Keita of Mali visits China.

October 16. China carries out her first nuclear test; the CPG issues a statement solemnly declaring that 'at no time and in no circumstances will China be the first to use nuclear weapons'. Mao Zedong, Liu Shaoqi, Zhu De and Zhou Enlai send cables to A. Kosygin and L. Brezhnev, congratulating them on being elected to the positions, respectively, of Soviet Prime Minister and First Secretary of the CPSU (Khrushchev's resignation from both positions had been announced the previous day).

17. Zhou Enlai cables all heads of government around the world explaining why China has exploded an atomic device and calling for a conference to ban and destroy all nuclear weapons.

November 1–7. President Keita of Mali revisits China, signing a Treaty of Friendship November 3.

4–5. Indonesian President Sukarno visits Shanghai.

5–13. Zhou Enlai leads a Chinese delegation to Moscow to attend the celebrations of the forty-seventh anniversary of the October Revolu-

negative) as a 'bourgeois literary notion'.
October 2. *Dongfang hong (The East is Red)*, a 'large-scale historical poem with music and dancing' is premiered in Peking.
3. The ballet *Hongse niangzi jun (Red Detachment of Women)* is premiered in Peking.
18–21. The Peking International Table Tennis Invitational Tournament is held.
November 26–December 29. The First National Mass Amateur Art Festival of the Minorities takes place in Peking.

D PUBLICATIONS

January. The Zhonghua Book Company publishes Hu Yujin's *Siku quanshu zongmu tiyao buzheng (Supplement to the Main Points in the Contents of the Complete Books of Four Treasuries)* in two volumes.
March. Aisin-Gioro Puyi's *Wo de qianbansheng (The First Half of My Life)*, the autobiography of the last emperor of China, is published in Peking. (The Foreign Languages Press publishes an English translation, *From Emperor to Citizen*, in two volumes 1964 and 1965.)
May. Chen Dengke's novel *Fenglei (Wind and Thunder)*, part 1, is published (part 2 appears May 1965).
July. Ruan Zhangjing's story-poem *Baiyun Ebo jiaoxiang shi (White Cloud Ebo Symphony)* is published.
September. Haoran's novel *Yanyang tian (Bright Sunny Skies)*, part 1, is published in Peking (part 2 appeared in March 1966). He Changqun's *Han Tang jian fengjian tudi suoyouzhi xingshi yanjiu (Studies on Feudal Land Ownership from Han to Tang)* is published in Peking.
22. *Peking Review* is published in German for the first time (*Peking Rundschau*).
30. The Foreign Languages Press publishes the official English version of *Selected Works of Mao Tse-tung*, Vol. I (Vols. II, III and IV appeared respectively December 1965, October 1965 and April 1961).

F DEATHS

February 5. Gan Siqi, deputy Director of the General Political Department of the PLA, d. aged 60.
22. Zhou Baozhong, CCPCC alternate member, d. aged 62.
March 30. Deng Xihou, deputy Governor of Sichuan, d. in Chengdu aged 75.
May 1. Professor Tang Yongtong, historian of Buddhism and deputy Vice-Chancellor of Peking University, d. in Peking aged 71.

1964–5

tion and holds talks with L. Brezhnev and A. Kosygin.

21. A *Red Flag* editorial 'Why Khrushchev fell' warns the new Soviet leaders that 'Khrushchevism without Khrushchev' is bound to fail.

December 21–January 4, 1965. The First Session of the Third NPC is held in Peking.

21–22. Zhou Enlai gives the report on the work of the government to the NPC. Among many other points he claims that China has repaid almost the whole of its foreign debt, and that the number of foreign countries having diplomatic relations with China has increased to fifty.

22. Nine Chinese are sentenced to ten years' imprisonment in Brazil for subversion and spying (see April 3 above).

1965 *China reacts strongly against the escalation of the Vietnam War and the coup in Indonesia*

January 10. The CPG issues a statement supporting Indonesia's decision to withdraw from the UN, announced by Sukarno January 7, because Malaysia had been made a member of the Security Council, as just, correct, and revolutionary.

14. A Central Work Conference, held January 1–14 and convened by the Politburo of the CCPCC, adopts 'The Twenty-three Articles' on the Socialist Education Movement: 'Some Problems Currently Arising in the Course of the Rural Socialist Education Movement', drafted by Mao Zedong. This begins a new stage in the movement in which indiscriminate attacks against basic local cadres are checked more carefully.

19. Liu Shaoqi promulgates regulations lengthening the period of active military service for the PLA's privates and non-commissioned officers.

29. Burundi 'temporarily suspends' diplomatic relations with China, accusing its embassy of interfering in Burundi's internal affairs, and ordering it to leave within forty-eight hours.

February 1. The Ministry of Public Security issues a communiqué that between July 1964 and January 1965, seven groups of US-NP agents, 196 men in all, were put out of action in Guangdong, Fujian, Zhejiang and Jiangsu provinces.

5–6, 10–11. Soviet Prime Minister A. Kosygin visits Peking on his way to and from Hanoi. The resultant talks yield no communiqué. Mao Zedong and Liu Shaoqi meet Kosygin February 11.

8–12. Over 11,000,000 people (in NCNA's claim) throughout China demonstrate against the extension of the war in Vietnam and the

26. Deputy Minister of Public Health Su Jingguan d. in Peking aged 58.

November 10. Yu Youren d. in Taibei aged 85.

First salvoes of the Cultural Revolution in **1965**
the literary sphere

A ECONOMICS

January 6. Direct civil air services are inaugurated between China and Indonesia.

February 18. In Karachi, China and Pakistan sign an agreement for a PRC loan and despatch of technicians and experts to Pakistan.

August 2. NCNA reports the 'recent' manufacture in Shanghai of China's first advanced electron microscope, with a magnification of 200,000 times.

9. Lee Kuan Yew, Prime Minister of Singapore, announces that the Singapore branch of the Bank of China, its last in South-east Asia, may continue operating. (Malaysia had tried to take over the branch, but Singapore seceded from Malaysia on August 9.)

25. The longest modern highway bridge ever built on the Tibetan plateau, over the Lhasa River, is opened to traffic.

December 5. In Peking, China and the DRVN sign an agreement for a PRC loan and a protocol for the mutual supply of commodities and payments in 1966.

B OFFICIAL APPOINTMENTS, RESIGNATIONS, DISMISSALS ETC.

January 3. The NPC reelects Liu Shaoqi as Chairman of the PRC, Song Qingling and Dong Biwu as deputy Chairmen of the PRC, Zhu De as Chairman of the Standing Committee of the NPC, and Zhou Enlai as Premier of the State Council; and elects Yang Xiufeng as President of the Supreme People's Court.

4. The NPC adopts Zhou Enlai's recommendations for the composi-

1965

bombing of the DRVN on February 7 and 8.

13. Direct radio telephone links between China and Pakistan are inaugurated.

16–23. President Julius Nyerere of Tanzania visits China. A Treaty of Friendship is signed February 20.

March 2–9. Pakistani President Ayub Khan visits China.

6. A hostile demonstration takes place outside the Soviet embassy in Peking – the first of its kind – following violence by Soviet troops and police against Chinese students demonstrating outside the US embassy in Moscow on March 4 over the war in Vietnam.

12. The CPG issues a statement denouncing the arrival of US marines in Vietnam on March 8 and 9.

23. A *People's Daily* article (signed by the editorial departments of both *People's Daily* and *Red Flag*) denounces the Moscow meeting of nineteen Communist Parties (held March 1–5): 'the new leaders of the CPSU have obstinately clung to the whole of Khrushchev's revisionist theories, general line and policies'.

23–27. Zhou Enlai visits Rumania. He then visits Albania (27–30), Algeria (30–April 1), United Arab Republic (April 1–2), Pakistan (2–3) and Burma (3–4), returning to Peking April 6.

24. In Kabul China and Afghanistan sign a protocol on the demarcation of their boundary.

26. In Rawalpindi China and Pakistan sign a protocol on the demarcation of the boundary between Xinjiang and 'contiguous areas under the actual control of Pakistan'.

April 16–26. Zhou Enlai and Chen Yi visit Indonesia for the celebrations of the tenth anniversary of the Bandung Conference.

26–28. Zhou Enlai visits Burma, returning to Peking on April 29.

May 12. Mao Zedong issues a statement called 'Supporting the Dominican People's Resistance to US Armed Aggression'. US marines had landed in the Dominican Republic April 28.

14. China conducts a second atomic explosion over its western areas.

22. President Liu Shaoqi issues an order promulgating the NPC Standing Committee's decision of the same day to abolish the system of ranks in the PLA. The order comes into effect June 1.

June. Zhou Enlai visits Pakistan (2–3) and Tanzania (4–8).

5. At a rally in Dar-es-Salaam Zhou Enlai declares that 'an exceedingly favourable situation for revolution prevails today not only in Africa but also in Asia and Latin America'.

10. Zhou Enlai arrives back in Peking from Tanzania, having made brief stops in Addis Ababa, Cairo and Damascus.

19. Zhou Enlai and Chen Yi arrive in Cairo on their way to the Second

tion of the State Council. These include: Vice-Premiers, Lin Biao, Chen Yun, Deng Xiaoping, He Long, Chen Yi, Ke Qingshi, Ulanfu, Li Fuchun, Li Xiannian, Tan Zhenlin, Nie Rongzhen, Bo Yibo, Lu Dingyi, Luo Ruiqing, Tao Zhu, and Xie Fuzhi. Reappointed ministers include Chen Yi, Minister of Foreign Affairs, Lin Biao, Minister of National Defence, and Xie Fuzhi, Minister of Public Security; new, Lu Dingyi, Minister of Culture.

March 31. NCNA announces Liu Shaoqi's appointment of Gu Mu as director of the State Capital Construction Commission (set up by the State Council March 27.)

September 8. The First People's Congress of the Tibetan Autonomous Region elects Ngapo Ngawang Jigme as Chairman of the Autonomous Region and Zhou Renshan and others deputy Chairmen.

C CULTURAL AND SOCIAL

January 15–27. The National Student and Youth Unions hold congresses simultaneously in Peking. (The National Youth Union is defined in its constitution of January 27, 1965 as 'a joint organization of various youth associations, with the Communist Youth League as the nucleus, under the leadership of the CCP'.

February 24. Premiere of the play *Chidao zhangu* (*Battle Drums on the Equator*), China's first major attempt to dramatize the African revolution.

25–April 5. The North China Festival of Modern Dramas and Operas, featuring 42 new spoken plays and operas, takes place in Peking.

March 7. *People's Daily* presses the 'new-style part-farming, part-study and part-work, part-study schools'. Two national conferences are held on these schools, in March for the rural, and in March–April for the urban. At each Liu Shaoqi makes a speech of strong advocacy.

April 15–25. China takes part in the Twenty-Eighth World Table Tennis Championships in Ljubljana, Yugoslavia, winning the men's singles, doubles and team events and the women's doubles and team titles.

May 3. The Ninth CC of the Communist Youth League issues a communiqué of the decisions of its Second Plenum (held March 29–April 19) which include lowering the minimum age of membership in the Young Pioneers from nine to seven.

June 12. In Shanghai, for the first time in China, surgeons successfully replace the mitral valve in a human heart (of a thirty-four-year-old woman) with an artifical valve.

1965

Afro-Asian Conference due to start in Algiers June 29. In a *coup* in Algiers, Houari Boumedienne overthrows Ben Bella as Prime Minister.

21–July 15. The Sixth Conference of Ministers of Posts and Telecommunications of Socialist Countries is held in Peking, attended by representatives from China, USSR, DRVN and ten other countries. A multilateral protocol is signed.

26. Despite Chinese opposition, a foreign ministers' meeting in Algiers decides to postpone the Afro-Asian Conference until November 5. (The Conference never took place.)

30. Zhou Enlai and Chen Yi leave Cairo for home, arriving in Urumchi July 3, having stopped briefly in Damascus and Karachi.

July 11–16. Ugandan Prime Minister Milton Obote visits China.

20. Li Zongren, last ROC acting President before liberation, returns to China and is greeted at Peking airport by Zhou Enlai and others. He meets Mao Zedong July 27.

21–28. Somali President Aden Abdulla Osman visits China.

24–August 1. The Chairman of Burma's Revolutionary Council, Ne Win, visits China.

26. In Nouakchott China and Mauritania issue an agreement to establish diplomatic relations at ambassadorial level.

August 1–6. D.N. Aidit, Chairman of the Indonesian Communist Party, visits China.

3. Mao Zedong and Liu Shaoqi meet visiting French Minister of State André Malraux.

5. A naval battle takes place south-west of Quemoy between NP and CCP forces, each side claiming to sink warships of the other.

September 1–9. The First Session of the First People's Congress of the Tibetan Autonomous Region is held in Lhasa. It ends with the formal declaration and establishment of the Tibetan Autonomous Region.

16, 19, 20. The Ministry of Foreign Affairs sends notes to the Indian embassy demanding that India discontinue intrusions into China and dismantle its military works on the Chinese side of the China-Sikkim boundary or on the boundary itself.

21–22. India replies to China's notes of September 16, 19, 20. Note follows counternote, accusation follows counter-accusation in the succeeding period.

22–October 4. Cambodian Prince Sihanouk visits China for the National Day celebrations, returning October 10–16.

October 18. The Ministry of Foreign Affairs hands a note to the Indonesian embassy protesting against the raid by Indonesian soldiers on the Chinese embassy in Jakarta on October 16.

19. For the first time NCNA reports the Indonesian *coup* of October 1

1965

13. A National Art Exhibition of 640 paintings by artists of Guangdong, Guangxi, Hubei, Hunan and Henan opens in Peking's Museum of Chinese Art.

26. Mao Zedong issues his later famous instruction: 'In medical and health work, put the stress on rural areas'.

July 1–August 15. The Central-South China Drama Festival is held in Guangzhou. In his closing speech Tao Zhu, First Secretary of the Central-South Bureau of the CCP, says operas on contemporary themes must completely and speedily take over the Chinese stage.

16–August 16. The North-west China Festival of Modern Spoken Plays, Operas and Peking Operas is held in Lanzhou.

September 11–28. The PRC's Second National Games are held in Peking.

17. For the first time in the world scientists, of Academia Sinica and Peking University, succeed in the total synthesis of insulin in crystalline form.

18. Tibet's first Youth Palace is formally opened.

November 1. A National Agricultural Exhibition opens in Peking showing 'the Dazhai spirit' in agriculture, i.e. strong emphases on self-reliance and ideological motivation.

6. The PLA's General Political Department issues a circular requiring adherence to Lin Biao's call to 'learn from Wang Jie', a young soldier of model revolutionary virtue who died by throwing himself on explosives, thus saving twelve others standing nearby.

10. Yao Wenyuan attacks Wu Han's historical drama *The Dismissal of Hai Rui* in Shanghai's *Wenhui bao* as an 'anti-Party poisonous weed' (see D, November, 1961): regarded during the Cultural Revolution as its first salvo.

25–December 14. A conference of more than 1100 'young activists in amateur literary creation', jointly sponsored by the CC of the Communist Youth League and the Chinese Writers Union, is held in Peking.

30. *People's Daily* reprints Yao Wenyuan's November 10 article, adding that it invites general participation in a debate on the issues Yao raises.

December 30. *People's Daily* publishes a long self-criticism by Wu Han, in which he admits to having falsified the character of Hai Rui.

D PUBLICATIONS

May. The Zhonghua Book Company publishes a modern edition of the *Hou Han shu* (*History of the Later Han*).

(which brought Suharto and the army to power), under the heading 'Sudden drastic changes in Indonesian political situation'. Direct postal services between China and Nepal are formally inaugurated.

November 4. The PRC embassy in Jakarta hands a note to the Indonesian Ministry of Foreign Affairs protesting over the raiding of the Chinese consulate in Medan on November 3 and over the persecution of Chinese nationals in general.

17. For the first time the vote in the UN over whether to seat the PRC in China's place is tied: 47 for, 47 against, 20 abstentions; but is lost on the two-thirds majority requirement.

19. The PRC embassy in Jakarta hands a note to the Indonesian Ministry of Foreign Affairs protesting over violent incidents against Chinese nationals and demands compensation and protection. Similar protests were made November 26, 27, December 9, 15, 18 and 20.

December 8. The CCPCC holds a conference in Shanghai, to criticize the 'many and serious wrongdoings of Luo Ruiqing'.

20. At a banquet given in honour of the fifth anniversary of the establishment of the NLF in southern Vietnam (December 20, 1960) Zhou Enlai again pledges total support for 'the fraternal Vietnamese people . . . until final victory'.

10. *Red Flag* publishes Luo Ruiqing's 'Jinian zhansheng Deguo faxisi, ba fandui Mei diguozhuyi de douzheng jinxing daodi' ('Commemorate the Victory over German Fascism! Carry the Struggle Against US Imperialism Through to the End!'). (*People's Daily* carries the article the next day.)

June. *Mingdai de juntun* (*Military Stations of the Ming Dynasty*), by Wang Yuquan, is published; the Zhonghua Book Company publishes a new edition of *Quan Songci* (*Complete Song Ci*) in five volumes, edited and supplemented from the 1940 Commercial Press edition.

September 3. Lin Biao's 'Renmin zhanzheng shengli wansui' ('Long Live the Victory of People's War') in commemoration of the twentieth anniversary of victory in the Chinese people's War of Resistance against Japan, is published in *Red Flag* and elsewhere. In it he compared North America and Western Europe to 'the cities of the world' and Asia, Africa and Latin America to 'the rural areas of the world'.

October. Liu Danian, *Zhongguo jindai shi zhu wenti* (*Problems in Modern Chinese History*). The Zhonghua Book Company publishes Yang Kuan's *Gushi xintan* (*New Explorations into Ancient History*).

November. The first collection of *Gongnongbing qingnian chuangzuo xuan* (*Selection of Creative Work by Young Workers, Peasants and Soldiers*) is published in Peking. The Zhonghua Book Company publishes a new edition of the Qing scholar Yan Kejun's *Quan shanggu Sandai Qin Han Sanguo Liuchao wen* (*Complete Prose of High Antiquity, the Three Dynasties, Qin, Han, Three Kingdoms, and Six Dynasties*), in five volumes.

December. The novel *Ouyang Hai zhi ge* (*The Song of Ouyang Hai*) by Jin Jingmai, is published in Peking.

F DEATHS

March 5. Chen Cheng d. in Taibei aged 67.
April 9. Vice-Premier Ke Qingshi d. aged 63.
May 7. Liu Yalou, Commander of the PLA air force, d. in Shanghai aged 55.
June 18. Musical composer and musicologist An Bo d. aged 49.
July 14. PLA hero Wang Jie d. in Jiangsu, aged 23.
December 21. Educationist Huang Yanpei d. in Peking aged 87.

1966 *Eleventh Plenum of the Eighth CCPCC formalizes the Cultural Revolution*

January 2. Cuban Prime Minister Fidel Castro accuses China of dislocating the Cuban economy through suddenly cutting sugar purchases and rice sales.
3. Dahomey breaks off diplomatic relations with China.
4. Deputy Minister of Foreign Affairs Wang Bingnan calls on the Soviet embassy and hands over a note formally denying accusations that China has obstructed the transport of Soviet military aid supplies to Vietnam.
6. The Central African Republic breaks off diplomatic relations with China following a *coup d'état* January 1.
12. The Chinese embassy in Jakarta hands a note to the Indonesian Ministry of Foreign Affairs protesting against the killing of Chinese nationals on Lombok Island at the end of December 1965. A similar protest follows January 17.
18. A twenty-day Political Work Conference, held in Peking by the General Political Department of the PLA, concludes. The conference 'stressed that the decisive factor in putting politics first was Party leadership'.
February 3. The Chinese Ministry of Foreign Affairs hands a note to the Indonesian embassy protesting against attacks on the Chinese embassy in Jakarta the same day. Further similar protests follow later in the year.
24–28. Ghanaian President K. Nkrumah visits Peking but a *coup* against his government succeeds in Ghana February 24.
March 6. The Chinese embassy in Accra hands a note to the Ghanaian government protesting against a note of March 4 accusing China of helping Nkrumah stage a counter-revolution, and denying the charge.
22. The CCPCC writes to the CPSUCC, refusing the latter's invitation (of February 24) to attend the Twenty-third CPSU Congress in Moscow.
26–31. Liu Shaoqi and his wife Wang Guangmei visit Pakistan.
April 4–8. Liu Shaoqi and Wang Guangmei visit Afghanistan.
15. A demonstration, described by Antara as the 'biggest and most violent against People's China' ever to have taken place in Indonesia, erupts at the Chinese embassy in Jakarta, ransacking the building.
15–17. Liu Shaoqi and Wang Guangmei visit East Pakistan.
16. The Indonesian ambassador in Peking, Mr Djawote, announces his resignation.
17–19. Liu Shaoqi and Chen Yi visit Burma.
18. The Chinese Ministry of Foreign Affairs announces the suspension of aid to and the withdrawal of Chinese experts from the Bandjaran textile mill in Indonesia.

Red Guards attack 'bourgeois and feudal remnants' 1966

A ECONOMICS

January 1. The New Year's day editorial in *People's Daily* claims that 'China has become a country that owes no debt to any country'. It describes 1966 as 'the first year of the Third Five-Year Plan'. The Wuhan–Junxian (Hubei) railway is opened to traffic.
August 1. A ceremony marks the opening to traffic of the first modernized highway bridge across the Tsangpo River (upper reaches of the Brahmaputra), south-west of Lhasa (Tibet).
10. *Red Flag* attacks the economic theories of Sun Yefang, former director of the Institute of Economics of the Academia Sinica, as 'revisionist' and 'reactionary'. In particular it denounces his view that 'profit quotas are "the very key link" in the entire system of planned targets'.
September 12. NCNA announces the opening of a new domestic airline from Shenyang (Liaoning) to Changchun (Jilin), Harbin (Heilongjiang) and Jiamusi (Heilongjiang).
20. The first plane of the new Air France Paris–Athens–Cairo–Karachi–Phnom Penh–Shanghai service arrives in Shanghai. (The air route is established under a Sino-French agreement signed in Paris on June 1, 1966).

B OFFICIAL APPOINTMENTS, RESIGNATIONS, DISMISSALS ETC.

May 16. The CCPCC Politburo formalizes the dismissal of Luo Ruiqing as Chief of the General Staff of the PLA (his deputy, Yang Chengwu, takes over the position).
25. The new (see below, June 3) Peking Municipal CCP Committee dismisses Fan Jin, editor of *Beijing ribao* (*Peking Daily*), and the entire editorial board.
June 3. NCNA announces the CCPCC's decision to appoint Li Xuefeng as First Secretary of the Peking Municipal CCP Committee, in place of Peng Zhen, and Wu De as Second Secretary.
4. *People's Daily* reports the decision of the Peking Municipal CCP Committee to dismiss Lu Ping as Vice-Chancellor and First CCP Secretary of Peking University.
July 10. NCNA reveals that Chen Boda is the 'leader of the group in charge of the Cultural Revolution under the Party's CC', and cites Tao Zhu as director of the Party Propaganda Department, indicating that the former occupant, Lu Dingyi, has been dismissed.
August 1–12. The Eleventh Plenum of the Eighth CCPCC elects Lin Biao sole deputy Chairman of the CCPCC and demotes Liu

1966

26–May 11. An Albanian delegation led by Mehmet Shehu, Chairman of the Albanian Council of Ministers, visits Peking. On the last day an anti-Soviet joint communiqué is issued.

May 4–18. The CCPCC Politburo holds an enlarged meeting in Peking. On May 16 it issues a circular letter announcing the CCPCC's decision to set up the Cultural Revolution Group under the Politburo's Standing Committee; and calling for criticism of reactionary ideas in academic circles and of 'all the representatives of the bourgeoisie who have infiltrated the Party, the government, the army and the cultural world'.

7. Mao Zedong writes to Lin Biao calling for the PLA to learn politics, military affairs and culture, as well as engaging in agriculture and other things; it should 'be a great school'. This is called the May 7 directive.

9. China conducts a nuclear test, its first containing thermonuclear material.

June (early). Liu Shaoqi assumes control of the Cultural Revolution for two months, sending 'work teams' into the organizations to exercise leadership.

2. *People's Daily* reproduces the big-character poster by Nie Yuanzi and others (see C, May 25) and describes it as the country's first Marxist-Leninist big-character poster.

16–24. Zhou Enlai visits Rumania.

24–29. Zhou Enlai visits Albania.

July 3. The CPG denounces the US bombing of Hanoi and Haiphong, begun June 29.

8. Mao Zedong writes to Jiang Qing privately, expressing doubts about Lin Biao's loyalty and his ideological purity.

16. Mao Zedong swims in the Yangzi at Wuhan to enormous publicity, setting off a wave of enthusiasm for swimming in China.

24. An enlarged meeting of the Cultural Revolution Group, held in Peking, decides to withdraw the work teams (see early June).

August 1–12. The Eleventh Plenum of the Eighth CCPCC is held in Peking. It issues a communiqué August 12.

5. Mao Zedong writes his own big-character poster called 'Bombard the Headquarters'.

8. The CCPCC Plenum adopts the Decision of the CCPCC Concerning the Great Proletarian Cultural Revolution, the so-called 'Sixteen Points', which are to guide the progress of the Cultural Revolution. 'The Great Proletarian Cultural Revolution' (GPCR), it states, 'is a great revolution that touches people to their very souls.'

18. A rally of over 1,000,000 in Tiananmen Square, Peking, ushers in a new phase of the Cultural Revolution. The rally is attended by Mao Zedong, Lin Biao, Zhou Enlai, Tao Zhu, Chen Boda, and Deng Xiao-

1966

Shaoqi from second to eighth place in the Politburo listings.

31. NCNA reveals Jiang Qing as first deputy head of the Cultural Revolution Group under Chen Boda.

November 17. *People's Daily* for the first time describes Li Fuchun as a member of the Standing Committee of the Politburo.

C CULTURAL AND SOCIAL

February 1. *People's Daily* attacks Tian Han's play *Xie Yaohuan* as a poisonous weed (see D, July-August 1961).

2–20. The Forum on the Work in Literature and Art in the Armed Forces, convened by Jiang Qing on the instructions of Lin Biao, takes place in Shanghai. Its 'Summary' is approved by the CCP's Military Affairs Committee March 30 and by the CCPCC Politburo at its May 4–18 meeting.

March 24. An article in *Red Flag* criticizes the well-known historian and CCPCC member Jian Bozan.

April 16. *Peking Daily* begins an attack on 'Notes from the Three-Family Village', by Deng Tuo, Wu Han and Liao Mosha (see D, October 10, 1961) and 'Evening Talks at Yanshan' (see D, August 1962). The attack continues throughout the following period.

18. A *Liberation Army Daily* editorial calls on literary and art workers in the PLA to take a leading role in eliminating bourgeois ideas in literature and art.

May 12. Newspapers in Peking begin to attack the film *Wutai jiemei* (*Sisters on the Stage*), produced by Xia Yan and others, for extolling bourgeois humanism and eliminating the class struggle. This was one of a number of films to be attacked at about this time.

25. A 'big-character poster' (*dazibao*) by Nie Yuanzi and six others of the Philosophy Department, appears in Peking University, denouncing Lu Ping, the Vice-Chancellor and First CCP Secretary, and others for sabotaging the Cultural Revolution at Peking University.

June 11. Shanghai's *Liberation Daily* declares some leading cultural organs are in the hands of the bourgeoisie. Among those attacked are famous actor Zhou Xinfang, President of the Shanghai Peking Opera Institute.

13. The CCPCC and State Council announce their decision to change the system of entrance examinations to tertiary educational institutions and to postpone 1966 enrolments of new students there.

20. *People's Daily* approvingly transmits Mao's view that 'posters written in big characters are an extremely useful new type of weapon'. (Big-character posters were an extremely important medium of

1966

ping, now the six top leaders in that order. The rally reveals the formation of the youth organization, the Red Guards, who play a vital role as the vanguard of the Cultural Revolution for the next two years. Mao Zedong attends enormous rallies in Tiananmen Square also on August 31, September 15, October 18, November 3, 10–11 and 25–26.

28. A *People's Daily* editorial calls on Red Guards to learn from the PLA, especially in its discipline, and to conduct the struggle through reasoning, not force.

September 5. The Chinese Ministry of National Defence protests to the USA against the bombing of Chinese cargo ships off the coast of Vietnam on August 29.

7. A *People's Daily* editorial urges Red Guards to organize themselves to take part in manual labour in the countryside to help with the autumn harvest. It stresses that the Cultural Revolution must not interfere with production.

16. NCNA reports that US aircraft intruded into Chinese air space near the border with Vietnam on September 9 and bombed Chinese villages.

19. A US State Department spokesman, Mr Robert McCloskey, for the first time admits that US combat planes have intruded into Chinese air space, but denies they attacked Chinese villages.

October 3. A Chinese ship leaves Medan, Indonesia, with 1005 passengers, 'persecuted Chinese nationals in Indonesia' returning home.

20. A *People's Daily* editorial praises a Red Guard group who walked from Dalian to Peking, covering 1000 km. within a month, to establish revolutionary ties and see Chairman Mao.

23. Liu Shaoqi and Deng Xiaoping submit self-criticisms to a Central Work Conference (held in Peking 8–25).

27. China successfully conducts a guided missile-nuclear weapons test.

28. *People's Daily* describes as a 'complete swindle' the suggestion that the USA should withdraw troops from Vietnam not later than six months after 'the other withdraws its forces to the North, ceases infiltration, and the level of violence thus subsides'. This proposal was contained in the Manila communiqué (October 25) at the end of the Manila Conference of the six nations supporting the USA (October 24–25).

November 5. Chinese diplomats leave Accra. China had announced on October 30 that it would recall its embassy in Ghana.

16. A joint CCPCC-State Council 'Urgent Notice on the Question of Revolutionary Teachers and Students Exchanging Revolutionary Experiences' orders that such people return home and be granted free

1966

information and propaganda in the Cultural Revolution.)

August 10. *Red Flag* denounces the well-known philosopher and historian Hou Wailu as a 'bourgeois reactionary "authority" of learning among historians'.

20. Red Guards begin destroying bourgeois and feudal remnants by changing the names of streets and shops with bourgeois or feudal overtones, forbidding various types of dress and literature etc. This process frequently involved violent ransacking of bookshops, private houses, and other places, and quickly spread throughout China. *Zhongguo qingnian bao* (*China Youth*, see D, April 27, 1951), organ of the Communist Youth League of China, ceases publication, one of a great many periodicals to do so at about this time.

22. The Red Guards begin the closure of Peking's churches and other religious establishments.

24. Red Guards ransack and close down all Christian churches in Shanghai.

26. The Peking Municipal People's Council announces the banning of the Franciscaines Missionaires de Marie, and decides to deport the last remaining eight foreign nuns in China, who were attached to the organization, for counter-revolutionary activities. (Red Guards took over their convent in central Peking the previous day.)

October 25. NCNA reports that some Shanghai surgeons 'have broken another world medical barrier' by reattaching completely severed fingers through a new technique of rejoining blood vessels.

November 25–December 6. The Games of the Newly Emerging Forces are held in Phnom Penh; China wins 113 titles.

28. At a rally in Peking the decision to incorporate the No. 1 Peking Opera Company of Peking and three other major cultural organs into the PLA, and Jiang Qing's appointment as cultural adviser to the PLA are announced.

D Publications

January. The People's Literary Publishing House publishes Yang Daqun's novel *Yizu zhi ying* (*The Eagle of the Yi People*).

February. The Commercial Press publishes *Luoji xue*, translation by Yang Yizhi of volume I of G. Hegel's *Wissenschaft der Logik*.

March. The Zhonghua Book Company publishes part one in two volumes of a re-edition of *Yuan yitong zhi* (*General Gazetteer of the Yuan*).

September. *Mao Zhuxi yulu* (*Quotations from Chairman Mao Zedong*) compiled by the General Political Department of the PLA, is published

travel only in a homeward direction.

December 4. The Portuguese impose a curfew in Macao following the eruption of bloody riots. On December 3 and 4 crowds had ransacked the City Hall and police fired on them to disperse them; several Chinese were killed.

12. The Macao administration announces its acceptance of demands made on December 10 by the Guangdong Provincial People's Council, in particular the banning of all NP activities in Macao.

26. A *People's Daily* editorial calls for the Cultural Revolution to be extended to industrial and mining enterprises, that is, to include workers as well as students.

28. China carries out her fifth nuclear test.

1967 The Cultural Revolution; the Wuhan Incident

January (early). Many Chinese diplomats are summoned home.

6. Large posters appear in Peking attacking Zhou Enlai, but are removed by January 8. A mass rally in Shanghai denounces the leaders of the CCP's East China Bureau and Municipal Committee, part of the move by rebel revolutionary organizations to seize power: the January Revolution.

13. The CCPCC issues Provisions on the Strengthening of Public Security Work in the GPCR. They forbid armed struggle, suppression of the revolutionary masses by the Party, government, military or public security. Also they declare anybody who attacks or humiliates Mao Zedong or Lin Biao will be punished on the basis of law.

23. The CCPCC, State Council, Military Affairs Committee and Cultural Revolution Group jointly issue an Urgent Notice on the

in Shanghai. The second edition has a foreword, dated December 16, 1966 by Lin Biao. (This work is often called *The Little Red Book*.)

E NATURAL DISASTERS

March 8. A strong earthquake strikes the area of Xingtai (Hebei).
22. Two further strong earthquakes strike the area of Shijiazhuang and Xingtai (Hebei). According to NCNA, though these earthquakes 'were stronger than that . . . on March 8, the loss of life was much less'.
July 12. *Yangcheng wanbao* (*Guangzhou Evening News*) reports major flooding in Guangdong from mid-June to early July.
December 27. NCNA reports drought in much of north China 'from spring right through into autumn, seven to eight months in duration' and 'torrential rains, typhoons and hailstorms' in the south succeeded by drought in the summer and autumn. It claims 'natural calamities in some districts have rarely been so severe'.

F DEATHS

February 18. Chen Shutong, Chairman of the Chinese National Industrial and Commercial Association, d. in Peking aged 90.
March 22. Philosopher Ai Siqi, d. aged 56.
May 18. Writer Deng Tuo d. aged 54.
August 24. Shu Qingchun (pen-name Lao She) d. aged 67.
September 19. Wan Xiaotang, First Secretary of the Hebei Provincial CCP Committee, d. aged 50.

The first Revolutionary Committees are set up **1967**

A ECONOMICS

January 1. NCNA claims 1966 had the best grain and cotton harvests in history and that the iron and steel, machine building, coal mining, petroleum, electric power, chemical, building materials, timber, textile and other industries exceeded the state plan. It claims China as self-sufficient in petroleum products.
9. Rebel groups in Shanghai and Fujian issue 'urgent notices' against economism, the doctrine of emphasizing material incentives among the workers in order to undermine their revolutionary fervour. Similar notices follow in other places in the next few days.
11. The CCPCC issues an Urgent Notice Opposing Economism, supporting the Shanghai and Fujian notices of January 9. A joint CCPCC-State Council Urgent Notice Restraining the Corruption

1967

PLA's Firmly Supporting the Revolutionary Left-Wing Masses. It calls on the PLA to intervene in the GPCR on the side of the 'broad left-wing masses'.

25. Chinese students attempting to lay wreaths on Lenin's mausoleum and Stalin's tomb in Moscow clash with Soviet police.

26. Mass demonstrations begin in front of the Soviet embassy in Peking. In Shihezi (Xinjiang), the August 1 Field Army, created by the First Secretary of the CCP North-west Bureau, Wang Enmao, opens fire on Red Guards trying to bring the GPCR to Xinjiang and seize power. Over 100 are killed, others tortured.

29. The Governor of Macao, José Nobre de Carvalho, signs an agreement for the Macao government admitting guilt for the death of several Chinese killed in recent riots and banning pro-NP activities in Macao.

February 11. According to a Red Guard report (of June 16, 1967) Vice-Premier Tan Zhenlin on this day 'deceived the CCPCC and Premier Zhou. He cleverly arranged that the representatives of five units ... in which false takeovers had taken place should be received by the Premier'. This was part of a temporarily successful attempt by Tan and others to prevent revolution and the seizure of power by mass organizations, known as the 'February Adverse Current'. The CCPCC, State Council and Military Affairs Committee jointly order that the GPCR be carried out in Xinjiang 'under military control'.

12. Wall-posters appear in Peking claiming that a PLA company has recently driven back an attack by a Soviet battalion on the border near Vladivostok.

17. *People's Daily* introduces the term 'three-way alliance' to indicate the fusion of revolutionary mass organizations, the PLA and cadres of Party and government organizations.

March 14–18. A meeting of the CCPCC's Politburo and Military Affairs Committee discusses measures against the February Adverse Current.

30. Broadcasts begin of articles in *Red Flag* (published April 1) attacking the 'top Party person in authority taking the capitalist road', or 'China's Khrushchev', i.e. Liu Shaoqi, and his book *How to be a Good Communist*: the beginning of a new radical phase of the Cultural Revolution.

April 1–4. Mass rallies take place all over China to denounce Liu Shaoqi.

6. The CCPCC's Military Affairs Committee issues a ten-point order, the first being 'as regards mass organizations, no matter whether they are revolutionary, or controlled by counter-revolutionary elements, or the situation is unclear, never open fire on them, but only carry out political work'.

of the Masses carries a similar intent.

March 18. NCNA releases the CCPCC's Letter to Revolutionary Workers, Staff and Cadres in Factories and Mines; it demands that they 'persist in the eight-hour work day' and confine GPCR activities to times outside that period.

April 13. In Damascus China and Syria exchange letters concerning PRC technical aid in building a cotton spinning mill in Syria.

16. Shanghai radio reports that congestion of goods on Shanghai wharves is seriously affecting the distribution of goods in China.

May 25. In Katmandu China and Nepal sign a protocol on PRC aid in building a power station and transmission line in Nepal.

August 5. In Peking, China and the DRVN sign an agreement on PRC economic and technical aid.

14. In Peking China and Mali sign an agreement on PRC economic aid to Mali.

28. NCNA announces the 'recent' inauguration of a direct air service between Chengdu and Lanzhou.

September 5. China, Tanzania, and Zambia sign an agreement in Peking under which China will assist in the construction of the Tanzania–Zambia railway.

October 5. NCNA reports the trial production by the Computer Technology Institute of Academia Sinica of a giant transistorized general-purpose high-speed computer.

November 15–December 15. The regular spring and autumn Guangzhou Export Commodities Fair is held, but one month later than usual owing to the GPCR.

25. At a meeting with representatives from railway bureaux in Peking, Zhou Enlai says there are serious problems in the railway transport situation: '3600 wagons are still not in operation; coal and petrol are not being transported from the north-east'.

December 10. Chengdu radio reports serious difficulties in railway transport in Sichuan because 'a number of workers of certain stations, sections and depots' have left their posts.

28. A rally marks the opening to traffic of a railway to Shaoshan (Hunan), the birthplace of Mao Zedong – a branch line of the Zhuzhou–Shaoyang railway.

B   OFFICIAL APPOINTMENTS, RESIGNATIONS, DISMISSALS ETC.

January 31. Pan Fusheng is inaugurated as Chairman of the Heilongjiang Provincial Revolutionary Committee, set up the same day as an alliance of revolutionary rebels, the PLA and revolutionary Party

1967

26. *People's Daily* denounces the 'anarchist trend of "suspect all, overthrow all"', which it claims 'has again appeared to scatter the targets of our struggle'.

May 1–6. Serious factional fighting takes place at the Sichuan cotton mill in Chengdu (Sichuan) in which workers, students and peasants are involved. For the first recorded time in the GPCR civilians use guns extensively, causing many casualties. On order from Peking the PLA intervenes and restores order May 6. This was only one instance of serious violence in Sichuan and other provinces at about this time.

15. The Ministry of Foreign Affairs protests to the British *chargé d'affaires*, D.C. Hopson, over arrests made in riots in Hongkong on May 6, 11, 12 and 14.

15–17. Demonstrations take place outside the British *chargé d'affaires'* office in Peking.

22. *People's Daily* editorializes: 'Of late a gust of sinister wind, the use of force in the struggle, has risen in some areas. ... We must be determined to check this sinister wind.' *People's Daily* reports that the revisionists have 'launched three major consecutive counterattacks' to seize back power in Shandong. Other reports claim similar happenings in other provinces at about this time.

29. An anti-Mao crowd of 30,000 raids an army college in Kunming, killing 266 men and wounding 1000, according to Peking wall posters appearing on June 7.

June 13. The Ministry of Foreign Affairs issues a statement again denouncing the British over their handling of the continuing unrest in Hongkong.

15. The Chinese Ministry of Foreign Affairs forbids foreign journalists and diplomats to copy or photograph wall posters.

17. China explodes her first hydrogen bomb.

21–25. Zambian President Kaunda visits China.

28. A Chinese is stabbed to death at the Chinese embassy in Rangoon during a siege of the embassy; this is part of anti-Chinese disturbances June 26–30 caused by the defiance by some Chinese students of a ban on the wearing of Mao badges.

29. The Chinese government accuses the Burmese of complicity in the anti-Chinese riots and announces its ambassador will not return to Burma.

July 14. Vice-Premier Xie Fuzhi and Wang Li, a member of the Cultural Revolution Group, arrive in Wuhan to arbitrate in a complicated struggle, involving Chen Zaidao, Commander of the Wuhan Military Region, and other factions.

19. Xie Fuzhi and Wang Li give their verdict on the struggle in Wuhan,

cadres. (This first provincial revolutionary committee became the GPCR's model for administration.)
February 3. Wang Xiaoyu is inaugurated as Chairman of the Shandong Provincial Revolutionary Committee, set up the same day.
  5. Zhang Chunqiao is inaugurated as First Secretary of the Shanghai People's Commune, set up the same day. (This leading organ of Shanghai is renamed Shanghai Municipal Revolutionary Committee on February 23, indicating the demise of the idea of the people's commune at municipal or provincial level.)
  14. Li Zaihan is inaugurated as Chairman of the Guizhou Provincial Revolutionary Committee, set up the same day.
March 18. Liu Geping is inaugurated as Chairman of the Shanxi Provincial Revolutionary Committee, established the same day.
April 20. Xie Fuzhi is inaugurated as Chairman and Wu De, Nie Yuanzi and others as deputy Chairmen of the Peking Municipal Revolutionary Committee, formally set up the same day.
May 7. The CCPCC issues its Decision on Handling the Sichuan Question, under which it dismisses Li Jingquan as First Secretary of the CCPCC's South-west Bureau and First Political Commissar of the Chengdu Military Region because 'he has made Sichuan into an independent kingdom which opposes the Party, socialism and Mao Zedong's thought'; it appoints Zhang Guohua to head a Preparatory Group of the Sichuan Provincial Revolutionary Committee.
August 4. At a rally in Wuhan, Zeng Siyu is referred to as Commander of the Wuhan Military Region in place of Chen Zaidao.
  12. Liu Xianquan is inaugurated as Chairman of the Qinghai Provincial Revolutionary Committee, set up the same day.
November 1. Teng Haiqing is inaugurated as Chairman of the Inner Mongolian Revolutionary Committee, set up the same day.
  12. The CCPCC issues its Decision on the Guangdong Problem, approving the establishment of a Preparatory Group of the Guangdong Provincial Revolutionary Committee, headed by Huang Yongsheng.
December 6. Xie Xuegong is inaugurated as Chairman of the Tianjin Municipal Revolutionary Committee, set up the same day.

C CULTURAL AND SOCIAL

January 10. Shanghai radio reveals 'an extremely serious dock strike' in the city. Rebel groups take over the docks January 17 and help restore normalcy.
  11. The CCPCC issues an Urgent Notice on Putting Military Control into Effect in Radio Stations, directing the PLA to take over in radio

1967

deciding against the supporters of Chen Zaidao, who promptly lay siege to their hotel.

20. Xie Fuzhi and Wang Li are kidnapped in Wuhan. Zhou Enlai flies to Wuhan.

21. Zhou Enlai secures their release and then flies back to Peking.

The Reuter correspondent in Peking, Anthony Grey, is placed under house arrest in retaliation for the arrest of three NCNA reporters in Hongkong.

22. Xie Fuzhi and Wang Li fly back to Peking. On about this day civil war breaks out in Wuhan between supporters of Chen Zaidao and of the central government.

23. A major battle erupts between two Red Guard factions in Guangzhou, called Red Flag and East Wind. According to its own claim, the former loses thirty-three dead and 'more than 400 sent to hospital for light or serious wounds'. (This is but one example of violent incidents in Guangdong at about this time. By the end of August, pro-Mao forces, supported by the PLA, are in control of Guangdong.)

August 4. A rally is held in Wuhan to celebrate the victory of the central forces in the civil war.

5. Indonesian youths attack the Chinese embassy in Jakarta and set fire to a building. Four demonstrators are shot. Liu Shaoqi, Deng Xiaoping, Wang Guangmei and Tao Zhu are denounced at rallies in Peking and make self-criticisms.

9. Lin Biao makes a speech on the Wuhan incident. He sums up the Cultural Revolution by saying 'the cost has been very slight, very slight indeed; the victory has been very great, very great indeed'. The Mongolian ambassador's car is burned in Peking; Red Guards invade the Mongolian embassy.

11. China protests to Burma over 'incessant land and air intrusions' into Yunnan 'in the past few years'. Red Guards board and damage the Soviet ship *Svirsk* at Dalian (Liaoning), beat up the crew and insult the captain.

20. The Ministry of Foreign Affairs, temporarily controlled by the ultra-leftist May 16 Group, issues an ultimatum to the British *chargé d'affaires*; it makes several demands on Britain to be fulfilled within forty-eight hours, including the release of some arrested Chinese in Hongkong.

22. After the expiry of the ultimatum (see previous entry), Red Guards attack and occupy the British *chargé d'affaires'* office in Peking and burn down the main building.

29. A violent incident takes place outside the Chinese *chargé d'affaires'* office in London.

1967

stations while the masses are asserting their control, and to broadcast, during this process, only items from central stations. On January 23 the CCPCC issued a supplementary urgent notice allowing local broadcasting stations to use some of their own items during the period of military control.

28. The Military Affairs Committee issues a directive prohibiting corporal publishment, parading people in dunces' hats and giving punishment runs, all common phenomena at this time.

29. Radio Peking announces the cancellation of the Spring Festival holidays.

31. The CCPCC issues its Preliminary Opinion on Reforming the Education System. Points include 'relaxing the restrictions on age for recruitment to universities or institutes, cancelling the restrictions on marriage, raising the proportion of workers, people's commune members (peasants), and demobilized army men', and 'abolishing all examination systems'.

February 17. The CCPCC issues the Regulations on the GPCR in Literary and Art Bodies: including that they should implement Mao Zedong's line on the arts and 'go to the countryside and factories in an organized and planned way, mingle with the workers and peasants and remould their own world outlook'.

21. Hefei radio announces that senior classes in Anhui primary schools have resumed work February 16, and that lower classes will resume February 25. This was but one among announcements indicating resumption of primary and middle-school classes, stopped owing to the Cultural Revolution.

22. The Congress of the Red Guards of Universities and Institutes in Peking is founded at a meeting of some 10,000 representatives in Peking. The inaugural meeting adopts a declaration in support of the GPCR and in opposition to 'the decadent customs and habits of the exploiting classes'.

March 6. NCNA announces that primary schools in Peking and Shanghai have reopened.

14. The CCPCC issues an Urgent Notice on the Question of the NCNA: that it may not be taken over by revolutionary mass organizations either within or without the NCNA, and that any changes in its leadership or staff must be decided on and approved by the CCPCC.

25. The Congress of the Red Guards of Secondary Schools in Peking is established at a meeting in Peking.

April 12. The USA grants political asylum to Ma Sicong, one of the PRC's most famous musical composers, after his departure from China.

October 14. The CCPCC issues an urgent notice that schools in the

1967

September 1. Addressing the Peking Municipal Revolutionary Committee, Zhou Enlai orders all Red Guards to 'stop exchanging revolutionary experiences' and return home; to cease violence and not to intrude into foreign embassies or missions.

5. The CCPCC, State Council, Military Affairs Committee and Cultural Revolution Group issue an order reinforcing earlier orders that army weapons not be handed over to mass organizations and allowing the PLA to use force against those who disobey the order. In an unprepared speech Jiang Qing tells representatives from two Anhui revolutionary groups that she 'resolutely supports Chairman Mao's call for "peaceful struggle, not armed struggle"' and blames abuses on the ultra-left May 16 group.

7. Fighting breaks out between Indian and Chinese troops on the Sikkim-Tibet border and continues for a week – the most serious series of incidents since October 1962.

13. Cambodian Prince Sihanouk announces his intention to withdraw the Cambodian embassy staff from Peking.

18. Sihanouk announces the reversal of his decision to withdraw Cambodian embassy staff from Peking, following the reception of a message from Zhou Enlai, through the Cambodian ambassador in Peking, Tuong Cang, expressing China's desire for friendly relations and mutual understanding with Cambodia.

20. Zhou Enlai, summarizing the situation, says: 'In the months of July and August, throughout the whole country, there were incidents of seizing weapons from our PLA, raiding arsenals and ambushing trains with military aid for Vietnam'.

24. NCNA reports Mao Zedong's return to Peking from a 'recent' tour of inspection of Hunan, Hubei, Henan, Jiangxi, Zhejiang and Shanghai.

October 1. The Chinese embassy in Jakarta is stormed by hundreds of youths.

7. The CCPCC issues a directive against harming foreigners or organizing demonstrations of any kind against them.

9. The Indonesian government decides to declare an official suspension of diplomatic relations with the PRC and instructs its embassy staff in Peking to return home.

17. Posters appear in Peking denouncing Wang Li as an ultra-leftist and leader of the May 16 group, and accusing him of ordering the attack on the British *chargé d'affaires*' offices (see August 22).

31. A Chinese aircraft drops all Indonesian embassy staff in Jakarta and picks up its own embassy staff, completing the rupture of diplomatic relations between the two countries.

whole country at all levels, primary, secondary and tertiary, should immediately resume classes and carry out reforms on the basis of actual practice and experience.

21. *People's Daily* releases a directive from Mao on cadres: 'The question of correct treatment of cadres holds the key to realizing the revolutionary three-way alliance, consolidating the revolutionary grand alliance, and implementing well the struggle-criticism-transformation in each unit, and it must be solved well.'

November 18. Shanghai's *Wenhui bao* (and NCNA on November 20) report that Chinese archaeologists have discovered a fossil skull cap of Peking Man at Zhoukoudian (Hebei).

30. NCNA reports that the Peking Observatory of Academia Sinica 'has just completed' and installed China's largest solar radio telescope.

D PUBLICATIONS

May 16. NCNA and other organs for the first time publish the 'Zhongguo Gongchan dang zhongyang weiyuanhui tongzhi (yijiuliuliu nian wuyue shiliu ri)' ('Circular of the CCPCC (May 16, 1966)').

28. NCNA publishes for the first time the 'Lin Biao tongzhi weituo Jiang Qing tongzhi zhaokai de budui wenyi gongzuo zuotanhui jiyao' ('Summary of the Forum on Literature and Art in the Armed Forces with which Comrade Lin Biao Entrusted Jiang Qing'). (See also C, February 2–20, 1966).

December 25. NCNA reports that in 1967 China has published 86,400,000 copies of the *Selected Works of Mao Zedong*, more than seven times the number published in the fifteen years before the Cultural Revolution began. It reports the number of copies of *Quotations from Chairman Mao Zedong* published in China as 350,000,000.

F DEATHS

February 2. Zhao Erlu, member of the CCPCC and NPC, d. aged 62.
May 2. Musician Wang Jianzhong d. aged 42.
June 22. Li Lisan d. aged 68.
27. Ye Jizhuang, Minister of Foreign Trade, d. aged 74.
August 15. Former NG Finance Minister Kong Xiangxi d. in the US aged 86.
September 5. Men He, PLA hero, d. aged 38.
October 17. Puyi, last Manchu emperor, d. aged 61.

1968 *The workers replace the Red Guards as the vanguard of the Cultural Revolution*

January 4. A ceremony in Phnom Penh marks the delivery of a consignment of Chinese military aid to Cambodia.
12. Shanghai's *Wenhui bao* lists 'ten crimes of factionalism', the first being 'the highest directives and the voice of the proletarian headquarters are not faithfully carried out ... '.
February 2. China and the People's Republic of South Yemen issue a joint communiqué establishing diplomatic relations at ambassadorial level. Zhou Enlai sends a message to Nguyen Huu Tho, President of the NLF of South Vietnam, congratulating the NLF on its victories in the Tet Offensive (begun January 31), involving large-scale attacks on major cities, and offering continued support.
6. *Wenhui bao* in Shanghai denounces anarchism and the lack of discipline among the masses; other media organs later follow suit.
22. The Chinese embassy in Rangoon protests over the sentencing of ten Chinese to prison terms on February 20.
March 15. In Lanzhou the Intermediate People's Court sentences the British engineer George Watt to three years in prison for 'carrying out espionage activities'.
21. In a talk to a reception for a delegation from Jiangsu and others, Zhou Enlai comments: 'Now the right has risen again, the February Adverse Current has made a comeback'. Jiang Qing makes a similar statement on the same occasion. This is a sympton of a general revival of GPCR radicalism at about this time.
29. The Ministry of Foreign Affairs issues a statement protesting against US bombing of the premises of the Chinese economic and cultural mission in Khang Khay, Laos, on March 21 and 22.
April 5. NCNA attacks US President Lyndon Johnson's speech of March 31 as a 'new fraud of inducing peace talks'. (Johnson had announced that he would not stand for re-election as President, and a partial suspension of the bombing of the DRVN. Peace talks began in Paris May 13.)
12. *People's Daily* reveals Mao Zedong's view that the Cultural Revolution is an extension of the struggle between the CCP and the NP, 'a continuation of the class struggle between the proletariat and the bourgeoisie'.
16. Mao Zedong, commenting on the assassination of Martin Luther King on April 4, issues a statement 'in support of the Afro-American struggle against violent repression'.
18. In Wuzhou (Guangxi), the forces of Wei Guoqing, called Alliance Command, begin wholesale attacks against a Red Guard organization, mobilized April 22, 1967, and called the April 22 Revolutionary Rebel

A Economics

April 27. In Dar-es-Salaam, China, Tanzania and Zambia sign a protocol on basic technical principles for the construction of the Tanzania–Zambia railway and an agreement on accounting procedures for the loans for the railway.

May 24. In Peking, China, Mali and Guinea sign an agreement on the construction of the Guinea–Mali railway.

July 23. In Peking, China and the DRVN sign an agreement and protocols on further economic and technical aid to the DRVN.

October 1. The rail section (lower tier) of the two-tiered bridge over the Yangzi at Nanjing is formally opened.

November 20. In Peking, China and Albania sign an agreement and protocols on a loan and other economic aid to Albania.

December 29. The road section (upper tier) of the bridge over the Yangzi at Nanjing is formally opened.

B Official Appointments, Resignations, Dismissals etc.

January 5. Cheng Shiqing is inaugurated as Chairman of the Jiangxi Provincial Revolutionary Committee, set up the same day.
24. Xian Henghan is inaugurated as Chairman of the Gansu Provincial Revolutionary Committee, set up the same day.
27. Liu Jianxun is inaugurated as Chairman of the Henan Provincial Revolutionary Committee, set up the same day.
February 3. Li Xuefeng is inaugurated as Chairman of the Hebei Provincial Revolutionary Committee, set up the same day with its capital in Shijiazhuang (transferred from Tianjin).
5. Zeng Siyu is inaugurated as Chairman of the Hubei Provincial Revolutionary Committee, set up the same day.
21. Huang Yongsheng is inaugurated as Chairman of the Guangdong Provincial Revolutionary Committee, set up the same day.
March 6. Wang Huaixiang is inaugurated as Chairman of the Jilin Provincial Revolutionary Committee, set up the same day.
22. The CCPCC, State Council, Military Affairs Committee and Cultural Revolution Group jointly dismiss Yang Chengwu as Chief of the General Staff of the PLA and replace him by Huang Yongsheng.
23. Xu Shiyou is inaugurated as Chairman of the Jiangsu Provincial Revolutionary Committee, set up the same day.
24. Nan Ping is inaugurated as Chairman of the Zhejiang Provincial Revolutionary Committee, set up the same day.
April 8. Li Yuan is inaugurated as Chairman of the Hunan Provincial

Grand Army. The attacks continue until May 6; and result in large-scale destruction of the city, extensive torture, the deaths of several thousand Red Guards, and the total annihilation of the April 22 Army.

June 13. The CCPCC issues an urgent cable demanding an end to violent clashes on the railway at Liuzhou (Guangxi). The instruction records that the railway system there has come to a halt and that reactionary forces have been stealing military materials destined for Vietnam and used them to attack the transport system.

July 3. Mao Zedong, the CCPCC, the Cultural Revolution Group and the State Council issue a joint Proclamation on the Guangxi Problem, demanding 'the immediate cessation of armed struggle' in Guangxi.

11. A *People's Daily* editorial note commends a county revolutionary committee in Henan for reducing its numbers, simplifying its administration, and allowing more time for cadres to work with the masses. The note thus asks others to follow suit.

17. An editorial in Guangzhou's *Nanfang ribao* (*Southern Daily*) claims 'counter-revolutionaries' have 'killed and robbed people of their goods and properties, created "white terror" and exercised dictatorship over the masses', suggesting continuing factional fighting in Guangdong at about this time.

24. The CCPCC, State Council, Military Affairs Committee and Cultural Revolution Group jointly issue a Proclamation on the Shaanxi Problem. Noting serious violence in the province, including the destruction of state banks, public buildings and granaries, and the theft of armaments from the PLA, it demands the immediate cessation of armed struggle.

27. A 'worker-peasant Mao Zedong thought propaganda team' is sent into Peking's Qinghua University.

28. From 3 a.m. to 8 a.m., Mao Zedong together with Zhou Enlai, Lin Biao and other top leaders, receives five Red Guard leaders including Nie Yuanzi of Peking University. He criticizes them severely for divorcing themselves from the people and indulging in armed fighting, and transmits a directive through Nie to stop all armed struggle. The net result of the meeting is that the chief role of the GPCR is transferred from the Red Guards to the workers, peasants and PLA. This meeting represents the effective end of the most radical phases of the GPCR and is one of its principal turning-points.

August 5. Mao Zedong sends a gift of mangoes to the worker-peasant Mao Zedong thought propaganda team at Qinghua University. This gift symbolizes Mao's approval for the work of the team in restoring order to the university, among other duties, and receives great coverage

Revolutionary Committee, set up the same day.
10. Kang Jianmin is inaugurated as Chairman of the Ningxia Hui Autonomous Region Revolutionary Committee, set up the same day.
18. Li Desheng is inaugurated as Chairman of the Anhui Provincial Revolutionary Committee, set up the same day.
May 1. Li Ruishan is inaugurated as Chairman of the Shaanxi Provincial Revolutionary Committee, set up the same day.
10. Chen Xilian is inaugurated as Chairman of the Liaoning Provincial Revolutionary Committee, set up the same day.
31. Zhang Guohua is inaugurated as Chairman of the Sichuan Provincial Revolutionary Committee, set up the same day.
August 13. Tan Furen is inaugurated as Chairman of the Yunnan Provincial Revolutionary Committee, set up the same day.
19. Han Xianchu is inaugurated as Chairman of the Fujian Provincial Revolutionary Committee, set up the same day.
26. Wei Guoqing is inaugurated as Chairman of the Guangxi Zhuang Autonomous Region Revolutionary Committee, set up the same day.
September 5. Long Shujin and Zeng Yongya are inaugurated as Chairmen, respectively of the Xinjiang Uighur and Tibetan Autonomous Region Revolutionary Committees, both set up the same day.
October 31. In its communiqué of the Twelfth Plenum (see October 13–31), the CCPCC announces its decision 'to expel Liu Shaoqi from the Party once and for all, and to dismiss him from all posts both inside and outside the Party'.

C CULTURAL AND SOCIAL

March 23. PLA surgeons successfully remove a 45-kg. tumour from the abdomen of a 37-year-old peasant woman.
May 7. The Heilongjiang Provincial Revolutionary Committee sends cadres to do manual labour on a farm at Liuhe in Qing'an (Heilongjiang). There they organize the first 'May 7' Cadre School, where cadres engage in agricultural and industrial productive labour according to Mao Zedong's May 7 directive (see May 7, 1966).
28. *People's Daily* begins a campaign to emulate Men He, an unselfish PLA cadre.
July 22. *People's Daily* releases a 'recent' directive from Mao Zedong. 'It is still necessary to have universities; here I refer mainly to colleges of science and engineering. However, it is essential to shorten the length of schooling, revolutionize education and put proletarian politics in command . . .'.
August 25. In an article in *Red Flag*, Cultural Revolution Group

1968

in the press. At about this time similar teams are sent to many other universities and schools throughout China.

15. *People's Daily* quotes a 'new directive' from Mao Zedong: 'Our country has 700,000,000 people and the working class is the leading class. Its leading role in the great Cultural Revolution and in all fields of work should be brought into full play. . . . '

23. *People's Daily* and Zhou Enlai both make strong attacks on the Soviet Union for its invasion of Czechoslovakia (begun in the night of August 20–21).

September 7. A mass rally is held in Peking to celebrate the 'establishment of revolutionary committees in all the provinces, municipalities and autonomous regions of China (except Taiwan)'. In his speech Zhou Enlai calls on the young to go and work in the countryside and settle there.

October 13–31. The Enlarged Twelfth Plenum of the Eighth CCPCC is held in Peking. On its last day it adopts a new draft CCP constitution and issues a communiqué on its decisions.

14. *Red Flag* calls for Party rebuilding and for 'fresh blood' in the CCP; this means mainly taking into the CCP 'a number of outstanding rebels, primarily advanced elements from among the industrial workers'.

November 3. *People's Daily* publishes, without comment, US President Johnson's speech of October 31 announcing a complete bombing halt over the DRVN.

9. An editorial in Shanghai's *Wenhui bao* calls for the continuation of the GPCR and assesses its achievements as 'greatest, greatest, greatest' and its losses as 'smallest, smallest, smallest'. The rebuilding of the Party proceeds.

27–December 3. A Chinese delegation headed by Huang Yongsheng visits Albania; Huang was the first major Chinese leader to go abroad since the beginning of the GPCR.

December 27. China conducts a hydrogen bomb test in Xinjiang.

member Yao Wenyuan releases another directive from Mao Zedong on education calling for working-class leadership: '... the workers' propaganda teams should stay permanently in the schools and take part in fulfilling all tasks in the schools of struggle-criticism-transformation, and they will always lead the school ...'

September 11. *Jiangxi Daily* puts forward as a model a new type of part tea-growing part study secondary school in Wuyuan (Jiangxi), the main features of which are (*i*) the students 'accept workers and peasants as their teachers', and (*ii*) 'they use workshops and farms as their classrooms, thus integrating learning with production'. The concept is later taken up nationwide.

October 5. *People's Daily* publishes, as part of an article on the model Liuhe May 7 Cadre School in Heilongjiang, a new Mao directive on cadres: 'Going down to do manual labour gives vast numbers of cadres an excellent opportunity to study once again.' The directive and article were followed by the establishment of many cadre schools to train cadres in ideology and in being one with the masses.

December 22. A directive by Mao urging that 'educated young people' be sent to the countryside for 're-education by the poor and lower-middle peasants' is broadcast (and printed in the press the next day).

D PUBLICATIONS

January 6. The essay 'Zhongguo xiang hechu qu?' ('Whither China?') by the Hunan Provincial Proletarian Alliance, is completed; distributed originally as a leaflet, it is published in March in *Guangyin hongqi* (*Guangzhou Printed Red Flag*). (The essay expresses the frustration of some Red Guards over the failure of the GPCR to produce a new political system.)

F DEATHS

July 15. CCPCC member Zeng Xisheng d. aged 64.
Cinema artist Cai Chusheng d. aged 62.
November 27. Deng Baoshan, deputy Chairman of the NP Revolutionary Committee, d. aged 75.
28. Xu Teli, Mao Zedong's former teacher and current CCPCC member, d. aged 91.
December 10. Dramatist Tian Han d. aged 70.
18. Historian Jian Bozan d. aged 70.
26. Peking Opera actor Xun Huisheng d. aged 68.

1969 *Border clashes with the Soviet Union; the Ninth CCP Congress*

January 24. The Chinese *chargé d'affaires* in The Hague, Liao Heshu, defects, leaving later for the USA.

27. US President Richard Nixon says, at his first press conference, that his administration's policy 'will be to continue to oppose Communist China's admission to the United Nations'.

February 19. The Chinese Ministry of Foreign Affairs issues a statement cancelling the 135th meeting of the Sino-US ambassadorial talks, scheduled for the following day, because of Liao Heshu's defection.

March 2. A Sino-Soviet armed clash breaks out at Zhenbao (Damansky) Island in the Ussuri River on the eastern border.

10. The Chinese Ministry of Foreign Affairs issues a long statement on the Sino-Soviet border, making clear its willingness to accept the *status quo*.

15. A second major clash erupts at Zhenbao Island, the Chinese claiming to have driven Soviet troops off the island.

29. The Soviet government proposes the reopening of talks on the border question 'in the nearest future'.

April 1–24. The Ninth National Congress of the CCP is held in Peking, attended by 1512 delegates. Lin Biao's report (made April 1) and a new CCP constitution are adopted on April 14, the latter reaffirming 'Marxism-Leninism-Mao Zedong Thought as the theoretical basis' guiding the CCP's thinking.

May 2. Lin Biao gives a talk at a reception for some of the delegates from Yunnan, Guizhou and Sichuan to the Ninth CCP Congress, and stresses the theme of unity.

24. China issues another statement on the Sino-Soviet border question.

June 10. Serious fighting breaks out on the Sino-Soviet border at Yumin (Xinjiang), the largest of many clashes on the western border at about this time.

13. The Soviet government issues a statement on the Sino-Soviet border question.

14. Zhou Enlai sends a message of support and recognition to Huynh Tan Phat, President of the Provisional Revolutionary Government of the Republic of South Vietnam, formed June 6.

July 8. An armed clash takes place between Chinese and Soviet troops on a border island in the Amur River near Khabarovsk.

19. Yang Qiliang and Wang Ruojie leave Peking to take up positions as Chinese ambassadors in Algeria and Yemen respectively; they make seventeen Chinese ambassadors sent abroad since May, following the withdrawal of almost all ambassadors during the GPCR.

21. The US government announces the lifting of many of the restrictions preventing travel to China on US passports.

A Economics

February 21. A *People's Daily* editorial, its first major statement on economic policy for some time, calls on the people to 'grasp revolution and promote production'. It urges taking agriculture as the basis of the economy and industry as the leading factor, and the setting of reasonable targets; it quotes a new Mao directive: 'in drawing up plans, it is necessary to mobilize the masses and see to it that there is enough leeway.'
April 2. The 15,000-ton oil tanker *Daqing No. 27*, the first of its kind built by China, is formally launched in Shanghai.
August 8. The Sino-Soviet Frontier Navigation Commission signs a protocol on the improvement of shipping.
24. A Chinese caravan of camels reaches Misgar in West Pakistan on the border with Xinjiang by way of the old Silk Route; the ancient road is thus reopened.
September 26. China and the DRVN sign in Peking an agreement for non-refundable economic and military assistance to the DRVN.
27. The 15,000-ton oil tanker *Daqing No. 28* is formally launched.
October 10. China and the Congo (Brazzaville) sign an Agreement on Economic and Technical Cooperation.
November 14. In Lusaka, China, Tanzania and Zambia sign a supplementary agreement on the Tanzania–Zambia railway, as preliminary work proceeds on the railway's construction.
December 19. The US State Department announces a partial lifting of the trade embargo with China, to take effect December 22; among other provisions it allows US tourists to make unlimited purchases of Chinese goods for private use.
26. The first ice-breaker designed and built in China is launched in Shanghai.

B Official Appointments, Resignations, Dismissals etc.

April 24. The Ninth National Congress of the CCP elects a CCPCC of 170 full and 109 alternate members.
28. The First Plenum of the Ninth CCPCC elects the Politburo: Mao Zedong (Chairman), Lin Biao (Vice-Chairman), Ye Qun, Ye Jianying, Liu Bocheng, Jiang Qing, Zhu De, Xu Shiyou, Chen Boda, Chen Xilian, Li Xiannian, Zhang Chunqiao, Zhou Enlai, Yao Wenyuan, Kang Sheng, Huang Yongsheng, Dong Biwu, Xie Fuzhi, and others. Lin Biao is elected sole Vice-Chairman. The Standing Committee of the Politburo is elected: Mao Zedong, Lin Biao, Chen Boda, Zhou Enlai and Kang Sheng.

1969-70

23. The CCPCC issues a proclamation demanding an end to factionalism and resistance to the central government in Shanxi; it notes that 'extremely serious counter-revolutionary crimes' have occurred, such as attacks on the PLA, occupation of state banks, and the destruction of railways.

August 13. A further Sino-Soviet armed clash takes place on the western border at Yumin (Xinjiang), the most serious incident since March, each side accusing the other of starting the clash and invading its territory.

September 4-5. Zhou Enlai visits Hanoi to pay respects to Ho Chi Minh, who died September 3.

11. Zhou Enlai and USSR Prime Minister Kosygin meet at Peking airport and discuss, among other things, the problems of the Sino-Soviet border.

23. China carries out its first successful underground nuclear test.

27. DRVN Prime Minister Pham Van Dong arrives in China, among many foreign dignitaries, for the National Day celebrations. He is followed by South Vietnamese NLF President Nguyen Huu Tho (September 29) and DPRK President Choi Yong Kun (September 30).

29. China carries out a hydrogen bomb test in the atmosphere.

October 4. Reuter correspondent Anthony Grey is released, following the release in Hongkong the previous day of the last of the 'patriotic' Chinese journalists. (See also July 21, 1967.)

8. The Chinese Ministry of Foreign Affairs issues a 'refutation of the Soviet government's statement of June 13, 1969' on the border problem. It calls for the conclusion of 'a new equal Sino-Soviet treaty to replace the old unequal Sino-Russian treaties', pending which the *status quo* should be maintained.

20. Talks on the Sino-Soviet border problem begin in Peking.

1970 *China establishes diplomatic relations with Canada and Italy*

January 20. The 135th session of the Sino-US ambassadorial talks takes places in Warsaw, the first for two years.

March 19. Cambodian Prince Norodom Sihanouk arrives in Peking

1969–70

C Cultural and Social

January 1. The New Year's editorial of the main media releases a new Mao directive on dealing with counter-revolutionaries and those who have made mistakes: 'the scope of attack must be narrow and more people must be helped through education. The stress must be on the weight of evidence and on investigation and study. It is strictly forbidden to extort confessions.'

May 12. *People's Daily* holds up as models the rural schools of Lishu (Jilin). Curricula are practical, flexible, and suited to peasants; school and family education are integrated with each other; primary schools are run by brigades, secondary by communes; examinations are abolished except for open-book tests.

November 28. NCNA reports from Peking that more than eighty blind people have regained their sight after new methods of treatment, involving acupuncture, at the clinic of a PLA battalion.

D Publications

October 29. The revised script of the 'model' Peking Opera *Zhiqu Weihushan* (*Taking Tiger Mountain by Strategy*) is published in *Red Flag*.

F Deaths

January 30. Li Zongren d. in Peking aged 78.
April 6. Zhang Zhizhong, deputy Chairman of the NPC and of the NP Revolutionary Committee, d. aged 78.
  23. Film director Zheng Junli d. aged 58.
June 9. He Long d. aged 73.
July 29. Historian and CCPCC member Fan Wenlan d. in Peking aged 76.
October 11. Historian Wu Han d. aged 60.
November 12. Former President Liu Shaoqi d. in Kaifeng (Henan) in prison aged 71.
  30. Tao Zhu d. aged 61.

The first post-GPCR Provincial Party Committees are set up 1970

A Economics

March 22. *Liaoning Daily* marks the tenth anniversary of the constitution of the Anshan (Liaoning) iron and steel works with an editorial strongly

1970

and is welcomed as head of state despite the successful *coup d'état* against him by Lon Nol the previous day.

April 5–7. Zhou Enlai visits the DPRK.

24. China successfully launches into orbit its first space satellite.

25. Zhou Enlai gives a banquet for the delegates of the Summit Conference of Indochinese Peoples, held 'in the locality of the Lao-Vietnam-China border areas' April 24–25.

28. The Chinese government issues a statement that the '700,000,000 Chinese people will always provide a powerful backing for the three Indochinese peoples in their war against US aggression and for national salvation'.

May 4. Norodom Sihanouk establishes his Royal Government of National Union of Kampuchea in Peking. The Chinese government issues a statement denouncing the US troop movement into Cambodia, announced by Nixon on April 30, as a 'provocation' to the Chinese people.

5. The Chinese government formally recognizes Sihanouk's Royal Government of National Union and declares its links with Lon Nol's government severed.

20. Commenting on the US invasion of Cambodia, Mao Zedong issues a statement denouncing US imperialism. He declares that 'the danger of a new world war still exists', but that 'revolution is the main trend in the world today'. He calls on the 'people of the world to unite and defeat the US aggressors and all their running dogs!'

21. Mao Zedong and Sihanouk attend a mass rally in Tiananmen Square to support the world's peoples against US imperialism, and to support Mao's statement of the previous day.

July 4. *People's Daily* describes the withdrawal of US troops from Cambodia, announced by US President Nixon June 30, as a smokescreen.

August 1–13. South Yemeni President Salem Robaya Ali visits China.

6–13. Sudanese President Gaafar Mohamed Nimeri visits China.

17. Huang Yongsheng for China and Duang Sam Ol for Cambodia (Royal Government of National Union) sign an agreement in Peking 'on the provision of military aid without repayment by China to Cambodia in 1970'. Full diplomatic relations at ambassadorial level with Yugoslavia are restored for the first time since 1958 with the arrival of the Chinese ambassador Zeng Tao in Belgrade. Yugoslavia's ambassador to China, B. Orescanin, had presented his credentials May 29.

23–September 6. The Second Plenum of the Ninth CCPCC is held on Lushan (Jiangxi). On August 23–25 several Lin Biao supporters

advocating it. This was a blueprint for industrial development suggested by Mao Zedong in a note of March 22, 1960, but not initially taken up. It emphasizes politics in command, Party leadership, mass participation and the technical revolution.

April 19. China and Japan sign the Memorandum Trade Agreement in Peking after much bargaining.

July 1. The 753.3-km. railway from Jiaozuo (Henan) to Zhicheng (Hubei) is completed; the 1085-km. Chengdu–Kunming railway is formally opened to traffic.

August 7. China and South Yemen sign an economic and technical agreement.

October 16. In Peking, China and Albania sign an agreement for a long-term interest-free PRC loan to Albania; and in addition a trade agreement and two economic protocols.

17. China and the DPRK sign two agreements, one on PRC economic and technical aid, the other on trade from 1971 to 1976.

19. *People's Daily* comments at length on 'the direction of China's socialist commerce'; it attacks too heavy a stress on balancing supply and demand and repeats that 'the fallacy "put profit in command" must be thoroughly criticized'.

26. President Kaunda of Zambia officially inaugurates the construction of the Tanzania–Zambia railway. Fang Yi, Director of the Commission for Economic Relations with Foreign Countries, attends.

B Official Appointments, Resignations, Dismissals etc.

September 2. For the first time, NCNA refers to Li Desheng as Director of the General Political Department of the PLA.

December 13. NCNA reports the election of Hua Guofeng as First Secretary of the Hunan Provincial CCP Committee by the Third Hunan Provincial CCP Congress (held November 24–December 4), the first Party Congress at province level since the GPCR.

26. The Third Jiangxi Provincial Party Congress (held 18–26), Third Guangdong Provincial Party Congress (held 18–26) and the Third Jiangsu Provincial Party Congress (held 19–26) elect Cheng Shiqing, Liu Xingyuan and Xu Shiyou as First Secretaries of the respective Provincial Party Committees.

C Cultural and Social

July 10. US citizen James Edward Walsh, formerly Bishop of Shanghai, is released from prison (see also C, March 18, 1960).

1970

try to reverse Mao's instruction that the Draft PRC Constitution omit reference to the position of PRC Chairman. Mao regards this attempt as a 'surprise attack' and it leads him to doubt Lin Biao's loyalty.

September 3. A joint *People's Daily* and *Liberation Army Daily* editorial marks the twenty-fifth anniversary of Japan's 1945 defeat by denouncing the revival of Japanese militarism.

15. Mao Zedong issues a 'letter to the whole Party' calling for a campaign to criticize Chen Boda.

October 13. Canada and China issue a joint communiqué on their decision to establish diplomatic relations at ambassadorial level; Canada 'takes note' of China's position that Taiwan is 'an inalienable part' of PRC territory.

14. A nuclear test is carried out in Xinjiang, according to non-Chinese sources.

15. China and Equatorial Guinea issue a joint communiqué establishing diplomatic relations; it makes no mention of Taiwan.

November 6. China and Italy issue a joint communiqué on their decision to establish diplomatic relations at ambassadorial level; Italy 'takes note' of China's claim to Taiwan.

10–14. Pakistani President Yahya Khan visits China.

16. Burma's new ambassador, U Thein Maung, the first since 1967, arrives in Peking.

20. The UN vote on the seating of China shows, for the first time, a majority in favour of the PRC (51–49, 25 abstentions), but the 'important question' issue (passed by 66 to 52 with 7 abstentions), demanding a two-thirds majority, prevents the PRC from being invited to join.

24. China and Ethiopia sign a joint communiqué (published by NCNA December 1) on their intention to establish diplomatic relations at ambassadorial level; Ethiopia makes no mention of Taiwan.

December 14. In New York, China and Cyprus sign a joint communiqué (issued January 12, 1971) on their decision to establish diplomatic relations.

15. In Paris, China and Chile sign a joint communiqué (published by NCNA January 5, 1971) on their intention to establish diplomatic relations at ambassadorial level; Chile 'takes note' of China's claim to Taiwan.

15. *People's Daily* carries a commentary calling for efficient effort 'to popularize model revolutionary theatrical works', beginning a campaign to expand performance of the operas both among professionals and amateurs.

21. *Red Flag* carries an article on Qinghua University as part of a special issue on education. It advocates running universities in close connection with factories: 'open door education'; and recruiting as students chiefly workers, peasants, the PLA, and young cadres. (The 1970–71 academic year was the first since the GPCR to have major university student enrolment.)

October 30. A *People's Daily* editorial lays down guidelines for studying Mao Zedong's philosophical works and in particular attacks the opinion that the masses cannot understand philosophy.

D Publications

May. *Red Flag* publishes revised scripts of the 'model' Peking operas *Hongdeng ji* (*The Red Lantern*) (May 1) and *Shajiabang* (May 25).

July 2. *Red Flag* publishes the revised script of the 'model' revolutionary ballet *Hongse niangzi jun* (*The Red Detachment of Women*).

E Natural Disasters

January 5. A strong earthquake strikes the region south of Kunming (Yunnan).

F Deaths

January 11. Zhou Shujia, deputy Chairman of the Chinese Buddhist Association and NPC deputy, d. aged 71.

March 29. Anna Louise Strong, longtime China resident, US writer and friend of Mao Zedong, d. in Peking aged 84.

May 4. Ma Xulun d. aged 85.

September 20. Mme Gong Peng, deputy Minister of Foreign Affairs, d. aged 56.

23. Writer Zhao Shuli d. in Taiyuan aged 64.

27. CCPCC member Li Tianyou d. aged 65.

November 15. Wang Jinxi, CCPCC member and deputy Chairman of the Daqing Oilfields Revolutionary Committee, d. aged 47.

December 18. Tan Furen, CCPCC member and Chairman of the Yunnan Provincial Revolutionary Committee, d. aged 60.

February 8. The Ministry of Foreign Affairs issues a statement strongly attacking the USA and their South Vietnamese 'lackeys' for the invasion of southern Laos, which began the same day.
10. China and Nigeria issue a joint communiqué agreeing to establish diplomatic relations at ambassadorial level.
25. US President Nixon's Foreign Policy Message to Congress uses the designation 'The People's Republic of China', being the first official US document to do so.
March 2. Zhou Enlai tells John Denson, British *chargé d'affaires* in Peking, that China will pay for the reconstruction of the British mission offices, destroyed by Red Guards (see August 22, 1967).
3. China launches its second satellite.
5–8. Zhou Enlai and other Chinese leaders visit Hanoi. On March 8 a joint communiqué is issued; China promises not to flinch 'even from the greatest national sacrifices' in its support and assistance to 'the Vietnamese and other Indochinese peoples'.
15. The US State Department announces the lifting of all restrictions on travel by US citizens to the PRC.
21. *People's Daily* reports the 'glorious victory of the Lao patriotic army and people' against the invasion of southern Laos by South Vietnamese troops, claiming that it marks the failure of Vietnamization (Nixon's policy of transferring war effort from US to Vietnamese soldiers).
22. China and Kuwait issue a joint communiqué agreeing to establish diplomatic relations.
22–24. According to documents issued on January 13, 1972 by the CCPCC within sections of the CCP and government, Lin Biao's son Lin Liguo and others draft the 'Outline of "Project 571"', a '*coup* programme' to overthrow Mao Zedong.
26. In Yaounde, capital of Cameroon, China and Cameroon sign a joint communiqué on their agreement to establish diplomatic relations.
April. A Central Work Conference takes place to extend criticism of Chen Boda to other Lin Biao supporters – part of the movement against the ultra-leftist May 16 group.
14. Zhou Enlai receives the US table tennis delegation visiting China (see also C, April 10–17), along with those of Canada, Colombia, UK and Nigeria.
May 26. In Bucharest, China and Austria sign a joint communiqué on their decision to establish diplomatic relations at ambassadorial level, effective as from May 28.
June 1–9. A Rumanian delegation visits China led by Nicolae Ceausescu, the General Secretary of the Rumanian Communist Party. On June 3,

Death of Lin Biao 1971

A Economics

January 1. *People's Daily* and other newspapers state that the 'Third Five-year Plan for developing the national economy has been successfully fulfilled', and announce the beginning of the Fourth Five-Year Plan.
April 14. US President Nixon announces the relaxation of the embargo on direct US trade with China and of US currency controls preventing the use of dollars by the PRC.
May 27. China and Ceylon sign an agreement for a PRC long-term interest-free loan.
August 22–28. A Chinese trade delegation, led by Zhang Guangdou, visits Malaysia. On the last day a joint statement is signed on the development of direct mutual trade.
October 9. In Peking, China and Ethiopia sign agreements on economic and technical cooperation, and trade.

B Official Appointments, Resignations, Dismissals etc.

January 10. The Fourth Shanghai Municipal Party Congress (held 4–10) elects Zhang Chunqiao as First Secretary of the Shanghai Municipal Party Committee, which it sets up the same day (all committees below are set up the same day as the election of the First Secretary).
13. The Fourth Liaoning Provincial Party Congress (held 9–13) elects Chen Xilian as First Secretary of the Party Committee.
21. The Third Anhui Provincial Party Congress (held 15–21) elects Li Desheng as First Secretary of the Party Committee.
28. The Fourth Zhejiang Provincial Party Congress (held 20–28) elects Nan Ping as First Secretary of the Party Committee.
February 16. The Third Guangxi Zhuang Autonomous Region Party Congress (held 9–16) elects Wei Guoqing as First Secretary of the Party Committee.
17. The Fifth Gansu Provincial Party Congress (held 11–17) elects Xian Henghan as First Secretary of the Party Committee.
March 5. The Fifth Shaanxi Provincial Party Congress (held February 28–March 5) elects Li Ruishan as First Secretary of the Party Committee.
8. The Third Henan Provincial Party Congress (held 2–8) elects Liu Jianxun as First Secretary of the Party Committee.
11. The Fifth Qinghai Provincial Party Congress (held 6–11) elects Liu Xianquan as First Secretary of the Party Committee.
15. The Fourth Peking Municipal Party Congress (held 10–15) elects Xie Fuzhi as First Secretary of the Party Committee.

1971

Mao Zedong and Lin Biao receive the delegation: Lin's last public appearance.

20. *People's Daily* denounces the US-Japan agreement to return Okinawa to Japan, signed on June 17, as 'a dirty deal, a despicable fraud', because the USA will continue, under the agreement, to maintain military bases in Okinawa.

July 9–11. US President Nixon's Assistant for National Security Affairs, Dr Henry Kissinger, visits Peking secretly and holds talks with Zhou Enlai.

15. US President Nixon announces that Zhou Enlai has invited him to visit China 'at an appropriate date before May, 1972' and that he has accepted the invitation. The meeting aims 'to seek the normalization of relations between the two countries'.

16. *People's Daily* and NCNA make the same announcement (see preceding entry).

29. China and Sierra Leone issue a joint communiqué on their decision to establish diplomatic relations at ambassadorial level.

August 4. In Paris, Turkey and China issue a joint communiqué on their decision to establish diplomatic relations and exchange ambassadors.

6–12. Burmese President Ne Win visits China.

16. In Islamabad, China and Iran sign a joint communiqué on their decision to establish diplomatic relations at ambassadorial level.

22. A Chinese delegation, led by Zhang Guangdou, visits Malaysia. (See A, August 22–28.)

September 12. Lin Biao's attempt to have Mao Zedong assassinated fails.

18. *People's Daily* uses the occasion of the fortieth anniversary of the Shenyang Incident (see September 18, 1931) to deliver, in its editorial, a sharp attack on Japan for its revival of militarism. This was only the strongest of many comments on this theme to appear at about this time.

22. A spokesman for the Chinese government announces the cancellation of the normal National Day parade on October 1.

29–October 1. An official Chinese government delegation led by Bai Xiangguo, Minister of Foreign Trade, visits France, the first Chinese group to visit Western Europe at full ministerial level since 1949.

October 5–13. Emperor Haile Selassie of Ethiopia visits China.

20–26. Dr Henry Kissinger of the USA revisits China.

25. In Paris, China and Belgium sign a joint communiqué on their decision to establish diplomatic relations at ambassadorial level.

24. The Third Jilin Provincial Party Congress (held 18–24) elects Wang Huaixiang as First Secretary of the Party Committee.
28. The Third Hubei Provincial Party Congress (held 23–28) elects Zeng Siyu as First Secretary of the Party Committee.
April 3. The Second Fujian Provincial Party Congress (held March 30–April 3) elects Han Xianchu as First Secretary of the Party Committee.
5. The Third Shandong Provincial Party Congress (held 1–5) elects Yang Dezhi as First Secretary of the Party Committee.
11. The Third Shanxi Provincial Party Congress (held 7–11) elects Xie Zhenhua as First Secretary of the Party Committee.
May 11. The Second Xinjiang Uighur Autonomous Region Party Congress (held 7–11) elects Long Shujin as First Secretary of the Party Committee.
14. The Third Guizhou Provincial Party Congress (held 7–14) elects Lan Yinong as First Secretary of the Party Committee.
18. The Third Inner Mongolian Autonomous Region Party Congress (held 13–18) elects You Taizhong as First Secretary of the Party Committee.
20. The Second Hebei Provincial Party Congress (held 17–20) elects Liu Zihou as First Secretary of the Party Committee.
26. The Third Tianjin Municipal Party Congress (held 22–26) elects Xie Xuegong as First Secretary of the Party Committee.
June 3. The Second Yunnan Provincial Party Congress (held May 31–June 3) elects Zhou Xing as First Secretary of the Party Committee.
August 12. The First Tibet Autonomous Region Party Congress (held 7–12) elects Ren Rong as First Secretary of the Party Committee.
16. The Second Sichuan Provincial Party Congress (held 12–16) elects Zhang Guohua as First Secretary of the Party Committee.
18. The Third Ningxia Hui Autonomous Region Party Congress (held 15–18) elects Kang Jianmin as First Secretary of the Party Committee.
19. The Third Heilongjiang Provincial Party Congress (held 16–19) elects Wang Jiadao as First Secretary of the Party Committee.

C CULTURAL AND SOCIAL

January 27. Premiere showings take place of the colour films of the 'model' Peking opera *The Red Lantern* and ballet *The Red Detachment of Women* (see also D, 1970).
March 21–April 30. A large table tennis delegation of sixty people, led by Zhao Zhenghong, visits Japan to take part in the World Table

1971-2

Belgium 'takes note' of China's claim to Taiwan. The PRC is admitted to the United Nations. The General Assembly votes on two resolutions. The first, sponsored by the USA and Japan and declaring the expulsion of the Republic of China (Taiwan) to be an important question requiring a two-thirds majority, is defeated by 59 votes to 55 with 15 abstentions. The second, sponsored by Albania and twenty-one other countries and calling for the restoration of all lawful rights of the PRC and the expulsion of 'the representatives of Chiang Kai-shek', is carried by 76 votes to 35 with 17 abstentions.

November 2. In Ottawa, China and Peru sign a joint communiqué on their decision to establish diplomatic relations at ambassadorial level.

9. In Paris, China and Lebanon sign a joint communiqué on their decision to establish diplomatic relations at ambassadorial level.

11. The Chinese UN delegation arrives in New York, headed by Qiao Guanhua, deputy Minister of Foreign Affairs.

12. China and Ruanda sign a joint communiqué on their decision to establish diplomatic relations at ambassadorial level.

18. China carries out a nuclear test in its western region.

December 7. China and Senegal sign a joint communiqué on their decision to establish diplomatic relations at ambassadorial level.

8. In Copenhagen, China and Iceland issue a joint communiqué on their decision to establish diplomatic relations at ambassadorial level.

16. The Chinese Ministry of Foreign Affairs sends a note to the Indian embassy protesting over two border crossings by Indian troops on the China-Sikkim frontier on December 10. The Chinese government issues a statement on the Indo-Pakistani War, condemning India as the aggressor. (The Indo-Pakistani War, November 21–December 17, resulted in the establishment of Bangladesh, formerly East Pakistan.)

1972 *US President Nixon and Japanese Prime Minister Tanaka visit China*

January 7. China carries out a further nuclear test.

22. In Peking, China and the DRVN sign a protocol for the 'supplementary gratuitous supply' of military and economic materials to the DRVN.

31. In Rome, China and Malta sign a joint communiqué on their decision to establish diplomatic relations (issued February 25).

31–February 2. Pakistani President Bhutto visits China.

Tennis Championships in Nagoya. It visits Osaka, Kyoto, Tokyo and other places.

April 10–17. A US table tennis team visits China after playing in the World Championships in Japan. This tour had the approval of both the US and Chinese governments. The group was the first from the USA at semi-official (or official) level to visit China for many years. See also April 14.

August 1. NCNA makes the first mention of the Cultural Group under the State Council (established the preceding month, headed by Wu De).

November 2–14. The Afro-Asian Table Tennis Friendship Invitational Tournament is held in Peking.

December 1. NCNA reports the excavation, during the GPCR, of numerous valuable ancient relics in Gansu, including over 340 well-preserved bronzes of the early Western Zhou dynasty (about 11th century BC) in September 1967.

D   PUBLICATIONS

November. The People's Literary Publishing House publishes Guo Moruo's *Li Bai yu Du Fu* (*Li Bai and Du Fu*), the first book on classical literature published in China since before the GPCR.

F   DEATHS

January 15. Actor Gai Jiaotian d. aged 83.
    27. Geologist Weng Wenhao d. aged 82.
April 29. Li Siguang, CCPCC member, d. aged 82.
June 21. Historian Chen Yuan d. in Peking aged 91.
September 13. Lin Biao is killed, aged 63.

Death of Chen Yi **1972**

A   ECONOMICS

January 1. *People's Daily* and other journals announce some statistics on economic production for 1971, the first official nationwide statistics for ten years. Total grain output was 246,000,000 tonnes; steel production 21,000,000 tonnes.

April 6. China and Rumania sign a civil air transport agreement in Bucharest.

1972

February 14. In New York, China and Mexico issue a joint communiqué on their decision to establish diplomatic relations at ambassadorial level.

16. In Bucharest, Argentina and China sign a joint communiqué on their decision to establish diplomatic relations at ambassadorial level as from February 19.

21. US President Nixon arrives in Peking, accompanied by his wife and an official party of thirteen, including William Rogers, the Secretary of State, and Dr Henry Kissinger. Nixon is met by Zhou Enlai and others and goes the same day for an audience with Mao Zedong.

26. Nixon and his party leave Peking for Hangzhou.

27. Nixon and his party go to Shanghai.

28. A joint US-China communiqué is issued in Shanghai, in which the US acknowledges that 'all Chinese on either side of the Taiwan Strait maintain there is but one China and that Taiwan is a part of China' and 'does not challenge that position'; it declares that it will 'progressively reduce' its forces 'as the tension in the area diminishes' with the 'ultimate objective' of total withdrawal of US forces and military installations from Taiwan. Nixon and his party leave China.

March 13. Britain and China reach agreement to raise the level of their diplomatic relations to that of ambassador. China and the USA begin ambassadorial meetings in Paris.

18. China carries out a nuclear test, reported by the US Atomic Energy Commission, but not by China.

April 1–8. Prime Minister Dom Mintoff leads a Maltese government delegation to China.

10. The Ministry of Foreign Affairs issues a strong statement supporting Hanoi's spring offensive in Vietnam (which began March 30). Several other similar statements are made at about this time.

12. The Prime Minister of Mauritius, Sir Seewoosagur Ramgoolam, arrives in Peking for a visit. On April 15 China and Mauritius sign a joint communiqué establishing diplomatic relations.

May 9. The Ministry of Foreign Affairs issues a statement protesting strongly against the USA's having bombed two Chinese merchant ships off the coast of Vietnam.

11. The Chinese government issues a statement denouncing US President Nixon's order for the mining of the harbours of the DRVN, announced by Nixon on May 8, and swearing continued support for the Vietnamese people.

14–18. The President of the Somali Democratic Republic, Mohamed Siad Barre, visits China.

1972

8. In Guangzhou, China and Malta sign an agreement for a long-term interest-free PRC loan to Malta.
July 24. China contracts to purchase two Anglo-French Concorde airliners.
26. China and Afghanistan sign a civil air transport agreement in Peking.
30. China and Ethiopia sign a civil air transport agreement in Peking.
August 16. A Japan Airlines airliner and All-Nippon Airways inaugurate air services between Shanghai and Japan.
September 9. China signs a contract with the US Boeing Aircraft Corporation to purchase ten 707 civilian jet airliners for $25,000,000.
14. The US Agricultural Department announces that China has purchased about 15,000,000 bushels of American wheat.
30. A ceremony marks the opening to traffic of a highway bridge over the Xiang River at Changsha (Hunan).
October 1. A ceremony marks the opening to traffic of the longest highway bridge over the Yellow River, 1394 m. long, at Beizhen (Shandong).
8. China and Italy sign a maritime transport agreement.
November 18. China and Iran sign a civil air transport agreement in Peking.
22. US President Nixon lifts the ban on the travel of American ships and aircraft to China.
December 29. China signs a contract with Japan's Tokyo Engineering Company for the purchase of an ethylene manufacturing plant, the first of a series of whole plant imports by China.

B OFFICIAL APPOINTMENTS, RESIGNATIONS, DISMISSALS ETC.

January 19. On the occasion of his attendance this day at a performance of a modern drama by a visiting Japanese troupe, Ji Pengfei is mentioned in a NCNA report (January 20) as Minister of Foreign Affairs.
February 24. Dong Biwu sends a message to the Emir of Kuwait as acting Chairman of the PRC, the first time he is mentioned in that capacity.
October 5. NCNA for the first time identifies Li Zhen as Minister of Public Security in succession to Xie Fuzhi.
18. NCNA for the first time identifies Yu Qiuli as Minister of the State Planning Commission.

C CULTURAL AND SOCIAL

January 10. Chinese surgeons in Peking successfully regraft the severed

1972

16. In Peking, China and the Netherlands sign a joint communiqué raising the status of their diplomatic relations from *chargé d'affaires* to ambassadorial level.

June 5. In Tirana, China and Greece sign a joint communiqué on their decision to establish diplomatic relations at ambassadorial level.

19–23. Dr Henry Kissinger visits Peking for talks with Zhou Enlai.

24–July 5. Sri Lanka Prime Minister Mrs Sirimavo Bandaranaike pays a state visit to China.

27. In London, China and Guyana issue a joint communiqué on their decision to establish diplomatic relations at ambassadorial level.

July 16–27. The Prime Minister of the Arab Republic of Yemen. Mohsin Ahmed Al Aini, visits China.

28. Reuter reports from Algiers the first official Chinese statement, issued by the Chinese embassy there, that Lin Biao had 'attempted a *coup d'état* and tried to assassinate Mao Zedong. After his plot was foiled, he fled on September 12 [1971] towards the Soviet Union on a plane which crashed in the People's Republic of Mongolia.'

August 1. An important article in *Red Flag* gives the first theoretical account of the fall of Lin Biao. It claims that class enemies have emerged within the Party every few years and that this pattern will continue. Similar articles appear over the next few months as the movement to criticize Lin Biao continues.

11–15. UN Secretary-General Kurt Waldheim pays a visit to China.

12. The Minister of Foreign Affairs, Ji Pengfei, announces Zhou Enlai's invitation to the Japanese Prime Minister, Tanaka Kakuci, to visit China.

24. The Ministry of Foreign Affairs issues a statement protesting to the USA for bombing the lifeboat of a Chinese merchant ship near an island off the DRVN coast on the 22nd, killing the five crew members.

25. China uses its UN Security Council veto power for the first time to bar Bangladesh from UN membership.

September 19. In Peking, China and Togo sign a joint communiqué establishing diplomatic relations (published September 26).

25–30. Japanese Prime Minister Tanaka Kakuei visits China, together with Minister of Foreign Affairs Ohira Masayoshi and others. Mao Zedong receives Tanaka and Ohira on the 27th, and on the 29th, Tanaka, Ohira, Zhou Enlai and Ji Pengfei sign a joint statement establishing diplomatic relations between the two countries 'as from September 29, 1972'; Japan 'fully understands and respects' China's claim to Taiwan. On the same day Ohira declares the treaty between Japan and the NP regime on Taiwan to be terminated (see April 28, 1952).

1972

leg of a peasant woman.

March 7. Xi'an radio reports general enrolment of students in its tertiary educational institutions for the first time since the Cultural Revolution. Similar reports emerge from other provinces at about this time.

April 1. In an article in *Red Flag* on language reform, Guo Moruo calls for the increased use of simplified characters but notes that phoneticization is the ultimate objective.

24. A *People's Daily* editorial advocates the policy of 'unity-criticism-unity' in dealing with cadres: only an extremely small number of incorrigible cadres should be dismissed, while the rest should be educated.

May 23. A joint editorial by the *People's Daily*, *Red Flag* and *Liberation Army Daily* celebrates the thirtieth anniversary of Mao Zedong's 'Talks at the Yan'an Forum on Literature and Art'. It lays stress on art 'for the workers, peasants, and soldiers', encouragement for amateurs, the policies of 'making the past serve the present', 'letting a hundred flowers blossom' and others.

July 24. *People's Daily* advocates that investigation reports and newspaper articles should be short, and criticizes verbosity. Other newspapers later print articles of similar content.

31. NCNA reports the excavation of a well-preserved tomb, about 2100 years old, on the outskirts of Changsha, containing the body of a woman and over 1000 burial accessories.

August 16. The Shanghai Dance-Drama Troupe arrives back home from a tour of Japan (on board the inaugural airliners, see A, August 16).

September 2–13. The First Asian Table Tennis Championships are held in Peking. Japan wins the men's singles, China the women's.

October 1. The Peking Man exhibition centre at Zhoukoudian (Hebei) is opened to the public.

November 17. The Shenyang Acrobatic Troupe leaves Peking on a tour of American countries, including the USA.

D PUBLICATIONS

The Foreign Languages Press publishes *Historical Relics Unearthed in New China*.

February 1. *Red Flag* publishes the revised version of the 'model' Peking opera *Haigang* (*On the Docks*).

March 1. *Red Flag* publishes the revised version of the revolutionary Peking opera *Longjiang song* (*Ode to Dragon River*).

May. The People's Literary Publishing House publishes *Jinguang dadao*

October 11. In Peking, China and the Federal Republic of Germany sign a joint communiqué on their decision to establish diplomatic relations at ambassadorial level.
14. China and the Maldives issue a joint communiqué agreeing to establish diplomatic relations at ambassadorial level.
November 6. China and Madagascar sign a joint communiqué establishing diplomatic relations.
19. China and Zaire sign a joint communiqué normalizing their relations as from November 24.
21. In Ottawa, China and Jamaica sign a joint communiqué establishing diplomatic relations.
28. China and Chad sign a joint communiqué establishing diplomatic relations.
December 20. The Ministry of Foreign Affairs issues a statement denouncing the US large-scale bombing of Hanoi, Haiphong and other areas of the DRVN (resumed December 18).
21. In Paris Australia and China, and in New York New Zealand and China sign joint communiqués on their decisions to establish diplomatic relations with effect from December 21 (Australia) and December 22 (New Zealand). Both countries 'acknowledge' China's claim to Taiwan.

1973 The Tenth Party Congress

January 1. The New Year's joint *People's Daily*, *Red Flag* and *Liberation Army Daily* editorial announces a new directive from Mao Zedong: 'dig tunnels deep, store grain everywhere and never seek hegemony'.
10–20. Zaire President Mobutu Sese Seko visits China.
28. A *People's Daily* editorial welcomes the signing in Paris the previous day of the Agreement on Ending the War and Restoring Peace in Vietnam.
29. CCP Chairman Mao Zedong, acting PRC Chairman Dong Biwu, NPC Standing Committee Chairman Zhu De and Premier of the State Council Zhou Enlai send a message to the leaders of the DRVN, NLF, and PRGSVN congratulating them on the signing of the Paris Accords.
February 14. The UN's *Demographic Yearbook 1971* is published, show-

1972–3

(*The Bright Golden Road*), a novel by Haoran.
November 1. *Red Flag* publishes the revised version of the 'model' Peking opera *Qixi baihu tuan* (*Raid on the White Tiger Regiment*).
December. *Shijie ditu ji* (*Atlas of the World*) is published.

E NATURAL DISASTERS

Autumn–June 1973. Serious drought conditions prevail in north China.

F DEATHS

January 6. Minister of Foreign Affairs Chen Yi d. aged 71.
9. Liang Sicheng, Professor of Architectural Engineering at Qinghua University, d. aged 71.
February 21. Zhang Guohua, First Secretary of the Sichuan Provincial Party Committee, d. aged 58.
March 26. Xie Fuzhi, Minister of Public Security and First Secretary of Peking Municipal Party Committee, d. aged 63.
April 6. Chen Zhengren, former Minister of the Eighth Ministry of Machine Building, d. aged 65.
16. Zeng Shan, CCPCC member, d. aged 73.
23. Li Dequan, former Minister of Public Health, d. aged 75.
September 1. He Xiangning, wife of Liao Zhongkai and Chairman of the NP Revolutionary Committee, d. aged 92.
November 23. El Hadj Yusuf Sha Mengbi, leading Moslem, d. aged 68.
December 10. Deng Zihui, CCPCC member, d. in Peking aged 76.

Deng Xiaoping returns to office 1973

A ECONOMICS

January 8. China and Italy sign a civil air transport agreement.
20. A Pakistan International Airlines Corporation airliner lands at Peking, officially inaugurating flights from Karachi to Peking and Shanghai.
February 22. Air services between Shanghai and Addis Ababa are formally inaugurated, the first between China and Africa.
May 23. China and Greece sign agreements on civil air transport, maritime transport and trade and payments.
June 11. China and Canada sign a civil air transport agreement in Ottawa.
13. China and the UK sign an agreement in Peking for direct air

1973

ing Shanghai in 1970 as the world's largest city with a population of 10,820,000 and Peking as the fourth largest (after Tokyo and New York) with a 1970 population of 7,570,000. China's total population in mid-1971 is given as 787,176,000.

15–19. Dr Henry Kissinger visits China.

18. The Cable and Wireless Company of Hongkong announces that it has signed an agreement with China to establish a coaxial telephone cable link between Hongkong and Guangdong.

22. The USA and China issue a communiqué that they will 'broaden their contacts in all fields' and to this end 'in the near future each side will establish a liaison office in the capital of the other'.

23. A *People's Daily* editorial welcomes the Agreement on Restoring Peace and Achieving National Concord in Laos (signed in Vientiane February 21).

28. The National Committee of the CPPCC sponsors a meeting in Peking to commemorate the Taiwan uprising (see February 28, 1947). Fu Zuoyi presides; in his speech he suggests talks with people on Taiwan to solve the Taiwan problem, and argues that his 'former colleagues' in the NP cannot rely on the USA for long.

March 9. In Paris, Spain and China sign a joint communiqué establishing diplomatic relations at ambassadorial level. Spain 'acknowledges' China's claim to Taiwan.

20. At the UN Seabed Committee, the chief representative of the Chinese delegation, Zhuang Yan, gives a speech on the PRC's policy; he claims that 'it is the sovereign right of each country to determine the limits of its territorial sea', and worldwide uniformity on this issue is undesirable.

25–April 2. Cameroon President El Hadj Ahmadou Ahidjo visits China.

April 16. Speaking on the question of population at a session of the UN Economic Commission for Asia and the Far East in Tokyo, China's spokesman gives China's growth of population since liberation at 'about 2 per cent' per annum.

19–24. Mexican President Luis Echeverria visits China. In the joint communiqué signed in Shanghai April 24 at the end of the trip China 'supports the Latin American countries in their just proposition concerning the establishment of a nuclear-free zone in Latin America'.

June 4–11. A large DRVN delegation visits China, led by Le Duan, First Secretary of the Vietnam Workers' Party Central Committee, and Pham Van Dong, DRVN Premier.

6–10. Chinese Minister of Foreign Affairs Ji Pengfei visits Britain.

10–14. Ji Pengfei visits France. He arrives in Teheran June 14, Karachi

services between the two countries.
July 4. The Chairman of the Chase Manhattan Bank, David Rockefeller, announces conclusion of a correspondent bank agreement with the Bank of China.
24. China and Australia sign a three-year trade agreement in Canberra.
November 4. In Huhehot China and Mongolia sign a new protocol on railway traffic.
12. China and Switzerland sign a civil air transport agreement in Bern.
December 26. The first 50,000-kW low-water-head turbo-generating set designed and built in China goes into regular operation at the Sanmen Gorge power station.

B OFFICIAL APPOINTMENTS, RESIGNATIONS, DISMISSALS ETC.

April 12. On the occasion of his presence at a banquet in honour of Norodom Sihanouk and other Cambodians, Deng Xiaoping is again mentioned as a Vice-Premier, after a long period in disgrace.
June 1. Dr Zhang Weixun of the PRC is appointed assistant Director-General of the World Health Organization.
August 29. The Tenth CCP Congress issues a press communiqué announcing that the Congress has elected a new CCPCC of 195 full and 124 alternate members.
30. The First Plenum of the Tenth CCPCC elects Mao Zedong as Chairman, and Zhou Enlai, Wang Hongwen, Kang Sheng, Ye Jianying and Li Desheng as deputy Chairmen. It elects, in addition to these, the following to the Politburo: Wei Guoqing, Liu Bocheng, Jiang Qing, Zhu De, Xi Shiyou, Hua Guofeng, Ji Dengkui, Wu De, Chen Xilian, Li Xiannian, Zhang Chunqiao, Yao Wenyuan, and Dong Biwu. Of these, nine are elected to the Standing Committee: Mao, Wang, Ye, Zhu, Li Desheng, Zhang, Zhou, Kang and Dong.
October 19. For the first time NCNA identifies Li Qiang as Minister of Foreign Trade, replacing Bai Xiangguo.

C CULTURAL AND SOCIAL

February 12–19. The Shanghai Municipal Congress of the Communist Youth League of China is held – the first at this level since the GPCR.
March 5–9. The Liaoning Provincial Congress of the Communist Youth League of China is held in Shenyang, the first at provincial level since the GPCR.
April 11–16. The Vienna Philharmonic Orchestra visits China.
16–21. Peking and Shanghai Municipal Trade Union Congresses

1973

June 17, and back in Peking June 19.

20–27. The President of Mali, Colonel Moussa Traore, visits China.

22. In the UN Security Council, China supports the proposal (accepted the same day by the Council) to admit both the German Democratic Republic and the Federal Republic of Germany.

27. A hydrogen bomb test in the two to three megaton range is carried out in Xinjiang.

July 27–August 1. Congolese President Major Marien N'gouabi visits China.

August 24–28. The Tenth National Congress of the CCP is held in Peking.

24. Zhou Enlai delivers his report to the Tenth CCP Congress giving the official version of the Lin Biao affair. Zhou claims Lin drew up his 'Outline of Project "571"' in March 1971 'for an armed counter-revolutionary *coup d'état*' to overthrow Mao, launched the *coup* on September 8 'in a wild attempt to assassinate our great leader Chairman Mao' and fled to the Soviet Union on September 13, but was killed in an air crash in the People's Republic of Mongolia. He also puts the CCP's membership at 28,000,000. On the same day Wang Hongwen's 'Report on the Revision of the Party Constitution', given to the Tenth CCP Congress, states that under the draft Constitution, cultural revolution will be a recurring phenomenon.

26. Tan Zhenlin, former Vice-Premier, and Ulanfu, former Vice-Premier and Chairman of the Inner Mongolian Autonomous Region, appear as spectators at the Asian-African-Latin American Table Tennis Friendship Invitational Tournament, their first public appearance for several years.

28. The Tenth CCP Congress adopts Zhou Enlai's and Wang Hongwen's reports, and a new CCP Constitution, under which the CCP 'takes Marxism-Leninism-Mao Zedong Thought as the theoretical basis guiding its thinking'.

September 11–17. French President Georges Pompidou visits China, the first time a West European head of state has ever done so, and meets Mao Zedong September 12.

15. China and Upper Volta issue a joint communiqué on their decision to establish diplomatic relations.

24. Mr L. Brezhnev of the USSR claims that in mid-June the Soviet Union proposed a treaty of non-aggression with China which it 'did not even take the trouble to answer'.

29. A joint editorial in the *People's Daily* and *Liberation Army Daily* calls for the further building up of militia forces.

October 8. Minister of Foreign Affairs Ji Pengfei, on behalf of the

both take place, the first sign of trade union activity since early in the GPCR. Beginning from late May, provincial-level trade union congresses follow.

May 25. Speaking at a banquet for a visiting group from Hongkong sporting circles, the table tennis champion Zhuang Zedong invites players, coaches and table tennis enthusiasts from Taiwan to visit Peking for the Invitational Tournament (see below August 25).

July 19. *Liaoning Daily* publishes a letter from a student called Zhang Tiesheng denouncing 'bookworms' as against practical knowledge and justifying himself for having handed in a blank examination paper because he had been working too hard on his commune. *People's Daily* reprints the letter in a prominent position August 10.

August 25–September 6. The Asian-African-Latin American Table Tennis Friendship Invitational Tournament is held in Peking.

September 12. The Philadelphia Orchestra, led by its conductor Eugene Ormandy, arrives in Peking for a concert tour in China.

October 1. A joint editorial in the *People's Daily*, *Liberation Army Daily* and *Red Flag* quotes a 'recent' directive from Mao Zedong on 'study classes for worker-peasant-soldier cadres': these should last 'a term of three months and with four terms a year; they [cadres] read books and at the same time take part in work'.

D PUBLICATIONS

July 1. *Red Flag* publishes the text of the newly revised revolutionary opera *Pingyuan zuozhan* (*Fighting on the Plains*).

August 7. *People's Daily* publishes 'Kongzi–wangude weihu nuli zhi de sixiangjia' ('Confucius – a Thinker Who Stubbornly Upheld the Slave System') by Yang Rongguo, Professor of Philosophy, Sun Yatsen University, Guangzhou. This article was the effective primary launching point of the Campaign to Criticize Lin Biao and Confucius.

September 15. The monthly *Xuexi yu pipan* (*Study and Criticism*) begins publication in Shanghai.

October 1. *Red Flag* publishes the text of the newly revised revolutionary opera *Dujuan shan* (*Azalea Mountain*).

December. The People's Literary Publishing House publishes *Honglou meng pinglun ji* (*A Collection of Commentaries on a Dream of Red Mansions*) by Li Xifan and Lan Ling; and republishes, in twenty volumes, the 1938 edition of *Lu Xun quanji* (*The Complete Works of Lu Xun*).

E NATURAL DISASTERS

February 6. An earthquake of 7.9 magnitude strikes the Ganzi Tibetan

1973–4

Chinese government, condemns Israel for launching the Middle East war (October 6).

10–17. Canadian Prime Minister Pierre Trudeau visits China. He meets Mao Zedong October 13.

19. The ashes of the American journalist on China, Edgar Snow, are buried at Peking University (he died February 15, 1972, in Switzerland).

31–November 4. Gough Whitlam makes the first visit of an Australian Prime Minister to China. He meets Mao Zedong November 2.

November 6–15. The President of Sierra Leone, Dr Siaka Stevens, visits China, meeting Mao Zedong November 7.

10–14. US Secretary of State Dr Henry Kissinger visits China. He meets Mao Zedong November 12. His visit results in a communiqué (November 14) that the activities of the liaison offices should continue to be expanded.

18–23. President Nguyen Huu Tho of the PRGSVN and Minister of Foreign Affairs Mme Nguyen Thi Binh visit China, meeting Mao Zedong November 19.

December 7–14. King Birendra and Queen Aishwarya of Nepal pay a state visit to China, meeting Mao Zedong December 9.

1974 *The Campaign to criticize Lin Biao and Confucius*

January 1. The joint *People's Daily*, *Red Flag* and *Liberation Army Daily* editorial states that 'criticizing Confucius is a component part of the criticism of Lin Biao'. The point is taken up and greatly expanded over the following months as the Campaign to Criticize Lin Biao and Confucius becomes a mass movement.

11. The Ministry of Foreign Affairs issues a statement claiming that the Nansha (Spratly), Xisha (Paracel), Dongsha (Pratas), and Zhongsha island groups 'have always been China's territory'.

19–20. A series of clashes takes place between Chinese and south Vietnamese forces in the Xisha Islands, ending in Chinese victory.

19. The Ministry of Foreign Affairs hands a note to the Soviet embassy expelling five of its members from China for espionage.

February 4. The Ministry of Foreign Affairs issues a statement protesting against military movements by south Vietnamese troops into the Nansha Islands on February 1.

21–March 2. Dr Kenneth Kaunda, President of Zambia, visits China, meeting Mao Zedong February 22.

25–March 2. Algerian President Boumedienne visits China, meeting

Autonomous District (Sichuan), causing considerable damage and some loss of life. After-tremors occur February 7 and 8.

F DEATHS

January 24. Xiong Jinding, Vice-President of the Chinese Red Cross Society and member of the CPPCC, d. aged 87.
March 9. He Wei, former Minister of Education, d. in Peking aged 63.
May 18. Zheng Tieru, NPC member and senior official of the Bank of China, d. aged 86.
   20. Chang Qiankun, Deputy Commander of the Air Force, d. aged 69.
July 1. Zhang Shizhao, educator, historian, journalist and member of the NPC Standing Committee, d. in Hongkong aged 92.
   8. Yuan Huabing, senior PLA cadre, d. in Peking aged 55.
   18. Zhang Xiruo, President of the Chinese People's Institute of Foreign Affairs, and former Minister of Education, d. in Peking aged 84.
   19. Former deputy Governor of Zhejiang Feng Baiju d. in Peking aged 69.
September 3. Zhang Tixue, CCPCC member, d. in Peking aged 58.

Significant advances in flood control **1974**

A ECONOMICS

January 30. The Civil Aviation Administration of China (CAAC) inaugurates its first direct flight from Peking to Moscow.
February 23. NCNA reports the completion of the first stage of a large and important water-control project near Danjiangkou (Henan) on the upper reaches of the Han.
April 20. China and Japan sign a civil aviation agreement in Peking.
June 3. In Peking the Nippon Steel Corporation of Japan signs a contract with China to build a giant steel plant in Wuhan capable of an annual production of 3,000,000 tonnes of hot rollings and 70,000 tonnes of silicon steel.
   24. NCNA reports that the ten-year-old projects to harness north China's biggest waterway system, the Haihe, 'have changed the temperament of this formerly rampant river. It is now made to serve the people according to their will.' (This indicates basic success in fulfilling a directive by Mao Zedong of November 17, 1963, 'the Haihe must be brought under permanent control'.)
August 19. NCNA begins daily releases of the Bank of China's exchange

1974

Mao Zedong February 25.

March 15. In Conakry, Guinea, China and Guinea-Bissau sign a joint communiqué establishing diplomatic relations.

23. The Ministry of Foreign Affairs issues a protest to the Soviet embassy against the Soviet Union's having sent a reconnaissance helicopter into Xinjiang on March 14. (The Soviet Union claimed it had strayed accidentally.)

23–31. Tanzanian President Julius Nyerere visits China, meeting Mao Zedong on March 25.

28. The Soviet Ministry of Foreign Affairs hands the Chinese embassy a note demanding the return by China of the helicopter which landed in Xinjiang earlier in March.

April 3. In a speech at a rally welcoming a Cambodian delegation led by the deputy Prime Minister of the Royal Government of National Union, Khieu Samphan, Wang Hongwen declares that, 'strategically, Europe is the focus of the contention' between the two superpowers, the USA and USSR.

10. Deng Xiaoping makes an important speech to the UN General Assembly as Chairman of the Chinese delegation to its Sixth Special Session, in which he declares that the two superpowers are 'vainly seeking world hegemony' but that 'the international situation is most favourable to the developing countries'; 'China is a socialist country and a developing country as well; China belongs to the Third World', he claims. (Deng left Peking April 6 and returned April 19.)

20. In Libreville, China and Gabon sign a joint communiqué establishing diplomatic relations.

May 6–13, 16–18. Senegalese President Leopold Senghor visits China, meeting Mao Zedong May 7.

11–14. Pakistani President Z.A. Bhutto visits China, meeting Mao Zedong May 11.

17–24. Cypriot President Archbishop Makarios visits China, meeting Mao Zedong May 18.

28–June 2. Malaysian Prime Minister Tun Abdul Razak visits China, meeting Mao Zedong May 29.

31. Zhou Enlai and Tun Abdul Razak sign a joint communiqué establishing diplomatic relations at ambassadorial level between China and Malaysia. China 'considers anyone of Chinese origin who has taken up of his own will or acquired Malaysian nationality as automatically forfeiting Chinese nationality' and enjoins those in Malaysia who have retained Chinese nationality to abide by Malaysian laws. Malaysia 'acknowledges' China's claim to Taiwan.

June 13. Posters attacking the Peking Municipal Revolutionary Com-

rates for the people's currency (*renminbi*).
September 14. NCNA reports the completion of the Danjiang canal project in the region of Xiangyang (Hubei)–part of the Danjiangkou water-control project.
   26. The Hunan–Guizhou railway from Zhuzhou (Hunan) to Guiyang (Guizhou) is formally opened to traffic.
   29. CAAC and Japan Airlines simultaneously inaugurate air services between Peking and Tokyo.
October 29. CAAC's Peking–Karachi–Paris air route is formally inaugurated.
November 13. In Tokyo, China and Japan sign a maritime transport agreement.
   27. CAAC's Peking–Teheran–Bucharest–Tirana air service is formally inaugurated.
December 20. NCNA reports that reconstruction work on the Sanmen Gorge dam (Henan), initially finished September 1960 but found inadequate, has been completed.
End of 1974. The Liujia gorge hydropower station (Gansu), China's largest, is declared completed.

B   OFFICIAL APPOINTMENTS, RESIGNATIONS, DISMISSALS ETC.

January 1. NCNA identifies important changes in the commanders of China's military regions. In the Guangzhou Military Region, Xu Shiyou replaces Ding Sheng; in the Fuzhou, Pi Dingjun replaces Han Xianchu; in the Lanzhou, Han Xianchu replaces Pi Dingjun; in the Nanjing, Ding Sheng replaces Xu Shiyou; in the Shenyang, Li Desheng replaces Chen Xilian; in the Ji'nan, Zeng Siyu replaces Yang Dezhi; and in the Wuhan, Yang Dezhi replaces Zeng Siyu; Chen Xilian is moved to the Peking Military Region.
November 15. The appointment of Qiao Guanhua to replace Ji Pengfei as China's Minister of Foreign Affairs is announced in Peking.

C   CULTURAL AND SOCIAL

January 14. *People's Daily* attacks certain European musical composers, such as Beethoven and Schubert, as bourgeois.
   18. *People's Daily* begins a campaign against the use of influence to gain admittance to higher education ('back-door entry').
   23–February 18. The North China Theatrical Festival is held in

1974

mittee are placed outside its committee offices, signalling a new phase of the Campaign to Criticize Lin Biao and Confucius.

17. China conducts a further nuclear test in Xinjiang.

20. In New York, China and Trinidad and Tobago sign a joint communiqué establishing diplomatic relations.

28. In Caracas, China and Venezuela sign a joint communiqué establishing diplomatic relations.

July 20. In Peking, China and Niger sign a joint communiqué establishing diplomatic relations at ambassadorial level.

August 15. In Brasilia, China and Brazil sign a joint communiqué establishing diplomatic relations at ambassadorial level.

21. Chinese representative Huang Shuze addresses the UN World Population Conference held in Bucharest (August 19–30) and criticizes the theory of the population explosion as a fallacy peddled by the superpowers.

September 2–7. Togolese President Gnassingbe Eyadema visits China, meeting Mao Zedong September 4.

8–15. General Y. Gowon, Prime Minister of Nigeria, visits China, meeting Mao Zedong September 10.

11. The Ministry of Foreign Affairs issues a statement denouncing India's constitutional amendment (ratified by India's Upper House September 7) making Sikkim an associate state as 'outright expansionism'.

17. President Moktar Ould Daddah of Mauritania arrives in China, meeting Mao Zedong September 19. After a visit to the DPRK he sees Zhou Enlai in hospital September 26 (Zhou having been seriously ill for several months) and leaves China September 27.

20–29. Mrs Imelda Marcos, wife of the Philippines President, visits China, meeting Mao Zedong September 27.

October 1. China holds lavish celebrations for the twenty-fifth anniversary of the founding of the PRC. The joint *People's Daily*, *Red Flag* and *Liberation Army Daily* editorial sums up the period optimistically: 'we have in the main completed the socialist transformation of the ownership of the means of production'.

4–9. The President of Gabon, El Hadj Omar Bongo, visits China, meeting Mao Zedong October 5, and Zhou Enlai the following day in hospital.

18–26. Danish Prime Minister Poul Hartling visits China, meeting Mao Zedong October 20.

November 5–11. Dr Eric Williams, Prime Minister of Trinidad and Tobago, visits China, meeting Mao Zedong November 6.

10–18. Salem Robaya Ali, Chairman of the Presidential Council of

Peking, featuring performances from Peking, Tianjin, Inner Mongolia, Hebei and Shanxi, including the spoken play *Liema he pan* (*On the Bank of the Liema River*) and the Shanxi opera *Sanshang Taofeng* (*Going Up Peach Peak Three Times*).

30. *People's Daily* attacks the film *China* by the Italian director M. Antonioni as anti-China and its appearance as 'a wild provocation against the Chinese people'.

February 28. *People's Daily* denounces *Going Up Peach Peak Three Times*, beginning an intense campaign against the opera as a political plot to negate class struggle.

March 8. International Working Women's Day is celebrated, with attacks on Confucius and Mencius because of their 'contempt for women'.

April 2–15. At the Second Asian Table Tennis Championships held in Yokohama, China wins the men's team event, the women's doubles and girls' singles.

May 1. New-style uniforms are introduced into the PLA.

1–23. A nationwide film festival of ten colour films of model revolutionary theatrical works takes place.

September 1–16. For the first time China takes part in the Asian Games, held in Teheran, sending its largest sports delegation ever to go abroad.

D PUBLICATIONS

The Foreign Languages Press publishes *Han Tang bihua* (*Murals from the Han to the Tang Dynasty*).

January 28. The People's Publishing House publishes *Pi Lin pi Kong wenzhang huibian* (*Collection of Articles in Criticism of Lin Biao and Confucius*), 2 vols.

March. The Peking People's Publishing House publishes Xie Bozhang, *Qingchunqi weisheng* (*Hygiene in Puberty*).

April. The Zhonghua Book Company publishes a modern, punctuated edition of the *Mingshi* in twenty-eight volumes.

June. The Shaanxi People's Publishing House publishes Zhang Qizhi's *Zhongguo zhexue shilüe* (*Historical Sketch of Chinese Philosophy*).

July 1. The quarterly *Zhongguo duiwai maoyi* (*China's Foreign Trade*) begins publication.

October. The People's Publishing House publishes *Jianming shijie shi* (*Concise History of the World*) by a group in the History Department of Peking University.

the People's Democratic Republic of Yemen, visits China, meeting Mao Zedong November 12.

25–29. US Secretary of State Dr Henry Kissinger visits China and arranges for President Gerald Ford to visit in 1975. (Ford became president on Nixon's resignation announced August 8.)

December 17. China and Gambia issue a joint communiqué on their decision to establish diplomatic relations at ambassadorial level as from December 14, 1974.

16–22. President Mobutu Sese Seko of Zaire visits China, meeting Mao Zedong December 17.

1975 *China hails the liberation of the three Indochinese countries*

January 6. In New York China and Botswana sign a joint communiqué establishing diplomatic relations at ambassadorial level.

7–10. Maltese Prime Minister Dom Mintoff visits China, meeting Mao Zedong January 9.

13–17. The First Session of the Fourth NPC takes place in Peking. On its last day it adopts (*i*) a new PRC Constitution, which differs from that of 1954, among other points, in that provision for the position of PRC Chairman is lacking; (*ii*) Zhang Chunqiao's 'Report on the Revision of the Constitution'; and (*iii*) Zhou Enlai's 'Report on the Work of the Government' (both reports delivered January 13).

31–February 6. Eric Williams, Prime Minister of Trinidad and Tobago, revisits China, meeting Zhou Enlai in hospital February 1.

February 27–March 8. President Henri Lopez of the People's Republic of the Congo visits China, meeting Zhou Enlai in hospital February 28.

March 12–17. Linden Forbes S. Burnham, Prime Minister of Guyana, visits China, meeting Zhou Enlai in hospital March 12.

1974–5

E NATURAL DISASTERS

May 11. An earthquake of 7.1 magnitude strikes Zhaotong (Yunnan) and nearby regions in Yunnan and Sichuan provinces, with aftershocks the following day.

F DEATHS

January 7. Wang Shusheng, CCPCC member, d. aged 69.
25. Wang Jiaxiang, CCPCC member, d. aged 68.
February 7. Zhu Kezhen, Vice-President of Academia Sinica and meteorologist, d. aged 84.
March 20. Zhang Qian, NPC Deputy and widow of Chen Yi, d. aged 52.
21. Chen Yu, CCPCC member, d. in Guangzhou aged 73.
27. Chen Shaoyu, former CCPCC member, d. in Moscow aged 69.
April 4. Ding Xilin, Vice-President of the Chinese People's Association for Friendly Relations with Foreign Countries, d. aged 81.
19. Fu Zuoyi d. aged 79.
July 4. Hu Jizong, CCPCC member and NPC deputy, d. in Lanzhou aged 54.
August 26. Chemical engineer Hou Debang d. aged 84.
November 29. Peng Dehuai d. aged 76.

Deaths of Chiang Kaishek and Dong Biwu 1975

A ECONOMICS

February 28. Royal Lao Airlines inaugurates services between Ventiane and Guangzhou.
April 7. Swissair inaugurates its Zurich–Geneva–Athens–Bombay–Peking–Shanghai air service.
June 23. An oil pipeline from Peking to Qinhuangdao (Hebei) comes into operation, completing the 1507-km. pipeline from Daqing (Heilongjiang) to Peking.
July 1. The electrification of the railway from Baoji (Shaanxi) to Chengdu (Sichuan) is completed, and the electric line formally opened to traffic, China's first electric railway.
August 18. China and Cambodia sign an agreement on economic and technical cooperation, under which China extends *gratis* aid.
September 15–October 19. The First National Conference on Learning from Dazhai in Agriculture is held in Xiyang (Shanxi). Attended by over 7000 people, including many major leaders, such as Deng

1975

17. The NPC Standing Committee decides to grant an amnesty to, and release, all war criminals in custody.
April 1–8. Tunisian Prime Minister Hedi Nouira visits China.
13. Ten of the war criminals released under the March 17 decision leave Peking for Taiwan via Hongkong, where they arrive April 14.
17. Mao Zedong, Zhu De and Zhou Enlai send congratulations to Sihanouk and Khmer Rouge leaders on the liberation of Phnom Penh (April 17).
18–26. DPRK President Kim Il Sung visits China, meeting Mao Zedong April 18.
19–27. Belgian Prime Minister Leo Tindemans visits China, meeting Mao Zedong April 20.
30. Mao Zedong, Zhu De and Zhou Enlai cable congratulations to NLF President Nguyen Huu Tho, and the NLF, PRGSVN and DRVN leaders on the liberation of Saigon (April 30).
May 3. According to *People's Daily*, October 25, 1976, a Politburo meeting takes place at which Mao Zedong warns Jiang Qing, Wang Hongwen, Zhang Chunqiao and Yao Wenyuan against 'functioning as a gang of four' and tells them 'Don't do it any more.'
8. China establishes official diplomatic relations with the European Economic Community during a visit of the Vice-President of its Commission, Sir Christopher Soames (May 4–11).
12–18. Deng Xiaoping and Qiao Guanhua visit France.
June 7–10. President F. and Mrs I. Marcos of the Philippines visit Peking, meeting Mao Zedong June 7.
9. Zhou Enlai and F. Marcos sign a joint communiqué by which China and the Philippines establish diplomatic relations at ambassadorial level. The Philippines 'fully understands and respects' China's claim to Taiwan.
11–17. Gambian President Sir Dawda Jawara visits China, meeting Mao Zedong June 12.
27–29. President Bongo of Gabon revisits China.
30–July 6. Thai Prime Minister Kukrit Pramoj visits China, meeting Mao Zedong July 1.
July 1. Zhou Enlai and Kukrit Pramoj sign a joint communiqué by which China and Thailand establish diplomatic relations at ambassadorial level. China enjoins Chinese residents in Thailand who elect to retain Chinese nationality to 'abide by the law' of Thailand, 'respect the customs and habits of the Thai people, and live in amity with them'. Thailand 'acknowledges' China's claim to Taiwan.
12. China and São Tomé and Principe sign a joint communiqué establishing diplomatic relations at ambassadorial level.

Xiaoping, Jiang Qing, Hua Guofeng and Yao Wenyuan, it makes vital decisions on the future direction of Chinese agriculture, including a determination to achieve basic farm mechanization by 1980. The summing-up report is given by Hua Guofeng.

25. In Peking China and the DRVN sign an agreement for a Chinese interest-free loan to the DRVN.

October 31. China and the Federal Republic of Germany sign a maritime and civil aviation agreement.

December 1. A 200,000-kW thermal power station is completed in the western suburbs of Peking.

13. Rolls-Royce of UK and China National Technical Import Corporation sign an agreement worth £100,000,000 for the supply and construction in China of Spey jet engines.

B OFFICIAL APPOINTMENTS, RESIGNATIONS, DISMISSALS ETC.

January 8–10. The Second Plenum of the Tenth CCPCC (held these days) elects Deng Xiaoping as deputy Chairman of the CCPCC and member of the Standing Committee of the Politburo.

17. The First Session of the Fourth NPC elects Zhu De as Chairman, and Dong Biwu, Song Qingling, Kang Sheng, Liu Bocheng, Wu De, Wei Guoqing, Saifudin, Guo Moruo, Tan Zhenlin, Li Jingquan, Ulanfu, Ngapo Ngawang Jigme and others as deputy Chairmen of the NPC's Standing Committee. The NPC appoints the following members of the State Council: Premier, Zhou Enlai; Vice-Premiers, Deng Xiaoping, Zhang Chunqiao, Li Xiannian, Chen Xilian, Ji Dengkui, Hua Guofeng, Chen Yonggui, Wu Guixian, Wang Zhen, Yu Qiuli, Gu Mu, and Sun Jian; Minister of Foreign Affairs, Qiao Guanhua; Minister of National Defence, Ye Jianying; Minister of the State Planning Commission, Yu Qiuli; Minister of Public Security, Hua Guofeng; Minister of Foreign Trade, Li Qiang; Minister of Economic Relations with Foreign Countries, Fang Yi; Minister of Culture, Yu Huiyong; Minister of Education, Zhou Rongxin; and other ministers.

October 8. On the occasion of the memorial meeting for his predecessor (see F, October 3) NCNA identifies Jia Qiyun as Yunnan Provincial First Party Secretary and Chairman of the Yunnan Provincial Revolutionary Committee.

28. Wei Guoqing attends a meeting in Guangzhou in the capacities of Chairman of the Guangdong Provincial Revolutionary Committee and of the First Secretary of the Guangdong Provincial Party Committee, the first time he is so identified.

19. Struggle over economic policy, bourgeois factionalism and other ills having led to a fall in production in Hangzhou, PLA units led by their commanders begin moving into certain factories to 'take part in labour', maintain production and overcome wrong policies.

26. China launches a satellite, which takes ninety-one minutes to go round the earth.

31. Luo Ruiqing, former Chief of the General Staff of the PLA, attends an Army Day reception, the first time he is seen in public since the GPCR.

August 15–19. A Cambodian government delegation led by deputy Prime Ministers Khieu Samphan and Ieng Sary visits China.

23. The Cambodian delegation now headed by Norodom Sihanouk, Cambodian Head of State, returns to Peking from Pyongyang. On August 27 Mao Zedong meets Sihanouk, Cambodian Prime Minister Penn Nouth, and Khieu Samphan, and on August 30 the delegation leaves Peking.

September 9. The tenth anniversary of the Tibetan Autonomous Region is celebrated in Lhasa; Huo Guofeng leads the delegation sent by the central government.

26. Qiao Guanhua, the head of China's UN delegation and Minister of Foreign Affairs, makes a major address to the UN General Assembly.

October 4. In New York, China and Bangladesh sign a joint communiqué establishing diplomatic relations at ambassadorial level.

6–12. D. Bijedic, President of the Yugoslav Federal Executive Council, visits China, meeting Mao Zedong October 8.

19. *People's Daily* commemorates the fortieth anniversary of the Long March, arguing that its victory proved correct Mao's notion that 'when the Party line is correct we have everything, if the line is incorrect we will lose what we already have'.

27. China carries out an underground nuclear test.

29–November 2. Helmut Schmidt, Chancellor of the Federal Republic of Germany, visits China, meeting Mao Zedong October 30.

November 5. In Canberra, China and Fiji sign a joint communiqué establishing diplomatic relations at ambassadorial level.

6. In Apia, China and Western Samoa sign a joint communiqué establishing diplomatic relations.

11–15. Burmese President Ne Win visits China, meeting Mao Zedong November 13.

13. In New York, China and Comoros sign a joint communiqué establishing diplomatic relations at ambassadorial level.

15. The Chinese Ministry of Foreign Affairs greets Angolan independence from Portugal (November 11) but denounces the Soviet Union

December 19. A Sichuan broadcast for the first time identifies Zhao Ziyang as First Secretary of the Sichuan Provincial Party Committee.

C Cultural and Social

January 13. In his 'Report on the Work of the Government' at the NPC Zhou Enlai states: 'Over a million barefoot doctors are becoming more competent. Nearly ten million school graduates have gone to mountainous and other rural areas'.

February 9. A *People's Daily* editorial announces an 'important instruction' of Mao Zedong: 'Why did Lenin speak of exercising dictatorship over the bourgeoisie? This question must be thoroughly understood. Lack of clarity on this question will lead to revisionism. This should be made known to the whole nation.' This heralds a new campaign based on the theory of the dictatorship of the proletariat.

11. A festival of theatrical works from the Xinjiang Uighur Autonomous Region, Shaanxi, Heilongjiang and Sichuan opens in Peking. From March 20 on, the areas of origin of the works in the continuing festival are the provinces of Guangdong, Hubei, Henan, Yunnan, Jilin and Gansu.

April 11. NCNA reports the excavation, beginning from winter 1973, of a large-scale settlement of the Shang dynasty in Qingjiang (Jiangxi).

27–30. China's national archery competition, held in Fujian, produces three world records.

May 27. A Chinese mountaineering expedition of nine, eight of them Tibetans including one woman, reaches the peak of Jomo Lungma (Mt Everest), the second to do so (see also C, May 25, 1960).

July 25. See C, November 5, 1976.

August 2–10. The Peking International Swimming and Diving Friendship Invitational Meet takes place, attended by some 300 swimmers and divers from twenty-three countries.

23. *Guangming Daily* carries several articles attacking the classical novel *Shuihu zhuan* (*Water Margin*). This begins a campaign against the novel based on an injunction from Mao Zedong 'that it be used as teaching material by negative example to help the people know the capitulationists'.

December 1. An article in *Red Flag* by the Criticism Group of Peking and Qinghua Universities reveals a major controversy over education policy. Some wish to retain GPCR policies, including the selection of students with worker-peasant-soldier backgrounds and practical experience; and the placing of major emphasis on revolutionary ideology. Opponents of the policies claim they produced bad academic standards.

1975

for interference and stirring up civil war.

24. *Guangming Daily* presents detailed historical evidence in support of China's claim to sovereignty over the islands of the South China Sea: Nansha, Xisha, Dongsha and Zhongsha Islands.

26. China launches a satellite, which NCNA reports on December 2 to have returned to earth after orbiting the earth normally.

December 1–5. US President Gerald Ford visits China, meeting Mao Zedong December 2.

5. Mao Zedong, Zhu De and Zhou Enlai send a message of congratulations to the Laotian leadership on the founding of the People's Democratic Republic of Laos, proclaimed at a meeting of the Laotian National Congress of People's Representatives held December 1–2.

9. *People's Daily* declares China's support for the Democratic Republic of East Timor, proclaimed November 28 but into which Indonesia had moved troops December 7.

16. China launches another satellite.

21–25. President Manuel Pinto da Costa of São Tomé and Principe visits China, meeting Mao Zedong December 23.

23. NCNA announces the release of all former NP officials of county or regiment level or above still held in custody.

26–31. Norodom Sihanouk visits Peking.

27. The Ministry of Foreign Affairs informs the Soviet embassy that China is releasing the Soviet helicopter and three crew-members captured in Xinjiang on March 14 (see March 23, 1974), and that the Chinese public security organs consider credible the statement of the three that the flight into China was unintentional.

20. Foreign newsmen visiting Qinghua University see big-character posters attacking university authorities as well as the Minister of Education, Zhou Rongxin, as opponents of revolution in education.

D PUBLICATIONS

January. The People's Publishing House publishes *Zhongguo zhexue shi jianghua* (*Lectures on the History of Chinese Philosophy*), by Yin Ming and others.
February. The Zhonghua Book Company publishes a modern punctuated edition of *Xin Tangshu* (*The New Tang History*) in twenty volumes.
May. The Zhonghua Book Company publishes a new punctuated edition of *Jiu Tangshu* (*The Old Tang History*) in sixteen volumes.
August. The Guangxi People's Publishing House publishes *Jintian qiyi* (*The Jintian Uprising*).
September. The People's Literary Publishing House publishes *Shaoshu minzu shige xuan* (*A Selection of Poems and Songs of the National Minorities*).
November. The Shanghai People's Publishing House publishes a new edition of *Shuihu quanzhuan* (*The Complete Water Margin*).

E NATURAL DISASTERS

February 4. A serious earthquake of 7.3 magnitude strikes the Haicheng-Yingkou area of Liaoning province. (According to a State Council circular of March 12, casualties and losses were lessened through predictions and observations of seismologists.)
August 7–8. During the night torrential rain in Zhumadian (Henan) causes floods affecting 5,490,000 people and sweeping away numerous homes.

F DEATHS

January 9. Vice-Premier and CCPCC member Li Fuchun d. aged 74.
March 8. Zhou Xinfang d. aged 80.
April 2. Dong Biwu d. in Peking aged 89.
   4. CCP member Zhang Zhixin d. aged 45.
   5. Chiang Kaishek d. aged 87.
October 3. Zhou Xing, Chairman of the Yunnan Revolutionary Committee and Yunnan Provincial First Party Secretary, d. aged 69.
December 16. Kang Sheng, Deputy Chairman of the CCPCC, d. aged 76.

1976 The Tiananmen Incident; the 'Gang of Four' is smashed

January 1. The New Year's Day *People's Daily*, *Red Flag* and *Liberation Army Daily* editorial signals a campaign against the restoration of capitalism and a renewed emphasis on continuing the GPCR; it carries a 'recent' new 'instruction' of Mao Zedong: 'Stability and unity do not mean writing off class struggle; class struggle is the key and everything else hangs on it'.
15. A solemn memorial ceremony is held for Zhou Enlai (see F, January 8).
23. China successfully conducts a nuclear test.
February 10. A wall poster campaign begins at Peking University attacking 'a capitalist roader' readily identifiable as Deng Xiaoping. The criticism grows more intense as time passes.
13. A rally of some 1800 people takes place in Shanghai, sponsored by the Municipal Revolutionary Committee, to denounce Deng Xiaoping.
21–29. Former US President Nixon revisits China, meeting Mao Zedong February 23.
March 15–24. A Laotian Party and government delegation led by Premier Kaysone Phomvihan visits China. Mao Zedong meets members of the delegation March 17.
April 4. Many thousands of people mourn Zhou Enlai in Tiananmen Square, central Peking, and place wreaths and placards in his honour.
5. Continuing demonstrations in honour of Zhou Enlai's memory and in protest against the removal of the wreaths and placards turn to rioting; police clash with the demonstrators and arrest many (including subsequent days), several cars are burned and a building ransacked and set on fire. This event is called the Tiananmen Incident.
6. Incidents similar to those in Peking on April 4–5 take place in Zhengzhou (Henan). At about the same time similar happenings occur in Kunming, Changchun, Shijiazhuang, Nanjing, Wuhan, Huhehot, Shanghai, Guangzhou, Taiyuan and possibly other places.
7. NCNA carries the current official interpretation of the April 4–5 events describing them as follows: 'a handful of class enemies, under the guise of commemorating the late Premier Zhou, ... engineered an organized, premeditated and planned counter-revolutionary political incident in Tiananmen Square in the capital.' The next two days enormous demonstrations are held in Peking in support of Hua Guofeng and against Deng Xiaoping while similar demonstrations take place elsewhere in China at about the same time.
15. China and Cape Verde sign a joint communiqué establishing diplomatic relations as from April 25.

Zhou Enlai and Mao Zedong die; Hua Guofeng **1976**
comes to power; the Tangshan earthquake

A ECONOMICS

January 3. A ceremony in Peking marks the formal opening of the China-Korea Friendship Oil Pipeline.

23. Fortnightly CAAC flights between Peking and Phnom Penh are inaugurated.

April 23. NCNA reports the sinking, in Sichuan, of an oil well, China's deepest to this date at 6011 m., and the collection of valuable data on oil and natural gas deposits in deep formations.

May 29. NCNA reports that China's first deep-water oil port capable of berthing 100,000-ton tankers has been 'recently' completed and put into operation in Dalian (Liaoning).

June 29. A ceremony marks the formal opening of the road section of a double-decker road-rail bridge across the Huangpu River in Shanghai (the rail section was opened September 11, 1975).

July 6. NCNA reports the formal opening of the 716-km. Yunnan–Tibet highway linking Xiaguan (Yunnan) with Mangkang (Tibet).

14. A ceremony in Kapiri Mposhi, Zambia, marks the formal handing over by China and opening to traffic of the PRC's largest aid project, the 1860-km. Tanzania–Zambia railway, from Dar-es-Salaam, Tanzania, to Kapiri Mposhi.

23. NCNA reports the opening to traffic of the second track of the Tianjin–Shanghai railway.

27. NCNA reports the discovery of large diamond deposits in Liaoning Province.

August 23. China's first 50,000-ton oil tanker, called *Xihu* (*West Lake*), is launched in Dalian.

October 25. Ceremonies in Tokyo and Peking mark the inauguration of the new China–Japan seabed cable.

November 1. *People's Daily* reiterates the economic slogan 'grasp revolution, promote production'; it accuses the 'gang of four' of distorting and opposing this principle and of sabotaging production, a common theme from this point on.

December 26. The large Shandong tractor plant goes into production in Yanzhou (Shandong).

B OFFICIAL APPOINTMENTS, RESIGNATIONS, DISMISSALS ETC.

February 3. The CCPCC appoints Hua Guofeng as acting Premier of the State Council.

April 7. The CCPCC Politburo resolves to appoint Hua Guofeng First Deputy Chairman of the CCPCC and Premier of the State

1976

21. In Peking, China and Egypt sign a protocol on military cooperation, during the visit of Vice-President Hosny Moubarek to China (April 18–24).

28–May 5. The New Zealand Prime Minister, Robert Muldoon, visits China, meeting Mao Zedong April 30.

29. Two Chinese guards are killed by an explosion outside the Soviet embassy in Peking.

30. According to Wu De's speech at the Tiananmen Square mass rally (see October 24), Mao Zedong writes down for Hua Guofeng the words: 'With you in charge, I'm at ease.' (Hua and his supporters later claim this as Mao's sanctioning Hua's succession to power.)

May 10–23. Singapore Prime Minister Lee Kuan Yew visits China, meeting Mao Zedong May 12.

14. NCNA reports the completion of a microwave communications line linking Peking with more than 20 provinces, municipalities and autonomous regions.

26–30. Pakistani Prime Minister Z.A. Bhutto visits China, meeting Mao Zedong May 27, the last high-ranking foreigner to do so.

28. In New York, China and Surinam issue a joint communiqué establishing diplomatic relations at ambassadorial level.

June 2–9. King Birendra of Nepal visits China, including Tibet, the first foreign ruler to visit the Autonomous Region.

11–15. Madagascar President Didier Ratsiraka visits China.

15. A Chinese government spokesman informs the foreign press that the CCPCC 'has decided not to arrange for Chairman Mao to meet foreign distinguished visitors'.

20–27. Australian Prime Minister Malcolm Fraser visits China.

30. China and the Seychelles sign a joint communiqué establishing diplomatic relations at ambassadorial level.

July 3. Mao Zedong, Zhu De and Hua Guofeng send a message of congratulations to the leaders of Vietnam on its reunification, proclaimed the same day.

7. K.R. Narayanan, the first Indian ambassador to China in 15 years, arrives in Peking, presenting his credentials July 24.

15–20. President Mathieu Karekou of Benin visits China.

26–August 9. President Sir Seretse Khama of Botswana visits China.

30. A delegation sent by the CCPCC and led by Hua Guofeng reaches the earthquake-devastated areas of Hebei to offer solicitude (see also E, July 28).

August 23. In Changsha and Taiyuan the 'gang of four' (see October 6) creates violent disturbances including looting and beating up, as part of a plot to undertake armed rebellion, according to later reports

Council. It also resolves to dismiss Deng Xiaoping 'from all posts both inside and outside the Party while allowing him to keep his Party membership'.

9. NCNA identifies Zhao Ziyang as Chairman of the Sichuan Provincial Revolutionary Committee.

October 7. The CCPCC appoints Hua Guofeng as its Chairman and as Chairman of its Military Affairs Committee in succession to Mao Zedong.

27. Su Zhenhua announces in Shanghai the decision of the CCPCC appointing him as First Secretary of the Shanghai Municipal Party Committee and Chairman of the Revolutionary Committee; and dismissing Zhang Chunqiao, Yao Wenyuan and Wang Hongwen from all posts held in Shanghai.

December 2. The third session of the Fourth NPC Standing Committee, held in Peking November 30 to December 2, appoints Deng Yingchao as deputy Chairman of the NPC Standing Committee, and Huang Hua as Minister of Foreign Affairs in place of Qiao Guanhua.

C CULTURAL AND SOCIAL

March 27. NCNA reports the excavation in Yunmeng (Hubei) of about 1000 bamboo slips, well preserved and legible, dating back some 2200 years.

April 29. For the first time scientists, from Academia Sinica, use Chinese-made instruments to observe an annular solar eclipse in the Karakorum Mountains in far western China.

May 13. Shanghai's Peking Opera Troupe gives its premiere, in Tokyo, at the beginning of a tour of Japan.

August 1. New romanized scripts officially come into use for the Uighur and Kazakh nationalities, replacing the old written scripts.

15–26. The Peking International Women's Basketball Friendship Invitational Tournament is held in Shanghai.

October 1. The public screening begins of forty-seven recently completed films, including feature films, film versions of operas, documentaries and science and educational films. They include *Lu Xun zhandou de yisheng* (*The Militant Life of Lu Xun*), among the many marks of respect to the great writer Lu Xun on the fortieth anniversary of his death (see F, October 19, 1936).

November 5. A *People's Daily* article gives the first major sign of cultural policy after the 'gang of four'. It reveals a directive by Mao Zedong of July 25, 1975, on behalf of the film *Chuangye* (*Pioneers*), about Daqing, and against 'nitpicking' in judging works of art. The

1976

(given at a rally in Changsha on December 22 and Shanxi radio December 7).

30. China launches its sixth satellite.

September 2–9. The Western Samoan head of state, Malietoa Tanumafili II, visits China.

11. A seven-day mourning period begins for Mao Zedong (see *F*, September 9).

14. A spokesman for the Ministry of Foreign Affairs reveals that condolences on the death of Mao Zedong were rejected from the CPSU and other communist parties having no relations with the CCP.

18. Memorial meetings are held in Peking and elsewhere in China for Mao Zedong.

26. China successfully conducts a nuclear test.

October 1. *Pravda* expresses the Soviet Union's willingness to repair relations with China.

6. On orders from Hua Guofeng, four members of the Politburo (Jiang Qing, Zhang Chunqiao, Yao Wenyuan and Wang Hongwen) and a number of their followers are secretly arrested and placed in detention. This event is later termed 'the smashing of the gang of four'.

8. The CCPCC, State Council, NPC Standing Committee and Military Affairs Committee decide to build a memorial hall in Peking for Mao Zedong and to place Mao's coffin in it 'so that the broad masses of the people will be able to pay their respects to his remains'. The CCPCC decides to publish *Mao Zedong quanji* (*Collected Works of Mao Zedong*) under the 'direct leadership' of the Politburo headed by Hua Guofeng, and Volume V of *Mao Zedong xuanji* (*Selected Works of Mao Zedong*).

11–17. The Prime Minister of Papua New Guinea, Michael Somare, visits China. On October 12, he and Hua Guofeng sign a joint communiqué establishing diplomatic relations at ambassadorial level between China and Papua New Guinea; it makes no mention of Taiwan.

15. Wall posters appear in Peking and Qinghua Universities, Peking, and in Shanghai, denouncing the 'gang of four' by name.

17. China successfully conducts an underground nuclear test.

21–25. Enormous demonstrations take place nationwide in support of Hua Guofeng's appointment as CCP Chairman (see B, October 7) and against the 'gang of four'.

24. A mass rally of 1,000,000 people is held in Tiananmen Square, Peking, in support of Hua Guofeng's appointment as the new Chairman of the CCP. At the rally Wu De reveals that Hua was Mao's choice as successor (see April 30) and attacks the 'gang of four' for trying to split the CCP and seize power, and for worshipping things foreign.

November 2. The CCPCC, NPC Standing Committee, State Council article attacks the 'gang of four's' regime strongly by saying 'what they enforced in literary and art circles was an out-and-out bourgeois dictatorship, a fascist dictatorship', and thus signals a more liberal policy; it also revives the slogan 'let a hundred flowers blossom, let a hundred schools of thought contend'.

D PUBLICATIONS

January. The People's Literary Publishing House publishes the novel *Yuhou qingshan* (*Blue Mountains, After Rain*), written by a group in Guangxi.
1. *Red Flag* and other journals publish two new poems by Mao Zedong, 'Chongshang Jinggangshan' ('Jinggang Mountains Revisited') and 'Niaoer wenda' ('Two Birds: A Dialogue', included also in the new edition of *Mao zhuxi shici* (*Chairman Mao's Poems*), published the same month.
March 25. The bimonthly *Meishu* (*Fine Arts*) and the bimonthly (from July monthly) *Renmin xiju* (*People's Theatre*) begin publication in Peking.
May 1. The Foreign Languages Press publishes the English-language edition of *Mao Tsetung Poems*.
August. The People's Literary Publishing House publishes *Lu Xun shuxin ji* (*Collection of Lu Xun's Letters*) in two volumes, among several of Lu Xun's works published to commemorate the fortieth anniversary of his death.
December. The Shanghai People's Publishing House publishes *Xin Yinghan cidian* (*A New English-Chinese Dictionary*). The second volume (in three parts) of Yao Xueyin's historical novel *Li Zicheng* is published in Peking (the first volume, in two parts, appeared in July 1963).
26. *People's Daily* publishes Mao Zedong's 'Lun shida guanxi' ('On the Ten Major Relationships'), also released for the first time in the PRC the previous day by NCNA (see also April 25, 1956).

E NATURAL DISASTERS

May 29. Two strong earthquakes, of magnitude 7.5 and 7.6, strike the Longling-Luxi area of Yunnan province.
July 28. A severe earthquake, of magnitude 7.5, strikes the Tangshan-Fengnan area of Hebei, strong shocks being felt in Tianjin and Peking. The earthquake devastates the city of Tangshan. On December 25, 1976, Hua Guofeng states at the Second National Conference on Learning from Dazhai in Agriculture that this earthquake 'inflicted

1976

and Military Affairs Committee make an announcement that Mao Zedong's domestic and foreign policies will be retained.

15–22. President Salah Addin Ahmed Bokassa of the Central African Republic visits China.

17. China successfully conducts a hydrogen bomb test.

24. Hua Guofeng formally lays the foundation stone for the memorial hall of Mao Zedong.

December 7. China successfully launches a satellite; its planned return to earth is reported by NCNA December 10.

10–27. The Second National Conference on Learning from Dazhai in Agriculture is held in Peking, convened by the CCPCC. Hua Guofeng makes a major speech December 25. Among many other points he calls for the achievement of the modernization of agriculture, industry, national defence, and science and technology by the end of the century; and claims that there would have been a 'major civil war' and 'foreign aggression' in China if the 'gang of four' had not been suppressed.

20. *People's Daily* carries a report from a Baoding delegate at the National Conference on Learning from Dazhai in Agriculture which says that armed clashes took place in the city because of the 'gang of four's' attempt to seize power there. It accuses the 'gang of four' of trying to create disorder in Baoding and surrounding Hebei province with the aim of threatening Peking's security. This is one of several similar reports at about this time, speaking of violent disturbances, sabotage and armed conflict in several of China's provinces, mainly those in the south. Most refer to the period of the 'gang of four's' arrest or before and blame the 'gang' and its supporters.

23. Sichuan radio reports that the 'gang of four' had 'conspired to organize a counter-revolutionary armed riot' in Yibin (Sichuan), causing serious loss of life and property. During the period of mourning for Chairman Mao they had 'created incidents in a planned and organized way, stormed funeral halls and beaten up and injured militia men on duty'.

25. Guizhou radio reports that the 'gang of four' and their supporters had caused serious trouble in the province by 'dragging out and struggling against leadership cadres at all levels'. It continues: 'They even went all out to beat, smash and loot, and sabotaged factories and communications', with the aim of seizing power amid the confusion.

a loss of lives and property that was rarely seen in history'. A report attributed to the Hebei Provincial CCP and Revolutionary Committees issued August 6 and published, through NP sources, in Hongkong's *South China Morning Post* January 5, 1977, gives the number killed in the earthquake as 655,237 and the number injured as 779,000. See also the PRC official figure under November 17–22, 1979.

August 16. The Songpan-Pingwu area of Sichuan is struck by an earthquake of 7.2 magnitude, strong shocks being felt in the provincial capital, Chengdu.

November 9. Yunnan province is struck by an earthquake (according to the Royal Observatory in Hongkong).

15. Another serious earthquake strikes the Tangshan area of Hebei province.

F DEATHS

January 8. Zhou Enlai d. of cancer in Peking at 9.57 a.m. aged 77.
31. Feng Xuefeng d. aged 74.
April 13. Zhou Rongxin, Minister of Education, d.
19. Peking Opera actor Shang Xiaoyun d. aged 76.
May 3. CCPCC member Li Dazhang d. aged 76.
July 1. Zhang Wentian d. aged 76.
6. Zhu De d. in Peking at 3.01 p.m. aged 89.
7. General Pi Dingjun d. aged 61.
21. Xu Jinqiang, Minister of Coal Industry, d. in Peking aged 61.
27. Musical composer Ma Ke d. in Peking aged 58.
September 9. Mao Zedong, Chairman of the CCP, d. in Peking at 12.10 a.m. aged 82.

1977   The Eleventh CCP Congress

January 2–6. The Bangladesh leader, Chief Martial Law Administrator Major-General Zia ur Rahman, visits China. On the last day a press communiqué announces that Hua Guofeng and Li Xiannian have accepted an invitation to visit Bangladesh at a time 'to be agreed upon later'.

6. A Chinese official spokesman denies reports, which have appeared in the world press, that disorder is continuing in China's provinces.

8. Commemoration meetings in honour of Zhou Enlai take place in Peking and elsewhere on the occasion of the first anniversary of his death.

9. A poster appears in Peking calling for Deng Xiaoping's appointment as Premier of the State Council.

February 5–11. A Chinese delegation led by Deng Yingchao, Zhou Enlai's widow, visits Burma.

8. US President Jimmy Carter (inaugurated January 20) receives Huang Zhen, head of the PRC's Liaison Office, and tells him that the aim of US policy is the normalization of Sino-US relations.

10. *Pravda* prints an article hostile to China, resuming polemics for the first time since the death of Mao Zedong.

17. In Monrovia, China and Liberia sign a joint communiqué establishing diplomatic relations at ambassadorial level.

28. A rally in Peking to commemorate the 1947 uprising in Taiwan (see February 28, 1947) signals the PRC's continuing determination to liberate Taiwan. The chief Soviet delegate to border talks with China, Leonid Ilyichev, leaves Peking after the failure of three months' negotiations on boundary problems.

March 19. *People's Daily* denounces the Soviet Union as the 'boss of the mercenary troops' from Angola, which moved into Shaba province of Zaire from March 8, and 'firmly supports' the Zairian 'armed forces and people in resisting foreign aggression'.

April 6–10. President Moktar Ould Daddah of Mauritania visits China.

7. In Washington, China and Jordan sign a joint communiqué establishing diplomatic relations at ambassadorial level (announced April 14). The CCPCC decides 'to launch a mass movement to study Volume V of the *Selected Works of Mao Zedong*' (see also D, April 15).

11. A *People's Daily* editorial, following Hua Guofeng, declares that 'the key link in running the country well' is 'to achieve stability and unity, consolidate the dictatorship of the proletariat and attain great order across the country in the acute struggle between the two classes'.

17–22. Deng Yingchao visits Sri Lanka.

18–30. President Raymond Chung of Guyana visits China.

27. The commentators of *People's Daily*, *Red Flag* and *Liberation Army*

A Economics

January 2. China's longest highway bridge so far, the 3500-m. bridge over the Yellow River at Luoyang (Henan), is opened to traffic.
4. In Peking, China and Bangladesh sign a trade agreement and an economic and technical cooperation agreement.
10–25. The National Conference of the Coal Industry to Learn from Daqing and Catch Up with Kailuan is held in Peking.
March 29. NCNA reports the discovery of a large coalfield in Suxian (Anhui).
April 20–May 13. The National Conference on Learning from Daqing in Industry is held at the Daqing oilfield and (from April 27 on) in Peking. Attended by some 7000 people, it is the biggest of its kind ever held in the PRC. Hua Guofeng and Ye Jianying give speeches May 9.
15. Shanghai–Lanzhou–Urumchi air services are inaugurated.
16. Shanghai–Hangzhou–Changsha–Guilin air services are inaugurated.
September 10. In Tunis, China and Tunisia sign a contract on the building of the Medjerda–Cape Bon canal for Tunisia.
October 23. In a major speech on the economy at the NPC Standing Committee, Yu Qiuli announces that 'on the basis of the gradual improvement in the economy . . . about 46 per cent of the total number of workers and staff' are to have their wages raised as from October 1.

B Official Appointments, Resignations, Dismissals etc.

January 13. For the first time, Chen Muhua is identified as Minister of Economic Relations with Foreign Countries.
25. On the occasion of the memorial service for Kang Jianmin, Chairman of the Revolutionary Committee of the Ningxia Hui Autonomous Region and First Secretary of its Party Committee, Huo Shilian is identified as his successor (see F, January 18).
29. For the first time, Liu Xiyao is mentioned as Minister of Education (in succession to Zhou Rongxin).
February 12. An Pingsheng is identified in a broadcast from Yunnan as the Chairman of the Provincial Revolutionary Committee and First Secretary of the Provincial Party Committee; on February 16 Qiao Xiaoguang as his Guangxi counterpart in a broadcast from Guangxi.
March 1. Harbin radio identifies Liu Guangtao as Chairman of the Heilongjiang Provincial Revolutionary Committee and First Secretary of the Party Committee; on March 3 Nanjing and Hangzhou radio identify Xu Jiatun and Tie Ying as his Jiangsu and Zhejiang counter-

1977

Daily declare that 'it has now been established, supported by an enormous amount of conclusive evidence, that Zhang Chunqiao was an NP special agent; Jiang Qing, a renegade; Yao Wenyuan, an alien class element; and Wang Hongwen, a new-born bourgeois element'.

27–May 12. Burmese President Ne Win visits China.

May 3–5. President El Hadj Omar Bongo of Gabon visits China.

5–11. An NPC delegation, led by Saifudin, deputy Chairman of the NPC Standing Committee, visits Rumania, proceeding to Yugoslavia (May 11–21), arriving back in Urumchi May 21.

24. The Chairman Mao Memorial Hall, in Tiananmen Square, Peking, is completed.

30. China and Barbados sign a joint communiqué in New York establishing diplomatic relations at ambassadorial level.

June 2–20. A Vietnamese military delegation, led by Minister of National Defence Vo Nguyen Giap, visits China.

6–16. Sudanese President Gaafar Mohamed Nimeri visits China.

13. The Ministry of Foreign Affairs issues a statement protesting to the Japanese government over the Diet's acceptance of the Japanese-Korean (South) Agreement on Joint Development of the Continental Shelf (signed January 30, 1974); the PRC, it states, enjoys sovereignty over the East China Sea continental shelf, and the Chinese government's consent is required for development of the shelf.

16–21. Congolese Prime Minister Louis Sylvain-Goma visits China.

18–20. Laotian Prime Minister Kaysone Phomvihan visits China.

July 7. The Albanian *Zeri i Popullit* (*Voice of the People*), official organ of the Albanian Party of Labour, indirectly criticizes China, by attacking the theory of the three worlds (see below, November 1).

22. The communiqué of the Third Plenum of the Tenth CCPCC (see B, July 21) is broadcast and enormous demonstrations begin in Peking and elsewhere in support of its resolutions.

August 1. A joint editorial in *People's Daily*, *Red Flag*, and *Liberation Army Daily*, and a large rally celebrate the fiftieth anniversary of the founding of the PLA. In a major speech at the rally Ye Jianying declares: 'We must ensure that the gun remains firmly in the hands of the Party', and·'we must speed up the revolutionization and modernization of our army.'

12–18. The Eleventh National Congress of the CCP takes place in Peking, attended by 1510 delegates. On August 12 Hua Guofeng gives a 'Political Report' covering all major aspects of Party policy, and it is adopted August 18. The Party Constitution is adopted August 18, Marxism-Leninism-Mao Zedong Thought remaining 'the guiding ideology and theoretical basis' of the CCP. Deng Xiaoping gives the

parts respectively.

6. Guiyang radio identifies Ma Li as Chairman of the Guizhou Provincial Revolutionary Committee and First Secretary of the Party Committee; the following day Xining radio identifies his Qinghai counterpart as Tan Qilong; and on March 30 Changchun radio his Jilin counterpart as Wang Enmao.

July 21. The Third Plenum of the Tenth CCPCC (held July 16–21) adopts a communiqué by which Hua Guofeng is confirmed as Chairman of the CCPCC and the CCPCC's Military Affairs Committee; Deng Xiaoping is restored to membership of the CCPCC, of the Politburo and of its Standing Committee, and to the posts of deputy Chairman of the CCPCC and of the CCPCC's Military Affairs Committee, Vice-Premier of the State Council and Chief of the General Staff of the PLA; and Zhang Chunqiao, Jiang Qing, Yao Wenyuan and Wang Hongwen are expelled from the Party and dismissed from all posts held.

August 19. The First Plenum of the Eleventh CCPCC elects Hua Guofeng as CCPCC Chairman, Ye Jianying, Deng Xiaoping, Li Xiannian and Wang Dongxing as deputy Chairmen, and these five (only) to the Politburo's Standing Committee.

C CULTURAL AND SOCIAL

February 15. The *geju* (opera) *Baimao nü* (*The White-haired Girl*) (see C, April 1945) is repremiered on the Peking stage after over a decade of suppression by the 'gang of four', one of numerous cultural items to be revived at about this time.

March 11. Chinese astronomers in Peking discover a ring system round the planet Uranus, similar to Saturn's.

14. Zhang Tiesheng is criticized at a rally in Shenyang and arrested as a fraud put forward by the 'gang of four'. (See also C, July 19, 1973.)

26. NCNA reports the 'recent' excavation of a bronze chariot and horse, about 2000 years old, in Xingyi (Guizhou).

April 17. NCNA reports the 'recent' discovery in Lufeng (Yunnan) of an almost complete lower jaw of an ape living some 8,000,000 years ago.

June 4. *People's Daily* reports that, to commemorate the thirty-fifth anniversary of Mao Zedong's 'Talks at the Yan'an Forum' (see C, May 2, 23, 1942), the historical Peking opera *Bishang Liangshan* (*Driven up Mt Liang*), based on the novel *Shuihu zhuan* (*Water Margin*), has been restaged (see C, January 9, 1944). This signals the return of public performances of classical Peking opera for the first time since 1966.

1977

closing address.
22–26. US Secretary of State Cyrus Vance visits China.
30–September 8. Yugoslav President Josip Tito visits China.
September 9. A meeting, attended by Hua Guofeng and other top leaders, takes place in front of the Chairman Mao Memorial Hall in Peking to commemorate the anniversary of Mao Zedong's death. Similar meetings are held in other places.
16–20. Burmese President Ne Win visits China.
17. China conducts another nuclear test.
18–23. Niger Head of State Seyni Kountche visits China.
20–27. President of Equatorial Guinea Masie Nguema visits China.
28. Kampuchean Prime Minister Pol Pot arrives in Peking for a visit to China at the head of a delegation. The delegation leaves for the DPRK October 4, returning to Peking October 8, and leaving China for home October 22.
29. China's Minister of Foreign Affairs, Huang Hua, makes a speech on the PRC domestic situation and foreign policy to the UN General Assembly. 'The factors for war', he states, 'are visibly growing and social-imperialism is the most dangerous source of war.'
October 4–6. Minister of Foreign Affairs Huang Hua visits Canada.
4–10. Cameroon President Ahmadou Ahidjo visits China.
6. A joint editorial in *People's Daily*, *Red Flag* and *Liberation Army Daily* commemorates the first anniversary of the smashing of the 'gang of four' with a call to those areas and units where the leadership is lagging behind the masses in uprooting the influence of the 'gang of four' to catch up quickly with the advanced units.
23–24. The Standing Committee of the NPC, held these days, decides to hold the Fifth NPC in spring 1978.
31. NCNA claims that locust plague, once a contributing factor to terrible famines, has been completely brought under control.
November 1. A very long *People's Daily* article (more than 35,000 characters) claims Chairman Mao's 'theory of the differentiation of the three worlds' as 'a major contribution to Marxism-Leninism'. In the theory, which Mao proposed February 1974, the USA and USSR are the first world, the second is Japan, Europe and Canada, and the third is Asia (except Japan), Africa and Latin America.
3–7. Maltese Prime Minister Dom Mintoff visits China.
20–25. A Vietnamese delegation led by Le Duan, General Secretary of the Vietnamese Communist Party Central Committee, visits China. At a banquet on November 20, Le Duan thanks both China and 'the Soviet Union and the other socialist countries' for their aid and support.
26–December 2. Deng Xiaoping visits Iran.

20–July 7. Academia Sinica holds a work conference in Peking to discuss the contribution of science and scientific expertise to the four modernizations (see December 25, 1976).

July 1. The Peking opera *Dielian hua* (*Butterflies' Attachment to Flowers*) dealing with Mao Zedong's former wife Yang Kaihui, is premiered in Peking.

1–13. A national conference of geological departments, the largest of its kind since 1949, takes place in Peking, one of numerous conferences held about this time.

October 5. The CCPCC issues its decision 'on running well Party schools at various levels'.

9. The Party School under the CCPCC, closed since the GPCR, is reinaugurated at a ceremony attended by Hua Guofeng and others.

12. NCNA reports the discovery of human bones about 100,000 years old west of Peking.

20. NCNA reports that a recent national work conference held by the Ministry of Education has decided to change enrolment policy for students of higher education in the interests of modernization, including the reintroduction of examinations to test the academic level of potential students.

D PUBLICATIONS

Early January. A group at the Second Foreign Languages Institute in Peking prints a not-for-sale run of poems on the Tiananmen Incident (see April 5, 1976) called *Tiananmen geming shichao* (*Revolutionary Poems on Tiananmen*), expanded and republished, also on a not-for-sale basis, in May 1977, renamed *Geming shichao* (*Revolutionary Poems*). It was formally published November 18, 1978, under the title *Tiananmen shichao* (*Poems on Tiananmen*).

April 15. The People's Publishing House publishes vol. V of *Mao Zedong xuanji* (*Selected Works of Mao Zedong*).

July. The Hubei People's Publishing House republishes the *geju Honghu chiweidui* (*Red Guards of Hong Lake*). (First published as a book May 1960, this opera was suppressed by the 'gang of four' and was among the most popular operas in the immediate post-'gang' period.)

August. The Shanghai People's Publishing House publishes a new punctuated edition of *Xi Han huiyao* (*State Regulations of the Western Han*) in two volumes.

November. The Tianjin People's Publishing House publishes the novel *Dihou zhanchang* (*Battleground at the Enemy Rear*), by Zhu Cong; the People's Literary Publishing House *Shenyang budui quyi zuopin*

1977–8

December 14–19. Pakistani Head of Government General Mohammad Zia Ul-Haq visits China.
31. Pich Cheang, Kampuchean ambassador in China, issues a statement that the Vietnamese army, since September 1977, 'has launched systematic and large-scale aggressive acts of invasion against Democratic Kampuchea'. The same day the Vietnamese embassy in China issues a statement proposing negotiations to solve the border issue between Vietnam and Kampuchea.

1978 *Sino-Japanese Treaty of Peace and Friendship;*
China and the USA decide on diplomatic relations

January 18–21. Deng Yingchao leads a Chinese delegation to Kampuchea.
19–24. French Premier Raymond Barre visits China.
26. China launches a satellite. NCNA reports its successful return to earth January 30.
26–31. Deng Xiaoping visits Burma.
February 3–6. Deng Xiaoping visits Nepal.
18–23. The Second Plenum of the Eleventh CCPCC takes place in Peking; it makes preparation for the Fifth NPC.
24. The Praesidium of the USSR Supreme Soviet writes to the Chinese NPC Standing Committee proposing 'a joint statement on the principles of mutual relations between the USSR and PRC'.
24–March 8. The First Session of the Fifth National Committee of the CPPCC is held in Peking. On its last day it adopts a Constitution which describes the CPPCC as 'an organization of the revolutionary united front under the leadership of the CCP'.

xuan (*Selection of Quyi Items by the PLA Units of Shenyang*).
December. The People's Literary Publishing House publishes the historical novel *Yihe quan* (*The Righteous and Harmonious Fists*), by Feng Jicai and Li Dingxing (final draft completed July 1, 1977).

E NATURAL DISASTERS

March 19. *People's Daily* describes the spring drought in China as the worst since 1949. The following day a State Council circular describes the drought as extremely severe in areas along the Yellow and Huai Rivers and a number of places in north China.

F DEATHS

January 18. Kang Jianmin d. in Yinchuan aged 60.
March 22. Peking Opera actor Tan Fuying d. aged 71.
June 17. Literary figure Aying d. aged 77.
July 24. He Qifang d. aged 65.
August 19. CCPCC member Lin Liming d. aged 67.
December 3. Specialist on Chinese theatre history Zhou Yibai d. aged 77.

Economic agreements and important conferences reach a peak ; **1978**
Guo Moruo dies

A ECONOMICS

January 4–26. A national conference on farm mechanization, convened by the State Council, takes place in Peking; it puts forward several goals to be reached by 1980, including 70 per cent increase in numbers of large and medium-sized tractors.
  15–22. A national conference on exchanging experience on technical innovations in industry and communications is held by the State Planning Commission in Yantai (Shandong), among a number of similar conferences held at about this time.
February 3. In Brussels, China and the European Economic Community initial a five-year trade agreement.
  16. In Peking, China and Japan sign a long-term trade agreement valid 1978 to 1985, under which China will export petroleum and coal, Japan technology, complete plants, and building materials; exports from each side will total US$10,000,000,000 in value.
  18. NCNA reports the completion of the first Chinese-designed and

26–March 5. The First Session of the Fifth NPC is held in Peking. On February 26, Hua Guofeng delivers the Report on the Work of the Government (adopted March 5). Among numerous other points he lays down the general tasks for the 'new period', including revealing a ten-year plan (1976–85) under which 'in each of the eight years from 1978 to 1985, the value of agricultural output is to increase by 4 to 5 per cent and of industrial output by over 10 per cent'; calls for a treaty of peace and friendship with Japan; and declares that 'how Sino-Soviet relations will develop is entirely up to the Soviet side'. On March 1, Ye Jianying delivers the Report on the Revision of the Constitution, and on March 5, the new PRC Constitution is adopted. Under it local revolutionary committees are 'local organs of state administration', and are thus abolished except at levels of political power, i.e. they cease to exist in factories or institutes, but remain in rural people's communes.

March 9. The Ministry of Foreign Affairs delivers to the Soviet ambassador in China, V.S. Tolstikov, a note rejecting the proposal of February 24 and calling instead, among other things, for 'an agreement on the maintenance of the *status quo* on the border'.

12–16. A delegation led by Vice-Premier Li Xiannian visits the Philippines.

15. China conducts a successful nuclear test.

18–21. Li Xiannian visits Bangladesh. On the last day, in Dacca, China and Bangladesh sign two agreements on economic and technical cooperation and on scientific and technical cooperation.

April 14–18. Somali President Mohamed Siad Barre visits China.

24. Prime Minister Ali Nasser Mohammed of the People's Democratic Republic of Yemen arrives in Peking for a visit, holding talks with Hua Guofeng April 26.

29. Seychelles President France Albert René arrives in Peking for a visit, holding talks with Hua Guofeng May 1.

May 1. Air Marshal Sir Neil Cameron, British Chief of the Defence Staff, in China to discuss Sino-British defence exchanges, says at a lunch in Peking that 'it must be good' that China and the UK are becoming more friendly, 'because we both have an enemy at our door whose capital city is Moscow'.

2–June 7. A Chinese delegation led by Vice-Premier Gu Mu visits France, Switzerland, Belgium, Denmark and West Germany.

5–10. Hua Guofeng visits the DPRK, his first trip outside China since the smashing of the 'gang of four'.

14–15. Nepalese King Birendra visits China.

15–20. Rumanian President N. Ceausescu visits China.

1978

built dry dock for 50,000-ton ships at Shanhaiguan (Hebei).
March 31. CAAC inaugurates a Peking–Karachi–Addis Ababa air service.
April 9. A *People's Daily* editorial on 'integrating moral encouragement with material reward' endorses the recent shift of emphasis towards material incentives.
May 4. CAAC inaugurates a Peking–Urumchi–Belgrade–Zurich air service.
19. Hua Guofeng and N. Ceausescu sign a long-term agreement on economic and technical cooperation between China and Romania.
June 1. The railway from Xiangfan (Hubei) to Chongqing (Sichuan) is opened to traffic.
18. A ceremony at Thakot, North-West Frontier Province, Pakistan, marks the opening to traffic of the Karakorum Highway, built with Chinese assistance and linking Thakot with the Chinese border area.
20–July 9. A National Finance and Trade Conference on Learning from Daqing and Dazhai, convened by the CCPCC, is held in Peking.
July 4. A *People's Daily* editorial calls for the implementation of the Draft Decision of the CCPCC Concerning Some Problems in Speeding Up the Development of Industry, recently issued to relevant organizations. Among thirty points it includes one on the responsibility of factory managers under the leadership of CCP committees.
17. The Japanese government-owned Japan National Oil Corporation announces that China and Japan have reached agreement on the joint development of oil resources in Bohai Bay.
28. In Peking the China National Technical Import Corporation and the Japanese Hitachi Ltd and Tokyo Shibaura Electric Co. sign a protocol and contract on a complete colour television plant for China.
August 21. In Bucharest, China and Rumania sign an agreement on economic and technical cooperation and eight other mainly economic agreements and protocols.
26. In Belgrade, China and Yugoslavia sign a long-term agreement on economic, scientific and technological cooperation.
September 5. A director of British Rolls-Royce, Sir Peter Thornton, announces that China has contracted Rolls-Royce, to the extent of possibly over £80,000,000, to help modernize China's aero-engine industry.
October 2. NCNA reports the completed construction of a high-yielding oilfield at Renqiu (Hebei).
12. Air services (on November 17 hovercraft services) are inaugurated between Hongkong and Guangzhou.
December 4. In Peking, China and France sign a seven-year agreement

1978

17. Minister of Foreign Affairs Huang Hua tells the Zairian embassy in Peking that China firmly supports 'the Zairian government and people in their just struggle to repulse the Soviet-Cuban mercenaries' invasion of the Shaba region'. (Troops moved from Angola into Zaire's Shaba province, entering the town of Kolwezi May 11–12.)

24. A State Council spokesman accuses Vietnam of 'unwarrantedly ostracizing and persecuting Chinese residents in Vietnam, and expelling many of them back to China'. He declares that more than 70,000 were expelled to China between early April and mid-May.

25. In London, China and Oman sign a joint communiqué establishing diplomatic relations. Mozambican President Samora Michel arrives in Peking for a visit, holding talks with Hua Guofeng May 28.

29. Minister of Foreign Affairs Huang Hua addresses the Special Session of the UN General Assembly on Disarmament. He declares that the Soviet Union is 'perniciously taking the offensive' in the arms race and 'seizing spheres of influence' on a worldwide scale.

June 2. In a speech to the All-Army Political Work Conference (held April 27–June 6), Deng Xiaoping advocates 'seeking truth from facts' not merely 'talking about Mao Zedong Thought every day'.

3. Huang Hua arrives in Kinshasa for a visit to Zaire; he holds talks with President Mobutu Sese Seko the next day.

8. President of Ruanda Juvenal Habyalimana arrives in Peking for a visit, holding talks with Hua Guofeng June 10.

9. The Ministry of Foreign Affairs issues a statement repeating earlier claims on the forced expulsion of Chinese from Vietnam (see May 24), attacking a Vietnamese Ministry of Foreign Affairs statement of May 27, itself attacking China's May 24 statement, and rejecting a proposal in the Vietnamese May 27 statement that 'representatives of the two governments meet soon to settle the differences' on the grounds that 'such a proposal was made purely out of propaganda needs'.

11. Fijian Prime Minister Ratu Sir Kamisese Mara arrives in China for a visit.

16. The Ministry of Foreign Affairs sends a note to the Vietnamese Ministry of Foreign Affairs notifying its decision to cancel the appointment of the Chinese consul-general in Ho Chi Minh City, Vietnam, and to close down the Vietnamese consulates in Guangzhou, Kunming and Nanning.

16–19. Spanish King Juan Carlos I visits Peking.

17. A *People's Daily* commentator places the ultimate blame for the 'campaign of ostracizing, persecuting and expelling Chinese residents' from Vietnam on the Soviet Union.

19. William Richard Tolbert, President of Liberia, arrives in Peking

on economic relations and cooperation; under it trade will amount to 60,000,000,000 francs.

6. In London, the Bank of China signs agreements with UK banks for seven separate 'deposit facilities' totalling US$1,200,000,000.

19. Boeing announces in Seattle that China has bought three Boeing 747 airliners. In Atlanta, Georgia, Mr J. Paul Austin, Chairman of Coca-Cola Co., announces that, on December 13, it reached agreement with China to sell Coca-Cola there and to open a bottling plant in Shanghai.

B OFFICIAL APPOINTMENTS, RESIGNATIONS, DISMISSALS ETC.

March 5. The First Session of the Fifth NPC elects Hua Guofeng as Premier of the State Council, Deng Xiaoping, Li Xiannian, Xu Xiangqian, Ji Dengkui, Yu Qiuli, Chen Xilian, Chen Yonggui, Fang Yi, Wang Zhen, Chen Muhua, and others as Vice-Premiers, Huang Hua as Minister of Foreign Affairs, Xu Xiangqian as Minister of National Defence, Huang Zhen as Minister of Culture, Liu Xiyao as Minister of Education, and others, and appoints Hu Qiaomu as President of the Chinese Academy of Social Sciences (set up in 1977).

8. The First Session of the National Committee of the CPPCC elects Deng Xiaoping as the Committee's Chairman.

October 13. The appointment of Lin Hujia as Mayor of Peking to replace Wu De is confirmed by an official Chinese spokesman. Wu De retains his place in the Politburo.

December 22. The communiqué of the Third Plenum of the Eleventh CCPCC announces its election of Chen Yun as a deputy Chairman of the CCPCC, and Deng Yingchao, Wang Zhen and Hu Yaobang as members of the Politburo.

C CULTURAL AND SOCIAL

January 1. The arranged classical Peking opera *Yangmen nüjiang* (*Women Generals of the Yang Family*) is restaged for the first time since before the GPCR.

21. China and France sign an agreement on science and technology, to include projects on medicinal plants, geology etc.

26. The Ministry of Education issues a circular on its decision, ratified by the State Council, to set up specially staffed and funded 'key' primary and secondary schools.

February 12–23. A national conference on mass cultural work, convened by the Ministry of Culture, takes place in Xiyang (Shanxi).

for a visit, holding talks with Hua Guofeng June 22.

26. The Ministry of Foreign Affairs issues a statement protesting against the exchange of ratifications (June 22) of the Japan-Republic of Korea Agreement on Joint Development of the Continental Shelf (see also June 13, 1977).

July 3. The PRC government sends a note to the Vietnamese government informing it of the Chinese decision to stop all economic and technical aid to Vietnam and to recall Chinese engineers and experts in Vietnam, because of the latter's 'anti-China activities and ostracism of Chinese residents in Vietnam'.

7. The Ministry of Foreign Affairs sends a note to the Albanian embassy in China that the PRC is suspending all aid to Albania and recalling its experts there because 'the Albanian leadership has decided to pursue the anti-China course' and 'sabotaged the economic and military cooperation' between the two countries.

10. The Vietnamese Ministry of Foreign Affairs lodges a strong protest with the Chinese embassy in Hanoi against the intrusion of Chinese aircraft into Vietnamese air space on July 8 (declared a fabrication by the Chinese Ministry of Foreign Affairs July 12).

19. The Ministry of Foreign Affairs sends a note to the Vietnamese Ministry of Foreign Affairs proposing negotiations at deputy foreign minister level on the Chinese residents in Vietnam. (The talks begin in Hanoi August 8.)

August 9. China and Libya sign a joint communiqué establishing diplomatic relations. NCNA announces that the CCPCC has 'recently' issued its Resolution Strengthening Political Work in the Army.

12. In Peking, Chinese and Japanese Ministers of Foreign Affairs Huang Hua and Sonoda Sunao sign the Sino-Japanese Treaty of Peace and Friendship. Under it, each declares it will not seek hegemony and 'each is opposed to efforts by any other country or group of countries to establish such hegemony'; also 'the present Treaty shall not affect the position of either Contracting Party regarding its relations with third countries.'

16–21. Hua Guofeng visits Rumania at the head of a delegation; he proceeds to Yugoslavia 21–29, and to Iran August 29–September 1, returning to Urumchi September 1 and to Peking September 5.

25. At Youyiguan (Friendship Pass) on the Sino-Vietnamese border, Vietnamese troops and police drive away many Chinese to the Chinese side of the border, killing four of them; over 200 men of the Vietnamese People's Army intrude into Chinese territory (the Chinese account). Vietnamese drive back Chinese who had 'rushed to cross the border into Vietnamese territory'; China was planning to send spies; two

1978

March 18–31. A National Science Conference is held in Peking. It discusses methods for making science advance the four modernizations. In his speech of March 18, Deng Xiaoping calls for the training of competent scientists and states 'we should give the heads and deputy heads of research institutes a free hand in the work of science and technology'.

April 15–21. The Third Asian Badminton Invitation Championships are held in Peking; China wins the men's singles and doubles, the women's singles and the boys' singles.

22–May 16. A National Conference on Educational Work, convened by the Ministry of Education, is held in Peking. In his speech on the opening day, Deng Xiaoping calls for better academic standards and greater respect for teachers among students. The conference adopts a draft outline programme for education 1978–85, including doubling the 1965 number of university students.

23. Radio France and the British Broadcasting Corporation transmit the stereophonic broadcast of a concert, given by the Chinese Central Philharmonic Society, live by satellite – China's first live concert broadcast to Europe.

May 27–June 5. The Chinese National Federation of Literature and Art Circles holds an enlarged national committee meeting in Peking, the first national conference on literature and art since the smashing of the 'gang of four'.

June 12. A ten-day national conference on medical science, the largest of its kind since 1949, closes in Peking.

15. The well-known Japanese conductor Ozawa Seiji conducts the Central Symphony Orchestra in a concert in Peking, the first time a foreigner has conducted a Chinese symphony orchestra since 1949.

September 8–17. The Fourth National Women's Congress takes place in Peking.

October 11. A ceremony marks the opening of classes at the Chinese Academy of Social Sciences' Postgraduate Institute.

11–21. The Ninth National Congress of Chinese Trade Unions takes place in Peking.

16–26. The Tenth National Congress of the Communist Youth League of China takes place in Peking.

31–December 10. A National Work Conference on Intellectual Youth Going to the Mountains and Countryside takes place in Peking.

November 16. The spoken play *Yu wusheng chu* (*Where the Silence Is*), about the Tiananmen Incident (April 5, 1976) is performed in Peking for the first time.

December 27. Twenty-eight youths in Tiananmen Square, Peking,

Vietnamese are killed in the incident (the Vietnamese account).
September 8–13. Deng Xiaoping visits the DPRK.
12–15. Tanzanian Prime Minister Edward Sokoine visits China.
20. The President of Chad, General Felix Malloum Ngakoutou Bey-Ndi, arrives in Peking for a visit and holds talks with Hua Guofeng September 23.
October 23. The instruments of ratification of the Sino-Japanese Treaty of Peace and Friendship are exchanged in Tokyo during a trip by Deng Xiaoping to Japan (October 22–29).
26. The Ministry of Foreign Affairs sends a note to the Vietnamese embassy in Peking protesting against alleged encroachments of Chinese territory on September 20, 24, 29 and 30, among other occasions. (Similar protests follow later in the year.)
November 5–9. Deng Xiaoping vists Thailand, proceeding to Malaysia 9–12, Singapore 12–14, and Burma 14, returning to Peking the same day November 14.
8. At a press conference in Bangkok, Deng Xiaoping declares that the Soviet-Vietnamese Treaty of Friendship and Cooperation (signed November 3) is aimed at China and threatens peace and security in the Asian-Pacific region.
15. NCNA reports a 'recent' declaration by the Peking Municipal CCP Committee that the Tiananmen Incident (see April 5, 1976) was a 'completely revolutionary action'.
19. A fourteen-page wall poster appears in Peking accusing Mao Zedong of supporting the 'gang of four' and being responsible for removing Deng Xiaoping in 1976. This was in the first batch of numerous posters on 'democracy wall' about this time.
26. Deng Xiaoping tells Sasaki Ryōsaku of the Democratic Socialist Party of Japan that 'it is a normal thing' to put up wall posters, 'and shows the stable situation in our country'.
December 4–6. President El Hadj Omar Bongo of Gabon visits China.
16 (15 in the US). The USA and China simultaneously release a joint communiqué on their decision to establish diplomatic relations as from January 1, 1979, and to exchange ambassadors on March 1, 1979. The US 'acknowledges' China's claim to Taiwan but 'the people' of the USA will still maintain 'unofficial relations with the people of Taiwan'.
16. The Ministry of Foreign Affairs issues a statement condemning Vietnam for 'producing on December 3, 1978, a so-called "Kampuchean national united front for national salvation"' and for calling for the overthrow of the government of Democratic Kampuchea; the statement supports the latter's 'just stand'.

claiming to represent 50,000 young people sent to do farm work in the far south-west of Yunnan after leaving school, hand out a leaflet reporting a general strike beginning December 9 among the 50,000 'to oppose the local leaders who trampled on the human rights and respect of intellectual youth'. The twenty-eight demand a meeting with Hua Guofeng or Deng Xiaoping.

D PUBLICATIONS

Early 1978. The Foreign Languages Press publishes *A Dream of Red Mansions*, Vol. I, a translation of part of *Honglou meng* by Gladys Yang and Yang Xianyi.

February. *Jinian Zhou Enlai zongli wenwu xuanbian* (*A Selection of Cultural Objects Commemorating Premier Zhou Enlai*), compiled by the Museum of Chinese History, is published in Peking.

April. The People's Literary Publishing House publishes *Moruo juzuo xuan* (*A Selection of Plays by Guo Moruo*), including four plays and explanatory material. The Zhonghua Book Company publishes its modern punctuated edition of all twenty-four standard histories, having completed publication of the individual works late in March.

June. The People's Literary Publishing House publishes the novel *Yunya chunuan* (*First Warmth on the Cloudy Cliffs*), by Gao Ying.

July 1. *Red Flag* and other papers publish Mao Zedong's 'Zai kuoda di zhongyang gongzuo huiyi shang de jianghua' ('Talk at an Enlarged Working Conference convened by the CCPCC') given January 30, 1962.

August. The Hunan People's Publishing House publishes *Cai Hesen wenji* (*The Collected Works of Cai Hesen*) in two volumes in Changsha.

13. NCNA reports that the People's Literary Publishing House has published *Shashibiya quanji* (*Complete Works of William Shakespeare*) in eleven volumes.

September 11. *Zhongguo qingnian* (*Chinese Youth*) resumes publication after a twelve-year break (see also D, October 20, 1923).

October. The Commercial Press publishes *Hanying cidian* (*Chinese-English Dictionary*), compiled by the English Department of Peking's Foreign Languages Institute.

November 18. See January 1977.

20. The periodical *Renmin wenxue* (*People's Literature*) publishes a new historical play by Cao Yu called *Wang Zhaojun*.

21–22. *People's Daily* publishes the long article 'Tiananmen shijian zhenxiang' ('The Truth about the Tiananmen Incident').

18–22. The Third Plenum of the Eleventh CCPCC takes place in Peking. It decides that 'since ... the large-scale nationwide mass movement to expose and criticize the "gang of four" has in the main been completed victoriously, the stress of the Party's work should shift to socialist modernization as of 1979'. It adopts a communiqué December 22 which rehabilitates Peng Dehuai and Tao Zhu (posthumously), among a number of other decisions.

1979 The Sino-Vietnamese War

January 1. Xu Xiangqian, Minister of National Defence, announces that as from this day, 'I have ordered the troops on the Fujian front to stop shelling the Greater and Lesser Quemoy ... and other islands', among other reasons 'to facilitate shipping, production and other activities in the Taiwan Straits'.
The USA and China formally establish diplomatic relations at ambassadorial level.
7. The Chinese government issues a statement denouncing the Vietnamese authorities for a 'new massive war of aggression against Democratic Kampuchea'. Large-scale Vietnamese forces had moved into Kampuchea December 25, 1978. (They seized Phnom Penh January 7, 1979.)
8. China and Djibouti establish diplomatic relations at ambassadorial level.
28. Vice-Premier Deng Xiaoping and his party arrive in Washington for an official visit to the USA, the first there by a senior PRC leader.

1978–9

Late December. The unofficial journal *Jintian* (translated as *The Moment* in the journal itself) begins publication in Peking.

E Natural Disasters

November 2. NCNA reports a nationwide serious drought in China in 1978: 'in length of time, breadth of scope, and seriousness of extent, it has surpassed the great droughts of 1934, 1959 and 1966. The drought in Hubei, Jiangxi, Henan, Shanxi, Shaanxi and other provinces has been the worst for fifty to seventy years, in Jiangsu for sixty to a hundred years and Anhui has suffered from a particularly bad drought not seen for 122 years.'

F Deaths

April 25. Deputy Chief of the General Staff of the PLA Peng Shaohui d. in Peking aged 72.
June 12. Scientist, writer and CCPCC member Guo Moruo d. in Peking aged 85.
July 16. Former deputy Minister of Finance Wang Xueming d. aged 61.
August 3. Luo Ruiqing d. aged 71.
13. Wang Zheng, CCPCC member and deputy Chief of the General Staff of the PLA, d. aged 70.

The NPC readjusts the economy 1979

A Economics

January 1. The completed Taiyuan (Shanxi)–Jiaozuo (Henan) railway, of 209 km., is formally handed over to the state for use.
14. In Peking, Chinese and Thai representatives sign a protocol under which China will supply Thailand with crude oil every year from 1979 to 1983.
20. The Chinese and Netherlands Ministers of Foreign Affairs, Huang Hua and C.A. van der Klaauw, sign a civil air transport agreement in Peking by which a regular air service will be established between the two countries.
March 4. In Peking, Chinese Minister of Foreign Trade Li Qiang and Eric Varley, British Secretary of State for Industry, sign an agreement on economic cooperation with a target of two-way trade worth a total of US$14,000,000,000 up to 1985.
June 7. The Bank of China opens a branch in Luxembourg, its first set up abroad since 1949.

1979

February 1. Deng Xiaoping and his party fly to Atlanta, Georgia, on their official visit to the USA. They arrive in Houston, Texas, the next day and Seattle, Washington, on February 4, visiting the Boeing 747 plant near Seattle the same afternoon. Deng and his party depart for Japan February 5.

6. Deng Xiaoping arrives in Tokyo for a visit to Japan. The next day he meets Japanese Prime Minister Ohira Masayoshi and, among other points, tells him that Vietnam must be punished for its expansionism against Kampuchea.

8. Deng Xiaoping returns to Peking from Japan.

Under a joint communiqué signed the same day in Paris by the Chinese and Portuguese ambassadors in France, the two countries formally establish diplomatic relations at ambassadorial level. The Portuguese Prime Minister, Dr Carlos Alberto Mota Pinto, states in Lisbon that the status of Macao will remain unchanged: 'Chinese territory under Portuguese administration'.

17. In the early hours of the morning a large Chinese force attacks Vietnam. The same day, the Vietnamese and Chinese governments issue statements. The first claims that the 'Chinese authorities have brazenly started a war of aggression against Vietnam, and mobilized many infantry, armoured and artillery divisions under air cover to mount a massive attack on the whole of the Vietnam-China border.' The second claims: 'All we want is a peaceful and stable border. After counterattacking the Vietnamese aggressors as they deserve, the Chinese frontier troops will strictly keep to defending the border of their own country.'

23. The NPC Standing Committee adopts the Regulations of the PRC Governing the Arrest and Detention of Persons Accused of Crimes.

March 1. The Chinese Ministry of Foreign Affairs sends a note to the Vietnamese embassy proposing 'concrete negotiations on ending the current border conflict' at the level of vice-minister of foreign affairs. China and the USA formally open embassies in each other's capitals.

5. Chinese troops complete the seizure of Langson in northern Vietnam. The Chinese government issues a statement that 'having attained the goals set for them' the Chinese troops in Vietnam will commence withdrawal the same day.

6. The Shanghai Municipal Security Bureau issues a notice, approved by the Shanghai Municipal Revolutionary Committee, ordering all those taking part in demonstrations to obey the police and preserve order, and to abstain from interfering with railway traffic or putting up posters except in designated places.

10. Han Nianlong, Chinese Vice-Minister of Foreign Affairs, hands

1979

21. Yu Qiuli, Vice-Premier and Minister in Charge of the State Planning Commission, gives a report on the economy to the Second Session of the Fifth NPC. He issues numerous detailed statistics and information.

July 1. The Second Session of the Fifth NPC endorses the policy of readjustment of the economy, in effect to scale down some aspects of the four modernizations and change the balance of the various sectors of the economy, for example by giving greater emphasis to agriculture.

7. Li Qiang, Minister of Foreign Trade, and US ambassador Leonard Woodcock sign a formal Sino-US trade agreement.

12. Hua Guofeng and Burmese Prime Minister U Maung Maung Kha (visiting Peking July 9-13) sign a Sino-Burmese economic and technical cooperation agreement in Peking.

September 9. NCNA announces that on May 11 the US and Chinese governments reached agreement whereby the USA would declare unfrozen all Chinese assets previously blocked by it. The same day the State Council decree authorizing the Bank of China to recover all unfrozen Chinese assets is made public.

28. Vice-Premier Gu Mu states at a press conference in Peking that China is 'ready to accept loans from all friendly countries and financial organizations provided they do not affect China's sovereign rights and the terms are appropriate'. The Fourth Plenum of the Eleventh CCPCC adopts the Decisions of the CCPCC on Some Questions Concerning the Acceleration of Agricultural Development.

October 24. NCNA announces that the State Council has raised the purchasing prices of eighteen major agricultural products since March, with an average price increase of 24.8 per cent.

December 6. A Sino-Japanese agreement on the joint exploration and exploitation of petroleum and natural gas resources in the Bohai Sea is signed in Peking.

B OFFICIAL APPOINTMENTS, RESIGNATIONS, DISMISSALS ETC.

February 23. The NPC Standing Committee appoints Peng Zhen as director of the Commission for Legal Affairs of the NPC Standing Committee, a body it sets up the same day. It also appoints Huo Shilian as Minister of Agriculture, among thirteen ministerial appointments.

June 5. The Standing Committee of the Fifth National Committee of the CPPCC endorses a list of 109 additional members of the Fifth National Committee of the CPPCC, including Lu Dingyi, Yang Xianzhen, adviser to the CCPCC Party School, Wang Guangmei,

1979

the Laotian ambassador to China, Thavone Sichaleun, a memorandum protesting against and denying allegations made in a Lao government statement of March 6 that China was massing troops along the Lao border.

15. The Vietnamese Ministry of Foreign Affairs issues a note to the Chinese Ministry of Foreign Affairs declaring Vietnam's willingness to begin vice-ministerial negotiations one week after the complete withdrawal of Chinese troops from Vietnam.

16. At a press conference in Peking Chinese Minister of Foreign Affairs Huang Hua announces that the withdrawal of Chinese troops from Vietnam has been completed the same day.

29. The Peking Municipal Revolutionary Committee adopts a public notice ordering public gatherings and demonstrations to obey the police and banning slogans, big-character posters, publications and photographs which oppose socialism or disclose classified information.

April 3. The NPC Standing Committee decides not to extend the Treaty of Friendship, Alliance and Mutual Assistance between the USSR and China (see February 14, 1950), due to expire on April 11, 1980. The same day Huang Hua, Minister of Foreign Affairs, transmits the decision to the Soviet ambassador to China, J.S. Shcherbakov, adding that the Chinese government was proposing negotiations to improve relations between the two countries.

14. A Chinese delegation, led by Vice-Minister of Foreign Affairs Han Nianlong, arrives in Hanoi for talks on relations between China and Vietnam.

23. *People's Daily* reports the discovery of Heilongjiang province's worst case of theft of state property since liberation. A group headed by a woman called Wang Shouxin had embezzled property worth 536,000 *yuan* since 1972.

May 2–6. Malaysian Prime Minister Datuk Hussein bin Onn visits Peking.

14. As part of the polemics with Vietnam an NCNA commentary presents China's case for claim to the Nansha and Xisha Islands (also claimed by Vietnam).

18. After five plenary meetings the first round of Sino-Vietnamese talks in Hanoi ends without positive result.

June 4. Soviet Foreign Minister Andrei Gromyko presents the Chinese embassy a memorandum offering negotiations on bilateral relations in July and August in Moscow.

5. President A. Sadat of Egypt announces the conclusion of a military arrangement with China. Western diplomats in Cairo believe this involved the sale of Chinese fighter aircraft to Egypt.

1979

widow of Liu Shaoqi, writer Ding Ling, and He Zizhen, former wife of Mao Zedong.

July 1. The final Plenum of the Second Session of the Fifth NPC elects Peng Zhen and others as deputy Chairmen of the NPC Standing Committee, and endorses Hua Guofeng's nomination of Chen Yun, Bo Yibo and Yao Yilin as Vice-Premiers of the State Council; and of Fang Yi as President of the Chinese Academy of Social Sciences.

25. The Peking Chinese Catholic Patriotic Association elects Michael Fu Tieshan as Bishop of Peking, the first since the Cultural Revolution. (He is consecrated December 21.)

30. The Standing Committee of the NPC appoints Vice-Premier Gu Mu as Minister in charge of two commissions, both of which it sets up the same day, one to regulate foreign investments, the other to supervise the PRC's imports and exports.

September 13. The Standing Committee of the Fifth NPC appoints Ji Pengfei as Vice-Premier of the State Council and Wei Wenbo as Minister of Justice, at the same time re-establishing the Ministry and two others.

28. A communiqué announces that the Fourth Plenum of the Eleventh CCPCC has elected Lu Dingyi, Zhou Yang, Bo Yibo and others to the CCPCC and Zhao Ziyang and Peng Zhen to the Politburo.

November 16. The Federation of Literary and Art Circles of China elects Zhou Yang as its Chairman.

December 13. The Seventh Municipal Congress of Peking elects Lin Hujia as Mayor of Peking.

C Cultural and Social

January 1. According to a decision of the State Council, all Chinese publications and documents in English, French, German, Spanish and other languages published in China, from this day start using the *Hanyu pinyin* system of romanization.

28. NCNA announces the 'recent' CCPCC Decision on the Question of Removing the Designations of Landlords and Rich Peasants and on the Class Status of the Children of Landlords and Rich Peasants, under which all people in the mentioned categories who have remoulded themselves shall be regarded as normal commune members, and not as bad elements.

31. Vice-Premier Deng Xiaoping and US President Jimmy Carter sign a scientific and technological cooperation agreement and a cultural agreement.

February. Wu Han's *Hai Rui baguan* (*The Dismissal of Hai Rui*) is

1979

15–July 2. The Second Session of the Fifth National Committee of the CPPCC takes place in Peking.

18–July 1. The Second Session of the Fifth National NPC takes place in Peking, attended by 3279 deputies. On the first day Hua Guofeng reports on the work of the government and issues a number of economic statistics, including the 1978 grain output (304,750,000 tons, an increase of 7.8 per cent over 1977) and claims that the 'per capita grain output surpassed the highest level of the past'. He states that China wants negotiations to improve relations with the USSR, but that the latter will have to change its stand.

22. Representatives of the governments of the PRC and Republic of Ireland sign a joint communiqué in New York announcing their decision to establish diplomatic relations at ambassadorial level. China and Vietnam complete the exchange of prisoners-of-war captured by each side during the February–March conflict.

26. At the Second Session of the Fifth NPC Peng Zhen explains seven draft laws for debate.

27. The State Statistical Bureau issues a communiqué announcing numerous economic, cultural and other statistics. It also states that at the end of 1978 China's population, including Taiwan province, stood at 975,230,000, and that the population growth rate was 12 per 1000.

28. The second round of Sino-Vietnamese peace talks begins in Peking.

July 1. The Fifth NPC adopts seven laws. They include the Electoral Law for the NPC and the Local People's Congresses of the PRC, the Criminal Law of the PRC, the Law of Criminal Procedure of the PRC, and the Law of the PRC on Joint Ventures with Chinese and Foreign Investment. (The last one came into operation on July 8, the others all on January 1, 1980.) In addition the session adopts several amendments to the Constitution, including the abolition of revolutionary committees at various levels.

8. Vice-Premier Li Xiannian and Mrs Imelda Marcos, wife of the Philippines President, sign Sino-Filipino agreements on (*i*) long-term trade, (*ii*) cultural understanding and exchanges, and (*iii*) civil air transport, for direct air service between Peking and Manila.

16. An incident on the Sino-Soviet border near Tacheng (Xinjiang) results in the death of a Chinese cadre. The Soviet and Chinese Ministries of Foreign Affairs issue mutual protests on July 17 and 24 respectively.

30. In Peking the Chinese delegation to the Sino-Vietnamese negotiations releases a pamphlet to the press containing documents in support of China's claim to sovereignty over the Xisha and Nansha Islands.

August 9. Having just defected to China, the Vice-Chairman of the Standing Committee of the National Assembly of Vietnam, Hoang

1979

restaged (see C, November 10, 1965).

12. *People's Daily* calls for a restoration of social order and the invocation of the law against trouble-makers, a warning against the demonstrations which had occurred in Shanghai over the previous week by youths protesting against being sent to the countryside.

March 15. NCNA reports a 'recent' national conference on the study of religion, the PRC's first, held in Kunming (Yunnan). Attended by over 100 scholars, teachers and cadres, it heard papers on Buddhism, Lamaism, Islam, Taoism and Christianity.

29. Wei Jingsheng, a major activist in the democracy and human rights movement, is arrested as a counter-revolutionary.

31. *Qielilüe zhuan* (*Leben des Galilei*, *The Life of Galileo*), a play by Bertolt Brecht, is premiered in Peking, the first contemporary foreign play to be performed in China by professionals since 1966.

April 5. In Peking Vice-Chancellor Zhou Peiyuan of Peking University and Alfred Bowker, Chancellor of the University of California, sign an agreement for academic exchange and cooperation between the two universities.

May 8. Li Qiang, Minister of Foreign Trade, and US Secretary of Commerce Juanita Krebs sign a five-year protocol on cooperation in science and technology.

June 1–5. A national forum on acupuncture, the largest ever held in China, takes place in Peking, attended by over 300 Chinese and 100 foreign specialists.

10–20. The Second World Badminton Championships take place in Hangzhou (Zhejiang).

July 3–5. Clashes between Chinese and foreign students in Shanghai result in injuries to some forty people.

September 15–30. The PRC's Fourth National Games take place in Peking's Workers' Stadium.

October 16. The Intermediate People's Court of Peking sentences Wei Jingsheng (see C, March 29) to fifteen years' imprisonment for passing on military intelligence to a foreigner and carrying out counter-revolutionary agitation. (An appeal by Wei against the judgment is rejected by the Peking Municipal High People's Court on November 6.)

19. Sixteen Chinese Moslems leave Peking on the first Chinese pilgrimage to Mecca since 1964.

30–November 16. The Fourth Congress of the Federation of Literary and Art Circles of China takes place in Peking, the first since 1960.

1979

Van Hoan, gives a press conference in Peking at which he reads his 'Message to Vietnamese Compatriots' denouncing the Vietnamese leadership, especially for having 'invaded and occupied Kampuchea... and mobilized tens of millions of our people for a war against China'.
13–20. Sri Lankan Prime Minister Ranasinghe Premadasa visits China, meeting Hua Guofeng August 14.
31. Near the end of a visit to China (August 25–September 1), US Vice-President Walter Mondale formally opens an American consulate-general in Guangzhou, the first in China for thirty years.
September 12. Queen Margrethe II of Denmark begins a ten-day official visit to China, the first by the head of state of a north-western European country.
23. A Chinese delegation headed by Vice-Minister of Foreign Affairs Wang Youping leaves Peking for Moscow for negotiations with the USSR on problems affecting bilateral relations.
25–28. The Eleventh CCPCC holds its Fourth Plenum in Peking.
29. In a long speech at a meeting of the CCPCC, the NPC Standing Committee and the State Council held in Peking to celebrate the thirtieth anniversary of the PRC's founding, Ye Jianying, Chairman of the NPC Standing Committee, states that, at the time the Cultural Revolution was launched, 'the estimate made of the situation within the Party and the country ran counter to reality', and that 'the havoc which the counter-revolutionary gang [of four] wrought for ten long years [1966–1976] spelt calamity for our people.' He thus declares the Cultural Revolution both unnecessary and disastrous.
October 7. At a press conference in Peking, Hua Guofeng states that the gang of four will go on trial, adding 'as to when this will take place, I can say that it probably won't be too far off. . . . We will not sentence them to death. They are now alive and well.'
12. Hua Guofeng leaves Peking for a visit to western Europe, the first there by a PRC government head. He visits France (October 15–21), the Federal Republic of Germany (October 21–28), Great Britain (October 28–November 3), and Italy (November 3–6). He returns to Peking November 10.
17. The first plenary meeting of the Sino-Soviet negotiations on bilateral relations takes place in Moscow. Chinese and French representatives sign in Paris three documents covering the expansion of economic and cultural cooperation.
24. In Bonn the Chinese and German Ministers of Foreign Affairs, Huang Hua and Hans-Dieter Genscher, sign two agreements on economic and cultural cooperation and a protocol on the mutual establishment of consulates-general.

1979

D PUBLICATIONS

January. The People's Publishing House publishes *Jianming Ouzhou zhexue shi* (*Concise History of European Philosophy*), by Zhu Desheng and others.

9. The magazine *Tansuo* (*Explorations*), editor Wei Jingsheng, goes on sale for the first time. The third and last issue is dated March 11 1979.

February. *Jinian Aiyinsitan yi wenji* (*Collected Translated Works in Memory of Einstein*), translated by Zhao Zhongli and Xu Liangying, is published in Shanghai.

4. Under the title 'Zai wenyi gongzuo zuotanhui he gushi pian chuangzuo huiyi shang de jianghua' ('Talk at a Forum on Literature and Art Work and Feature Film Creation Conference') *People's Daily* publishes, for the first time, a speech on literature and art made by Zhou Enlai on June 19, 1961 to participants of a forum on literature and art work and a meeting on scenario writing.

April. *Gudai baihua xiaoshuo xuan* (*A Selection of Ancient Vernacular Short Stories*) is published in two volumes in Shanghai. *Weida de daolu, Zhu De de shengping he shidai*, a translation by Mei Nian of Agnes Smedley's *The Great Road, the Life and Times of Chu Teh*, is published in Peking. The People's Publishing House publishes Fan Wenlan's *Tangdai Fojiao* (*Tang Dynasty Buddhism*).

May. The Zhonghua Book Company publishes *Zhongguo jindai shi* (*Modern History of China*) by a number of scholars from the History Department of Shandong University and other places.

15. The periodical *Wenyi yanjiu* (*Studies in Literature and Arts*) begins publication; the inaugural issue includes two speeches by Zhou Enlai.

August. The Jiangsu People's Publishing House publishes *Zhongguo xiandai wenxue shi* (*History of Modern Chinese Literature*) by scholars from Peking University and various other institutions.

September. The Shanghai People's Publishing House publishes the *Lunheng* (*Critical Essays*) by Wang Chong of the first century AD. The 1979 edition of the *Cihai* (*Sea of Terms*) is published in Shanghai in three volumes. Liang Bin's novel *Bohuo ji* (*Spreading Fire*), the successor to *Hongqi pu* (see December 1957), is published in Peking.

9. Under the title 'Tong yinyue gongzuozhe de tanhua' ('Talk to Music Workers') *People's Daily* publishes, for the first time, a talk Mao Zedong gave to music workers on August 24, 1956.

October. The Zhonghua Book Company publishes in five volumes *Dushi xiangzhu* (*Comprehensive Notes on Du Fu's Poems*), a modern punctuated republication of a Qing dynasty annotated edition, com-

1979–80

November 1. In London, Chinese and British representatives sign agreements on education, culture and civil air transport.
6. Chinese and Italian representatives sign documents covering economic and cultural relations and the mutual establishment of consulates-general.
12–16. Greek Prime Minister Constantine Karamanlis pays an official visit to Peking.
15. Elections by secret ballot take place in Peking's East City District, the first step towards a general election. Out of 592 candidates standing, 348 are elected.
17–22. In Dalian (Liaoning) the Chinese Seismological Society's inaugural meeting, held over these six days, reports that casualties in the great Tangshan earthquake (see E, July 28, 1976) were an estimated 242,000 people killed and 164,000 seriously injured.
30. The first round of the Sino-Soviet negotiations concludes without positive result.
December 6. The Peking Municipal Revolutionary Committee issues a notice, to take effect from December 8, banning the posting of big- or small-character posters in public places other than one site in one specified park in the city.
7. The China-Japan Joint Press Communiqué on the Occasion of Prime Minister Ohira Masayoshi's Official Visit to China (December 5–9) is issued in Peking. It announces specific expansions in economic and cultural relations between the two countries.
9–15. Djibouti President Hassan Gouled Aptidon visits China.
24. In New York, Chinese and Ecuadorean representatives sign a joint communiqué announcing their decision to establish diplomatic relations at ambassadorial level as from January 2, 1980.
30. The Chinese government issues a statement condemning the Soviet 'massive military invasion of Afghanistan' and demands 'the withdrawal of all Soviet armed forces'. (On December 27, Soviet troops had brought Babrak Karmal to power as President of Afghanistan. Further Soviet troops moved into Afghanistan on subsequent days.)

1980   *The Trial of the Ten*

January 1. Six new laws come into effect (see July 1, 1979). They include the Organic Law of the Local People's Congresses and Local People's Governments, which, among other matters, restores the posts of provincial governors and mayors.

pleted in 1693, of the Tang poet's works.

November. *Yilin* (*Forest of Translations*), a journal devoted to the translation of foreign literature, begins publication by the Jiangsu People's Publishing House. The two-volumed novel *Ji Lu chunqiu* (*Spring and Autumn in Hebei and Shandong*) by Guo Minglun and Zhang Zhongtian is published in Peking. The People's Publishing House publishes Chen Jingpan's *Zhongguo jindai jiaoyu shi* (*History of Modern Chinese Education*) in Peking.

E   NATURAL DISASTERS

July 9. An earthquake strikes Liyang (Jiangsu), killing 41 people, injuring some 2000, and destroying many houses.

August 25. An earthquake strikes Wuyuan (Inner Mongolia), destroying over 400 houses and injuring over 100 people.

F   DEATHS

January 25. Author Zheng Boqi d. aged 84.
February 7. Politburo member Su Zhenhua d. in Peking aged 67.
March 30. Embryologist Tong Dizhou d. aged 77.
August 18. Li Bendong is executed by firing squad, aged 43, for the rape and murder of a twenty-six-year-old woman. (The announcement of the event in the press was part of an admission of the existence of serious crime in China and an attempt to reduce its incidence. Such executions were frequently announced at about this time and later.)
September 25. Author Zhou Libo d. in Peking aged 71.
December 3. Zhang Guotao d. in Toronto aged 82.

Zhao Ziyang replaces Hua Guofeng as Premier   **1980**

A   ECONOMICS

January 7. Passenger shipping services resume between Shanghai and Hongkong for the first time for twenty-eight years.
    22–February 6. A national work conference on electric power is

1980

2. China and Ecuador establish diplomatic relations at ambassadorial level.

5–13. US Secretary of Defence Harold Brown visits China, the first formal contact between Chinese and American military leaders. On January 8 he meets Deng Xiaoping who tells him 'all the world's countries should enter into an alliance' against Soviet global expansionism.

20. A spokesman for the Ministry of Foreign Affairs informs an NCNA correspondent of China's decision not to hold a second round of Sino-Soviet negotiations because of the Soviet invasion of Afghanistan.

24. In Washington the US Defence Department announces its willingness to sell non-offensive military equipment to China.

30. The Ministry of Foreign Affairs issues a document giving historical evidence in support of China's claim over the Xisha and Nansha islands.

February 1. The Ministry of Foreign Affairs announces that, because of the Soviet invasion of Afghanistan, China supports the call of the International Olympic Committee to move the summer Olympic Games from Moscow or cancel them altogether.

7. China and Colombia establish diplomatic relations at ambassadorial level.

23–29. The Eleventh CCPCC holds its Fifth Plenum.

25. In Peking, the Mayors of Peking and New York, Lin Hujia and Edward Koch, sign a 'sister city' agreement between the two cities.

28. The Fifth Plenum adopts a resolution to reestablish the Party secretariat.

29. The Fifth Plenum adopts a communiqué which announces (*i*) that the Twelfth CCP Congress will be held 'before the due date'; (*ii*) that it has approved the 'guiding principles for inner-Party political life'; (*iii*) that it has rehabilitated Liu Shaoqi posthumously, removed 'the labels "renegade, traitor and scab"' and cancelled 'the erroneous resolution expelling him "from the Party once and for all and dismissing him from all posts both inside and outside the Party"' (see B, October 31, 1968); and (*iv*) that it has decided to amend Article 45 of the Constitution to eliminate the rights of 'speaking out freely, airing views fully, holding great debates and writing big-character posters'.

March 9. During a banquet for the Prime Minister of Democratic Kampuchea, Khieu Samphan, Hua Guofeng pledges China's continuing support for the struggle against the Heng Samrin regime imposed by Vietnam.

20. A memorial meeting is held in Peking to commemorate and rehabilitate Li Lisan.

24–31. President Mobutu Sese Seko of Zaire visits China.

held in Peking.
26. NCNA issues a State Council circular prohibiting the circulation of foreign currencies in China, except in specifically designated places.
28. NCNA reports the completion of the Liaohe oilfield in the area between Shenyang, Yingkou and Jinzhou (Liaoning).
February 1. The Ministry of Foreign Affairs and the US Embassy in Peking exchange notes to bring into effect a trade agreement (signed July 7, 1979, approved by the US Congress January 24, 1980) under which both sides will do all they can to strengthen 'economic and trade relations between the two countries'.
March 19. Representatives of three companies, one Chinese, one Swiss, one Hongkong, sign an agreement in Peking to establish the joint China-Schindler Elevator Co. Ltd.
April 2. A spokesman for the Chinese customs announces that goods from Taiwan will be exempt from duty since Taiwan is part of China.
17. The International Monetary Fund formally decides to admit China as a member.
May 15. The World Bank formally decides to admit China to representation in the World Bank Group.
June 20. The Tibetan government issues a notice announcing a series of new economic policies, including exemption for two years from all taxes on agriculture and animal husbandry, allowing local teams to set their own production quotas, and encouraging trade in the border regions, so that people may come to the markets from India, Nepal, Bhutan, Sikkim and Burma to exchange goods.
26. In Peking Chinese and Thai representatives sign a civil air transport agreement.
July 1. The highway bridge over the Yangzi near Chongqing (Sichuan) opens to traffic.
2. France's Aérospatiale announces an agreement to sell 50 Dauphin-2 helicopters to China and eventually to manufacture them under a licensing arrangement.
4. Chinese and Portuguese representatives sign a trade agreement in Peking.
24. Representatives of China and Bangladesh sign agreements on loans and civil air transport.
August 7. The US Central Intelligence Agency releases a study claiming that China's defence expenditure rose by an average annual 10 per cent from 1967 to 1971, but only 1 to 2 per cent annually since 1972.
30. Vice-Premier Yao Yilin, Minister in Charge of the State Planning Commission, delivers a report on the national economic plans for 1980 and 1981 to the Third Session of the Fifth NPC.

1980

April 9–15. Dr Kenneth Kaunda, President of Zambia, visits China. On April 11 Chinese and Zambian representatives sign a protocol on economic and technical cooperation and a cultural agreement.

18. China and Zimbabwe establish diplomatic relations at ambassadorial level. Zimbabwe proclaimed independence of Great Britain at a ceremony at midnight April 17–18.

24. The Chinese Olympic Committee formally decides to boycott the Moscow summer Olympic Games unless the Soviet Union withdraws its troops from Afghanistan before May 24, the date entries for the Games officially closed.

28. The US consulate-general in Shanghai is formally opened.

30. The State Statistical Bureau issues a communiqué announcing economic, cultural and social statistics for 1979, and giving China's population, not including Taiwan, as 970,920,000 at the end of 1979. The rate of birth was 17.9 per thousand, of death 6.2, and of population growth 11.7 per thousand.

May 2–6. Pakistan President Zia Ul-Haq visits China.

3–6. Guinean President Sekou Touré visits China.

5. Hua Guofeng, Ye Jianying and Deng Xiaoping send messages of condolence on the death of President Josip Tito of Yugoslavia, which had occurred on May 4.

6–9. Hua Guofeng visits Yugoslavia for Tito's funeral, which took place May 8. He arrives in Bucharest, Romania, on May 9 and back in Peking May 11.

12–18. Head of State and Government of Mauritania Mohamed Khouna Ould Haidalla visits China. On May 14 representatives of the two countries sign an agreement on economic and technical cooperation.

15. At a meeting of the Tibetan CCP committee, the contents of a CCPCC circular on Tibet are made known. It calls for more consideration to be given to Tibet's special needs, and more efforts to train cadres of Tibetan and other minority nationalities. From May 22 to 31, Hu Yaobang and others make an inspection tour of Tibet.

17. A memorial meeting is held in Peking to commemorate the rehabilitated Liu Shaoqi (see also F, November 12, 1969).

18. China successfully launches its first carrier rocket to a landing zone in the Pacific Ocean. Another follows May 21.

27–June 1. Hua Guofeng pays an official visit to Japan, the first time a Chinese government head has done so. A joint press communiqué is issued May 29. On the same day Hua repeats at a news conference that China supports the DPRK's position for the peaceful reunification of Korea.

1980

September 10. The Third Session of the NPC approves, and Ye Jianying, Chairman of the NPC Standing Committee, promulgates, the Income Tax Law Concerning Joint Ventures With Chinese and Foreign Investment of the PRC; and the Individual Income Tax Law of the PRC, by which personal incomes over 800 *yuan* per month are subject to taxation.

October 6. China and Kuwait sign a trade agreement.

November 4. Direct air services between Peking and Hongkong are formally inaugurated.

8. Chinese and Yugoslavian representatives sign an agreement on cooperation in marine shipping.

12. The inaugural British Airways flight to Peking leaves London; the inaugural CAAC flight from Peking arrives in London on November 16.

20. *People's Daily* publishes the Provisional Regulations on the Control of Resident Representative Offices of Foreign Enterprises in China, promulgated by the State Council on October 30.

December 30. *People's Daily* publishes the Provisional Regulations for Exchange Control of the PRC, promulgated by the State Council on December 18.

B OFFICIAL APPOINTMENTS, RESIGNATIONS, DISMISSALS ETC.

January 9–17. The Hubei Provincial People's Congress, held these days, decides upon Han Ningfu as provincial governor. (The other provinces, municipalities and autonomous regions also held congresses at about this time and selected governors or mayors.)

February 29. The communiqué of the Eleventh CCPCC's Fifth Plenum announces that the Plenum has elected Hu Yaobang and Zhao Ziyang to the Standing Committee of the Politburo, elected Hu Yaobang as Secretary-general of the CCPCC and approved the requests of Wang Dongxing, Ji Dengkui, Wu De and Chen Xilian to resign from the CCPCC.

August 25. The State Council accepts the request of Song Zhenming, Minister of Petroleum Industry, to be relieved of his post because of responsibility for the collapse of an oil rig in Bohai Bay (see July 22).

September 10. The Third Session of the Fifth NPC approves a number of changes in the leadership. They include (*i*) Zhao Ziyang replaces Hua Guofeng as Premier of the State Council; (*ii*) Deng Xiaoping, Li Xiannian, Chen Yun, Xu Xiangqian, and Wang Zhen resign as Vice-Premiers of the State Council because of old age; (*iii*) Chen Yonggui is relieved of his post as Vice-Premier of the State Council;

1980

June 5–10. Argentinian President Jorge Videla visits China. On June 7 Chinese and Argentinian representatives sign two agreements on economic, scientific and technical cooperation.

11–18. John Adams, Prime Minister of Barbados, visits China.

14. China and Singapore sign an agreement in Peking to establish commercial representative offices.

15. *People's Daily* criticizes Xiyang County, home of Dazhai Brigade, for mounting an 'excessively costly and unprofitable' water diversion project, which it describes as 'folly'. This begins the discrediting of the former model agricultural unit.

17–23. The Prime Minister of Western Samoa, Tupuola Efi, visits China.

25. China establishes diplomatic relations with Kiribati, a South Pacific nation independent of Britain since July 12, 1979.

July 3. The Vietnamese Ministry of Foreign Affairs sends a note to its Chinese counterpart suggesting a revival of Sino-Vietnamese negotiations.

4. The Vietnamese Ministry of Foreign Affairs sends a note to the Chinese embassy in Hanoi, protesting against 'recent Chinese armed provocations in the border area'. It cites incidents on June 28, July 1, 2 and 3. This is one of a number of similar protests at about this time.

5. The Chinese Ministry of Foreign Affairs issues a note to the Vietnamese embassy in Peking protesting strongly against continuing armed Vietnamese incursions into China; it cities incidents on July 1, 2 and 3. This is one of a number of similar protests at about this time.

6–11. The President of the People's Republic of the Congo, Denis Dassou-Nguesso, visits China. On July 8 agreements between China and the Congo on economic, technical and cultural cooperation are signed in Peking.

8–10. Hua Guofeng again visits Japan. On July 9 he attends the funeral of Japanese Prime Minister Ohira Masayoshi who had died June 12. The same day he meets with several other leaders, including Thai and Australian Prime Ministers Prem Tinsulanond and Malcolm Fraser. On July 10, he meets US President Jimmy Carter.

12. At a memorial meeting for An Ziwen (see F), Hu Yaobang publicly denounces Kang Sheng by name.

21–24. Ziaur Rahman, President of Bangladesh, pays a state visit to China.

22. *People's Daily* reveals that on November 25, 1979, an oil rig had collapsed in Bohai Bay killing seventy-two people and causing enormous petroleum losses. *People's Daily* declares that an investigation has indicated responsibility to lie with leaders of the relevant oil-

1980

and (*iv*) Yang Jingren, Zhang Aiping and Huang Hua are appointed Vice-Premiers of the State Council.

29. The NPC Standing Committee appoints Huang Huoqing as chief of the special procuratorate and Jiang Hua chief of the special court to prosecute and try the 'gang of four' and six others.

October 31. The CCPCC posthumously expels Kang Sheng and Xie Fuzhi from the Party.

C Cultural and Social

January 5–10. A conference on the theory of particle physics takes place near Guangzhou; eighty-five scholars present papers.

5–23. The Ministry of Education holds an educational work conference to discuss immediate tasks.

23–February 13. A forum on writing plays is held in Peking, sponsored by the Chinese Writers' Union and other bodies; it discusses juvenile delinquency and bureaucratic privilege as themes for dramas.

February 5. The International Law Society of China is formally founded in Peking.

12. The Standing Committee of the NPC, at its meeting of February 5–12, approves regulations to award the academic degrees of bachelor, master and doctor, to come into effect January 1, 1981.

March 13–19. The Ministry of Education holds a national work forum on physical culture and hygiene in schools.

15–23. The Chinese Scientific and Technical Association holds its Second National Congress. On the last day Hu Yaobang makes a speech.

April 8–12. The Chinese Society of History is re-established at a major meeting in Peking, at which Hu Qiaomu gives the main speech.

21–28. The Chinese Society for the Study of the World Economy is founded at a major meeting in Shanghai, at which Gu Mu gives the main speech.

May 3. The Japanese Katō Yasuo reaches the peak of Mt. Everest, the first non-Chinese to do so from the Tibetan side.

5–8, 19–22. The International Laser Conference is held in Shanghai (first four days) and Peking.

7–13. The Chinese Taoist Association holds its third national conference in Peking.

22–30. The Chinese Catholic Patriotic Association holds its third national conference in Peking.

23. The results of the 'hundred flowers' cinema poll are announced. *Ji Hongchang* receives first award for features.

drilling bureau under the Ministry of Petroleum Industry. It also claims their negligence to have been at least partly to blame for other accidents.

August 10. In written replies to questions from the Yugoslav correspondent Dara Janekovic, Hua Guofeng states that Mao Zedong 'was indeed the most outstanding figure in Chinese history. . . . But he was a man, not a god, and he was not immune to mistakes.'

11. NCNA reports a 'recent' directive by the CCPCC to the whole Party 'to propagate the individual less'.

28–September 12. The Third Session of the Fifth National Committee of the CPPCC is held in Peking.

30–September 10. The Third Session of the Fifth NPC is held in Peking. On September 7 Hua Guofeng delivers a speech on the work of the government. Among other points he calls for younger, more educated and more proficient government leaders, and the incorporation of family planning into the long-term development programme, so that each couple, except in minority areas, should have a single child only. On September 10, the NPC follows the CCPCC's lead by approving the suggestion to amend Article 45 of the Constitution (see under February 29).

September 11. New Zealand Prime Minister Robert Muldoon arrives in Peking for a visit. The same evening the new Premier Zhao Ziyang gives him a banquet. He leaves Peking September 14.

14–19. Kenyan President Daniel Arap Moi visits China. On September 15 he holds talks with the new Premier Zhao Ziyang who tells him that 'the key to the settlement of the Kampuchean issue' is immediate withdrawal of Vietnamese troops.

17. In Washington Vice-Premier Bo Yibo and President Jimmy Carter sign Sino-US agreements on civil aviation, maritime transportation and textiles, and a consular convention.

18–26. Italian President Sandro Pertini visits China.

22–29. Norwegian Prime Minister Odvar Nordli visits China.

23. The Ministry of Foreign Affairs sends a note to the Vietnamese embassy in Peking stating that the necessary conditions do not exist for reviving Sino-Vietnamese negotiations.

24. Vice-Premier and Minister of Foreign Affairs Huang Hua addresses the UN General Assembly. Among other points he states China's support for a general election in Kampuchea, if necessary supervised by the UN Secretary-General or his representative, but only after the withdrawal of Vietnamese troops from Kampuchea.

October 2. The American Institute in Taiwan and Taiwan's Coordination Council for North American Affairs sign an agreement granting each other's staffs diplomatic privileges and immunities. The following

1980

28. Chinese and Japanese representatives sign in Tokyo an agreement on scientific and technological cooperation.

June 13. Representatives of China and Barbados sign a cultural agreement in Peking.

27–July 7. A national work conference on cultural relics is held in Peking.

July 21. Three Americans, led by Ned Gillette, reach the peak of Muztagh Ata (Xinjiang) (see also C, July 7, 1959).

August 2–7. The CCPCC holds a national labour and employment conference in Peking. It adopts a new employment policy which allows individuals to seek work they prefer instead of awaiting assignment by the state.

26. The NPC Standing Committee adopts the Provisional Regulations on Lawyers of the PRC, to come into effect on January 1, 1982.

September 10. The Third Session of the NPC approves, and Ye Jianying promulgates, the revised Marriage Law of the PRC, which raises the marriage age to 22 for men and 20 for women; and the Nationality Law of the PRC, which disallows dual nationality for any Chinese national.

20–October 20. The National Minority Arts Festival takes place in Peking. Some 2000 performing artists take part, and audiences for the 109 sessions are about 168,000.

26–27. A large-scale international track and field invitational competition takes place in Peking, with eight nations taking part.

October 16. United Press International reports that students in Changsha have ended a protest and hunger strike against official interference in a local election. The demonstration ended when it was announced that the CCPCC would send representatives to investigate the students' charges.

November 12. NCNA reports the discovery in October and early November of a well-preserved human skull dating back 300,000 to 400,000 years in a cave in Hexian (Anhui).

December 1. Chinese scientists discover the well-preserved skull of an early pre-man, dating back 8,000,000 years, in Lufeng (Yunnan). NCNA announces the discovery on December 27.

9. At the trial of the ten, it is alleged that Jiang Qing, in collaboration with Lin Biao's wife Ye Qun, had the homes of five artists, including the film director Zheng Junli and the film star Zhao Dan, searched in Shanghai in October 1966 in order to seize material with which they could discredit her (Jiang Qing). The latter denies responsibility for the search. Zheng Junli's widow, Huang Chen, testifies that Jiang Qing had Zheng arrested in September 1967 and that he died in prison

day, an NCNA correspondent in Washington is told that the US government is 'quite aware of what the agreement is', i.e. that it implies government-to-government relations, and has made 'no objection to it'.

6. The Ministry of Foreign Affairs sends a note to the Soviet embassy in Peking protesting strongly against an intrusion by Soviet armed personnel into the Inner Mongolian Autonomous Region on October 5; a Chinese herdsman and Soviet soldier had been killed.

9 *People's Daily* protests against the October 2 agreement as 'an inadvisable move' which breaks the US government's own commitment and runs 'counter to the principles governing the establishment of diplomatic relations with China'.

13–14. Robert Mugabe, the Prime Minister of Zimbabwe, visits China on his way home from the DPRK.

15–21. French President Giscard d'Estaing visits China. On October 17, a Sino-French agreement to establish mutual consulates-general in Shanghai and Marseilles is signed. On October 21, the French consulate-general in Shanghai is formally opened.

16. China carries out a nuclear test in the atmosphere.

20–23. Burmese President U Ne Win visits Peking.

27–30. Thai Prime Minister Prem Tinsulanond visits Peking. At a banquet in his honour on October 27, Zhao Ziyang states that 'tension in South-east Asia has been caused entirely by the Soviet-backed Vietnamese invasion and occupation of Kampuchea', and that China 'supports the principled stand of the ASEAN countries on the Kampuchean question'.

28–November 4. Dutch Prime Minister Andreas van Agt visits China. On October 30 Sino-Dutch agreements on economic, technological and cultural cooperation are signed.

29. An explosion at Peking Railway Station, deliberately set off by a dissatisfied worker from Shanxi, kills ten people, including the worker himself, and injures eighty-one others.

November 6. Premier Zhao Ziyang sends a message of congratulations to Ronald Reagan on his election as President of the USA on November 4. He expresses the hope that relations between China and the USA 'will continue to move forward on the basis of the principles of the joint communiqué on the establishment of diplomatic relations between the two countries'.

6. Veselin Djuranovic, President of the Federal Executive Council of Yugoslavia, arrives in Peking for an official visit.

9–24. Singapore Prime Minister Lee Kuan Yew visits China.

10. The special court serves copies of the indictment drawn up by

(see F, April 23, 1969).

16–23. The Chinese Buddhist Association holds its Fourth National Congress in Peking.

D PUBLICATIONS

January. The Zhonghua Book Company publishes *Lu Jiuyuan ji* (*Lu Jiuyuan's Works*), a punctuated edition of works by Lu Jiuyuan (1139–93). *Chengbao*, a translation by Tang Yongkuan of Franz Kafka's *Das Schloss* (*The Castle*), is published in Shanghai.

March. The Shaanxi People's Publishing House publishes *Huaian shishe shixuan* (*A Selection of Poems from the Huaian Poetry Society*), compiled by Li Shihan. The People's Publishing House publishes *Xingxiang siwei ziliao huibian* (*A Compendium of Material on Thought through Images*). *Social Sciences in China, A Quarterly in English* begins publication.

14. Liu Shaoqi's *Lun Gongchan dangyuan de xiuyang* (*How to Be a Good Communist*) is republished.

April. The People's Publishing House publishes *Li Ji shixuan* (*A Collection of Poetry by Li Ji*); the Commercial Press *Yuyan lun*, a translation of Leonard Bloomfield's *Language* by Yuan Jiahua and others.

6. *Zhongguo nongmin bao* (*The Chinese Peasant*) formally begins publication.

May. The Peking Publishing House publishes Gu Ligao's novel *Longdong* (*The Depth of Winter*). The novel *Pobi ji* (*Breaking the Wall*), by Chen Dengke and Xiao Ma, and *Zhongguo xiandai wenxue shi* (*A History of Modern Chinese Literature*), in two volumes by the Language and Literature Department of the People's University and others under the general editorship of Lin Zhihao, are published in Peking, and *Mao Dun lun chuangzuo* (*Mao Dun on Creation*) in Shanghai.

12. The monthly *Huanqiu* (*The World*) begins publication.

June. *Kexue huanxiang xiaoshuo xuan* (*Science Fiction Collection*) and *Zhongguo shangye jingji guanlixue* (*Commercial and Economic Management in China*), both collectively written, are published in Peking.

July. Yang Xianzhen's *Shenma shi Weiwuzhuyi?* (*What is Materialism?*) is published by the Hebei People's Publishing House in Shijiazhuang, and Wang Ying's novel *Liangzhong Meiguo ren* (*Two Kinds of American*) in Peking.

August. Yang Qianru's novel *San* (*Umbrella*) is published in two volumes in Peking; the Hunan People's Publishing House publishes Ren Guangchun's historical novel *Wuxu diexie ji* (*The Flow of Blood in the 1898 Reform Movement*). The PRC's first encyclopedic yearbook

1980

the special procuratorate (see B, September 29) on Jiang Qing, Zhang Chunqiao, Yao Wenyuan, Wang Hongwen (the 'gang of four'), Chen Boda, Huang Yongsheng and four others. The indictment, dated November 2, makes charges under four headings: (*i*) 'Frame-up and persecution of Party and State leaders and plotting to overthrow the political power of the dictatorship of the proletariat'; (*ii*) 'the persecution and suppression of large numbers of cadres and masses'; (*iii*) 'plotting to assassinate Chairman Mao Zedong and engineer an armed counter-revolutionary *coup d'état*; and (*iv*) 'plotting armed rebellion in Shanghai'.

20. Jiang Hua declares open the special court trying the ten; Huang Huoqing reads the indictment.

24, 26. Wang Hongwen turns evidence against Jiang Qing over a charge that on October 17, 1974, she arranged a meeting of the 'gang of four' which sent Wang to Changsha to report to Mao Zedong against Zhou Enlai and Deng Xiaoping with the aim of seizing state power.

25–December 1. Romanian Prime Minister Ilie Verdet visits China.

29. Chen Boda pleads guilty to a charge of having framed the CCP organization in eastern Hebei during the Cultural Revolution, as a result of which 84,000 people were persecuted, and 2,955 died.

December 3. The Chinese government makes a serious representation to the Dutch government to reconsider the Cabinet decision of November 29 approving the sale of two submarines to Taiwan. Notwithstanding, the Dutch Parliament ratifies the Cabinet's decision on December 18.

5. Jiang Qing agrees that, in cooperation with Chen Boda and Kang Sheng, she organized a public meeting which took place on July 18, 1967, to denounce Liu Shaoqi, that his house was searched and ransacked, and that he himself was physically hurt. She argues that the actions were 'reasonable and lawful' and 'did not constitute criminal offences'.

12. At the trial of the ten, Jiang Qing is ordered to leave the courtroom for disrupting the court by interrupting the judges and prosecutors and abusing a witness.

14. Hu Yaobang tells Vasilis Konstantinidis, the editor of a Greek Communist newspaper, that the Cultural Revolution decade, 1966 to 1976, was one of catastrophe: 'Nothing was correct or positive during these ten years. The whole thing was negative. Tremendous damage was done to our economy, culture, education, political thinking and Party organization.'

22. *People's Daily* states that Mao Zedong made serious mistakes in his last years; especially the Cultural Revolution, which he personally

1980

Zhongguo baike nianjian 1980 (*Chinese Encyclopedic Yearbook 1980*) is published in Peking and Shanghai, covering the year 1979.
1. The weekly *Zhongguo fazhi bao* (*China's Legal System*) begins publication.

E NATURAL DISASTERS

June 26–27. Severe hurricane, wind and hail storms strike twenty-six coastal counties and cities in Zhejiang. As a result, 151 people are killed, some 260 injured, 23 are missing, serious damage is done to crops and many houses are destroyed.
September 2. The water level of the Yangzi at Wuhan reaches 27.76 metres, apart from 1931 and 1954 its highest since the beginning of records in 1865, but damage is minimal owing to efficient flood prevention measures.

F DEATHS

March 8. Poet Li Ji d. in Peking aged 57.
May 26. Lawyer Tan Shengbin d. in Peking aged 69.
30. Noted journalist Wang Yunsheng d. in Peking aged 79.
June 25. An Ziwen, former Director of the CCPCC's Organization Department, d. in Peking aged 70.
July 3. Senior PLA and alternate CCPCC member Deng Hua d. in Shanghai aged 70.
10. Noted journalist and former NCNA head Chen Kehan d. in Peking aged 63.
17. Noted historian Lu Zhenyu d. aged 80.
October 10. Film actor Zhao Dan d. aged 65.
30. Zhang Chongtong, Vice-Chairman of the CPPCC's National Committee, d. aged 81.
December 25. Historian Gu Jiegang d. in Peking aged 86.

initiated and led, was a great misfortune. However, the newspaper distinguishes between mistake and crime; Mao was guilty of the former, but not the latter.

29. The special court trying the ten ends its investigations with the prosecution demanding that Jiang Qing be punished according to Article 103 of the Criminal Law, which allows the death sentence for those who cause 'particularly grave harm to the state and the people'. Jiang Qing continues to insist that she is not guilty of the charges against her.

1981 *Jiang Qing and Zhang Chunqiao are sentenced to death with two-year reprieves*

January 10–14. DPRK Premier Li Jong Ok visits China.

19. The Ministry of Foreign Affairs hands a note to the Dutch ambassador to China, J. Kneppelhout, asking for a downgrading of Sino-Dutch diplomatic relations to the level of *chargé d'affaires*. This followed Holland's public reaffirmation on January 16 of its decision to sell two submarines to Taiwan.

20. Zhao Ziyang cables greetings to Ronald Reagan on his assumption of office as US President the same day.

25. At the last session of the special court, sentences are pronounced on the ten on trial. Jiang Qing and Zhang Chunqiao are sentenced to death with two-year reprieves, Yao Wenyuan to twenty years' imprisonment, Wang Hongwen to life imprisonment, Chen Boda and Huang Yongsheng to eighteen years' imprisonment, and the others to terms of sixteen to eighteen years.

Zhou Enlai's works are published **1981**

A ECONOMICS

January 1. The Sichuan Foreign Trade Corporation is established in Chengdu to develop business relations between Sichuan and foreign countries.
7. CAAC inaugurates its Peking–New York air route.

B OFFICIAL APPOINTMENTS, RESIGNATIONS, DISMISSALS ETC.

January 25. The Peking Municipal People's Congress Standing Committee decides to appoint Jiao Ruoyu as acting Mayor of Peking to replace Lin Hujia.

C CULTURAL AND SOCIAL

January 9. The Chinese Energy Research Society is formally established in Peking.

D PUBLICATIONS

January 1. The People's Publishing House publishes Volume I of *Zhou Enlai xuanji* (*Selected Works of Zhou Enlai*).

E NATURAL DISASTERS

January 24. A strong earthquake strikes the region of Dawu County (Sichuan); in the county seat almost all buildings collapse, killing some 150 people and injuring over 300 others.

CHINA
100 0 100 200 300 km.
RUSSIA
AKTOGAI
TARBAGATAI (TAERBAHATAI)
ALTAI
TACHENG
YUMIN
KARAMAI
ALMA-ATA
YILI
YINING
WUSU
SHIHEZI
MANAS
DUSHANZI
URUMCHI (DIHUA)
TURFAN
USH
AKSU
KUCHA
KARASHAR
HAMI
XINJIANG
UIGHUR
AUTONOMOUS
REGION
KASHGAR (KASHIHEER)
YANGI HISSAR
MUZTAGH ATA
PAMIR
YARKAND
KARGILIK
KOKONOR LAKE
KARAKORUM MTS
MISGAR
HUNZA
PAKISTAN
KHOTAN
DUNHUANG
GANSU
SUZHOU
GANZHOU
LIANGZHOU (WUWEI)
DATONG
XINING
LIUJIA GORGE
LANZHOU
HEZHOU
DIDAO
QINGHAI
Ladakh
KASHMIR
GARTOK
SIMLA
JINSHA
YUSHU
MAOERGAI
SONGPAN
TIBET
AUTONOMOUS
REGION
DELHI
DEGE
CHANGDU
RIVER
DAWU
TSANGPO
SHIGATSE
LHASA
Ganzi
Tibetan
Autonomous
Region
MANGKANG (MARKAM)
DADU R
MT GOSAINTHAN
GYANTSE
NAIDONG
RIVER
NEPAL
KHAMBAJONG
JOMO LUNGMA
(MT EVEREST)
TSENG JONG
DHOLA POST
THAGLA RIDGE
McMAHON LINE
KATMANDU
TUNA
YADONG
LONGJU
SIKKIM
Chumbi Valley
BHUTAN
BOMDI LA (BOMDIRA)
(N E F A)
WALONG
LEDO
RIVER GANGES
BRAHMAPUTRA
WEIXIN
LIJIANG
JIANCHUAN
HEQING
TARO
INDIA
BANGLADESH
DACCA
MYITKYINA
MOGAUNG
LANGQIONG
DALI
XIAGUAN
YONGCHANG
TENGCHONG (TENGYUE)
LONGLING
LUFENG
KUNMING
BHAMO
LUXI
YUNZHOU
SHUNNING
NAMKHAM
WANDING
YUNNAN
BURMA
LASHIO
MANDALAY
VIETNAM
PHONG SALY
YENANGYAUNG
LAOS
TOUNGOO
THAILAND
CHIANGMAI
KHANG KHAY
Provincial Capital
Prefecture (fu)
District (zhou)
County (xian)
Other
Mountain
Provincial boundaries are those of the date of compilation (1981). The administrative status shown for each place is generally that of the time of reference in the text.

Map 1

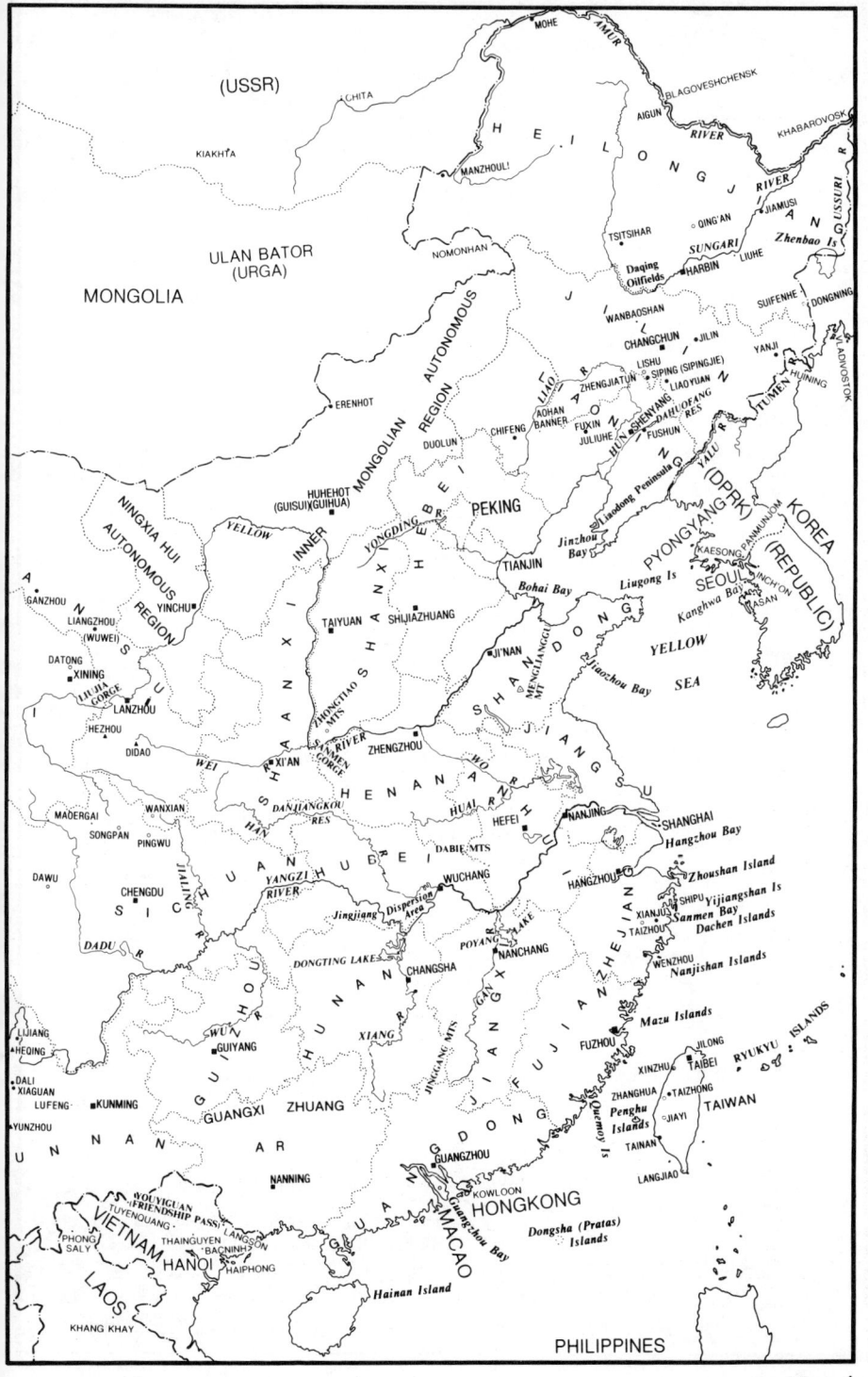

INNER
MONG
BAILINGMIAO
HUHEHOT
(GUISUI)(GUIHUA)
WUYUAN
BAOTOU
JINING
ZHANGJIAKOU
FENGZHEN
DATONG
HEBEI
CHANGXINDIAN
ZHOUKOUDIAN
PINGXINGGUAN
ZHUOXIAN
MANCHENG
BAODING
BOYE
SHENXIAN
FU
SHIJIAZHUANG
YUXIAN
JINXIAN
YANGQU
SHANXI
NINGXIA (CITY)
YINCHU
LINGZHOU
JINJIBAO
ZHONGWEI
JIAXIAN
TAIYUAN
YUCI
XIYANG
DAZHAI
XINGTAI
(SHUNDE)
SUIDE
TAIGU
FENZHOU
WAYAOBAO
QIUXIAN
SHANCHENGBAO
WUQIZHEN
ANDING
BAOAN
YAN'AN
YANCHANG
KAIZHOU
GUAN-
DONGZHIYUAN
GUYUAN
QINGYANG
YICHUAN
JIZHOU
ANYANG
(ZHANGDE)
HUINING
ZHENYUAN
LUOCHUAN
PUYANG
PINGLIANG
NINGXIAN
SHANXIAN (SHANZHOU)
JIAOZUO
CHANGYUAN
XIANGFU
TONGCHUAN
HUAYUANKOU
ZHONGMOU
FUQIANG
CHUNHUA
RUICHENG
KAIFENG
LINPINGZHEN
LUOYANG
TIANSHUI
(QINZHOU)
BAOJI
WEINAN
ZHENGZHOU
ZHU-
XIANYANG
XI'AN
XUCHANG
ZHOUZHI
DAOLINGGANG
LUSHAN
SHAANXI
NANZHAO
YANGXIAN
HENAN
ZHUMADIAN
HANZHONG
DENGZHOU
QUESHAN
XING'AN
JUNXIAN
GUANGYUAN
XIANGFAN
XINYANG
TONGJIANG
XIANGYANG
ZAOYANG
GUANG-
CANGXI
HUBEI
MACHENG
JINGMEN
ZHONGXIANG
HANKOU
HUANGPI
WANXIAN
YICHANG
YUNMENG
WU-
CHANGYANG
JINGZHOU (JIALING)
GUANG'AN
ZHICHENG
GONGAN
SHASHI
DAYE
ENSHI
CHANGLE
JIANGBEI
HONGHU

NORTH CHINA

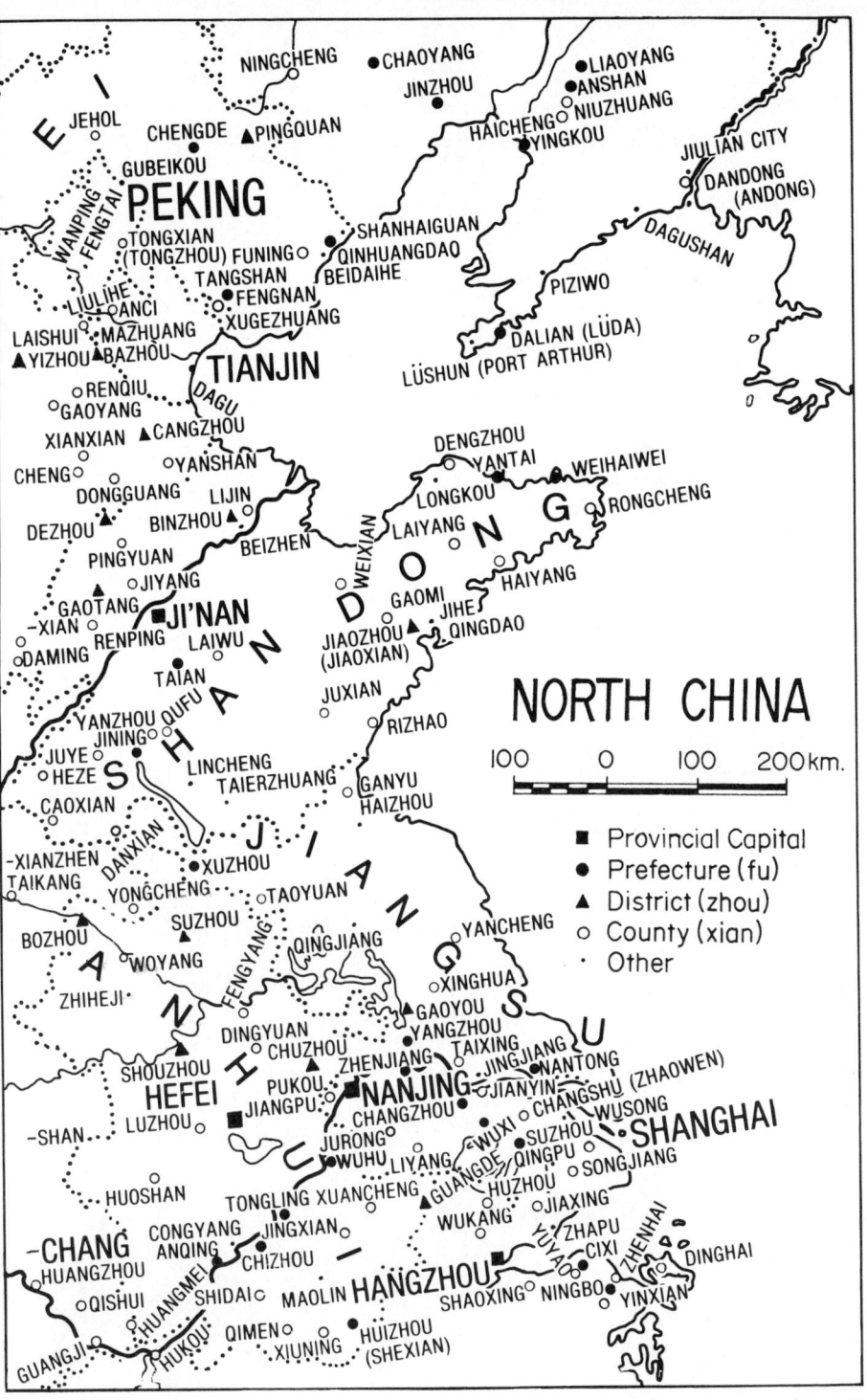

Map legend:
- ■ Provincial Capital
- ● Prefecture (fu)
- ▲ District (zhou)
- ○ County (xian)
- · Other

Scale: 100 0 100 200 km.

Map 2

SICHUAN
HUBEI
HUNAN
GUIZHOU
GUANGXI ZHUANG AR
GU
VIETNAM
LAOS
TONGJIANG
CANGXI
MOUGONG
CHENGDU
GUANG'AN
CHANGYANG
KANGDING
YAAN
LUDING
TONGLIANG
NEIJIANG
DAZU
JIANGBEI
ENSHI
CHANGLE
CHONGQING
RONGCHANG
SANGZHI
YONGSHUN
CHANGDE
YIBIN (XUZHOU)
LUZHOU
QIJIANG
NANCHUAN
YOUYANG
JIANG'AN
GAOXIAN
JIANGNAN
XICHANG
YUNLIAN
DAGUAN
RENHUAI
SINAN (SIXIAN)
SONGTAO
TONGREN
BIJIE
ZUNYI
ZHAOTONG
SHAOYANG
QIANXI
WEINING
HUANGPING
TAIGONG
WUGANG
HUILI
GUIYANG
KAILI
GUANGSHUN
LIPING
XINNING
DONGCHUAN
DINGFAN
DUYUN
QUANZHOU
XIAJIANG
GUANYANG
FUMIN
LINGCHUAN
KUNMING
GUILIN
CHENGJIANG
XINGYI
ANNING
LUOCHENG
LIUCHENG
PINGLE
XILIN
DONGLAN
LIUZHOU
LIPU
QINGYUAN
XIUREN
SHIPING
XIANGZHOU
LIN'AN
GUOHUA
WUXUAN
PINGNAN
GEJIU
MENGZI
TIANBAO
QIANJIANG
JINTIAN
LITANG
GUIPING (XUNZHOU)
KAIHUA
HEKOU
YONGKANG
NANNING
BEILIU
ZUOZHOU
GUIXIAN
TAIPING
YONGNING
YULIN
ZHENNANGUAN (YOUYIGUAN)
LONGZHOU
LUCHUAN
TUYENQUANG
NINGMING
QINZHOU
JIANGNING
HUAZHOU
LANGSON
THAINGUYEN
BEIHAI
BACNINH
ZHAN-
HANOI
HAIPHONG
QIONGZHOU

SOUTH CHINA

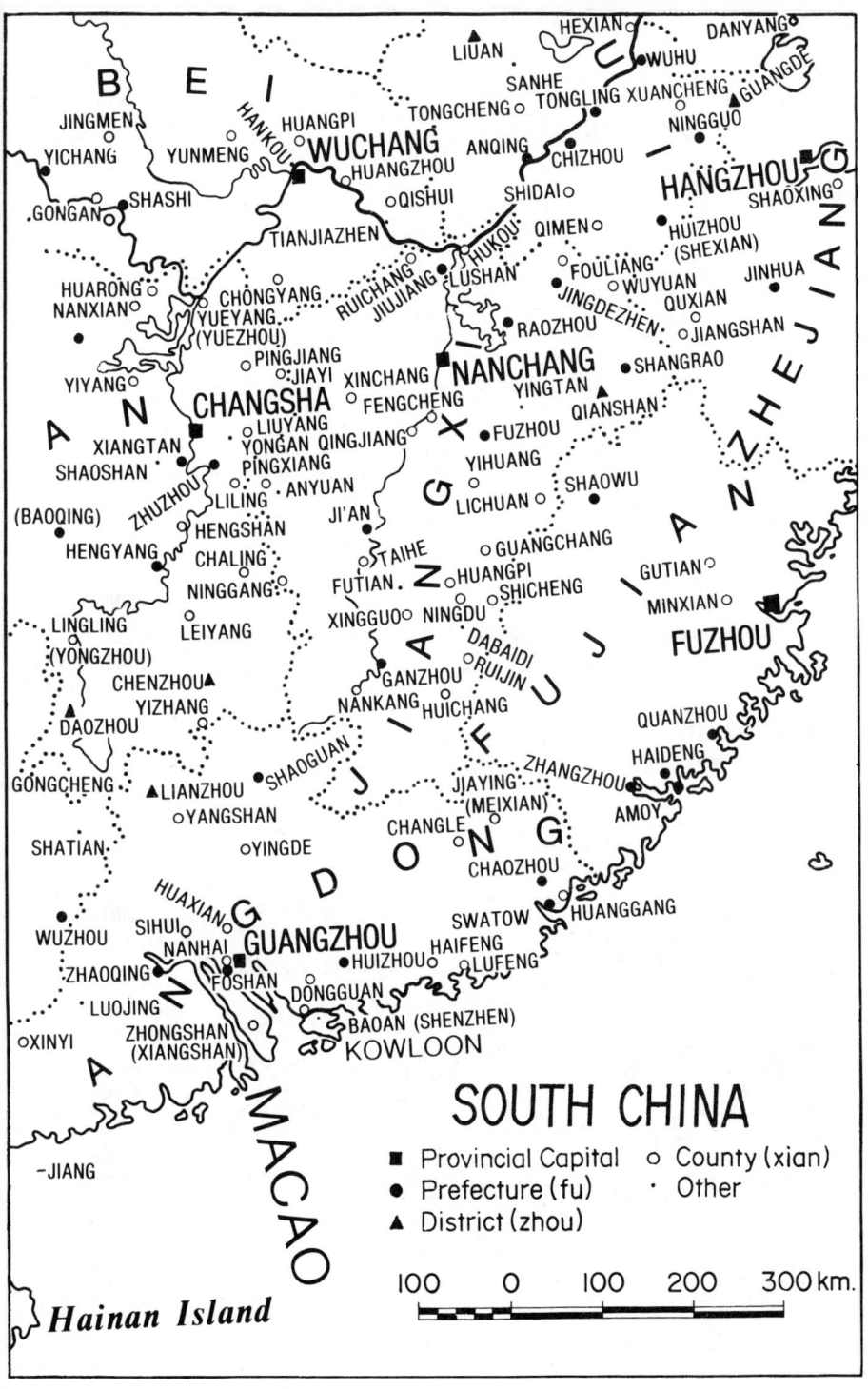

- ■ Provincial Capital
- ● Prefecture (fu)
- ▲ District (zhou)
- ○ County (xian)
- · Other

Map 3

GLOSSARY OF TITLES AND TECHNICAL TERMS

Adviser in the Administration of Government — Yizheng wang 議政王
Alliance Command — Lianzhi 聯指
Army Corps — Juntuan 軍團
Army Group — Jituan jun 集團軍
Assistant Grand Secretary — Xieban da xueshi 協辦大學士
Assistant Military Commander — Fu dutong 副都統
Assistant Resident in ... — zhu ... Bangban dachen 駐 ... 幫辦大臣
(General Commander of) Bandit Suppression — Jiaofei (Zong zhihui) 剿匪 (總指揮)
(Hereditary) Baron — Nan 男
Brigadier-General — Zongbing 總兵
Bureau (provincial) — Ting 廳
Censor — Yushi 御史
Chairman — Zhuxi 主席
Chief Commandant (Taiping) — Zheng zhangshuai 正掌率
Chief Executive (Manzhouguo) — Zhizheng 執政
Chief Executive — Zong zhizheng 總執政
Chief-of-Staff — Canmou zhang 參謀長
Chief of the General Staff — Zong canmou zhang 總參謀長
Colonel — Canjiang 參將
Commander — Junzhang 軍長
Commander (post-1949) — Silingyuan 司令員
Commander-in-Chief — Zong siling 總司令
(Naval) Commander-in-Chief (of a province) (Qing period) — (Shuishi) Tidu (水師) 提督
Control Yuan — Jiancha yuan 監察院
Council (at prefecture, district or county level) — Yishi hui 議事會
County — Xian 縣
County Magistrate — Zhixian 知縣
Deputy Commandant — Fu zhangshuai 副掌率
Director — Zhuren 主任
Director-General — Dongshi zhang 董事長
Director-General of the Conservancy of the Yellow River and Grand Canal — Hedong Hedao zongdu 河東河道總督
District — Zhou 州
District Court — Difang fayuan 地方法院
District Magistrate — Zhizhou 知州
Earl — Bo 伯
East King — Dongwang 東王
Examination Yuan — Kaoshi yuan 考試院
Executive Yuan — Xingzheng yuan 行政院

The characters of the glossary were prepared by Mr Peter Chang of Griffith University.

Glossary

Extraordinary President	Feichang da zongtong 非常大總統
Field Army	Ye zhanjun 野戰軍
Financial Commissioner	Buzheng shi 布政使
Friendship Association	Youhao xiehui 友好協會
Gang of Four	Siren bang 四人幫
Garrison Commander (NP period)	Jingbei siling 警備司令
Garrison Commander (early Republic)	Zhenshou shi 鎮守使
General	Shangjiang 上將
General-in-Chief	Jiangjun 將軍
Generalissimo	Da yuanshuai 大元帥
Governor (provincial, May 23, 1914 to July 6, 1916)	Xun an shi 巡按使
Governor (provincial, July 6, 1916, and after 1949)	Shengzhang 省長
Governor (provincial, Qing)	Xunfu 巡撫
Governor of Shuntian Prefecture	Shuntian fuyin 順天府尹
Grand Guardian to the Heir to the Throne	Taizi taibao 太子太保
Grand Secretariat	Neige 內閣
Grand Secretary	Da xueshi 大學士
Grand Tutor to the Heir to the Throne	Taizi taifu 太子太傅
High Court	Gaodeng fayuan 高等法院
Higher Normal College	Gaodeng shifan xuexiao 高等師範學校
Imperial Commissioner	Qinchai dachen 欽差大臣
Inspector-General	Xunyue shi 巡閱使
Inspector-General of Maritime Customs	Zong shuiwu si 總稅務司
Intendant (of a Circuit)	Daotai 道台
Jiangbei Command	Jiangbei daying 江北大營
Jiangnan Command	Jiangnan daying 江南大營
Judicial Yuan	Sifa yuan 司法院
Junior Guardian to the Heir to the Throne	Taizi shaobao 太子少保
Land, Naval and Air Forces	Luhaikong jun 陸海空軍
Legislative Yuan	Lifa yuan 立法院
Manager (of a Bank)	Hangzhang 行長
Managing Director	Zongcai 總裁
Marquis	Hou 侯
Marshal	Yuanshuai 元帥
Military Commander	Dutong 都統
Military Government	Jun zhengfu 軍政府
Military Governor (1912-16)	Dudu 都督
Military Governor (from July 6, 1916)	Dujun 督軍
Mr	Xiansheng 先生
North King (Taiping)	Beiwang 北王
Pacification Commissioner (NP period)	Suijing zhuren 綏靖主任
Pacification Commissioner (early Republic)	Xuanfu shi 宣撫使
Picul	Dan 石
Plenipotentiary	Quanquan dachen 全權大臣
Political Adviser	Zhengzhi guwen 政治顧問

645

Glossary

Political Commissar	Zhengzhi weiyuan 政治委員
Praesidium	Zhuxituan 主席團
Prefectural Magistrate	Zhifu 知府
Prefecture	Fu 府
Premier	Zongli 總理
Premier (of the State Council)	Guowu zongli 國務總理
President (of a Board or Ministry, *bu*)	Shangshu 尚書
President (of a Yuan or Court)	Yuanzhang 院長
President (of the ROC)	Da zongtong 大總統
Prime Minister (end Qing)	Zongli dachen 總理大臣
Prince of the Second Degree	Junwang 郡王
Provincial Graduate	Juren 舉人
Pure and True King	Qingzhen wang 清真王
Regent	Jianguo shezheng wang 監國攝政王
Resident in ...	zhu ... Banshi dachen 駐 ... 辦事大臣
Second Chief Commandant (Taiping)	Youzheng zhangshuai 又正掌率
Second-Degree Examinations	Xiangshi 鄉試
Second Deputy Chancellor of the Earth Department (Taiping)	Diguan youfu chengxiang 地官又副丞相
Secretary (to the Grand Council or Zongli yamen)	Zhangjing 章京
Secretary-General	Zong shuji 總書記
Sir	Jun 君
South King (Taiping)	Nanwang 南王
String of large cash	Daqian 大錢
Sub-Chancellor	Neige xueshi 內閣學士
Superintendent of Educational Affairs	Guanxue dachen 管學大臣
Superintendent of Trade	Tongshang dachen 通商大臣
Tartar General (Qing)	Jiangjun 將軍
Vice-President (of a Board, *bu*)	Shilang 侍郎
Viceroy (Qing)	Zongdu 總督
Viscount	Zi 子
West King (Taiping)	Xiwang 西王

646

INDEX

A Q zhengzhuan 阿Q正傳 285
Abstinence Sect, *Zhaijiao* 齋教 48
Academia Sinica 321, 525, 537, 543, 591, 601, *see also* Central Research Institute
academies, *shuyuan* 書院 191, 203
Academy: Datong 大同 243; Chinese National 223; Guangya 廣雅 159; Hanlin 翰林 146; Japanese (East Asia Common Culture) 203; Lianchi 連池 91; Sino-Western, *Zhongxi xuetang* 中西學堂 179
acupuncture 553, 619
Administrative Committee, *Xingzheng weiyuanhui* 行政委員會 457
Admiralty, Board of, *Haijun shiwu yamen* 海軍事務衙門 155, 156, 162
Afghanistan 402, 464, 476, 480, 494/6, 512, 522, 528, 565, 622, 624, 626
African People's Friendship Association, Sino-, *Zhongguo Feizhou renmin youhao xiehui* 中國非洲人民友好協會 495
Afro-Asian Conference, Bandung 466, 514, 522/4
Afro-Asian Society of China, *Zhongguo Yafei xuehui* 中國亞非學會 505
Aftermath Conference 296, 298, 300
agriculture 435, 455, 457, 466/8, 470, 477, 480, 482, 496, 498, 504, 509, 515, 525, 530, 535, 547, 551, 581/3, 594, 603, 604, 615, 625, 628; Agricultural Producers' Cooperatives 457, 470
Agriculture, Industry and Commerce, Ministry of, *Nonggongshang bu* 農工商部 218, 267, 293
Ai Siqi 艾思奇 535
Aiqing sanbuqu 愛情三部曲 355

air: lines, routes, services 393, 461, 471, 515, 521, 529, 563/5, 567, 575/7, 581, 589, 597, 605, 613, 616, 618, 625, 627, 637; -craft 461, 477, 483, 489, 583, 605, 607; China National Aviation Corporation, *Zhongguo hangkong gongsi* 中國航空公司 331, 335, 365, 377, 393; Chinese Society of Aeronautics, *Zhongguo hangkong xuehui* 中國航空學會 517; Civil Aviation Administration of China, *Zhongguo minhang* 中國民航 575; Eurasia Aviation Corporation 335, 349, 365, 377, 389; Nanyuan 南苑 Aviation School 251, 264; Sino-Soviet Aviation Corporation 377
Albania 438, 459, 460, 461, 489, 499, 500, 503, 506, 512, 514, 522, 530, 548, 555, 562, 598, 608; *Zeri i Popullit* 598
Albert 44
Alexander II, Tsar of Russia 136; III 176
Algeria 486, 509, 512, 522/4, 550, 574/6
allied powers, troops 196-202, 276
Alute 阿魯特 129
Amau Eiji 天羽英二 348
American *see* US
American International Corporation 263
Amur Company 73
An Bo 安波 527
An Dehai 安德海 110, 113
An Pingsheng 安平生 597
An Ziwen 安子文 628, 635
Anfu 安福 clique, Club 266, 268, 276, 278
Angola 584/6, 596, 606
Anhui 安徽 clique 296
Ann 22, 23
Annam, Vietnam 122
Anti-Communist Autonomous Com-

Apart from Japanese and Koreans, foreign personalities must generally be sought through their country of origin.

Index

mittee of Eastern Hebei, *Jidong fanggong zizhi weiyuanhui* 冀東防共自治委員會 356
Anyang fajue baogao 安陽發掘報告 323
April 17 Declaration 348
April 22 Revolutionary Rebel Grand Army, *Sierer geming zaofan dajun* 四二二革命造反大軍 544/6
Archimede 28
Argentina 410, 564, 628
Army, Ministry of the, *Lujun bu* 陸軍部 218, 288
Arrow 68
arsenal 83, 99, 103, 123, 156, 159; Fujian 109; Hanyang 225, 249; Jiangnan 江南 91, 99, 107, 113, 123, 149, 157, 165, 246, 256, 299; Jinling 金陵 105; Suzhou 95; Tianjin 105, 113
artists 525, 531, 541; acrobatic troupes 567; actors 481; amateurs 519, 525; *see also* literature
Asian Students' Sanatorium 463
Asiatic Quarterly Review 161
atomic, bomb, explosion 412, 480, 484, 504, 518, 522; reactor 484
August 7 Conference 316
Australia 388, 390, 499, 568, 571, 574, 590, 628
Australian Wireless Corporation 392
Austro-Hungarian, Austria 196, 202, 245, 264, 558
Authors, Association of Chinese, *Zhongguo zhuzuoren xiehui* 中國著作人協會 407
Autumn Harvest Uprising 313, 316
Aying 阿英 603

Ba Jin 巴金 329, 347, 355, 361/3, 373, 385, 417, 427, 504
Ba Jin wenji 巴金文集 507
Bai Chongxi 白崇禧 326-7, 359/61, 365, 371, 382-6, 419, 432
Bai Lang 白狼 250-3
Bai Xiangguo 白相國 560, 571
Bai Yanhu 白彥虎 106, 110, 118, 120, 130, 132, 134, 142, 144
Baimao nü 白毛女 *(The White-haired Girl)* 415, 599
Baisui 柏葰 67, 69/71, 75
Baiyun Ebo jiaoxiang shi 白雲鄂博交響詩 519
Bak Hun Yung 450

Baliqiao 八里橋 (Zhili) 80
banditry, bandits 38, 45
Bandung Conference 466, 514, 522/4
Bangladesh (formerly East Pakistan) 562, 566, 584, 596, 597, 604, 625, 628
Bank, *yinhang* 銀行 : Central, of China, *Zhongyang* 中央 319, 353, 371, 379, 409, 413, 425, 429, 435; Central, of Guangzhou government 295; Chase Manhattan 571; Chinese Agricultural, *Zhongguo nongye* 中國農業 465; Chinese People's, *Zhongguo renmin* 中國人民 431, 441, 465, 571; Deutsch-Asiatische 181, 225, 231, 245; Exchange, of China, *Zhonghua huiye* 中華匯業 267; Export-Import 371; Farmers', of China, *Zhongguo nongmin* 中國農民 379, 389, 403/5; Federal Reserve 371; First National, New York 231/3; Great Qing, *Da Qing* 大清 227, 241; Imperial, of China, *Zhongguo tongshang* 中國通商 185; Industrial, of Japan 263, 267; Jehol National, *Rehe guan* 熱河官 221; National City, New York 233; of China, *Zhongguo* 中國 241, 353, 379, 403/5, 441, 521, 575/7, 605/7, 613/15; Bank of Chosen 263, 267; of Communications, *Jiaotong* 交通 221, 263, 353, 379, 403/5; of Construction, Chinese People's, *Zhongguo renmin jianshe* 中國人民建設 461; of Guangzhou 241; of Taiwan 263, 267, 419; Russo-Asiatic 233, 237, 245, 259, 277; Russo-Chinese 183, 237; Savings, of Chicago 281; Xinhua 新華 Savings 255; Yokohama Specie 245, 263, 267, 371; Zhonghua 中華 Savings 271
Banking Corporation: Hongkong and Shanghai, *Huifeng yinhang* 匯豐銀行 99, 123, 133, 153, 181, 231, 245; Jincheng 金城 263; Oriental 37
Banque: de l'Indo-Chine 231, 245; du Nord 237; Industrielle de Chine 247, 251
Banxing zhaoshu 頒行詔書 51
Bao Chao 鮑超 74, 82, 97, 100, 159
Baofeng zouyu 暴風驟雨 433

648

baojia 保甲 35, 99, 334
Baoting 寶廷 109, 167
Baoxing 寶興 30
Baoxue yuekan 報學月刊 329
Baoyun 寶鋆 85, 125, 140, 141, 151
Barbados 598, 628, 631
Bayue de xiangcun 八月的鄉村 357
Beg Kuli Beg 132, 134
Beidaihe Conference 484
Beijing ren 北京人 385
Beijing ribao 北京日報 529
Beijing wenyi 北京文藝 501
Beitang 北塘 (Zhili) 76, 80
Beiyang 北洋: Army 218; Fleet 162, 166, 174-8; General Minting Office, *zhuzao yinyuan zongju* 鑄造銀元總局 205; group 260, 271
Beiyang junfa tongzhi shiqi shihua 北洋軍閥統治時期史話 487
Beiying 背影 323
Belgium 31, 189, 191/3, 202, 227, 228, 241, 282, 298, 301, 302, 322, 334, 400, 562, 582, 604; Tram Company 343
Benin 590
Bethune, Dr Norman 373, 379, 381
Bhutan 625
Bian yaoxue wei zuili lun 貶妖穴為罪隸論 55
Bianbaodi 卞寶第 149
Bianbaoquan 邊寶泉 175
Bichang 璧昌 29
big-character posters, *dazibao* 大字報 530, 531/3, 587, 614, 616, 622
Big Sword Society, *Dadao hui* 大刀會 183, 195, 196
Bishang Liangshan 逼上梁山 (Driven Up Mt Liang) 405, 599
Bixie jishi 辟邪紀實 87
Biyun 碧雲 Temple 300, 304
Black Flag Army, *Heiqi jun* 黑旗軍 122, 142, 148, 150
Bloomfield, Leonard 633
Bo Wenwei 柏文蔚 246, 247
Bo Yibo 薄一波 389, 431, 450, 451, 515, 523, 617
Bogue, the (Guangdong) 38; Treaty of 24
Bohuo ji 播火記 621
'Bolshevism de shengli' 的勝利 271
Book Company: Kaiming 開明 347; Tongwen 同文 153; Zhonghua 中華

351; bookshop, official Qing 清 183; New China Bookshop, *Xinhua shudian* 新華書店 379, 417, 427; see D sections
Botswana 580, 590
Boxer(s) 190, 194-9, 203; Indemnity 227, 274, 294, 297, 299/301, 331; Protocol 202, 396
boycott 214/16, 217, 224/6, 228/30, 254, 272/4, 302, 308, 427, 440
Brazil 139, 142, 244, 333, 514, 520, 578
Brecht, Bertolt 619
Bretton Woods Conference 403
Brief History of Chinese Fiction 491
Britain *passim*, especially lefthand pages 22/334, 376/414 and A sections; during Cultural Revolution 540; raises mission to embassy 354, 564; recognizes PRC 440
British-American Tobacco Company 269, 283, 317
British and Chinese Corporation 247, 251
British International Export Company 303
British Museum 115, 223
broadcast(s), -ing 536, 539/41, 459, 609; Central Station, *Zhongyang guangbo diantai* 中央廣播電臺 343, 415; Xinhua Station 415; see also radio
Bu Huanyu fangbei lu 補寰宇訪碑錄 97
Buddhist 297, 511, 619; Chinese Association, *Zhongguo Fojiao xiehui* 中國佛教協會 457, 479, 505, 633; Academy 475; Republican Society of the Ten Thousand Buddhas, *Wanfo gonghe hui* 萬佛共和會 253
budget 233, 435
Bulgaria 438, 459
Buren 不忍 249
Burhan 433, 436, 437, 457
Burhanuddin 94/6, 98
Burlingame, Anson 88, 106-12, 115
Burma 124/6, 392/4, 404/8, 440, 625; agreements, contracts with China 175, 465, 496, 498, 499, 615; border with China, delimitation of 168, 184, 388, 498; Chinese leaders visit 508, 514, 516, 522, 528, 610; leaders visit China 462, 492, 496, 524,

649

560, 584, 598, 600, 632; relations with China 156, 442, 506, 538, 556
Burma road 371, 382-4, 394
Burundi 512, 520
Burut Moslems 34, 35
Buyantai 布彥泰 31, 35
Buzurg Khan 98-100

cabinet system 234, 237, 238, 250, 258
Cable and Wireless Company 570
cadres 385, 393, 401, 405, 446, 490, 518, 520, 536, 537/9, 543, 546, 547, 557, 567, 573, 594, 618, 626, 634
Cai Chusheng 蔡楚生 549
Cai E 蔡鍔 147, 237, 256, 258, 261
Cai Gongshi 蔡公時 325
Cai Hesen 蔡和森 269, 281, 325
Cai Hesen wenji 蔡和森文集 611
Cai Jun 蔡鈞 206
Cai Shaonan 蔡紹南 218-20
Cai Yuanpei 蔡元培 109, 207, 212, 243, 259, 270, 273, 307, 313, 321, 327, 387
Cairo Conference, Declaration 400/2
Cambodia 470, 471, 484, 496, 506, 508, 524, 542, 544, 552/4, 571, 576, 581, 582, 584; *see also* Kampuchea
Cameroon 558, 570, 600
Campaign to Criticize Lin Biao and Confucius, *Pi Lin pi Kong yundong* 批林批孔運動 573, 574, 576/8
Canada 390, 402, 499, 556, 558, 569, 574, 600
Canton (Guangzhou) Commune 316/18
Cao Kezhong 曹克忠 102
Cao Kun 曹錕 91, 240, 266, 276/8, 280, 291, 295-7, 375
Cao Rulin 曹汝霖 259, 267, 271-3
Cao Yu 曹禺 pen name of Wan Jiabao 萬家寶 357, 363, 367, 385, 401, 611
Cao Yuying 曹毓瑛 85, 89, 103
Cape Verde 588
Carter, Jimmy 596, 617, 628
Catholic(s), Church 99, 119, 157, 445, 447; Chinese Patriotic Association, *Zhongguo Tianzhujiaoyou aiguohui* 中國天主教友愛國會 479/81, 485/7,

495/7, 505, 617, 629; converts condemned under PRC 457/9, 495/7; hostilities 46, 47, 89, 93, 111, 114, 121, 167/9, 187, 199; Legion of Mary 449; officially approved 29, 195; Pope's attitude to Chinese Catholics 379, 463
CCP *see* Chinese Communist Party
Cen Chunxuan 岑春煊 205, 209, 219, 237, 268/70, 269, 277
Cen Yuying 岑毓英 92, 104, 110, 116, 120, 121, 126/8, 145, 148, 149, 152, 165
Censorship of Books and Periodicals, Central Commission for the, *Zhongyang tushu zazhi shenchahui* 中央圖書雜誌審查會 401, 407
census 456, 462
Central African Republic 518, 528, 594
Central China United League *see* United League
Central Executive Committee, *Zhongyang zhixing weiyuanhui* 中央執行委員會 295
Central News Agency, *Zhongyang tongxun she* 中央通訊社 297
Central People's Government (CPG), *Zhongyang renmin zhengfu* 中央人民政府 436, 438, 440, 442
Central Research Institute (Academia Sinica), *Zhongyang yanjiu yuan* 中央研究院 313, 317
Central Supervisory Committee, *Zhongyang jiancha weiyuanhui* 中央監察委員會 295
Ceylon 440, 453, 472, 476, 493, 503, 506, 508, 514, 559
Chad 568, 610
Chai Degeng 柴德賡 481
Chamber of Commerce, *Shangwu zonghui* 商務總會 214, 309
Chang Qiankun 常乾坤 575
Chang'an huogu bian 長安獲古編 217
Changgeng 長庚 161, 229
Changjiang ribao 長江日報 488
Changshi ji 嘗試集 279
Changxu 長敘 161
Chaoyong 超勇 143
Chatu ben Zhongguo wenxue shi 插圖本中國文學史 343
Chefoo Convention 130, 153
Chefoo Daily News 265
Chen Bingkun 陳炳焜 264

Index

Chen Boda 陳伯達 529, 530-2, 551, 556, 558, 634, 636
Chen Bulei 陳布雷 167, 435
Chen Cheng 陳誠 193, 405, 419, 425, 432, 527
Chen Decai 陳得才 88, 90/2, 94/6, 97
Chen Dengke 陳登科 519, 633
Chen Duxiu 陳獨秀 139, 257, 265, 271, 281, 288, 289, 290, 312-16 *passim*, 319, 327, 342, 346, 397
Chen Fuen 陳孚恩 35
Chen Geng 陳賡 503
Chen Gongbo 陳公博 405, 423
Chen Guangyuan 陳光遠 273
Chen Guofu 陳果夫 171, 451
Chen Jiageng see Tan Kah Kee
Chen Jing 陳靖 491
Chen Jingpan 陳景磐 623
Chen Jiongming 陳炯明 137, 246, 247, 258, 266/8, 277, 278, 280, 284-6, 291, 298, 300, 304, 347
Chen Kai 陳開 60, 62/4, 84
Chen Kehan 陳克寒 635
Chen Kuilong 陳夔龍 223, 227, 229
Chen Lanbin 陳蘭彬 119, 122, 124, 127, 145
Chen Li 陳澧 147
Chen Lifu 陳立夫 399, 405
Chen Lu 陳籙 381
Chen Mingshu 陳銘樞 346, 347
Chen Muhua 陳慕華 597, 607
Chen Qimei 陳其美 137, 236, 237, 256, 257, 261
Chen Sanli 陳三立 369
Chen Sen 陳森 41
Chen Shaobai 陳少白 198, 353
Chen Shaoyu (Wang Ming) 陳紹禹 (王明) 332, 337, 349, 373, 581
Chen Shufan 陳樹藩 258, 260, 262
Chen Shuren 陳樹人 435
Chen Shutong 陳叔通 535
Chen Tanqiu 陳潭秋 403, 413
Chen Xilian 陳錫聯 547, 551, 559, 571, 577, 583, 607, 627
Chen Yannian 陳延年 319
Chen Yagui 陳亞貴 42
Chen Yi 陳宜 258/60
Chen Yi 陳毅 (CCP) 318, 384, 389, 424, 426, 432, 436, 437; d. 569; as Minister of Foreign Affairs 482-6, 488, 490, 496, 498, 504, 508, 512, 514, 516, 522, 523; widow d. 581

Chen Yi 陳儀 (NP) 349, 416, 422, 425, 447
Chen Yonggui 陳永貴 583, 607, 627
Chen Youren 陳友仁 312, 409
Chen Yu 陳郁 581
Chen Yuan (historian) 陳垣 563
Chen Yuan (Xiying) 陳源 (西瀅) 323
Chen Yucheng 陳玉成 62, 64/6, 68/70, 71, 72/4, 76/8, 77, 78, 84, 88, 91
Chen Yuchuan 陳玉川 194, 195
Chen Yun 陳雲 471/3, 523, 607, 617, 627
Chen Zaidao 陳再道 538/40, 539
Chen Zhengren 陳正人 569
Chen Zhongming 陳鐘明 158
Chenbao 晨報 *(Morning Post)* 275, 285
Cheng Biguang 程璧光 263, 264, 271
Cheng Dequan 程德全 237, 246, 247
Cheng Jingyi 誠靜怡 381
Cheng Qian 程潛 436
Cheng Shiqing 程世清 545, 555
Cheng Xingling 程星齡 479
Cheng Xueqi 程學啟 92/4, 97
Cheng Yanqiu 程硯秋 481, 487
Cheng Yucai 程禹采 28, 41, 45, 49
Chengbao 城堡 *(Das Schloss)* 633
Chenglin 成林 111
Chennault, General Claire 388/90, 394, 400, 413
Chiang Kaishek 蔣介石 286-438 *passim*, especially left-hand pages and B sections; attacks trade unions 315; as author 401; b. 161; d. 587; launches New Life Movement 351
Chiang Kaishek, Soldier and Statesman: Authorized Biography 369
Chidao zhangu 赤道戰鼓 523
Childers 36
Chile 295, 556
China Bookshop, *Zhonghua shuju* 中華書局 245
China Development Company 189
China Inland Mission 109, 111/13
China Mail 31, 97
China Merchants' Steam Navigation Company, *Lunchuan zhaoshang ju* 輪船招商局 119, 121, 131, 289
China National Import and Export Company, *Zhongguo jinchukou gong-*

651

Index

si 中國進出口公司 455
China Revival Society, *Huaxing hui* 華興會 210, 212
China Shipping Company 105
China-Schindler Elevator Co. Ltd. 625
'China: the Sleep and the Awakening' 161
China Times 206
China's Destiny by Chiang Kaishek 401
Chinese Border Studies Society, *Zhongguo bianjiang xuehui* 中國邊疆學會 379
Chinese Central Railways Company 225
Chinese Changchun Railway Company 411, 441, 442, 451/3
Chinese Communist Party (CCP), *Zhongguo Gongchan dang* 中國共產黨 initiated 276, 279-635 *passim*
Chinese Democratic League, *Zhongguo minzhu tongmeng* 中國民主同盟 406, 414, 422, 426, 428, 430, 478
Chinese Eastern Railway Company 183, 202, 205, 209, 216, 264, 268, 274, 276-8, 288, 294, 296, 326-8, 332, 352, 411
Chinese Expeditionary Force 392, 394, 404, 406, 408
Chinese Literature 451
Chinese National Relief and Rehabilitation Administration, *Shanhou jiuji duban zongshu* 善後救濟督辦總署 409
Chinese Nationalist Party (NP), *Zhongguo guomin dang* 中國國民黨 274; see Nationalist Party
Chinese People's Political Consultative Conference (CPPCC), *Zhongguo renmin zhengzhi xieshang huiyi* 中國人民政治協商會議 436, 437, 453, 454, 602, 607, 615, 630
Chinese People's Volunteers, *Zhongguo renmin zhiyuanjun* 中國人民志願軍 444, 446, 448, 456, 482, 486
Chinese Revolutionary Party, *Zhonghua geming dang* 中華革命黨 250, 252, 254, 258, 260, 274, 275
Chinese Seamen's Union, *Zhonghua haiyuan gongye lianhehui* 中華海員工業聯合會 287
Chinese Social Education Association, *Zhongguo shehui jiaoyu she* 中國社會教育社 343
Chinese Society of History, *Zhongguo lishi xuehui* 中國歷史學會 401
Chinese Soviet Republic (CSR), *Zhonghua suweiai gongheguo* 中華蘇維埃共和國 337-40, 342, 344, 348-52
Chinese United League see United League
Chinese Youth 511
Choi Yong Kun 510, 552
Ch'olchong 40
Chonghou 崇厚 85, 103, 113-19 *passim*, 134, 135, 136, 138, 140, 141, 173
Chongli 崇禮 137, 167, 187, 199, 209
Chonglun 崇綸 60, 85, 129
'Chongshang Jinggangshan' 重上井岡山 593
Chongshi 崇實 79, 93
Christian(s) 67, 93, 111, 165, 183, 191, 199, 203, 207, 213, 223, 251, 445, 533, 619
Chuangye 創業 591/3
Chuangzao jikan 創造季刊 289
Chun 春 375, 385
Churchill, Winston 384, 390, 400, 408, 412
Cihai 辭海 363, 621
Civil Affairs, Ministry of, *Minzheng bu* 民政部 218
Civil Appointments, Board of, *Libu* 吏部 29
class struggle 504, 510, 517, 531, 588, 596
coal mines 125, 143, 153, 167, 205, 249, 455, 477, 597, Anyuan 安源 287/9, 303/5, Jilong 雞龍 125, Kailuan 開灤 279, 289, 597, Kaiping 開平 135, 143, 147, 167, Zhongxing 中興 257; Fuzhong Corporation 255; Hanyeping Coal and Iron Company, *Hanyeping meitie gongsi* 漢冶萍煤鐵公司 227, 305; Kaiping Mining Company 201; see also mines
Coca-Cola Co. 607
Cochinchina 122
College of Foreign Languages, *Tongwen guan* 同文館 89, 93, 103, 111, 207; Guangzhou 97
Columbia 558, 624
Comintern 270, 276, 282, 284, 286, 288, 310, 314, 332
Commerce, Ministry of, *Shangbu*

商部 208
Commercial Press, *Shangwu yinshuguan* 商務印書館 187, 309, 351, 355, 357, 363, 369, 385, 407/9, 427/9, 527, 533
Commission for Economic Relations with Foreign Countries, *Duiwai jingji lianluo weiyuanhui* 對外經濟聯絡委員會 515, 555
Committee for the Establishment of Constitutional Government, *Xianzheng shishi xiejin hui* 憲政實施協進會 399
Committee of Three 418, 422
Common Programme, *Gongtong gangling* 共同綱領 435, 436, 439
commune(s) 482, 484, 486, 490, 498, 504, 539, 553, 573, 604, 617
Communications, Ministry of, *Jiaotong bu* 交通部 259, 267, 283, 327, 342, 397
Comoros 584
Compagnie Générale Bruxelles de Chemins de Fer et de Tramways en Chine 271
Confucius 221, 251, 255, 323, 351, 379, 499, 505, 573, 574, 579
Cong yuantou dao hongliu 從源頭到洪流 453
Congo 190, 498, 500, 514, 518, 551, 572, 580, 598, 628
Congshu jicheng 叢書集成 355
Congwen zizhuan 從文自傳 401
constitution(al) 214, 216, 218, 226, 238, 250, 260, 454, 460, 461, 580, 604, 618, 630; Compact 250; Compilation, Bureau of, *Xianzheng biancha guan* 憲政編查館 222, 226; Drafting Committee 248; Provisional of the Political Tutelege Period, *Xunzheng shiqi yuefa* 訓政時期約法 336
contradictions 476, 481
Convention of Citizens' Representatives, *Guomin daibiao dahui* 國民代表大會 256
cooperative(s) 435, 457, 466/8, 470
Cooperative League of China 383
Cornwallis 22
Costa Rica 404
Council of State, *Canzheng yuan* 參政院 250, 256
counter-revolutionary 446, 469, 476, 479/81, 488, 491, 495, 536,

546, 552, 553, 588, 594, 620, 634
Court: Mixed 109, 313; of Colonial Affairs, *Lifan yuan* 理藩院 34; People's Intermediate 495, 544, 619; Supreme People's, *Zuigao renmin fayuan* 最高人民法院 437, 439, 461, 481, 521
Creation Society, *Chuangzao she* 創造社 289
crime, criminal 616, 618, 623
Criminal Code 323
Crisp, C. Birch and Co. 241
CSR *see* Chinese Soviet Republic
Cuba 124, 132, 246, 396, 494, 496, 499, 506, 509, 528, 606
Cui Yinghe 崔英河 166
cultural 445, 449, 495, 591/3, 599, 607, 631; Cultural Circles' National Salvation Association, *Wenhua jie jiuwang xiehui* 文化界救亡協會 367; Group, *Wenhua zu* 文化組 563; Relations with Foreign Countries, Chinese People's Association for, *Zhongguo renmin duiwai wenhua xiehui* 中國人民對外文化協會 463; Revolution (GPCR) 525, 528-49, 555, 557, 563, 567, 571-3, 582, 588, 607, 617, 620, 634/6; Revolution Group, *Wenhua geming xiaozu* 文化革命小組 529, 530, 531, 534, 538, 545, 546
Culture, Ministry of, *Wenhua bu* 文化部 453
currency 221, 229, 233, 345, 353, 429, 465, 475/7, 625
Currency, Bureau of, *Bizhi ju* 幣制局 273
customs, duty 24, 39, 53, 73, 124, 137, 188, 193, 263, 285, 301, 304, 311/13, 331, 341, 447, 625; appointments 85, 186, 188; Bureau of Customs Affairs, *Shuiwu chu* 稅務處 218; Customs Postal Department 136; rates set 65, 127, 205, 321; *see also lijin*
cyclone *see* E sections
Cyprus 556, 576
Czechoslovakia 268, 438, 459, 476, 506, 548

Da Qing huidian 大清會典 157
Da Qing Muzong Yi huangdi shengxun 大清穆宗毅皇帝聖訓 139
Da Qing Muzong Yi huangdi shilu

Index

大清穆宗毅皇帝實錄 139
Da Qing Wenzong Xian huangdi shengxun 大清文宗顯皇帝聖訓 107
Da Qing Wenzong Xian huangdi shilu 大清文宗顯皇帝實錄 107
Da Qing Xuanzong Cheng huangdi shilu 大清宣宗成皇帝實錄 67
Da Qing yitong zhi 大清一統志 27
Da Zhonghua 大中華 257
Dachen 大陳 Islands (Zhejiang) 464
Dacheng 大成 64
Dagong bao 大公報 207, 217, 391
Dahomey 528
Dahonga 達洪阿 22, 23, 24, 25
Dahuangjiang 大黃江 (Guangxi) 46
Dai Hongci 戴鴻慈 216, 221, 229, 235
Dai Jitao 戴季陶 321, 355, 399, 425, 441
Dai Li 戴笠 423
Dai Wangshu 戴望舒 447
Dai Xi 戴熙 83, 173
Dalai Lama 212, 230, 232, 347, 383, 448, 467, 471, 479, 488, 489, 517
dance 449; ballet 519, 557, 561
Danmaoqian 單懋謙 119, 139
Danyang 丹陽 (Jiangsu) 66
Daoguang 道光 22, 43, 48
Daqing lichao shilu 大清歷朝實錄 369
Darjeeling, India 164, 172, 232
Date Munenari 伊達宗城 116, 117
Dazhai spirit 525, 581/3, 593-5, 605, 628
Dazhong shenghuo 大眾生活 391
De 德 Prince (Demchukdonggrub) 346, 359, 360/2, 365, 379
De Zhuangguogong nianpu 德壯果公年譜 75
debt(s), indebtedness 325, 520, 529
December 9 Movement 356
Democratic League *see* Chinese Democratic League
Democracy Wall 479, 610
Deng Baoshan 鄧寶珊 549
Deng Chengxiu 鄧承修 151
Deng Fa 鄧發 423
Deng Hua 鄧華 635
Deng Keng 鄧鏗 284/6, 291

Deng Tingzhen 鄧廷楨 33, 35
Deng Tuo 鄧拓 501, 507, 531, 535
Deng Xiaoping 鄧小平 436, 478, 480, 496, 498, 510, 511, 530/2, 540, 576, 581-627 *passim*, 634; appointments 471/3, 509, 523, 571, 599, 607, 627
Deng Xihou 鄧錫侯 519
Deng Yanda 鄧演達 341
Deng Yingchao 鄧穎超 416, 591, 596, 600, 602, 607
Deng Zeru 鄧澤如 295, 353
Deng Zihui 鄧子恢 569
Deng Ziyu 鄧子瑜 222
Denmark 30, 91, 143, 183, 301, 442, 578, 604, 620
Deshou 德壽 205
Dexing'a 德興阿 66, 67, 74, 77
Dezong huangdi shilu 德宗皇帝實錄 231
Dian (Thunder) 電 355
Dianying yishu 電影藝術 475
Dielian hua 蝶戀花 601
Dihou zhanchang 敵後戰場 601
Ding Baozhen 丁寶楨 55, 110, 127, 129, 159
Ding Bing 丁丙 197
Ding Fubao 丁福保 283, 373
Ding Ling 丁玲 347, 433, 479, 615/17
Ding Richang 丁日昌 91, 125, 147
Ding Ruchang 丁汝昌 143, 146, 156, 163, 176, 181
Ding Sheng 丁盛 577
Ding Wenjiang 丁文江 363
Ding Zhenduo 丁振鐸 205, 208, 213, 219, 223
Ding'an wen(xu)ji 定盦文(續)集 109
DIXIE, US Military Mission 404, 406
Diyi wutai 第一舞臺 (First Stage) 251
Djibouti 612, 622
dockyard(s): Fuzhou 103, 111, 152; Jiangnan 261, 495; Shanghai 239; *see also* shipyard
Dominica 522
Dong Biwu 董必武 417, 424, 568; appointments 411, 413, 431, 461, 489, 521, 551, 565, 571, 583; d. 587
Dong Fuxiang 董福祥 180, 182, 196/8, 199, 203, 229
Dong Kang 董康 288
Dong Pei 董沛 181
Dong Xun 董恂 81, 85

Dongfang hong 東方紅 519
Dongfang zazhi 東方雜誌 213
Dongfeng 東風 495
Dongping 東平 Association School 23
Dongsha 東沙 (Pratas) Islands (Guangdong) 574, 586
Dongxi wenhua ji qi zhexue 東西文化及其哲學 285
Dorrock, John 335
Double Sword Society, *Shuangdao hui* 雙刀會 54
drama(s) 51, 277, 445, 449, 473, 481, 485, 491, 511, 517, 523, 565, 567, 629; Festivals 453, 513, 525; *yangge* 秧歌 399; Central Institute, *Zhongyang xiju xueyuan* 中央戲劇學院 443; Chinese Research Institute, *Zhongguo xiqu yanjiu yuan* 中國戲曲研究院 449; Reform Committee 445; Chinese Publishing House, *Zhongguo xiju chubanshe* 中國戲劇出版社 487; see also dance, opera, play, theatre
Dream of Red Mansions (Honglou meng) 459, 463, 611
drought see E sections
Du Fu 杜甫 621/3
Du Han 杜翰 59, 85
Du Shoutian 杜受田 43, 53
Du Wenlan 杜文瀾 101
Du Wenxiu 杜文秀 64, 90, 101, 106, 108, 118, 121
Du Xigui 杜錫珪 307, 310
Du Yuesheng 杜月笙 451
Du Yuming 杜聿明 434
Du Zhongyuan 杜重遠 354
dual nationality 466, 480, 491, 496, 631
Duan 端 Prince 197
Duan Qirui 段祺瑞 240, 246, 262/8, 296/306, 297, 307; b. 101; 243/77 B sections *passim*; d. 363
Duan Xipeng 段錫朋 341, 343, 435
Duan Zhigui 段芝貴 246, 247
Duanfang 端方 87, 205, 214, 216, 219, 221, 226, 227, 229, 231, 236, 239
Duanhua 端華 85, 87
Dujuan shan 杜鵑山 (*Azalea Mountain*) 573
Duke of Argyle 34
Dumbarton Oaks Proposal 405, 406
Dumen jilüe 都門紀略 31
Duolong'a 多隆阿 74, 88, 93, 94, 97
Dushi xiangzhu 杜詩詳註 621
Dutch 120, 160, 302, 632, 634, 636; see also Holland, Netherlands

earthquake(s) see E sections
East Pakistan, later Bangladesh 528
East Turkestan Republic see Turkestan
Eastern Expedition 300, 301, 304
economic(s) see A sections
Economic Aid Agreement 429
Economic Committee of the Northeast Headquarters 411, 413
Economic Council, Supreme, *Jingji zuigao weiyuanhui* 經濟最高委員會 411, 413
Economic Emergency Discipline Regulations 429/31
Economics, Ministry of, *Jingji bu* 經濟部 397
economism 529, 535
Economy, the World, Chinese Society for the Study of, *Zhongguo shijie jingji xuehui* 中國世界經濟學會 629
Ecuador 622, 624
education 207 and later C sections *passim*; China Foundation for the Promotion of, and Culture, *Zhonghua jiaoyu wenhua jijin dongshihui* 中華教育文化基金董事會 297, 309; China Vocational Society, *Zhonghua zhiye jiaoyu she* 中華職業教育社 265, 269; Chinese New Promotion Society, *Zhonghua xin jiaoyu gongjin she* 中華新教育共進社 273, 275; Ministry of, *Jiaoyu bu* 教育部, *Xuebu* 學部 (Qing) 216, 218, 219/303, C sections *passim*, 311, 337, 343, 379, 397; National Union, *Quanguo jiaoyu lianhehui* 全國教育聯合會 239; Educational Associations, National Union of, *Quanguo jiaoyu hui lianhehui* 全國教育會聯合會 255, 261
Egypt 470, 472, 522, 590, 616
Eighth Route Army, *Balu jun* 八路軍 366, 378, 384, 402, 404
Eisenhower, Dwight 454, 464, 490
Elder Brothers Society, *Gelao hui* 哥老會 106, 116, 154, 164, 168, 169, 170, 192, 194, 195, 214, 236, 382

Index

election(s) 226, 228, 242, 266, 456, 458, 482, 508, 618, 622, 631; Electoral Law of the PRC for the National People's Congress and the Local People's Congresses at All Levels 456, 618
electric power, generation 571, 583, 623/5; hydro- 477, 489, 493, 577; railway 581
Elehebu 額勒和布 151
Elements of Geometry (by Euclid) *(Jihe yuanben)* 71
Elements of International Law (by Henry Wheaton) *(Wanguo gongfa)* 101
Emperor, *huangdi* 皇帝 Daoguang 道光 22, 40, 43, d. 45; Guangxu 光緒 136, 155-204 *passim*, ascends throne 127, b. 117, d. 229; Puyi 溥儀 296, 298, 300, 338, 341, abdication 240, 241, 265, ascends throne 227, 263, 351, author 519, b. 221, d. 543, Emperor of Manzhouguo 351, 382, 414; Tongzhi 同治 113, 118, 120, 123, 125, ascends throne 85, b. 69, d. 127, 129; Xianfeng 咸豐 72, 80, 81, 82, 85, ascends throne 42, 43, d. 87
Empress Dowager, *huang taihou* 皇太后 Cian 慈安 85, 86, 145, *see also* Xiaozhen; Cixi 慈禧 110, 136/204 *passim* left-hand pages, carries out *coup* 86, 192, d. 229, set up girls' schools 219, and theatre 151; *see also* Xiaoqin
Empress Longyu 隆裕 249
Encheng 恩承 151
Encirclement Campaign, *Weijiao* 圍剿 332-6, 342-50
Energy Research Society, Chinese, *Zhongguo nengyuan yanjiu hui* 中國能源研究會 637
Ershi nian mudu zhi guai xianzhuang 二十年目睹之怪現狀 231
Ershi shiji zhi Zhina 二十世紀之支那 217
Ershisi shi 二十四史 355
Ershiwu shi 二十五史 351, 355
Ethiopia 514, 522, 556, 559, 560, 565
European Economic Community (EEC) 582, 603
Ever Victorious Army, *Changsheng jun* 常勝軍 88-94, 140
Everest, Mt 629, *see also* Jomo Lungma
examinations 135, 191, 203, 213, 217, 343, 531, 541, 553, 601
excavations 327, 499/501, 563, 567, 585, 591, 599, 601, 631

'Fa E geming zhi bijiao guan' 法俄革命之比較觀 269
Falü da cishu 法律大辭書 363
Family 347, 385
family planning 511, 630
famine *see* E sections
Fan Jin 范瑾 529
Fan Qiguang 范其光 327
Fan Wenlan 范文瀾 427, 459, 553, 621
Fan Yaonan 樊燿南 325
Fang Dongshu 方東樹 39, 49
Fang Yi 方毅 515, 555, 583, 607, 617
Fang Zhimin 方志敏 337, 357
Fanyu ji 飯餘集 355
Fei Kaishou 費開綬 42
Feng Baiju 馮白駒 575
Feng Guifen 馮桂芬 49, 87, 125, 133
Feng Guozhang 馮國璋 79, 238, 264, 265, 266-8, 275
Feng Jicai 馮驥才 603
Feng Xuefeng 馮雪峰 595
Feng Youlan 馮友蘭 351, 507
Feng Yunshan 馮雲山 27, 29, 35, 36, 38, 39, 46-8, 53
Feng Yuxiang 馮玉祥 147, 258, 295-7, 304-7, 314, 321, 326-33, 341, 345, 435, 450
Feng Zicai 馮子材 116, 134, 138, 154, 158, 211
Feng Ziyou 馮自由 421, 427
Fenglei 風雷 519
Fengtian Army, clique 276/8, 280, 284/6, 296, 300, 303, 304, 308, 309
Fiji 584, 606
film(s) 185, 337, 355, 447, 505, 511, 531, 579, 591, 629/31
Finance, Ministry of, *Caizheng bu* 財政部, *Duzhi bu* 度支部 (Qing) 218, 221/419, A sections *passim*
Finland 444
fire(s) *see* E sections
Five-Antis Movement, *Wufan yundong* 五反運動 450/2
Five Year Plan(s) 453, 455, 465, 471, 483, 509, 529, 559; *see also*

656

Index

Ten Year Plan
floods(s) *see* E sections; Flood Dispersion Area, Jingjiang 荊江(Hubei) 451; Flood Relief Commission, National 357
Food, Ministry of, *Liangshi bu* 糧食部 387
foot binding 191, 207, 243
Ford, Gerald 580, 586
foreign affairs, left-hand pages *passim*; Ministry of, *Waijiao bu* 外交部 , *Waiwu bu* 外務部 (Qing) set up 202, later left-hand pages *passim*; *see also* individual countries and *Zongli yamen*
foreign languages 82, 89, 93, 207, 273; Foreign Languages Institute, *Waiguo yu xueyuan* 外國語學院 601, 611; Foreign Languages Press 519, 567; School of Foreign Languages, *Guang fangyan guan* 廣方言館 93, 113; *see also* College of Foreign Languages
Foreign Policy Association of China 415
Foreign Trade Association of China, *Zhongguo jinchukou maoyi xiehui* 中國進出口貿易協會 407
Four-power Consortium 233, 241, 263, 277
Foxue da cidian 佛學大辭典 283
France 26-302 *passim*, especially left-hand pages, 330; economic ties 177, 241, 299/301, 321, 529, 605/7; and missionaries 39, 93, 99, 101, 111, 121, 149, 191, 199, 213, 219, 223; recognizes PRC 514; in World War II 372, 376, 384
From Emperor to Citizen 519
Fu Bingchang 傅秉常 400
Fu Liangzuo 傅良佐 264
Fu Sinian 傅斯年 185, 447
Fu Tieshan 傅鐵山 , Michael 617
Fu Yiling 傅衣凌 475
Fu Zuoyi 傅作義 360, 382, 434, 570, 581
Fuji 福濟 85
Fukun 福錕 151, 171
Fuli ji 伏櫪集 513
Funiyang'a 富呢揚阿 23, 24
Fuqi 孚琦 239
Fushi 腐蝕 391

Futian Incident 332
Fuxian guan tihua shi 芙仙館題畫詩 39

Gabon 576, 578, 582, 598, 610
Gai Jiaotian 蓋叫天 563
Gaizao 改造 275
Gambia 580, 582
Games, National 233, 333, 491, 525, 619, 631; Asian 579; Far Eastern 247, 255, 283; of Newly Emerging Forces 513, 533; Olympic 624, 626
Gan Siqi 甘泗淇 519
gang of four 582, 589-94, 599-601, 604, 609, 612, 620, 629, 634
Gangyi 剛毅 175, 193, 197-9, 201
Gansu ribao 甘肅日報 439
Gao Gang 高崗 435, 453, 457, 458, 461, 465
Gao Ying 高纓 611
Gao Yubao 高玉寶 487
Gao Zongwu 高宗武 380
Ge Gongzhen 戈公振 359
geju 歌劇 (opera) *see* opera
Geming jun 革命軍 209
Geming shichao 革命詩抄 601
Geming yishi 革命逸史 427
General Conference of Workers, Peasants and Soldiers 316
Geneva Agreement, Conference (on Laos) 498, 500, 504; (on Vietnam) 458/60, 466, 476, 518; Convention 452
Genghiz Khan 181
Genü Hong mudan 歌女紅牡丹 337
geological 599, 607; Geophysical Association, Chinese, *Zhongguo diqiu wuli xuehui* 中國地球物理學會 479
Germany 110, 120, 131, 178/206 *passim*, 240/84 *passim*, 360, 368/88 *passim*; A sections 83, 193, 231, 235/7, 241, 263, 295, 319; Democratic Republic of 438, 443, 468, 488; Federal Republic of 416, 568, 620
Gezhi guwei 格致古微 185
Ghana 494, 500, 506, 514, 528, 532
Giaogong, Sikkim 206
Gnatong, Sikkim 160
God Worshippers Society, *Bai Shangdi hui* 拜上帝會 35, 42-4, 46, 50
Golden Elixir Sect, *Jindan jiao*

657

Index

金丹教 168, 169
Gong Chuntai 龔春台 218, 220
Gong Peng 龔澎 557
Gong Pinmei 龔品梅 495
Gong 恭 Prince, Yixin 奕訢 82-4, 103, 119/21, 126, 188; appointments 43, 55, 79, 85, 99, 125, 151, 175; d. 193
Gong Zizhen 龔自珍 109
Gongchan dang 共產黨 279
'Gongchan dang de xuanyan' 共產黨的宣言 275
Gongchan dangren 共產黨人 381
gongche shangshu 公車上書 179
Gongnongbing qingnian chuangzuo xuan 工農兵青年創作選 527
Goto Shimpei 後藤新平 268
Government Administrative Council (GAC), *Zhengwu yuan* 政務院 437, 438, 450, 452, 456, 461
Government Affairs, Bureau of, *Duban zhengwu chu* 督辦政務處 202, 203, 216
grain 31, 37, 73
Grand Canal, *Da yunhe* 大運河 102, 104, 263, 329
Grand Council, *Junji chu* 軍機處 218, for appointments to see B sections to 233
Great Leap Forward 482, 483, 485, 486, 490
Great Proletarian Cultural Revolution (GPCR) see Cultural Revolution
Great Wall 194, 286, 344, 346
Greece 566, 569, 622, 634
Grey, Anthony 540, 552
Gu Jiegang 顧頡剛 391, 401, 635
Gu Ligao 古立高 633
Gu Mu 谷牧 523, 583, 604, 615, 617, 629
Gu Weijun 顧維鈞 270, 276, 287, 288, 294, 366, 405, 406, 411, 412
Gu Xiegeng 顧諧賡 44
Gu Zhenggang 谷正綱 433
Gu Zhenghong 顧正紅 300, 305
Guan Hanqing 關漢卿 487
Guan Linzheng 關麟徵 413
Guang fangyan guan 廣方言館 93; Shanghai 113
Guangbao 廣報 157
Guangdong Army 295, 300
Guangdong Victorious Army 152
Guangming ribao 光明日報 439,

484
Guangu tang suozhu shu 觀古堂所著書 207
Guangxi Army 300
Guangxi ribao 廣西日報 439
Guangyin hongqi 廣印紅旗 549
Guangzhou Merchants' Corps, *Guangzhou shangtuan* 廣州商團 294, 296
Guangzhou Minguo ribao 廣州民國日報 293
Guanwen 官文 63, 68, 75, 85, 101, 105, 117
'Guanyu Hu Feng fangeming jituan de cailiao' 關於胡風反革命集團的材料 469
Guanyu nüren 關於女人 401
'Guanyu zhengque chuli renmin neibu maodun de wenti' 關於正確處理人民內部矛盾的問題 ('On the Correct Handling of Contradictions among the People') 481
Gudai baihua xiaoshuo xuan 古代白話小說選 621
Gudai Hanyu 古代漢語 507
Gudai zhengzhi sixiang yanjiu 古代政治思想研究 293
Gui Wencan 桂文燦 93
Guichun 桂春 191
Guiliang 桂良 55, 67, 72, 73, 80, 85, 91
Guinea 486, 490, 496, 514, 545, 556, 574, 620, 626
Gulang 鼓浪 Island (Fujian) 390
Guixiang 桂祥 161
Guizhou Army 118
Gujin tushu jicheng 古今圖書集成 153, 351
Guo Baiyin 郭柏蔭 107
Guo Liang 郭亮 325
Guo Minglun 郭明倫 623
Guo Moruo 郭沫若 313, 361/3, 415, 466, 480, 567, 583; as author 283, 333/5, 369, 395/7, 417, 563, 611; b. 171; d. 613
Guo Songlin 郭松林 104, 106
Guo Songling 郭松齡 304, 305
Guo Songtao 郭嵩燾 35, 127, 130, 134, 135, 155, 169, 171
Guo Taiqi 郭泰祺 389, 455
Guo Tingyi 郭廷以 9, 16, 385, 421
Guochao xianzheng shilüe 國朝先正事略 103
Guocui xuebao 國粹學報 217
Guofeng bao 國風報 235
Guomin bao 國民報 203

658

Guomin ri ribao 國民日日報 211
Guomin yuekan 國民月刊 249
Guomin zazhi 國民雜誌 (*Citizens' Magazine*) 275
Guomin zazhi 國民雜誌 (*Nationalist Magazine*) 249
Guoshi dagang 國史大綱 385
Guowen bao 國聞報 187, 199
Guoyin luomazi pinyin fashi 國音羅馬字拼音法式 311
Guoyin zidian 國音字典 279
Guqian da cidian 古錢大辭典 373
Guquan conghua 古泉叢話 119
Guquan hui 古泉匯 97
Guquan zayong 古泉雜詠 203
Gushi bian 古史辨 391
Gushi xintan 古史新探 527
Guyana 566, 580, 596
Guyu tukao 古玉圖考 165
Guzhou shiyi 古籀拾遺 163

Habeas Corpus Act (Regulations for Safeguarding the Freedom of the Human Person) 407
Hai Rui baguan 海瑞罷官 501, 525, 617
Haigang 海港 (*On the Docks*) 567
Haiguo sishuo 海國四說 33
Haiguo tuzhi 海國圖志 27, 51
Haihe 海河 River 575
Hamengleite 哈夢雷特 (*Hamlet*) 335
Han, non-Han 32, 34, 36, 66, 88, 98/100, 180, 207, 223, 243, 420, 425, 505
Han Fuju 韓復榘 326, 375
Han Nianlong 韓念龍 614/16
Han Ningfu 韓寧夫 627
Han Tang bihua 漢唐壁畫 579
Han Tang jian fengjian tudi suoyouzhi xingshi yanjiu 漢唐間封建土地所有制形式研究 519
Han Xianchu 韓先楚 547, 561, 577
Hanlin compiler, *bianxiu* 編修 207
Hanshi cunmu 漢石存目 163
Hanshu 漢書 507
Hanshu zhu jiaobu 漢書注校補 147
Hanye 寒夜 427
Hanying cidian 漢英詞典 611
Hanyu pinyin 漢語拼音 473, 485, 617
Haoran 浩然 519, 567/9

Havana, Cuba 34
Hayashi Gonsuke 林權助 224, 320/2
He Changling 賀長齡 31, 33
He Changqun 賀昌群 519
He Guiqing 何桂清 71, 73, 78, 79, 91
He Haiming 何海鳴 246
He Jian 何鍵 324, 325/7, 330, 335, 475
He Jing 何璟 119, 129
He Long 賀龍 313, 314, 316, 337, 342, 350, 356, 358/60, 378, 467, 523; d. 553
He Lu 何祿 60
He Mengxiong 何夢雄 339
He Qifang 何其芳 417, 603
He Qiutao 何秋濤 31, 81, 91, 181
He Ruzhang 何如璋 109, 133, 134
He Shaoji 何紹基 123
He Shuheng 何叔衡 269, 357
He Wei 何偉 575
He Xiangning 何香凝 569
He Yaozu 賀耀祖 320
He Yingqin 何應欽 334/6, 345, 354, 371, 382, 384/6, 400, 405, 414, 432, 435/7
He Zhongshi 郝中士 477
He Zizhen 賀子珍 615/17
health 337, 525; Health Programme 415; public 479; Public Health Work Conference 445; Health Station, Central Field, *Weisheng shiyan chu* 衛生實驗處 339
Heaven and Earth Society, *Tiandi hui* 天地會 28, 36/8, 40-8, 56, 60-4, 68, 74, 212, 214, 222; see also Three Harmonies Society and Triads
Heavenly Kingdom of Ascending Peace, *Shengping tianguo* 昇平天國 64, 74
Hebei-Chahar Political Affairs Committee, *Jicha zhengwu weiyuanhui* 冀察政務委員會 355, 356
Hechun 和春 64, 67, 77, 83
Hegel, G. 533
Heinu yutian lu 黑奴吁天錄 223
Helsinki 466
Hengchun 恒春 63, 71
Hengfu 恒福 76, 77
Hengqi 恒祺 85, 107
Hengxing chidao jingwei du tu 恒星赤道經緯度圖 63

Hengxuan suojian suocang jijin lu 恒軒所見所藏吉金錄 157
Hermes, HMS 54
'heterodox bandits', *xiefei* 邪匪, religions 33, 45, 46, 47
highway(s) 341, 397, 399, 405, 451/3, 461, 521, 529, 565, 589, 597, 605, 625
Highway Administration, *Gonglu zongju* 公路總局 397, 409
Hioki Eki 日置益 252, 254
Hiroshima 廣島 412
Hirota Kōki 廣田弘毅 352, 358
Historical Relics Unearthed in New China 567
history, historical 195, 391, 611; History, Chinese Society of 629
Hitachi 日立 Ltd. 605
Ho Chi Minh 460, 466, 478, 488, 490, 496, 508, 552
Ho Chi Minh City, Vietnam 606; *see also* Saigon
Holland 202, 298; *see also* Dutch, Netherlands
Hong Ji 洪紀 48
Hong Jun 洪鈞 159, 167, 173
Hong Renda 洪仁達 73
Hong Renfa 洪仁發 73
Hong Ren'gan 洪仁玕 27, 35, 51, 76, 77-9, 81, 82, 85/7, 89, 96, 97
Hong River Society, *Hongjiang hui* 洪江會 218, 220
Hong Shen 洪深 401, 469
Hong Tianguifu 洪天貴福 41, 95, 96, 97
Hong Xiuquan 洪秀全 27-9, 34-55 *passim*, 67-77 *passim*, 82, 94, 95; d. 97
Hongdeng ji 紅燈記 (*Red Lantern*) 517, 557, 561
Honghao 紅號 rebellion 64
Honghu chiweidui 洪湖赤衛隊 601
Hongjun ribao 紅軍日報 335
Hongkong 香港 38, 44, 62, 70-6 *passim*, 158, 171, 180, 192, 200, 204, 219, 288, 425, 428, 466, 582; appointments to 28, 36, 58; becomes British colony 24; communications 365, 605, 623; in Cultural Revolution 538, 552; declared free trade port 23; refugees 502; site of publications 57, 75; strikes in 287, 302, 308; water 495; in World War II 378, 380, 390; *see also* Banking

Corporation, Hongkong and Shanghai
Honglou meng 紅樓夢 (*Dream of Red Mansions*) 459, 463, 611
Honglou meng pinglun ji 紅樓夢評論集 573
Honglou meng yanjiu 紅樓夢研究 455
Hongqi 紅旗 487
Hongqi pu 紅旗譜 481, 621
Hongse niangzi jun 紅色娘子軍 (*Red Detachment of Women*) 519, 557, 561
Hongse Zhongguo 紅色中國 339
Hongxian 洪憲 256
Hongxue yinyuan tuji 鴻雪因緣圖記 41
Hongyan 紅岩 501
Hou Debang 侯德榜 581
Hou Han shu 後漢書 525
Hou Wailu 侯外廬 533
House of Legislature, *Lifa yuan* 立法院 250, 256
House of Representatives, *Zhongyi yuan* 眾議院 242, 244-8, 262, 266
How to be a Good Communist 381, 507, 536, 633
Hu Feng 胡風 453, 467/9
Hu Fu 虎符 397
Hu Hanmin 胡漢民 139, 237, 247, 295, 301, 307, 321, 327, 334, 337, 346, 355, 363
Hu Jizong 胡繼宗 581
Hu Linyi 胡林翼 63, 64, 66, 68, 70
Hu Qiaomu 胡喬木 607, 629
Hu Ruoyu 胡若愚 312, 313
Hu Shi 胡適 169, 265, 275, 279, 411, 415, 507
Hu Tinggan 胡廷幹 219
Hu Weide 胡惟德 228
Hu Yaobang 胡耀邦 607, 626, 627, 628, 634
Hu Yepin 胡也頻 211, 341
Hu Yihuang 胡以晃 44, 54, 58
Hu Youlu 胡有祿 60, 62, 64
Hu Yujin 胡玉縉 519
Hu Zhan'ao 胡占鰲 128
Hu Zongnan 胡宗南 197, 410, 424, 428, 507
Hua Guofeng 華國鋒 555, 571, 581-630 *passim*
Hua Luogeng 華羅庚 509/11
Hua zhi si 花之寺 323
Huabei ribao 華北日報 329
Huai Army, *Huaijun* 淮軍 88, 92, 94, 106, 146

660

Huaian shishe shixuan 懷安詩社詩選 633
Huang Chen 黃晨 631
Huang Demei 黃德美 54
Huang Fu 黃郛 143, 297, 320, 363
Huang Gonglüe 黃公略 320
Huang Hua 黃華 591, 600, 606, 607, 608, 616, 620, 629, 630
Huang Huoqing 黃火青 629, 634
Huang Jiguang 黃繼光 451
Huang Jingyuan 黃靜原 305
Huang Kecheng 黃克誠 485, 491, 505
Huang Maosong 黃茂松 204, 206
Huang Mingtang 黃明堂 224, 226
Huang Musong 黃慕松 369
Huang Qing jingjie 皇清經解 111
Huang Shuze 黃樹則 578
Huang Tifang 黃體芳 93, 197
Huang Xing 黃興 208, 212, 224, 226, 234, 243, 244, 246, 261
Huang Yanpei 黃炎培 137, 527
Huang Yongsheng 黃永勝 539, 545, 548, 551, 554, 634, 636
Huang Zhen 黃鎮 515, 596, 607
Huang Zirong 黃子榮 166
Huang Zonghan 黃宗漢 59, 73
Huang Zunxian 黃遵憲 139, 167, 185, 217
Huangchao bingzhi kaolüe 皇朝兵制考略 127
Huangchao fanshu yudi congshu 皇朝藩屬輿地叢書 209
Huangchao xu wenxian tongkao 皇朝續文獻通考 235
Huangchao zhanggu huibian 皇朝掌故彙編 207
Huanghe da hechang 黃河大合唱 (Yellow River Cantata) 379
Huangpu 黃浦 River (Shanghai) 53, 589
Huangzhuqi 黃竹岐 (Guangdong) 36
Huanqiu 環球 633
Huaqiao ribao 華僑日報 305
Huasha'na 花沙納 72, 73, 75
Huazi ribao 華字日報 97
Hubei xuesheng jie 湖北學生界 209
Hué, Vietnam 148
Hui 回 486, 597
Huibao 匯報 125
Huicheng 彗成 55
Huiji 惠吉 31
Huimin 惠民 Corporation 258
Huinian 惠年 173
Hunan Army, *Xiangjun* 湘軍 56/118 left-hand pages *passim*
'Hunan nongmin yundong kaocha baogao' 湖南農民運動考察報告 317
Hunan Provincial Proletarian Alliance, *Hunan shengwulian* 湖南省無聯 549
Hunan tongzhi 湖南通志 155
'Hundred Days' Reform' 190, 192
hundred flowers campaign 473, 476, 479, 499, 505, 567, 591
Hundred Regiments Offensive 384, 388
Hungary 438, 459, 472/4, 476, 478, 488
Huo 火 417
Huo Shilian 霍士廉 597, 615
Hurley, Brigadier-General Patrick 406, 408, 410, 411, 413, 414
Huxley, Thomas 185
hydrogen bomb 538, 548, 552, 572, 594

Iceland 562
illiteracy 467, 487
Imperial College, *Guozi jian* 國子監 162
Incense Burners' League, *Fenxiang jiemeng* 焚香結盟 76, 86, 88
indebtedness *see* debt
India 162, 212, 516, 562, 578, 625; border conflict 502/6, 542; border disputes 158, 490, 492, 494, 508, 510/12, 524; British 114, 122, 156, 164, 172; China-India Friendship Association, *Zhongyin youhao xiehui* 中印友好協會 453; Chinese leaders visit 392, 476, 494; contracts 451; diplomatic relations 440, 442, 590; leaders visit China 378; and Tibet 164, 172, 444, 460, 488
Indochina 382, 444, 458/60, 476, 488, 518, 554, 558; *see also* Cambodia (Kampuchea), Laos, Vietnam
Indonesia 442, 466, 467, 480, 490/8 *passim*, 506, 508, 512, 518/32 *passim*, 540/2, 586
industry, industrialization 455, 461, 471, 477, 489, 493, 498, 534, 535, 547, 551, 553/5, 565, 594, 597, 603-5; Industrial and Commercial Association, Chinese National, *Zhonghua quanguo gongshangye lianhehui* 中華全國工商業聯合會 455, 535; In-

661

Index

dustrial Reconstruction Programme 409
Institute of Chinese History, *Guoshi guan* 國史館 253, 261, 265
Institute of History and Philology, *Lishi yuyan yanjiusuo* 歷史語言研究所 323
Interior, Ministry of the, *Neizheng bu* 內政部 291, 424
International: Bank for Reconstruction and Development (World Bank) 403, 625; Group 241; Labour Organization (ILO) 333; Monetary Fund 403, 625; Settlements, *Gonggong zujie* 公共租界 92, 110/12, 184, 194, 300, 302, 313, 333, 390, 400
Iran 560, 565, 600
Iraq 392, 484
Ireland 618
Irkutsk, USSR 441
iron mines, -works 29; Anshan 鞍山 457, 553/5; Daye 大冶 173; Chongqing 崇慶 29; Hanyang 漢陽 165, 179; Wuhan 武漢 489; Hanyeping Coal and Iron Company, *Hanyeping meitie gongsi* 漢冶萍煤鐵公司 227, 305; *see also* mines
Islam 619; Islamic Association, Chinese, *Zhongguo Yisilanjiao xiehui* 中國伊斯蘭教協會 457, 511; Islamic Society, Chinese, *Zhongguo Huijiao gonghui* 中國回教公會 323; *see also* Moslem
Israel 574
Italy 194, 256, 270, 384, 400; agreements 565, 569, 622; Boxer Protocol 202; demands on China 192, 206; diplomatic relations 248, 298, 388, 556; leaders' visits 620, 630; recognizes Manzhouguo 360; troops in China 196, 198; war against 390; Washington Conference 282, 301
Itō Hirobumi 伊藤博文 154, 172/4, 176, 208, 231

Jamaica 568
Japan 116/56 *passim*, 174-414 *passim*, especially left-hand pages, 503, 555, 565, 566, 577, 603-15 *passim*; Japanese Kwantung Army 320, 336, 338; Japanese People's Liberation League, *Riben renmin jiefang tongmeng* 日本人民解放同盟 402; *see also* individual Japanese
Ji Chaoding 冀朝鼎 211, 513
Ji Dengkui 紀登奎 571, 583, 607, 627
Ji Hongchang 吉鴻昌 (film) 629
Ji Lu chunqiu 冀魯春秋 623
Ji Pengfei 姬鵬飛 565, 566, 570/4, 577, 617
Ji Zhichang 季芝昌 47, 48
Jia 家 (*Family*) 347, 385
Jia Deyao 賈德耀 307
Jia Qiyun 賈啓允 583
Jia Zhen 賈楨 63, 76, 125
Jiading 嘉定 (Jiangsu) 56, 80, 88
Jian Bozan 翦伯贊 10, 531, 549
Jian tianjing yu Jinling lun 建天京於金陵論 55
Jiang Biao 江標 187
Jiang Fangzhen 蔣方震 375
Jiang Guangci 蔣光慈 305, 343
Jiang Hua 江華 629, 634
Jiang Jingguo 蔣經國 416, 431
Jiang Menglin 蔣夢麟 333, 413
Jiang Qing 江青 511, 530, 531, 533, 542, 544, 551, 571, 581/3, 582, 592, 598, 599, 631, 634, 636
Jiang Wei 江暐 293
Jiang Weiguo 蔣緯國 261
Jiang Wenqing 蔣文慶 46
Jiang Yong 江永 27
Jiang Zhaozong 江朝宗 263
Jiang Zhongyuan 江忠源 50, 53, 54, 55, 61
Jiangbei yuncheng 江北運程 81
Jiangsu 江蘇 489
Jiangwan 江灣 (Shanghai) 128, 129
Jianming Ouzhou zhexue shi 簡明歐洲哲學史 621
Jianming shijie shi 簡明世界史 579
Jianshe 建設 (journal) 275; (ship) 515
Jiao Dafeng 焦達峰 237
Jiao Ruoyu 焦若愚 637
Jiao Youying 焦祐瀛 79, 85
Jiaobin lu kangyi 校邠廬抗議 87
Jiaoji ribao 膠濟日報 339
Jiaoping Nianfei fanglüe 剿平捻匪方略 119
Jiaoping Yuefei fanglüe 剿平粵匪方略 119
Jiaoyu shijie 教育世界 203
Jiaoyu yu zhiye 教育與職業

Jiaoyu zazhi 教育雜誌 231
Jiayin zazhi 甲寅雜誌 253
Jiefang 解放 381
Jiefang bao 解放報 419
Jiefang jun bao 解放軍報 475, see also Liberation Army Daily
Jiefang ribao 解放日報 391, see also Liberation Daily
Jiefang yu gaizao 解放與改造 275
Jierhang'a 吉爾杭阿 62, 69
Jihe yuanben 幾何原本 (Elements of Geometry by Euclid) 71
Jiliu sanbuqu 激流三部曲 385
'Jin' 今 269
Jin Deshun 金得順 34
Jin Jingmai 金敬邁 527
Jin Shuren 金樹仁 320, 321, 325
Jin Yunpeng 靳雲鵬 273, 277, 278
Jinchaji ribao 晉察冀日報 369
Jingbao 京報 279, 309
Jingji yanjiu 經濟研究 469
Jinglian 景廉 123/5, 129, 140, 151
Jingshou 景壽 85
Jinguang dadao 金光大道 567/9
Jingxin 敬信 175, 189, 209
Jingxue congshu 經學叢書 93
Jingxue tonglun 經學通論 225
Jinian Aiyinsitan yi wenji 紀念愛因斯坦譯文集 621
'Jinian zhansheng Deguo faxisi, ba fandui Mei diguozhuyi de douzheng jinxing daodi' 紀念戰勝德國法西斯把反對美帝國主義的鬥爭進行到底 527
Jinian Zhou Enlai zongli wenwu xuanbian 紀念周恩來總理文物選編 611
Jinpin 瑾嬪 Gem Concubine 161
Jinse de qunshan 金色的群山 501
Jinsha jiang pan 金沙江畔 491
jinshi 進士 degree 31, 35
Jinshi yuan 金石苑 39
Jinshun 金順 127, 130
Jintian 今天 613
Jintian qiyi 金田起義 587
Jiu Tangshu 舊唐書 587
Jiuguo ribao 救國日報 347
Jiuwang ribao 救亡日報 369
Jiuyizhao shengshu 舊遺詔聖書 (Old Testament) 55
Johnson, Lyndon B. 544, 548
Jomo Lungma (Mt Everest) 497, 585

Jordan 596
Ju Zheng 居正 258, 304, 355, 399, 425
Juben 劇本 487, 501
'Junxian jiuguo lun' 君憲救國論 257
Jurists, International Commission of 488
Justice, Ministry of, *Fabu* 法部 218
Juwai pangguan lun 局外旁觀論 101

Kabaodi 卡賓第 161
Kafka, Franz 633
Kaiser Wilhelm I 112; II 182, 186
Kampuchea, as from 1970 552, 600, 602, 610, 612, 614, 618/20, 624, 630, 632; see also Cambodia
Kang daodi 抗到底 373
Kang Guangren 康廣仁 193
Kang Jianmin 康建民 547, 561, 597, 603
Kang Liang shichao 康梁詩鈔 253
Kang Nanhai wenji 康南海文集 261
Kang Sheng 康生 367, 505, 551, 571, 583, 628, 629, 634; d. 587
Kang Youwei 康有爲 162, 169, 178-80, 187-93, 212, 262-3; b. 75; d. 319
Kang Zhili 康芷林 115
Kangxi 康熙 33
Kangzhan wenyi 抗戰文藝 375
Kantanzhe zhi ge 勘探者之歌 513
Kaocha zhengzhi riji 考察政治日記 227
Kaopan ji 考槃集 39
Karachi 474
Karakhan, Leo 274, 276, 278, 288, 294, 298, 300, 332
Katō Yasuo 藤保男 629
Katsura Tarō 桂太郎 208
Kawagoe Shigeru 川越茂 362, 370
Kazakh minority 408, 495, 507
Ke Qingshi 柯慶施 485, 513, 523, 527
Ke Shaomin 柯紹忞 275
Kennedy, John F. 506, 512
Kenya 512, 630
Kexue huanxiang xiaoshuo xuan 科學幻想小說選 633
Kexue zazhi 科學雜誌 257
Khabarovsk Protocol 328
Khmer Rouge 582
Khrushchev, Nikita 462, 470, 484,

663

Index

489, 490, 494, 500, 502-6, 518/20, 522
Kienphuoc 148
Kim Il Sung 448, 456, 458, 482, 486, 490, 498, 582
Kim Okkyun 177
Kiribati 628
Kissinger, Henry 560, 564, 570, 574, 580
Kojong 172, 174
Komura Jutarō 小村壽太郎 208, 210, 216
Kong Xiangxi (H.H. Kung) 孔祥熙 347, 349, 353, 365, 371, 379, 403, 405, 413; d. 543
'Kong Yiji' 孔乙己 275
Kongjiao hui zazhi 孔教會雜誌 249
Kongzi gaizhi kao 孔子改制考 187
'Kongzi - wangude weihu nuli zhi de sixiangjia' 孔子一頑固地維護奴隸制的思想家 573
Konoye Fumimaro 近衛文麿 374
Korea pre-1945 142, 402, appointments 40, 155, China intervenes 146, 152, 154, economic relations 145, 153, 194, and Japan 126/8, 136, 146, 152, 154, 172/4, 178, 204, 208, 228, 408, and Russia 182, 208/10, Wanbaoshan Incident 336; 1945-81 Democratic People's Republic of 438/46 passim, 454/60 passim, 468, 482, 486, 498, 503/7, 510, 524, 555, 608, 626, Korean War 440/6 passim, Republic of 446, 598; see also individual Koreans
Kosygin, A. 518, 520, 552
Kowloon 九龍 190, 194, 221, 237
Kowshing 高陞 174
Kuang Qizhao 鄺其照 157
Kuangren riji 狂人日記 269
Kuangyuan 匡源 75, 85
Kuijun 奎俊 189
Kungang 崑岡 179, 183
Kunshan 崑山 (Jiangsu) 92, 94, 220
Kuwait 558, 565, 627

labour 457, 631; All-China Labour Federation Congress, Quanguo laodong dahui 全國勞動大會 287, 303, 309, 317, 329, 433, 481; Insurance Regulations 447; Laws 339; Programme 415; China Labour Union Secretariat, Zhong-

guo laodong zuhe shujibu 中國勞動組合書記部 283
Lai Hanying 賴漢英 54
Lai Jiu 賴九 42-4
Lai Ruoyu 賴若愚 487
Lai Wenguang 賴文光 80, 88, 90-106, 109
Lan Chaogui (Dashun) 藍朝貴 (大順) 76, 86, 88, 92, 94, 97
Lan Ling 藍翎 573
Lan Yinong 藍亦農 561
land (reform) 347, 389, 395, 419, 427, 433, 453, 496
language, Chinese 265, 277, 279, 567, 591, 617; characters 467, 469, 473, 567; Chinese Character Reform Association, Zhongguo wenzi gaige xiehui 中國文字改革協會 439, 469, -Research Committee 449, 467, 473; Hanyu pinyin 漢語拚音 473, 485, 617; National Association for the Promotion of Teaching of the National Language, Quanguo guoyu jiaoyu cujin hui 全國國語教育促進會 309; Preparatory Committee for the Unification of the Chinese Official Language, Guoyu tongyi choubei weiyuanhui 國語統一籌備委員會 273, 311, 327; putonghua 普通話 473
Lao Can youji 老殘遊記 221
Lao Chongguang 勞崇光 77, 87, 93, 107
Lao Naixuan 勞乃宣 319
Lao She 老舍 pen name of Shu Qingchun 舒慶春 317, 347, 375, 401, 535
Laodong jie 勞動界 279
'Laodong yu ziben' 勞動與資本 275
Laos 472, 488, 498, 500, 503-5, 508, 509, 514, 516, 554, 558, 568, 586, 588, 598, 614/16
Latin American Friendship Association, China- 495
law(s) 233, 239, 449, 618, 619, 622, 627; Agrarian Reform 433, 445; Anti-Opium 327; County Bank 381; Criminal 618; Customs 447; Electoral 456, 508, 618; Labour 333, 339; Land 333, 339, 427; Marriage 333, 443, 631; Nationality 631; Organic of the CPPCC, and of the CPG 436; Publication 253; Trade Union 443/5
Law Society of China, International, Zhongguo guoji fa xue-

hui 中國國際法學會 629;
Studies Research Institute,
Chinese New, *Zhongguo xin faxue
yanjiu yuan* 中國新法學研
究院 443
lawyers 631
League of Nations 276, 336, 338,
340, 344, 345, 346, 376, 380;
Association, *Guoji lianmeng
tongzhi hui* 國際聯盟同志會
273; Report of the Commission
of Enquiry into the Sino-Japanese Dispute 345
Lebanon 484, 562
Lei Boli 雷波里 142
Lei Boyi 雷波夷 164, 166
Lei Feng 雷鋒 507, 511
Lei Yixian 雷以諴 53
Lei Zaihao 雷再浩 34
Leiyu 雷雨 (*Thunderstorm*) 357
Lend-Lease Agreement 394, 419
Lenin 270, 469, 492/4, 536, 585
Li Bai yu Du Fu 李白與杜甫 563
Li Baojia 李寶嘉 221
Li Bendong 李本東 623
Li Bingheng 李秉衡 155, 186, 187, 201
Li Chun 李純 281
Li Chunfa 李春發 73, 74
Li Ciming 李慈銘 177
Li Dazhang 李大章 595
Li Dazhao 李大釗 163, 261, 269/71, 278, 295, 307, 312, 317
Li Dequan 李德全 450, 479, 569
Li Desheng 李德生 547, 559, 571, 577
Li Dingxing 李定興 603
Li Feigan 李芾甘 *see* Ba Jin
Li Fengbao 李鳳苞 133, 135
Li Fuchun 李富春 437, 465, 523, 531, 587
Li Gongpu 李公樸 423
Li Guozhen 李國珍 168
Li Hanzhang 李瀚章 113/15, 126, 129, 163, 179
Li Henian 李鶴年 117
Li Hongzao 李鴻藻 51, 99, 103, 129, 140, 141, 143, 151, 175, 179, 183, 189
Li Hongzhang 李鴻章 88-202 *passim*; awarded degree 35; d. 205;
Li-Fournier Convention 150, 154;
Li-Itō Convention 154
Li Houji 李厚基 273
Li Hui 李輝 34
Li Ji 李濟 323, 327
Li Ji 李季 (poet) 635

Li Ji shixuan 李季詩選 633
Li Jiannong 李劍農 429
Li Jingfang 李經方 165
Li Jinglin 李景林 304
Li Jingquan 李井泉 453, 485, 539, 583
Li Jingxi 李經羲 229, 236/8, 262-4
Li Jishen 李濟深 153, 347, 359, 425, 437, 493
Li Kaifang 李開芳 50, 52, 58, 62, 63, 65
Li Kenong 李克農 507
Li Lianying 李蓮英 239
Li Liejun 李烈鈞 246, 247, 256, 423
Li Lisan 李立三 303, 313, 321, 324, 330-4, 337, 543, 624
Li 禮 Prince (Shiduo 世鐸) 151
Li Qiang 李强 571, 583, 613, 615, 619
Li Ruishan 李瑞山 547, 559
Li Sanwen 李三文 46
Li Shanlan 李善蘭 71, 147
Li Shihan 李石涵 633
Li Shixian 李世賢 78-82, 90, 98, 101
Li Shizhong 李世忠 74, 76, *see also* Li Zhaoshou
Li Shuchang 黎庶昌 141, 159
Li Siguang 李四光 563
Li Tangjie 李棠階 89, 101
Li Tianyou 李天佑 557
Li Weihan 李維漢 446/8
Li Wenmao 李文茂 60-4
Li Xiannian 李先念 461, 523, 551, 571, 583, 596, 599, 604, 607, 618, 627
Li Xifan 李希凡 573
Li Xingrui 李興銳 209
Li Xingyuan 李星沅 33, 35, 41, 45, 49
Li Xiucheng 李秀成 64/96 *passim*, 97; appointments 71, 73, 77
Li Xubin 李續賓 74, 75
Li Xuefeng 李雪峰 529, 545
Li Xuyi 李續宜 76, 95
Li Yangcai 李揚才 134, 138
Li Yiyuan 李一原 30
Li Youcai banhua 李有才板話 401
Li Yuan 黎原 545/7
Li Yuandu 李元度 103, 161
Li Yuanfa 李沅發 40, 42, 43, 45
Li Yuanhong 黎元洪 237-41, 246-7, 255, 259-64 *passim*, 287, 291; b. 97

Li Zaihan 李再含 539
Li Zhaolin 李兆麟 423
Li Zhaoluo 李兆洛 63
Li Zhaoshou 李昭壽 60, 66-70, 74, see also Li Shizhong
Li Zhen 李震 565
Li Zhengpin 李正品 250
Li Zhenguo 李珍國 129
Li Zhilong 李之龍 306
Li Zhun 李準 234, 236
Li Zicheng 李自成 593
Li Zongren 李宗仁 316, 326, 327, 331, 337, 359/61, 365, 370, 431, 432, 435/7, 524, 553
Li Zongxi 李宗義 121
Li Zuoxian 李佐賢 97
Liang Bin 梁斌 481, 621
Liang Fa 梁發 65
Liang Hongzhi 梁鴻志 373, 378
Liang Qichao 梁啟超 123, 179, 185, 191-3, 196, 207, 212, 224, 257, 258, 275, 329
Liang Shangquan 梁上泉 513
Liang Shiyi 梁士詒 258, 260, 271, 281, 284, 285, 286
Liang Shuming 梁漱溟 285
Liang Sicheng 梁思成 569
Liang Tingnan 梁廷枏 33
Liang Zhangju 梁章鉅 41
Liangbi 良弼 245
Liangzhong Meiguo ren 兩種美國人 633
Lianyuan 聯元 191, 201
Liao Chengzhi 廖承志 503, 511
Liao Heshu 廖和叔 550
Liao Mosha 廖沫沙 501, 531
Liao Shouheng 廖壽恒 151, 187, 188, 189, 190, 195, 211
Liao Zhongkai 廖仲愷 139, 291, 301, 305, 569
Liaoning Daily 553/5
Liberation Army Daily 531, 556, 567, 600; *Liberation Daily* 421; *Liberation Daily* (of Yan'an) 396, 397, 401; Liberation News Agency 417, 567; Liberation Press, *Jiefang she* 解放社 381
Liberia 596, 606/8
Library Association, Chinese, *Zhonghua tushuguan xiehui* 中華圖書館協會 303; Library, Eastern, *Dongfang tushuguan* 東方圖書館 309; Library, Peking, now National 309, 383, 491
Libya 608
Liehuo jingang 烈火金鋼 487
Liema he pan 烈馬河畔 579

Liening quanji 烈寧全集 469
Lihun 離婚 347
lijin 厘金 53, 63, 75, 123, 153, 313, 335, see also customs, duty
Lin Baoyi 林葆懌 269
Lin Biao 林彪 361, 366, 418, 424, 430, 432, 436, 525-74 *passim*, especially left-hand pages, 631; appointments 337, 413, 443, 457, 467, 471, 485, 491, 523, 529/31, 551; d. 563
'Lin Biao tongzhi weituo Jiang Qing tongzhi zhaokai de budui wenyi gongzuo zuotanhui jiyao' 林彪同志委托江青同志召開的部隊文藝工作座談會紀要 543
Lin Boqu 林伯渠 365, 404, 406, 413, 497
Lin Botong 林伯桐 33
Lin Fengxiang 林鳳祥 50, 52, 65
Lin Hujia 林乎加 607, 617, 624, 637
Lin Liguo 林立果 558
Lin Liming 林李明 603
Lin Sen 林森 109, 304, 337
Lin Shaonian 林紹年 219
Lin Shaozhang 林紹璋 58, 73
Lin Shi 林侍 40
Lin Shu 林紓 47, 53, 253
Lin Wanli 林萬里 309, 311
Lin Xiangqian 林祥謙 295
Lin Xu 林旭 189, 193
Lin Zexu 林則徐 23, 31, 33, 35, 36, 43, 45
Lin Zhihao 林志浩 633
Ling Shiba 凌十八 42, 46, 50, 53
Ling Shuhua 凌叔華 323
Linggui 靈桂 141, 143
Lingtu, Sikkim 158, 160
Linkui 麟魁 49, 89
Linqing 麟慶 41
Linshu 麟書 137, 171, 179
Linsu laoren nianpu 鄰蘇老人年譜 257
Linyi xiaoshuo congshu 林譯小說叢書 253
Lishan 立山 201
Lishi yanjiu 歷史研究 463
literature, literary 463, 499, 505, 511, 517/19, 525, 531, 541, 591/3, 609; Literary Association, *Wenxue yanjiu hui* 文學研究會 281, 283; Literary Institute, Central, *Zhongyang wenxue yanjiusuo* 中央文學研究所 447; Literary and Art Cir-

cles of China, Federation of, *Zhongguo wenxue yishu jie lianhehui* 中國文學藝術界聯合會 439, 459, 467, 497, 511, 617, 619; Literary Society, *Wenxue she* 文學社 234; *Literature and Art*, see *Wenyi bao*; Literature and Art Circles, Chinese National Anti-Japanese Association of, *Zhonghua quanguo wenyi jie kangdi xiehui* 中華全國文藝界抗敵協會 373, 375; Literature and Art Circles, Chinese National Federation of, *Zhonghua quanguo wenxue yishu jie lianhehui* 中華全國文學藝術界聯合會 609; Literature and Art Workers, Congress of 437/9, 459; Literature and Art, Yan'an Forum on 395, 401, 405
Little Red Book, The 535, 543
Liu Baonan 劉保楠 65, 103
Liu Bingzhang 劉秉璋 157
Liu Bocheng 劉伯承 424, 426, 436, 457, 467, 551, 571, 583
Liu Changyou 劉長佑 76, 89, 93, 105, 127, 161
Liu Chaodong 劉朝棟 192
Liu Cunhou 劉存厚 259
Liu Danian 劉大年 527
Liu E 劉鶚 71, 209, 221, 231
Liu Fu 劉復 353
Liu Geping 劉格平 539
Liu Guangdi 劉光第 189, 193
Liu Guangtao 劉光濤 597
Liu Hua 劉華 305
Liu Jianxun 劉建勳 545, 559
Liu Jie 劉傑 113, 114, 115
Liu Jintang 劉錦棠 112, 114, 118, 130, 132, 134, 135, 151
Liu Jinzao 劉錦藻 235
Liu Kunyi 劉坤一 127, 136, 137, 165, 169, 175, 194, 198, 207
Liu Lichuan 劉麗川 56, 65
Liu Liu 劉流 487
Liu Mingchuan 劉銘傳 102, 106, 108, 141, 143, 185
Liu Pu 劉璞 180
Liu Ruifen 劉瑞芬 159
Liu Shaoqi 劉少奇 appointments after 1949 437, 461, 473, 489, 521; author 381, 507, 633; career before 1949 287, 289, 321, 337, 349, 389, 413; career 1949-66 439, 445, 452/4, 458, 472, 496, 500, 507-11, 515-23 *passim*; and Cultural Revolution 529-31, 536, 540, 547, 634; d. 553; rehabilitated 624, 626
Liu Shipei 劉師培 275
Liu Shu 劉書 34
Liu Shutang 劉樹堂 194
Liu Songshan 劉松山 104, 112, 115
Liu Wenhui 劉文輝 342, 344, 377, 438
Liu Xiang 劉湘 342, 344, 352, 375
Liu Xianquan 劉賢權 539, 559
Liu Xianshi 劉顯世 258, 259, 277
Liu Xihai 劉喜海 39, 217
Liu Xihong 劉錫鴻 130
Liu Xingyuan 劉興元 555
Liu Xiyao 劉西堯 597, 607
Liu Yalou 劉亞樓 527
Liu Yishun 劉儀順 72, 108
Liu Yongfu 劉永福 122, 146, 148, 267
Liu Yuanhao 劉源灝 79
Liu Yuezhao 劉嶽昭 107, 108, 127
Liu Yunke 劉韻珂 25, 28
Liu Zihou 劉子厚 561
Liuhe congtan 六合叢談 71
Liuli 琉璃 Pagoda 61
loan(s), domestic and foreign see A sections *passim* from 99 on
locusts 71, 131, 135, 171, 253, 257, 493, 600
Long Jiguang 龍濟光 246, 247, 254, 258, 260
'Long Live the Victory of People's War' 527
Long March 350, 354, 358/60, 584
Long Shujin 龍書金 547, 561
Long Yun 龍雲 312, 507
Longdong 隆冬 633
Longjiang song 龍江頌 567
Lu Dahuang 路大荒 507
Lu Deming 盧德明 319
Lu Dingyi 陸定一 416, 478, 489, 495, 505, 517, 523, 529, 615/17
Lu Diping 魯滌平 325, 327, 357
Lu Han 盧漢 438
Lu Jianying 陸建瀛 41, 47, 57
Lu Jianzhang 陸建章 260, 271
Lu Jiuyuan 陸九淵 633
Lu Jiuyuan ji 陸九淵集 633
Lu Ping 陸平 495, 529, 531
Lu Rongting 陸榮廷 258, 259, 265, 266, 267, 280
Lu Runxiang 陸潤庠 233
Lu Shunde 陸順德 98, 100
Lu Xialing 陸遐齡 54

Lu Xinyuan 陸心源 167, 169, 177
Lu Xun 魯迅 145, 269, 275, 285, 293, 361/3, 363, 491, 591, 593
Lu Xun Memorial Hall, *Lu Xun jinian guan* 魯迅紀念館 447
Lu Xun quanji 魯迅全集 375, 573
Lu Xun shuxin ji 魯迅書信集 593
Lu Xun zhandou de yisheng 魯迅戰鬥的一生 591
Lu Yafa 陸亞發 208, 212
Lu Yongxiang 盧永祥 296, 297, 298
Lu Zhengxiang 陸徵祥 243, 254, 270, 272
Lu Zhonglin 鹿鐘麟 306
Lu Zhuanlin 鹿傳霖 179, 195, 199, 223, 229
Lu Zongyu 陸宗輿 273
Lugou 蘆溝 Bridge (Peking) 163, 215, 364
'Lun chijiu zhan' 論持久戰 375
Lun Gongchan dangyuan de xiuyang 論共產黨員的修養 381, 507, 536, 633
Lun lianhe zhengfu 論聯合政府 417
'Lun renmin minzhu zhuanzheng' 論人民民主專政 439
'Lun shida guanxi' 論十大關係 470, 593
Lunheng 論衡 621
Lunyu zhengyi 論語正義 103
Luo Bingzhang 駱秉章 105, 107
Luo Changpei 羅常培 455, 481, 487
Luo Dagang 羅大綱 44, 52, 60, 62
Luo Fuxing 羅福星 253
Luo Guangbin 羅廣斌 501
Luo Jialun 羅家倫 341
Luo Ming 羅明 344
Luo Raodian 羅饒典 49
Luo Ronghuan 羅榮桓 437, 513
Luo Ruiqing 羅瑞卿 489, 491, 505, 523, 526, 527, 529, 582, 613
Luo Shilin 羅士琳 57
Luo Yinong 羅亦農 325
Luo Zenan 羅澤南 31, 41, 60, 69
Luo Zhenyu 羅振玉 103, 249, 387
Luoji xue 邏輯學 533
Luomiou yu Zhuliye 羅密歐與朱麗葉 (Romeo and Juliet) 335
Luotuo Xiangzi 駱駝祥子 375
Lushan Plenum (1959) 490, 491
Lü Tiaoyuan 呂調元 293

Lülü xinlun 律呂新論 27

Ma Fuxiang 馬福祥 323
Ma Fuyi 馬福益 214, 217
Ma Hualong 馬化龍 90, 92, 110, 114, 117
Ma Junguang 馬峻光 130
Ma Ke 馬可 595
Ma Lan 馬蘭 433
Ma Lanhua 馬蘭花 473
Ma Li 馬力 599
Ma Liang 馬良 381
Ma Mouyuan 馬茂元 497
Ma Rulong 馬如龍 70, 86
Ma Sicong 馬思聰 541
Ma Wanxuan 馬萬選 116
Ma Wenlu 馬文祿 98, 122
Ma Wucheng 馬武成 46
Ma Xinyi 馬新貽 35, 107/9, 114, 115
Ma Xulun 馬叙倫 333, 419/21, 445, 557
Ma Yanbang 馬彥邦 94
Ma Yinchu 馬寅初 357, 484, 487, 495
Ma Yonglin 馬永琳 180
Ma Zhaoyuan 馬兆元 94
Ma Zhenghe 馬政和 106, 110
Ma Zhongying 馬仲英 350
Macao 28, 30, 39, 40, 42, 126, 137, 156, 158, 211, 434, 452, 536, 614
McMahon line 490, 492, 502
Madagascar 568, 590
Makesi Engesi quanji 馬克思恩格斯全集 475
Malaysia, formerly Malaya 478, 520, 521, 559, 576, 610, 616
Maldives 568
Mali 496, 514, 518, 537, 545
Malraux, André 524
Malta 562, 564, 565, 580, 600
Manchu(s) 218, 223, 237, 243
Manchuria 178, 235, 406, 433, 450; appointments 229, 413; and CCP 416, 418, 424, 428, 430; floods 257; independence 286, 340; and Japan 208, 210, 214, 216, 227, 232, 320, 336, 338, 389; loyal to NG 322, 400; plague epidemic 235, 239; railways 177, 182, 186, 219, 230, 288, 411; reorganization 220; and Russia or USSR 188, 198, 202, 204, 208, 216, 232, 408, 417/19, 443; *see also* Manzhouguo
Manzhouguo 滿洲國 340-8 *passim*

351, 353, 354, 360, 368, 370, 388, 390, 414
Mao Anying 毛岸英 451
Mao Changxi 毛昶熙 111, 141
Mao Dun 茅盾 391, 401, 417, 505, see also Shen Yanbing
Mao Dun lun chuangzuo 茅盾論創作 633
Mao Hongbin 毛鴻賓 93
Mao Memorial Hall, Chairman, Mao zhuxi jinian tang 毛主席紀念堂 598, 600
Mao Tsetung Poems 593
Mao Zedong 毛澤東 316-54 passim, 378-484 passim, 530-601 passim; b. 173; d. 595; early activities 269, 278-83 passim, 291, 295, 307; reevaluation 610, 630, 634/6
Mao Zedong quanji 毛澤東全集 592
Mao Zedong xuanji 毛澤東選集 (Selected Works of Mao Zedong) 449, 453, 459, 463, 497, 592, 601
Mao Zedong Thought 606
Mao Zedong, Quotations from Chairman 543
Mao Zemin 毛澤民 394, 403
Mao Zetan 毛澤覃 357
Mao zhuxi shici 毛主席詩詞 513, 593
Mao Zhuxi yulu 毛主席語錄 533/5
'Maodun lun' 矛盾論 369
Margary, Augustus Raymond 124-30
Maring, G. (pseudonym of H. Sneevliet) 280, 284, 288
Marshall, George C. 413, 418, 420, 422, 430
Marx(ism), (ist) 275, 454, 472
Marxism-Leninism 391, 511/13, 530, 600; -Mao Zedong Thought 550, 572, 598
masses 312, 401, 447, 544, 546
Mauritania 524, 578, 596, 626
Mauritius 564
May Day 279, 430
May Third Incident 320, 326
May Fourth Movement 272
May 7 directive 530, 547; May 7 Cadre School 547, 549
May 16 group 558
May Thirtieth Incident 300, 302, 303
Mazu 馬祖 Islands (Fujian) 484
medicine, medical 191, 445, 497,

511, 523, 525, 533, 565, 607, 609; barefoot doctors 585; Medical Association, Chinese National, Zhonghua yixue hui 中華醫學會 261; Medical College, Peking Union 283; Research Institute of Chinese, Zhongyi yanjiu yuan 中醫研究院 469; Traditional Chinese, Peking Hospital of 473
Mei Lanfang 梅蘭芳 177, 299, 367, 481, 503
Mei Nian 梅念 621
Meishu 美術 593
Meiyun 湄雲 111
Meizhou pinglun 每週評論 271, see also Weekly Critic
Men He 門合 543, 547
Mencius 579
Meng De'en 蒙得恩 71, 73, 77
Meng Yuqi 孟毓奇 176
Menggu youmu ji 蒙古遊牧記 107
Menghua suobu 夢華瑣簿 25
Mengzi jie 孟子解 31
Metamorphosis 385
Mexico 196, 244, 406, 564, 570
Miao 苗 minority 36, 64, 66, 104, 110, 114, 118, 168, 352
Miao Peilin 苗沛霖 86, 88, 95
Miewang 滅亡 329
military 207, 218, 260, 418, 520, 572; academy 155, 156, 183; Academy, Whampoa, Huangpu lujun junguan xuexiao 黃浦陸軍軍官學校 295, 296, 297, 300; Affairs Committee, Junshi weiyuanhui 軍事委員會 295, 301, 307, 321, 340, 345, 413, 419, 534, 536, 541, 545; Affairs Control Committee, Junshi guanzhi weiyuanhui 軍事管制委員會 449, 453, 455; Affairs Council, Junwu yuan 軍務院 258, 260; Revolutionary Affairs Committee, Geming junshi weiyuanhui 革命軍事委員會 432, 437; and Political Committee, Junzheng weiyuanhui 軍政委員會 438, 443; Hubei Preparatory School, Wubei xuetang 武備學堂 187; Training, Bureau of, Lianbing chu 練兵處 210
mill(s), textile 183, 185, 217, 219, 231, 237/9, 287/9, 301/3, 309, 323, 347, 427, 433, 457, 538; cotton mill, zhibu ju 織布局, Dasheng 大生 175, 193, Huasheng 華盛 175, Huaxin 華新

669

219, 259, Jicheng 集成 217, Laogongmao 老公茂 185, Shanghai 135, 163, 173, Sulun 蘇綸 187, Wuchang 169, Yihe 怡和 185; mechanical woollen mill *jiqi zhibu ju* 機器織布局, Lanzhou 139; paper mill 477; silk mill, Qinchang 勤昌 231, Xiehe 協和 237, 239
Min, Queen of Korea 174
Min Dianchen 閔殿臣 124, 129
Minbao 民報 217, 227
mine(s), mining 29, 53, 185, 186, 188, 204, 218/20, 221, 272, 534; diamond 589; gold 161, 267; lead 31, 65; silver 29, 53, 65; see also coal, iron
Ming Qing shidai shangren ji shangye ziben 明清時代商人及商業資本 475
Mingdai de juntun 明代的軍屯 527
Minglun 明倫 Hall 23
Mingshi 明史 579
Minguo ribao 民國日報 299
minorities 446, 448, 449, 452, 456, 457, 516, 519, 626, 631; see also nationalities
Minsheng bao 民生報 317
mint, minting 53/5, 59, 73, 75, 111, 123, 135, 163, 205, 215, 251, 252, 345
Minzu yanjiu 民族研究 487
missionaries 179/81; government policy 93, 99, 101, 195, 203, 251, 533; hostility to 93, 99, 111-13, 121, 149, 167/9, 179, 186-7, 191/3, 195, 199, 213, 219, 223; social activity 85, 203
Mo Dehui 莫德惠 332
Mo Youzhi 莫友芝 117
modernization 91, 119, 549, 598, 601, 612; four modernizations 609, 615
monarchy 256, 257, 262
Mongol Alliance, autonomous government of, *Menggu lianmeng zizhi zhengfu* 蒙古聯盟自治政府 367, 379
Mongolia 186, 242, 248, 254, 274, 280-2, 388, 408, 418; Mongolian Joint Committee, *Mengjiang lianhe weiyuanhui* 蒙疆聯合委員會 368; language 463, 507; nationality 505; People's Republic 298, 358, 360, 368, 376, 388, 451, 452, 454, 459, 467,

494, 503, 506, 510, 516, 540, 566, 571, 572
Mori Arinori 森有禮 128
Morning Post Supplement 275
Morocco 470, 486, 512
Morrison, G.E. 243
Moruo juzuo xuan 沫若劇作選 611
Moscow Declaration 400
Moshushi de qiyu 魔術師的奇遇 505
Moslem(s): disturbances 34, 36, 66, 98; intermarriage 243; to Mecca 619; National Institute, *Guoli Huimin xueyuan* 國立回民學院 439; strike 213; uprisings 30, 33, 64, 70, 88/124 *passim*, 117, 130/4, 180/2
mountaineering 491, 517, 585
Mozambique 606
Mule mingxue 穆勒名學 (*The System of Logic* by John Stuart Mill) 217
Muqin 母親 347
museum(s) 485, 491, 499; of Chinese Art 525; of Chinese History, *Zhongguo lishi bowuguan* 中國歷史博物館 499, 611; of the Chinese Revolution, *Zhongguo geming bowuguan* 中國革命博物館 499; Imperial Palace, *Gugong bowuyuan* 故宫博物院 305
music 443, 449, 475, 577, 609, 621; Central Institute, *Zhongyang yinyue xueyuan* 中央音樂學院 443; National Conservatory, *Guoli yinyue yuan* 國立音樂院 317; see also orchestra
mutiny 236-42, 332, 338
Mutsu Munemitsu 陸奧宗光 176
Muyin 穆蔭 47, 79, 85
Muzhang'a 穆彰阿 43

Naerjing'e 訥爾經額 49, 55
Nagasaki 長崎 Japan 156, 255, 412
Nan Ping 南萍 545, 559
Nanfang ribao 南方日報 546
Nanguo yuekan 南國月刊 329
Naniwa 174
Nanjishan 南麂山 Islands (Zhejiang) 464
Nansha 南沙 (Spratly) Islands 470, 574, 586, 616, 624
Nanyang Public Institute, *Nanyang gongxue* 南洋公學 207
Napoleon III 110

National Assembly (1946-9) *Guomin dahui* 國民大會 418-22, 426, 430/1; (Qing) *Zizheng yuan* 資政院 222, 223, 232-4; (ROC) *Guohui* 國會 244-50, 259/69, 277, 282, 291
National Bureau of Compilation and Translation, *Guoli bianyi guan* 國立編譯館 343, 345
National Chinese Theatre World Association to Resist the Enemy, *Zhonghua quanguo xiju jie kangdi xiehui* 中華全國戲劇界抗敵協會 367
National Convention, *Guomin huiyi* 國民會議 336
National Day 242, 438, 518, 524, 560
National Defence Council, Supreme, *Guofang zuigao weiyuanhui* 國防最高委員會 379, 399, 425
National Defence, Ministry of, *Guofang bu* 國防部 419, 506
National Economic Council, *Quanguo jingji weiyuanhui* 全國經濟委員會 335
National Food Administration, *Quanguo liangshi guanliju* 全國糧食管理局 383, 387
National Government (NG), *Guomin zhengfu* 國民政府 307-436 *passim*, especially left-hand pages; set up 302
National Liberation Front (NLF) of Vietnam 518, 526, 544, 552, 568, 582
National Pacification Army, *Anguo jun* 安國軍 307, 314
National People's Congress, *Quanguo renmin daibiao dahui* 全國人民代表大會 454, 456, 458, 462
National Protection Army, *Huguo jun* 護國軍 256-8
National Relief Commission, *Zhongyang zhenji weiyuanhui* 中央賑濟委員會 411
National Revolutionary Army (NRA), *Guomin geming jun* 國民革命軍 301, 302, 308-12, 318-21, 346
National Salvation Society, *Jiuguo hui* 救國會 355
Nationalist Army, *Guomin jun* 國民軍 304, 306-7, 314, 326-8, 332
Nationalist Party (NP), *Guomin dang* 國民黨 242-429 *passim*, especially left-hand pages and B sections
nationalities 505; Central Institute, *Zhongyang minzu xueyuan* 中央民族學院 445; Publishing House, *Minzu chuban she* 民族出版社 457; Research Institute, *Minzu yanjiu suo* 民族研究所 485
Natong 那桐 197, 209, 215, 219, 229
naval, navy 152, 166, 174-8, 228, 426; academy 141; Fuzhou Dockyard Naval Academy, *Fujian chuanzheng xuetang* 福建船政學堂 133, 143/5, 157; Jiangnan Naval Academy, *Jiangnan shuishi xuetang* 江南水師學堂 167; Ministry of the Navy, *Haijun bu* 海軍部 234, 245, 264
Nepal 468, 472, 476, 492, 494, 500, 509, 524, 537, 574, 590, 604, 625
Nerbudda 22, 23
Netherlands 91, 282, 301, 321, 333, 398, 410, 442, 462, 566, 613; *see also* Dutch, Holland
Netherlands'Syndicate 271
New Army, *Xinjun* 新軍 232, 234-42
New China News Agency (NCNA), *Xinhua tongxun she* 新華通訊社 founded in Yan'an 367
New Fourth Army, *Xinsi jun* 新四軍 384, 386, 388, 389
New Life Movement 351
New People's Study Society, *Xinmin xuehui* 新民學會 269
New Sect, *Xinjiao* 新教 117
New Testament 45
New Youth 265, 269, 275, 279; *see also Xin qingnian*
New Zealand 568, 588, 630
newspapers 191, 567
Ni Sichong 倪嗣沖 262, 264
Ni Yingdian 倪映典 232, 235
Nian 捻 rebels 24, 28-34 *passim*, 46, 50, 54, 60, 62, 66, 74, 78, 84-8, 92-108 *passim*, 119/21
Nianjun 捻軍 459
'Niaoer wenda' 鳥兒問答 593
Nicholas II, Tsar of Russia 176, 182, 186, 262
Nie Er 聶耳 245, 359
Nie Rongzhen 聶榮臻 523
Nie Shicheng 聶士成 174, 196, 201

671

Index

Nie Yuanzi 聶元梓 530, 531, 539, 546
Niger 578, 600
Nigeria 558, 578
'night-bird bandits' (salt smugglers), *xiaofei* 梟匪 104, 106
Nikolaievsk, Russia 43
Nine Power Treaty 284, 285
Nishihara 西原 loans 263, 267
Nishio Juzō 西尾壽造 380
Niu Jian 牛鑑 22, 23
Niu Shixiu 牛世修 192
Nixon, Richard 550, 554, 558, 559, 560, 564, 565, 580, 588
North China Daily News 87, 97
North China Herald 45, 192, 335
North China People's Government 430, 431
North Korea *see* Korea, Democratic People's Republic of
North-east Frontier Agency (NEFA) 490, 506
North-east People's Government 437
Northern Expedition, *Beifa* 北伐 282-8, 296, 308-20 *passim*
Norway 35, 301, 333, 440, 630
NP *see* Nationalist Party
NPC *see* National People's Congress
nuclear, weapons, tests 510, 518, 530-4, 552, 556, 562, 564, 576, 584, 588, 592, 600, 604, 632
Nuclear Research, Joint Institute (with USSR) 473
Nüshen 女神 283

Observance Sect, *Zaili jiao* 在理教 149, 169
Ohira Masayoshi 大平正芳 566, 612, 622, 628
oil field(s), pipeline(s), well(s) 251, 403, 447, 489, 515, 581, 589, 605, 613/15, 625, 628/30; Daqing 大慶 Oilfield 515, 597, 605; Liaohe 遼河 Oilfield 625
Okinawa 沖繩 Ryukyu Islands 136, 560
Ōkubo Toshimichi 大久保利通 124
Oman 606
On Coalition Government 410, 417
'On Contradiction' 369
'On New Democracy' 385
'On Protracted War' 375
'On the Correct Handling of Contradictions among the People' 481
'On the People's Democratic Dictatorship' 439
'On the Ten Major Relationships' 470, 593
'Open Door Policy' 194-8, 204
opera(s) 449, 473, 505, 517, 523, 525, 579, 591, 599; 'model' 553, 557, 561; Peking opera 299, 405, 517, 531, 533, 553, 557, 561, 599, 601, 607, Company of China, *Zhongguo Jingju yuan* 中國京劇院 467, No. 1 Company of Peking, *Beijing Jingju yituan* 北京京劇一團 533; Sixi 四喜 Peking Opera Company 81
opium 149; agreements on 153, 156, 158, 239, 243; conferences on 228, 273, 323, 385; government bans 27, 131, 221, 243, 245, 273, 327; and Taipings 55; tax on 153; traffic in 31;
Opium War 22
oracle bones 195
orchestra(s) 609; Central Symphony, *Zhongyang yuetuan jiaoxiang yuedui* 中央樂團交響樂隊 609; Ozawa Seiji 小澤征爾 609; Philadelphia 573; Philharmonic Society, Chinese Central 609; Vienna Philharmonic 571
Organization Department, *Zuzhi bu* 組織部 321
Oriental Travel Bureau, *Dongfang lüxing she* 東方旅行社 349
Ōtori Keisuke 大鳥圭介 174
Oumei zhengzhi yaoyi 歐美政治要義 221
Ouyang Hai zhi ge 歐陽海之歌 527
Ouyang Shan 歐陽山 491
Ouyang Wu 歐陽武 247
Ouyang Yuqian 歐陽予倩 165, 223, 401, 443, 507
Overseas Chinese 142, 160, 170, 576, 606, 608; Overseas Chinese Affairs Commission, *Huaqiao shiwu weiyuanhui* 華僑事務委員會 508
Ōyama Ikuo 大山郁夫 456

Pakistan 473, 562; border 506, 508; Chinese leaders visit 514, 528; communications 515, 516, 522, 569, 605; establishes relations with China 448; leaders visit China 508, 556, 562, 576,

590, 602, 626
palace(s) 174, 228; Imperial Palace Museum, Gugong bowuyuan 故宮博物院 305; Imperial Palaces 157, 198, 200, 264, 347; Old Summer Palace, Yuanming yuan 圓明園 79, 81, 123; Summer Palace, Yihe yuan 頤和園 171, 190, 192
Pan Dingxin 潘鼎新 108, 152, 155
Pan Duo 潘鐸 85, 95
Pan Fusheng 潘復生 537
Pan Guangdan 潘光旦 351
Pan Shien 潘世恩 41, 43, 61
Pan Shihuang 潘世璜 65
Pan Zuyin 潘祖蔭 51, 89, 119, 147, 167
Panchen Lama 405, 440, 467, 488, 489, 496
Pangu lou yiqi kuanshi 攀古廎彝器款識 119
Papua New Guinea 592
Paris, Accords (1973) 568; Peace Conference (1919) 270-2
parliament 226, 228, 230-4, 237, 242, 262
Pathet Lao (Neo Lao Hak Xat) 488, 498
Patriotic School, Aiguo xueshe 愛國學社 207
peaceful coexistence 460, 470, 484
Pearl River (Guangdong) 28, 286, 442
peasants: in the Cultural Revolution 538, 546, 549, 553, 557; and culture 459, 495, 567; in the economy 435; land reform 419, 433, 445; move to cities 456, 481; role in the revolution 309, 314-18, 331, 426; in Tibet 496
Pei Wenzhong 裴文中 329
Peiping Chronicle 343
Peking and Tientsin Times 175
Peking Man 317, 329, 543, 567
Peking Review 487, 519; *Peking Rundschau* 519
Peking Union of Students of Secondary Schools and Above (Peking Students Union), Beijing zhongdeng yishang xuexiao xuesheng lianhehui 北京中等以上學校學生聯合會 273
Peng Dehuai 彭德懷 320-6, 330/2, 337, 365, 443, 448, 456, 457, 467, 478, 486, 491, 612; d. 581

Peng Pai 彭湃 286, 291, 300, 316, 329
Peng Shaohui 彭紹輝 613
Peng Yulin 彭玉麟 58, 78, 88, 167
Peng Yunzhang 彭蘊章 47, 67
Peng Zhen 彭真 447, 510, 512, 517, 529, 615, 617, 618
Penghu 澎湖 Islands 154, 464, see also Pescadores
People's Anti-Japanese Allied Army, Minzhong kangri tongmeng jun 民衆抗日同盟軍 345, 346
People's China 445
People's Daily 433, 439; see also 452, 455, 457, 469 and many other editorials or articles on policy
People's Liberation Army (PLA), Renmin jiefang jun 人民解放軍 418-442, 448, 453, 464, 486, 488, 500, 508-16, 522, 525, 528-47, 550, 553-9, 584, 598, 608
People's Literary Publishing House, Renmin wenxue chuban she 人民文學出版社 463, 481, 487, 497, 507, 513, 533, 563, 567/9
People's Publishing House, Renmin chuban she 人民出版社 475, 493; Guangdong 491; Shanghai 481, 493, 501, 507
People's Republic of China (PRC) 436-637
Persia 276, see also Iran
Peru 124, 126, 127, 562
Pescadores 154, 178, 400/2, see also Penghu Islands
Philippines 424, 578, 582, 604, 618
Phnom Penh, Cambodia 474, 484, 494, 515, 529, 533, 544, 582, 589, 612
Pi Dingjun 皮定鈞 577, 595
Pi Lin pi Kong wenzhang huibian 批林批孔文章匯編 579
Pi Shushi 皮漱石 479, 505
Pi Xirui 皮錫瑞 45, 225, 229
Pingding Yuefei jilüe 平定粵匪紀略 101
Pingyuan zuozhan 平原作戰 573
Pinhua baojian 品花寶鑑 41
pinyin, Hanyu 473, 485, 617
piracy 38
PLA see People's Liberation Army
plague 41, 177, 235, 239
Planning Commission, State, Guo-

jia jihua weiyuanhui 國家計劃委員會 453, 465, 565, 615, 625
play(s), spoken, *huaju* 話劇 223, 449, 473, 505, 517, 523, 525, 579, 609, 619, 629
Pobi ji 破壁記 633
Poland 392, 438, 446, 459, 476, 482, 483
Police, General Office, *Xunjing zongting* 巡警總廳 218; Ministry of, *Xunjing bu* 巡警部 215; Security Acts 250
Politburo (of the CCP) 592; appointments to 353, 485, 551, 571, 583, 599, 607, 617, 627; major decisions, policies 330, 332, 350, 356, 394, 446, 530, 589; major meetings 352, 354; set up 313; speeches at 470
Political Affairs, Board of, *Zhengshi tang* 政事堂 250; Committee of the North-east Headquarters 413; Consultative Conference, *Zhengzhi xieshang huiyi* 政治協商會議 416, 418, 420, 430, 434; Council, *Zhengzhi huiyi* 政治會議 248, 327; Information Society, *Zhengwen she* 政聞社 224
Polytechnic Institute, *Gezhi shuyuan* 格致書院 155
Pope 479/81; Pius XII 379, 463, 485/7
population: of China 30, 42, 170, 456, 512, 568/70, 578, 618, 626; control 484, 630; of Hongkong 74; UN World Congress 578
Portugal 38, 87, 126, 158-60, 208, 211, 282, 301, 302, 322, 614, 625
postal system 250, 288, 327, 342, agreements 282, 440, 454, 515, 524, appointments 183, established 22, 180, strikes 341/3; Postal Bureau, General of CPG 444; Posts and Communications, Ministry of, *Youchuan bu* 郵傳部 218, 229, 235, 236
Press Association, Chinese National, *Zhongguo xinwen xuehui* 中國新聞學會 391, 407
Procuratorate, Supreme People's, *Zuigao renmin jianchashu* 最高人民檢查署 437, 439, 449, 461
Progressive Party, *Jinbu dang* 進步黨 246

Progressive Society, *Gongjin hui* 共進會 236
proletariat, dictatorship of the 585, 596
propaganda 385, 447
Propaganda Department, *Xuanchuan bu* 宣傳部 321, 401, 478, 495, 517
Protect the Country Society, *Baoguo hui* 保國會 191
Protestant(s) 167, 199
provincial assembly(ies), *ziyi ju* 諮議局 224-34, 242, 248, 260
Pu Fa zhanji 普法戰記 123
Pu Songling ji 蒲松齡集 507
Public Health, Ministry of, *Weisheng bu* 衛生部 479
Public Order, Provisional Measures for the Maintenance of 427
Public Security, Ministry of, *Gongan bu* 公安部 510, 512, 516, 520
Pujun 溥儁 197, 203
Pulun 溥倫 223
Punishments, Board of, *Xingbu* 刑部 214
puppet(s) 467
Putong yuyinxue gangyao 普通語音學綱要 481
putonghua 普通話 473
Puxing 溥興 197
Puyi see Emperor

Qi Baishi 齊白石 97, 419, 483
Qi Baishi yanjiu 齊白石研究 491
Qi Baishi zuopin ji 齊白石作品集 513
Qi Gong 祁墳 27
Qi Junzao 祁雋藻 43, 75, 105, 107
Qi Xieyuan 齊燮元 296-300
Qian Jiang 錢江 23, 25
Qian Mu 錢穆 385
Qian Nengxun 錢能訓 269, 270, 273
Qian Sanqiang 錢三強 509/11
Qian Xuesen 錢學森 509/11
Qian Yiji 錢儀吉 45
Qian Yingpu 錢應溥 179
Qian Zhongshu 錢鍾書 421
Qianfeng 前鋒 293
Qianfo 千佛 Caves 195, 233
Qiangfa zhunsheng 槍法準繩 153
Qiangxue bao 強學報 185
Qianlong 乾隆 Emperor 22
Qianpi ting guzhuan tushi

千甓亭古塼圖釋 169
Qiantang 錢塘 River (Zhejiang) 311
Qianxian 前綫 487, 501
Qiao Guanhua 喬冠華 562, 577, 582, 583, 584, 591
Qiao Xiaoguang 喬曉光 597
Qielilüe zhuan 伽俐略傳 (*Leben des Galilei*, *Life of Galileo*) 619
Qiling 耆齡 89
Qin Bangxian 秦邦憲 337, 349, 423
Qin Dingsan 秦定三 68
Qin Lishan 秦力山 203
Qin Rigang 秦日綱 56, 60-6
Qinding junci shilu 欽定軍次實錄 87
Qinding shijie tiaoli 欽定士階條例 85
Qinding yingjie guizhen 欽定英傑歸眞 87
Qing 慶 Prince 151, 203, *see also* Yikuang
'Qingchun' 青春 261
Qingchun zhi ge 青春之歌 487
Qingchunqi weisheng 青春期衛生 579
Qingdao ribao 青島日報 439
Qinghe 清河 (Zhili) 84
Qinglian 青蓮 sect 30
Qingming qianhou 清明前後 417
'Qingnian yu nongcun' 青年與農村 275
Qingnian zazhi 青年雜誌 257
Qingqi 慶祺 75
Qingru xuean 清儒學案 373
Qingrui 慶瑞 77
Qingshi gao 清史稿 323
Qingtong shidai 青銅時代 417
Qingyi bao 清議報 193
Qinming wenheng zhengzongcai jingzhong junshi Ganwang baozhi 欽命文衡正總裁精忠軍師干王寶製 77
Qishan 琦善 35, 37, 41, 54, 56, 59, 61
Qiu 秋 385
Qiu Jin 秋瑾 222, 225
Qiu Qingquan 邱清泉 441
Qiu Zhonghui 邱鐘惠 499
Qixi baihu tuan 奇襲白虎團 569
Qixiu 啟秀 191, 197
Qiying 耆英 22-37 *passim*, 43, 72; d. 75
Qu Hongji 瞿鴻璣 205, 271
Qu Qiubai 瞿秋白 197, 313, 320, 332, 337, 357
Qu Qiubai wenji 瞿秋白文集 463
Qu Yuan 屈原 395
Quan shanggu Sandai Qin Han Sanguo Liuchao wen 全上古三代秦漢三國六朝文 527
Quan Songci 全宋詞 527
Quanguo xinshu mu 全國新書目 449
Quanqing 全慶 119, 135, 141
Quanshan yaoyan 勸善要言 169
Quanshi liangyan 勸世良言 27
Quanxue pian 勸學篇 193
Quemoy 金門 Island and Little Quemoy 小金門 Island (Fujian) 462, 484, 486, 524, 612
quyi 曲藝 (ballads) 373

radio(-telephone) 358, 376, 392, 396, 398, 415, 452, 484, 502, 511, 539/41; Radio Administration 392; *see also* broadcasting
railways 128/30, 186, 188, 194, 202, 204, 208, 228/30, 234/6, 272, 284, 290, 326, 356; strikes 283, 293, 295; *see also* A sections *passim*
Railway(s): Cooperation Organization of Socialist Countries 515; General Trade Union, Peking-Hankou, *Jing Han lu zong gonghui* 京漢路總工會 291, 293, 295; Ministry of, *Tiedao bu* 鐵道部 441, 489; Protection League, *Baolu tongzhi hui* 保路同志會 236; Protection League Army, *Baolu tongzhi jun* 保路同志軍 236; Workers' General Union, All-China, *Quanguo tielu zong gonghui* 全國鐵路總工會 297
Rangoon, Burma 376, 392, 460, 471, 474, 492, 499, 514, 538, 544
Rao Shushi 饒漱石 443, 457, 458, 461
Rawalpindi, Pakistan 522
Records of a Historian 491
Rectification Campaign 395, 399, 401, 476-80, 498, 517
Red Army 314/56 *passim*, 321; reorganized into Eighth Route Army 366
Red Cross 212, 213, 450, 453
Red Detachment of Women 561, *see also Hongse niangzi jun*
Red Flag: as exponent of policy

675

Index

statements 494, 499, 512, 520, 522, 529, 531, 536, 547/9, 568, 573, 574, 578, 585, 588, 596/8, 600; as source of articles or dramas 527, 553, 557, 567, 569, 573, 611; see also *Hongqi*
Red Guards 532, 533, 536, 540-6, 549
Red Lantern see *Hongdeng ji*
Red Spears Society, *Hongqiang hui* 紅槍會 306
Red Turbans, *Hongjin* 紅巾會 60/4
Ren Bishi 任弼時 213, 350, 356-60, 413, 447
Ren Guangchun 任光椿 633
Ren Kecheng 任可澄 256
Ren Rong 任榮 561
Ren, shou, gui 人獸鬼 421
Renmin ribao 人民日報 see *People's Daily*
Renmin wenxue 人民文學 469, 611
Renmin xiju 人民戲劇 593
Renmin yinyue 人民音樂 445
'Renmin zhanzheng shengli wansui' 人民戰争勝利萬歲 527
renminbi 人民幣 575/7
Republic of China (ROC), *Zhonghua minguo* 中華民國 240-437
Republic of China People's Government 346, 348
'Republic or Monarchy?' 257
Republican Party, *Gonghe dang* 共和黨 240
requisition 447, 453, 455, 457
reservoir(s) 461, 483; Dahuofang 大夥房 483; Danjiangkou 丹江口 575; Guanting 官廳 461, 467; Ming Tombs 483; Sanmen 三門 Gorge 483; Shenzhen 深圳 493, 495
Restoration Society, *Guangfu hui* 光復會 212, 222
Revenue, Board of, *Hubu* 户部 63, 211, 214, 215, 227
revisionism(ists) 508, 510, 511/13, 517, 522, 529, 538, 585
Revive China Society, *Xingzhong hui* 興中會 176, 180
revolution(ary) 314, 516, 517, 525, 532, 534-6; Committee (of NP) 428, 430; Committees (in Cultural Revolution), *Geming weiyuanhui* 革命委員會 537/9, 545/7, 548, 557, 588, 604; January Revolution 534
Riben fangshu zhi 日本訪書志 187
Riben guozhi 日本國志 167
Riben zashi shi 日本雜事詩 139
rice 105, 220/2, 232, 423, 451, 453, 493, 503, 528
Richu 日出 363
rickshaw(s) 121, 234
Rickshaw Boy 375
Righteous and Courageous Army, *Yiyong jun* 義勇軍 342
Righteous and Harmonious Militia, *Yihe tuan* 義和團 190, 253, see also Boxers
Righteous People's Society, *Yimin hui* 義民會 190
rightists, anti- 477, 478, 479, 480, 483/5, 490
Rites, Board of, *Libu* 禮部 146, 214
ROC see Republic of China
Rong Hong (Yung Wing) 容閎 81, 91, 119, 122, 124, 125, 127
Ronglu 榮禄 175, 183, 188, 189, 192, 211
Rongqing 榮慶 209, 211, 213, 215, 219
Rongquan 榮全 116
Roosevelt, Franklin D. 365, 390, 392, 393, 395, 396, 398, 400, 402, 405, 406, 408, 410
Royal Asiatic Society 75
Ruan Lingyu 阮玲玉 357
Ruan Yuan 阮元 43
Ruan Zhangjing 阮章竟 513, 519
Ruanda 462, 606
rubber 453, 493, 503
Ruichang 瑞常 82, 117
Ruilin 瑞麟 55, 79, 80, 99, 103, 117, 122
Ruizheng 瑞澂 229, 233, 236
Rumania 494; agreements 459, 563, 605; Chinese leaders visit 522, 530, 598, 608; establishes diplomatic relations 438; leaders visit China 482, 514, 558/60, 604, 634
Russell, Bertrand 279
Russia 58/72 *passim*, 96, 108/20 *passim*, 130/48 *passim*, 166/278 *passim*; A sections 37, 43, 45/7, 109/11, 169, 177, 193, 241, 251, 259; see also USSR
Russian Academy of Sciences 415
Russo-Japanese War 210, 214/16
Ryukyu Islands 105, 136

Sa Bendong 薩本棟 441

Index

Sa Zhenbing 薩鎮冰 277
Sa'id Yakub 132
Saifudin 467, 583, 598
Saigon, Vietnam 122, 582, *see also* Ho Chi Minh City
Saishang'a 賽尚阿 43, 47, 49
salt 35, 137, 145, 247, 393
Samoa, Western 584, 592, 628
San 傘 633
Sanbamen 三巴門 (Guangdong) 28
'Sanjia cun zhaji' 三家村札記 501, 531
Sanjia xiang 三家巷 491
Sanli wan 三里灣 469
Sanshang Taofeng 三上桃峰 579
Sanxia wuyi 三俠五義 139
Sanzijing 三字經 51
São Tomé and Principe 582, 586
Saodang bao 掃蕩報 375
Sasaki Ryōsaku 佐佐木良作 610
satellite 554, 558, 584, 586, 592, 594, 602
Saying'a 薩迎阿 43
Schantung-Eisenbahn-Gesellschaft 193
school(s) 203, 219, 231, 233, 237, 269, 323, 343, 523, 541/3, 548, 549, 553, 599, 607, 629; of the Association of Approaching Peace, Shengping *shexue* 昇平社學 27, 29; Beiyang Women's Normal 219; for Gathering Talent, *Chucai xuetang* 儲才學堂 183; Girls' Normal, *Nüzi shifan xuetang* 女子師範學堂 227; Jingye 敬業 Middle 213; Nantong 南通 Normal 209; Sanjiang 三江 Normal 209; Self-Strengthening, *Ziqiang xuetang* 自強學堂 171/3; Wenhua 文華 243
science(s), -tists 517, 525
Science and Technology, Council for the Promotion of 399
Science Publishing House 481
Sciences, Hall of 517
Scientific and Technical Association, Chinese, *Zhongguo kexue jishu xiehui* 中國科學技術協會 629
secret societies 36/8, 40, 46, 47, 50, 106, 166, 220, 222
Secretary of State, *Guowu qing* 國務卿 250, 258
Seismological Society, Chinese, *Zhongguo dizhen xuehui* 中國地震學會 622
Selected Works of Mao Tse-tung 519, 596

self-criticism 525, 532, 540
Self-Study University, *Zixiu daxue* 自修大學 283
Senate, *Canyi yuan* 參議院 240-4, 262, 266
Senegal 562, 576
Senggelinqin 僧格林沁 58, 62, 63, 73, 79, 80, 92-8, 101
'Serve the People' 403, 407
Seychelles 590, 604
Sha Mengbi 沙夢弼 El Hadj Yusuf 569
Sha Wenhan 沙文漢 477/9, 483
Shadi Mirza 108
Shajiabang 沙家濱 557
Shandong Army, clique 306, 308, 309, 312
Shandong Peninsula 65
Shang Xiaoyun 尚小雲 201, 595
Shanghai Steam Navigation Company 87, 131
Shanghai Steamship Company 105
Shanghai xinbao 上海新報 87, 119
Shanquan ji 山泉集 513
Shao Can 邵燦 49
Shao Piaoping 邵飄萍 279, 309, 311
Shao Youlian 邵友濂 173, 176
Shaonian piaobozhe 少年飄泊者 311
Shaoshu minzu shige xuan 少數民族詩歌選 587
Shashibiya quanji 莎士比亞全集 (*Complete Works of William Shakespeare*) 611
Shehui ribao 社會日報 309
Shen Baozhen 沈葆楨 35, 123-8, 131, 135, 137-9
Shen Bingcheng 沈秉成 155
Shen Bingkun 沈秉堃 237
Shen Chong 沈崇 421
Shen Guifen 沈桂芬 99, 105, 111, 140, 145
Shen Jiaben 沈家本 249, 513
Shen Junru 沈鈞儒 428, 437, 513
Shen Yanbing 沈雁冰 pen name Mao Dun 茅盾 283, 347, 466
Shen Zhaolin 沈兆霖 85, 89, 91
Shenbao 申報 119, 353
Sheng Shicai 盛世才 348, 350, 353, 383, 394-8, 403, 405
Sheng Xuanhuai 盛宣懷 29, 121, 179, 183, 185, 194, 225/7, 235, 261
Shengbao 勝保 54-8, 63, 72-4, 75, 93, 95
Shengshi weiyan 盛世危言 173

677

Index

Shengtai 升泰 162-4
Shengwu ji 聖武記 25
Shengyun 升允 215, 229
Shenma shi weiwuzhuyi? 甚麼是唯物主義？ 633
Shenyang 沈陽 Incident 336, 560
Shenyang budui quyi zuopin xuan 沈陽部隊曲藝作品選 601/3
Shenzhou ribao 神州日報 225
Shi Dakai 石達開 46, 47, 52, 56, 62/6, 70/92 *passim*; appointments 47, 67; d. 95
Shi Liangcai 史量才 353
Shi pipan shu 十批判書 417
Shi Tuo 師陀 pen name of Wang Changjian 王長簡 433
Shi Yukun 石玉昆 139
Shi Zhaoji 施肇基 (Alfred Sze) 135, 282, 336, 487
Shi Zhenxiang 石貞祥 56/8
Shigemitsu Mamoru 重光葵 331
Shiji 史記 491
Shijie ditu ji 世界地圖集 569
Shijie ribao 世界日報 305
Shijie wanbao 世界晚報 299
Shijie zazhi 世界雜誌 339
Shikan 詩刊 481
ship(s), shipping 215, 261, 465, 483, 489, 495, 499, 515, 551, 598, 603/5, 623, 627; shipyard 207, 261; Yesong 耶松 shipyard 207; *see also* dockyard
Shishi yuebao 時事月報 335
Shishido Tamaki 宍戶璣 136
Shiwu bao 時務報 185, 191
Shixu 世續 211, 215, 219, 231
Shouchang wenji 守常文集 439
Shu Qingchun 舒慶春 *see* Lao She
Shuangmei ying'an congshu 雙楳景闇叢書 225
Shuangye hong si eryue hua 霜葉紅似二月花 401
Shuibian 蛻變 385
Shuihu quanzhuan 水滸全傳 587
Shuihu zhuan 水滸傳 (*Water Margin*) 47, 405, 585, 599
Shuji tang jinyue 庶幾堂今樂 81
'Shumin de shengli' 庶民的勝利 271
Shumu dawen 書目答問 129
Shuntian fuzhi 順天府志 157
Shuntian shibao 順天時報 279
Shuofang beisheng 朔方備乘 81
Shuowen guzhou bu 説文古籀補 153
Shuxing'a 舒興阿 47

Siberia 266-70, 276, 288
Sichuan guanyun yan an leibian 四川官運鹽案類編 145
Sidalin xuanji 斯大林選集 381
Siems Carey Railway and Canal Co. 259
Sierra Leone 560, 574
Sihanouk, Norodom 470, 484, 496, 508, 518, 524, 542, 552/4, 571, 582, 584, 586
Sikkim 158-64, 172, 206, 524, 542, 562, 578, 625
Siku quanshu 四庫全書 351
Siku quanshu zongmu tiyao buzheng 四庫全書總目提要補正 519
Silk 113, 157; Silk Route 551; *see also* mills, textile
Sima Guang 司馬光 475
Singapore 392, 521, 590, 610, 628, 632
Sino-Soviet Friendship Association, *Zhongsu youhao xiehui* 中蘇友好協會 439
Sleeping Dragon Society, *Wolong hui* 卧龍會 30
Small Sword Society, *Xiaodao hui* 小刀會 56, 62, 65
Smedley, Agnes 364, 621
Snow, Edgar 358/60, 574
Social Affairs, Ministry (Bureau) of, *Shehui bu (ju)* 社會部 (局) 433
Social Sciences, Chinese Academy of, *Zhongguo shehui kexue yuan* 中國社會科學院 607, 609, 617
Social Sciences in China 633
socialism, socialist 471, 482, 485, 497, 509, 578
Socialist Education Movement, *Shehuizhuyi jiaoyu yundong* 社會主義教育運動 504, 510, 512, 518, 520
Society for Planning Peace, *Chouan hui* 籌安會 254, 257
Society for the Diffusion of Knowledge, *Guangxue hui* 廣學會 179
Society for the Study of Marxist Theory, *Makesi xueshuo yanjiu hui* 馬克斯學説研究會 279
Society for the Study of National Strengthening, *Qiangxue hui* 強學會 179, 183
Society for the Study of Socialism, *Shehuizhuyi yanjiu hui*

678

社會主義研究會 273
Society for the Study of Sun Yat-sen's Principles, *Sun Wen zhuyi xuehui* 孫文主義學會 303
Society of Arts and Drama, *Yishu jushe* 藝術劇社 333
Soejima Taneomi 副島種臣 120
Somalia 496, 509, 510, 514, 524, 564, 604
Song Jiaoren 宋教仁 147, 208, 236, 243, 244, 249, 275
Song Jin 宋晋 119
Song Jingshi 宋景詩 84, 90, 92, 98
Song Meiling 宋美齡 316, 367, 415, 431
Song of Youth, The 487
Song Qingling 宋慶齡 313, 316, 437, 480, 489, 521, 583
Song Shaowen 宋劭文 371
Song Yuan xiqu shi 宋元戲曲史 245
Song Zhenming 宋振明 627
Song Zheyuan 宋哲元 326, 345, 355, 356, 364, 387
Song Ziwen 宋子文 (T.V. Soong) 308, 331, 425; appointments 295, 347, 389, 411, 413, 431; as Minister of Foreign Affairs 392, 394, 396, 400, 408/10
Songfan 松番 179, 199, 215
Songshou 松壽 223, 239
Sonoda Sunao 園田直 608
South Korea *see* Korea, Republic of
South-east Asia, Collective Defence Treaty 462; Treaty Organization (SEATO) 498
Southern Manchurian Railway Company 219, 411
Souphanouvong 498
Souvanna Phouma 472, 498, 508, 514
soviet areas 316, 318, 322/6, 330-8 *passim*, 342, 345-52 *passim*
Soviet Union *see* USSR and Russia
Spain 95, 127, 132, 160, 202, 301, 322, 570, 606
Sparks from the Lantern Sect, *Denghua jiao* 燈花教 72
spoken play *(huaju) see* play
Sri Lanka 566, 596, 620, *see also* Ceylon
Stalin, Josef 310, 314, 381, 408, 410, 412, 438, 452, 456, 470, 536
Standard Histories 153, 351, 611
Standard Oil Company 251

State Capital Construction Commission, *Guojia jiben jianshe weiyuanhui* 國家基本建設委員會 523
State Council (of PRC) 509, 563, 603; appointments to 461, 521/3, 599; directives, notices etc. 481, 505, 534/6, 542, 546; policy decisions 473, 477, 478, 488, 511, 607, 615, 617, 625; reorganized 470
Statistical Bureau, State, *Guojia tongji ju* 國家統計局 462, 618, 626
statistics 615, 618, 626
Stein, Dr Mark Aurel 201, 223
Stilwell, General Joseph 395, 398, 400, 404, 405, 406, 408
strikes 311; arsenals 165, 249; banned 427; Belgian Tram Company 343; British-American Tobacco Company 269, 317; British International Export Company 303; CCP to organize 330; dockyards 261, 539; general 213, 272, 300, 312, 315, 611; Hongkong 151, 287, 308; iron and steel works 179; mills 217, 219, 231, 237, 239, 287, 289, 301/3, 309, 323, 347, 433; mines 147, 289, 303/5; postal workers 341/3; printing offices 261; railways 283, 293; students 272, 273, 283, 293, 302, 303, 415, 422, 427, 433; teachers 277, 283, 433
Strong, Anna Louise 420, 557
student(s) 557, 567, 585, 609, 619; in CCP campaigns 479, 534, 538; demonstrations against Japan 338, 356; demonstrations against US 430, 522; and examinations 573; female raped 421, 422; government or official action against 277, 315/17, 339, 413, 433, 437; protests against authorities 355, 425/7, 631; and USSR 480, 510, 536; *see also* strikes
Student(s): Associations, National Union of, *Quanguo xuesheng hui lianhehui* 全國學生會聯合會 273; Christian Federation 287; Federation, Chinese National, *Zhonghua quanguo xuelian* 中華全國學聯 437; in Japan, National Salvation Corps of, *Liu Ri xuesheng jiuguo tuan* 留日

679

學生救國團 269; Union, Chinese, *Zhongguo xuesheng lianhehui* 中國學生聯合會 427; Union, National, *Quanguo xuesheng lianhehui* 全國學生聯合會 273, 274, 276, 523
Su Jingguan 蘇井觀 521
Su Yu 粟裕 485
Su Zhenhua 蘇振華 591, 623
Subao 蘇報 187, 209
Sudan 470, 486, 514, 554, 598
Sugiyama Akira 杉山彬 196, 202
Summer Palace *see* palace
Sun Baoqi 孫寶琦 251, 295
Sun Chuanfang 孫傳芳 300, 301, 304, 307, 308/10, 312
Sun Daoren 孫道仁 237
Sun Dezhang 孫德彰 257
Sun Fo 孫科 341, 355, 377, 399, 425, 431/3, 435
Sun Jiagu 孫家穀 105, 106, 114
Sun Jian 孫建 583
Sun Jia'nai 孫家鼐 183, 185, 189, 191, 205, 211, 223, 231
Sun Juxian 孫菊仙 341
Sun Liangcheng 孫良誠 394
Sun Wen xueshuo 孫文學說 271
Sun Yatsen 孫逸仙 179, 210, 240-301 *passim*, 317, 326, 436; author 271, 293, 475; b. 105; d. 305; 'father of the country' 385; first revolts 178, 180, 198, 200, 222/6, 232, 234; kidnapped in London 182; provisional President of ROC 237; sets up United League 214, 216; student 137, 171; suggests reform 175
Sun Yefang 孫冶方 529
Sun Yirang 孫詒讓 39, 163, 229
Sun Yue 孫岳 307
Sun Yuwen 孫毓汶 151, 155, 179
Sun Zhongshan xiansheng xuanji 孫中山先生選集 417, 475
Sun Zhongshan xuanji 孫中山選集 475
Sunrise 363
Supreme State Conference, *Zuigao guowu huiyi* 最高國務會議 470, 473, 476, 478
Surinam 590
Sushun 肅順 85, 87
Suxie sanpian 速寫三篇 401
Suzuki Kantarō 鈴木貫太郎 412
Sweden 35, 171, 227, 301, 321, 408/10, 442
Switzerland 382, 442, 516, 571, 604
Syria 472, 522, 537

Ta shi yige ruo nüzi 她是一個弱女子 343
Table Tennis 499, 519, 523, 558, 561/3, 567, 572, 573, 579; Afro-Asian Tournament 563
Taewongun 146, 156, 174
Taicang 太倉 (Jiangsu) 52, 130, 376
Taidong ribao 泰東日報 227
Taiping(s) 27, 46-102 *passim*, 119/21
Taiping jiushi ge 太平救世歌 55
Taiping lizhi 太平禮制 51, 75
Taiping tianguo 太平天國 455
Taiping tianguo shishi luncong 太平天國史事論叢 357
Taiping tianguo shishi rizhi 太平天國史事日誌 16, 421
Taiping tianri 太平天日 89
Taiping tiaogui 太平條規 51
Taiping zhaoshu 太平詔書 51
Taixu 太虛 297, 429
Taiyang zhaozai Sanggan he shang 太陽照在桑乾河上 433
Taiyong 台勇 59
Takahira Kogorō 高平小五郎 228
Takasaki Tatsunosuke 高碕達之助 503
Takezoe Shinichirō 竹添進一郎 140, 152
'Talks at the Yan'an Forum on Literature and Art' 401, 567, 599
Tan Furen 譚甫仁 547, 557
Tan Fuying 譚富英 603
Tan Haoming 譚浩明 264, 278
Tan Kah Kee 陳嘉庚 (Chen Jiageng) 125, 283, 503
Tan Pingshan 譚平山 475
Tan Qilong 譚啓龍 599
Tan Renfeng 譚人鳳 236, 238
Tan Shaoguang 譚紹光 86, 88, 92-4, 95
Tan Shengbin 譚生彬 635
Tan Sitong 譚嗣同 101, 189, 192, 193
Tan Tingxiang 譚廷襄 71, 99
Tan Xinpei 譚鑫培 37, 267
Tan Yankai 譚延闓 246, 278, 291, 307, 321, 327, 335
Tan Zhen 覃振 429
Tan Zhenlin 譚震林 485, 489, 523, 536, 572, 583
Tan Zhonglin 譚鐘麟 143, 171, 175, 179, 180
Tanaka Giichi 田中義一 320/2
Tanaka Kakuei 田中角榮 566

Tang Caichang 唐才常 198, 200, 201
Tang Hualong 湯化龍 125, 271
Tang Jingxing 唐景星 155
Tang Jinzhao 湯金釗 69
Tang Jiong 唐炯 146
Tang Jiyao 唐繼堯 256, 259, 260, 265-9 *passim*, 277, 296, 312, 313, 319
Tang Mingzhao 唐明照 512
Tang Shaoyi 唐紹儀 125, 262, 270, 276, 278; appointments 211, 243, 269, 277, 287, 337; b. 87; d. 377; discussions on Tibet 214, 218
Tang Shouqian 湯壽潛 237
Tang Xianzu ji 湯顯祖集 507
Tang Yihe 唐一和 409
Tang Yixun 唐義訓 82
Tang Yongkuan 湯永寬 633
Tang Yongtong 湯用彤 519
Tanganyika *see* Tanzania
Tangdai Fojiao 唐代佛教 621
Tanggu 塘沽 (Hebei) 350, 414, 451; Truce Agreement 346, 348
Tangshi xuan 唐詩選 497
Tansuo 探索 621
Tanzania 500, 522, 537, 545, 576, 598, 610
Tao Enpei 陶恩培 65
Tao Jingsun 陶晶孫 455
Tao Juyin 陶菊隱 487
Tao Mo 陶模 168, 171, 183, 199
Tao Xinchun 陶新春 104
Tao Xingzhi 陶行知 423
Tao Xisheng 陶希聖 380, 397
Tao Zhu 陶鑄 523, 525, 529, 530/2, 540, 553, 612
Tao-ism, -ist 47, 619; Chinese Association, *Zhongguo Daojiao xiehui* 中國道教協會 479, 501, 629
Taoyuan 桃園 production brigade 516
Taozhai cangshi ji 陶齋藏石記 231
Taozhai jijin lu 陶齋吉金錄 227
Taqibu 塔齊布 58, 65
Tariff Revision Committee 285, 291
Tashkent, Russia 276
Tatsu maru 辰丸 224, 226
tax, -ation 218, 281, 311/13, 319, 349, 381, 389, 409, 509, 627
telegraph, -gram 132, 147, 153, 509; Chengdu-Geneva 382; cut 197, 311; Imperial Telegraph Administration, *Dianbao zongju* 電報總局 142, 145; international agreements or contracts 153, 197, 255, 454, 515, 524; loan for 267; schools 141; Shanghai-Colombo 514; Shanghai-Havana 502; Shanghai-Hongkong 115; Shanghai-London 115/17; *see also* telephone
telephone(s) 142, 440, 444, 522, 570, *see also* telegraph
television 511, 605; Peking 487
'Ten-thousand-word letter' 162, 179
ten-year plan 604
Teng Haiqing 滕海清 539
Thailand 390, 582, 610, 613, 625, 628, 632
Thakot, Pakistan 605
theatre(s) 81, 115, 251, 585; children's 473; North China Festival 577/9; Sanqing 三慶 Company 81; *see also* drama, opera
Thistle 68
Three-Antis Movement, *Sanfan yundong* 三反運動 448, 450, later Five-Antis
Three Autonomies Movement, *Sanzi yundong* 三自運動 445, 447, 463
Three Family Lane 491
Three Harmonies Society, *Sanhe hui* 三合會 30, 42; *see also* Heaven and Earth Society and Triads
three people's principles 290, 486
Three People's Principles Youth Corps, *Sanminzhuyi qingnian tuan* 三民主義青年團 373
'Three Principles of the People are the Tool for Creating a New World', '*Sanminzhuyi wei zaocheng xin shijie zhi gongju*' 三民主義爲造成新世界之工具 283
Thunder 355
Thunderstorm 357
Tian Han 田漢 193, 329, 333/5, 367, 401, 487, 501, 531, 549
Tian Jiyun 田際雲 305
Tiananmen geming shichao 天安門革命詩抄 601
Tiananmen 天安門 Incident 588, 601, 609, 610, 611; Square 438, 530/2, 554, 590, 592, 598
Tiananmen shichao 天安門詩抄 601

681

'Tiananmen shijian zhenxiang'
天安門事件真相 611
Tianchao tianmou zhidu 天朝
田畝制度 55
Tianfu huangshangdi yanti huang-zhao 天父皇上帝言題皇詔
51
Tianfu shi 天父詩 71
Tianfu xiafan zhaoshu 天父
下凡詔書 51
Tianji 恬吉 107, 108
Tianjin shibao 天津時報 159
Tianli yaolun 天理要論 61
Tianming zhaozhi zhu 天命詔
旨書 51
Tianqing daoli shu 天情道
理書 61
Tiantiao shu 天條書 51
Tianyan lun 天演論 (*Evolution and Ethics* by Huxley) 185
Tianye de feng 田野的風 343
Tibet 497, 503; appointments 161, 211, 453, 467, 488, 509, 516, 523, 547, 561; Autonomous Region 511, 516, 523, 547, 584; set up 524; and Britain 156, 158, 164, 206, 214, and non-interference 218, 222, 242, trade 34, 172, 227, troops to 160, 240, Younghusband expedition 208, 210; China sends troops to 230, 232, 266, 268, 448; communications 405, 451/3, 461, 465, 471, 521; democratic reforms 490, 496; floods in 463; intermarriage 243; and Mongolia 244; negotiations with China on 446/8, 448; and Nepal 472, 590; Panchen Lama on independence 440; rebellion in 488; reforms in 1980 625, 626; schools in 501; Simla conference 248, 250
Tie Ying 鐵瑛 597
Tieliang 鐵良 215, 218, 219
T'ien Hsia Monthly 357
Tieyun canggui 鐵雲藏龜 209
Timor, East 586
Tōa dōbun shoin 東亞同文書院
(East Asia Common Culture Academy) 203
Togo 566, 578
Tokyo Shibaura 芝蒲 Electric Co. 605
Tong Dizhou 童第周 623
Tong, Hollington K. 369
'Tong yinyue gongzuozhe de tanhua' 同音樂工作者的談話 621

Tonghak (Eastern Learning) 172
Tongking, Indochina (French) 126, 146, 148, 150, 158
Tongxiang Lao xiansheng yigao 桐鄉勞先生遺稿 319
trade, trade agreements: Albania 489, 499, 503, Australia 499, 571; Austria 111; Bangladesh 597; Belgium 31; Brazil 139; British 25, 73, 184, 205, 455, 613, *see also* Tibet; Burma 184, 465; Canada 499; Ceylon 453, 493, 503; Chile 295, 451; and China Open Door Policy 194; cities opened for trade 25, 49, 79, 83, 87, 129, 130, 211, 216, 251, 255, 285; Cuba 494, 499, 509; Denmark 30, 91; Ethiopia 559; European Economic Community 603; fairs 483, 537; French 73, 150, 154, 156, 158, 605/7; Germany 83, 443; Ghana 500; Greece 569; India 451, 460; Indonesia 457; inland 137; Italy 103; Japan 117, 178, 209, 284, 457, 483, 503, 505, 555, 603; Korea 145, 194, 503, 555; Kuwait 627; Malaysia 559; Ministry of Trade, *Maoyi bu* 貿易部 443; Netherlands 91; Norway 35; Poland 483; Portugal 87, 211, 625; Russia (or USSR) 109, 138, 337; Spain 95; stopped 65, 111; superintendent of trade, *tongshang dachen* 通商大臣 82, 85, 103, 114, 119, 121, 142, 151; Sweden 35, 227; US 73, 77, 209, 615, 625; Vietnam 154, 156, 158, 477, 489, 505
trade union(s) 439, 443/5; Act 327/9, 401; All-China General, *Zhonghua quanguo zong gonghui* 中華全國總工會 312, 313, 315/17, 433; Congress 571/3, 609; General, *Zong gonghui* 總工會 303/5, 315/17; Law 443/5; World Federation of 497
tram system 225, 343
Trans-Continental Offensive (1944) 402, 404, 406, 408
Treaty: of Amity, Sino-Afghan 402, Sino-Costa Rican 404, Sino-Mexican 406; of the Bogue 24; Boundary, Sino-Burmese 496, 498; of Commerce and Navigation, Sino-Albanian 499; Concerning the Question of Dual Nationality, Sino-Indonesian 466, 496;

of Friendship and Alliance, Sino-Soviet 412; of Friendship, Alliance and Mutual Assistance, Sino-Soviet 440/2, 616; of Friendship and Cooperation, Sino-Czechoslovakian 496, Sino-German 468, Sino-Hungarian 488, Soviet-Vietnamese 610; of Friendship and Mutual Assistance, Sino-Mongolian 494; of Friendship and Mutual Non-Aggression, Sino-Afghan 494/6, Sino-Cambodian 496; of Kuldja 47; of Livadia 138/42; of Mutual Defence, Sino-American 462; of Nanjing 22, 24, 26; New, Sino-American 396, 398, Sino-British 396, 398, Sino-Canadian 402, Sino-Dutch 410, Sino-Swedish 410; of Peace and Friendship, Sino-Japanese 608, Sino-Nepalese 494; of Portsmouth 214/16; of St Petersburg 142; of Shimonoseki 馬關 178, 179; Sino-Japanese 450; of Tianjin 72, 74, 82; of Versailles 274; of Wangxia 望廈 28, 30; of Whampoa 黃埔 28, 30
Triads 28, 42-6, 54-64, 84, 200, 218/20; see also Heaven and Earth Society and Three Harmonies Society
Trinidad and Tobago 578, 580
Truman, Harry S. 410, 412, 413, 424, 426, 429, 442
Tunisia 470, 478, 514, 582, 597
Tuoming 妥明 96, 98, 112, 114, 117
Tuoming'a 托明阿 59, 64, 67, 88
Turkestan 130/2, 134; East Turkestan Republic 408, 416
Turkey 348, 560
Tushu pinglun 圖書評論 345
Twenty-one demands 254, 290, 303
typhoon *see* E sections

Uganda 524
Uighur minority 408, 425, 495, 507
Ulanfu 425, 523, 572, 583
Umezu Yoshijirō 梅津美治郎 354
Union of Soviet Socialist Republics (USSR) 358; border clashes 328, 550, 552, 632; Chiang Kaishek's hostile policy 306, 312, 314, 318, 326; invaded by Germany 388; and Japan 372, 412; Khabarovsk Protocol 328; recognizes PRC 438; relations with PRC 440-632 *passim*; and Sheng Shicai's Xinjiang 348, 353; Sino-Soviet: Agreements (1924) 294, beginnings of conflict 470, 484, 490, 494, 496, 500, 508, 510, Treaty of Friendship and Alliance 411, 412, 414, Treaty of Friendship, Alliance and Mutual Assistance 440/2, 616; and Sun Yatsen 268, 290, 301; war booty in Manchuria 417/19; *see also* Russia
unions *see* trade unions
United Arab Republic (UAR) 482, 506, 512, 522
united front 602; first 284, 286, 290, 310, 312; to resist Japan 344, 348, 354, 356, 364, 378, 386
UK *see* Britain
United League, *Tongmeng hui* 同盟會 214, 220, 222, 225, 236, 240, 242, 243
United Nations (UN) 438, 550; during World War II 392, 400, 406; established 410/12, 411; and Korean War 442, 446, 448, 456, 486; PRC presence in 562, 570, 572, 576, 578, 584, 606, 630; Secretary-General visits China 464, 566; Security Council 406, 520; UNESCO 415; UNRRA 399; votes against PRC's entry 440, 444, 500, 526, 556
United States of America (USA): anti-US activities 46, 121, 140, 421, 445, 454/6, 486, 522, 560; audience with Emperor 120; Boxers 198, 199, 202, 226; Chinese leaders visit 108, 116, 182, 431, 576, 612/14; cultural and student relations 111, 119, 121, 127, 203, 227; Dumbarton Oaks Conference 406; economic relations with PRC 565, 571, 607, 615; economic relations with Qing 24, 53, 59, 63, 91, 105, 153, 209, 231; economic relations with ROC 277, 365, 371, 383, 387/9, 393, 429; establishment of diplomatic relations 127, 596, 610, 612, 620; general relations with Qing 127, 174, 214, 216, 230; and Japan 214, 230, 264, 368, 372, 390; Korean War 442, 444, 446, 450, 454; leaders or others visit China 136/8, 560, 563, 564, 574, 588,

624; Mao on 420, 600; migration 140, 160, 162, 172; negotiations with PRC 460, 466, 468, 486, 550, 552, 570; Open Door Policy 194, 196; recognizes ROC 244, relations with NG 354, 382, 390, 394, 400, 414, 418, 419, 422, 426, 430, 462, 630/2; relinquishes extraterritorial rights 396, 398; and Shanghai 54, 92, 110, 184; treaties, and revision 28, 30, 60, 66, 72, 319; and UN 400; and USSR 490; and war in Indochina 504, 516, 518, 520/2, 530, 532, 544, 548, 554, 558, 564, 568; Washington Conference 282; Yalta meeting 408
United States Relations with China 439
universities 203, 268, 272, 339, 367, 395, 415, 427, 491, 541, 546/8, 547, 557, 609
University, *daxue* 大學: Agricultural, *Nongye* 農業 291; Amoy 283; Anti-Japanese, *Kangri* 抗日 361; *Beiyang* 北洋 209; Communications, *Jiaotong* 交通 283; Hunan 309; Imperial, *Jingshi daxuetang* 京師大學堂 185, 191, 205, 207, 208; Inner Mongolian 481; Lingnan 嶺南 315; Nankai 南開 213, 415; National Central, *Guoli zhongyang* 國立中央 341/3, 427; National Chiang Kaishek, *Guoli Zhongzheng* 國立中正 385; National Guangdong 299; National Ji'nan 395; National Jiangsu 323; National Sichuan 339; National Sun Yatsen, *Guoli Zhongshan* 國立中山 309, 573; National Taiwan 415; National Wuchang 299; National Yingshi 英士 395; Nationalist, *Guomin* 國民 303; North-eastern, *Dongbei* 東北 293, 367; Peking 265, 268, 269, 279, 415, 484, 487, 525, 574, 579, 585, 592, 619, 621, and coeducation 277, and the Cultural Revolution 529, 531, 546, and 'Hundred Flowers' 479, and the May Fourth Movement 272, 275, Vice-Chancellor of 307, 495, 529, 619; People's, *Renmin* 人民 445, 633; Qinghai 497; Qinghua 清華 231, 287, 367, 415, 546, 557, 585, 587, 592; Self-Study, of Hunan 283; Shandong 621; Shanghai 303; Shanxi 213,

395; Southern, *Nanfang* 南方 443; Southwest Associated, *Xi'nan lianhe* 西南聯合 415; Suzhou, *Dongwu* 東吳 203; Tongji 同濟 367; Wuhan 427; Xinjiang 497; Yanjing 燕京 367, 449; Zhejiang 321/3; Zhonghua 中華 249
Upper Volta 572

Venezuela 578
Victoria, Queen of England 24, 108, 130, 182
Vientiane, Laos 570, 581
Vietnam 116, 134, 161, 165, 177, 183, 185, 188, 208, 220, 224, 226, 231, 399, 408, 410; hostilities with France over 122, 126, 142-58; Democratic Republic of (DRVN) (1945-76) 440, 460, 464, 471, 546, 548, 566, 568, 602, agreements 466, 473, 477, 489, 499, 503, 505, 537, 545, 551, 562, 583, and southern Vietnam 518-32, 554, 558, 564, 568, 582, 590, Tet Offensive 544, visits of leaders 462, 474, 478, 488, 496, 508, 552, 570; Republic of South 550, 552, 568, 574, and northern 518-32, 544, 558, 564, 568, 582, 590, Tet Offensive 544; Socialist Republic of (1976-) 590, hostilities with China 606-20, 628, 630, 632, visits of leaders 598, 600; *see also* trade

Wage, Labour and Capital by Marx 275
Waijiao da cidian 外交大辭典 369
Wan Xiaotang 萬曉塘 535
Wanbaoshan 萬寶山 Incident 336
Wang (Taoist monk) 195, 223
Wang Bingnan 王炳南 468, 528
Wang Chong 王充 621
Wang Chonghui 王寵惠 243, 270, 278, 321, 365, 369, 388, 411, 487
Wang Daxie 汪大燮 222, 273, 287
Wang Dongxing 汪東興 599, 627
Wang Enmao 王恩茂 536, 599
Wang Guangmei 王光美 508, 516, 528, 540, 615/17
Wang Guangqi 王光祈 351
Wang Guowei 王國維 135, 203, 245, 319
Wang Haiyang 汪海洋 100, 103
Wang Heshun 王和順 222
Wang Hongwen 王洪文 571, 572,

684

576, 582, 591, 592, 596, 599, 634, 636
Wang Huaixiang 王淮湘 545, 561
Wang Jiadao 汪家道 561
Wang Jianzhong 王建中 543
Wang Jiaxiang 王稼祥 437, 581
Wang Jie 王傑 525, 527
Wang Jingwei 汪精衞 351, 394; appointments 295, 301, 307, 327, 331, 337, 341, 347, 373, 383; b. 149; d. 409; early career 232, 304; head of Wuhan government 312, 314, 316, 317; and Japan 352, 374, 376, 380, 383, 386, 398, 405; leaves for France 306/8, 318; opposes Chiang Kaishek 330, 331, 337; wounded in assassination attempt 355, 356
Wang Jinxi 王進喜 557
Wang Jun 王均 481
Wang Kaiyun 王闓運 261
Wang Kemin 王克敏 367, 378
Wang Kuiyi 王揆一 50
Wang Li 王力 (leftist leader) 538/40, 542
Wang Li 王力 (linguist) 507
Wang Mingluan 汪鳴鑾 175
Wang Qingyun 王慶雲 71, 77
Wang Renjun 王仁俊 185
Wang Ruofei 王若飛 423
Wang Ruojie 王若傑 550
Wang Shaoguang 王韶光 23
Wang Shiduo 汪士鐸 165
Wang Shijie 王世傑 404, 411, 412, 413, 418
Wang Shiwei 王實味 395, 397
Wang Shizhen 王士珍 265, 335
Wang Shouhua 王壽華 313
Wang Shouxin 王守信 616
Wang Shunu 王書奴 351
Wang Tao 王韜 123
Wang Wenshao 王文韶 135, 137, 163, 177/9, 189, 195, 199, 203, 204, 215
Wang Xianqian 王先謙 147, 271
Wang Xiaoyu 王效禹 539
Wang Xueming 王學明 613
Wang Yaowu 王耀武 430/2
Wang Yide 王懿德 59, 77
Wang Ying 王瑩 633
Wang Yirong 王懿榮 163
Wang Yitang 王揖唐 266
Wang Youping 王幼平 620
Wang Yuanfang 汪元方 103
Wang Yuanlin 王元林 132
Wang Yunsheng 王芸生 635
Wang Yuquan 王毓銓 527
Wang Zhaojun 王昭君 611
Wang Zhaowen 王朝聞 491
Wang Zhen 王震 583, 607, 627
Wang Zheng 王靜 613
Wang Zhengting 王正廷 243, 287, 291, 322, 326, 330, 331, 503
Wang Zhichun 王之春 176, 206
Wang Zhongmin 王重民 513
Wanguo gongbao 萬國公報 125, 165
Wanguo gongfa 萬國公法 (*Elements of International Law* by Henry Wheaton) 101
Wangzhang cixiong qinmu qiner gongzheng fuyinshu 王長次兄親目親耳共證福音書 81
Wannianqing 萬年青 111
Wanyan shu 萬言書 see 'Ten-thousand-word letter'
War: Board of, *Bingbu* 兵部 179, 214; European 378, 404, 410; of Liberation 424, 428-32; Ministry of, *Junzheng bu* 軍政部 354; Pacific 390, 412/14; Russo-Japanese 210-16; Sino-French 148-54; Sino-Japanese (1894-5) 174-8; Sino-Japanese (1937-45) 364-414; Transport Board, *Zhanshi yunshu guanliju* 戰時運輸管理局 409; World I 250, 270; World II 414
warships 55, 146, 152, 218, 426
Washington Conference 282, 284, 285, 301
water, control of 443, 575/7
Water Margin see *Shuihu zhuan*
Wealth of Nations by Adam Smith, translation of see *Yuanfu*
Weekly Critic 273, 275
Wei Changhui 韋昌輝 46-8, 66, 67, 69
Wei Daoming 魏道明 396, 411, 425
Wei Guangtao 魏光燾 151, 195, 199, 211, 215
Wei Guoqing 韋國清 477, 544, 547, 559, 571, 583
Wei Jingsheng 魏京生 619, 621
Wei Jun 韋俊 62, 76/8
Wei Wenbo 魏文伯 617
Wei Yuan 魏源 25, 27, 31
Weida de daolu, Zhu De de shengping he shidai 偉大的道路，朱德的生平和時代 621
Weida de shinian, Zhonghua renmin gongheguo jingji he wenhua jianshe chengjiu de tongji 偉大的十年，中華人民共和國經濟和文化建設成就的統計 491/3
Wen Shengcai 溫生才 239
Wen Yiduo 聞一多 423
Weng Tonghe 翁同龢 67, 151, 162,

175, 179, 187-91, 213
Weng Tongjue 翁同龢 127, 129
Weng Wenhao 翁文灝 431/3, 563
Weng Xincun 翁心存 67, 75, 77
Wenhui bao 文匯報 525, 543, 544, 548
Wenqing 文慶 35, 63, 67, 69
Wenwei 文蔚 22, 23, 25
Wenxiang 文祥 31, 75, 85, 117, 119, 131
'Wenxue gailiang chuyi' 文學改良芻議 265
'Wenxue geming lun' 文學革命論 265
Wenxue jikan 文學季刊 357
Wenyan 文碩 160, 161
Wenyi bao 文藝報 439, 463, 517/19
Wenyi fuxing 文藝復興 427
Wenyi yanjiu 文藝研究 621
Wenyu 文煜 85, 93, 143
Western Hills clique, Conference 304, 306, 316
Whampoa 黃埔 (Guangdong) 39, see also Treaty of
White-haired Girl, The see *Baimao nü*
White Lotus sect, *Bailian jiao* 白蓮教 84, 90, 92, 102, 149
White Signal sect, *Baihao jiao* 白號教 72, 98, 100, 102, 108
wireless 293, 317, 335, 376, see also radio
Wo de jingji lilun zhexue sixiang he zhengzhi lichang 我的經濟埋論哲學思想和政治立場 487
'Wo de Makesizhuyi guan' 我的馬克思主義觀 275
Wo de qianbansheng 我的前半生 519
Wo 渦 River (Henan, Anhui) 387
women 439, 447, 457, 579; Beiyang 北洋 Normal School 219; Chinese League for Participation in Politics, *Zhonghua nüzi canzheng tongmeng hui* 中華女子參政同盟會 279; Chinese National Association for War Relief, *Zhongguo funü weilao ziwei kangzhan jiangshi zonghui* 中國婦女慰勞自衛抗戰將士總會 367; International Day for Working 579; Nanjing Union College, *Jinling nüzi daxue* 金陵女子大學 255; National Congress 437, 481, 609; Peking Higher Normal College, *Beijing nüzi gaodeng shifan daxue* 北京女子高等師範大學 289, 297; Rights League, *Nüquan yundong tongmeng hui* 女權運動同盟會 289
Woren 倭仁 89, 117
workers: in the Cultural Revolution 538, 546, 549, 557; and culture 459, 567; role in the revolution 312, 316/18, 315/17, 330, 331; *see also* strikes
Workers' and Peasants' Red Army, *Gongnong hongjun* 工農紅軍 see Red Army
Workers' and Peasants' Revolutionary Army, *Gongnong gemingjun* 工農革命軍 316
Works, Board of, *Gongbu* 工部 179, 214
World Bank see Bank, International for Reconstruction and Development
World Health Organization (WHO) 571
World Peace, Assembly 466; Council 512
Writers: Afro-Asian Conference 505; Chinese Association, *Zhongguo wenyijia xiehui* 中國文藝家協會 361; Chinese Union, *Zhongguo zuojia xiehui* 中國作家協會 463, 467, 479, 525, 629; League of Leftwing, *Zuoyi zuojia lianmeng* 左翼作家聯盟 333, 341; Publishing House, *Zuojia chubanshe* 作家出版社 459
Wu 霧 355
Wu Bingjian 伍秉鑑 68
Wu Changqing 吳長慶 146
Wu Chaoshu 伍朝樞 353
Wu Chongyue 伍崇曜 68, 95
Wu Dacheng 吳大澂 109, 153, 157, 165, 207
Wu De 吳德 529, 563, 571, 583, 590, 592, 607, 627
Wu Dunyuan 伍敦元 27
Wu Guangmo 吳光漠 46
Wu Guixian 吳桂賢 583
Wu Han 吳晗 501, 525, 531, 553, 617
Wu Jianzhang 吳健彰 52, 59
Wu Jiezhang 吳介璋 237
Wu Jingheng 吳敬恒 see Wu Zhihui
Wu Kedu 吳可讀 136, 139
Wu Liutang xiansheng leiwen 吳柳堂先生誄文 141
Wu Mei 吳梅 381
Wu Peifu 吳佩孚 125, 266-8, 276, 280-6, 295-7, 306-10, 381
Wu Qijun 吳其濬 24
Wu Rulun 吳汝綸 205
Wu Shiying 武士英 249

686

Wu Tang 吳棠 103, 107, 129
Wu Tiecheng 吳鐵城 163, 459
Wu Tingfang 伍廷芳 25, 189, 196, 215/17, 263, 266/8, 269, 276-8, 285
Wu Tingfen 吳廷芬 149, 195
Wu Wenrong 吳文鎔 45, 49, 55, 61
Wu Woyao 吳沃堯 231
Wu xiao yi 五小義 165
Wu Xiuquan 伍修權 444, 506
Wu Xun zhuan 武訓傳 449
Wu Youxun 吳有訓 509/11
Wu Yuanzhi 吳源植 501
Wu Yue 吳越 216, 217
Wu Zancheng 吳贊誠 141
Wu Zhenyu 吳振棫 67, 71
Wu Zhihui 吳稚暉 101, 206, 307, 327
Wu Zhongxin 吳忠信 153, 405, 419, 493
Wu Zongci 吳宗慈 299
Wu Zonglian 吳宗濂 239
Wu Zuxiang 吳組緗 355
Wuhan ribao 武漢日報 329
Wulantai 烏蘭泰 53
Wutai jiemei 舞台姐妹 531
Wuxing jinshi ji 吳興金石記 167
Wuxu diexie ji 戊戌喋血記 633

Xi Baotian 席寶田 108, 114
Xi Han huiyao 西漢會要 601
Xia Gong 夏恭 365
Xia Jiagao 夏家鎬 119
Xia Ruifang 夏瑞芳 187
Xia Yan 夏衍 531
Xiaer guanzhen 遐邇貫珍 57
Xian Henghan 冼恒漢 545, 559
Xian Xinghai 冼星海 217, 379, 417
Xianfeng yuannian zhongxing biao 咸豐元年中興表 49
Xiang Da 向達 455
Xiang Jingyu 向警予 325
Xiang Rong 向榮 43, 46, 47, 52, 55, 66, 67, 69
Xiang Ying 項英 337, 349, 365
Xiang Zhongfa 向忠發 321, 332, 337, 341
Xiangdao 響導 289, 309
Xiangjiang pinglun 湘江評論 275
Xiangqi lou riji 湘綺樓日記 317
Xiangxue xinbao 湘學新報 187
Xianzhi tang gao 顯志堂稿 133
Xiao Chaogui 蕭朝貴 46, 47, 50, 53
Xiao Erhei jiehun 小二黑結婚 401
Xiao Hua 蕭華 515
Xiao Jinzhong 蕭錦忠 31
Xiao Jun 蕭軍 357

Xiao Ma 肖馬 633
Xiao Qijiang 蕭啓江 83
Xiao San 蕭三 513
Xiao Yaonan 蕭耀南 281, 311
Xiaoqin 孝欽 67, 85, 125, 127, see also Empress Dowager Cixi
Xiaoshuo yuebao 小説月報 283, 317
Xiaozhen 考真 85, 127, see also Empress Dowager Cian
Xie Bingying 謝冰瑩 363
Xie Bozhang 謝柏樟 579
Xie Chenglie 謝承烈 39
Xie Chi 謝持 381
Xie Fuzhi 謝富治 491, 523, 538/40, 551, 559, 565, 569, 629
Xie Wanying 謝婉瑩 401
Xie Wuliang 謝无量 293
Xie Xingyao 謝興堯 357
Xie Xuegong 謝學恭 539, 561
Xie Yaohuan 謝瑤環 501, 531
Xie Zhenhua 謝振華 561
Xiguo jinshi huibian 西國近事彙編 123
Xihu 西湖 589
Xiku zhai huaxu 習苦齋畫絮 173
Xiliang 錫良 209, 211, 213, 223, 229
Ximing jiangyi 西銘講義 41
Xin chenbao 新晨報 323
Xin jiaoyu 新教育 275
'Xin minzhuzhuyi lun' 新民主主義論 385
Xin Qian ribao 新黔日報 439
Xin qingnian 新青年 257, 261, see also New Youth
Xin shiji 新世紀 225, 227
Xin Tangshu 新唐書 587
Xin Yinghan cidian 新英漢詞典 593
Xin yinyue 新音樂 385
Xin Yuanshi 新元史 275
Xinbao 新報 131
Xinchao 新潮 275
Xing de jiaoyu 性的教育 351
Xingjun zongyao 行軍總要 63
Xingming guizhi 性命圭旨 47
Xingshi wen 醒世文 75
Xingxiang siwei ziliao huibian 形象思維資料匯編 633
Xinhai geming 辛亥革命 481
Xinhai geming huiyi lu 辛亥革命回憶錄 513
Xinhua ribao 新華日報 373, 381, 425
Xinhua ribao 新華日報 439
Xinhua yuebao 新華月報 439
Xinjing ribao 新京日報 329
Xinmeng 新夢 305

687

Xinmin congbao 新民叢報 207
Xinqiang 新墙 River (Hunan) 390/2
Xinsheng zhoukan 新生週刊 354
Xinwen bao 新聞報 173
Xinwen xue 新聞學 275
Xinxue weijing kao 新學偽經考 169, 175
Xinyizhao shengshu 新遺詔聖書 57
Xinyue 新月 323
Xiong Chengji 熊成基 226
Xiong Jinding 熊瑾玎 575
Xiong Shihui 熊式輝 413, 425
Xiong Xiling 熊希齡 247, 251, 270
Xisha 西沙 (Paracel) Islands 574, 586, 616, 624
Xixue shumu biao 西學書目表 185
Xiying xianhua 西瀅閒話 323
Xizang ribao 西藏日報 475
Xizhen 錫珍 151
Xu Baohuang 徐寶璜 275
Xu Beihong 徐悲鴻 181, 419, 459
Xu Fu 徐郙 199
Xu Gengshen 許庚身 151
Xu Guangjin 徐廣縉 37, 38, 40, 41, 49, 55
Xu Guangqi ji 徐光啓集 513
Xu guwen ci leizuan 續古文辭類纂 147
Xu Haidong 徐海東 354
Xu Jiatun 許家屯 597
Xu Jingcheng 許景澄 33, 109, 165, 189, 201
Xu Jinqiang 徐今強 595
Xu Jiyu 徐繼畬 39, 99
Xu Liangying 許良英 621
Xu Qian 徐謙 387
Xu Run 徐潤 121
Xu Shichang 徐世昌 214, 270, 272, 274, 278, 280, 287; appointments 215, 219, 223, 233, 251; as author 373; b. 65; d. 381
Xu Shiying 許世英 301, 307, 357, 370
Xu Shiyou 許世友 545, 551, 555, 571, 577
Xu Shou 徐壽 95, 155
Xu Shuofang 徐朔方 507
Xu Shuzheng 徐樹錚 305
Xu Song 徐松 39
Xu Teli 徐特立 549
Xu Tingjie 徐廷傑 64
Xu Tong 徐桐 163, 183
Xu Xiangqian 徐向前 607, 612, 627
Xu Xilin 徐錫麟 222, 225
Xu Xinliu 徐新六 375
Xu Xueqiu 許雪秋 220
Xu Yingkui 許應騤 187, 190
Xu Yongyi 徐用儀 151, 175, 179

Xu Yuntan 徐允襢 440
Xu Zechun 徐澤醇 41
Xu Zhimo 徐志摩 189, 341
Xuantong 宣統 226, *see also* Emperor: Puyi
Xuchang 續昌 155
Xue Fucheng 薛福成 163, 168, 170, 177
Xue Huan 薛煥 86, 93, 126
Xue Zhiyuan 薛之元 74
Xuexi yu pipan 學習與批判 573
Xujiahui 徐家匯 (Zikawei) near Shanghai 80
Xujing zhai yunyan guoyan lu 須靜齋雲烟過眼錄 65
Xun Huisheng 荀慧生 201, 549
Xushou tang wenji 虛受堂文集 201

Yakub Beg 98-104, 108, 112-18, 121, 122, 128-30, 132, 135
Yan Botao 顏伯燾 23
Yan Fu 嚴復 61, 185, 187, 201, 285
Yan Huiqing 嚴惠慶 (W.W. Yen) 285, 295, 297, 301, 307, 344
Yan Jingming 閻敬銘 31, 151, 171
Yan Kejun 嚴可均 527
Yan Xishan 閻錫山 149, 237, 312, 313, 321, 326, 330-3, 341, 430, 437, 497
Yang Changxun 楊昌濬 141, 151, 161, 170
Yang Chengwu 楊成武 529, 545
Yang Dapeng 楊大鵬 28
Yang Daqun 楊大群 533
Yang Dezhi 楊得志 561, 577
Yang Du 楊度 257, 260
Yang Fuqing 楊輔清 68, 71, 76-80
Yang, Gladys 491, 611
Yang Guozhen 楊國楨 23
Yang Hansheng juzuo xuan 陽翰笙劇作選 481
Yang Hsien-yi and Gladys 491, *see also* Yang Xianyi and Yang, Gladys
Yang Hucheng 楊虎城 362, 441
Yang Jingren 楊静仁 629
Yang Kaihui 楊開慧 205, 335, 451, 601
Yang Kuan 楊寬 527
Yang Mo 楊沫 487
Yang Moujian 楊懋建 25
Yang Pei 楊沛 59, 62, 63
Yang Qianru 楊纖如 633
Yang Qiliang 楊琪良 550
Yang Quyun 楊衢雲 180, 205
Yang Rongguo 楊榮國 573
Yang Ru 楊儒 182, 202
Yang Rui 楊銳 189, 193

688

Yang Sen 楊森 308
Yang Shenxiu 楊深秀 193
Yang Shixiang 楊士驤 223, 227
Yang Shoujing 楊守敬 141, 187, 257
Yang Shu 楊樞 210
Yang Wending 楊文鼎 234
Yang Wenhui 楊文會 239
Yang Wenzheng 楊文政 102
Yang Xianyi 楊憲益 491, 611
Yang Xianzhen 楊獻珍 517, 615/17, 633
Yang Xiaolou 楊小樓 135, 375
Yang Xitang 楊習堂 42
Yang Xiufeng 楊秀峰 389, 521
Yang Xiuqing 楊秀清 39, 44-8, 52, 54-6, 63, 66, 69
Yang Yiyan 楊益言 501
Yang Yizeng 楊以增 69
Yang Yizhi 楊一之 533
Yang Yuebin 楊岳斌 95, 167
Yang Yuechun 楊悅春 168
Yang Yuke 楊玉科 118, 155
Yang Zengxin 楊增新 276, 325
Yangcheng wanbao 羊城晚報 535
Yangmen nüjiang 楊門女將 607
Yangwei 揚威 143
Yangwu yundong 洋務運動 501
Yangzhi shuwu quanji 養知書屋全集 171
Yanshan yehua 燕山夜話 507, 531
Yantai 烟台 83
Yanyang tian 艷陽天 519
Yanzhi jikan 言治季刊 271
Yao minority 34
Yao Wenyuan 姚文元 525, 547/9, 551, 571, 581-3, 591-2, 598, 599, 632/6
Yao Xueyin 姚雪垠 593
Yao Yilin 姚依林 617, 625
Yao Ying 姚瑩 22, 23, 25
'Ye baihehua' 野百合花 397
Ye Changchi 葉昌熾 41
Ye Dehui 葉德輝 203, 207, 225, 391
Ye Gongchao 葉公超 (George Yeh) 462
Ye Gongzhuo 葉恭綽 283
Ye Jianying 葉劍英 416, 443, 551, 571, 583, 597-9, 604, 620, 626, 627, 631
Ye Jizhuang 葉季壯 543
Ye Mingchen 葉名琛 52, 65, 66, 70/2; appointments 37, 41, 49, 55, 67; and *Arrow* Incident 68; buy foreign cannon 63; d. 79; dismissal 73; and God Worshippers 50; taken to Calcutta as prisoner 72
Ye Qun 葉群 551, 631
Ye Ting 葉挺 314, 316, 365, 384/6, 432
Ye Zhichao 葉志超 174
Yege 夜歌 417
Yellow River Cantata 379
Yemen 472, 516, 544, 550, 554, 555, 566, 578/80, 604
Yetaishan 爺台山 (Shaanxi) 412
Yi 憶 363
Yi Si-eung *see* Taewongun
Yifei 懿妃 67
Yige nübing de zizhuan 一個女兵的自傳 363
Yihe quan 義和拳 603
Yihuan 奕譞 155, 156, 162, 169
Yijiangshan 一江山 Island (Zhejiang) 464
Yijing 奕經 22, 23, 25
Yikuang 奕劻 160, 167, 190, 202-4, 209, 223, 226, 237, 267
Yiliang 怡良 23, 24, 25, 53, 55, 60, 65, 71
Yilibu 伊里布 22, 23, 24, 27
Yilin 譯林 623
Yin Changheng 尹昌衡 242
Yin Ming 尹明 587
Yin Rugeng 殷汝耕 356
Yinggui 英桂 109, 133
Yinghan 英翰 125
Yinghuan zhilüe 瀛寰志略 39
Yinqi cuibian 殷契粹編 369
Yinxu shuqi qianbian 殷虛書契前編 249
Yinyue cidian 音樂辭典 357
Yinyue yanjiu 音樂研究 487
Yishan 奕山 35, 45, 72, 77
Yitang 易棠 67
Yiwen yuebao 益文月報 161
Yixiang kaocheng xubian 儀象考成續編 31
'Yizai suowei guoti wenti zhe' 異哉所謂國體問題者 257
Yizhu 奕詝 *see* Emperor Xianfeng
Yizu zhi ying 彝族之鷹 533
Yong'an [Wing On] 永安 Co. Ltd. 315
Yonglu xianjue 勇盧閒詰 113
Yoshizawa Kenkichi 芳澤謙吉 300, 326, 336
You Taizhong 尤太忠 561
Young China Study Society, *Shaonian Zhongguo xuehui* 少年中國學會 269
Young Pioneers, Chinese, *Zhongguo shaonian xianfengdui* 中國少年先鋒隊 459, 523

Younghusband, Major Francis 208-12
youth 511, 521, 609, 619; Chinese National Federation of Democratic, Zhonghua quanguo minzhu qingnian lianhe zonghui 中華全國民主青年聯合總會 439, -World Federation 463; Chinese New Democratic League, Zhongguo xin minzhuzhuyi qingnian tuan 中國新民主主義青年團 437, 459, 469, 479; Chinese Party, Zhongguo qingnian dang 中國青年黨 292; Chinese Socialist Corps, Zhongguo shehuizhuyi qingnian tuan 中國社會主義青年團 279, 287, 293; Communist League of China, Zhongguo gongchanzhuyi qingnian tuan 中國共產主義青年團 301, 469, 479, 517, 523, 525, 533, 571, 609, -of Tibetan Autonomous Region 511; National Congress 457, 485; National Games 473; National Union, Quanguo qingnian lianhehui 全國青年聯合會 523; Palace 525
Youxue shi 幼學詩 51
Yu 雨 355
Yu Dafu 郁達夫 343, 417
Yu Dongchen 余棟臣 170, 190-2
Yu Hongjun 俞鴻鈞 (O.K. Yui) 405, 413, 431
Yu Huiyong 于會泳 583
Yu Jicheng 余濟成 222
Yu Pingbo 俞平伯 455
Yu Qiuli 余秋里 565, 583, 597, 607, 615
Yu Shuyan 余叔岩 167, 403
Yu Wanqing 余萬清 50
Yu wusheng chu 於無聲處 609
Yu Youren 于右任 139, 355, 399, 521
Yu Yue 俞樾 225
Yu Zhi 余治 81
Yuan Baoling 袁保齡 149
Yuan Chang 袁昶 189, 201
Yuan Huabing 苑化冰 575
Yuan Jiahua 袁家驊 633
Yuan Jiasan 袁甲三 66, 72, 95
Yuan Shengwu qinzheng lu 元聖武親征錄 181
Yuan Shikai 袁世凱 179, 183, 206, 238; appointments under Qing 195, 197, 203, 205, 223, 237; b. 79; becomes ROC President 241/3; calls for constitutional government 214; d. 261; declares support for the Republic 240; dismissed 229; in Hundred Days' Reform 192; inspects military manoeuvres 218; in Korea 152, 155, 156, 172; as ROC President 240-59 passim; sends military students to Japan 207
Yuan Shuxun 袁樹勳 229
Yuan yitong zhi 元一統志 533
Yuanfu 原富 (Wealth of Nations by Adam Smith) 201
Yucheng 裕誠 47, 49
Yude 裕德 209, 211
Yuebin 樂斌 67
Yuejin 躍進 483
Yugoslavia 464, 523, 554, 598, 600, 605, 608, 626, 627, 630, 632
Yuhou qingshan 雨後青山 593
Yulang 毓朗 233
Yulu 裕祿 155, 187, 189
Yung Wing, see Rong Hong
Yunnan zazhi 雲南雜誌 221
Yunya chunuan 雲崖初暖 611
Yurui 裕瑞 49, 55
Yutai 裕泰 43, 45, 47
Yuxian 毓賢 195, 196
Yuyan lun 語言論 (Language) 633
Yuzhi qianzizhao 御製千字詔 61

Zai chengshi li 在城市裡 369
'Zai kuoda de zhongyang gongzuo huiyi shang de jianghua' 在擴大的中央工作會議上的講話 611
'Zai wenyi gongzuo zuotanhui he gushi pian chuangzuo huiyi shang de jianghua' 在文藝工作座談會和故事片創作會議上的講話 621
'Zai Yan'an wenyi zuotanhui shang de jianghua' 在延安文藝座談會上的講話 ('Talks at the Yan'an Forum on Literature and Art') 401, 567
Zaichun 載淳 85, 86, see also Emperor Tongzhi
Zaifeng 載灃 223, 227, 228, 232, 237
Zailing 載齡 133, 135
Zaire 568, 580, 596, 606, 624
Zaitian 載湉 117, 127, see also Emperor Guangxu
Zaixun 載勳 197, 203, 205
Zaiyi 載漪 197, 198, 203
Zaiyuan 載垣 79, 85, 87
Zaize 載澤 214, 216, 227
Zaizhen 載振 209
Zambia 537, 538, 545, 551, 555, 598, 626
Zanzibar 512

690

Zeiqing huizuan 賊情彙纂 65
Zeng Dao 曾道 441
Zeng Guofan 曾國藩 55, 56, 58; advances modernization 91, 95, 99, 115, 117; appointments 35, 79, 89, 95, 99, 103, 105, 113; brother d. 75; d. 121; diplomatic activities 108, 114; father d. 71; given leave 71; and Nian 102; and Taipings 52, 58, 64, 82, 96, 97
Zeng Guohua 曾國華 75
Zeng Guoquan 曾國荃 76, 83, 84, 88-96 *passim*, 143, 145, 146, 150, 151, 167
Zeng Huimin gong quanji 曾惠敏公全集 173
Zeng Jize 曾紀澤 135, 140-4, 153-7, 161, 167
Zeng Linshu 曾麟書 71
Zeng Ruzhu 曾如炷 24
Zeng Shan 曾山 569
Zeng Siyu 曾思玉 539, 545, 561, 577
Zeng Tao 曾濤 554
Zeng Tianyang 曾天養 61
Zeng Wangyan 曾望顏 77
Zeng Xisheng 曾希聖 549
Zeng Yongya 曾雍雅 547
Zeng Zhongming 曾仲鳴 376, 381
Zengqi 增祺 205, 208
Zhan Tianyou 詹天佑 275
Zhang Aiping 張愛萍 629
Zhang Binglin 章炳麟 113, 204, 209, 210, 219, 363
Zhang Bishi 張弼士 261
Zhang Bojun 章伯鈞 478, 485
Zhang Boling 張伯苓 131, 451
Zhang Boxi 張百熙 205, 207, 213, 225
Zhang Chongtong 張沖同 635
Zhang Chunqiao 張春橋 539, 551, 559, 571, 580, 582, 583, 591, 592, 598, 599, 634, 636
Zhang Dejian 張德堅 65
Zhang Dingcheng 張鼎丞 461
Zhang Ertian 張爾田 125, 417
Zhang Guangdou 張光斗 559, 560
Zhang Guangzao 張光藻 113, 115
Zhang Guohua 張國華 453, 467, 539, 547, 561, 569
Zhang Guoliang 張國樑 66, 70, 74, 78, 83
Zhang Guotao 張國燾 281, 282, 283, 299, 313, 337, 342, 344, 349-54 *passim*, 360, 365, 371, 623
Zhang Huaiyi 張懷一 331

Zhang Huizan 張輝瓚 332, 334, 339
Zhang Ji 張繼 147, 211, 429
Zhang Jia'ao 張嘉璈 411, 413, 425
Zhang Jian 張謇 57, 193, 209, 270, 311
Zhang Jiashu 張家樹 495
Zhang Jiluan 張季鸞 391
Zhang Jingyao 張敬堯 276, 349
Zhang Jizhi 張際治 295
Zhang Kaisong 張凱嵩 105, 107
Zhang Lan 張瀾 437, 469
Zhang Liangji 張亮基 55, 77
Zhang Luoxing 張洛行 50, 62, 66-8, 72, 78, 92
Zhang Mingfeng 張鳴鳳 67
Zhang Mu 張穆 43, 107
Zhang Peilun 張佩綸 146, 149, 211
Zhang Qian 張茜 581
Zhang Qilong 張啓龍 331
Zhang Qizhi 張豈之 579
Zhang Qun 張群 362, 383, 414, 418, 425
Zhang Renjie 張人傑 307, 327
Zhang Renjun 張人駿 323, 229
Zhang Shaoceng 張紹曾 291
Zhang Shizhao 章士釗 211, 253, 301, 303, 575
Zhang Shouyong 張壽鏞 207
Zhang Shusheng 張樹聲 119, 137
Zhang Side 張思德 407, 409
Zhang Tailei 張太雷 316, 319
Zhang Tianyi 張天翼 369, 401
Zhang Tiesheng 張鐵生 573, 599
Zhang Tixue 張體學 575
Zhang Weiping 張維屏 79
Zhang Weixun 張煒遜 571
Zhang Wentian 張聞天 595
Zhang Xigong 張錫恭 299
Zhang Xiruo 張奚若 575
Zhang Xiumei 張秀眉 64, 110, 118
Zhang Xueliang 張學良 302, 320-2, 326, 331, 332, 341, 345, 355, 361, 362, 367
Zhang Xun 張勳 247, 248, 260-4
Zhang Yinhuan 張蔭桓 160, 163, 176, 189, 201
Zhang Yinwu 張蔭梧 376, 378
Zhang Zhidong 張之洞 163, 169, 179; appointments 145, 151, 163, 205, 215, 223; as author 129, 193; calls for constitutional government 214; d. 231; and economic, educational and military establishments 152, 159, 165, 169, 171/3, 183, 189, 209; on educational reform 213; on foreign policy issues 138, 144, 148, 160, 198; *jinshi* degree 93;

691

and loans 153, 219
Zhang Zhijiang 張之江 306, 307
Zhang Zhiwan 張之萬 35, 89, 117, 151, 163
Zhang Zhixin 張志新 587
Zhang Zhizhong 張治忠 373, 404, 406, 416, 417, 419, 434, 553
Zhang Zhongtian 張重天 623
Zhang Zizhong 張自忠 387
Zhang Zongchang 張宗昌 298-309 *passim*, 318, 320, 345
Zhang Zongxiang 章宗祥 267, 268, 271-3
Zhang Zongyu 張宗禹 88, 92, 94-106 *passim*, 109
Zhang Zuolin 張作霖 129, 280, 281, 286, 295, 296, 302-10 *passim*, 313, 314, 320, 321, 325
Zhao Bingjun 趙秉鈞 243, 244, 245, 247, 253
Zhao Dan 趙丹 631, 635
Zhao Erfeng 趙爾豐 227, 228, 230, 236, 237
Zhao Erlu 趙爾陸 543
Zhao Ersun 趙爾巽 29, 223, 227, 237, 319
Zhao Haoran 趙浩然 86
Zhao Hengti 趙恒惕 276, 287
Zhao Qilin 趙啓霖 223
Zhao Shenxian 趙神仙 158
Zhao Shuhan 趙舒翰 191
Zhao Shuli 趙樹理 401, 469, 557
Zhao Shuqiao 趙舒翹 195
Zhao Zhenghong 趙正洪 561
Zhao Zhiqian 趙之謙 97, 113, 153
Zhao Zhongli 趙中立 621
Zhao Ziyang 趙紫陽 585, 591, 617, 627, 630, 632, 636
Zhao Ziyue 趙子曰 317
Zhaoshu gaixi banxing lun 詔書蓋璽頒行論 57
Zhenbao 珍寶 Island (Damansky Island) 550
Zheng Boqi 鄭伯奇 623
Zheng Guanying 鄭觀應 173
Zheng Junli 鄭君里 553, 631/3
Zheng Rucheng 鄭汝成 257
Zheng Shiliang 鄭士良 200
Zheng Tieru 鄭鐵儒 575
Zheng Xiaoxu 鄭孝胥 341
Zheng Zhenduo 鄭振鐸 343, 375, 487
Zheng Zhengqiu 鄭正秋 359
Zhengyi 正誼 253
Zhenpin 珍嬪 Pearl Concubine 161
Zhigang 志剛 105, 106, 114
Zhili Army, clique 276-80, 286, 291, 296, 306, 308, 309, 312

Zhiping baojian 治平寶鑑 89
Zhiqu Weihushan 智取威虎山 553
Zhixin bao 知新報 187
Zhong Renjie 鍾人杰 22
Zhongguo baike nianjian 1980 中國百科年鑒 633/5
Zhongguo changji shi 中國娼妓史 351
Zhongguo congshu zonglu 中國叢書綜錄 501
Zhongguo dianying 中國電影 475
Zhongguo duiwai maoyi 中國對外貿易 579
Zhongguo fazhi bao 中國法制報 635
Zhongguo geming he Zhongguo gongchan dang 中國革命和中國共產黨 381
Zhongguo geming shi 中國革命史 293
'*Zhongguo geming zhanzheng de zhanlüe wenti*' 中國革命戰爭的戰略問題 363
Zhongguo Gongchan dang diqici quanguo daibiao dahui wenxian 中國共產黨第七次全國代表大會文獻 417
'*Zhongguo Gongchan dang zhongyang weiyuanhui tongzhi (yijiuliuliu nian wuyue shiliu ri)*' 中國共產黨中央委員會通知（一九六六年五月十六日）543
Zhongguo gongren 中國工人 299, 385
Zhongguo gudai shehui yanjiu 中國古代社會研究 333/5
Zhongguo gudai yinyue shiliao jiyao (diyi ji) 中國古代音樂史料輯要（第一輯）507
Zhongguo gudian xiqu lunzhu jicheng 中國古典戲曲論著集成 497
Zhongguo Guomin dang shigao 中國國民黨史稿 407/9
Zhongguo huaju yundong wushi nian shiliao ji 中國話劇運動五十年史料集 487
Zhongguo jiaohui xinbao 中國教會新報 109, 125
Zhongguo jin bainian zhengzhi shi 中國近百年政治史 429
Zhongguo jindai jiaoyu shi 中國近代教育史 623
Zhongguo jindai shi 中國近代史 385
Zhongguo jindai shi 中國近代史 427
Zhongguo jindai shi 中國近代史 621
Zhongguo jindai shi zhu wenti 中國近代史諸問題 527
Zhongguo jindai shishi ji 中國近代史事記 493

692

Zhongguo jindai shishi rizhi 中國近代史事日誌 9
Zhongguo jingji gaizao 中國經濟改造 357
Zhongguo nongmin bao 中國農民報 633
Zhongguo qingnian 中國青年 293, 611, see also *Chinese Youth*
Zhongguo qingnian bao 中國青年報 449, 533
Zhongguo ribao 中國日報 195
Zhongguo shangye jingji guanlixue 中國商業經濟管理學 633
Zhongguo shaonian bao 中國少年報 451
Zhongguo suwenxue shi 中國俗文學史 375
Zhongguo wenhua 中國文化 385
Zhongguo wenhua shi congshu 中國文化史叢書 369
Zhongguo wenxue shi 中國文學史 487
Zhongguo xiandai wenxue shi 中國現代文學史 621
Zhongguo xiandai wenxue shi 中國現代文學史 633
'*Zhongguo xiang hechu qu?*' 中國向何處去？549
Zhongguo xiaoshuo shilüe 中國小說史略 293
Zhongguo xiju shi 中國戲劇史 459
Zhongguo yinyue shi 中國音樂史 351
Zhongguo yuwen 中國語文 455
Zhongguo zhengzhi sixiang shi 中國政治思想史 397
Zhongguo zhexue shi 中國哲學史 351
Zhongguo zhexue shi dagang 中國哲學史大綱 275
Zhongguo zhexue shi jianghua 中國哲學史講話 587
Zhongguo zhexue shi lunwen 中國哲學史論文 507
Zhongguo zhexue shilüe 中國哲學史略 579
Zhongguo zhi mingyun 中國之命運 401
Zhonghua minguo kaiguo qian geming shi 中華民國開國前革命史 421
Zhonghua minguo xianfa shi 中華民國憲法史 299
Zhonghua Police Research Society 383
Zhonghua ribao 中華日報 343
Zhonghua xinbao 中華新報 257

Zhongsha 中沙 Islands 574, 586
Zhongshan 中山 S.S., Incident, 306, 307
Zhongsu youhao 中蘇友好 439
Zhongwai jiwen 中外紀聞 181
Zhongwai xinbao 中外新報 75
Zhongwai xinwen qiri lu 中外新聞七日錄 101
Zhongwai zazhi 中外雜誌 89
Zhongxing ribao 中興日報 225
Zhongyang ribao 中央日報 329, 338, 381
Zhongyang zhengfa gongbao 中央政法公報 445
Zhou Baozhong 周保中 519
Zhou Enlai 周恩來 : advocates destruction of nuclear weapons 510, 518; appointments (post-liberation) 521, 571, 583, Premier and Minister of Foreign Affairs 437; attends domestic conferences 469; as author 621, 637; b. 193; career before liberation, appointments 313, 321, 337, 349, 413, army occupies Swatow 316, attends Political Consultative Conference 416, defends Li Lisan line 332, negotiates for CCP with NG 362, 382/4, 414, 416, 418, 420/2, 436; correspondence with Nehru 490, 492, 506; and the Cultural Revolution 534, 540/8; d. 595; diplomatic activities, as Minister of Foreign Affairs (1949-58) 438/82 left-hand pages *passim*, post-1958 496, 518, 548, 552, 558, 586; gives report to the National Party or People's Congress 520, 572, 580; honoured after death 588, 596; on intellectuals 473; interviews with foreigners 456/8, 578, 580; issues joint statements with foreign leaders 464, 470, 472, 480, 484, 486, 498, 582; and Japan 566; orders Three-Antis Movement 448/50; signs treaties and agreements for China 440, 441, 488, 492, 496, 499, 509, 566; succeeded as Minister of Foreign Affairs 485; trips outside China 474/6, 492/4, 498, 516, 522, 530, 558, Africa 512/14, 522, Bandung Conference 474/6, Cairo 522/4, DPRK 482, 554, Geneva Conference etc 458/62, Mongolia 494, Moscow 440-2, 452,

693

Index

456, 488, 500; and US 560, 564; and Vietnam War 526, 544, 550, 558, 582; votes in elections 484
Zhou Enlai xuanji 周恩來選集 637
Zhou Fohai 周佛海 281, 435
Zhou Fu 周馥 211, 214, 219
Zhou Jiamei 周家楣 135, 143
Zhou Jianren 周建人 483
Zhou Libo 周立波 433, 623
Zhou Lichun 周立春 56
Zhou Peiyuan 周培源 619
Zhou Renshan 周仁山 523
Zhou Rongxin 周榮鑫 583, 587, 593, 597
Zhou Shouchang 周壽昌 147
Zhou Shujia 周叔迦 557
Zhou Shuren 周樹人, *see* Lu Xun
Zhou Tianjue 周天爵 46, 47, 54, 57
Zhou Xineng 周錫能 49
Zhou Xinfang 周信芳 481, 531, 587
Zhou Xing 周興 561, 587
Zhou Xuehui 周學輝 259
Zhou Xuexi 周學熙 259, 429
Zhou Yang 周揚 361/3, 505, 511/13, 617
Zhou Yibai 周貽白 401, 459, 603
Zhou Yichun 周詒春 435
Zhou Yunxiang 周雲祥 208
Zhou Ziqi 周自齊 285
Zhou Zuomin 周作民 475
Zhou Zuoren 周作人 281
Zhou Zupei 周祖培 75, 85
Zhouli zhengyi 周禮正義 217
Zhoushan 舟山 Island (Zhejiang) 32, 442
Zhu Chengxiu 朱承修 176
Zhu Cong 竹叢 601
Zhu De 朱德 appointments before 1949 313, 337, 365, made Commander of the Red Army 321, 337; b. 159; career from 1949 440, 445, 518, appointments 437, 461, 467, 471/3, 489, 521, 551, 571, 583, attends Twentieth Congress of the CPSU 470, sends messages of congratulations to Indochina 568, 582, 586, 590; d. 595; defends CCP against Chiang Kaishek from 1945 412, 414; and Long March 350, 354, 360; military leader pre-1934 318, 321, 322, 324, 330, 332, 338; orders countrywide advance 436; united front against Japan 364, 384, 386
Zhu De shixuan ji 朱德詩選集 513

Zhu Desheng 朱德生 621
Zhu Fengbiao 朱鳳標 107
Zhu Hongdeng 朱紅燈 194, 195, 197
Zhu Hongying 朱洪英 62, 64, 68, 74
Zhu Jiahua 朱家驊 405, 513
Zhu Junsheng 朱駿聲 75
Zhu Kezhen 竺可楨 581
Zhu Peide 朱培德 163, 317, 369
Zhu Qiqian 朱啓鈐 270
Zhu Ruhang 褚汝航 58, 60, 61
Zhu Xizu 朱希祖 409
Zhu Zhixin 朱執信 155, 281
Zhu Ziqing 朱自清 323, 435
Zhu Ziqing wenji 朱自清文集 459
Zhuang 僮 minority 477, 482
Zhuang Yan 莊焰 570
Zhuang Zedong 莊則棟 499, 573
Zhuangzi yizheng 莊子義證 333
Zhushi suoyan 諸史瑣言 513
Zhuyao xiwen 誅妖檄文 85/7
zhuyin fuhao 注音符號 333
Zimbabwe 626, 632
Ziye 子夜 347
Zizheng xinpian 資政新篇 79
Zizhi tongjian 資治通鑑 475
Zongli yamen, *Zongli geguo tongshang shiwu yamen* 總理各國通商事務衙門 ('office for the general management of affairs and trade with every country') 105, 111, 130, 139; becomes Ministry of Foreign Affairs 202; and the Boxers 196; and Britain 86, 90, 108, 112, 113, 188, 196; and Cuba 124; and customs duty 87, 127, 137; established 84; and France 86, 104, 108, 144, 148, 150, 184, 188/90, 196; and Germany 186, 196; and Japan 124, 128, 136/8, 190; and reform 188; role in modernization 89, 97; and Russia 108, 134; and the Taipings 86, 98; and the US 108, 111, 143
Zou Hanxun 鄒漢勳 61
Zou Lu 鄒魯 304, 407/9
Zou Rong 鄒容 209, 210, 217
Zuo Baogui 左寶貴 177
Zuo Quan 左權 397
Zuo Zongtang 左宗棠 108, 153; advocates modernization 101/3; appointments 93, 97, 103/7, 111, 121, 123, 127, 135, 143, 151; attitude to foreign affairs 132, 138, 140; d. 155; and Moslem rebels 110, 114, 118, 122, 126, conquest of Xinjiang 127-36, 140

694

GEOGRAPHICAL INDEX

Aigun (Heilongjiang) Map 1, 251, 259; Treaty of 72, 77, 82, 514
Aksu (Xinjiang) Map 1, 98, 104, 132, 350
Alma-Ata, USSR, Map 1, 377, 441, 471
Amoy (Fujian) Map 3, 34, 48, 214, 272, 348, 400, 438, 477; and Britain 25, 26, 30, 334; and Japan 194, 370, 390; and Triads 54, 56
Amur River (Heilongjiang) Map 1, 43, 66, 72, 198, 471, 550
Andong (Fengtian) Map 2, 230, 444, see Dandong
Anqing (Anhui) Maps 2, 3, attacked by Japanese 370; communications 331; missionaries 111; modernization 83, 87, 91, 95; and Taipings 54, 56, 66, 74, 82, 84; uprisings in 222, 226
Anshan (Liaoning) Map 2, 428; iron works 259, 457, 553/5
Anyang (Henan) Map 2, 195, 327, see Zhangde
Anyuan (Jiangxi) Map 3, coal mines 287, 303/5

Bailingmiao (Inner Mongolia) Map 2, 346, 360
Baoding (Hebei) Map 2, 197, 199, 240, 292, 364, 366, 404, 432, 594
Baoji (Shaanxi) Map 2, 397, 411, 430, 471, 581
Baoqing (Hunan) Map 3, 76, 264, 276, see Shaoyang
Baotou (Inner Mongolia) Map 2, 477, 483
Bazhou (Hebei) Map 2, 104, 171, 199
Beihai (Guangxi) Map 3, 130, 131, 360, 366, 380
Beiliu (Guangxi) Map 3, 29, 280
Beiping, 1928-49, Maps 1, 2,

319, 329, 342, 346, 347, 372, 437; banks in 371; and CCP 419, 434; communications 335, 349, 350; and Japanese army 356, 360, 364, 408; labour movement 341, 427; name changed 320, 436; political activities 330, 331, 354, 367, 378; student activities 338, 355, 361, 422, 427, 430, 433; US troops 390, 421; see also Peking
Bhamo, Burma, Map 1, 124, 408
Bohai Bay (Hebei) Map 1, 605, 615, 627, 628
Bozhou (Anhui) Map 2, 24, 50, 54, 62

Caozhou (Shandong) Map 2, 30, 98, 186, 187, see Heze
Changchun (Jilin) Map 1, 274, 340, 351, 414, 529, 588, 599; as industrial centre 483, 493; as NG headquarters 413, 416, 418, 430; and railway 216, 241, 255, 263; see also Chinese Changchun Railway Company in General Index
Changde (Hunan) Map 3, 235, 239, 344, 400
Changdu (Tibet) Map 1, 230, 266, 444, 451/3
Changle (Hubei) Maps 2, 3, 191, 192
Changsha (Hunan) Maps 1, 3, 487, 567, 634; and CCP 283, 314, 330, 331; in civil wars 264, 266, 276, 308; communications 267, 515, 565, 597; disturbances in 233, 590/2; fires, floods 299, 372-5; and Japanese 290, 297, 372, 390, 392, 404; labour movement 315/17; revolution 210, 236, 269; student protest 631; and Taipings 50, 52, 56, 58
Changxindian (Peking) Map 2, 286, 289, 293
Changyuan (Henan) Map 2, 351,

Places which do not appear on the maps may be found in the General Index; those mentioned only once in the text are not indexed here.

695

Geographical Index

357, 429
Changzhou (Jiangsu) Map 2, 78/80, 94
Chaozhou (Guangdong) Map 3, 77, 79, 110, 220, 221, 239
Chengde (Hebei) Map 2, 53, 493
Chengdu (Sichuan) Maps 1, 3, 342, 404, 438, 637; communications 376, 382, 392, 398, 451, 471, 537, 555, 581; Conference 482; disturbances 179, 360, 423, 538; earthquake 595; in 1911 revolution 236, 238; student protest 430, 433; universities 339
Chita, Russia, Map 1, 270, 441
Chizhou (Anhui) Maps 2, 3, 77, 78
Chongqing (Sichuan) Map 3, 213, 404, 425, 436; bombed 376; communications 251, 335, 365, 377, 393, 397, 451, 509, 605; falls to PLA 438; fire 441; and missionaries 93, 115; NG capital 374, 378-96 *passim*, 405, 407, 410, 415, 418, moved from 420, moved to 368; negotiations 414; opened for trade 130, 165; student protest 422
Chongyang (Hubei) Map 3, 22, 64
Chuzhou (Anhui) Map 2, 54, 74
Cixi (Zhejiang) Map 2, 22, 233

Dagu (Tianjin) Map 2, 60, 76, 80, 143, 156, 159, 197, 306; and the Boxers 198, 202; and Japan 178, 358, 364
Daguan (Yunnan) Map 3, 76, 265
Dali (Yunnan) Map 1, 36, 64, 118, 120, 305
Dalian (Lüda) (Liaoning) Map 2, 188, 193/5, 210, 282, 290, 411, 532, 540, 589, 622
Dandong (Liaoning) Map 2, 444, *see* Andong
Datong (Shanxi) Map 2, 365, 366
Daye iron mines (Hubei) Map 2, 173, 225
Dazhai (Shanxi) Map 2, 525, 581, 593, 594, 605, 628
Dazu (Sichuan) Map 3, 165, 170, 191
Dege (Sichuan) Map 1, 228, 266
Delhi, New, India, Map 1, 474, 476, 492, 504
Dengzhou (Shandong) Map 2, 82, 85, 127, 176
Dinghai (Zhejiang) Map 2, 22, 23, 442
Dongguan (Guangdong) Map 3, 60, 220
Dongting Lake (Hunan) Map 1, 50, 435
Dunhuang (Gansu) Map 1, 219, 223, 233
Duolun (Inner Mongolia) Map 1, 346, 430
Duyun (Guizhou) Map 3, 72, 110, 114

Fengtai (Peking) Map 2, 197, 360
Foshan (Guangdong) Map 3, 34, 60, 62, 70
Fumin (Yunnan) Map 3, 106, 166
Fuzhou (Fujian) Maps 1, 3, 73, 288, 505, 577; and Britain 32, 42; communications 159; falls to PLA 436; fire, floods in 131, 231; and Japan 274, 278, 388, 406; seat of ROC People's Government 346, 348; student activities 273, 274; as trade port 25, 43; *see also* General Index under dockyard, and naval academy
Fuzhou (Jiangxi) Map 3, 205, 346

Ganzhou (Jiangxi) Map 3, 223, 224, 286, 308, 330, 340
Guangchang (Jiangxi) Map 3, 336, 348
Guangde (Anhui) Maps 2, 3, 78, 96
Guangzhou (Guangdong) Maps 1, 3, 246, 254, 279, 290, 303, 312, 471, 525, 565, 588; appointments in 23, 265, 269, 281, 291, 577, 583; banks in 295; and Britain 22-5, 28, 30, 34, 42, 68/74, 86, 140, 142, 148, 455; and Chen Jiongming 278, 298; Commune 316; communications 113, 255, 362, air 349, 515, 581, 605, rail 189, 215, 219, 221, 235, 245, 263, 267, 359, 441, 477, *see also* Hankou; conferences or congresses in 294, 306, 309, 498, 505, 629; in Cultural Revolution 537, 540, 546; falls to PLA 438; foreign entry into walled city 30, 32, 38, 40, 42; and French 70, 72, 86, 152; government 264-6, 270, 280, 281, 284, 287, 291, 338; and Japan 224, 361, 370, 408; modernization 123, 159, 163; natural disasters in 177,

696

Geographical Index

231; and Red Turbans 60, 62; and revolution 178, 232, 234; strikes, student protests 302, 309, 361; and Taipings 29, 35, 36; trade fairs 483, 537; as trade port 25, 65; universities 315, 443; and US 30, 46, 52, 68, 153, 214, 620
Guangzhou Bay (Guangdong) Map 1, 188, 194, 414
Guanyang (Guangxi) Map 3, 60, 62
Guilin (Guangxi) Map 3, 41, 48, 206, 282-4, 288, 374, 377, 408
Guiping (Xunzhou) (Guangxi) Map 3, 35, 39, 42-8 *passim*
Guiyang (Guizhou) Maps 1, 3, 365, 438, 489, 502, 577, 599
Gutian (Fujian) Map 3, 179, 328
Gyantse (Tibet) Map 1, 208, 210, 230, 240, 448, 463, 465

Haicheng (Liaoning) Map 2, 176, 587
Haifeng (Guangdong) Map 3, 286, 291, 300, 316, 318
Hainan Island (Guangdong) Maps 1, 3, 129, 146, 158, 177, 184, 376, 442
Haizhou (Jiangsu) Map 2, 258, 271, 411, 451
Hami (Xinjiang) Map 1, 122, 140, 377
Hangzhou (Zhejiang) Maps 1, 2, 3, 113, 238, 252, 321, 498, 564; boycotts, demonstrations, disturbances 22, 214, 220, 292, 423, 427, 584; CCP meetings in 288, 508/10; communications 225, 245, 477, 515, 597; falls to Japanese 368; falls to PLA 436; floods 133; sports held in 333, 619; and Taipings 78, 82, 86; trade port 43
Hangzhou Bay (Zhejiang) Map 1, 366
Hankou (Hubei) Maps 2, 3, 100, 191, 200, 302, 342, 371; air routes 331, 335; concessions 180, 234, 236, 262, 310, 360, 364; highways 341; and Japan 254, 367, 373; natural disasters 229, 339; in Northern Expedition 308, 311; railways 211, 235, Guangzhou-Hankou 189, 219, 245, 267, 283, 359, 408, Peking-Hankou 163, 215, 228, 289, 291, 372, 402, 408, 441, 489; in revolution of 1911 236, 238; and Taipings 50, 56, 58, 62, 74; as trade port 87; *see also* Wuhan
Hanoi, Vietnam, Maps 1, 3, 477, 503, 564, 608; bombed by US 530, 568; communications 365, 377, 465; and the French 122, 142, 144, 148, 150; visited by Chinese or Soviet leaders 474, 508, 520, 552; and Wang Jingwei 374, 376
Hanyang (Hubei) 236, 238, 308; and Taipings 50, 56, 58, 60, 62, 68; *see also* Wuhan
Hanzhong (Shaanxi) Map 2, 92, 94, 113
Harbin (Heilongjiang) Map 1, 433, 455, 483, 597; communications 201, 259, 411, 529; falls to CCP 418; and Japan 268, 340; and Russia or USSR 256, 264, 326, 411, 414
Hefei (Anhui) Maps 1, 2, 146, 423, 541
Hengshan (Hunan) Map 3, 264, 276, 299, 315
Hengyang (Hunan) Map 3, 266, 308, 377, 406
Hengzhou (Hengyang) (Hunan) Map 3, 56, 58
Heze (Shandong) Map 2, 357, 420, *see* Caozhou
Hezhou (Gansu) Map 1, 96, 112, 124, 180
Hezhou (Hexian) (Anhui) Map 3, 70, 76
Huai River (Anhui) Map 1, 102, 375, 603
Huangzhou (Hubei) Maps 2, 3, 56, 84, 236
Huaxian (Guangdong) Map 3, 27, 28, 29, 38
Huayuankou (Henan) Map 2, 370, 375, 423
Huhehot (Guihua) (Guisui) (Inner Mongolia) Maps 1, 2, 251, 366-7, 372, 460, 481, 571, 588
Huizhou (Shexian) (Anhui) Maps 2, 3, 82, 84
Huizhou (Guangdong) Map 3, 200, 222, 258, 278, 292, 300, 304, 372
Hukou (Jiangxi) Maps 2, 3, 70, 246, 372
Hunza, India (now in Pakistan) Map 1, 166, 170
Huoshan (Anhui) Map 2, 60, 96
Huzhou (Zhejiang) Map 2, 22, 88, 96

697

Geographical Index

Jehol (Hebei) Map 2, 80, 81; *also* province, 344, 432
Ji'an (Jiangxi) Map 3, 84, 205
Jianchuan (Yunnan) Map 1, 102
Jiang'an (Sichuan) Map 3, 258
Jiangpu (Jiangsu) Map 2, 76, 78
Jiaozhou (Jiaoxian) (Shandong) Map 2, 186, 195, 211, 216, 284, 428
Jiaozhou Bay (Shandong) Map 1, 184-8
Jiaozuo (Henan) Map 2, 555, 613
Jiaxing (Zhejiang) Map 2, 22, 80, 94, 229, 280
Jiayi (Taiwan) Map 1, 28, 39, 48
Jilin (Jilin) Map 1, 200, 208, 241, 255, 263
Jilong (Taiwan) Map 1, 125, 150, 154, 178
Ji'nan (Shandong) Maps 1, 2, 239, 242, 303, 330, 505, 577; communications 188, 193, 211, 241, 258, 267, 291; and Germany 188, 193; and Japan 252, 256, 267, 272, 284, 291, 320, 326, 368; and Nian 86, 104; PLA captures 428, 430/2
Jingdezhen (Jiangxi) Map 3, 76, 84
Jinggang Mountains (Jiangxi) Map 1, 316, 318, 324
Jingzhou (Hubei) Map 2, 264, 266
Jinhua (Zhejiang) Map 3, 84, 137, 394
Jining (Inner Mongolia) Map 2, 451, 467
Jining (Shandong) Map 2, 104, 142, 368, 420
Jinjibao (Ningxia) Map 2, 110, 112, 114
Jinsha River, part of Yangzi River, Map 1, 354, 358
Jintian (Guangxi) Map 3, 42, 46
Jinzhou (Liaoning) Map 2, 176, 210, 338, 340, 416, 432
Jiujiang (Jiangxi) Map 3, 56, 62, 68, 72, 255, 308, 312, 314, 331, 372
Jiyang (Shandong) Map 2, 108, 171
Jomo Lungma (Mt Everest) Tibet-Nepal border, Map 1, 497, 585
Juye (Shandong) Map 2, 30, 187

Kaifeng (Henan) Map 2, 23, 84, 102, 213, 255, 314, 332, 370, 432, 462, 505
Karakorum Mts (Xinjiang) Map 1, 591, 605

Kashgar (Kashiheer) (Xinjiang) Map 1, 31, 34, 37, 43, 45, 83, 98/100, 108, 122, 134, 180, 214, 219
Katmandu, Nepal, Map 1, 472, 476, 494, 509, 537
Khabarovsk, Russia, Map 1, 328, 550
Khang Khay, Laos, Map 1, 516, 544
Khotan (Xinjiang) Map 1, 104, 134, 201
Kiakhta, Russia, Map 1, 252, 254, 274, 280
Kucha (Xinjiang) Map 1, 94, 98, 104, 112, 132, 219
Kunming (Yunnan) Maps 1, 3, 256, 358, 392, 514, 557, 588, 606, 619; air battle 390; communications 365, 371, 376, 398, 471, 515, 555; in Cultural Revolution 538; police raid in 415; student activities in 415, 422, 430; *see also* Yunnan

Ladakh, Tibet-India border, Map 1, 490, 506
Laiyang (Shandong) Map 2, 232
Langfang (Anci) (Hebei) Map 2, 198, 202, 264, 364
Langjiao (Taiwan) Map 1, 122, 126
Langson, Vietnam, Map 1, 116, 152, 614
Lanzhou (Gansu) Map 1, 102, 139, 393, 404, 411, 436, 451, 471, 477, 483, 489, 515, 525, 537, 544, 577, 597
Lhasa (Tibet) Map 1, 158, 162, 383, 440, 471, 506, 511, 584; and Britain 212; Chinese troops occupy 232, 448; communications 461, 465, 471, 509, 521, 529; hydroelectricity 493
Liangzhou (Wuwei) (Gansu) Map 1, 98, 180, 319
Liao River (Liaoning) Map 1, 206, 329
Liaodong Peninsula (Liaoning) Map 1, 178, 216
Liaoyang (Liaoning) Map 2, 212, 268
Lijin (Shandong) Map 2, 181, 185, 201, 207, 211, 213
Lingzhou (Ningxia) Map 2, 90, 94, 110
Liuan (Anhui) Map 3, 68, 72, 92
Liuyang (Hunan) Map 3, 220, 316, 330, 331
Liuzhou (Guangxi) Map 3, 68, 74,

Geographical Index

377, 408, 412, 489, 546
Longju (Tibet) Map 1, 490, 502
Longkou (Shandong) Map 2, 252, 255, 426
Longling (Yunnan) Map 1, 408, 593
Longzhou (Guangxi) Map 3, 42, 183, 282, 410
Lufeng (Guangdong) Map 3, 316, 318
Lufeng (Yunnan) Map 1, 599, 631
Luoyang (Henan) Map 2, 88, 241, 328, 332, 340, 404, 426, 428, 489, 597
Lushan (Jiangxi) Map 3, 297, 316, 332, 490, 554
Luzhou (Anhui) Map 2, 58, 64, 70, 74, 88
Lüda (Dalian) (Liaoning) Map 2, 418, 454
Lüshun (Liaoning) Map 2, 165, 176; communications 201, 227; fortifications 149, 156, 166; and Japan 180, 210, 214, 227, 290; and Russia (or USSR) 186, 188, 192, 210, 442, 452, 462, 466

McMahon Line, China-India border, Map 1, 490, 502
Macheng (Hubei) Map 2, 96, 102, 171
Manas (Xinjiang) Map 1, 96, 130
Mandalay, Burma, Map 1, 394, 471
Manzhouli (Heilongjiang) Map 1, 268, 326, 335, 411
Muztag Ata (Xinjiang) Map 1, 491, 631

Nanchang (Jiangxi) Maps 1, 3, 238, 246, 308, 330, 351; Chiang's anti-CCP headquarters 344, 346; communications 255, 477; disturbances in 89, 218, 219, 242; falls to Japanese 376; falls to PLA 436; flooding 133; and Taipings 54, 56, 64, 84; Uprising 314, 318
Nanjing (Jiangsu) Maps 1, 2, 105, 108, 110, 112, 298, 419, 493, 577, 588, 597; boycotts, demonstrations, strikes etc 214, 303, 423, 427, 433, 437; capital: of NG (1927-37) 312, 324, 331, 334, 338, 339, 342, 362, 366, of NG (1946-49) 420, 422, 430, of Republican government (1912) 238, 240, 241, 243, of Taipings (1853-64) 52-96 *passim*, of Wang Jingwei 394, 396; communications 251, 296, 331, 335, 489, 545; conferences 308, 326, 333, 336, 349, 356; educational institutions 167, 183, 209, 323, 341, 431; falls to PLA 436; and Japanese 368, 373, 378, 382, 404, 414; Treaty of 22
Nankang (Jiangxi) Map 3, 223, 224, 330, 336
Nanning (Guangxi) Maps 1, 3, 153, 221, 280, 380, 386, 408, 410, 606
Ningbo (Zhejiang) Map 2, 22, 26, 29, 43, 86, 88, 89, 122, 211, 225, 245, 388
Ningdu (Jiangxi) Map 3, 338, 342, 350
Ningguo (Anhui) Map 3, 66, 80, 82, 235
Niuzhuang (Liaoning) Map 2, 82, 83, 85, 104, 178, 208, 214

Pamir, Xinjiang-Russian border, Map 1, 166, 168, 491
Panmunjom, Korea, Map 1, 448, 456
Peking, Maps 1, 2; capital of PRC 436-637 *passim*; capital of Qing 28-230 *passim*; capital of various governments (1916-27) 312 *passim*; capital of Yuan Shikai 240-61 *passim*; place of publication, see D sections, 271, 299, 305, 439-527 *passim*, 593-635 *passim*; *see also* Beiping, and Peking-Hankou railway under Hankou
Phong Saly, Laos, Map 1, 503, 509
Pingjiang (Hunan) Map 3, 320, 330, 331, 376, 404
Pingliang (Gansu) Map 2, 92, 96
Pingnan (Guangxi) Map 3, 44, 46, 48
Pingxiang (Jiangxi) Map 3, 170, 218, 225
Pingyuan (Shandong) Map 2, 194, 195
Pukou (Jiangsu) Map 2, 78, 225, 233, 241, 247, 255, 290, 359, 368, 430, 489
Puyang (Henan) Map 2, 253, 257
Pyongyang, Korea (DPRK) Map 1, 174, 461, 482, 584

Qianjiang (Guangxi) Map 3, 42, 121
Qianxi (Guizhou) Map 3, 98, 102
Qingdao (Shandong) Map 2, 272,

699

427, 473; communications 291, 299; and Germany 186, 193, 216, 250; and Japan 250, 252, 284, 288, 291, 314, 318, 360, 368, 414; and PLA 430, 436; strikes 301/3, 363
Qingjiang (Jiangsu) Map 2, 141, 143, 232
Qingjiang (Jiangxi) Map 3, 585
Qingpu (Shanghai) Map 2, 36, 39
Qingyang (Gansu) Map 2, 106, 110
Qingyuan (Guangxi) Map 3, 78, 212
Qinhuangdao (Hebei) Map 2, 195, 202, 366, 432, 581
Qinzhou (Guangxi) Map 3, 222, 226, 250, 251, 380
Qiongzhou, Hainan Island (Guangdong) Map 3, 129, 146, 156, 222
Quanzhou (Fujian) Map 3, 310, 491

Raozhou (Jiangxi) Map 3, 60, 205
Renhuai (Guizhou) Map 3, 194, 195
Renping (Shandong) Map 2, 62, 108
Ruichang (Jiangxi) Map 3, 121, 218, 372
Ruijin (Jiangxi) Map 3, 74, 324, 338, 345, 348
Ryuku Islands, Map 1, 46, 50, 56, 116, 126, 134, 136, 140

Sanmen Gorge, Yellow River, Shanxi-Henan border, Map 1, 483, 571, 577
Seoul, Korea (Republic) Map 1, 146, 152, 174, 194, 336
Shanghai, Maps 1, 2, 39, 118, 309, 447, 459, 495, 509, 513, 521, 523, 542; anti-inflation campaign 431; appointments 237, 313, 443, 495, 559, 591; arsenals etc 99, 157, 299; bishops of 495, 555; boycotts 215, 254; British presence: cultural 75, 155, 279, diplomatic 26, 36, 52, 73, 76, 108, 206, military 22, 54, 58, 86, 206, 384; CCP activities, pre-1949 276, 280, 286, 300, 308, 334, 344, 422; Chiang Kaishek's *coup* 312; Coca-Cola 607; commerce 37, 215, British 25, 53, 105, 125, US 24, 87, 105, 185, 447; communications with other places 43, 311, 502, 623, air 331, 335, 529, 565, 569, 581, 597, radiotelephone 358, 364, railways 91, 101, 125, 128, 129, 133, 211, 229, 245, 296, 477, 589, telegraph 132, 142, 143, 147, 514, wire cables 113, 115, 141, 197; Concessions 58, 60, British 30, French 40, 122; conferences or congresses 228, 261, 265, 319, 329, 559, 571, 629; cotton cloth mills 135, 163, 173, 175, 185, 217, 219, 301; and Cultural Revolution 525, 531, 534, 535, 539; currency 69, 365; customs duty 53, 73; demonstrations 184, 254, 290, 292, 300, 419, 422, 425, 430, 433, 534, 588, 614, 619; education/training 89, 93, 155, 203, 243, 395, 541; epidemic 91; falls to PLA 436; films 185; French presence 121, diplomatic 46, 52, 56, 73, 76, 146, 148, 632, expelled 457, military 62, 86, 206; and India 506; International Settlement 110, 184, 194, 225, 300, 333, 400; Japanese presence 203, 367, military 206, 340, 360, 364, 366, 368; law courts 101, 206, 333; libraries 491; May Day 279; mint 345; motor cars 205; NP bombs 440; observatory 119; peace talks 270; political parties or societies 212, 236, 240, 279; population 456, 570; port to leave China 127, 130, 134, 182; and Portugal 38; and rebels 52, 56, 62, 80, 86, 92, 198; residents' committees 463; and revolution of 1911 238; rice riots 423; rickshaws 121, 184, 273; robbers 31; ships launched 465, 489, 495, 551; social services or charity in 47, 213; socialist transformation 471, 473; sport 255; strikes 269, 273, 287, 289, 341, 422, dock 207, 539, textile workers 217, 219, 231, 237, 301/3, 347, 363; translation bureau 191; uprisings in 308, 312; US presence: diplomatic 58, 66, 106, 564, 626, military 54, 58, 390; and USSR 290; visited by foreign leaders 518, 564; volunteer corps 54, 58
Shanhaiguan (Hebei) Map 2, 174, 175, 178, 202, 286, 306, 344, 349, 432, 605

Geographical Index

Shaoguan (Guangdong) Map 3, 284, 286, 408
Shaowu (Fujian) Map 3, 70, 71
Shaoxing (Zhejiang) Maps 2, 3, 22, 86, 90, 220, 311
Shaoyang (Hunan) Map 3, 537, see Baoqing
Shashi (Hubei) Maps 2, 3, 335, 339, 382, 400
Shenyang (Liaoning) Map 1, 199, 293, 342, 427, 463, 489, 571, 577, 599, 625; communications 221, 329, 349, 350, 515, 529; falls to PLA 430, 432; Incident 334, 336, 560; and Japan 214, 228/30, 254, 334, 336; NG troops in 416, 418; and Russia 200, 208, 214, 296, 358, 414, 443; US bombing 406; and Zhang Zuolin 296, 320
Shigatse (Tibet) Map 1, 463, 465
Shijiazhuang (Hebei) Map 1, 402, 426, 430, 431, 535, 545, 588
Shiping (Yunnan) Map 3, 161, 208
Shouzhou (Anhui) Map 2, 46, 54, 86, 88
Shunning (Yunnan) Map 1, 34, 128
Simla, India, Map 1, 248, 250
Sinan (Sixian) (Guizhou) Map 3, 72, 108
Siping (Sipingjie) (Jilin) Map 1, 267, 418, 424, 428
Songjiang (Shanghai) Map 2, 38, 46, 52, 80, 86, 130, 368
Sungari River, Russia-China border (Heilongjiang) Map 1, 64, 293
Suzhou (Suxian) (Anhui) Map 2, 24, 597
Suzhou (Gansu) Map 1, 98, 122, 128, 142, 165
Suzhou (Jiangsu) Map 2, 31, 43, 52, 80, 81, 88, 90, 91, 92, 113, 142, 300, 304, 376
Swatow (Guangdong) Map 3, 214, 221, 278, 287, 289, 298-304, 316, 318, 378

Taibei (Taiwan) Map 1, 128, 173, 180, 370, 422, 435, 438, 450, 486
Taigong (Guizhou) Map 3, 66, 114
Taikang (Henan) Map 2, 387, 391
Taiping (Guangxi) Map 3, 42, 116, 220
Taixing (Jiangsu) Map 2, 384, 420
Taiyuan (Shanxi) Maps 1, 2, 333, 368, 430, 436, 495, 505, 588, 590, 613
Tangshan (Hebei) Map 2, 143, 159, 161, 249, 279, 283, 432, 593
Tarbagatai (Taerbahatai) (Xinjiang) Map 1, 34, 37, 43, 47, 49, 96, 102, 148
Tianbao (Guangxi) Map 3, 38, 444
Tianjiazhen (Hubei) Maps 2, 3, 56, 60
Tianjin, Maps 1, 2, 37-311 passim, 341-78 passim, 390, 414-33 passim, 449, 463, 489, 539, 545, 561, 579; earthquake 593; falls to PLA 434; newspapers use simplified characters 467; takeover of enterprises and properties 453, 471, 473
Tianshui (Qinzhou) (Gansu) Map 2, 411, 451
Tongcheng (Anhui) Map 3, 68, 78, 226
Tongjiang (Sichuan) Maps 2, 3, 344, 352
Tongling (Anhui) Map 2, 70, 249
Tongzhou (Tongxian) (Peking) Map 2, 80, 198, 242, 293, 356
Tsitsihar (Heilongjiang) Map 1, 200, 251, 338, 418
Turfan (Xinjiang) Map 1, 98, 114, 130, 142, 219

Ulan Bator (Urga) Mongolia, Map 1, 242, 274, 280, 358, 451, 462, 467, 494, 510, 516
Urumchi (Dihua) (Xinjiang) Map 1, 65, 404, 497, 524, 598, 608; appointments 123, 127, 467; communications 376, 377, 597, 605; Moslem rebellions 96, 98, 112, 130; and USSR 383, 396, 514
Ush (Xinjiang) Map 1, 104, 132, 134
Ussuri River, Russia-China border (Heilongjiang) Map 1, 82, 550

Vladivostok, Russia, Map 1, 268, 536

Wanding (Yunnan) Map 1, 371, 394, 408
Wanxian (Sichuan) Maps 1, 2, 166, 308, 335, 369
Wayaobao (Shaanxi) Map 2, 356, 358, 361
Weihaiwei (Shandong) Map 2, 127, 156, 174, 176, 190, 330, 332, 426, 430

Weixian (Shandong) Map 2, 252, 258, 430
Wenzhou (Zhejiang) Map 1, 130, 131, 394
Woyang (Anhui) Map 2, 192, 222
Wuchang (Hubei) Maps 1, 2, 3 (provincial capital under Qing) 76, 112, 169, 186, 258, 308, 372; communications 247, 263, 267, 441; educational institutions 171/3, 187, 243; Plenum 486; and Taipings 52, 55, 58-68 *passim*, 76, 84; Uprising 234, 236; *see also* Wuhan
Wuhan (Hubei) provincial capital, triple city Hankou, Hanyang and Wuchang, 326, 327, 330, 373, 453, 483, 488, 489, 539, 577, 588; communications 263, 477, 529; conferences 370, 372; falls to NRA 308; falls to PLA 436; flooding 465; Incident (1967) 538/40; and Japanese 368, 372, 382, 404, 575; labour, student movements 272, 422, 427, 430; seat of a government (1927) 310, 313, 317; *see also* Hankou, Hanyang, Wuchang
Wuhu (Anhui) Maps 2, 3, 52, 130, 131, 167, 235, 239, 292, 368, 423
Wusong (Shanghai) Map 2, 24, 86, 125, 128-30, 133, 255, 264, 340, 366
Wuxi (Jiangsu) Map 2, 80, 94, 169, 183, 368, 423
Wuxuan (Guangxi) Map 3, 46, 47
Wuxue (Guangji) (Hubei) Map 2, 167, 232
Wuyuan (Jiangxi) Map 3, 380, 549
Wuzhou (Guangxi) Map 3, 280, 299, 365, 406, 544

Xiaguan (Yunnan) Map 1, 371, 589
Xi'an (Shaanxi) Maps 1, 2, 88, 92, 104, 200, 204, 241, 260, 355, 362, 377, 404, 436, 483, 485, 501, 567
Xiang River (Hunan) Map 1, 50, 477, 565
Xiangfu (Henan) Map 2, 46, 213
Xiangtan (Hunan) Map 3, 55, 58, 89, 170, 173, 214, 292, 299, 314, 315
Xiangyang (Hubei) Map 2, 39, 98, 264, 266, 382, 577
Xiangzhou (Guangxi) Map 3, 35, 46, 47

Xilin (Guangxi) Map 3, 66, 67
Xingtai (Shunde) (Hebei) Map 2, 370, 535
Xingyi (Guizhou) Map 3, 206, 599
Xining (Qinghai) Map 1, 118, 122, 180, 405, 436, 461, 489, 497, 599
Xinning (Hunan) Map 3, 40, 42, 76
Xinyang (Henan) Map 2, 247, 382, 402
Xiyang (Shanxi) Map 2, 581, 607, 628
Xinyi (Guangdong) Map 3, 42, 48
Xuancheng (Anhui) Maps 2, 3, 220, 232
Xunzhou (Guiping) (Guangxi) Map 3, 64, 84
Xuzhou (Jiangsu) Map 2, 255, 260, 262, 285, 314, 318, 370, 426, 430, 432

Yadong (Tibet) Map 1, 160, 172, 210, 240
Yalu River, Korea-China border (Liaoning) Map 1, 174, 210
Yan'an (Shaanxi) Map 2, 380, 402; CCP headquarters 362, 367, 376, 396, 410, 424; culture 361, 367, 379, 395, 399, 405, 415, 567; falls to NG forces 424; speeches by Mao in 391, 395, 410
Yangi Hissar (Xinjiang) Map 1, 34, 98, 132
Yangzhou (Jiangsu) Map 2, 52, 53, 54, 56, 59, 64, 67, 74, 106, 108, 109, 434
Yangzi River, Maps 1, 2, 3, 112, 193, 253, 366, 375, 509; bridges over 247, 477, 545, 625; and British 22, 74, 188, 194; CCP troops 414/16, 436; floods 115, 239, 261, 311, 339, 357, 435, 465, 635, control 451; and Japanese 372, 382, 398; and Taipings 54, 62, 74, 78, 83, 90
Yantai (Chefoo) (Shandong) Map 2, 83, 86, 104, 127, 130, 178, 227, 370, 426, 430, 603
Yarkand (Xinjiang) Map 1, 102, 108, 114, 170
Yellow River, Maps 1, 2, 54, 90, 204, 384, 402, 424, 483, 603; bridges over 215, 241, 368, 493, 565, 597; floods 23, 71, 141, 149, 351, 357, changes course 57, 65, 375, in Henan 27, 109, 253, 257, 387, 391, 397, 429, in Shandong 155, 159, 171, 181,

Geographical Index

185, 193, 201, 205, 207, 211, 213, 271, 349, 357; and Nian 102, 106; NP troops burst dykes 370, 375
Yichang (Hubei) Maps 2, 3, 130, 131, 169, 335, 382, 398
Yihuang (Jiangxi) Map 3, 344, 346
Yili (Xinjiang) Map 1, 23, 31, 34, 37, 41-9 *passim*, 102, 116, 118, 132-46 *passim*, 240, 396, 512
Yingde (Guangdong) Map 3, 40, 44, 46
Yingkou (Liaoning) Map 2, 342, 587, 625
Yining (Xinjiang) Map 1, 276, 377, 408, 416/18
Yiyang (Hunan) Map 3, 50, 116
Yizhang (Hunan) Map 3, 318, 350
Yong'an (Hunan) Map 3, 48, 380
Yongchang (Yunnan) Map 1, 30, 32, 33, 34, 36
Yongcheng (Henan) Map 2, 24, 434
Yongding River (Hebei) Maps 1, 2, 173, 461, 477; floods 27, 67, 109, 117, 149, 171, 173, 213, 299, 329
Youyang (Sichuan) Map 3, 99, 111, 115
Yueyang (Yuezhou) (Hunan) Map 3, 263, 390
Yuezhou (Yueyang) (Hunan) Map 3, 49, 50, 58, 60, 195, 266, 276, 282, 308, 372, 390
Yulin (Guangxi) Map 3, 44, 46
Yunnan (Yunnan) name of provincial capital in Qing dynasty 70, 90, 106, 108, 110, 112, 185, 249, *see also* Kunming
Yunzhou (Yunnan) Map 1, 120, 128
Yuyao (Zhejiang) Map 2, 22, 86, 90, 220

Zaoyang (Hubei) Map 2, 94, 382
Zhanghua (Taiwan) Map 1, 33, 39
Zhangjiakou (Hebei) Map 2, 229, 251, 255, 366, 368, 379, 420
Zhangzhou (Fujian) Map 3, 96, 98, 348
Zhaoqing (Guangdong) Map 3, 60, 62, 258, 290
Zhaotong (Yunnan) Map 3, 76, 581
Zhapu (Zhejiang) Map 2, 22, 23, 38
Zhengjiatun (Jilin) Map 1, 260, 262, 267
Zhengzhou (Henan) Maps 1, 2,

161, 291, 314, 328, 332, 370, 402, 426, 432, 462, 493, 501, 588
Zhenjiang (Jiangsu) Map 2, 22, 43, 64, 70, 83, 162, 168
Zhennanguan (Youyiguan) (Guangxi) Map 3, 152, 165, 224
Zhiheji (Anhui) Map 2, 66, 92, 98
Zhongshan (Xiangshan) (Guangdong) Map 3, 300, 386, 452
Zhongwei (Ningxia) Map 2, 51, 158
Zhoukoudian (Peking) Map 2, 317, 329, 543, 567
Zhouxian (Zhouzhou) (Hebei) Map 2, 196, 278
Zhouzhi (Shaanxi) Map 2, 92, 94
Zhuzhou (Hunan) Map 3, 251, 477, 537
Zunyi (Guizhou) Map 3, 111, 352, 353

Note: The provinces, autonomous regions or cities given in brackets in this index for the location of places are generally those of the date of compilation (1981), whereas the provinces (or province-level regions) given in the text in every case follow that appropriate to the date of reference.

703

951.04 20052
JEN Jenner, W. J., editor
     Modern China

DATE DUE			
JA 22 '90			
NOV 19 1997			
JAN 20 1999			
JAN 28 2002			